S0-AIX-429

Da Capo Press Music Reprint Series

GENERAL EDITOR

FREDERICK FREEDMAN

VASSAR COLLEGE

HISTORY OF
ENGLISH MUSIC

By

HENRY DAVEY

*Second Edition
Revised & Rewritten
With Appendix to
1921*

𝄞 DA CAPO PRESS • NEW YORK • 1969

ML
285
.D25
1969

A Da Capo Press Reprint Edition

This Da Capo Press edition of Henry Davey's
History of English Music is an unabridged
republication of the second edition,
revised and rewritten, published in London in
1921 by J. Curwen & Sons Ltd. It is reprinted
by special arrangement with the original
publisher.

Library of Congress Catalog Card Number 69-15620

Published by Da Capo Press
A Division of Plenum Publishing Corporation
227 West 17th Street
New York, N. Y. 10011
All rights reserved

Printed in the United States of America

HISTORY OF
ENGLISH MUSIC

A Choir-book of Henry VIII (see p. 87)

HISTORY OF
ENGLISH MUSIC

Curwen Edition 8217

By
HENRY DAVEY

Second Edition
Revised & Rewritten
With Appendix to
1921

J. CURWEN & SONS LTD
24 Berners St., London, W.1
Price 25s. Net Cash

PREFACE TO THE FIRST EDITION

A FEW words concerning the origin of this book are
necessary. It was already begun during an illness in
1892, and arrangements were made for its publication.
But upon further investigation, especially of the early
MSS., I perceived that the wealth of most valuable
material still unexamined was far greater than I had sus-
pected; so great, in fact, as to modify my previous opinions
concerning English music in the fifteenth and sixteenth
centuries. What I had previously written had largely to
be rejected, and the whole plan of the work was altered;
while three years' study has been necessary before I could
let the book be printed. A variety of accidents unfortunately prevented a systematic comparison of every
proof-sheet with the original sources of information, a test
I had intended to apply; should any mistakes have arisen
thereby, they will be duly published as they are discovered,
and corrected in future editions. The main hindrance,
in this and other respects, has, of course, been my living
away from London and the other great repositories of
MSS.; but I am able in consequence to have a clearer
view of the condition of music in the whole country,
of our defects and their causes, than I should probably
have acquired had I been a London musician, when it
would have been difficult or impossible for me to perceive
the effects of centralisation upon our musical life.

A minor but a very real hindrance has been the unsystematic indexing of many important publications. In
Bullen's catalogue of the Early English Books in the
British Museum, the subject-index under *Music* mentions
only the treatises of Bathe, Morley, and Butler, and Barley's 'Pathway'; Campion's treatise is put under *Counterpoint*, Ravenscroft's under *Harmony*, while Dowland's
translation of Ornithoparcus is concealed under *Singing!*
As for the musical compositions (which are included in
Bullen's catalogue), almost the only ones I have as yet
discovered in the index are Tye's setting of the 'Acts of
the Apostles,' indexed under *Bible*, and Leighton's 'Tears

or Lamentations of a Sorrowful Soul,' indexed under
Sorrowful. Any one who is making researches, not as yet
knowing what he may find, is seriously impeded by these
eccentricities, and risks altogether overlooking something
of importance. As a proof of this possibility, I may point
to the catalogue of the Cambridge University MSS.,
where the index has a heading *Music*, under which are
placed the lute-books and some other MSS.; but the part-
book of masses and motets (see page 85) is not there,
though it may be discovered by reading the index through,
for it is placed under *Anthems!* In fact, it was only by
reading that whole catalogue through that I discovered the
valuable MSS. 235, 1354, and 1940; two of these I have
mentioned in the Appendix, the other I observed just in
time to correct the proof of page 180. These are by no
means the only indexes whose defects have hindered
me.

At last, however, I have judged it expedient to let the
work appear, without waiting for further discoveries; and
English musicians can now obtain a clear and connected
idea of the great musical deeds of our forethers in the fifteenth, sixteenth, and seventeenth centuries. I have given
space to the account of works and performances rather
than to biographical details; and some fact not yet published in any History will be found on almost every page,
until I reach the account of Handel. Doubtless much
other material will yet be found; and may throw light on
various doubtful points. Another such choir-book as that
at Eton would indeed be welcome.

I have, unfortunately, not been able to give much help
towards elucidating the obscure origin of composition.
Since it is now certain that the polyphonic style was invented in England, it is especially the duty of Englishmen
to investigate this matter; as F. X. Haberl wrote in 1885
(*Bausteine fuer Musikgeschichte*, vol. i, p. 114), 'Through
the undeniable origination of Polyphony by Dunstable,
the interest in England for this period will, perhaps, be
quickened, so that the necessary materials for the origin of
Polyphony there (no doubt in the period when England
invaded France) may be obtained partly from theorists,

partly from archives and libraries, with that tranquility and perseverance which adorn the English race.'

This matter should, of course, have been the chief feature of my work; but I have discovered few new facts of importance concerning that period. I have, however, been able to show that the earliest known free instrumental compositions are also English, and this is in some respects the most important addition to general musical knowledge which I have been able to make.

On one point I much fear strong opposition, also misquotation and misapprehension. The standpoint I have taken up regarding the Puritans will, I doubt not, startle and offend very many; and careless readers will not apprehend my statements. Should any one think me wrong, I hope he will set forth his reasons at length; and he may do useful work by issuing a detailed Monograph on the subject.

Some may, perhaps, be surprised at not finding greater space given to the latest English works. When I published my *Student's Musical History* I found that a large proportion of critics opened the book at the end, and judged the whole work according to their agreement or disagreement with my opinions concerning living composers. All such will be disappointed in this book, from which, indeed, I should have been glad to exclude all mention of living men.

Objection may be brought, and with reason, to the complete absence of all practical illustrations; but if I had used examples, I should have required a great number, which would have increased the cost of the work to a price beyond the reach of many, and I wished to produce a work which all English musicians would read. Also, as so many of the early compositions are in separate parts, it would have been necessary to postpone the work still longer until I had copied and scored at least some hundreds of pieces from which to make a representative selection. Such a selection can be better made afterwards, when MSS. now unknown are brought to light. I hope to make a systematic examination of all known English works of the fifteenth and sixteenth centuries, and, perhaps, to issue a selection of the most important. It is because the early

music exists generally in separate parts that I have so
seldom inserted critical remarks.

The details of the work call for some allusion. I have
endeavoured to condense everything as much as possible,
and in archæological matters to simply indicate how those
interested in the subject may find what they seek; had I
minutely detailed my discoveries I should have filled
several volumes. Especially to facts which have been previously published I have allotted little space. I have
thought it advisable, in naming notes, to use the acoustical
notation, universal in Germany and always convenient; it
is very much simpler to use, for instance, d'', than 'D on
the fourth line of the treble stave.' Influence of the German language may, perhaps, be detected in the construction of some sentences; and I may also mention that I use
the word *Polyphony* (which in England is seldom and not
definitely employed) in the restricted technical sense in
which Continental musicians and writers use the word, to
denote *a style of artistic composition*, not a fortuitous or ex-
perimental conjunction of notes such as we may find in
some English and French MSS. of the thirteenth and
fourteenth centuries. To prevent any misunderstanding
on this point I appended a footnote to page 46 giving references to Grove's *Dictionary*, where Polyphony is thus
defined; but I think it advisable to distinctly state my
meaning here also, besides the remarks on page 69.

As regards authorities for my statements, I have not
usually quoted any which are taken from standard works,
such as Hawkins's and Burney's *Histories*, Grove's *Dictionary*, or Neal's *History of the Puritans*. Other references,
especially fresh discoveries, will be found in the Appendix. But the earlier chapters consist so largely of original
matter that few authorities are necessary.

I have not attempted to be systematic in spelling names;
I prefer archaic forms (such as Banastir, Fayrfax, Whyte,
Byrd, Sympson) in naming old musicians, but the variety
they used was very great.

I hope that at least some improvement may take place
in the attitude of our literary men to music, especially
music of the past. It is, indeed, not probable that

Macaulay, if writing now, would omit music from his description of the State of England in 1685; nor would Carlyle now write as if Italian Opera and ballet-divertissement constituted the whole music of the nineteenth century. Yet even lately, Mr. Maunde Thompson and Mr. Falconer Madan have written elaborately of Palæography without once mentioning musical MSS.; and our historians of literature still display unpardonable ignorance of the early songs, while our great Reviews generally employ half-learned amateurs for their occasional articles on music. A Monograph on the connection between English poetry and music, in the period from Chaucer to Spenser, is very much needed by students of both arts.

I have still remaining the very agreeable task of thanking those who have assisted me. Above and before all I must mention Mr. Taphouse, of Oxford, who, accidentally hearing that I was engaged upon this work, wrote in the kindest manner to place the whole of his magnificent library at my disposal. From the officials of the British Museum (especially from Mr. W. B. Squire and Mr. Hughes-Hughes), of the Bodleian Library, and of the Cambridge University Library, I have received most valuable help bestowed with every courtesy. To the librarians of Eton College, of Sion College, of several colleges at the Universities, and of the Fitzwilliam Museum, my warm thanks are due for permitting access to the treasures under their charge. Dr. F. X. Haberl (whom England must ever gratefully remember for his finally proving that Dunstable invented composition) very kindly sent me the poem discovered by Coussemaker, with his own varying readings, which I have inserted on page 55. For information sent or obtained through their assistance I must tender my sincere thanks to Mrs. Arthur Sassoon, Miss Middleton, Mr. Kidson, Dr. Alfred King, Dr. C. Wells, my old and endeared friends Mr. F. Corder and Mr. J. W. Nias, with many another who has rejoiced to add one stone to the work. Nor must I forget the publishers, who have done everything possible to produce the book in a style worthy of its purpose, yet at a price within the reach of all.

Finally, I leave the book, such as it is, to the judgment of the public, and especially of the professional musicians of England. Previously we have had no connected account of England's musical achievements; and now that I have undertaken the task, the greatest reward I could obtain would be the knowledge that my fellow-professionals appreciated my endeavours. With the hope that I may obtain that reward, I dedicate this History of English Music to the Incorporated Society of Musicians.

HENRY DAVEY.

GRAND PARADE, BRIGHTON,
   August 21*st*, 1895.

PREFACE TO THE SECOND EDITION

THIS History of English Music was completed in 1894, and published in September 1895. The edition was sold out several years since, but various causes, besides the World War, have combined to delay the reissue till a full quarter of a century after the original appearance. Much retouching in details has been effected; the principal additions will be found on pages 27–9 (early MSS.); 45–7, 56, 64–8 (Dunstable and his school); 135, 153 (Elizabethan sacred music); 159, 162, 164, 169–72 (madrigals and instrumental works); 184 (Catholics); 201 (Wilbye); 236–7, 243–6, 252, 271, 278 (Puritan doings); 392, and 395–7 (hymn-tunes). The Appendix brings the record up to date.

Though serious research had preceded writing and publication, a rather longer period of incubation would have been advantageous. The year 1896 saw the rising of Edward Elgar to a foremost place; and in 1900 the Old Hall MS. was first described. Little of real moment has occurred since, except that several very promising composers and performers appear annually.

Immediately on the publication, a number of enthusiastic appreciations, with or without qualification, recognised the additions the book had made to the knowledge of general musical history. Foreign and American critics were especially eulogistic. A rival historian, Dr. Willibald Nagel, who had already published his first volume, contributed a criticism to the *Monatshefte fuer Musikgeschichte*, not without carping, but paying me the highest compliments for the discoveries; and such authorities as Adler, Haberl, Riemann, Bewerunge, Koller, Ecorcheville, Soubies, Eitner, were equally appreciative. To be called *ein gediegener Historiker* by Riemann I consider a compliment which atones for any ignoring or cavilling from ordinary critics. I had never expected attention from foreign scholars, or that any applications for review copies would arrive from foreign periodicals, or that I should be complained of for not expounding

English matters sufficiently for foreigners' comprehension. But such things were. Professor Koller came from Vienna specially to study the MSS. I had described. Yet the book did not reach some authors occupied with English music, notably Van den Borren.

The reception at home was more qualified. There were some depreciations, even attacks; the points where I had feared attack were, however, left untouched. I feared complaints that I had but slightly noticed the manufacture of instruments, and musical journalism; but no critic alluded to these. Almost all discussed compositions only. Little allusion was made to my slight mention of living composers, and it was recognised that I had treated the entire course of our history. Yet, just then, adulation of our living men was pronounced. Such works as Mackenzie's *Rose of Sharon* and *Colomba*, Stanford's *Eden*, above all, Parry's *Judith* and English Symphony, were looked upon as almost of immortal value. So, twenty years earlier, had been Macfarren's oratorios! But contemporary work is, as a rule, outside the scope of a History; I discussed Sullivan's works only, as some of them displayed intrinsic novelty.

Rather to my surprise my defence of the Puritan attitude towards our art was accepted almost universally. There were but two dissentient voices in England; and elsewhere, every critic professed himself fully satisfied. Even those who had already stated contrary opinions—Nagel, for instance—came round to my view. But there have since been repetitions of the old slanders; it is sad to find Sir C. V. Stanford joining in that chorus.

But it would be affectation to ignore that serious objection was taken to my advocacy of the old statement that Dunstable solved the problem of musical composition. Not only ordinary journalists, but such authorities as Professor Niecks, declared themselves in opposition. They held by the theory that, to use Professor Niecks's phrase, 'there are no beginnings'; nobody ever 'invents' anything. This, I submit, is word-catching only. If I made the true assertion that Elias Howe invented the sewing machine, it would be idle to object that sewing without a machine existed earlier; and equally idle to say that photography was never invented, because the sun casts a shadow. *Invention*, the creation of an organism previously non-existent, is distinct from *Discovery*—the making known what previously existed. Columbus *discovered* America; Howe *invented* the sewing machine; as Dunstable solved the problem of musical composition. The word *invention* is justly applied to his achievement. And, similarly, though much less distinctly, with Hugh Aston's introduction of a definite style of composition for instruments.

'Sumer is icumen in' was, of course, adduced by my opponents. This objection falls to the ground if the Rota was in two handwritings, as many have supposed; but in any case the repetition of an unbroken tune does not solve the general problem, and unpleasant consecutives show the composer had not escaped from the thraldom of 'diaphony.' The very complete English treatises of the thirteenth and even the fourteenth century (see *infra*, pages 31, 45–7) show no knowledge of canonic devices or independent part writing generally. We must be content to accept the Rota as a mystery or a later work. Its existence, even if entirely in one handwriting, does not invalidate Dunstable's claim.

The few really venomous attacks on the History may now be forgotten. But it was remarkable that several quite favourable notices misnamed me strangely or gave a wrong account. Even Dr. Riemann said (and his blunder has been copied) that the book treated of our musical history 'since Purcell'! In conversation he expressed his regret for this strange slip of the pen, the more inexplicable as he used me for authority.

Some critics, looking upon the book as a literary production only, took the facts for granted, and condemned the want of style. I had not written for such readers, but for our native musicians; and devoted myself to the disinterring of new facts, and placing on record the gist of what we had done and what we had omitted to do.

Some points in this new edition may be noted. As in the original, I have not attempted to modernise or systematise old names. Though we have nothing to compete with the four thousand spellings of Shakespeare, we have a vast variety in such names as Cornysshe, Philipps, Shepherd, Whyte, Hingeston, and many others. The original Index was complained against, especially by Germans, as too detailed; it has been considerably shortened, only the material references being given.

Original investigators find their results appropriated by others, often without acknowledgment; naturally I have shared that fate. Those who have thus acted need not be specified. Dr. R. R. Terry has followed the opposite course, and has plainly stated that when asked where he discovers all the old English music, replies, 'In Mr. Davey's History.' Perhaps the most satisfactory result of my labours is that Dr. Terry was impelled to examine, score, and bring into practical use many unknown works I had mentioned.

We need not speculate on the future. The appearance of Elgar in 1896 discounted much of what I had written in 1895. We desire a British-born composer (also poet and painter) of the very first rank; such a composer may never appear again. Arts, like nations, rise, flower, decay, and die; it may now be the turn of music, as Rubinstein feared. In the meantime very much may be done to push forward our own productions if our composers will help. Ceremonial compositions have been left to foreigners. When an English couple are married, music of Wagner's precedes their arrival and music of Mendelssohn's accompanies their march out. Spohr's and Chopin's music is heard at funerals. At Florence Nightingale's burial the music, except 'Handel's Largo,' was all by Gounod. At Christmas every street resounds with a tune by Mendelssohn. Even after the World War the Armistice was greeted with 'Nun danket alle Gott.' In some cathedrals our dead warriors were commemorated by 'Brahms's Requiem.' British composers seem helpless to amend all this neglect. Elgar alone has done something; he has set us singing 'Land of Hope and Glory'; this is the single exception. Nor do our most ambitious efforts find their way to foreign concert-rooms.

France and Belgium suffered far more from the German invasion than England did; but German music is the staple of their concerts, English works being quite neglected. Most regrettable of all, many of our own greatest performers, pianists especially, ignore our own music entirely; it is common to see recital-programmes without one British item. Remembering all these unpleasant facts I cannot join in the usual expressions of complete satisfaction with present conditions; peace is cried when there is no peace.

But we can cherish the master-works of past centuries; and we can hope for the future.

HENRY DAVEY.

MONTPELIER ROAD, BRIGHTON.
May, 1921.

CONTENTS

CHAPTER I

BEFORE THE INVENTION OF COMPOSITION .. 2-44

Introduction.—The respective attitudes of the Anglo-Saxon and the Keltic races towards the arts.—The intimate connection between poetry and music in all ages till the invention of counterpoint, and even later.—Early allusions to Keltic skill.—Ecclesiastical music during the Anglo-Saxon period—Instruments delineated.—Proofs of the high advance of music in the twelfth century.—'Sumer is icumen in.' —Other remains of the thirteenth and fourteenth centuries.—Mediæval theorists.—Popular music.

CHAPTER II

THE INVENTION OF COMPOSITION (1400-53) 45-70

John Dunstable solves the problem of composition.—The fundamental novelty of his works.—A New Art.—Henry V's Chapel Royal. —Renown of the English musicians on the Continent.—The treatise of Gulielmus Monachus.—Faulxbourdon and Gymel.—Lionel Power's treatise.—This earliest school of composition rediscovered in the nineteenth century.—The known remains.

Chief Composers: Dunstable, Power, Benet, Hothby.

CHAPTER III

THE PERIOD OF THE INVENTION OF INSTRU-
MENTAL COMPOSITION (1453-1536) 71-105

After Dunstable.—The Chapel Royal.—Musical Degrees.—The Flemings surpass the English in Ecclesiastical Music.—Account of the existing MSS.—Biographical Notices of the Fayrfax School.—Instrumental Composition invented by Hugh Aston.

Representative Composers: Banester, Fayrfax, Aston, Taverner.

CHAPTER IV

THE REFORMATION: FROM THE DISSOLUTION
OF THE MONASTERIES TO THE DEFEAT OF
THE ARMADA (1536-88) 106-153

Immediate effects of the dissolution of the monasteries and the religious changes under Henry VIII, Edward VI, Mary, and Elizabeth. —Concentration of talent in the Chapel Royal.—The earliest English

CHAPTER V

CHAPTER VI

CHAPTER VII

anthems disused.—French models followed.—Concerts.—Celebrations of St. Cecilia's Day.—Sacred music.—Catches.—The dramas with music, or English operas.—Purcell follows Italian models and unites contrapuntal writing with intellectual declamation and melodic beauty, thus becoming the greatest English composer.—The age of the Restoration especially the greatest in English dramatic music.

Representative Composers: Child, Rogers, Lock, Humfrey and Purcell.

CHAPTER VIII

After Purcell.—Ruinous effects of centralisation.—Ecclesiastical composers of Queen Anne's reign.—Establishment of Italian opera.—Arrival of Handel; his English life, and invention of the concert-oratorio.—The Academy of Ancient Music, and the Madrigal Society.—The ballad operas.—Handel's successors.—Arne and his contemporaries.—Evolution of the glee.—Historians, and editors of old music.—The Handel Commemoration.—Folk-tunes written for by the Scotch and Irish poets.—The only enduring eighteenth-century secular music an outcome of the patriotic enthusiasm.

CHAPTER IX

Infant Prodigies.—Samuel Wesley.—Field and his Nocturnes.—Song-Composers.—The Philharmonic Society.—Choral Societies.—Hullah's Classes.—Tonic Sol-fa.—The Handel Festivals.—Choral Services become general.—English Opera.—Sterndale Bennett and Macfarren.—A dull period.—Organist-Composers.—Performers.—Concert Institutions.—Sullivan.—Fresh activity.—Defects to be amended.

APPENDIX

Changes in public taste.—Advances in the study of musical literature and science.—The present social position of the art and its professors.—The alterations and developments in surroundings.—Choral concerts and Church oratorio.—Orchestral concerts.—Chamber music.—Opera and operetta.—Great performers, vocal and instrumental.—Composers and compositions.

History of English Music

CHAPTER I

BEFORE THE INVENTION OF COMPOSITION

Introduction.—The respective attitudes of the Anglo-Saxon and the Keltic races towards the arts.—The intimate connection between poetry and music in all ages till the invention of counterpoint, and even later.—Early allusions to Keltic skill.—Ecclesiastical music during the Anglo-Saxon period—Instruments delineated.—Proofs of the high advance of music in the twelfth century.—'Sumer is icumen in.' —Other remains of the thirteenth and fourteenth centuries.— Mediæval theorists.—Popular music.

THE art of musical composition is an English invention. From the earliest dawn of history the necessary materials had been accumulating; but the secret of using them so as to create a structural art more than equal to any other art in its emotional power still lay hidden. In the Middle Ages the ecclesiastics of Western Europe began to perceive that something of hitherto unknown capabilities might be created; but during three or four centuries they could not exactly discover how to set about what they intuitively felt might be done. They were groping for a new art of which they had an inkling only. At last the secret was discovered in England by John Dunstable, who, by making each voice-part independent, raised music to the rank of a *structural* art, about 1400–20; and there is some reason to believe that we owe this to the patronage of the hero-king Henry V. Instrumental music first became artistic a little later, and this was accomplished by making it a specialised independent art, expressing what vocal music cannot express; and here again the achievement was one of English invention. Something had indeed been apparently attempted in Germany for the organ; but the specifically-instrumental florid style was, as far as we know, first adopted by Hugh Aston about 1500–20.

Of the many glories of England, the creation of artistic

music must be reckoned among the highest. Since it has not been well followed up, especially after 1700, the fact has been little known; and though the evidence is more than sufficient, and was fully admitted in the 18th century, yet it was afterwards doubted. Careful research has dispelled all objections, and musical historians now admit that the ancient statements were correct. A History devoted solely to English music is therefore necessary, to throw light on the origin of the whole art of composition, as well as for the record of subsequent deeds. Musical history may be divided into three periods, each of 161 years. The first (1400–1561) was the English period, although the Flemings surpassed the English in the middle portion; the second (1561–1722) was the Italian period, beginning with the composition of Palestrina's 'Improperia'; the third (1722–1883) was the German period, lasting from the completion of Bach's 'Wohltemperirtes Klavier' to the death of Wagner.* These rough divisions of course admit of modification in detail; thus in the Italian period, the English were still superior in instrumental music for many years, and afterwards Purcell was greater than any contemporary Italian composer; yet my divisions are in the main sufficiently descriptive. Since the original invention was English, the history of English music is longer than that of any other nation, and all through the period of Italian supremacy it remains important; but in the eighteenth and nineteenth centuries it is of little interest except as regards the performances of foreigners' works; and a General History of Music might after 1700 omit the compositions of Englishmen almost entirely.

Since England was distinguished so early, but afterwards fell behind, it has happened that a great deal of early music has remained quite a household possession. Not to mention hymn-tunes, some of which date from the Reformation, there are Rounds known to every child, which were, nevertheless, printed in Shakespeare's lifetime, or under the Commonwealth. Some of our most familiar folk-tunes are still older. And in a higher style,

* Then Dvořák and the Russians brought the Slavonic school to the front.

there are sacred and secular works (anthems and madrigals) which are over 300 years old, yet not antiquarian matters, but as alive as Shakespeare's words; while our choirs daily sing the harmonies of Tallis, and all our patriotic tunes, though later than these, are yet much older than the tunes of any other nation.

I may here mention that I do not in this work use the words 'England' and 'English' with scientific accuracy; by England I sometimes mean the forty English counties, sometimes England and Wales, sometimes all the British Islands. It is a fact, not without political significance, that there is no special name for the entire cluster of islands, nor for their inhabitants. There is no word which includes Englishman, Welshman, Scotchman, and Irishman, them all, and them only. In the previous paragraphs I have used England in the most restricted sense of the word, even excluding Wales. These considerations naturally lead to the question of ethnological differences among the various inhabitants of the British Islands.

The earliest inhabitants of Ireland were apparently Basques, and there are not wanting thinkers who suggest that the bulk of the population is still Basque, and that the Kelts were conquering intruders who formed an aristocratic caste. Cæsar found various nations in Britain; we may suppose they were principally Keltic. During the great movement of the Teutonic nations in the fifth century, successive invasions of Danish and Frisian immigrants drove the Christianised Keltic inhabitants of Southern Britain into the western and northern mountains, while many were forced over the Irish Sea, and others crossed the Channel to Brittany. After about 150 years of turmoil, we find Angles and Saxons possessing the fertile plains, and divided into several kingdoms. Christianity was introduced at the end of the sixth century, and prevailed everywhere before the end of the seventh. How far the English and Kelts intermarried is unknown; but there is evidence that Kelts abounded in the northern and south-western counties, besides their special mountain refuges in Wales and Scotland. In process of time the races doubtless intermingled, and their descendants have to this day a higher average of musical gifts than the more Teutonic inhabitants of the eastern and southern counties.

The two races, English and Kelts, who thenceforth shared the British Islands, are in many respects singularly opposed in temperament and capabilities. Many competent authorities hold that they are far more mingled than is usually supposed, and that the differences are climatic rather than racial; but for convenience I here take the rough popular line of demarcation which assigns England and the Scotch Lowlands to the Anglo-Saxons; and Wales, the Scotch Highlands, and almost all Ireland to the Kelts. As regards music, and indeed all culture, the difference is very perceptible, and may be stated as follows: The Kelts all have a decided gift for music and poetry, and even in earliest times were celebrated for it; the English are usually much less gifted, but when they possess the gift they can cultivate it to a much higher point than any Kelt ever can. It may be assumed that, as a rule, a high general average does not produce the highest genius; and the Teutonic race, both in England and Germany, is distinguished especially by the individuality and isolation of its constituents; while the Kelts— in France as in our islands—follow a general type, and are social, coherent, cultivated, easily polished into similarity. Thence proceeds the result that the average Englishman—especially of the south and east—is, in culture, inferior to the average Scotchman or Irishman; but our great geniuses, even the greatest men the world has even produced, come from the English. Shakespeare, the top and crown of the human race, came from Warwickshire; Newton,* the greatest of all philosophers, from Lincolnshire; Chaucer, Spenser, and Milton from London; Shelley from Sussex. The rest of the world can show no poet equal to Shakespeare, no philosopher equal to Newton, although the average Englishman has talent neither for poetry nor for abstract reasoning. The idea should be completely apprehended by all my readers; and it forms 'a good working hypothesis' in all branches of study. Many mistakes in practical matters have been

---

* See Goethe upon Newton's personality, *Zur Geschichte der Farbenlehre.*

made through a supposition that where there is occasional
high genius, there is necessarily also a high general
average; any one who supposed that a countryman of
Shakespeare necessarily has the poetic and dramatic sense
would certainly be mistaken, but not more so than those
who imagine that every compatriot of Beethoven is
musical. A visit to London killed all Heine's enthusiasm
for England, because he found the average Englishman
quite deficient in the qualities distinguishing the greatest
Englishmen. I allude, be it remembered, to intellectual
qualities only. The contrast between the English and the
Kelts need not be pushed too far; nor should we forget
that the Kymric Kelts vary somewhat from the Gaelic
Kelts. The Welsh have not the dramatic gift of the
Irish. But the various tastes of the races must not be
overlooked. In particular the delight of the English in the
forest and the ocean solitude finds no counterpart among
the Kelts. As our ancient ballad has it:

> ' In summer when the shawes be sheen,
>   And leaves be large and long;
> It is full merry in fayre forèst
>   To hear the foulës song.'

Nothing of this feeling is perceptible in the Keltic nature.
Our love for the sea, though not marked before the
Reformation, has been the greatest characteristic since,
and is likewise quite unshared by the Kelts. 'I have
loved thee, Ocean,' said Byron, and spoke the nation's
voice; and our songs utter the same note. With all its
commonplace of thought and clumsiness in expression,
Byron's 'Address to the Ocean' at once fixed itself in
the national heart as the utterance of the English feeling,
'I have loved thee, Ocean'; while the Irish imagination
shrinks from the destroying power.

A comparison between the different races should not
omit reference to their popular heroes, who embody at
least one side of the national ideal. England has evolved
a certain legendary Robin Hood, who lived with his
merry men under the greenwood tree; there is, indeed,
a story of his death by treachery, but it does not interest
the popular mind, which remembers only his jovial life.

Sharply opposed is the Keltic hero, Ossian, with the typical line: 'They went to the war, but they always fell.' Every Irish national hero has failed, and died picturesquely.

We may sum up all the foregoing disquisition in the result that the Teutonic races favour individuality often pushed into eccentricity; while the Kelts endeavour to conform to a fixed standard. The class distinctions loved by the English, and their multitudinous religious sects, as opposed to the equality and Catholic unity in France, are all symptoms of the tendency; also the dwelling in separate houses instead of flats. One Frenchman is fundamentally like all other Frenchmen; each Englishman is fundamentally different from every other Englishman in intellectual matters, all the separate units being fused into a nation by the consciousness that England expects each to do his duty.

It is, therefore, not a surprising fact that the English invented the art of musical composition, and the Germans carried it to its highest point; while neither the English nor the Germans are, as a rule, specially musical. In each nation the work done has been rather the deeds of separate individualities than the outcome of the general artistic life, and this has been so even more in Germany than in England, as far as our knowledge shows us. But while the adding of the loftiest spires—the German share of the edifice—is done last and in full sight of the world, the laying the foundations was done first and in silence; so that we have almost no particulars of the earliest stages, and must count ourselves extremely fortunate in not having lost all traces.

The ancient Kelts were passionately fond of poetry recited to harp accompaniment. Let it be remembered that lyric and narrative poetry were originally always sung, or rather chanted; in consequence, the criticism of poetry has been very much confused and entangled with musical terms. The words 'melodious,' 'tuneful,' 'singing,' 'harmonious,' are applied to the structure of verse in a sense quite different from their meaning in the tone-art; it is only since the invention of composition that music has acquired an *independent* life of its own, and any references to music in previous ages must be taken to mean, not an art of sounds, but an art of delivering words effectively. The connection between poet and musician has been sundered since the seventeenth century; previously they were not only closely connected, but were even identical in most cases. I shall have occasion to return to this matter repeatedly; it is of the greatest importance in literary as well as musical history, but has hitherto been overmuch neglected. Probably it will not be possible to discover the connection between music and the various forms of poetry used in the Middle Ages, as regards the constructive influence.

The bards of Wales and the Scottish Highlands, and their counterparts in Ireland, were held in the highest respect. The Irish bards had a legal right to free quarters; and both in Ireland and Wales a slave was not allowed to play the harp. O'Curry (in his 'Manners and Customs of the Ancient Irish') argues that the earliest forms of Irish lyric verse exactly fit certain Irish tunes, which had therefore a contemporary origin. His contention is plausible, though we have no indication of the oldest form of the tunes. The Welsh also claim that some of their tunes are of extraordinary antiquity, one, Morva Rhuddlan, having been traditionally produced just after the battle of Rhuddlan in 795. Whether traditional or even written evidence refers to poems or tunes is always doubtful. The oldest document dealing with Welsh music (now in the British Museum as Additional MS. 14,905) was written 1620–30, though professedly copied from a rather older MS.; it contains an account of the congress of bards, summoned in 1040 by Griffyd ap Conan, and mentioned by Giraldus Cambrensis. The Kelts used a peculiar stringed instrument called in Ireland the 'Crut,' in Wales the 'Crwth,' and in mediæval English the 'Crowd.' Venantius Fortunatus (a bishop of Poitiers), writing about 600, mentioned it in the famous lines: 'Romanusque lyra plaudat tibi, Barbarus harpa, Græcus achilliaca, *chrotta* Brittanna canat.' At a later period, the Crwth was a bowed instrument; but in earliest times it was apparently a harp of some kind. W. K. Sullivan, in his elaborate introduction to O'Curry's work, says that the allusions to the instrument in ancient Irish MSS. suggest that the Crut 'was a true harp, played upon with the fingers and without a plectrum.' The ancient Irish also had an instrument called 'Timpan'; at what period it was in use does not appear. W. K. Sullivan calls it a bowed instrument; in an Anglo-Saxon MS. the 'Timpanum' is a bagpipe. The Irish and Welsh harps were played by the pointed finger-nails. The names used by the two branches of the Keltic race are quite unlike, the Irish and Scotch Gaels calling the harp *Clairsach*, while the Kymry in Wales, Cornwall, and Brittany called it *Telyn*. The earliest known illustration of the Irish harp shows no front pillar; but later delineations all have this important addition. The folk-music of the Irish has been justly celebrated, though we know nothing of it before the English conquest; it was famous all over Europe during the Middle Ages. Students should not forget that Erse (ersche) does not mean specifically Irish, but Gaelic generally.

Of the Anglo-Saxon appreciation of music we hear less. A MS. of the eighth century (formerly at St. Blaise, but burnt in 1768) contained a representation of the 'Cythara Anglica,' which had fortunately been copied, and was published in Gerbert's *De Cantu Sacra*. It shows a true harp; the 'Cythara Teutonica' being a psaltery. But we know almost nothing of the life of our pagan forefathers during their settlement here. After the Christianising of the Anglo-Saxons in the seventh century, ecclesiastical music occupied nearly all attention. In 668 Theodore of Tarsus and Adrian of Naples came to England and taught the ecclesiastical plain-song. A story of Bishop Aldhelm's singing like a minstrel on the bridge at Malmesbury, and Bede's account of Caedmon's escaping from the revel as the harp was passed round, show a certain practice of the bardic art. In Beowulf the harp is called 'the wood of joy.' Since the Anglo-Saxon name *hearp* is the same as the Teutonic (which has been adopted by the Romance nations), there may have been some independent origin of the Clairsach, Telyn, Hearpe, and Cithara. The Horn was a favourite with the Anglo-Saxons.*

Some of the earliest Anglo-Saxon MSS. have representations of musical instruments. The Psalter from Canterbury, written about 700 (now British Museum, Cotton MS. Vespasian *a* 1), shows a representation of David playing a psaltery, with other performers blowing horns and dancing. Another drawing of David playing a psaltery is in a MS. at Durham, by tradition the work of Bede's own hands. The wonderful Lindisfarne Gospels of the same date afford us only a hornblower standing behind the figure of St. Matthew. Yet when St. Boniface was in Germany, the abbot of York wrote asking if the missionary could send him a player 'on that kind of harp which we call *rotta*,' as he had an instrument, but no performer. There is here a very fair proof that the 'Rote' was not a bowed instrument; nor a hurdy-gurdy, as Burney supposed it was. The word Rotta is probably a form of Chrotta, or Crwth; and it is only reasonable to suppose that the old name would be retained even after the bow had been used for the vibrating agent.

The Anglo-Saxons were at a very early period acquainted with organs, which are mentioned even in Aldhelm's poem, 'De Laude Virginitatis.' Not long after Aldhelm's death (A.D. 709) was written the celebrated Psalter containing the Athanasian Creed, and formerly among the Cotton MSS., but lent and not returned, and since 1718 at Utrecht; this Psalter contains a representation of an organ played by two monks. The illustrations to this MS. were copied in a later psalter, now at Trinity College, Cambridge; the picture of an organ has been often engraved. The Utrecht Psalter has been facsimiled; its date has been much discussed, but all authorities, except one—Sir T. D. Hardy—agree that it is not older than the eighth century. The exception assigned it to the sixth, and believed it to be one of the books brought to Canterbury by Augustine, and not Anglo-Saxon work; no other palæographer agrees with this.

Bede makes happy references to harp-playing, to the

* See J. F. Hodgett's ' Older England,' Vol. II.'

consonances of the octave, fourth, and fifth, and to the
semitones 'in the high as well as the low strings,' in
his Commentary on the Fifty-second Psalm. The treatise
on 'Mensurable Music,' which in some mediæval MSS.
was attributed to him, is obviously of a much later date,
and was written by a Frenchman under the pseudonym
of Aristote. Bede refers to organs twice.

Alcuin, of York, who died in 804, and was the great
restorer of learning in the West, wrote on all the seven
liberal arts. His catechism of music is preserved in a MS.
at Vienna, and was printed by Gerbert in 1784; it
describes the eight modes, authentic and plagal.

The story which assigns to King Alfred the foundation
of a Professorship of Music at Oxford University, and
the appointment of Friar John, from St. David's, is taken
from the Annals of Winchester; it is probably a pure myth.

In the tenth century we hear much of music in connection with Dunstan. He made an organ 'with brass
pipes,' and was also skilled in secular minstrelsy. The
story of his harp which vibrated of itself is familiar, and
sounds in no way unreasonable when we remember the
draughty Saxon houses. Count Elwin at this period gave
an organ which cost thirty pounds to Ramsey Abbey;
one was given to Abingdon Abbey by Dunstan, and other
churches and abbeys were furnished by him.

The most remarkable account of any organ ever written
refers to one built at Winchester by Bishop Elphege (who
died in 951), and was written by Wulstan, a monk who
died in 963. He says that *seventy* men were required to
blow it, that there were 400 pipes, and forty tongues,
'twice six' bellows above, and fourteen below. As it was
'on a double ground' there may have been differing
effects of wind-pressure. It was played by two monks,
'each of whom manages his own alphabet. . . . They
strike the seven differences of joyous sounds, adding the
music of the lyric semitone,' that is, B♭; a fact of interest
as showing the system followed. Of course no execution
was possible on an instrument played by slides, though
the two organists may have sometimes tried two-part
harmony.

The oldest known Neums are in the Codex Amiatimus, a copy of the Vulgate prepared by Ceolfrid, Abbot of Wearmouth, for his journey to Rome in 716; they are written above the Lamentations and Benedicite. The oldest printed by Gerbert were from a MS. of Aldhelm; they were also facsimiled in A. Schubiger's treatise. Aldhelm mentions that he used signs over the words. Among the Cotton MSS. containing Neums are Nero *a* 1–2; the remains of Otho *a* 3; and Vespasian *d* 12. The fire of 1731 robbed the world of Arts. 1, 3, and 4 in Vitellius *a* 6 (which contained Hymns to the Virgin, Augustine of Canterbury, Theodore, and Adrian, 'notulis musicalibus insigniti'), and of Art. 3 in Vitellius *d* 20, which contained a Hymn to St. Cuthbert. Harley MSS. 110, 863, 1117, 1772, 2637, 3020, and 3091; Arundel MS. 340; the Winchester Tropary at Oxford, Bodley MS. 775; Nos. 190 and 473 of the Parker MSS. at Corpus Christi College, Cambridge, and the Pontifical of Dunstan (MS. lat. 943 in the Bibliothèque Nationale at Paris) have Neums of the usual kind. But some Anglo-Saxon MSS. have Neums quite unlike these; they are squarely drawn, often consisting of perpendicular strokes, and are very carefully placed as to height above the words. So distinct are they that the stave-lines are not needed. While, as a rule, it may be taken that these carefully-heighted Neums are later than the others, it does not appear that they are a development of the older notation; they seem like an independent growth, and I have seen no such Neums in MSS. of other countries. The Anglo-Saxon MSS. containing these angular care-fully-heighted Neums are: No. 267 of the Parker MSS. at Cambridge; and (in the British Museum) Royal MSS. 1 *d* 3, 5 *e* 7, and 8 *c* 13; Cotton MSS., Julius *a* 6 (the last leaf), Tiberius *b* 8; Caligula *a* 14, the remains of Galba *a* 14, Vitellius *a* 19, Cleopatra *b* 13; Harley MSS. 2961, 3033; Addit. MS. 15461. I have seen no instances of stave-lines before the Conquest; even Vitellius *e* 12, which contains a litany in which the Conqueror's queen Matilda is mentioned, is quite without them. This MS. was badly damaged by the fire of 1731; and the writing

was so altered by the heat that one cannot know whether
the Neums were carefully-heighted or not. Formerly the
Winchester Tropary in the Bodleian Library was thought
to exhibit the earliest known use of a four-lined stave;
the microscope shows that this portion of the MS. is a
superimposed later addition. A five-lined stave appears
in the middle of the Cotton MS. Vespasian *d* 12; but
it is obviously a later insertion to fill up a blank space.
In Caligula *a* 14, carefully-heighted Neums are used as
far as folio 36; then a four-lined stave follows.

There are some slight indications that harmony was
known. A remarkable Winchester Tropary of the tenth
century (now No. 473 in the Parker MSS.) has been
thought to exhibit traces of harmony, as it is really a
double Tropary, and the Neums in the two portions
of the book do not agree; but they are not carefully-
heighted, or sufficiently comprehensible to enable us to
judge whether they were used for two-voiced singing.
Hucbald, it must be remembered, lived from 840–930;
and his treatise doubtless soon found its way into England.
In the Bodleian Library is a MS. (Codex Bodley 572)
which on one page has two lines of letter-notation above
the words; there is no indication of the length of the notes,
nor is there any evidence that the two lines were intended
to be sung simultaneously. The MS. was written about
A.D. 1000, probably in Cornwall. Although the two
organists whom we see depicted in the Utrecht Psalter,
and are mentioned by Wulstan as required at Winchester,
may have tried the effect of simultaneous sounds, it is
probable that the use of any other note besides the one
prescribed by the ritual would for a long time be supposed
heretical. We have no evidence as to the tuning employed;
with the Pythagorean and Boethian tuning, thirds are too
discordant to be used in harmony. This point is important, as will be seen later.

Towards the end of the Anglo-Saxon period there are
some most interesting matters to chronicle in connection
with secular music. The Saxon word *gligg* (modern
English *glee*) refers to all kinds of entertainment, as was
natural in the days when a minstrel sang, played, danced,

and did anything else to please or astonish. We read of King Alfred disguising himself as a minstrel, to gain admittance to the Danish camp; and a Danish king retorted the stratagem on Athelstan, but was discovered. The Cotton MS. Tiberius *c* 6, probably written about the year 1000, or later, contains a description of musical instruments, with figures. The Nabulum, Psalterium, Tympanum (bagpipe), Cythara, Tintinnabulum, Sambuca, Pennola, Bombylium, and Corus are briefly mentioned. Some are delineated; there is a large picture of David playing a psaltery. Later in the same MS. is a representation of David and his 'gleemen'—Asaph, Jeduthun, Ethan, and Heman. In the middle sits David playing a psaltery; one of his gleemen is tossing knives and balls; the other three have musical instruments, one of which is bowed. This is the earliest representation of the *fithele* known, and has been repeatedly engraved; in Strutt, Chappell, and 'Grove' (*Art.*, Violin) accurate copies may be seen. The bridge is not shown. The other two gleemen have a bagpipe and a horn.

This introduction of the bow marks an enormous advance in instrumental music. Whether it was brought from India, whether it was an original Anglo-Saxon invention, whether it was another of the artistic discoveries of the Irish, we have no evidence. All we can say is that one of the earliest known representations of a musician playing a bowed instrument is in an Anglo-Saxon MS. of the tenth or eleventh century.

There are also illustrations of harps and trumpets in Harl. MS. 603; of a harp and a double-flute in Cotton MS. Cleopatra *c* 8; both of the tenth or eleventh century. Lansdowne MS. 431 contains a calendar apparently written about 1064; one would judge the work to be rather later. The initial letter of the psalter contains a harpist and a figure playing a fithele with a very long bow. These long bows are usual in later illustrations, but I have seen no other as ancient as the eleventh century.

The Norman Conquest assisted the progress of music in England by increasing the communication with the Continent, and bringing here many leading foreign

ecclesiastics, who must have spread the knowledge of
foreign advances in harmony and notation. As already mentioned, the litany praying for Queen Matilda, and probably
actually used at her coronation in 1067, is without even
a stave-line. No English instances of transitional notation
(with one or two lines) are known to me; but Guido
d'Arezzo's treatises were already brought here directly
after the Conquest, as one exists at Durham in a MS.
which belonged to William (first bishop of Durham), who
died 1096. Guido's use of two lines would be quickly
appreciated. There are other treatises in the Durham
MS., including one on the Chromatic and Enharmonic
Genera, and one on the Monochord 'secundum Boetium
et Guidonem.'

The Norman Conquest had, however, a permanently
mischievous effect on the English language, musically
considered. Long after the separation of England from
Normandy in 1205, French still remained the language of
the Court and upper classes; it was not till the fourteenth
century that English was officially recognized. The
literary classes in the monasteries wrote in Latin or French
only; Anglo-Saxon was left to the ignorant for 200 years,
and when it finally prevailed it had become considerably
different from the tongue of Alfred; declensions and
conjugations had disappeared, auxiliary verbs had taken
the place of inflexions. The worst change, as regards
music, was the introduction of the French hissing plural;
the Teutonic plural *en* was retained only in a few elementary cases (*men, women, children, oxen*). The feminine
inflexion *ess* is another unmusical introduction; also the
change of the Latin termination *tion*, now pronounced
zhon. We have, *per contra*, lost the gutturals, which were,
beyond doubt, as much a feature of Anglo-Saxon as of
other Teutonic languages; we have, for instance, softened
Ecgberht into Egbert. Yet the losses have far outweighed
the gains. The English of Chaucer's time still remained
a very good language for music, far superior to that which
Shakespeare knew; Chaucer would have written 'the
freshë streamës' where Shakespeare wrote 'the fresh
streams.' But our language has, since Shakespeare's time,

worsened yet further. Milton wrote of 'the mild o-ce-an,' which we now call the *oshun*; and we turn *talk-ed* into *talkt*, and say that a mourner *watcht thro' the night*, and that *wasps sting*. Handel (in *Solomon*) had to set *obeys the artist's string*. At what time the vowel sounds were changed is not known; the almost complete disuse of the broad *a* is a serious loss, but not so fatal a defect as the masses of consonants, especially sibilants, which are the greatest stumbling-blocks in modern English speaking and singing.

Directly after the Conquest we hear of advances in musical art. Osbern of Dover is said to have invented 'new points of music,' and wrote a treatise; William of Malmesbury calls him 'Musica certe omnium sine controversia maximus.' He was patronized by Lanfranc, who made him precentor of Canterbury Cathedral; Boston of Bury supposes he flourished about 1074, which agrees with this fact. Johannes [Cotto], more particularly mentioned later in this chapter, left a treatise, printed by Gerbert; it is almost certain that Cotto was English. He mentions Guido d'Arezzo.

Osmund, Bishop of Salisbury, established Sarum Use in 1077; it is said to have been the result of a quarrel at Glastonbury between the Norman abbot and the English monks, who objected to any change in the ancient ritual. Osmund's compilation in time prevailed over nearly all England. The Bishop of Salisbury, by ancient custom, claimed the office of precentor at the College of Bishops of Canterbury Province.

The twelfth century, excepting the anarchy of Stephen's reign, was a period of very great advance and prosperity in England. The reaction from the Norman Conquest was perceptible at the beginning of the century, when Henry I strengthened his right by marrying an Anglo-Saxon princess. Before the end of the century, Gothic architecture had been completely established. The Crusades had opened up communications with the Eastern world. The vast Continental possessions of the Angevin kings promoted intercourse. Science was cultivated, however timidly. But in England, as elsewhere, the arts were especially followed. Poetry, painting, and, above all, architecture, were materially improved; while music seems to have been so much cultivated that the ire of precisians was aroused. Secular music was not yet independent of poetry; but ecclesiastical music is referred to by two writers in a manner which shows that already attempts were made to establish that independent art which was finally invented 300 years later.

The word *minstrel* came into England with the Normans. Taillefer, the Conqueror's minstrel, rode singing before the Norman army at the battle of Hastings, and made a preliminary single attack such as we read of in Homer, and as Commissioner Romilly had the singular fortune to behold in our days in the South Sea. Henry I's minstrel, Rahere, founded the hospital and priory of St. Bartholomew, Smithfield, one of the finest remains of old London. John of Salisbury spoke severely of the riches heaped upon the amusement-makers of every kind. When Becket visited Paris in 1159 he entered the French towns in great state, the procession being headed by 250 boys, in groups of six, ten, or more, who walked singing in English 'according to the custom of his country.'

The allusions to ecclesiastical music are more essential to musical history than the stories of minstrelsy, which concern poetry rather than music. There is a very striking account in the *Speculum Charitatis* of Ailred, or Ethelred (1109–66), Abbot of Rivaulx Abbey, Yorkshire. The passage clearly proves the use of harmony, and of the 'Hocket,' which implies the interspersing of rests, and the knowledge of time-divisions. The words 'Unde in ecclesia tot Organa, tot Cymbala?' point to the use in the ritual of other instruments besides the organ; and the whole account is the clearest evidence that all possible elaboration was employed in the Church music of the twelfth century. Prynne quoted the passage in *Histriomastix*, translating it as follows:

'Let me speake now of those who, under the show of religion, doe obpalliate the business of pleasure. . . . Whence hath the Church so many Organs and Musicall Instruments? To what purpose, I pray you, is that terrible blowing of Belloes, expressing rather the crakes

of Thunder, than the sweetnesse of a voyce? To what purpose serves
that contraction and inflection of the voyce? This man sings a base,
that a small meane, another a treble, a fourth divides and cuts
asunder, as it were, certaine middle notes. One while the voyce is
strained, anon it is remitted, now it is dashed, and then againe it is
inlarged with a lowder sound. Sometimes, which is a shame to
speake, it is enforced into a horse's neighings; sometimes, the mascu-
line vigour being laid aside, it is sharpened into the shrilnesse of
a woman's voyce; now and then it is writhed, and retorted with a
certaine artificiall circumvolution. Sometimes thou may'st see a
man with an open mouth, not to sing, but, as it were, to breathe out
his last gaspe, by shutting in his breath, and by a certaine ridiculous
interception of his voyce, as it were to threaten silence, and now
againe to imitate the agonies of a dying man, or the extasies of such
as suffer. . . . In the meantime, the common people standing by,
trembling and astonished. admire the sound of the Organs, the noyse
of the Cymballs and Musicall Instruments, the harmony of the
Pipes and Cornets.'

Prynne's translation is slightly influenced by the
musical practice of his own age; but Ailred's words,
'Hic succinit, ille discinit, alter supercinit, alter medias
quasdam notas dividit et incidit,' show that attempts had
been made at independent voice-parts. The ecclesiastics
of the twelfth century were clearly on the right path for
musical progress; yet it was not till 250 years after
Ailred's death that the problem was finally solved.

Almost exactly contemporary with Ailred was John
of Salisbury (1120–80), who wrote in the same vein
against the elaborate Church music, in his *Polycraticus*,
Book I. His words give no exact information, but he
speaks of 'proecinentium et succinentium, canentium et
decinentium, intercinentium et occinentium proemolles
modulationes'; he abuses the Phrygian Mode.

The treatise from Bury St. Edmunds known as Coussemaker's Anonymus 4, which he believed of the twelfth
century, is of the late thirteenth or fourteenth, as it
quotes Odington; it is accordingly examined later in this
chapter.

We have now to turn to another side of twelfth-century
art. There remain most important accounts of Keltic
folk-music. Ireland, where early art had worked wonders
in the seventh century, was first invaded by the Normans

in 1169, partially subjugated, and brought more into connection with the rest of Europe. John of Salisbury and Giraldus Cambrensis (1146–1220) have told us much of the island and its inhabitants. Giraldus, in his *Topographica Hibernica* III, 10, inserted an admirable account of Irish playing. He found nothing to praise in Irish life, except the music:

'Only in musical instruments I find commendable the diligence of that nation; in these it is incomparably superior to every nation we have seen. For the performance is not heavy and gloomy (as among the Britons, to whom we are accustomed), but is rapid and dashing, yet a gentle and pleasing tone-effect. It is astonishing that in so great a rapidity of fingering, musical proportion should be retained, and art in everything satisfied, through involved changes, and harmonies of manifold complication; swift in delicacy, equal in equality, concordant in dissonance, the consonant melody is adhered to and completed. Whether the chords are taken by the fourth or the fifth, they yet always preserve the scale.' (So I understand the words, 'Semper tamen ab B.')

Giraldus, however, adds that Scotland and Wales were then striving to equal Ireland; and in the opinion of many Scotland had not only equalled, but far surpassed its teacher. He says the Irish used two instruments—cithara and tympanum; the Scotch three—cithara, tympanum, and chorus; the Welsh also three—cithara, tibiæ, and chorus. What he meant by tibiæ and chorus we cannot exactly decide; almost certainly, the tympanum was the bagpipe.

In a later work, *Descriptio Cambriæ*, Giraldus repeats this account. He then proceeds to the celebrated description of Welsh singing, one of the best known passages in musical history. The Welsh, he relates, do not sing their folk-tunes in unison, as other nations do, but in harmony, so that there are as many different parts as there are singers, 'and at length the diversities are united in one soft consonance and organic melody under the sweetness of B flat,' by which he doubtless means to say that everything sounded well, and in its proper key. Then he mentions that the inhabitants of northern England sing in two parts, and even the children naturally fall into the same habit. Since the English elsewhere do not sing in harmony, he judges that the Northerners learnt the style from the 'Dacians' and Norwegians who settled in that part of Britain.

Gerald's account is the more valuable as he was a restless, active, able man, who repeatedly visited France and Italy; and consequently speaks with authority upon the contrast between the harmonious singing of Wales and northern England, and the unisonous singing of other countries and the rest of England. Bold conjectures have been built upon this foundation; some have argued that harmony was a British invention, and the discovery of the laity, not of the Church. The account has also been linked with a story that harmony was invented by Bede, from whom it may have been supposed to spread over Northumbria. Some have said that the 'sweetness of B flat' proves that the Welsh folk-music was in the modern key-system, instead of the modal system of the Church. The use of thirds as harmonies by the organists of 'that part of England which is called West-country' (see p. 32) should be remembered in connection with this description.

In considering the ancient accounts of music, as of other matters, the dates at which these accounts were written should be borne in mind. We must remember that Giraldus visited Ireland 500 years after the 'Book of Kells' was illuminated. There is a natural tendency to confound all ages of a distant past; and doubtless in the future, if musical history be still studied, the time of Dunstable will seem practically contemporaneous with the time of Elgar. Musicians, unless they are antiquaries, will think of the two as contemporaneous. It was for this reason that I have deferred the accounts of Welsh and Irish folk-music till now, instead of inserting them early in the chapter.

Before quitting the twelfth century, I must quote evidence that an artistic conception of style in musical composition was inchoate. The mysterious personage Alain de L'Isle, or Alanus de Insulis (who wrote under the name 'Anticlaudianus'), may have been English; a poem by him is printed in the collection of Anglo-Norman

satirists which forms Part 59 of the Rolls Series. This
poem describes how Music (as second in the Quadrivium)
was entrusted with the fabrication of the second wheel
for Wisdom's chariot; and incidentally touches upon the
powers of the art, among which is included its variety—
'the mingling of laughter with tears, gravity with fun,
now it sounds enharmonically, now feigning sadness it
mourns in ditonic song, now it sports in chromatics.'*
Here again we have evidence of the use of the major
third; it was evidently considered a plaintive interval,
whether of harmony or melody does not appear.

Alexander Neckam (1157–1217), foster-brother of
Richard I, wrote on the scholastic aspect of the liberal
arts. In a poem, 'De Laudibus Divinæ Sapientiæ,' he
includes among the functions of music the explaining
why man has two eyes, two nostrils, two arms, etc.; but
in a more important prose treatise on the same subject,
he turns against these subtleties, asking why such matters
should be included in the art of sound. This question,
one would think, must have entered the minds of many,
but probably the philosophers of that age were only too
eager to work out a verbal connection between the most
diverse matters.

At this time the intellectual centre of the world was
certainly Paris, which was in great prosperity and celebrity
from 1000–1300. Neckam wrote most enthusiastically
of the University. English students were so numerous
there that they formed one of the four schools into which
the University was divided. If the composers of Paris
were in advance of the rest of Europe, as has been argued,
then their works must have been familiar to thousands
of students who subsequently returned to England; but
all the accounts of early Parisian musicians depend upon
the anonymous treatise from Bury.

We may now sum up the results attained by the end
of the twelfth century. Harmony was in use in the Church
music, with syncopation and the Hocket, and apparently

---

* 'Quomodo mutato se mutat Musica cantu
  Cum lacrimis risus, cum ludis seria texens
  Nunc inharmonice resonat, nunc tristia fingens
  Ditonico cantu luget, nunc chromate ludit.'

some variety of instrumental accompaniment. The folk-music of Wales was in harmony, and that of northern England in two-voiced harmony. In instrumental performance the Irish had been notably superior to other nations, but the Scotch were beginning to rival them. The organ, bagpipe, harp, and various kinds of stringed instruments were in use; the bow was applied to the latter.

Chappell claims that even Canonic Imitation 'seems to be comprised in the words *præcinentium et succinentium, canentium et decinentium*,' used by John of Salisbury; but they give us no clear idea of anything except complication of some unknown kind. A more striking passage occurs in the *Contra Avaros* of Walter Mapes (born 1143, and last mentioned in 1196); he had been at Rome in 1179, and saw much of the venality of the Pope's officers. His satire is principally aimed at them. Puns abound in the poem; for instance, in line 62 there are three:

'Libra libros, reos res, Marcum vincit marca.'

Ten lines later occurs the passage here in question, punning upon Canons and Rounds:

'Commissus notario, munera suffunde;
Statim causæ subtrahet quando, cur, et unde,
Et formæ subjiciet canones rotundæ.'

There is no meaning apparent, unless Canons and Rounds were familiar forms. Yet no Canon is known older than the fifteenth century, except one now to be discussed.

We pass into the thirteenth century, which saw the building of Salisbury, Chartres, Rheims, and Amiens Cathedrals; which was adorned by the piety of Francis of Assisi and of Hugh Grosseteste, the intellect of Roger Bacon, the culture and magnificence of Frederick the Second; and which was finally crowned with the glory of Dante's Vision. And in this thirteenth century appeared, for one moment, the art of musical composition. How this came about we shall never know, nor yet whether the piece that is left us is the one survivor of many such, or was a solitary inspiration. So inexplicable is its production that in a simpler age one might have supposed some miraculous agency had interposed, and a tale such as Bede tells of Caedmon might have grown around the work. To fully appreciate the historical importance of this piece, one must know the other remains of the thirteenth century—such helpless groping after good effect as may be seen in the Montpellier MS., the works of Adam de la Hale, or the Tournay Mass.* Unlike all these, the Rota written at Reading Abbey is an artistic composition, and may be performed at the present day, or centuries hence, without antiquarian thought or intention, as a piece of music heard for its beauty alone.

The Rota is contained in Harley MS. 978. The first allusion to it was made about 1710, when the MSS. were catalogued; Wanley, a good musician as well as a learned antiquary, described it as the oldest Canon he had seen; Hawkins referred it to the fifteenth century; Burney was inclined to give an older date. Both these historians, and afterwards Forkel, provided solutions; very many writers have discussed the mystery. Some argue that the directions for singing in canon are in a later handwriting. All authorities upon mediæval manuscripts unhesitatingly declared that the writing was of the thirteenth century, and of the earlier or middle part. An autotype facsimile may be seen in Plate 125 of the Palæographical Society's publications, with the date 1240. Chappell has printed a facsimile in colours,† and gave much study to the matter, in the course of which he noticed the allusion in Walter Mapes's satire, and also that the handwriting of the early part of the MS. is that of JOHN OF FORNSETE, who kept the Cartulary of Reading Abbey (now in the Cotton MSS. as Vespasian *e* 5). Fornsete (now Forncett) is a village in Norfolk. John of Fornsete's handwriting is still found in the Cartulary, in an entry dated 1238; then it disappears, and his successor has written in the calendar for 1239, on St. Wulstan's day, 'Ora, Wulstane, pro nostro fratre, Johanne de Fornsete.' The leaf containing the Rota was probably written in or about 1226. There is, of course,

---

* Specimens sung at Paris in June, 1914, were unbearably discordant.

† Another facsimile was given in an English edition of Naumann's work where the Rota is, without evidence, called a ' Northumbrian ' Round. Mr Hurry, of Reading, published another.

no proof that the Rota had not been written at an earlier
date, but the language shows it cannot be much older.
In default of further evidence, we must accept the theory
that the English words, the Latin words, and the music
were all alike due to the inspiration of John of Fornsete.

The MS. begins with some Antiphons on a five-lined
stave. Then follow pieces without words on two staves,
marked *Cantus Superior* and *Cantus Inferior*. Next is a
motet, 'Ave gloriosa mater,' with a second text in very
old French; the music is written in score upon three
staves so placed as to resemble one stave with fifteen lines.
This motet is also to be found in the Montpellier MS. A
separate fourth voice has been added in this Reading MS.

On the next page appears the Rota, which (like the
motet) is written in the notation given in Franco's tract
on Mensurable Music, but is without a time-signature.
The Rota has several special features, which both add to
its musical value and, from an historical point of view,
make it yet more inexplicable. It is not in any of the eight
ecclesiastical modes, but in the modern key of F major,
having a B flat marked on each stave, just as in a modern
composition in one flat. The letter C is also written as
a clef. The staves are six-lined. The melody has the
compass of a ninth, more than most tunes have even now.
The composition is a double Canon for six voices; no
other composition for more than four voices, and no
Canon at all, is heard of for two centuries after. There
are exact directions for singing it, from which it may be
argued that Canons were at that time unfamiliar. It is
a secular piece (though a sacred poem is also given), in
the midst of ecclesiastical music for the use of the
monastery. The words express the genuine English
delight in nature, in the cheerful life of sweet Maytime,
in the happiness of animals, in the song of the cuckoo;
and John of Fornsete must have fully shared that sentiment which has created Robin Hood and his merry men.
Very fitting is it, that the earliest composition, being
English, should be inspired by the thoroughly English
sentiment, joy in country life.

How did such a complicated piece of real music, fresh

and welcome even now, come into being in the early thirteenth century?* Evolution is the one formula which our age applies to all things—inorganic and organic nature, religion and politics, science and art. But here the law of evolution seems to fail; a completely organized complex art-form suddenly appears in existence, without any known previous attempts, though the words of Mapes, and even of Ailred, are some little evidence that attempts had been made.

At a miraculous command, we are told, Caedmon began the strain of English poetry. But he did not begin a new art. John of Fornsete did more than Caedmon; he for a moment created an absolutely new art, an art of which ancient Greece knew even less than the carver of the Easter Island idols knew of the art of Phidias, or the woad-stained Briton knew of the art of Titian. Supernatural assistance was more called for in the uniting of harmony, rhythm, and melody, which John of Fornsete first achieved, than in transferring the existing art of poetry to another language and the service of another religion; and rather than to the watcher in the stable at Whitby, it was to the monk in the scriptorium above the Thames, that One came, not by night, but by a spring morning, and the Presence said to him, 'Compose.' John of Fornsete knew not that hundreds of years afterwards his music would be sung, and be sung again at the demand of the listeners; still less could he have imagined how mighty an art he had called into being, and to what dizzy heights of sublimity men would arise on its magic pinions. But he obeyed the command to compose, and wrote down the 'Sumer is icumen in' which we all love.

And then the art of music, made independent and structural for one moment, died again, and came not into life for another 200 years. What an Englishman had begun no other Englishman took up and carried on. Still the art of sound remained timidly subservient to

---

* Even its faults are remarkable ; the ground-bass or burden sung by the two basses often produces consecutive fifths with the upper parts. Rimbault, indeed, said there was an ancient copy without the ground-bass in the Pepysian library, and published the piece thus, as a Canon for four voices ; but Rimbault is untrustworthy.

ecclesiastical ritual and minstrels' verses all through the thirteenth and fourteenth centuries. No other canon is known, until the little round made in 1453 to honour John Norman, Lord Mayor of London; a piece child-like in simplicity when compared with 'Sumer is icumen in.' None of the exhaustive treatises on music, whether English or Continental, mentions such a resource. These considerations make the Rota all the more an inexplicable production; it appears as the morning-star of musical composition, rising resplendent but solitary, and long before the full glory which dawned in England during the fifteenth century, which reached its meridian in Germany long afterwards, and which now seems distinctly declining.

Of other attempts during the thirteenth century, the most remarkable are preserved in Arundel MS. 248. Though interesting historically, they have not absolute permanent musical value, as the Rota has. The MS. was written towards 1300. There is a piece for two voices, 'O labilis, O flebilis hominum conditio'; antiphons; then the 'Angelus ad Virginem' mentioned by Chaucer, with an English version, 'Gabriel, from ebene king,' to an un-harmonized tune of some merit. Two more tunes follow, with English words. The most important musical relics of the MS. are a two-voiced 'Jesu Cristes milde moder,' and a three-voiced 'Salve virgo virginum,' with both Latin and French words. There are other songs; and at the end some two-voiced harmony without words. All the harmonized pieces are written with the voice-parts in score, looking like a continuous many-lined stave, though not really such. The exact correspondence between the lines of music and lines of poetry raises a doubt whether harmony was intended. Similarly in Lambeth Palace MS. 457. There is another setting of 'Angelus ad Vir-ginem' in Cotton MSS. App. 29.

Some exceedingly crude and elementary songs are preserved in MSS. of the thirteenth century; one from the Douce Collection was printed in J. Stafford Smith's *Musica Antiqua*; there is another, to almost Anglo-Saxon words, in a MS. at the Guildhall, London. A comparison

of these, or of the Tournay Mass, or of Guillaume
Machaut's 'Coronation Mass,' or of Adam de la Hale's
remains, all unbearable to modern ears, with 'Sumer is
icumen in,' will show how far superior to all music of the
thirteenth and fourteenth centuries was the Rota from
Reading Abbey. A song from Harley MS. 1717, and
one (for two voices) from the Bury St. Edmunds' treatise,
are a little less barbarous than the other attempts; they
were printed in *Musica Antiqua.*

There are a few distinct simple tunes in triple time
left from the thirteenth century. 'Samson, dux fortissime,'
which opens the Reading MS., is a specimen; there is
another to French words in Ashmole MS. 1285; and two,
also to French words, in Cotton MSS. Vespasian *a* 18.
The last-named are followed by two lines of music much
barred, with the words 'Et gaudebit,' forming a Mutetus.*

Until the time of Dunstable attempts at real composition are very few, in England as elsewhere; and none
which remain are pleasant to hear, excepting the Rota.
Burney MSS. 357 has a piece of two-part harmony of the
clumsiest kind; the staves are barred through.† In a
thirteenth-century Cotton MS. (Titus *a* 21) there is a
hymn, 'Virtute numinis non natura,' which is written as
if for three voices, all barred; they continually produce
barbarous fifths or octaves, or both. Another more important piece of three-part harmony is written at the
beginning of a Cartulary of Bury St. Edmund's Abbey,
now in the Cambridge University MSS. It is much older
than the Cartulary, and begins in late Neums on a four-
lined stave, above a bass singing 'Alleluja.' Then other
short responses follow, 'Sancte ingenite ingenitor,' etc.;
the bass is in long notes, regularly barred after every
three, while the upper parts are both very florid. This is
possibly a descant written out for pupils. In these three
MSS. the bass alone has the words; the staves are four-
lined, and all are in the C clef. Another singularly florid
vocal piece is in the British Museum at the end of
Arundel MS. 505; it ranges over a ninth (from d to e'),

* Compare Addit. MS. 30,091.
† 'Veri floris,' in Harley MS. 524, is a rather more successful attempt.

and is also probably a descant written out. In a very defective thirteenth-century collection of tracts (Addit. MSS. 25,031), probably from Cirencester, there are several chants, one of which, 'Deus de supremis sedibus,' may be a Quadruplum. Some important attempts from the fourteenth century have been discovered.* There is a fragment of a 'Gloria in excelsis' for two voices, in Tiberius *a* 7; and two leaves of music which looks like two-voiced writing with organ accompaniment in Addit. MS. 28,550, from the Abbey of Robertsbridge, East Sussex. The latter is stiff descant, as far as is legible.† In the MSS. of the town of Bridport are the archives of a Guild, apparently about 1400, in which occurs some music for two voices with the remark, 'Tenor de A toute hure' (Tenor always on A); it is to French words, and has been written over.

In 1897, after the original appearance of this History, the Plain-song and Mediæval Music Society facsimiled the pieces mentioned above, with some later compositions, and published them in a volume entitled *Early English Harmony*. A translation was published in 1913. It was assumed that simultaneous singing was invariably intended. But there are foreshadowings of complete polyphony in the Cambridge University MS. 1354 (Ff. vi. 16), and still more in MS. 1940 (Kk. i. 6), which contains three short pieces, 'Deo gratias,' 'Paradisi porta,' 'Sancta Maria,' and part of a Magnificat, all for three voices in correct solid chords, without consecutive fifths or octaves. Gonville and Caius College MS. 334 (now 727) contains eleven complete hymns in the same style: 'Mater Christi,' 'Mutato modo genituræ,' 'Maria mater,' 'O Stella,' 'Includimur nube cœli,' 'Glacio putas,' 'Quid melius,' 'Stella maris illustrans,' 'Dei non frustra,' 'Sit cornute munda,' 'Archa Noe,' and some fragments. Both MSS. were probably written about 1350. MS. 7 E Musæo in the Bodleian Library contains a piece whose construction goes a step further, using a fourth voice, a bass, in

---

* In MS. 457, at Lambeth Palace, there are five lines of two-staved music; I believe harmony is not intended.

† See Haberl's Kirchemusikalisches Jahrbuch for 1899; from the facsimile issued by the Plain-song and Mediæval Music Society.

fragments of plain-song; this is the nearest approach
I know to the solution of that problem which had been
dimly apprehended by musicians all through the thirteenth and fourteenth centuries, the creation of a
structural tone-art. The piece is facsimiled and translated in *Early Bodleian Harmony*. The three-voiced
pieces from Cambridge (University Library and Caius
College), most important historically, still await publication.

MEDIÆVAL THEORISTS

A considerable number of treatises upon the theory
of music were produced in the monasteries, and many of
these are still preserved. None of those written in
England, except Alcuin's, are equal in antiquity to those
of Hucbald and Guido, but several are of very high
importance.

The oldest known, written apparently about the year
1100, is not certainly, although most probably, by an
Englishman. It was included in the second volume of
Gerbert's collection, published at Hornau in 1784. Gerbert's copy was destroyed by fire; but there are several
ancient manuscripts still in existence at London, Paris,
Leipzig, Antwerp, Rome, Munich, and Vienna. Two
MSS. ascribe the treatise to Johannes Cotto, who appears
in the Dictionary of National Biography as JOHN COTTON.
But Burney showed that Cotto was probably only the
possessor. The chronicler of Mölk mentions that a
learned English musician named Johannes wrote an excellent treatise on music. The dedication, 'Domini et
patri suo venerabili Anglorum antistiti Fulgentio,' suggests an English interest. Fulgentius was the name of
an abbot who ruled over the monastery of Afflighem,
near Brussels, 1088–1122; it had close connection with
England. Cotto or Cotton is now received as the author's
name. The treatise is repeatedly quoted by Hieronymus
de Moravia. A German translation was given in Haberl's
Jahrbuch for 1888.

Cotto does not allude to Mensurable Music; whence it
may be argued that Franco lived at a later period than
1100. In his first chapter, Cotto states that the English

French, and Germans use the syllables *ut, re, mi, fa, sol, la,* in solmization; but the Italians have others. The twenty-third chapter contains a very singular and precise account of the style of harmony then in vogue; from this it may be gathered that the *diaphonia* (which was vulgarly called *organum* from its resemblance to organ effects) consisted of a florid variation on the plain-chant melody.* A direction that 'where there is an elevation in correct modulation, there should be a depression in the *organum,* and conversely,' has been used by some historians as ground for asserting that Cotton enjoins contrary motion instead of the consecutive fifths and octaves previously used. But, just as the ancient Greek treatises give us no help in conceiving how Greek music really sounded, so also does Cotton give us no help in conceiving the *organum.* Could we hear a single chorus of Æschylus or ode of Pindar performed as they were originally performed; could we hear a single plain-chant sung as it was sung when the massive-pillared, round-arched architecture had not yet flowered into the Gothic style—then, probably, all the treatises of classical antiquity and the Dark Ages would immediately become perfectly clear. This, at least, we may affirm—that Cotton did not describe the consecutive perfect concords whose use is apparently enjoined by Hucbald and Guido. His words† best agree with the description of a florid variation.

The next English writer on music was Johannes de Garlandia, formerly confused with a Gerlandus of Besançon, who flourished about 1150. In the earlier volumes of Coussemaker's collection, the mistake still appears; but it was rectified in the third volume, though since repeated by several writers. Johannes de Garlandia, who in the Dictionary of National Biography is called JOHN GARLAND, tells us in his poem, 'De Triumphis Ecclesiæ,' that he was born in England, apparently about 1180, and studied at Oxford under John of London, then under Alain de L'Isle at Paris. He has been claimed

---

* The Munich MS. contains a specimen of this florid accompaniment, subsequently called *organum purum.*

† See also, for this conception of the *Organum,* an anonymous treatise in Coussemaker, Vol. II, p. 494.

for a Devonshire man, as there was a family of that name settled at Chudleigh. He assisted in founding the University of Toulouse in 1229; subsequently he came into conflict with the Dominicans, and escaped to Paris, where he seems to have remained in safety and celebrity. He was still alive in 1252. Garlandia's works are principally upon others of the seven liberal arts; but he has left several upon music. Two fragments upon acoustical proportions, entitled *De fistulis* and *De nolis*, were printed in the first volume of Gerbert's collection. His most important musical work is entitled *De Musica Mensurabili Positio*, and contains specimens of double counterpoint, which he defines to be the same phrase repeated by different voices at different times, giving an example. He also distinguishes three kinds of dissonances, calling them perfect, imperfect, and middle; a chapter on the *Organum* is worthy of consultation in connection with the account of Cotton. An 'Introductio Musice secundum Magistrum de Garlandia' is entirely devoted to plainchant. These, and a shorter work, *De Musica Mensurabili*, are printed in the first volume of Coussemaker's collection. A tract of two chapters preserved at Einsiedeln, and entitled *Johannis de Garlandia Optima Introductio in Contrapunctum pro Rudibus*, seems almost too advanced for the thirteenth century. It may be found in Coussemaker's third volume. It is also printed with a German translation in Riemann's *Geschichte der Musiktheorie*. It recommends contrary motion, forbids consecutive fifths and octaves, and permits consecutive thirds and sixths. But only note-against-note two-voiced harmony is described.

Next in time comes the treatise of WALTER ODINGTON, *De Speculatione Musices*, preserved in Parker's MSS. at Corpus Christi College, Cambridge. Walter Odington was probably from Oddington in Gloucestershire; he was a monk of Evesham Abbey, whence he is also called Walter de Evesham. He is not mentioned in the Chronicle of Evesham Abbey, and Tindal could find no contemporary account for his 'History of Evesham.' He has been confused with the Walter de Einesham who was elected Archbishop of Canterbury, but disallowed by the

Pope in 1228; and, consequently, a too early date has been ascribed to his treatise. Leland describes him as a man of extraordinary learning, who wrote many works, giving 1280 as the date when he flourished. Even this date is too early, for a list of mathematicians living at Oxford in 1316 includes 'Walter de Evesham,' and a calendar written by him for the use of Evesham Abbey begins with 1301. He was still living at Merton College about 1330. Some of his mathematical tracts are in Cambridge University MSS., and the Digby MSS. at Oxford. The date of his musical treatise may be given as after 1300.

Odington's *De Speculatione Musices* was very fully discussed by Burney, who describes it as sufficient to replace the loss of all other mediæval treatises. It is divided into six books, the first three dealing with acoustics, the fourth with Latin prosody, the fifth with the Gregorian plain-chant, and the sixth giving a most interesting account of Mensurable Music and the art of 'composition.' He gives directions* for composing Rondels, prescribing that the best possible melody should be invented (with or without words), one or two other parts should be fitted to it in contrary motion, and that each of the melodies should then be sung by each voice. Riemann has pointed out that Odington was the first theorist who plainly asserted the consonance of thirds, major or minor; and maintained that the entire common chord, with doublings in the octave, should be considered consonant. Odington admitted that the ratios he proposed for thirds are not in exact agreement with mathematical calculation, but argued that the voices naturally temper the intervals, producing a pleasant combination; and yet the little motet he gives as a specimen is discordant. He dimly apprehended that music might become a structural art, but could not quite hit on the solution of the problem. There is no allusion to canons or imitation; the mystery of 'Sumer is icumen in' gets no light.

* Rondelli sicsunt componendi: excogitetur cantus pulchrior qui possit, et disponatur secundum aliquen modorum predictorum, cum littera vel sine, et ille cantus a singulis recitetur; tamen aptentur alii cantus in duplici aut triplici procedendo per consonantias, et dum unus ascendit, alius descendit, vel tertius ita ut non simul descendat vel ascendat, nisi forte tamen majoris pulchritudinis, et a singulis singulorum cantus recitentur.

Among other noteworthy features of *De Speculatione Musices* may be mentioned an allusion to minims* (generally said to be invented by Philippe de Vitry) and a chapter upon bells, a very early treatment of that subject. Lengthy extracts from the treatise may be seen in Burney's 'History of Music'; and the whole has been printed in Coussemaker's collection, Vol. I. Walter Odington's name deserves to be remembered with Johannes de Garlandia's as an honour to English music; and when we remember that the thirteenth century had already seen the creation of 'Sumer is icumen in,' it may justly be claimed that England was beyond question the most musical of nations during the flower-time of Gothic art.

A very valuable anonymous treatise from Bury St. Edmunds is preserved in the Royal MSS., British Museum. Both Burney and Hawkins described it in detail; and it was published by Coussemaker. The author was an Englishman or a foreigner who had settled here. It was written after 1272, probably after 1300, as Odington is quoted. Coussemaker reckoned it quite a century too early. The special peculiarity of this work is its most welcome historical information, in which respect it stands quite alone among early musical treatises; especially it tells us of Parisian musicians. The writer was evidently a much-travelled man. He describes the inhabitants of England, France, and Navarre, as specially musical; of English singers he names 'Johannes Filius Dei, Makeblite of Winchester, and Blakismet, a singer in the palace of our Lord Henry the last.' His most important allusion is that to the ditone and semi-ditone, or major and minor thirds, which, he says, are generally reckoned dissonances; but 'in some places, for instance, in that part of England which is called West-country,' they are thought the best of consonances, and are much used by the organists. This confirms Odington's arguments.

We may judge from this account that the Pythagorean tuning was not followed in the West of England; and there is accordingly some reason to believe that harmony

---

* Ita Semibrevem primo divido in tres partes quos Minimas voco, Figuras retinens Semibrevis, ne ab aliis musicis videar, discedere.

was matured there. Harmony has become second nature to modern European ears; and musicians can hardly conceive the art without it. Yet Orientals still do not employ it; and it appears certain that long centuries went by in Western Europe without any simultaneous sounds other than octaves, and possibly occasional fourths and fifths. With the Greek tuning, major thirds were much too sharp, and could not have been used simultaneously; we may suppose that the West-country organists used tuning nearer our own. When thirds were made consonant a harmonic basis was secured; and it is not surprising that the country where this was done should have been musically in advance of other countries.

In the Bury St. Edmunds treatise there are valuable accounts of Leoninus, Perotinus, and other Parisian musicians. The title, *De Mensuris et Discantu*, at once indicates an advance on the treatise of Cotton. Mensurable music was now in existence. The 'Hocket' is distinctly described. Franco Primus and Franco de Colonia are mentioned; a little more positive information concerning this mysterious person or persons would have been most welcome to historians. At the end is a separate chapter—'De Synnemenis'—on the introduction of accidentals into plain-chant. This valuable treatise, Royal MS. 12 *c* 6, is printed in Coussemaker's 'Scriptorum de Musica nova series,' Vol. I; but Mr. Chappell complained at a meeting of the Musical Association that, owing to French unfamiliarity with English writing, this and the other treatises in Coussemaker's collection were very inaccurately printed. Its date depends on the words, 'King Henry the last'; Henry the Third is intended, as Odington is named at the end.

Among the treatises burnt in the Cottonian library was one by ROBERT DE HANDLO, which bore the date 1326. It had, fortunately, been transcribed for Dr. Pepusch, whose copy is now in the British Museum. The title is 'Regulæ cum Maximis magistri Franconis, cum additionibus aliorum musicorum, compilatæ a Roberto de Handlo.' Garlandia is quoted, but in the main the work is a commentary upon Franco. It is included in Coussemaker's first volume. Nothing is known of the author, but a pedigree of the De Handlo family is preserved in the Lansdowne MSS.

The very important treatise, *De Quatuor Principalibus, in quibus totius musicæ radices consistunt*, exists in three manuscripts—two at the Bodleian Library, Oxford, and one in the British Museum. One has a short prologue and a different title, whence it has been supposed that the works are different; but there is no other material variation. One is dated 1351, 'Simon Tunsted being Regent of the Minorites at Oxford.' Bale, followed by Pits, ascribed the treatise to Tunsted; Burney repeated the statement, which has no real ground. Simon Tunsted was born about 1300, at Norwich; his father came from Tunsted, whence the surname was derived. Simon, after living at Oxford as a Minorite Franciscan, rose to be the head of the English branch of the order. He died in 1369 at a nunnery in Bruisgard, Suffolk. The treatise *De Quatuor Principalibus* forms, according to Coussemaker, a link between the harmonic systems of the thirteenth and fourteenth centuries. By far the most important part is the section on Mensurable Music, which forms 'Quartum Principale.' It has given rise to an interesting speculation.

In Ravenscroft's *Briefe Discourse* (published in 1614), a work on 'Mensurabilis Musica,' by John Dunstable, is quoted six times. No such treatise is now known, nor is Dunstable's name included in Bale's 'Scriptores Majoris Britanniæ,' published in 1550. But Ravenscroft's allusions are plain; and it has also been said, though incorrectly, that Gaforius and Morley quote the treatise. It will be found, upon examination, that Ravenscroft was really quoting Tunsted's 'Quartum Principale,' both words and the number of the chapters coinciding. A single example will be sufficient. Ravenscroft begins by defining ' Mensurable Music '; then proceeds:

' As Jo. Dunstable, the man whom Joan. Nucius in his " Poeticall Musicke " (and divers others), affirme to be the first that invented composition, saith, it hath his beginning at an Unite, and increaseth upward by two and by three infinitely, and from the highest decreaseth in like manner downe againe to an Unite.'

The marginal reference is to Jo. Dunstable's 'Mensurabilis Musica,' Cap. I. Compare Dunstable's alleged words with the following from Tunsted's 'Quartum Principale,' cap. I:

'Crescere autem potest per binarium vel ternarium numerum usque in infinitum, ut inferius patebit; decrescit vero ad illum in unitatem.'

Another of the resemblances may be seen in the noteworthy assertion in Tunsted's sixth chapter that 'Phillippus de Vitriaco, who was the flower of musicians of all the world in his time, invented the minim'; and the remaining four cases are nearly parallel.

De Quatuor Principalibus is printed in Coussemaker's collection, Vol. IV; but the section on Mensurable Music had already appeared in Vol. III, pages 334–54. It was from the latter that I first observed the coincidences with Ravenscroft's quotations. At first I thought I had discovered Dunstable's work, but the chapters are here divided differently, and it was not till I found the supposed anonymous treatise to be identical with Tunsted's, where the chapter-numbers agree with Ravenscroft, that I was satisfied that Ravenscroft was mistaken in ascribing a treatise to Dunstable. Morley mentions *De Quatuor Principalibus* among the works he had studied, but without any author's name.*

The Bodleian Library has also preserved a treatise by THEINRED, who was apparently precentor of the Benedictine monastery at Dover. It is dated 1371, and is curious in using the antiquated letter-notation for the gamut. Coussemaker had intended to include this treatise in his collection, but was unable.†

Hawkins claims JOHANNES DE MURIS (1300–70) as an Englishman, on the strength of a passage in a fifteenth-century treatise:

'Pausas juncturas, facturas, atque figuras
  Mensuratarum formavit Franco notarum
Et Jhon de Muris variis floruitque figuris
  Anglia cantorum omen gignit plurimorum.'

---

* Tunsted makes no allusion to canons or imitative writing.
† For Odington (Walter of Evesham), Tunsted, and Theinred, see *Dictionary of National Biography*.

Pits and Tanner had also counted de Muris as English, but the claim was waived by Burney, and does not rest on sufficient grounds. A modern investigator (Hirschfeld) has pronounced that the only genuine work of De Muris is the *Speculum Musicæ*, two books of which are printed in Coussemaker's Vol. II. Six short tracts under his name may be seen in Gerbert's Vol. III; and three others in Coussemaker's Vol. III.

Other treatises are preserved in the British Museum, one of which (Addit. MS. 21,455) concludes with a page of fifteenth-century English. In the same MS. (Cod. Bodley 842), which contains Theinred's, is a short tract by RICHARD CUTELL, with the date 1420; and with Odington's at Cambridge is another of about that date, and in the same style, but without an author's name. Both are similar to Lionel Power's, described in Chap. II; and, like his, are in English.

In the catalogues of Bale, Pits, and Tanner are recorded many other writers whose works are now lost. The earliest was WOLSTAN, a Saxon monk of Winchester, who wrote *De Tonorum Harmonia* about the year 1000. OSBERN of Canterbury, already mentioned, flourished about 1070; he wrote *De Re Musica*. ADAMUS DORENSIS, Abbot of the Cistercian monastery at Door, Herefordshire, was born at Dover, and died 1200; his treatise was called *Rudimenta Musices*. GREGORY, of Bridlington, is mentioned a little later. ALPHREDUS ANGLICUS seems to have been an ecclesiastic of standing in the thirteenth century, and was with Cardinal Ottoboni in England about 1270; Bale ascribes to him a treatise, *De Musica*. SIMON TAILLER, a Scot, contributed four treatises about 1240. No theoretical attempts from the Keltic parts of the British Islands have been recorded.

JOHN HANBOYS is usually ascribed to the reign of Edward IV on the authority of Bale and Holinshed; the latter, however, plainly says that he copies Bale. I am inclined to think Hanboys lived at an earlier period, perhaps in the fourteenth century. His known treatise is, like Handlo's, a commentary upon Franco; Garlandia is quoted. Robert of Brunham, William of Doncaster, and

Robert Trowell (? Orwell) are mentioned as authorities upon notation. According to Hanboys, the minim and crotchet were distinguished by the differing lengths of their tails; the tail of the minim was drawn through two lines of the stave, that of the crotchet through one. The treatise, printed by Coussemaker, is in the British Museum with Tunsted's, as Addit. MS. 8866.

POPULAR MUSIC OF THE MIDDLE AGES

During the twelfth and succeeding centuries, down even to the Stuart period, the popular music is constantly alluded to by writers of all kinds; and many quaint customs existed, in which music formed a considerable part. In London there existed a musical society in the thirteenth century called 'Le Pui.'

Every town was walled; and a number of men called the Waits regularly patrolled the town every night. *Wait* is evidently a corruption of the Norman-French *guet*. The Waits used a kind of large, shrill oboe for signalling; the name passed from the men to their instruments. The statutes given by Edward I to the City of London (before 1296) prescribe that each gate 'shall be shut at night by the Servant dwelling there; and each Servant shall have a Wayte at his own expense.' The watchman at Edward IV's palace was required to keep *Bon Gate*, and to sound his Wait every three hours. The watch of a city formed the municipal band, which played at civic functions; there is a representation on the tomb of Robert Braunch (died 1364) in St. Margaret's, King's Lynn. Naumann ('Illustrated History,' Fig. 166) gives it as from a MS. at Paris.

The Minstrels are still more frequently mentioned than the 'Waytes.' There were grades in them; and each country had its 'king.' There was, no doubt, nearly as great a difference between the minstrels attending on the Court or a great noble and the wanderers who tramped about amusing the populace, as there is now between an ennobled leading musician and the peripatetic nuisances who grind organs or 'sing' with blackened faces.*

* The 'nigger minstrel' has fortunately disappeared in the twentieth century.

A singular story is told of the minstrels of John's reign. In 1212 the Welsh besieged the Earl of Chester in his castle; but De Lacy, Constable of Chester, 'making use of the Minstrels of all sorts, then met at Chester fair, by the allurements of their music assembled such a vast number of people, who went forth under the conduct of a gallant youth named Dutton (his steward and son-in-law), that he intimidated the Welsh,' who raised the siege. From this story we see that a fair, even in those days, attracted a crowd of itinerant minstrels. The story is confirmed by the charters granted to De Lacy and Dutton, with authority over the minstrels of the County Palatine of Chester; it will again be referred to.

Warton and Percy did full justice to the minstrels, who were savagely attacked by Ritson. None of these writers, however, sufficiently considered the differing ranks and standing among them, and speak as if one minstrel was like every other. It must also be remembered that between the time when Aldhelm sang 'like a minstrel' on the bridge at Malmesbury and the time when minstrels were included in a statute against rogues and vagabonds, no less than nine hundred years had elapsed, a longer period than the interval from the Norman Conquest to the present day.

Certain ancient records give curious glimpses of a minstrel's life. Very remarkable is the account of the gathering at the marriages of Edward I's daughters Joan and Margaret, in May and July, 1290. On the latter occasion four hundred and twenty-six minstrels were present, and £100 was bestowed upon them. Yet more extraordinary was the gathering at the *Cour plénière* kept at Whitsuntide, 1306. Six 'kings' were present, Le Roy de Champaigne, Le Roy Capenny, Le Roy Boisescue, Le Roy Marchis, Le Roy Druet, and Le Roy Robert (of England). Each of these, except Le Roy Druet, received five marks, equal perhaps to a gift of £50 at the present day. Among the others were some distinguished by such familiar names as 'Reginald le menteur,' 'Guillaume sans manière,' 'Makejoye,' 'Perle in the eghe,' while others were called after their town or patron. The total sum paid them was about £200, equal to about £3,000 of our money.

In those days, when there was little or no accumulation of property, practical work was found for all; and the minstrels, it may well be thought, were not allowed to be idle. Those in the service of the court or nobility may have had duties similar to those of the Waits, who not only formed the city bands, but also had to keep watch. Offenders were condemned to be taken to the pillory 'with minstrels' to attract attention; and minstrels headed processions at public festivals. The minstrels of Beverley were rich enough to contribute a pillar to St. Mary's Church; five men are carved upon it, some holding instruments.

What music they played and sang is very difficult even to guess. There is a specimen of a dance-tune in Douce MS. 139, dating about 1300. J. Stafford Smith, in *Musica Antiqua*, printed a version of this tune, which was copied in the publications of Crotch, Chappell, and Ouseley; in Wooldridge's new edition of Chappell quite a different rhythm is given. Probably the minstrels sang tunes such as those in the Cotton MS., Vespasian *a* 18; alternately a semibreve and a minim, with a dotted semibreve at the end of each line. 'We've got no work to do' is a too-familiar example of such a tune, though less simple.

As regards their singing, I have to put forward a matter of the greatest importance in literary as well as musical history, and for which I ask the closest attention. The connection between poetry and music was originally far closer than at present, and all through the Middle Ages this lasted, being again specially important during the Shakespearian age. What modern readers are apt to forget is that even very long narrative poems were *sung*, not recited; a minstrel's audience apparently did not object to the continual repetition of the same series of notes. Even at the present day traces of this may be found; clumsy ballads with several dozen stanzas may yet be heard in out-of-the-way villages. In narrative song the words alone are listened for, and the monotonous repetition of a short tune does not weary. The elementary music of savage and half-civilized nations is similar, and is intolerably monotonous and dreary to our ears. It must be remembered that such poems as 'Chevy Chase' were sung in the streets, and familiar to all. Thus Sir Philip Sidney wrote: 'I never heard the old song of Percy and Douglas, that I found not my heart moved more than with a trumpet; and yet it is sung but by some blind crowder, with no rougher voice than rude style'; while his contemporary, Puttenham, wrote still more to this point in the passage—

'The over busy and too speedy return of one manner of tune doth too much annoy, and, as it were, glut the ear, unless it be in small and popular musicks sung by these *Cantabanqui* upon benches and barrels' heads, where they have none other audience than boys or country fellows that pass by them in the street; or else by blind harpers, or such-like tavern minstrels, that give a fit of mirth for a groat; and their matter being for the most part stories of old time, as the Tale of Sir Topas, Bevis of Southampton, Guy of Warwick, Adam Bell, and Clym of the Clough, and such other old romances or historical rhimes, made purposely for the amusement of the common people at Christmas dinners and bride-ales, and in taverns and alehouses, and such other places of base resort. Also they be used in Carols and Rounds, and such-like.'

We possess one example of the notes to which the minstrels chanted their lays, preserved in a song-book published by the Percy Society, then stolen, and in 1887 bought by the Bodleian Library; it contains (among other pieces) a long poem beginning 'Of all the enimyes,' with above it eighteen notes in even lengths. The notes are a, c', d', e', e', e', f', f', e', e', f', e', d', c', a, d', b, a.

If students apprehend the idea that even long poems were in the Middle Ages chanted in the streets, there will be fuller appreciation of the early music and poetry; and the custom lasted into modern times. Hannay's *Philomela*, published 1622, contains music for the first stanza, which is evidently intended to be sung to all the others (about a hundred); and even later, under the Commonwealth, Davenant expressed a hope that cantos of his *Gondibert* might be sung at village feasts. These considerations lead to a result of importance in literary history. Narrative or lyric poetry, meant to be sung, was written in stanzas; dramatic poetry, meant to be spoken, was written in 'riding rhyme,' afterwards in blank verse. No one ever wrote a narrative poem in blank verse until Milton, who had previously only used it in his masque *Comus*, tried it in *Paradise Lost*; and after a part of the first edition had been printed an extra leaf was added containing an explanation and defence of the versification. This matter concerns literary even more than musical history, but has hitherto been overlooked. It is probable that the strolling musicians knew only narrative poems, with perhaps a few carols for Christmas and Easter, while the higher classes, especially after the Renaissance, favoured lyrics.

The variety of instruments known in the Middle Ages was considerable. The celebrated and much discussed Crut, Crwth, or Crowd* was certainly a bowed instrument in the Middle Ages; it was still heard in Wales at the end of the eighteenth century, and a few specimens remain. It had six strings. Among its successors was the Rebeck, or Ribible, which was nearer the Fithele. We also read of the lute, harp, psaltery, fiddle, gittern, cithern, citole, and rote; the organistrum, or hurdy-gurdy; the flute, horn, trumpet, shalm, sackbut, hautboy or wayte; the bagpipe and shepherd's pipe; and, of course, the organ. Some of these require a description. The flute was a large instrument, sometimes over four feet long, and was played with a mouthpiece. The gittern and the cithern, or cittern, were instruments of the guitar family; the gittern was gut-strung, the cithern wire-strung. The psaltery (Sautry), and probably the citole, were dulcimers plucked by the fingers. The shalm, or shawm, was a powerful wood instrument, probably the cornet of the seventeenth century, and the cornetto used by Bach and Gluck.

Some MSS. contain representations of mediæval instruments. Besides the Anglo-Saxon MSS. described previously, I may mention Lansdowne MS. 383, which contains a fiddle and longbow; and Royal MS. 2 *a* 22,

---

* Some ancient English Primers translate Ps. cxlix. 3, 'Herie thei His name in a crowd'; others . . . 'in a cornmuce.'

which has a thirteen-stringed harp. These are of the twelfth century. Among the later delineations specially remarkable are Harl. MSS. 6563 (fourteenth century), which has many grotesques of animals playing instruments; and Harl. MSS. 1892 (fifteenth century), where may be seen a beautiful harp, also a psaltery, a rote, handbells, and a choir singing under guidance. Others which must not be omitted are Royal MSS. 2 *b* 6 and 19 *b* 15; the Cotton MS., Tiberius *a* 7; Addit. MSS. 21,926 and 24,686; Harl. 745 and 1896; and especially the Bodley MS. 248. Many are engraved in the works of Strutt and J. R. Green, and in T. Wright's *Domestic Manners of the Middle Ages*.

A good epitome of mediæval musical resources is in Richard of Maidstone's poem (published in the Rolls Series, XIV 293) on the reconciliation of Richard II with the City of London in 1393. He thus describes the scene outside St. Paul's:

> 'Organa pulsat ibi, mentem rapit hœc melodia
> Vocibus angelicis dum canit ille chorus.
> Hinc decor, hinc dulcor oculos recreatur et aures,
> Singula cernentes obstupuere simul.
> Quot putas hic musas, quot et instrumenta canora
> Quam quoque multimodum hic genus organicum!
> Fistula, cistula, tibia, timpana, cum monacordo,
> Organa, psalteria, cimbala, cumque lyra
> Zambuca, citharæ, situlæque, tubæque, viellæ,
> Buccina cum nablis, simphonicisque choris.'

Besides these, there may have been another known. Musical antiquaries are now inclined to look for the invention of keyed stringed instruments in England. The only evidence, however, is from a poem by Guillaume de Machaut, who, in *Li temps pastour*, speaks of 'Eschaqueil d'Angleterre'; in *La Prise d'Alexandrie*, Machaut speaks of an 'Esquaquiel'; while Molinet's *Chanson sur le jour de Guinegate* includes 'Bons échiquiers' among musical instruments. Vander Straeten has ingeniously linked these allusions with his discovery that King John of Aragon in 1387 heard and desired an instrument like an organ, but stringed, and called 'Exaquir.' Since instrumental composition was developed in England so much earlier than elsewhere, it is natural to infer the spinet, virginal, clavicimbalum, etc., were invented in England; but it is a guess only, and I can offer no evidence beyond Vander Straeten's.

Taking now a few miscellaneous matters, I wish to point out that in England, as in France and Germany, 'music' was, and is still, restricted in common speech to instrumental music as distinguished from *singing*. Mistakes have been made through ignorance of this usage; English musicians never employ it now, but the rest of the world very commonly does, and cases may be seen in Mendelssohn's letters. 'I am going to give up my music and go in for singing,' said a pupil at the Royal Academy of Music recently; and though such a phrase is most laughable to a musician, it sounds quite natural to the public. In older times the distinction was correctly applied, which antiquaries should not forget.

The peculiar English word *Treble* deserves an allusion; in the Middle Ages, the words *Quadrible* and *Quinible* were also used. What their signification may then have been is disputable; in the fifteenth century, *Quadrible* meant a higher voice-part than the *Treble*, as will be seen in the next chapter. They are not heard of later; and Shakespeare has for ever fixed the appellation *childish treble* to denote a boy's high voice.

Nothing of remarkable interest to musical history in Scotland or Ireland is recorded after Giraldus Cambrensis. There is one piece of music in a Welsh MS. (of the seventeenth century) stated to have been played at the court of King Arthur! It is certainly very primitive, and is written in letter-notation; clumsy as the harmonies are, it is, historically, of value, and was published* in 1807. The MS. is now in the British Museum as Addit. 14,905. The regulations of the Welsh Bards show that they were poets first, and their music was only accessory. 'A singer should know how to tune a harp or Crwth, and to play several essays and embellishments, two preludes, a *cwlwm*, a *caniad*, and the thirteen principal tunes, with all their flats and sharps. He should understand likewise the

* By the Cymrodorion Society. It is an elementary set of variations.

thirteen principal styles of expression, and accenting them with his voice to several tunes; he should know the twenty-four metres of Poetry and twenty-four measures of Music, and be capable of composing in two of the *Englyn* metres and one of the *Cywyd* metres. He should read Welsh with propriety, and write it with exactness, and be skilful in correcting and restoring any old poem or song that has been corrupted by transcribers.'

The Welsh bards were certainly a higher order than the minstrels, yet their powers led to no lasting result. The Kelts, with all their gifts of tone and expression, have never been able to superadd science, and make themselves great musicians. The glory of creating an independent art of sound was therefore not achieved by them, but by the English, as I now proceed to describe.

CHAPTER II

THE INVENTION OF COMPOSITION
(1400–53)

John Dunstable solves the problem of composition.—The fundamental novelty of his works.—A New Art.—Henry V's Chapel Royal.—Renown of the English musicians on the Continent.—The treatise of Gulielmus Monachus.—Faulxbourdon and Gymel.—Lionel Power's treatise.—This earliest school of composition rediscovered in the nineteenth century.—The known remains.
Chief Composers : Dunstable, Power, Benet, Hothby.

AS with a sound of trumpets, announcing the arrival of high personages or the preparation for solemn ceremonies, even so should this chapter begin; for now I have to relate how Englishmen led musicians out of the arid desert where for centuries they had wandered since escaping from the bondage of Greek theories, still wistfully remembered. England may well be proud that the one evergreen refreshing spot in the long wilderness is the Rota of Reading Abbey; and England may well be proud that the Pisgah-sight into the Promised Land, and the first footing on its pastures, were granted to a school of English musicians, of whom the chief was John-Dunstable.

This school invented the art of musical composition; and English, French, Spanish, Flemish, and German writers alike mention Dunstable as the first and greatest of the band. So immediately did their superiority appear that all previous attempts at once fell into disuse; and one result is that the attempts at composition have seldom been preserved, and generally by accident; but more are known than when I wrote in 1894. Two MSS. at Cambridge I mentioned in the original Appendix; and there are others at both universities, described in the previous chapter. To judge by these, the problem of euphonic chord-succession had been solved in England about 1350–80; but only solid chords were used. On the

45

Continent barbarous cacophony was still perpetrated. We were given practical experience at the International Musical Society's Paris congress in June, 1914; a number of twelfth to fifteenth-century pieces were sung in the Sainte Chapelle, and more unpleasantly discordant combinations are inconceivable. The 'Motez' of the French composers, two songs simultaneously sung in consecutive fifths, with a third voice repeating two or three words, are hideous as music. An Italian motet, written about 1370, and published by J. Stafford Smith, is just as unbearable. From these helpless attempts up to Dunstable's works, the change is immeasurable. Musicians had long tried to compose satisfactorily, and failed; he tried again and succeeded in solving the problem. He made each voice-part independent, cutting the succession by rests, thus breaking the continuous flow into phrases; and he used suspensions, passing-notes, and imitative passages, all combined in euphony. Naturally, as the inventor of Polyphony, he used the style with less skill than did those who entered into his labours.* Ambros has well pointed out how Dunstable's best work, 'O rosa bella,' was composed by setting an upper voice-part to an existing song, the middle voice-part being subsequently inserted, not awkwardly, and even with some short imitations, yet the whole is still rather stiff; in the songs of Dufay and Binchois the subsequent addition of the Contratenor is also perceptible, but in Okeghem's the voice-parts become entirely independent.

For three or four centuries musicians apparently had a dim perception that some hitherto unknown possibilities lay dormant in the art of sound; but they could not find out exactly what to do. They had the mathematical speculations of Boethius, the plain-song of the Church ritual, and the tunes (whatever they may have been) sung by the minstrels; how to fuse these various elements into a plastic art was the problem they could not solve. Not even Odington, or the musicians represented in the

---

* For the technical sense of the word ' Polyphony,' which is here intended, see the articles ' Polyphonia ' and ' Schools of Composition ' in Grove's *Dictionary of Music and Musicians* (original edition).

Montpellier MS., had succeeded; and their attempts had not established a school. To one man only—to John of Fornsete in the scriptorium of Reading Abbey—came the light of inspiration, and but for one moment; so far as we know, not a piece endurable by modern ears existed before 1400, or ever did exist, save and except only 'Sumer is icumen in.' But now at last the genius of John Dunstable had thrown back the veil, and musicians found before them a vast and fertile region, waiting only the cultivator's hand. Dunstable was thus the originator of the whole art of composition, and is in one sense the most important figure in the whole range of musical history.

Dunstable's invention was at once taken over by the Flemings; Jules Didiot eulogizing Dufay's compositions in the *Revue de l'Art Chrétien* says:

'Grâce à l'Anglais Dunstaple, les parties sont devenues plus mélodiques, plus alertes, plus concertants; elles savent se répondre, dialoguer, faire des dessins et des broderies sur un thème donné.'

F. du Menil, in *L'école contrapuntique flamande*, has also testified in favour of Dunstable's priority, calling Dufay creator, with Dunstable, of modern counterpoint; and confessing that Dunstable may have taught Dufay, though the fact is improbable. But du Ménil knew practically nothing of Dunstable's English contemporaries and successors.

Victor Lederer, through mistranslating a passage in Capgrave's Chronicle, has in his *Ueber Heimat und Ursprung der mehrstimmigen Tonkunst* elaborated a fancy that Polyphony began in Wales, afterwards sank, and was re-created by Dunstable, 'der Ahnherr unser Tonkunst.' The *Nova Ars*, says Lederer, was born 3rd September, 1416. On that day the Emperor Sigismund and John of Burgundy left England, the Emperor making a speech at Dover which Lederer has mistranslated, and which is the sole foundation for his theory.

In examining the origin of an art, or of any special department of an art, historians should continually bear in mind the resources at the original inventor's command. Before his time there has been a mechanical application of undeveloped resources, for useful purposes; these resources in time are improved, and then a man appears who uses them artistically. The *art* is now created; the resources are further improved and enlarged, the creative artists use them better and better until the culminating point is reached, and the natural decline follows. The practical side of the art has been, in the meantime, so developed that the youngest student knows more of it than the greatest genius did during the early stages; and historians (artists still more) are apt to forget that the art originally arose through the attempts to practically use undeveloped resources. Instances may freely be taken from the history of music, as it is by so many degrees the youngest of the arts that we possess exact details of nearly every advance; thus we may see how Stamitz's improvement of orchestral playing led to the orchestral symphony; how the improvements in the pianoforte led to Clementi's, then to Beethoven's, then to Chopin's and Liszt's styles of pianoforte compositions; how Tourte's improvement of the violin-bow led to Paganini's bowing. We may see, too, how each successive improvement in stage matters affected Shakespeare's plays. Architecture affords, perhaps, as good an instance as any; the Anglo-Saxons learnt the use of stone in church-building from the Normans, and their first attempts (so far as we can judge) show great unskilfulness and waste of material, while the only ornaments were hewn by the axe. During the twelfth century the masonry improved as the workmen acquired experience, and the chisel was brought into use for sculpturing ornaments of great variety. Then quickly appeared the art of Gothic architecture; and in the choir of Canterbury Cathedral can be seen the rude early Norman work, supplying a practical want as well as it could, side by side with the artistic creation just a century later, when the practical requirements were better understood and better tools were in use. In later times the original practical requirements are apt to be overlooked, and artistic treatment is alone valued. We may take as axioms that at the creation of an art, or any department of an art, the artistic composition was only one feature of general practical improvements; and that without knowing the resources at the artist's command we cannot understand what his deeds were, nor appreciate his standpoint relatively to his predecessors and contemporaries.

In the present instance, unfortunately, exact records are scanty; still, we have one distinct statement confirming what I have just set forth, and some collateral evidence may be gleaned in support. Tinctor, the best theorist of the fifteenth century, has in the dedication of his *Proportionale* told us that the institution of Chapels Royal attracted gifted men to cultivate music, and the improvement thus occasioned was so great that a new art seemed to be created. He then proceeds: 'This new art, if I may so speak, had its fount and origin among the English, of whom Dunstable was the principal.'

Dunstable died in 1453, and had a European reputation in 1430–40; we may therefore date the rise of English music about 1400–20, and suppose that a Chapel Royal was first set up by Henry IV or V. No records remain, though there are some allusions which prove that Henry V had one. Thomas of Elmham tells us that Prince Hal was exceedingly given to music in his youth, a touch which Shakespeare has missed; and that at the hero-king's coronation the number of minstrels was exceedingly great. John Clyff and seventeen other minstrels were, long after the king's death, still claiming twelve pence a day for their services at Agincourt. It is not to be wondered at, then, if it was this music-loving monarch who first established a choir for his delectation, though of course he may have but followed the example of his father, or even of Richard II. A passage from a contemporary eulogistic poem seems to indicate that a Chapel Royal was, at least, not usual in a king's establishment:

> 'Est ut odor nardi, sed et hospitium bene sanum
> Non ibi Lollardi, non est ibi digna profanum.
> Psallit plena Deo cantoribus ampla capella,
> Carmine siderio laudabilis est ea cella.'

No eulogy of a subsequent monarch puts forward the maintaining a Chapel Royal as a meritorious deed; and I think any one who reads this poem (which was printed in the Rolls Series, Part XI) will come to the conclusion that Henry V's 'plena cantoribus ampla capella' was a novelty. During the king's second expedition to France he sent over for his Chapel in order to celebrate the Easter of 1418 with full splendour. Already, on October 28th, £5 was paid by the Exchequer to Walter Wodehall, one of the organists of St. Paul's, going to France with five other organists. These, who received £25 on November 22nd, were 'William Thorley, chaplain, William Dyolet, Richard Laudewarnake, Thomas Wodeforde, and Gerald Hesyll, clerks and singers.' By 'organists' I understand singers of the *organum*—extemporizing descantists. These are the only names known in connection with Henry V's Chapel Royal; and whether they were regular members or special additions is doubtful. Fifty years later the Chapel Royal consisted of twenty-four clerks and eight boys ; afterwards of thirty-two clerks and some boys.

On January 26th 1418–19, Rouen surrendered. John Page's poem thus describes Henry V's triumphal entry:

> ' So to the Mynster did he fare,
> & of hys hors he lyght there
> His Chapylle met him at the doore
> And went byfore him in the floore
> And songe a responde gloryus
> That ys namyd, Quis est magnus ?'

We, however, hear nothing more of the king's musical tastes, except that in 1421 a harp was sent over to him, for which John Bore was paid £2 13s. 4d. It is not till Edward IV's reign that anything definite of the Chapel Royal is known.

Did John Dunstable walk in Rouen Cathedral before Henry V? I believe we may take this as nearly certain. Dunstable's renown was so rapidly spread that it seems probable he was personally known on the Continent. Tinctor's statement, and the other evidence, justify us in supposing that Henry V, on coming to the throne, gratified his love of music and his anti-Lollard predilections by establishing a Chapel Royal; that among the priests was John of Dunstable, whose inventive genius was aroused by the large body of voices, and who speedily devised various novel means of displaying their powers, to the wonder and delight of every hearer. He would have followed the conqueror's progress in France, perhaps then going to Italy; for Landino boasted that Florence possessed an organist so skilled that 'many most excellent English musicians' were drawn thither by his fame. If Dunstable visited France and Italy, the singularly rapid diffusion of his works is easily explicable.

And he was only one, though the greatest, of the English composers. During his own lifetime, his works, with those of seven other Englishmen, were copied into a large choir-book for the use of the Cathedral of Trent in the Tyrol; and other MSS. at Bologna, Dijon, Piacenza (now at Bologna), Rome, and Modena, have preserved these venerable relics to show us that France and Italy knew of the English creation of polyphonic composition as soon as they know of new English music now, in fact sooner, for they then obtained and performed many English works.

A very singular and most valuable testimony to the supremacy of English musicians in the early fifteenth century is obtained in the treatise of Gulielmus Monachus, entitled *De Preceptis Artis Musice et Practice Compendiosus Libellus*, and preserved in the library of St. Mark's, Venice. It was printed in Coussemaker's 'Scriptorum de Musica nova series,' III 273–306. The author was apparently an Italian pupil of the English musicians, and inserts chapters *De modis Anglicorum* and *Regule contrapuncti Anglicorum*. These are, in fact, instructions in 'composition in the English style,' just as a modern English musician might write upon 'vocalization in the true Italian style.' There is also a chapter giving examples of both English and French styles. The two principal chapters, which are much alike, tell us that 'according to the English themselves counterpoint is practised in two styles. The first style, which is common among them, is called *Faulxbourdon*; which *Faulxbourdon* is sung by three voices—namely, tenor, contratenor, and soprano. The second style, which is called *Gymel*, is sung by two voices—namely, soprano and tenor.'

Gulielmus Monachus then gives rules for both styles; but he was writing for those who were accustomed to hear extempore descant, and his description gives us little more idea of the effect of a fifteenth-century *Faulxbourdon* or *Gymel* than Johannes Cotto gives us of the twelfth-century *Organum*. There are, however, several examples; and we may gather from his words that both styles were used as extempore descant upon an ecclesiastical plain-song. The *Faulxbourdon* was to be sung in successions of 6–3, except the first and last chords, which were to consist of 8–5 from the plain-song; while the *Gymel*, much less clearly described, was apparently a succession of thirds or sixths.

From this most important treatise we learn that *Faulxbourdon* (Fa-Burden) was not a Flemish, but an English invention; and that there was another English style called *Gymel*. This word puzzled me very much at first; but I have since found it used as a direction in several MSS. of the fifteenth and sixteenth centuries, the latest I have seen being in two motets by Robert Whyte, copied by Sadler in 1585. It is variously spelt *Gymell*, *Gymel*, *Gimel*, and (in the great Eton MS.) *Gemellum*. The Eton MS. also contains *Semellum*, both directions sometimes appearing in the same piece, and suggesting that they are in some way connected. *Gymel* may be a form of *gimmal* = anything that revolves (as a gimlet, a gimmal-bit); in Digby's *Of Man's Soul* is an allusion to 'set gimals or strings.' Or it may be derived from *gemellum*, thus expressing duplicity of harmony. I have not seen it directed in secular music. As far as I can judge, it means that the choir were to sing in thirds, or that only two voice-parts were being employed.* In a long motet by Prowett (in the Cambridge part-books), the direction occurs three times in the tenor part. Other instances may be found in the Pepysian MS. 1236, the Lambeth volume of Masses, etc., the choir-book at Gonville-and-Caius College, Cambridge, and the Forrest-Heyther collection in the Bodleian Library, all described in my next chapter. In the works of Dunstable's period,

* Sometimes it seems equivalent to *divisi*.

I have not seen this rubric, but it may be present in the original MSS.; in Mr. W. B. Squire's transcript of the Modena choir-book there are frequently sections for two voices only, marked *Duo*.

We find some further account of the musical practice of this period in a treatise by Lionel Power; it forms part of a volume brought by Tallis from the monastery of Waltham Holy Cross, containing several treatises founded upon Guido and de Muris, also the rules of Thomas Walsingham and Torkesey, Power's treatise, a supplement to it, and another upon the time-table by Chilston. As this MS. (now in the British Museum as Lansdowne MS. 763) was described by both Hawkins and Burney with extensive quotations, there is no need to speak of it in detail; the main point which Power establishes is the use of sixths and thirds, and the distinct prohibition of consecutive unisons, fifths, and octaves. He uses the word *sight* apparently to signify interval from the plain-song; *sight* is thus used by several writers, down even to 1620. A specimen of Power's counterpoint, written like a figured-bass, confirms Gulielmus Monachus by consisting entirely of 6–3, except the first and last chords, which are marked 8–5. Power does not use the word *Gymel*; neither does the following treatise. The latter, perhaps also his, is very similar, but in clearer language; it declares that of the nine 'accordis' (concords), the 'Mene,' the 'Trebill,' and the 'Quadrible,' each used five. The Mean (Contratenor) used the five concords ranging from a unison with the plain-song to an octave above; the Treble, the five ranging from a fifth to a twelfth above the plain-song; the Quadrible, the five starting from an octave above the plain-song. Consecutive 'perfect acordis of one kynde' are here also forbidden; and many 'imperfite acordis together' are said to be 'ful mery and swete.'

These treatises are both in English of the fifteenth century; and another upon Mensurable Music (Addit. MS. 21,455) has one page of English, clearly and practically expressed. All the rest is in Latin, as are also the earlier treatises of the Waltham Holy Cross MS.

One of these—*De Origine et Effectu Musice speculative*—attacks the singers of the time for using semitones in the wrong places, as for instance in singing *sol, fa, sol,* or *re ut re*; and in finishing *re mi fa sol*. This shows that there was a feeling for the modern scale with its leading-note. The writer—evidently one of the 'old school'—tells us that the singers sheltered themselves under 'the authority of singers in Chapels Royal, who (say they) would not sing so without reason, as they are the best singers. . . . There are others who will have it that this method is sweeter and more pleasing to the ear.' This last argument the writer attacks, asserting, on the authority of Boethius, that the reason is a safer guide than the ear. I regard this passage as of considerable importance, from its evidence as to the repute of Chapels Royal, and the novelty of the requirement that music should *sound well*.

In imitation of Henry V's Chapel Royal, other musical establishments appear during this period; and a few isolated facts are of interest, helping us to get some little idea of the state of musical matters. Archbishop Chicheley (1414–43) organized the musical service of Canterbury Cathedral. At Easter, 1448, William of Boston, clerk of the upper choir and instructor of the choristers at King's College, Cambridge, received money from the Exchequer. There are several references to organs; one, of which the account remains, was built at Ely in 1407, at a cost of £3 17s. 8d., £2 being charged for 'fetching the organ-builder, and his board thirteen weeks.' There were twelve springs, showing the compass was an eleventh with one 'lyric semitone.' A grand organ which cost* £50 was given to St. Alban's Abbey by Abbot Wheat-hamstead in 1448; the Abbey chronicles boast of its superiority to every other in England. The regulations for the choir of this Abbey are still preserved. More important than all these facts is the record of an inventory made at St. Paul's Cathedral in 1445; besides plain-song books, there were, altogether, nine choir-books 'de cantu organico,' and one 'pro organis.' The Kyries, the Glorias,

* But in Cotton MS. Nero D 7 : ' ultra libras 17.'

and the Credos seem to have been written in separate
volumes. The extra organ copy is of special interest,
suggesting that the organist played polyphonically from
a score.

Turning now to personal details, I can but regret that
practically nothing remains which casts the faintest light
on the biography of the men who created the art of
composition. Even of Dunstable nothing is recorded
beyond his two epitaphs, one on his tomb, another written
by Abbot Wheathamstead. Of Lionel Power (who seems
to have ranked next in celebrity), of John Benet,
Bedingham, Stanley, Stove, Richard Markham, John
Alain, and Gervasius de Anglia, all of whose names
appear in the Modena, Trent, and Bologna MSS.,
absolutely nothing is known. John Alain wrote a poem,
alluding to several musicians, not one of whom is otherwise heard of; it is sung by two voices, while the tenor
sings Ps. xix. 3, 'In omnem terram ivit sonus eorum, et in
fines orbis terræ verba eorum.' This work is found in a
MS. belonging to the Duc d'Aumale; and twice in a MS.
at Bologna, one of the latter versions having yet another
text which gives a musical history, as it was understood
in those days, i.e. mentioning Jubal, Pythagoras, Boethius,
and Guido, with a few incomprehensible lines concerning
contemporary music.*

* Coussemaker supposes the names in Alain's poem are those of a princely
establishment under his own direction; I cannot see any reason for this, but
the reader may judge for himself, if he can understand the barbarous diction:

'Sub Arturo plebs vallata
  Plaudat melos ; laus ornata
    Psallatur Altissimo;
Anglis conferuntur (*conferentur*) grata
  Eventu piissimo.

'En milicia cum clero
  Floret, musicorum vero
    Chorus odas jubilat
E quibus modo sincero
  J. de Corbensi (*Torbrez emicat*)
    micat.

'Cujus non previsas pacto
  Res, quas J. de Alto Bosco
    Reserat theorica.
Qua fungens vernat, ut nosco,
  G. Martini practica.

'Piis placent ac tyrannis
  Res Ricardi Blith (*Blich*), Johannis
    Necnon de Oxonia;
Arte cujus multis annis
  Fulsit Cantuaria.

'Sed G. Mughe radix florum
  Det generibus melorum.
    Edmundus de Buria,
Basis aurea tenorum
  Est quem fovet curia.

'Princeps bellicus probavit
  Quas ex Blith (*Blich*) G. res creavit
    Rutilantes oculo;
Ex Ipswich (*epis. Wich.*) J. quas
    gustavit
  Mire vocis modulo.

Robert Morton, who is mentioned by several writers, has an unmistakably English name; nothing is known of him except that in 1474 he visited Cambrai with the Netherland composer Hayne, and was received with great honour, as is related in a chanson of the Dijon MS. Robertus de Anglia, choirmaster at Bologna 1467–72; Robertus Anglicus, in the choir of St. Peter's at Rome in 1485, may have both been identical with Robert Morton.

John Hothby (Otteby, Ottobi) is better known personally than any other English musician of the period.* He was also of the second generation of composers, and in a treatise mentions Okeghem. After lecturing at Oxford in 1435 he travelled, and settled in Italy; he lived first at Florence, then in the Carmelite monastery at Ferrara. In 1467 he went to Lucca, and, as he was sought for by other towns, his salary was raised in 1469. A MS. (now at Paris) was copied for him in 1471 by his pupil, Mathæus de Testadraconibus, who has inserted a highflown poem by 'Ferrabos':

'Musica si quis adest dederit cui nomen, et ipse
Ex apii meruit fronde operire comas
Ottobi, cedat tibi.   Si lustraveris orbem
A Gange ad Gades par tibi nullus erat;
Nam rerum natura parens effudit in uno
Quidquid erat forme, quidquid honoris erat.'

In 1486 Henry VII summoned Hothby back to England; the Lucchese gave him leave of absence for eighteen months, and a very flattering testimonial, but he died soon after, as they were informed on November 6th, 1487.

Four sacred and five secular compositions by Hothby, all three-voiced, were long preserved at Ferrara; the MS. is now lost, but a transcript by Padre Martini remains.

'Flos Oxonie miratur
Nicolaus qui vocatur
De vade (*Valde*) Famelico.
E. de Muristo jungatur
His triplo mirifico.

'Prepollet G. de Horarum
Fonte lira ; vox non parum
Mulcet aures Symonis;
Clementis os cujus clarum
Manus nitet organis.

'Practicat Adam Levita
Precellenter, quorum vita
Sane diu vigeat,
Ut ex (*et*) illis qua finita
Porta coeli pateat.'

* See Kornmüller's monograph in Haberl's *Jahrbuch*, 1893.

Three short treatises were published in Coussemaker's third volume. There are copies of these at Bologna, Venice, Paris, the British Museum, and Lambeth Palace. *Dialogus de Arte Musica*, as yet unprinted, is at Florence. The published works are: *Regulæ super Proportionem, De Cantu Figurato, Regulæ super Contrapunctum*; and three little tracts, in *Cecilia* for 1850. Hothby is described as a Carmelite; if he had been a Benedictine I should have been inclined to identify him with John Benet. Under his direction Lucca became a musical centre of importance.

All these, even Lionel Power, were but as satellites around the great JOHN DUNSTABLE. It is singular that we know nothing personal of so celebrated a man, beyond his two epitaphs. He was doubtless from the little Bedfordshire town, where there was a wealthy and important Dominican monastery. Stow, in his *Survey of London*, p. 245, tells us that in the church of St. Stephen's, Walbrook, Dunstable's epitaph was to be seen on 'two fayre plated stones in the Chancell, each by other.' Fuller also quotes the epitaph, which runs as follows in his version:

> ' Claudit hoc tumulo, qui Cœlum pectore clausit
> Dunstable I. juris, astrorum conscius ille
> Judice novit hiramis abscondita pandere cœli.
> Hic vir erat tua laus, tua lux, tua Musica princeps
> Quique tuas fulces (dulces) per mundum sparserat artes.
> Anno Mil. Equater, semel L. trias jungito Christi.
> Pridie natale sidus transmigrat ad astra,
> Suscipiant proprium civem cœli sibi cives.'

Stow reads 'illo' for 'ille' in line 2; and in line 5, 'dulces' for 'fulces,' and 'sperserat onus' for 'sparserat artes.'

The other epitaph was one of a number written by the famous John of Wheathamstead, then Abbot of St. Albans; it was printed[*] in Weever's *Funeral Monuments*. It adds nothing to our knowledge of the composer, save the high character it ascribes to him, but must be quoted:

> ' Upon John Dunstable, an astrologian, a mathematician,
> a musitian, and what not.
> Musicus hic Michalus alter, novusque Ptholomeus,
> Junior ac Athlas supportans robore celos
> Pausat sub cinere; melior vir de muliere

---

[*]From Cotton MS. Otho *b* 4, damaged in 1731, and practically destroyed in 1865.

Numquam natus erat; vicii quia labe carebat,
Et virtutibus opes possedit vincus omnes.
Cur exoptetur, sic optandoque precetur
Perpetuis annis celebretur fama Johannis
Dunstapil; in pace requiescat et hic sine fine.'

The epitaphs tell us only of a man who died in 1453
(apparently December 24th), of remarkable skill in
astronomy, and unrivalled in music, being, in fact, *the
man who dispersed the knowledge of music through the
world.* They do not mention Dunstable's age, but they
suggest that he was well advanced in years. He was
probably born between 1380 and 1400, and the earlier
date seems the more probable.

The earliest known reference to Dunstable is in *Le
Champion des Dames* of Martin le Franc, a French poet
who became Papal notary in 1439 and died in 1460.
His poem was written in or about 1437; it declares that
the best Parisian singers had been surpassed by Dufay
and Binchois, who had modelled themselves upon the
English, especially Dunstable:

'Car ilz ont nouvelle pratique
    De faire frisque concordance
En haulte et en basse musique,
    En fainte, en pause, et en muance,
Et ont prins de la contenance
    Angloise et ensuy Donstable;
Pour quoy merveilleuse playsance
    Rend leur chant joyeux et stable.'

At the same time works by Dunstable, Power, Benet,
Forest, and Markham had penetrated into the Tyrol;
other MSS. of this period contain works of Dunstable's.
We know no other reference to him during his lifetime.

The next allusion is probably that in Hothby's *Dialogus
de Arte Contrapuncti*, and is noteworthy from the patriotic
pride of the insertion, 'that Englishman,' the Latin words
reminding one of the construction, 'Alexander ille.' It was
first printed by Morelot; subsequently by Coussemaker,
who misprinted Leonel [Power] *Iconal.* Hothby says:

'In quamplurimis . . . aliis cantilenis recentissimis, quarum
conditores plerique adhuc vivunt, Dunstable anglicus ille, du Fay,
Leonel, Plumeret, Frier, Busnoys, Morton, Ockinghem, Pelagultus,
Bicheleth, Baduin, Forest, Stane, Fich, Caron, etc.'

Tinctor, the best Flemish theorist, mentions Dunstable in three of his treatises, all probably written about 1475–80. The earliest, from *De Arte Contrapuncti*, is:

'Neque quippiam compositum, nisi citra annos quadraginta, extat, quod auditu dignum ab eruditis existimetur. Hac vero tempore infiniti florent compositores, ut Okeghem, Regis, Busnois, Caron, Faugues, qui novissimis temporibus vita functos, Dunstable, Binchois, Dufay, se præceptores habuisse in hac arte divina gloriantur.'

This may imply that Dunstable actually taught Okeghem, etc., or only that the younger school followed the style of the recently deceased masters. Tinctor's allusion in his *Complexus Viginti Effectuum Nobilis Artis Musices* is of less importance, as it simply names Dunstable first among a list of famous composers, concluding with 'Obrechts,' thus showing its later date than the preceding quotation:

'Nostro autem tempore, experti sumus quanti plerique musici gloria sint effecti. Quis enim Joannem Dunstable, Guillermum Dufay, . . . Jacobum Obrechts non novit?'

The most famous allusion, and also the most important in every respect for the historian of the origin of composition, is in the Prohemium to Tinctor's *Proportionale*, and has already been partly quoted on p. 49. The entire passage (omitting a compliment to the King of Naples) is as follows:

'Denique principes christianissimi, . . . cultum ampliare divinum cupientes more davidico capellas instituerunt, in quibus diversos cantores per quos diversi vocibus (non adversis) Deo nostro jocunda decoraque esse laudatio, ingentibus expensis assumpserunt; et quoniam cantores principum (si liberalitate, quæ claros homines facit prædicti sint) honore, gloria, divitiis afficiuntur, ad hoc genus studii ferventissime multi incenduntur. Quo fit ut hac tempestate, facultas nostræ musices tam mirabile susceperit incrementum quod ars nova esse videatur, cujus, ut ita dicam, novæ artis fons et origo, apud Anglicos quorum caput Dunstaple exstitit, fuisse perhibetur, et huic contemporanei fuerunt in Gallia Dufay et Binchois quibus immediate successerunt moderni Okeghem, Busnois, Regis, et Caron, omnium quos audiverim in compositione præstantissimi. Hæc eis Anglici nunc (licet vulgariter jubilare, Gallici vero cantare dicuntur) veniunt conferendi. Illi etenim in dies novos cantus novissime inveniunt, ac isti (quod miserrimi signum est ingenii) una semper et eadem compositione utuntur.'

This invaluable account (printed in Coussemaker's great collection, IV 154) was the ground on which Dunstable secured a fitful remembrance during the sixteenth and seventeenth centuries. The English composers apparently did not influence Germany; neither Adam of Fulda nor Ornithoparcus mentions Dunstable. Sebastian Heyden was the first to introduce his name there; in *De Arte Canendi* (1537) he says, evidently quoting Tinctor, that Dunstable was the inventor of counterpoint. This statement is true as regards what we now call counterpoint; the word existed before Dunstable's time, but it had not meant the use of *independent* voice-parts as it has done since. The master was also known in Spain, for a MS. (at the Escurial Palace*) written at Seville in 1480 contains a history of the art, beginning with Dunstable; I have, unfortunately, not been able to procure the exact words. Gaforius twice mentions Dunstable in his *Practica Musica* (Naples, 1496); once quoting the tenor of a 'Veni sancte spiritus,' and once as an authority for the use of passing-notes. Even in Guillaume Crétin's *Deploration de Jehan Ockeghem* the poet mentions Dunstable among the musicians whom he sees in his dream. Eloy d'Amerval's *Livre de la Diablerie*, published in 1508, contains a vision of Paradise; there the poet saw the great musicians, directed by Dunstable and Dufay, composing hymns of praise for the saints and angels to sing. Afterwards nothing was heard of Dunstable till Sebastian Heyden gave him his due credit as the inventor of counterpoint, Nucius and later German writers copying the statement. For fifty years after his death he had been in the highest repute as the creator of a new art, and still a leading authority.

Who was he, then? I like in fancy to trace his life through; to see him as a boy mounting the grassy Chilterns to the barrows of the sea-kings who sleep high above his native town at the crossing of the Watling Street and the Icknield Way; watching the stars as they passed over him; hearing the organists as they added fifths to the plain-song of the monks in the monastery

* Codex C III 23.

church, and wondering why it offended his ear, perhaps even supposing such a thought to be a sin which needed confession and penance; pitying deposed Richard as the unhappy monarch was led northward to his fate at Pontefract; joining in the crowds applauding Prince Hal returning from Shrewsbury fight; then becoming a great clerk, entering the newly-founded Chapel Royal, finding that the large body of skilled singers there continually suggested untried effects to him, and inventing novelties which amazed and delighted every hearer; arranging music for the celebrations when the Londoners welcomed the victor of Agincourt; following the hero-king to Normandy, singing at the head of the procession before him in Rouen Cathedral, in Notre Dame de Paris, in Troyes; passing on into wealthy and cultivated Italy; ever improving music by making the ear a higher authority than arithmetical calculation, and everywhere bringing older attempts into disuse by the obvious superiority of his own; returning in honour and renown to English-ruled Paris, and after perhaps a lengthened stay there, through English Calais to his native country; settling in London under the evening shadow of the lofty spire which crowned its famous cathedral; surrounded with reverent pupils, and passing into the decline of life comforted by 'all that should accompany old age,' and with the consciousness that he had done what scarce any man may do in creating a new art, had led musicians out of the arid desert, and both by precept and example had indicated the true path; finally, paying the debt of nature, and being buried with rare pomp, amid universal sorrow at the loss of a great and good man, who was remembered and honoured throughout all Europe.

So for a time he continued in remembrance. Some of his works were copied into the Old Hall and Eton MSS., and a volume of Henry VIII's contains another. Then he was forgotten. The unlucky absence of theoretical English treatises prevents us from hearing more of him; and Bale, whose *Scriptores Britanniæ* might have given us full information, seldom mentions musicians, and never without a sneer. Morley, in 1597, was acquainted with

some of Dunstable's works, and of Power's; though he
mentions Dunstable only to make a wretched pun on his
name, and to ridicule a motet of his in which there are
rests between syllables. Ravenscroft, however, in 1614
reasserted Dunstable's claim to the invention of composition, on the authority of 'Nucius, and divers others.'
Thus England already had to use the authority of Germans
to prove her own glory! Ravenscroft repeatedly quoted
a treatise, which, as I have previously said, I believe was
Tunsted's; and since Ravenscroft himself was proposing
to go back to the clumsy Proportional notation, his book
had little success, and no subsequent English musician
seems aware of Dunstable's place in history. The epitaphs
were ridiculed by Fuller, who said they must refer to the
same wonderful man, as 'it would bankrupt the exchequer
of nature to afford two such persons, one Phœnix at
once being as much as any would believe.' H. Lawes,
writing during the Commonwealth, knew nothing of
pre-Reformation music, and supposed that Henry VIII
had sent to Italy for musicians. Then the Great Fire of
London destroyed Dunstable's grave; and not for another
century, not until the researches of Hawkins and Burney,
aided by Padre Martini, was Dunstable's name again
heard in his native country.

Elsewhere he had been only remembered in Germany.
One writer after another had copied Heyden's statement;
but even this had been confused by the senseless blunder
of Lustig, a Dutch historian, who confused Dunstable
with St. Dunstan, and had been copied by Printz,
Marpurg, and Walther. Others had been more exact;
and by far the most striking mention of the old composer
occurred when D. Venzky, librarian at Halberstadt, wrote
to Mizler's *Musikalische Bibliothek* proposing that the
tercentenary of Dunstable's invention of composition
should be celebrated in 1740, together with the tercentenary of Gutenberg's invention of printing. Venzky's
suggestion was not adopted; and the year would have been
rather too late. Nevertheless, his idea should be acted
on in future; and the year 1415 may conveniently be
taken as the date which deserves remembrance.

Yet again, after Hawkins and Burney had reasserted Dunstable's claim, he fell for a time into the background. Forkel, discussing the subject at length, decided against the claim. Then came a mistake of Baini's, who casually mentioned Dufay as a member of the Papal choir from 1380–1432. Kiesewetter (followed by every writer for forty years) at once, without examination, gave the credit of inventing composition to Dufay. Friedrich W. Arnold, Houdoy, and others corrected this by discovering the details of Dufay's life; and the full biography by Haberl finally showed that Dufay was of a later generation, and died in 1474. Thus the evidence of Martin le Franc, Tinctor, and the other fifteenth-century writers, is confirmed. The question is now settled; and as long as musical history is studied, John Dunstable will be affectionately remembered as the man who invented the art of composition.

We are also at last in possession of some of his works. Hawkins and Burney knew only the fragments quoted by Gaforius and Morley; in 1847 a secular piece was discovered at Rome, and since then the choir-books at Bologna, Trent, and Modena have yielded up many relics of English genius preserved for 400 years. In England there is also a little by him or his school, generally anonymous.

The following is a complete list of the works by Dunstable and his contemporaries, as far as they are at present known:

Thirteen pieces for two or three voices, in a vellum roll at Trinity College, Cambridge. They are all Christmas carols, except a song on the battle of Agincourt. The latter is found in other MSS., and was printed both by Burney and J. Stafford Smith, but in an inferior version. The whole thirteen were printed in 1891. They are anonymous, but both words and music are probably by Dunstable or Power. The Agincourt song was written in Henry V's life, and soon after the victory, and the MS. can hardly be dated after 1430.

Six secular songs in Ashmolean MS. 191, Bodleian Library. They are of later date than the Cambridge roll, probably about 1430–50. The poetry is of more value than the music, which is clumsy and roughly noted. The songs are for two or three voices; the last is in open-note notation, the others in the 'black-full.' Ashmolean MS. 1393 has another song very similar in style; on the opposite page is an Antiphon for two voices. All these are anonymous. They are facsimiled, with a translation into modern notation, in E. W. B. Nicholson's *Early Bodleian Music*.

A Christmas Carol—published (with harmony) by Chappell, three lines of Latin ecclesiastical music, and a succession of eighteen notes as a minstrel's reciting chant are in the song-book edited by the Percy Society, and now at the Bodleian Library, as mentioned on p. 40.

Lansdowne MSS. 462, a fine Sarum Gradual from Norwich Cathedral, has at the end some pages of music, Kyries, a Magnificat, etc., some of which are inscribed 'Dunstable' and 'Lyonel' (Power). They are probably intended as descant upon the plain-song.

A collection of fifty-two anonymous pieces is in Selden MS. *b* 26, Bodleian Library. One is ascribed to Dunstable in the Modena MS. There are a few secular pieces, including the Agincourt Song; the rest are hymns in Southern English dialect, with Latin refrains. All are facsimiled and translated in *Early Bodleian Music*.

Additional MSS. 5666, formerly belonging to Ritson, has six tunes for Christmas Carols. It was written by Friar John Brakley of Norwich, who died about 1465 The tunes are very roughly scribbled.

The part of the Eton MS. which contained a five-voiced 'Gaude flore virginali' by Dunstable has disappeared. In British Museum MS. 10,336, and also in a MS. at Lambeth, a treatise on Mensurable Music is followed by some notes and figures marked 'Qd. Dunstable'; this has been called an enigma, but is more probably a chorister's exercise. In Addit. MS. 31,922 there is a piece of music (without words) for three voices, by Dunstable; a translation has been made by Mr. J. F. Stainer, and published. This volume, which contains many pieces by Henry VIII, was doubtless the last in which a piece of Dunstable's music was included. I do not think that the motet at which Morley sneered was No. 3 in Royal MSS. 8 *g* 7, but this is not impossible. Morley evidently knew some choir-books containing works by Dunstable, Power, a certain Robert Orwell, now unknown, besides other composers dealt with in the next chapter. There is a motet by ' John Bedingham ' in the Royal Collection.

The three songs in the Shearmen and Taylors' Pageant at Coventry, 'As I rode out this enders night,' 'Lullay, lullay,' 'Downe from heaven so hie,' all three-voiced, are printed in T. Sharp's *Coventry Mysteries*. They are probably of this period; so also is the Boar's Head Carol, still sung at Queen's College, Oxford, every Christmas Day, and undeniably a very early relic. The little round, 'Row the boat, Norman,' celebrates John Norman, in 1453 Lord Mayor of London. A MS. written at Hendon about 1420 contained three carols, apparently two-voiced; it was sold at Sotheby's in 1904 to Mr. Oldfield.

These pieces, it is obvious, are all small and unambitious, only short flights of song; no Mass or large connected work is prseerved in England.* But on the Continent the discoveries since 1847 have been really wonderful, and show how great the fame of the English musicians must have been.

'O rosa bella,' a three-voiced love-song by Dunstable, was discovered at Rome, and afterwards, in a different version, at Dijon. It is evidently counterpoint on a popular song. Both versions were printed by Morelot in 1856; the one from the Vatican Library also by Ambros, and by Ritter. It is the most interesting to a modern hearer of Dunstable's works, as far as I know.

In six choir-books, written 1430–70, for Trent Cathedral, and now at Vienna, there are in all forty English works; fifteen of these are by Dunstable, and eleven by Power. The oldest of these books was written before 1440; it contains twenty-four English works, ten of which are by Dunstable and eight by Power. The other books, except the latest, all have some contributions from

*But see p. 67.

England. In one there is a secular song, 'Puis que m'amour,' by Dunstable. Bedingham, Markham, Forest, Stanley, and John Benet are all represented. In these choir-books there are three Masses constructed on 'O rosa bella'; it is used in each movement except the Benedictus. Unfortunately, no composer's name is given. With many other English and Flemish excerpts they were published in 1904 by the Austrian Government, edited by Professors Adler and Koller.

In the library of Bologna University there is a MS. with two Glorias and a Motet, 'Ave maris stella,' by Dunstable. A still more important MS. from Piacenza, now at the Liceo Comunale, Bologna, has fifteen works by Dunstable, Power, Alain, Benet, and Gervasius de Angliâ.

Most important of all is the great MS. at Modena,* written 1470–80. Besides many Flemish works, there are forty-eight by English composers; of these, a Magnificat and thirty motets are by Dunstable, and eight by Power, the rest being by Benet, Forest, Sandley or Stanley, and Stove. Four of Dunstable's and one of Power's are for four voices; all the others for three. Mr. W. Barclay Squire, of the British Museum, in April, 1892, went to Modena, and made a complete copy of Dunstable's thirty-one works, with a Thematic catalogue of the other seventeen; this is now in the British Museum, Addit. MS. 36,490.

Including the contents of the Old Hall MS. we now possess over 300 compositions of this period. 'O rosa bella,' the carols of the Trinity College roll, the Selden MS., and the Ashmole MS., some of the motets found in Italy, and the Trent excerpts edited at Vienna, are published, and accessible. Miss Cecie Stainer in 1900 contributed to the International Musical Society's publications a Thematic catalogue of the forty-six known compositions of Dunstable, not including the three Masses on 'O rosa bella.' Every great library should possess a complete copy of these works in modern notation. To the musical historian, not only of England, a knowledge of this earliest school of composition will be necessary in future.

* Bibl. Estense VI H 15.

At Old Hall, near Ware, is preserved a rather later MS., a choir-book containing no less than 138 compositions. Although it belonged to John Stafford Smith it was first described in the second volume of the International Musical Society's publications (1900–1), on pp. 342 and 719, by Mr. W. Barclay Squire. It contains thirty-seven settings of the Gloria; then fifteen Antiphons; thirty-seven settings of the Credo, with three motets by Dunstable and Forest; thirty of the Sanctus, with three hymns; fifteen of the Agnus Dei, and four other pieces. There are no Kyries. Nearly every piece is complete, but carelessly written. Many are anonymous; the composer most frequently named is Leonel (Power), to whom twenty-one pieces are ascribed. The names Thomas Damett and Nicholas Sturgeon point to a connection with St. George's Chapel, Windsor.

Other composers named are Cooke, Burell, Gyttering, J. Tyes, J. Excetre, Pycard, Rowlard, Queldryk, Pennard, Gervays (probably the 'Gervasius de Anglia' of the Italian choir-books), Fonteyns, Olyver, R. Chirbury, W. Typp, Swynford, Lambe, Mayshuet; and a Gloria and Sanctus are ascribed to 'Roy Henry,' who is naturally supposed King Henry VI. The monk-monarch's testament shows he was almost an architect; it had not been known that he was skilled in music. To Mr. Squire's exhaustive account I can only add the suggestion that 'Swynford' may have been Thomas Swynford (1408–65), a nephew of John of Gaunt's third wife; a place in the Chapel Royal might be expected for a relation of the king's.

Most of the complete pieces are three-voiced. Some of Power's are four-voiced. There are remarkable complications in Pycard's and some of the anonymous, where two free upper parts are accompanied by three-voiced canons. Exact directions are given for the performance of No. 71, which contains all the varieties arising from the use of black-full, black-void, red-full, red-void, and even blue notes.* In No. 107, by Damett, the upper parts

* Blue notes, it is directed, are to be sung 'according to double proportion'; they are also explained in Tucke's treatise.

are accompanied by a canon four-in-one in the tenor; the first answer is in diminution, the next is in one-third the original length, and the last one in one-sixth. Here and in a few other instances, even in Mass-movements, different words are sung simultaneously. Two Glorias by Pycard, and a Credo by Pennard, have an extra voice-part, marked *Solus Tenor*.

This important volume is sadly marred by the care-lessness of the scribe. Mr. Squire quoted specimens by Henry VI, Power, Damett, and Mayshuet; and they are decidedly inferior to the earlier works by Dun-stable and Power in the Modena and Trent choir-books. Dunstable had 'scattered the sweet arts of music through the world,' but it would almost appear that he had left none at home. Some thirty years of weakness began, so far as we can judge from the relics preserved. Then English musicians began to revive once more and invent.

One reference to Scottish musical history is here required. James I's long captivity and education in England occurred just in the time when Dunstable flourished. On the young king's return with an English wife he introduced the new music into his own realm, and himself composed 'Cantilenas Scoticas' and sacred music. These are, unfortunately, all lost. Even Bale forgets to sneer at music when he mentions the king's compositions, and their traditional fame reached Italy, for they are mentioned by Tassoni.

A complete critical examination of the Dunstable school is not possible until all the works preserved are accessible. A point which to me seems deserving of special study is the varying treatments respectively allotted to works consisting entirely of free voice parts, and works in which a measured plain-song is throughout sung by the tenor. Liturgical knowledge will here be useful. The French and English musicians of the thirteenth century had indeed felt that music could be made a structural art, but their attempts had failed, because they could not discover the right means. The Italians of the fourteenth century had (according to Ambros) felt their way towards the expressive side of music, but could not advance, because the structural laws were still unknown; and Italy then gave up the cultivation of music to foreigners. At last (1400–20) the laws were discovered, and in fundamentals they rule music to the present day. Dunstable, rejecting the arguments of Boethius, made the ear a higher authority than the 'reason,' and abjured consecutive fifths. It is especially interesting to note how his plan of using separate phrases cut by rests, so that each voice part is silent unless it is indispensable to the effect, is essentially the same as that of all the Polyphonic Schools to Palestrina himself, and not only of these, but also of Bach's fugues, of Haydn's quartet-writing, of Beethoven's orchestration. With discordant progressions forbidden, and suspensions, passing-notes, and imitations in regular use, the art of composition could begin; Dunstable began it, and it has never ceased.

As regards the influence of the earliest English school upon the general course of musical history, Haberl has clearly shown that the improvements which Fétis had ascribed to Dufay were really the inventions of Dunstable; and Haberl reasonably supposes that Dufay, before he went to Rome in 1428, was already acquainted with Dunstable's 'new art.' We know that Dufay graduated at Paris; and Paris was under English rule from 1420–36. We have seen how Henry V sent to England for his Chapel Royal in 1418; and the Duke of Bedford, Regent of France after the king's death, doubtless continued the establishment. Thus Dufay, without visiting England, could learn how immeasurably superior English music then was to all other; indeed, to any music which had ever existed. Binchois, in his youth a soldier, would naturally follow his lord, the Duke of Burgundy, the English ally; and would also come in contact with English music. There is thus nothing inexplicable in Martin le Franc's statement that Dufay and Binchois surpassed all the Parisians, by taking the English, especially Dunstable, as models.

Should anything further come to light regarding any of the school, it will probably turn up in Paris or in Northern Italy. In the long Regency of the Duke of

Bedford, traces of their presence may have been left at Paris, or the archives of some Italian city may give us a distinct account of some one among them, as of Hothby at Lucca. Especially of Dunstable we would gladly learn something; in spite of all his just celebrity he remains a singularly shadowy figure. There is an astronomical tract in the Bodleian Library, dated April, 1438, apparently in his handwriting; that, his epitaphs, and Hothby's 'Dunstable anglicus ille,' alone have personal associations, such as we should love to find in the case of so gifted a man, one of the great benefactors of the human race. High in the roll of England's worthies must his place ever be; and whatever may be achieved in the future, let it never be forgotten that the original invention of musical composition was the work of an Englishman, that without John Dunstable there could have been no Palestrina, no Handel, no Bach, no Mozart, no Beethoven. The day may come, may possibly come soon, when England will fall from its place among nations. The future historian who then sums up the tale of the nation's achievements will not begin with musical matters, nor even with the discovery of the laws of gravitation and evolution, nor with the conquest of India and the empire of the sea, but with the creation of *King Lear*, *Macbeth*, *Hamlet*, and *Othello*. Yet let him not put much below these the invention of musical composition by John Dunstable.

CHAPTER III

THE PERIOD OF THE INVENTION OF INSTRUMENTAL COMPOSITION (1453-1536)

*After Dunstable.—The Chapel Royal.—Musical Degrees.
—The Flemings surpass the English in Ecclesiastical Music.
—Account of the existing MSS.—Biographical Notices of
the Fayrfax School.—Instrumental Composition invented
by Hugh Aston.*

*Representative Composers : Banester, Fayrfax, Aston,
Taverner.*

IN 1453, the year when John Dunstable was borne to
his last resting-place in London City, the Eastern
Roman Empire finally ended, and the last attempt of the
English to retain their French conquests was frustrated.
Gutenberg and Faust were printing Bibles. The Middle
Ages were closing, and the Renascence of classical learning and arts, quickly followed by the discovery of America,
by the circumnavigation of Africa, and a generation later
by the Reformation, brought the modern world into being.
England passed through a period of fearful turmoil, of
murderous battles, excitement, unrest. The Wars of the
Roses began in 1455, and did not altogether cease even
at the Union of the Roses thirty years later. In those
thirty years England lost her pre-eminence in the art of
music; the English themselves did not believe so, but on
the Continent their renown was quite eclipsed, the last
choir-book which contains English works being that at
Modena. For sixty or seventy years afterwards Netherland composers ruled the world in musical matters. But
in the meantime the English, surpassed in ecclesiastical
music, turned their attention especially to instruments;
and they quickly found how to use the resources of the
keyboard, perceiving that an entirely new style of music
was required, that the styles neither of Dunstable nor of
his Flemish successors were sufficient for these novel
powers. Musical antiquaries are at present inclined to
look for the origin of the spinet, virginal, clavicytherium,
etc., in England; but we have no evidence other than

that mentioned on p. 43, which is far too slight to be sufficient by itself. The first mention of keyed instruments, other than the organ, is in 1477, at Lincoln, where William Horwode was appointed to teach choristers singing and playing on the 'clavychordes.' In Germany the organ had been long provided with a chromatic keyboard; Paumann (*d.* 1473) made an attempt to set running accompaniments to sustained notes. The earliest known instrumental *compositions* are, however, English, and are to be found in a MS. of the Arundel collection (Appendix to Royal MSS. 58); they are three in number, and are for the virginals. A number of short dance-tunes and some arrangements in lute-tablature follow in the MS.; they are probably of rather later date than the virginal compositions, which must have been transcribed about 1510. Only one of them all has a composer's name attached; it is the longest and most difficult, though not the most musical, of the three keyboard compositions— a Hornpipe. However, I do not doubt that all three were by the same composer; and his name, almost equally important with John Dunstable's, was Hugh Aston.

It was during the forty or fifty years after Dunstable's death that the Flemish composers were especially superior to the English; and so much of the Flemish work remains, and so little of the English work, that the English appear to be more inferior than they really were. Of that period, after the Old Hall MS. described in Chap. II, the only English MSS. are one in the Pepysian Library at Cambridge, and a Mass, also at Cambridge. About 1500 there are several, some of very great importance, and thenceforward we have opportunity of knowing the composers' works; but let it never be forgotten that we do not *exactly* know the original style of performance.

What were the causes of the failure to keep ahead in the race which had been started so splendidly? Some writers have laid the blame to the charge of the Wars of the Roses; but the strife was not incessant, and after 1471 Edward IV reigned undisturbed, the later struggle being brief. Periods of turmoil are also not unfavourable to literature, and the tranquillity succeeding them has

often matured high creative genius.   As will be seen,
musicians had full encouragement and opportunity; yet
there was evidently a period of weakness.   Tinctor's words
tell us the secret why the Flemings quickly and decidedly
surpassed their English models; the quotation* from his
Proportionale states that 'the French invent novelties,
while the English continually employ one and the same
method of composition.'   The craven imitators of Dunstable were soon left hopelessly behind.   Okeghem's
science brought forth the genius of Josquin des Pres, who,
as early as 1480 had produced that *Stabat Mater* which to
this day commands admiration, while the English were
still doing what had been done before.   Let English
musicians ever bear in mind that England once led the
world in music, and lost the position because our composers no longer invented, but copied.

No other reason seems perceptible, nor is any other
required.   The kings of the House of York and their
Tudor successors were munificent in support of the art;
and we have now documentary evidence of this.   In
1469 Edward IV issued letters patent establishing a
perpetual guild of minstrels, with power over all in the
realm except those of Chester, where the descendants of
Dutton still held the hereditary rule conferred in 1212.
This guild, or Fraternity and Sisterhood of Minstrels,
was enjoined to restrain all unqualified musicians, who
were only to practise at home until they were considered
duly qualified.   The Marshal, appointed for life, was
Stephen Haliday; while John Cliff, Robert Marshall,
Thomas Grene, Thomas Calthorn, William Christian, and
William Eynsham formed the Court of Assistants, two
being annually elected wardens.   Every minstrel was
required to join the Guild, and to pay three shillings
and fourpence on being admitted.   The Marshal and
Court of Assistants were all in the service of the king,
and previously of Henry VI.

The first definite account of the Chapel Royal is in
the *Liber Niger Domus Regis* recording Edward IV's
household expenses; there were twenty-four chaplains and

* See p. 59.

clerks; the food and regulations for the thirteen minstrels, the 'Wayte' who was to sound three times nightly during summer and four times during winter, and for the eight choir-boys, with their 'Master of the Song,' are all duly directed in this Black Book, which may be seen in Harleian MSS. 293 and 610; the passages in question are given in Hawkins and Burney. There were also strangers who assisted at the principal feasts, and doubtless on state occasions; and we have other evidence of the strength and skill of Edward IV's musicians. In 1466 Leo von Rozmital, brother-in-law of George Podiebrad, King of Bohemia, made a tour through Western Europe, of which an account, written by Schassek, his secretary, still exists; it was published at Olmütz in 1577, and reprinted at Stuttgart in 1844. The visitors were entertained by Edward IV with a banquet, followed by a state ball and concert. Schassek describes the ceremony, saying: 'We heard in no country more agreeable and sweeter musicians than these; their chorus consists of about sixty voices.' A German member of the suite, Gabriel Tetzel, also recorded his opinion: 'After the ball came the king's singers and sang; I believe that there are no better singers in the world.'

There were other princely establishments besides the Chapel Royal, though we only know of their existence at a rather later date. The Duke of Buckingham in 1508 had a choir of eighteen men and nine boys; and the Northumberland Household-Book, which begins in 1512, shows another large musical establishment. Cardinal Wolsey had thirty-two singers. Magdalen College, Oxford, founded in 1458 by Waynflete, has a choir of twenty-four; and it was especially provided that, in case of diminished revenue, the choir should not suffer. This College and its organists have had an important share in the musical history of England.

In maintaining these and other choirs the daily musical Mass was the principal object, but there was also other work for them. The connection between musical and literary history here again is intimate; for out of the Chapel Royal and the other establishments grew the

English drama. The principal officials, such as the Master of the Children, the organist and almoner (posts commonly united), were expected to provide entertainments of all kinds. They wrote *Interludes* for the amusement of their patrons, introducing music and everything likely to please; Gilbert Banastir in 1482, Cornysche in Henry VIII's reign, Heywood, Redford, and Edwards, are all recorded as writing dramas, and even in Shakespeare's time the connection between choir-boys and the stage had not ceased. The Northumberland Household-Book provides that if the Almoner were a 'maker of interludys,' he should have a servant to copy the parts. It should be noted that the earliest known piece of music printed in England is a song in an Interlude by Rastell. It appears to me that the rise of English lyric poetry is largely due to the introduction of songs into Interludes, Moralities, and Mysteries; every student of our dramatic literature before Shakespeare, and of our poetic achievements until 1700, should have a close acquaintance with music and our musical history.

Richard III granted powers for forcibly bringing to the Chapel Royal any competent singers, boys or men. This was long practised; Tusser mentions it, and Queen Elizabeth gave similar powers, exempting only St. Paul's Cathedral and Windsor Castle; the latter had an establishment of its own in St. George's Chapel, which must not be confounded with the Chapel Royal in London. Testimony concerning the splendid efficiency of the Chapel Royal may be gathered from the reports of foreign visitors all through the sixteenth century. Henry VII, and Elizabeth of York still more, were thorough lovers of music, and the king's parsimony apparently did not affect his choir. The Venetian ambassadors to Henry VIII, and German nobles who visited Elizabeth, spoke as enthusiastically of the Chapel Royal as the Bohemian travellers of the fifteenth century had done. Henry Abyngdon was made 'Master of the Song' (trainer of the children) in 1465; in 1482 Gilbert Banastir appears in that post, subsequently William of Newark, who died in 1509, and was succeeded by William Cornysch till 1524.

It is at the beginning of this period that we first hear of a special feature of English musical life—namely, university degrees. The first distinct mention is that Thomas Saintwix (Saintriste), Doctor of Music, was made Warden of King's Hall, Cambridge, in 1463; and in the same year Henry Habyngton (Abyngdon?) was made Bachelor of Music. Hanboys, according to Bale, was made Mus. Doc. about the same time. Whether any exercise was demanded is doubtful: the later admissions recorded sometimes mention an exercise, sometimes not. Probably the study of Boëthius was considered more essential than skill in practical music. Robert Fayrfax, who took the higher degree at Cambridge in 1502, had composed 'for his forme in proceeding to his degree' the five-voiced Mass, *O quam glorifica*; Richard Ede, who supplicated for Mus. Bac. Oxon. in 1506, was required to compose 'a Mass with an Antiphona,' to be sung on the day of his admission.

We may suppose that the school of which Dunstable was the chief master was still in vigour when he died. Hothby and Morton are known to have been alive many years later, possibly also Lionel Power and John Benet. They were doubtless held in all honour, and the aged masters were perhaps surrounded with pupils who thought that nothing could be nobler than to imitate them, and continue the glorious traditions of the earlier generation.

HENRY ABYNGDON is greatly celebrated as a singer and organist in two epitaphs by Sir Thomas More. I suppose him to have been from Abingdon, and to be the Henry Habyngton who took the degree of Mus.Bac. in 1463. In 1465 he was appointed 'Master of the Song' in the Chapel Royal, at an annual salary of forty marks. He had already (1447) received an appointment in Wells Cathedral, and subsequently enjoyed other preferments. He died September 1st, 1497, and was succeeded at Wells by ROBERT WYDOW, who seems to have been distinguished rather as a poet than a musician, though Leland tells us he had been made Bachelor of Music at Oxford. This must have been about 1470, as Wydow, after succeeding his father as schoolmaster at his native place, Thaxted,

Essex, was made vicar there in 1481. He is therefore the earliest known holder of a musical degree at Oxford. He died in 1505. No composition by either of these is known. It is worth mentioning here that the names Cornysch and Lovell, both important in our musical history about 1500, occur in the staff of Wells Cathedral, and that a canon of Wells copied a poem by William Cornysch.

The last allusion suggests a matter of great importance. I have in the previous chapter laid stress on the improvements in practical performance which led up to Dunstable's invention of the polyphonic style, and I must now draw attention to the musical instruments then known, before I describe the music composed for them. It is too often forgotten that in the early stages of an art practical improvements are an essential part of the advance.

Happily we possess some little knowledge on this point, through a poem by Cornysch, and another which I am certain is also his. They occur together in a MS. written by the Duke of Northumberland's secretary, T. Peeris; it is now Royal MS. 18 *d* 2. (See *Antiquarian Repertory* IV 405.) The poem with Cornysch's name is also in Harleian MS. 43; it was composed in July, 1504, and is a satire on informers and slanderers, the most interesting verse being:

> ' Any instrument mistunyd shall hurt a true songe,
> Yet blame not the clavycord, the wrester doth wronge.'

The anonymous poem (in language, spelling, style, and clumsiness of versification exactly similar) consists of thirty-two stanzas, which were formerly on the walls of a lodge in Leckingfield Park, and speak throughout of music and instruments. The most interesting parts are:

> ' Perfect vowellynge of a songe to the eere is delectable,
> He that quadribilith too hye his voice is variable.

> ' He that fingereth well the keyes of the clavicordis makithe a
>   good songe
> For in the meane is the melodye with a rest longe
> If the tewnye be not pleasant to hym that hath no skill
> Yet no lac to the Clavicord, for he doth his good will.

' He that is a perfyte musicion
    Perceyvith the lute tewnce and the good proporcion;
    In myddest of the body the stryngis soundith best
    For stoppid in the freytis they abyde the pynnes wrest.

' A slac strynge in a virgynall soundithe not aright
    It doth abyde no wrastinge, it is so loose and light.

' He that covetithe in clavisymballis to make goode concordaunce
    Ought to finger the keyes with discrete temporaunce
    Too muche wyndinge of the pipes is not the best
    Whiche may cause them to sypher where Harmony shulde rest.

' A shawme makithe a swete sounde, for he tunyth basse
    It mountith not too hye, but kepith rule and space.'

There are also verses upon the Clarion, 'the swete orgayne
pipis,' and the Recorder which 'the meane doth desyre.'
Both here and in a later poem (by Redford or Heywood)
the 'meane' appears as the most important voice part.
In the Expenses of Henry VII there are records of
payments for music, including £30 for an organ in 1493,
and 10s. for 'setting' a clavichord in 1502. There are
many references to organs in cathedral and parish
accounts during the whole of this period; the earliest
specification known is in 1519, when 'Antony Duddyngton, citizen of London,' contracted to build an organ
for Allhallows, Barking, which was to have twenty-seven
'playne keyes,' the lowest note to be 'double C-fa-ut.'
I suppose this to denote a compass from eight-foot C up
to f^{ll}, with three black notes for the 'lyric semitones';
but it is also possible that all the semitones were understood, and that a compass of twenty-seven white notes
was meant. Yet there was to be a 'Diapason of ten foot
or more.' Here again the connection between the
musician's invention and the resources at his command
must be borne in mind; and the chromatic keyboard, the
compass of the organs, and the pitch to which they were
tuned, are matters of importance in considering the
earliest instrumental music. This organ was to have
stops and a soundboard, and to cost £50. Schlick in 1511
had written that German organs always had the same
length of pipe for the lowest note, whether that note were
F or C; this illustrates the 'ten foot or more' diapason of

Duddyngton's C organ. The extreme compass of Hugh Aston's virginal music is from F to a^{11}, three octaves and a third; this is one note higher than Virdung mentions in his *Musica getutscht und auszgezogen* (Basel, 1511). The oldest organ music known to me is of rather later date, and is of the Reformation period.

In studying the biographical details of musicians' lives, the frequent recurrence of the same surnames is very confusing. We do not know the names of Edward IV's Chapel Royal, who sang through 'the holl sauter' over his corpse; but Richard III gave many rewards (the names being preserved in Harleian MS. 433), as did also Henry VIII; and we find these surnames elsewhere in connection with music, but with other Christian names. Musical skill commonly is hereditary (partly because children in a musical family hear much music from infancy), and the Middle Ages were specially times of craft-guilds, which indeed are in every way favourable to the development of an art until its culmination; afterwards mischievous. We may then reasonably suppose that musicians with the same surnames were of the same family. Also it is to be remembered that professional musicians must have been very few, and were either in the pay of the king, the great nobles, or the cathedral and monastic establishments, in the latter case being doubtless in holy orders. There were also wandering minstrels, who were now falling into disrepute, and were looked upon with great contempt by the scientific musicians; and there were the town bands of watchmen, the *waits*. Of musicians such as we know, who get their living by teaching, there can have been none; and the highest ambition of a musician must have been a post in the Chapel Royal (which admitted of other appointments also) or in the Royal Household.

I turn now to the actual musical remains. Some of the most important of these were known to Hawkins and Burney; the Fayrfax Boke has been in great part printed by them and Stafford Smith; and Burney has given important extracts from the Forrest-Heyther collection of Masses. But, very strangely, Hawkins did not look at the Royal MSS., then already in the British Museum; a glance at the index to Casley's catalogue would have shown him several MSS. I have to mention. Burney began to examine these, but went no farther than scoring one piece. Stafford Smith, in *Musica Antiqua* (1812), somewhat repaired the omission. The great choir-book at Lambeth Palace was also unknown to them; and there are others at Cambridge and Eton of the highest importance.

But also there is a MS. which Burney did see, and has described in an inexplicable way. He speaks of a MS. in the Pepysian Library containing two-voiced unimportant fragments by John Gwinneth and Robert Davis, in which red notes are used to indicate diminution. I have carefully examined the only MS. of this period mentioned in Pepys's catalogue, and could see in it neither the name Gwinneth nor the name Davis. There are some fifteen or twenty compositions in it, with red notes, by Banastir, Corbronde, Tuder, Hawt, Nesbet, Fowler, and Garnesey, and, as usual, there is a *Gymel*. It is possible that Burney carelessly turned over the leaves, and confused *Gymel* with *Gwinneth*; he must have evolved *Davis* from his inner consciousness, having seen the names together in Morley's list. Repeated examination showed nothing but what I had seen at first.

It is to be remembered that while the remains of the later fifteenth century are few and not important, those of the early sixteenth are numerous and valuable. There was evidently a very great advance as the weak imitators of Dunstable died out, and their place was taken by inventive men, of whom (in ecclesiastical music) the principal was Dr. Fayrfax. At the same time we might judge more favourably of Edward IV's musicians if we had more of their works preserved. The weak period I judge to have begun about 1450, and to have lasted till 1480 at least. Before 1500 new life had appeared in the ecclesiastical music; and above all there then appeared the study of keyed instruments, quickly, with extraordinary results. That most splendid period of English music, the sixteenth century, now began; about 1530 the Flemings were equalled, and England was again the most musical of nations until Palestrina in 1561 began the 161 years of Italian supremacy. The period covered by this chapter, therefore, consists of two sections, 1453 to about 1490, a little known and weak time; and 1490–1536, an age of extraordinary advance, in which we for the first time know of instrumental composition. The whole period was especially the time of Flemish music; but the English (certainly after 1500) were quite the equals of the Flemings in secular art, and by the end of the period in ecclesiastical music also.

Cambridge University MS. Ii. V 18.

The date of this MS. is only a guess, but I suppose it to be 1480 at latest. It is an anonymous Mass for three voices—medius, contratenor, and tenor—the latter being generally measured plain-song. The leaf containing the medius and tenor of the 'Et resurrexit,' and the contratenor of the 'Sanctus' and 'Osanna,' has been torn out. The 'Benedictus' and part of the 'Agnus' are for two voices only. The first movement is to the words, 'Kyrie, rex genitor ingenite, vera essencia, eleyson,' showing that the Mass was intended for certain festivals. The music is stiff and rather crude counterpoint on the plain-song.*

The Pepysian MS. 1236.

This is a small well-written and well-preserved volume, which in Pepys's catalogue is assigned to the reign of Edward IV. I should prefer the date 1480–1500. The music is interspersed with other matters; it is mostly at the beginning and end of the book. There are in all some fifteen or twenty pieces, among them being a two-voiced 'In manus tuas' and a 'Confitemini' by WILLIAM CORBRONDE; three-voiced pieces by GILBERT BANASTIR; several by JOHN TUDER; a five-voiced 'Benedicamus Domino' by SIR WILLIAM HAWT; and other pieces by NESBET, HAWT, FOWLER, FRYE, and GARNESEY. The most singular piece is a 'Lamentations' (beginning 'Aleph')

---

* I understood from the late Dr. Koller that this Mass is found in the Trent choir-books, with Dunstable's name. I cannot confirm this.

by Tuder for one voice; with a *Gymel*, apparently to be
repeated after each verse.

The Eton College MS.

This is the most important of the musical remains
of Henry VII's reign. According to the original index,
it contained ninety-five works by twenty-six composers;
ninety leaves are missing, but 149 remain, with fifty-eight
works, some of which are imperfect. There is an index
at the beginning; and another (not containing the
Magnificats) at the end. The volume is a large parchment
full-choir-book.* From internal evidence (the mention
of Richard Davy of Magdalen College, and the omission
of Fayrfax's degree) the date is between 1490 and 1504.
The binding bears the portcullis and initials of Henry VII;
and there is every reason to believe that the book was
originally written for Eton College. When the missing
parts disappeared is not easy to guess; the binding is not
loose. The volume is mentioned in Stafford Smith's
Musica Antiqua.

Originally the MS. contained sixty-six motets and
twenty-eight Magnificats. There are now forty-three
motets and four Magnificats; with five motets each
wanting a page, and four imperfect Magnificats. There
are also at the end an imperfect Passion according to
Matthew; and the Apostles' Creed, each clause allotted
to one of the Apostles, apparently forming a thirteen-
voiced riddle-canon. At the first place where there are
missing leaves, a nine-voiced 'Salve Regina' has been
inserted. This is without the composer's name, and is
not in the index.

The music, as far as it remains, approaches the style
of the early sixteenth century; and in one important
particular is quite unlike the works from the Modena MS.
and the Cambridge MS. Ii. V 18. It is never written on
a plain-song; but all the parts are free. The concluding
Creed is the only canon. There are many red notes, but
ligatures are not common. The music is mostly for five
voices, or more.

* I have invented this word to denote a volume containing all the voice-
parts, displayed at once upon opposite pages, in *cantus lateralis*.

The Passion is for four voices, and was composed by Richard Davy; it contained the twenty utterances of the Turba, or 'Crowd.' Specimens may be seen in the Oxford History of Music. Two pages of the triplex and contra, and one of the tenor and bass, seem lacking. The Creed is by Wilkinson; there is another by him in the Royal Collection.

The rest of the MS. consists almost entirely of Hymns to the Virgin. There are in all nine pieces by JOHN BROWNE, six by R. DAVY, seven by WALTER LAMBE, four each by HORWUD, CORNYSCH, and WYLKYNSON; two each by STURTON, HUGO KELLYK, EDMUND TURGES, FAWKYNS, and FAYRFAX; with one each by BRIDGMAN, JOHN SUTTON, HACOMPLAYNT, NICHOLAS HUCHYNS, RICHARD HYGONS, JOHN HAMPTON, GILBERT BANESTER, HOLYNGBOURNE, SYGAR, and WILLIAM STRATFORD, monachus Stratfordie. The missing twenty Magnificats included specimens by NESBET, BRYGEMAN, MYCHELSON, and BALDWYN; we have also lost an 'Ascendit Christus' by HUCHYN; and, alas, a five-voiced 'Gaude flore virginali' by DUNSTABLE.

This MS. is also peculiarly interesting on account of its singular directions for performance. Several pieces have a *Gymel*; but here it is always written *Gemell* or *Gemellū*; and is generally followed by *Semel* or *Semellū*. The latter occurs alone in a 'Salve Regina' by Lambe; and in the tenor of a Magnificat by Horwud. These directions seem to point to the use of solo voices, and it is possible that in large choirs *Gymel* and *Semel* were used as the words *Verse* and *Full* have been since.

It is most desirable that this precious volume should be completely copied out in modern notation. Several pieces were scored by John Travers in the eighteenth century; his copy subsequently became No. 1737 in the library of the Sacred Harmonic Society, now at the Royal College of Music. Hawkins and Burney do not mention the volume. M. R. James's catalogue of the Eton MSS. contains a detailed list of the contents. Mr. W. Barclay Squire published a valuable monograph in *Archæologia* for 1898, with a list of the complete pieces.

With so royal a foundation and endowment as Eton College received, it may readily be believed that music was enthusiastically cultivated there. The sad havoc worked in the library during the Reformation has probably for ever robbed us of other volumes of music as important as this one; there were beyond doubt many Masses composed or copied there, besides the motets, Magnificats, and Matthew-Passion, preserved in this splendid volume. Lyte's 'Eton College' unfortunately gives no particulars of musical matters.

Kirby's 'Annals of Winchester College' also gives but few particulars concerning the organs and organists of William Wykeham's foundation.

The Fayrfax Boke.

Since many of the pieces in this MS. have been published (by Hawkins, J. Stafford Smith, Burney, afterwards by Rimbault, and the Plain-song and Mediæval Music Society), and it has been repeatedly described, it requires less mention than its importance would suggest. The music is to secular words, some of which seem to refer to the Union of the Two Roses; and one to Prince Arthur Tudor. The volume, which belonged to, and was probably written by, Dr. Robert Fayrfax, must have been written in or before 1504, when he became Doctor, which he is not styled in it; the Yorkshire Fairfaxes owned it in the seventeenth century, subsequently Thoresby the antiquary, and it is now in the British Museum as Addit. MS. 5465. The songs are for three or four voices, in *cantus lateralis* on opposite pages; this style of notation I distinguish as a *full-choir-book*. Five of the songs are by Fayrfax himself; there are also seven by William of Newark, two by Sheryngham, one by Hamshere, four by R. Davy, four by Turges, one by Tutor (doubtless the 'Tuder' of the Pepysian MS.), one by Sir John Phelyppis, three by Browne, three by Cornysshe, and one by Banastir, with seventeen anonymous; in all forty-nine. Red notes are freely used. On the first page is some florid keyboard music, apparently of rather later date.

The Lambeth MS. 1

This is a large full-choir-book containing several Masses and motets, and is peculiarly interesting, as the second of the Masses is superscribed—'Doctor Fayrfax for his forme in proceeding to his degree.' The whole of the movements are on the same theme, *O quam glorifica*. The Gloria opens for two voices, the other three joining at 'Laudamus Te.' There is also a five-voiced Magnificat by Fayrfax, and an 'Eterne laudis' for six voices. The only other author-named piece is an 'Ave Maria' by Stourton; one Magnificat is superscribed 'Regale.' At the end there are three Masses in a different writing, making eighteen works in all, mostly by Fayrfax.

It is remarkable that neither Hawkins nor Burney thought of examining the Lambeth Palace Cambridge MSS. They thus missed Fayrfax's degree-exercise, and many other important works yet to be mentioned, belonging to Henry VIII's reign.

Gonville and Caius College MS. 667.

This huge full-choir-book measures twenty-eight inches by twenty inches. It is a parchment MS. written and presented to some cathedral or college by Edward Higgons, one of the canons. The contents are ten masses and five Magnificats. The masses are *O bone Jesu, Regali, O quam glorifica, Tecum principium,* and *Albanus,* by Fayrfax; *Cristi virgo, Videte miraculi, Benedicta,* and *Lapidaverunt,* by Ludford; and *Criste resurgens* by PASCHE. The Magnificats are by Cornysh, Fayrfax, Turges, Trentes, and Ludford. This invaluable MS. is in perfect preservation; there is no clue to the exact date, but I should guess 1510–20. Mr. Frere pointed out that it seems to be in the same handwriting as the Lambeth MS.

The Cambridge Part-Books.

A set of parchment part-books, numbering five or six originally, became dispersed and partly lost. One drifted into the Cambridge University Library (MS. Dd XIII 27); another is at St. John's College. They contain

ten motets: by Fayrfax (three), Prowett (two), R. Davy
(one), Lovell (one), Austen or Aston (one), and Taverner
(two); with a Stabat Mater by Davy, and a Magnificat
by Fayrfax. There are also five Masses: by Fayrfax
(two), Austen, William Pasche, and Ashwell; these are to
be found complete elsewhere, except Ashwell's, which is
superscribed 'God save King Herry.' In one of the
motets Queen Katherine is also mentioned; and the
appearance of Taverner's name proves a rather later date,
perhaps 1525–30. One can but hope that the others of
this fine set of part-books may yet come to light. The
detailed list of works may be seen in the Catalogue of
MSS. in the Cambridge University Library, V 588.

Harleian MSS. 1709.

This is unfortunately only a medius part-book. The
set contained twenty-six motets, some by Fayrfax, Davy,
Cornysshe, Ludford, Ashwell, Pygott, and T. Hyllary;
the sixteen others are anonymous. Some are included
in the Cambridge part-books; I think nearly all can be
identified.

Additional MSS. 5665.

No less than 117 pieces are preserved in this book;
copies of documents dated 1510 and 1511 occur. At the
beginning are carefully written and rubricated pieces by
Richard Smert (de Plymptre), John Trouluffe, R. Mower
(More?), John Cornysshe, Sir Thomas Packe; afterwards,
in various handwritings, works by Sir William Hawte,
Edmund Sturges (Turges), W. P. (Pasche?), and a Mass
by Henricus Petyre. The words are mostly Latin; there
are some ballads. This MS. was discovered by Ritson;
a few pieces were printed in *Musica Antiqua.*

Additional MSS. 31,922.

This fine volume perhaps belonged to King Henry VIII;
it contains 112 pieces, but many are very incorrectly
transcribed. The enigma by Dunstable has been mentioned in the previous chapter; there is also one by

Fayrfax, the other composers being principally of Fayrfax's period. No less than thirty-three songs (either
arrangements or original) are by the King; the rest
largely by Cornish and Thomas Farthing, with three each
by Dr. Cooper, John Fluyd (Lloyd), and single specimens
by William Daggere, Pygott, Kemp, and Rysbye. The
date cannot be before 1509, probably soon after; Gilbert
Banastir and William Newark were passing out of
remembrance. Many pieces have no words; but they
are not, I believe, instrumental.

Royal MSS. 8 g 7.

How this most beautiful MS. has hitherto escaped the
notice of writers I cannot divine. It is a splendidly
illuminated full-choir-book containing thirty-eight motets,
all for four voices, in which respect it differs from the
other existing choir-books, which were written for five or
six voices. Most unfortunately no composer's name is
given. In the second motet, Henry VIII and Queen
Katherine are mentioned. No. 3, a 'Nesciens virgo mater
virum,' suggests the work of Dunstable's at which Morley
sneered. In No. 16, the tenor and bass sing 'Tota
pulcra es,' etc., while the triplex and contratenor have
only the word 'Salve' in long notes. In No. 17, 'O
pulcherrima mulierum,' this treatment is inverted. On
the flyleaf is a riddle-canon on 'Honi soit qui mal y
pense.'

Royal MSS. 11 e 11.

Though less elaborate and splendid than the preceding,
this is also a work of art. It is dated 1516, and has two
motets by RICHARD SAMPSON (who in that year became
Dean of the Chapel Royal), and one by BENEDICTUS DE
OPICIIS, with others, anonymous. One of Sampson's
motets—'Psallite felices'—is in honour of Henry VIII.

Royal MSS. Appendix 45-8.

This is a very curious set of small part-books, the
covers bearing the arms of Henry VIII and Katherine
of Aragon. The contents are seven Masses (one for each

day in the week) for three voices. These Masses, unlike all the others of this period, begin with a 'Kyrie Eleison';* and between the Gloria and Credo there are a Hymn to the Virgin and an Alleluia. The fourth book has no 'Sanctus,' 'Benedictus,' nor 'Agnus Dei,' and the words in the Gloria and Credo are apportioned differently. These Masses deserve attention from liturgiologists; and the music is of easier notation than the other choir-books. At the end is the composer's name, NICHOLAS LUDFORD. I guess these books to have been written for a small establishment, possibly the Queen's private chapel. The date must be between 1509 and 1533; probably early rather than late in the period, about 1510–15.

Royal MSS. Appendix 58.

It is this MS. which enables us to claim for England the glory of having invented instrumental as well as vocal composition; and apart from its national interest, it is one of the most important in the whole range of musical history. The contents are miscellaneous, as it was originally intended as a tenor part-book; other pieces have been added by various hands. There are about sixty pieces in all, of which twenty are tenor parts of secular songs, perhaps written before 1500; then follow various sacred and secular pieces, some complete, and some with the names John Ambrose, John Cole, Parker (monk of Stratford), Dr. Coper, and Ralf Drake; and the Medius part of a Mass. The instrumental music begins at fol. 38. There are three solos for the virginals; some short dance-tunes; and pieces for the lute, in tablature, of rather later date. The keyboard pieces are entitled: 'A Hornpipe'; 'My Lady Carey's Dompe' (dump); 'The short mesure off my Lady Wynkfyldes Rownde.' The two former are both attempts at the variation-form; and for such early examples the success of the experiment is really wonderful. The Hornpipe is the more ambitious and elaborate in its treatment of the keyboard, and is

---

* The English composers seem to have not treated the *Kyrie* as a part of the musical Mass, probably leaving it for extempore descant. Lambeth MS. 438 contains three settings of the *Kyrie*, by William Dendy. Compare p. 64.

also much longer and altogether more remarkable; but the 'Dompe' is more musical. There are long scale passages for each hand in the Hornpipe, also wide skips, combinations of various rhythms, appreciation of the contrasts between close and dispersed harmonies and between the different registers of the keyboard; while the 'Dompe,' less difficult, has similar merits, and is in addition touchingly pathetic in its graceful melancholy. I have no doubt that they were by the same composer, and ascribe the honour of inventing the instrumental style of composition to the composer of the Hornpipe, HUGH ASTON.

In *Musica Antiqua* all three pieces are printed,* with the dance-tunes and several of the older songs. The date of the keyboard music is about 1510; of the dance-tunes, probably 1522; the lute-music is still later.

There are many collections of music in the Appendix to Royal MSS.; but they are generally Flemish or anonymous compositions.

The Forrest-Heyther Collection.

These six part-books were written in 1530 by (or for) William Forrest, subsequently known as a rigid Papist. There are eleven Masses in very thick and black ink, which has in places eaten away the paper; later hands have added seven more. The volumes came afterwards into the possession of Dr. Heyther, who presented them to the Music School, Oxford, where they still remain. Burney scored some of the Masses, and has printed five movements.

The eleven Masses in the older writing are: Taverner's *Gloria tibi Trinitas;* Avery Burton on the Hexachord; Merbecke's *Per arma justitiæ*; Fayrfax's *Regali* and *Albanus*; Rasar's *Cristi Jesu*; Hugh Aston's *Te Deum Mass*; Fayrfax's *O bone Jesu* and *Tecum principium*; Ashwell's *Jesu Cristi*; and John Norman's *Resurrexit.* The later additions, which Tye's title prove were written at earliest in 1545, are: Taverner's *Corona spinea*;

---

* Pages 39, 42, 82–4. Some of the songs have also been printed by the Plain-song and Mediæval Music Society.

Ashwell's *Ave Maria Mass*; Aston's *Videte manus meæ*; Taverner's *O Michael*; Shepparde's *Cantate*; Dr. Tye's *Euge bone*; and *Praise Him praiseworthy*, by Richard Alwood, priest. These part-books offer a very late instance of a *Gimel*, which occurs in Dr. Tye's *Euge bone*; this Mass has been published by Mr. Arkwright. The Gloria, printed by Burney, was included in Hullah's *Vocal Scores*, and sung by his classes. The latest hand-writing in the books is that of John Baldwin of Windsor.

Cambridge University MS., Nn. VI 46.

This is a large full-choir-book containing a Mass without composer's name. It is long and elaborate, with many red notes, sometimes the Longs being half black, half red. I should have supposed the music to date about 1500* were it not for the first two pages, on which there are paintings which I believe are intended for Henry VIII and Cranmer, the King holding keys and the Archbishop the Tudor rose. Below each portrait is a stanza apparently for directions to the performers; the rest of the page is occupied by a tenor voice-part beginning 'Regina celorum.' Opposite are two other voice-parts to different words; and the three pieces may be riddle-canons, or a motet for three voices. The large use of red notes points to an earlier date than the picture of Henry VIII with the keys would imply. The verse below it says: 'Of this Tenor I have the kayes, Who list to know ensue my wayes.' The bishop's verse says: 'Dyapentes ye must have three, That with this Rose ye shall agree,' suggesting a riddle-canon, especially as the tenor is inscribed 'multiplex.'

The Peterhouse Part-Books.

Although this collection includes works by Tye, Whitbroke, and four by Tallis, I believe it to be not later in date than 1530–40; and as most of the compositions are earlier, I prefer to catalogue it in the present chapter. It is a fine set of four part-books, containing seventy-two

* I am now inclined to prefer this earlier date.

Masses and motets, most unfortunately quite useless through the absence of the tenor volume. The first twelve leaves of the triplex volume are also missing. The catalogues of this and a later collection in the same library* were published in the *Ecclesiologist* for 1859. Among the most interesting works are a 'Sancta Maria' and two Magnificats by Pashe; a Mass, *Spes nostra*, and a Magnificat by Robert Jones; and a Stabat Mater by Robert Hunt. In addition there are five works by Aston, ten by Fayrfax, seven by Ludford, two by Lupus Italus, four by John Mason, three by Pygott, and eleven by Taverner; a Magnificat and Mass by Appleby; Masses by Rasar, Knight, and Tye; and motets by Wm. Alen, Bramston, John Catcott, Arthur Chamberlayne, John Dark, Edwards, Walter Erell, Edward Martyn, Merbecke, Norman, James Northbroke, Hugh Sturmes, and an anonymous 'Te Matrem.' Many anonymous works elsewhere may perhaps be identified by this collection, by far the most important of the earlier Reformation period in England.

Addit. MS. 34,191 in the British Museum is a part-book containing the bass of three Masses by Robert Jonys and Pygott, and ten other pieces by Taverner, R. Davy, Pygott, Aston, Ashwell, and Fayrfax. Some English Church music and much scribbling and memoranda were subsequently inserted; singularly enough, the name Thomas Mulliner occurs in eighteenth-century writing.

There is a Magnificat in the MSS. of the town of Dartmouth.

Of later MSS. containing works of this period, Addit. MSS. 17,802–5, and John Sadler's part-books (now in the Bodleian Library), are deserving of notice. The latter set, written 1585, include motets by Fayrfax and Aston; the others, by Dr. Cooper, Bramston, Appleby, and Knight. We find that through the reign of Elizabeth this school was not forgotten. Wodde, of St. Andrews, apparently regarded Fayrfax as unrivalled; Morley reckoned Fayrfax among the English musicians in no way inferior to the best on the Continent; and

* See Chap. VI.

Meres in 1598 began his list of England's 'excellente
musitions' with Cooper and Fayrfax. But with the prevalence of madrigals, taste grew more refined, the simplifi-
cation of notation made the older works unintelligible,
and seventeenth-century musicians knew nothing older
than Tye and Tallis, till even the existence of the Fayrfax
school was well-nigh forgotten, as is shown by the preface
to Lawes's *Ayres and Dialogues*, published 1653. Their
Flemish contemporaries, Josquin himself, shared the
same fate, and did not receive their due recognition till
the nineteenth century. I do not claim for any of the
English ecclesiastical music between Dunstable and Tye
a merit at all comparable to that of the best works of
Josquin; but in secular music the English are, in my
opinion, decidedly the superior of the two nations.
None of the earlier songs published in Van Maldeghem's
Trésor Musical seem to me equal to the best of those in
the Fayrfax Boke; and we have still to add to the over-
weight Hugh Aston's instrumental music. The opening
of the period covered by this chapter was certainly a
weak time in English music; and since the only existing
remains are so few, we are unable to exactly trace the
rise of the Fayrfax-Aston-Ludford-Cornysshe school.
The advance shown in Fayrfax's degree exercise, composed in 1504, upon the works of Corbronde and Banastir
in the Pepysian MS., is really great, and the intermediate
progress does not seem discoverable, except perhaps from
the Eton MS. The style of Fayrfax is not more like the
Flemings than must be always the case with contemporary
practical musicians; and the English have left few examples of the enigmas and combinations of different
words in which the Flemings delighted.

In another department nothing is left to show, though
it is hard to believe that nothing was produced. Not a
single theoretical work is known after Hothby. Tucke (of
New College) made a collection* in 1500 which Chelle
(of Hereford) copied† in 1526; but they added nothing
to older writers. This was the period when Tinctor,

---

* Now in the British Museum as Addit. MS. 10,336.
† Lambeth MS. 466.

Gaforius, Pareja, Burtius, Sessa, Virdung, Ornithoparcus, and Agricola produced valuable treatises in Italy and Germany; but with the possible exception of a work on the Monochord (in Lincoln Cathedral library), everything English has disappeared, and the record of printed music is almost a blank. Caxton set up a printing press about 1475; in 1482 he printed Trevisa's translation of Ralph Higden's Polychronicon: in this the legendary Pythagorean discovery of the consonances is mentioned. Caxton printed an eight-lined stave, leaving the notes to be filled in by hand; in Wynkyn de Worde's reprint of 1492 the notes were inserted. Ten years later Petrucci was publishing music at Venice, but the English printers were long in following his example. In or before 1529 John Rastell published *The Four Elements*, an interlude in which a song is introduced; the music is for three voices, and was reprinted in *Musica Antiqua*. Next year followed the first printed collection of English music.

Wynkyn De Worde's Song-Book (1530).

This was a splendid commencement of music-publishing, as the specimen remaining to us is at least equal to any musical typography ever produced. It is, alas! a single bass part-book, bound with the title-page of the triplex and some blank pages and writing. The index shows that, of the twenty songs, nine were for four voices and eleven for three.

The 'songes of four partes' were: A 'Paternoster' by Cornysshe; a 'By-by' (carol?) by Pygot; Ashwell's 'She may be callyd'; Taverner's 'The bella'; Gwynneth's 'My love mourneth'; Cornysshe's 'Pleasure it is,' and 'Concord as musicall'; with two pieces on the Hexachord by Dr. Fayrfax and Dr. Cooper. The three-voiced pieces are partly anonymous. Dr. Cooper contributed 'In youth' and 'So great unkyndness'; Jones, 'Who shall have my fayre ladye?' Taverner, 'My heart, my mynde,' and 'Love wyll I'; Fayrfax, 'My hertes lust'; and Cornysh, 'Fa la sol.' The anonymous pieces are 'Beware my lytyll finger,' 'Mynyn goo trym,' 'Joly felow,' 'And wyl ye serve me soe?'

This volume, unknown to Hawkins and Burney, was discovered by Ritson. In 1864 it was purchased by the British Museum, and has been exhibited in a show-case, with Rastell's Interlude, and many other musical rarities. Let us hope the other volumes will some day come to light; even for the typography alone they will be precious.

Biographically, we are better informed concerning the principal musicians of this period than might be expected; in fact, we know more of them than of some leaders of the next generation. It will be convenient to quote here the list of Englishmen which Morley gives among the 'Practicioners' at the end of his treatise (1597):

Mr. Pashe, Robt. Jones, Jo. Dunstable, Leon. Power, Rob. Orwell, Mr. Wilkinson, Jo. Guinneth, Rob. Davis, Mr. Risby, Dr. Farfax, Dr. Kirby, Morgan Grig, Thomas Ashwell, Mr. Sturton, Jacket, Corbrand, Testwood, Ungle, Beech, Bramston, Jo. Mason, Ludford, Fording, Cornish, Pyggot, Taverner, Redford, Hodges, Selby, Thorne, Oclande, Averie, Dr. Tye, Dr. Cooper, Dr. Newton, Mr. Tallis, Mr. White, Mr. Persons, Mr. Byrde.

This list reaches to Morley's own time; but it will be seen that most of the names have already occurred. The order is evidently not quite chronological; we may infer that Morley copied out the earlier names from some old choir-books, just as they happened to occur. Certainly Pashe and Jones did not live before Dunstable and Power. A few names are now only known by their appearance in this list.

WILLIAM PASHE (Pasche) may have been the Pashe whose will was proved in 1525; but I should have supposed his period rather earlier, perhaps 1430–1500. His only complete remaining work is the Mass at Caius College (and also in the two part-books at Cambridge mentioned above); the incompleteness of the Peterhouse MSS. is particularly to be regretted for Pashe's sake, as his 'Sancta Mater' seemed (judging from my *very* hasty glance) to be an attractive piece allied in spirit to Josquin's 'Ave vera virginitas.'

ROBERT JONES (Jonys) is still less fortunate, though one

of his pieces was included in Wynkyn de Worde's collection, and three are in the Peterhouse MSS. All are imperfect.

Omitting Dunstable, Power, and the unknown Orwell, we find next in Morley's list the name of Mr.WILKINSON, doubtless the Robert Wilkinson, four of whose works are preserved in the Eton MS.

JOHN GWYNNETH was of a later generation. He was licensed to proceed Mus.Doc. Oxon. in 1531. He had then 'published three five-voiced masses, and five four-voiced, as also certain symphonas, antiphonas, and divers songs for the use of the Church'; and had also composed 'all the responses for a whole year in cantis chrispis aut fractis ut aiunt.' So says Anthony à Wood, quoting from the Oxford registers; but 'published' can hardly mean *printed*. Gwinneth, a secular priest, was presented to a London vicarage—St. Peter's, Cheap—in 1543; he resigned in the reign of Mary, when he published tracts against the Protestants. His only known work is the song in Wynkyn de Worde's book.

ROBERT DAVIS is unknown, unless, as I suspect, RICHARD DAVY is intended. The mistake which Burney made concerning Gwynneth and Davis has already been mentioned. Mr. RISBY is repeatedly quoted in Morley's work, and there is a song by him in Addit. MS. 31,922.

Of the later fifteenth-century musicians omitted by Morley, the most important were doubtless GILBERT BANASTIR (Banester) and RICHARD DAVY. The former was in 1482 Master of the Children in the Chapel Royal; he died 24th August, 1487. In 1499 WILLIAM NEWARK was appointed; he died in 1509. Banastir's remaining works are few; the principal is an 'O Maria et Elizabeth' in the Eton MS. Newark (who received an annuity of £20 from Richard III) has left only the seven songs in the Fayrfax MS.

RICHARD DAVY (Davys) became choirmaster and organist of Magdalen College, Oxford, in 1490. He is said in the Eton MS. to have composed a piece for Magdalen College in a single day; it is a very long motet, 'O Domine celi et terræ.' There are five other works at Eton, and the four in the Fayrfax Boke, with a Stabat Mater and some motets in the incomplete part-books; he has the honour of composing the earliest known Passion music.

EDMUND TURGES, by whom there are works at Eton, in the Fayrfax Boke, the Caius College MS., and Addit. MS. 5665, was doubtless related to the Turges, whose name occurs among the minstrels of Henry VI. THOMAS LOVELL, whose motet in the Cambridge part-books looks good work, had the 'ordering and guyding of the trompettes and ministrelles' who were to be stationed 'on high in the vawtes' of St. Paul's at the marriage of Prince Arthur Tudor and Katherine of Aragon in 1501, and was probably the Sub-dean of Wells who died 1524. HENRY PETRE, having studied music thirty years, supplicated for the degree of Mus.Bac. Oxon. in 1516; he was a secular chaplain, but his Mass in Addit. MS. 5665 looks uninteresting. RICHARD PARKER, organist of Magdalen College in 1500, received the degree in 1502. His song in Royal MSS. App. 58 is only a few two-part chords. In the Pepysian MS. there is an 'Alleluia' by 'Gilbert,' whom I believe to be Gilbert Banastir; but a certain JOHN GILBERT was admitted Mus.Bac. Oxon. in 1510. Nothing is known of the other musicians of the Pepysian and Eton MSS.

ROBERT FAYRFAX (Fairfax) is the typical composer of the school, and was probably its greatest man, though his ultimate influence on the art was far inferior to Hugh Aston's. According to Anthony à Wood, he was of the Yorkshire family celebrated in the wars of the seventeenth century, but was born at Bayford, Hertfordshire. This must have been between 1450 and 1470. His earliest known compositions are those in the Eton MS. and his own volume. Burney conjectured that his song, 'That was my woe,' was composed to congratulate Henry VII on attaining the crown in 1485. Fayrfax took the degree of Mus.Doc. Cantab. in 1504, and in 1511 supplicated for incorporation at Oxford. He belonged to the Chapel Royal, receiving a grant from Henry VIII in 1509, and subsequently others. In 1520 he headed the choir of the Field of the Cloth of Gold, dying next year. Wood states

that Fayrfax was either organist or precentor at St. Alban's
Abbey, where he was buried under a stone subsequently
covered by the Mayor's seat; the Fayrfax Boke says, by
the Mayoress's. He was long remembered, as two motets
are copied in Sadler's part-books; and both Morley and
Meres mentioned Fayrfax among England's greatest
musicians. His Masses entitled *Albanus* and *Regali* are
found in nearly all the choir-books of his time; the Mass
in the Lambeth MS., composed for his degree exercise
in 1504, is specially interesting. In Addit. MS. 29,246
there are two motets and a Mass of his in lute-tablature.

To Fayrfax more than any other single man appears
due the enormous advance made toward 1500; the
difference between the unpretending stiff counterpoint of
Corbronde and Banastir in the Pepysian MS. and the
elaborate and lengthy development of the best of Fayrfax's
motets and Mass-sections would seem to require a century
of progress rather than twenty or thirty years. The Eton
MS., when scored, may bridge over the gap which seems
at present to separate the two styles.

Dr. ROBERT COOPER is mentioned by Meres before
Fayrfax; but the few pieces I have seen by him in Addit.
MS. 31,922, Royal MSS. App. 58, and Addit. MSS.
17,802–5, do not warrant the belief that he was one of
England's most 'excellente Musitions.' A MS. at Cambridge states that he graduated there in 1502, which
helps to fix the date of the two old MSS. In 1516 Cooper
received two benefices from the Archbishop of Canterbury.
Why Morley mentioned him so late in his list does not
appear.

Among the group Morley places after Fayrfax, we
know nothing of Dr. Kirby or Morgan Grig, nor of
Ungle and Beech. Mr. STURTON (Stourton) has compositions at Lambeth and Eton; THOMAS ASHWELL, at Oxford,
in the Cambridge part-books, and the Harl. MS. 1709;
Corbrand was doubtless the William Corbronde of the
Pepysian MS., or his son; JACKET (Jakett) was organist
of Magdalen College, Oxford, in 1537; TESTWOOD, one
of the Windsor Chapel Royal, became a fiery Reformer,
and was burnt for heresy in 1544. No compositions by

the two latter are known. BRAMSTON has a good motet, 'Recordare Domine,' in Addit. MSS. 17,802–5, and another in the Peterhouse part-books; a Richard Smyth, alias Bramston, was a Vicar-Choral of Wells in 1531, when he received an annuity. JOHN MASON graduated Mus.Bac. Oxon. in 1508; Anthony à Wood has given an account of his life and his death as treasurer of Hereford Cathedral in 1547. I somewhat question the accuracy of Wood's statements; there was more than one John Mason of some note at the time, and the composer is in the Peterhouse MSS. described as *Cicestriensis*—of Chichester. There seems no remains of his works besides the four at Peterhouse. All these composers presumably flourished early in Henry VIII's reign, but are less important than the following group on Morley's list.

NICHOLAS LUDFORD is quite unknown; but was probably connected with the King's (or perhaps Queen Katherine's) Chapel. His four Masses and Magnificat at Caius College, and the seven in the Royal MSS. Appendix 45–48, show admirable powers; Dr. R. R. Terry has performed them at Westminster Cathedral. There are incomplete works in the Peterhouse and Harleian MSS.

FORDING (Farthing, Farding) appears only in Addit. MSS. 31,922, where there are seven of his songs. RICHARD PYGOTT (Pigot)* was Master to Cardinal Wolsey's choir-boys, as appears from a letter written in 1518; there are three pieces by him at Peterhouse, and one in Addit. MS. 31,922. One was printed by Wynkyn de Worde. Pygott afterwards entered the Chapel Royal, and received an annuity of £20 till November, 1549.

WILLIAM CORNYSSHE (Cornish, Cornysche) was a very important musician during the early sixteenth century. In Addit. MS. 5665 we find the name John Cornysch, and in the Fayrfax Boke 'William Cornish, junior'; father and son may be indicated. The name first appears in the Expenses of Henry VII for 1493; in 1502 William was paid 13s. 4d. for a carol. In July, 1504, he was in the Fleet prison, having been accused of writing a satire upon

* There is a poem by ' Pigott,' as clumsy as Cornysshe's, in Lansdowne MS. 205.

Empson; while there he wrote the poem in clumsy verse (already quoted), called 'The Treatise between Truth and Enformacion.' It is preserved in the Royal MSS., and also in the Harleian. He was soon restored to favour, and under Henry VIII succeeded Newark as Master of the Children, receiving large gifts from the King. Cornysshe's duties were multifarious, and by no means confined to music. Perhaps the most remarkable was the devising the pageants at the Field of the Cloth of Gold. In November, 1524, he was dead.

Less of Cornysshe's music is left than one would expect; there are four works at Eton, three in the Fayrfax Boke, and one at Caius College, with twelve songs in Addit. MS. 31,922. In the index of the Eton MS., *bonus cantor* has been scribbled after his name; possibly he was more at home as a performer and a choir-trainer than as a composer. The bass part of his 'Paternoster,' printed 1530, looks particularly good.

CHRISTOPHER WODDE supplicated Mus.Bac. Oxon. in 1513; the name appears in Addit. MS. 15,233, and in Paston's lute-books.

JOHN TAVERNER may be regarded as closing this period, and connecting it with the next, as his name stands first in Forrest's book of Masses, and he contributed to Wynkyn de Worde's book, though evidently living on till later than 1530. Fox, the martyrologist, states that 'Taverner, of Boston, the good musician,' was called to Oxford by Wolsey for the newly-founded Cardinal College, now Christ Church. As 'only a musician,' he escaped the persecution which soon followed. It is said that he afterwards returned to Boston and died there. Fox says 'Taverner bitterly repented the Popish ditties he had made in the time of his blindness.'* John Taverner seems to belong to the Fayrfax school rather than the Tye and Tallis; his style looks back rather than forward. He is the earliest composer whose works are represented in the immense collection at Christ Church, Oxford, where there are seventeen of his motets. There are also eleven works at Peterhouse, and others are to be

* For particulars, see the 'Dictionary of National Biography.'

found in Sadler's part-books and various collections.
In Addit. MSS. 17,802–5 is a very interesting specimen
of his compositions, a Mass on the popular song, 'Western
Wind, why dost thou blow?' It is the most advanced
work of Taverner's I know. In Thomas Mulliner's book,
Addit. MS. 30,513, is a piece called 'Taverner's In
Nomine.' This is the earliest instance of an ' In Nomine'
which I have seen, though doubtless it was not a novelty
to compose pieces without particular words.

The rest of the names on Morley's list are left to the
next chapters. I will now give a few particulars concerning
others, and especially one who apparently had a greater
influence upon the art than all the rest put together.

In the Eton MS. is a 'Salve Regina' by JOHN HAMPTON,
who was perhaps the 'Hampton of Worcester' paid 20s.
'for making of Balades' by Henry VII in 1495. In
1495, 6s. 8d. was paid to 'Frenshman, player of the
organes'; this may have been Clement Frengham of
Rolvenden, who in 1523 bequeathed all his 'pryksong
bookes' to Rolvenden Church, and whose son John
Frencham built the organ at Rye in 1540. JOHN DYGON
graduated Mus.Bac. Oxon. in 1512; he was prior of St.
Augustine's, Canterbury, at the Dissolution. There is
a fine motet of Dygon's in a MS. of the Royal Collection,
whence it was printed by Hawkins. JAMES NORTHBROKE,
a secular chaplain, graduated Mus.Bac. Oxon. in 1531;
there is a motet by him at Peterhouse. WALTER ERELL,
also represented there, is said in a MS. of Immyns's to
have been a Gentleman of the Bedchamber to Henry VIII.

KING HENRY VIII himself claims a not obscure place
among English musicians. Having been originally intended for the Church, he probably began the study of
ecclesiastical music in childhood, continuing it when he
became Prince of Wales. A small volume of Flemish
music, which then belonged to him, fell into the hands of
Pepys, and finally to Magdalen College; the music is
mainly by Fevin, partly by Josquin, Brumel, Mouton,
and others. Hall's Chronicles tell us that the King composed two complete Masses, sung in the Chapel Royal.
A motet is preserved in a volume in the Royal Library,

and was printed by Hawkins, while Burney says that Hayes had a different copy. Most of the King's known works are to be found in Addit. MS. 31,922; there are eighteen with words, and fifteen without words. An anthem, 'O Lord, the Maker of all things,' was ascribed to him by Aldrich and some subsequent writers; it is still sung, but Burney truly judged the music too advanced in style to be of Henry VIII's reign. The words are from his Primer; the music was composed by Mundy or Shepherd. It may be assumed that his compositions were the work of his earlier years; after 1530 he had to steer the ship of State in the most tremendous crisis of the national life, and could have had little leisure for composition.

At the King's death he possessed a 'pricksong book of Masses and anthems,' 'four books of pricksong Masses,' and three 'lutyng bookes,' besides 'musica ecclesiastica,' probably plain-song.

An early work of Henry VIII was a ballad, 'Pastime with good company,' which is frequently referred to. He seems to have been very proud of his powers, and of this ballad in particular. I prefer his 'Green grows the holly' in Addit. MS. 31,922. The Venetian ambassadors reported in 1515 that he played on almost every instrument, and composed tolerably. Pasqualigo, the Ambassador-extraordinary, said that he 'plays well on the lute and virginals, and sings from book at first sight.' Holinshed speaks in the same style; and of the excellence of his Chapel Royal, Sagudino wrote: 'Their voices are really divine rather than human; *non cantavano ma giubilavano*; and as for the deep basses, I do not believe they are equalled in the world.' Francis I's queen and embassy were entertained in 1527 by a grand pageant, at which some of the Chapel Royal sang English songs; and the visitors were also taken to hear the Princess Mary, then aged eleven, play on the spinet. If the child could play Aston's Hornpipe she must indeed have astonished the strangers, who could hardly have known that such passages existed.

The whole number of Henry VIII's musicians amounted to seventy-nine; the list may be seen in the

Historical MSS. Commission's Fourth Report, p. 404.
A list of the musical instruments bequeathed by him is
in Harl. MSS. 1419. In the regulations made for the
Royal Household in 1526, six choir-boys and six Gentlemen of the Chapel were ordered to attend royal journeys
and progresses, and daily perform a Mass of Our Lady,
with also a 'Mass of the day' and an anthem in the afternoon on Sundays and holydays. It may have been for
some such purpose that Ludford composed the seven
Masses in the Arundel collection.* We have no exact
list of the thirty-two Gentlemen of the Chapel Royal,
but by the reckless prodigality of Henry VIII's early
years several of them profited, especially Fayrfax and
Cornysshe. We also hear of John Fyssher, John Fluyd or
Lloyd (who died in 1523 after a pilgrimage to Jerusalem),
and William Lambe, who died in 1540, and had a very
quaint punning epitaph.

Cardinal Wolsey also maintained a splendid establishment, consisting of a Subdean 'repeater of the Quire,'
Gospeller, Epistler, ten singing priests, a Master of the
Children, twelve lay choristers, and ten boys, with extra
assistance on Festivals. Indeed, Erasmus, in his bitter
censures on the costly Church choirs (see p. 74), was
particularly severe on the English fondness for sumptuous
and ornate musical services.

It does not appear that any of the great Flemish
composers came to England, though both Flemish and
Italian lutenists and a Venetian organist were in the
service of Henry VIII. The style of the English composers differs from the Flemish mainly in the rarer use
of rhythmic subtleties, and in the very rare appearance
of canons. There is no reason to think the few MSS.
preserved are other than fairly representative of the time.

Admitting that the highest flights of Josquin were
beyond the reach of Fayrfax, Davy, and Cornysshe, yet
it must not be forgotten, in fairness to our musicians,
that they were practically the *only* composers in Europe
except the Flemings. The attention of Italy was occupied
with the Renaissance; and in the full splendour of the

* See p. 88

Medicean age singers had to be imported from the Netherlands. With passionate avidity the Italians flung themselves upon the newly-discovered ancient literature; the fine arts reached their acme; but no Italian music as yet existed. The great and the small musicians in Italy were, almost without exception, Flemings. Adam of Fulda was the only good composer of Germany; Isaak has been proved a Fleming, and his pupil Senfl was not born till 1492. We read of one Spanish composer— Vaqueras. From Lisbon to Cracow, from Paris to Naples, there were Flemish chapelmasters everywhere. In England alone the native school held its ground, both in performance and composition.

There are a few traces of music in Scotland during the period covered by this chapter. James III (whom Lindsay of Pitscottie accuses of delighting more in music and architecture than 'in the governance of his realm') founded a Chapel Royal, and a discussion concerning jurisdiction in 1508 shows that James IV maintained the establishment. In 1489 'Wilzean, sangster of Lithgow,' was paid ten pounds for a song-book. Records of payments to wandering English and even Italian minstrels are preserved, and in 1497 is noted a charge for transporting James IV's 'monichordis.' Under James V composers are heard of, who belong rather to the next period. It should be noticed that four Frottole in Petrucci's Seventh Book, and one in his Eighth, were by 'Paulus Scotus.'

I have left till last the most important name of this entire chapter, HUGH ASTON (also Ashton, Ayston, Austen, Asshetone), whom I claim as the inventor of instrumental composition. His 'Hornpipe' in Royal MSS. Appendix 58 is an extraordinary piece of keyboard execution, and 'Lady Carey's Dompe' is probably also his. They, with the other pieces for the keyboard in the same MS., are all written on seven-lined staves, and barred; J. Stafford Smith printed them all in *Musica Antiqua* (pp. 39–43, 82–4), adding sharps to make a leading-note in the 'Dompe' and altering the end.* Aston's insight into the

---

* This modernised version was reprinted in Stainer & Barrett's *Dictionary of Musical Terms*, but with a wrong date.

necessary difference between the styles for vocal and for instrumental music was wonderfully correct; and all the effects known* to the older school of players may be traced in these pieces, excepting double-runs. 'Lady Carey's Dompe' is quite worthy a place in recital-programmes; the 'Hornpipe,' though much more advanced in executive requirements, and three times as long, would be found old-fashioned and strange by an ordinary audience. 'The short measure of my Lady Wynkfyld's Rounde' has a singular five-bar rhythm, and though a slighter work than the others, is quite musical and interesting. The same may be said of the short dance-pieces in the MS., which were probably used at Charles V's visit in 1522.

Aston's invention of instrumental composition was an English achievement only excelled by John Dunstable's invention of the polyphonic style, and it was better followed up. Unlike Dunstable's successors, the successors of Aston advanced. Redford and Blithman carried on the work until Byrd, Bull, and Philipps at the end of the sixteenth century attained a really extraordinary mastery of instrumental performance; and their pupils transplanted it in Germany, where, in the hands of Scheidt, it coalesced with Italian forms to produce the German instrumental music which, two centuries after Aston's death, culminated in Bach.

Of Aston's other works, the one most frequently occurring in the choir-books is a 'Te Deum Mass,' found entire in Forrest's collection, and imperfectly in the Cambridge part-books; the Gloria alone is at Peterhouse. There is also another Mass at Oxford; a 'Te Matrem' and four other motets at Peterhouse and elsewhere; and an 'Ave Domina' in a later and very defective part-book, Harl. MSS. 7578. Even two generations later he was not forgotten, as Sadler included his 'Te Deum' and 'Gaude Mater' in the part-books now at the Bodleian Library. But these works, though they seem very good for their period, sink into insignificance in comparison with the really novel instrumental music.

At once the question occurs, who was Hugh Aston?

* Compare p. 89.

I have little doubt, though there is no distinct connecting evidence, that he was the Hugh Aston who was born in Lancashire, graduated M.A. at Cambridge in 1505, was incorporated at Oxford in 1507, became Comptroller to Lady Margaret Countess of Richmond, and finally Archdeacon of York; dying December, 1522, and buried under an elaborate monument in St. John's College, Cambridge, where every day visitors gaze on his effigy in sumptuous robes above, with a skeleton beneath. He passed away, but his work remains yet, and his influence is felt all over the world to this moment. When a child practises a scale, when a great pianist plays a Beethoven concerto, they are repeating passages which were first used by Hugh Aston.*

* Mr. Grattan Flood argues there were two of the name; and the composer died in 1521.

CHAPTER IV

THE REFORMATION: FROM THE DISSOLUTION OF THE MONASTERIES TO THE DEFEAT OF THE ARMADA
(1536-88)

Immediate effects of the dissolution of the monasteries and the religious changes under Henry VIII, Edward VI, Mary, and Elizabeth.—Concentration of talent in the Chapel Royal.—The earliest English psalters.—The Anglican Prayer Books.—Establishment of the English form of 'Service.'—The principal existing MSS.—Great advance in instrumental music.—Appearance of the English madrigal. —Publications.—Biographical notices.—This period the greatest in our ecclesiastical music.

Representative Composers :—Instrumental : Redford and Blithman.—Vocal : Tye, Shepherd, Edwards, Whyte Tallis, Byrd.

IT is now necessary to take a glance at the religious history of England, upon which the musical history, always closely connected, was especially dependent at this period, as it was again a century later. A series of accidents brought the English King to declare himself independent of the Pope, and to be the personal Head of the English Church. Then followed the dissolution of the smaller monasteries in 1536; and the larger quickly shared this fate, their enormous possessions mainly falling into the hands of the King's favourites. This was a serious blow to the art of music, as every monastery was a permanent choir, maintaining singers and an organist. And, sad to relate, the great change, tremendous both politically and socially, as well as religiously, was carried out without care to preserve what was worth preserving. The nobles pulled down magnificent buildings for the sake of selling the materials. In many cases the huge stores of manuscripts accumulated during several centuries were used as waste paper, and the parchments were sent 'by ships' full,' says Bale, to the bookbinders abroad. When it is remembered that more than 600 monasteries and nunneries were dissolved, and that in the previous chapters all the known remains of pre-Reformation compositions are catalogued, it will be seen how extraordinary the destruction must have been.* How many *hundreds* of Masses and Magnificats and motets by Dunstable and Power and Benet and Pasche and Banester and Davy and Cornish and Ludford and Fayrfax and Cooper, and their compeers, must have at this time for ever perished!

The zealots on the reforming side soon began to show a dislike to ecclesiastical music. Thomas Bilney, burnt at Norwich in 1531, is said to have had 'an almost insane antipathy' to music, but music of all kinds may be meant. In 1536 the Lower House of Convocation included ecclesiastical music and organ-playing among the Eighty-four Faults and Abuses of Religion. The same feeling was coarsely expressed in 1546, in a tract entitled *The Supplication of the Poor Commons*. But in the meantime a temporary reaction had been felt, and the Six Articles had been passed; in this Act both vocal music and organ-playing are defended in well-chosen language. During Henry VIII's reign there was an attempt made to bring the Lutheran choral into use in England. At this time the Lutheran choral was different from the choral we know in the works of Bach. It was not in notes of even length, the syllables being quantitative, not accentual; and the voice-parts were in independent polyphony. In 1539 or 1546 Coverdale published *Goostly Psalms and Spiritual Songs*, founded on the Lutheran collections, and including fifty-one tunes, mostly from the same source. It was suppressed by order of Henry VIII, but one copy had found its way to Queen's College, Oxford, where it lay forgotten for three hundred years; in the nineteenth century it was noticed and examined, and in 1846 reprinted by the Parker Society.

On May 27th, 1544, the Litany was published in English; and Cranmer wrote to the King, 'I have travailed to make the verses in English, and have put the Latin note unto the same.' On June 16th appeared an edition with 'the Latin note'—that is, the plain-song

* See Gasquet's *Henry VIII and the English Monasteries*, II 423–5. A specimen of the destruction may be seen in Addit. MS. 30,520, two imperfect leaves of what was once a grand full-choir-book.

of the Roman service; and soon followed a setting harmonised by Robert Stone for five voices, 'according to the notes used in the Kynge's Chapel.'

Henry VIII died, and his sceptre came into the hands of a child. The nobility were eager to continue the spoliation which had brought them the wealth of the monasteries, and took the side of the Reformers. The Protestant party now had the upper hand, and many zealots pressed for extreme courses. Unfortunately neither Luther nor Zwingle had any following in England, but the stern logical Calvin had already a party here; several of his followers came to England, and obtained great influence. The attacks on ecclesiastical music were renewed, and in 1552 the organ in St. Paul's was silenced. Cranmer succeeded in preserving liturgical forms, in spite of the Genevan opposition; the Anglican Prayer Book appeared in 1549, and a revised form, the one used since, in 1552. But throughout the reign of Edward VI there was much havoc wrought with liturgical works. On the issue of the Anglican Prayer Book, all existing service-books, excepting Henry VIII's Primers, were ordered to be delivered up and destroyed. At the same time important libraries, such as that of Eton College, were much despoiled, and the Oxford University Library disappeared altogether. Stow's *Survey of London* asserts that three cart-loads of rare MSS. were taken from the Guildhall Library. Cathedral ornaments were in some cases removed, and the greedy nobles melted down the church bells.

The Chapel Royal, however, was kept on the same scale as in the previous reign; the household musicians numbering seventy-three besides the Children, and the Gentlemen of the Chapel thirty-two with nine subordinates, in all 114, at an annual cost of £2,209. Burney and Hawkins have given an exact list of the thirty-two without specifying their authority. The names are, I feel certain, placed in order of seniority. The oldest is Emery Tuckfield, who (with the next six on the list) is otherwise unknown. The eighth is Richard Farrant; the twentieth, Tallis; the twenty-first, Wright; the twenty-second,

Robert Stone; the twenty-seventh, John Sheppard; the twenty-eighth, William Hunnis. Afterwards Dr. Tye and Thomas Causton were added.

Under Mary the same establishment was maintained. The intemperate zeal of the Reformers had brought the natural reaction, and a return to the old worship was welcomed. Froude, describing Mary's triumphant entry into London, tells how 'the Lords, surrounded by the shouting multitude, walked in state to St. Paul's, where the choir again sang a Te Deum, and the unused organ rolled out once more its mighty volume of music.' Mary herself had been musical from earliest childhood—it is said from two years old. A splendidly bound Virginal Book in the British Museum (Addit. MS. 31,392), bears the arms and names of Philip and 'Marie,' but thirty-two leaves have been cut out, and the music which remains is of a later date. Mary bestowed a lease of crown lands upon Tallis and Bowyer.

One of the earliest results of the return to the older worship was the revival of Sunday evening singing from the spire of St. Paul's. As can be testified by all who have stood on Magdalen Bridge on May morning, the effect of music thus floating down from a great height is exquisite beyond description.

The Queen sanctioned a terrible persecution; the excesses of Edward VI's reign were speedily forgotten in the four black years which passed over England. The Government was in everything unpopular; the last of the Continental possessions was surprised and lost; and all welcomed the accession of Elizabeth with unfeigned delight, though the great majority of the nation were still scarcely Protestants. The persecution was immediately stopped, but there was no change in the form of worship until the next year, when English was used at the funeral of the Duchess of Suffolk. The Protestant exiles returned, ardently longing to model the English Church after the Genevan pattern, but Queen Elizabeth was inflexibly opposed to them, preserving a crucifix and lights in her chapel, and always speaking with disgust and horror of the marriage of priests, which she would never formally

permit. The Second Prayer Book of Edward VI was
again enjoined, and apparently the great bulk of the
nation were satisfied by this compromise. At this critical
moment a gentle, conciliatory Pope might have kept
England in alliance with the Roman Church, but the
stern Paul IV ruled at the Vatican, and refused all
compromise. Soon the breach was complete, and the
Anglican Church was settled as it still remains.

But the Genevan school, who now acquired the name
of Puritans, continually pressed for the abolition of all
ceremonies, the choral service being one of their special
stumbling-blocks. A motion to put down 'curious
singing' and organs was made in Convocation on February
13th, 1562–3; and it was only lost by one vote. Where
a Genevan disciple obtained ecclesiastical preferment,
there the choral service was suppressed; and a tract,
'The Praise of Musick' (in the Royal MSS.), says that
about 1567 'not so few as one hundred organs were taken
down, and the pipes sold to make pewter dishes.' In the
homily on the 'Place of Prayer,' organs and curious
singing are ranked with image-worship.

Almost all the greatest musical talent of the kingdom,
after the suppression of the monasteries, was concentrated
in the Chapel Royal, where, through all the changes in
the form of worship, a body of most gifted musicians
were to be found. To the names already mentioned must
be added (Robert?) Persons, Richard Edwards, William
Blithman, and William Mundy, who joined during the
early years of Elizabeth's reign. None of them all seems
to have been troubled by the religious changes, unless it
were William Hunnis, who in 1557 was implicated in a
Protestant plot. Each received sevenpence-halfpenny a
day. Their duties were still not musical alone; they
assisted in the Court amusements in various ways. The
Gentlemen acted a play before Queen Mary at Christmas,
1557, and the Children were frequently employed in the
same service. The Master of the Children was expected
to superintend pageants and revels. Gilbert Crane had
succeeded Cornysshe in 1524; Arundel MS. 97 records
payments. Richard Bowyer (Bower) followed. From

1563 to 1566 the dramatist and poet Richard Edwards was the master; then William Hunnis, till 1597. The great popularity of dramas brought the rise of a special class of actors; this, according to Stow, began about 1583. Before the period allotted to this chapter had closed, the Chapel Royal received further strength from the accession of William Byrd and John Bull. Every important musician of this great period was thus a member, excepting John Redford (choirmaster of St. Paul's), Robert Johnson, and Robert Whyte (organist of Westminster Abbey); of these no connection with the Chapel Royal is recorded. In this period begins the oldest known Cheque-book of the Chapel Royal, starting in 1561; it gives us many dates of entries and deaths, and was edited by Dr. Rimbault for the Camden Society.

At the opening of the English Reformation the Flemish school was still supreme on the Continent, but its ecclesiastical music was falling into a labyrinth of scientific ugliness; while the secular music had made a wonderful advance, and Willaert, Arcadelt, and others were producing madrigals still sung. The Italians and Spaniards were also competing with the Flemings; and even the Pope's own chapelmaster was now, for the first time, an Italian. The English school, when this period began, was regaining its lost position in the forefront of all musical art; and the composers of the Chapel Royal were once more the greatest in the world, during the middle of the sixteenth century. Then, in 1561, Palestrina's 'Improperia' showed decisively that the sceptre had passed to Italy; the 161 years of English and Netherlands supremacy were over, and the 161 years of Italian supremacy began. In instrumental music, however, the English retained the pre-eminence for at least half a century longer.

The great improvement in English (as in Continental) music during this period consisted in the disuse of needless complication. This was largely affected by the desire of the Reformers to make the *words* more prominent than the music; and also by the introduction of psalters, and the consequent simple settings necessary for congregational singing. The Reformers, alike of Trent as of Geneva, in their zeal against the florid complications of ecclesiastical music, were not aware that the changes they insisted upon were exactly the changes required to perfect the art of polyphonic music itself, as well as to make it subservient to devotion. Calvin's introduction of unisonous congregational singing is said to have been taken from the Hussite practice. Louis Bourgeois fitted tunes to the Genevan Psalter (written by Marot and Beza), and also published them with four-voiced harmony; but harmony was not permitted in the Swiss worship, and this prohibition remained in full force to the nineteenth century. The rhythmical even notes of the Genevan tunes set the model for the English psalm-tunes, and in time prevailed also over the polyphonic style at first used by the Lutherans.

The suppression of Coverdale's *Goostly Psalms* has been already related; they contained many of the celebrated Lutheran hymns, such as 'Ein' feste Burg,' 'Mit Fried und Freud,' and 'Nun freut euch, lieben Christen g'mein.' Soon after Edward VI's accession English psalters began to appear; and at Brasenose College, Oxford, is a copy of one issued in September, 1549, complete in 'common measure,' and with a single harmonised tune. Another, by Francis Seagar, contains nineteen Psalms, and two tunes in polyphony; it was published in 1553, in which year Dr. Tye issued a similar work—a metricised version of the Acts of the Apostles, with a separate tune for each chapter. Tye's tunes were also slightly polyphonic. The accession of Queen Mary was hailed in verse, about equal to that of the psalters, by Richard Beard, a London clergyman; the hymn is set to a simple four-voiced tune, much more resembling a modern hymn-tune than the polyphony of Seagar and Tye. The whole is reprinted in Huth's *Fugitive Tracts*; the tune alone in J. T. Lightwood's *Hymn-Tunes and their Story*. The exiles of Geneva issued psalters upon the Genevan model, with unharmonized tunes; in 1556 appeared a new edition of Sternhold with a tune for each Psalm. Two of the tunes are attempts to adapt the

Genevan tune which finally became settled in popular favour as the 'Old Hundredth.' As the tune originally appeared, the notes at the beginning and end of each line were semibreves, the others minims; subsequently all were made of even length, but latterly the old version has been reintroduced. In Bach's cantata No. 130 it is used both in common and triple time. The Lutheran choral, 'Nun lob mein' Seel den Herren,' begins with the same series of notes.

With the return of the Genevan exiles, psalm-singing reappeared in England. Strype mentions its effect at St. Paul's Cross after Nowell's sermon on March 17th, 1560. Enlarged editions of the Genevan Psalter of 1556 were published, followed by a complete Psalter which has immortalised the names of Sternhold and Hopkins. In 1563 John Day also printed a harmonised edition in four beautiful part-books, with extra anthems and canticles; the harmonisings were by Causton, Southerton, W. Brimle, Hake, and W. Parsons, anthems by Tallis, Shepherd, and Edwards being included in the Appendix. This work was first noticed by Todd in 1822; a complete score (Addit. MS. 31,855) was made by Joseph Warren from the supposed unique copy at Brasenose College, Oxford. The British Museum now contains another and considerably different copy, beginning with 'Veni, Creator,' and the canticles of the Morning and Evening Service in metre. The latter part is the same in both copies.

Day also printed in 1567 a complete Psalter for Archbishop Parker, apparently the versifier, though it has also been claimed for John Keper; it was never published, and is known only by a few presentation copies. The music consisted of nine masterly tunes by Tallis; one, a canon, is now among the most familiar of melodies as the 'Evening Hymn.' They are longer than modern tunes, occupying two stanzas; the canon is sung twice through. There is no complication of parts; even the canon is at present turned into a part-song. Tallis's tunes are composed in an original style, unlike those in the Genevan Psalter: 'in four parts, broad, simple, and effective, and suitable for congregational singing; and, from the technical point of view, finer than anything of the kind that has been done since.'*

Hunnis published some devotional poetry, in each book of which appeared a few good but unharmonised tunes. In 1585 JOHN COSYN published a Psalter containing forty-three six-voiced pieces and fourteen five-voiced; unfortunately no complete copy is known. The harmonised Psalter of Day put the *Church Tunes*, as they were now called, in the tenor; and Tallis did the same with his tunes for Parker's Psalter. Daman's polyphonic setting partly used the upper voice.

The English Prayer Books also had considerable influence in the perfecting English polyphony, by the disuse of needless complication owing to the desire of the Reformers for distinctness in the words; unfortunately the desire was obeyed to such a point that the exaggerated simplicity had unfavourable influence upon the service-music itself. Cranmer's Litany and Robert Stone's harmonising were the beginnings. In 1550, John Merbecke, organist of the Chapel Royal at Windsor, adapted the ancient plain-song to the First Prayer Book of Edward VI; he included the Benedictus and Agnus Dei omitted in the Second Prayer Book, though, since the Lincoln judgment of 1892, it has become lawful to use these also. Merbecke omitted the Litany, doubtless because it had been already published; and his work consists of the Venite and Psalms, the Te Deum, Benedicite omnia opera, Benedictus, Magnificat, and Nunc Dimittis, and a very complete setting of the Communion Service, besides the Athanasian Creed, the Burial Service, and the Communion at Burials. The Nicene Creed is the part of Merbecke's service most frequently sung at present. There is no harmony in the book; it follows Sarum Use very closely.

With the accession of Elizabeth came a speedy return to the Second Prayer Book of Edward VI. The forty-ninth of the 'Injunctions' of 1559 prescribes 'a modest and distinct song so used in all parts of the Common Prayer, that the same might be understanded as if it were

* G. A. Crawford in 'Grove.'

read without singing'; and also that 'for the comforting
of such as delight in music, it may be permitted that in
the beginning or at the end of the Common Prayer there
may be sung an hymn or such-like song, to the praise of
Almighty God, in the best melody and music that may
be devised, having respect that the sentence of the hymn
may be understood and perceived.'

These words, designedly or undesignedly, include both
congregational and choral singing. The sentences concerning due comprehension of the words show the spirit
of the age, and must be carefully noticed, as their influence
may be traced in all our cathedral music.

The form of the Anglican 'Service' differs from the
the musical 'Mass' of the Latin church in that the Office
of Lauds, on which was founded the Order of Morning
Prayer, gradually became more important than the Communion Service; music was in time disused altogether in
the latter, and not revived until the Oxford movement
of 1840. Consequently, though a complete setting
originally included even more than Merbecke had set
(the alternative canticles, 'Jubilate,' 'Cantate Domino,'
and 'Deus misereatur' having been added in the Prayer
Book of 1552), yet a 'Service' soon began to mean only
the 'Te Deum' and 'Benedictus,' the 'Magnificat' and
'Nunc Dimittis,' with at most the alternative canticles in
addition. The anthem has always been independent of
the rest of the 'Service,' and is, in fact, a mere excrescence
which can be contracted to a congregational hymn, or
expanded to a long and elaborate concert-work. The
Preces, Versicles, and Responses were harmonised by
Tallis (with the ancient plain-song in the tenor) in a
manner never likely to be surpassed, and they also lie
outside what musicians call the 'Service.'

The musical results of the English 'Service' are
certainly not so high as might be reasonably expected
from the splendid powers of the men who created the
style. In an article by Chrysander (Vierteljahrsschrift
für Musikwissenschaft for 1891) the continuity of the
Anglican Church, and its favourable result upon the
music, are well pointed out, and contrasted with the

differing conditions of the Lutheran Church, where each
composer contributed separate work, and did not continue
the line of tradition.   Yet from the first, the Anglican
'Service' has laboured under serious restrictions, which
have been seldom broken through with success; and it is
well to examine the reason of its inferiority to the best
music of other churches.

Cranmer, in issuing his Litany, wrote to Henry VIII
that the harmonising should be note-against-note, one
note to a syllable—that is, in plain chords.   Now, in the
Litany and Responses, the shortness of the sentences
causes no difficulty in using this style.   But the desire
for distinct articulation caused Tallis, Patrick, and others
to treat the entire Service in the same style, and the
result is dull.   With one exception (a contrapuntal Evening
Service by Tye) all the original models of the Anglican
Service are from beginning to end heavy successions of
full chords without imitation or figuration.   The model
and type is undoubtedly Tallis's in the Dorian Mode;
and the constraint which the new requirement set upon
Tallis is obvious in the longer pieces—the Te Deum, the
Nicene Creed, and the Gloria.   The same may be said
of Patrick's equally fine Service; and with men of lesser
abilities—such as Bevin, Barcroft, Stonard—the longer
pieces become absolutely tedious.   During the seventeenth
century there were two distinct attempts to establish a
new model; the first by Orlando Gibbons, who composed
contrapuntally; the second by the Restoration school.
Other attempts have been made since, but the shadow
of the original limitation hangs over English cathedral
music more or less to this day.   It seems to have pleased
Elizabethans, if we may judge from this sentence in
Harrison's *Description of England*:

'In Cathedrall and Collegiate churches is so ordered that the
psalmes onlie are sung by note, the rest being read (as in common
parish churches) by the minister with a loud voice, saving that in
the administration of the communion the quier singeth the answers,
the creed, and sundrie other things appointed, but in so plaine,
I saie, and distinct manner, that each one present may understand
what they sing, every word having but one note, though the whole

harmonie consist of manie parts, and those verie cunninglie set by the skilfull in that science.'

This passage may be taken as a commentary upon the services of Tallis, Patrick, and their contemporaries. It appears to me that the same restriction, though to a less extent, fettered the anthem, and that the magnificent contrapuntal anthems of Elizabethan composers are really adaptations of Latin motets, in which the composer's skill had full play. This was certainly so in many instances, of which we still possess the original forms; and I believe it was the general rule, though the older Latin versions have usually disappeared.

I have dealt specially with this matter because it had, in my opinion, a baneful effect upon Anglican music, and consequently upon English art generally. Not Palestrina, nor Bach, nor Mozart, nor Beethoven could, I believe, have produced interesting *lengthy* pieces with the restriction under which the Tallis school laboured. In so divinely perfect a short piece as Mozart's 'Ave verum corpus' there is yet one point of imitation—the motet is not all solid chords.

It is, however, very remarkable with what skill the Elizabethan composers used their heavy style; it is only in the longer pieces that the restriction is felt. As examples of the power of the unfigurated style, we need only mention Tallis's 'Responses,' and his little anthem, 'Remember not, Lord, our old iniquities,' which concludes Day's harmonised Psalter, and is a veritable masterpiece. Still, let it be remembered that the greatest ecclesiastical music of this and the subsequent period was of a different character.

In 1560 Day published 'Certaine notes set forth in 4 and 3 parts to be sung at the morning communion and evening praier . . . and unto them be added divers godly praiers and psalms.' I have only seen the Bassus part of this, which is in the Douce Collection, Bodleian Library. It contains two services, at the end of which is the name T. Cawston. After the four-part service is an anthem, 'Let all the congregation'; and after the three-part eleven anthems, by Johnson, Tallis, Okeland,

Shephard, and Causton. On the last page is a different
date—1565, but both title-page and last page are quite
unlike those of Day's other collection, published 1565,
with the title 'Morning and Evening Prayer and Communion, set forth in 4 parts.' The settings are four-
voiced throughout, the Medius, Secundus Contratenor,
and Tenor parts being at Oxford bound up with the
Bassus part of 1560. In the collection of 1565 some
canticles are ascribed to Caustun, Whitbrooke, Heath,
Stone, and Knyght; there are also an anthem by Hasylton,
the eleven anthems of the older book, and three others
by Causton. In all four parts nearly every piece is marked
'This Mean is for children,' 'This Bassus is for children,'
'This Tenor is for men,' etc.

Having now described the change which came over
English ecclesiastical music and musicians during the
thirty years following the dissolution of the monasteries,
I revert to the beginning of the period, and resume the
story of music in general. As previously asserted, the
cry of the early Reformers for distinct articulation in the
words, and the introduction of psalm-singing, caused a
sudden disuse of the over-florid and complicated part-
writing of the Fayrfax school, and there was at once an
increase in beauty of effect, which makes the works of
Tye an enormous improvement upon his immediate
predecessors. We therefore find that works of the
earlier Reformation period have always remained in use.

The contemporary MSS. are singularly few, and the
publications consisted almost entirely of the psalters.
What few MSS. remain are, however, of very great value,
and in particular the one I am now about to describe is
one of the most important in existence.

Thomas Mulliner's Book.

This is an oblong MS. which belonged, as John
Heywood's signature testifies, to Thomas Mulliner. No
information seems procurable about Mulliner, though
J. Stafford Smith has written on the flyleaf that he was
master of St. Paul's school; there seems no proof of this.
In 1564 a Thomas Mulliner was organist of Corpus

Christi, Oxford. J. S. Smith lent the volume to Hawkins, who has inserted several pieces from it in the Appendix to his History. After the sad dispersal of Smith's library it was acquired by Dr. Rimbault, at whose sale it was most fortunately secured (for £84) by Mr. W. H. Cummings, and transferred to the British Museum, where it is numbered Addit. MS. 30,513. Full particulars (except of the pieces published by Hawkins from the MS.) are given in Mr. Hughes-Hughes's Catalogue of MS. Music.

There are more than a hundred pieces in this MS., consisting of instrumental music (mostly founded upon plain-song), and vocal music in score. Some lute arrangements by Mulliner himself and Churchyard (the poet?) have been added at the end. The keyboard music is usually on seven-lined staves. It was probably composed for the organ, but as the English organs had no pedals it is playable on the pianoforte. Historically, these seventy instrumental pieces are of great interest, and the examples printed in Hawkins's History and Rimbault's 'History of the Pianoforte' show the advance made upon Aston's execution, though they are not musically the best in the MS. The instrumental pieces are mainly by Redford and Blithman; there are also examples by Nicholas Carleton, Alwood, Farrant, Sheppard, and Tallis, and two very difficult ones by Shelbye. There is also a 'Fansye of Master Newmans'—the first instance I know of the use of this title—and a Pavin by Newman. The vocal music is mainly in the second half of the book, and includes two pieces which, having been printed by Hawkins, are on the repertory of cathedral choirs and choral societies; one of them is even quite familiar. It is singular that they are both anonymous in the MS. One, the anthem, 'Rejoice in the Lord alway,' was ascribed by Hawkins to Redford, and reprinted as Redford's by the Motet Society. It is still sung, especially during Advent, at St. Paul's Cathedral. Whose it may be I cannot guess; it is not quite like any other composer's work with which I am acquainted, Causton's being perhaps nearest in style.* But there can be no doubt that it is a singularly

* Mr. Arkwright, whose judgment is entitled to all respect, would prefer Tye for the composer.

beautiful example of the contrapuntal anthem; the subjects are melodious and charmingly treated, while the
long inverted tonic pedal at the conclusion has an
exquisite effect, and must have been strikingly novel.
The other piece is the admirable madrigal, 'In going to
my naked bedde,' now for grace's sake known as 'In
going to my lonely bed,' and quite familiar to all madrigal
unions. The words appear in 'The Paradyce of Dainty
Devyces' as Richard Edwards's. Another piece in the
Mulliner MS. was composed by Edwards, and Hawkins
has accordingly ascribed the music also of this piece to
him, probably correctly.

There are also two anthems and three secular pieces
by Tallis; 'In Nomines,' by Taverner and Johnson; 'The
syllye man,' by Edwardes; 'Defyled is my name,' by
Johnson; 'I lift my heart,' by Tye; and sixteen anonymous pieces. Many of the latter are of great interest.
One is a setting of Surrey's 'Ye happy dames.' The last
piece before the lute-music is a canon by Mundy.
A 'Quia fecit' by Sheppard 'of the Queenes Chappell'
helps to fix the date, which cannot be earlier than 1553,
and is probably several years later, as Tallis's anthems
are to be found in Day's Prayer Book and Psalter, whence
they were perhaps taken, though they may have been
older. 1560 is a convenient date, and must be nearly or
quite correct. It is much to be regretted that this splendid
proof of English musical skill in the middle of the
sixteenth century has not yet been completely published.

It is possible that the anonymous pieces were of
Mulliner's own composition. The vocal music is generally
indicated by the first words only, and some poems I am
not acquainted with, including 'Fond youth is a bubble'
(Tallis), and the anonymous pieces, 'Like as the chayned
wight,' 'The wretched wandering prince of Troye,'
'When Cressyde went from Troye,' and 'The bitter
sweet.' These and the other secular works are the
earliest English madrigals known, but they are not so
entitled in the MS. Thomas Mulliner did not quite do
what it was his duty to do—he should have recorded the
composers of 'Rejoice in the Lord alway,' 'In going to

my naked bedde,' and all the other pieces; but we must
be grateful to him for having preserved some of the best
vocal music of his age, and instrumental music which,
for its time, stands quite alone. The titles 'In Nomine,'
'Fancy,' and 'Voluntary' all occur here for the first time.

Additional MS. 29,996.

This is scarcely less valuable than Mulliner's book,
and is much larger, but is entirely instrumental. There
is more personal interest attached than to any other of
our early MSS., as it was begun by Redford, probably
continued by Tallis, then by Byrd; it was completed in
the seventeenth century by T. Tomkins, who annotated
the earlier portions. The composers who appear in
Redford's writing are Thomas Preston, Phillips ap Rice
of St. Paul's, Robert Corsum, Avere, Richard Winslate,
Kinton, Thorne of York, and Redford himself. This
part of the MS. has been damaged by damp. Among the
best pieces are a 'Precatus est Moyses' and a 'Justus erit
palma' by Redford, and Thorne's 'Exultabunt sancti';
these appear to be literal transcriptions of vocal works.
At the opening there are many arrangements of plain-
songs, each verse treated differently.

The later portions of this book are of less historical
interest; but a duet for two players on one virginal or
organ, by N. Carleton, deserves mention; and a clever
set of Variations on a Ground, by Arthur Phillips, is of
value.

Additional MS. 15,233.

In 1848, Mr. Halliwell (-Phillipps) edited the literary
part of this MS. for the Shakespeare Society. It contains
a Morality of Redford's, and many poems by Redford,
Heywood, Thorne, and other musician-poets of Henry
VIII's reign. Before the Morality there are several pieces
of music by Redford, some of them original, while one
appears to be an organ arrangement of a Te Deum.
The others are short settings of plain-chants, similar to
those at the beginning of Addit. MS. 29,996.

Royal MSS., Appendix 56.

This MS. belongs to the beginning of the period, perhaps even to the previous chapter. It contains organ pieces and the score of some part-songs. The right-hand stave is six-lined; the left-hand, seven-lined. The music (anonymous, possibly Heywood's) is less florid than usual.

Additional MS. 4900.

This is the earliest collection of solo songs I have seen. It contains twenty tunes in the treble clef, with a lute accompaniment in tablature on the opposite page. Some are by Taverner, Tallis, Sheppard, and John Heywood; and at the end is a 'Madonna' marked 'M(r.) Edward,' and some canons. One melodious piece, 'My little pretty one,' was published by Chappell. I am not certain that this MS. was intended for a solo-singer; it may have been a part-book containing the treble voice-part and the accompaniment. Some of the pieces are sacred, two being by R. Johnson. Very few are complete.

Harleian MS. 7578.

A much mutilated part-book, containing secular and sacred pieces, among them one by Hugh Aston. The other composers named are Heath, More, Mundy, and R. Johnson. Other part-books may be found, when this one might be of service in completion or identification; alone it is almost useless.

Additional MS. 17,802–5.

In musical value this is the most important set of Latin part-books in the British Museum; it is, fortunately, intact. It was written after the Reformation had finally prevailed in England, and may have been intended for a private chapel where the Romish rites were adhered to. There are pieces in it by Byrd, at once indicating a later date than the Mulliner MS.; J. Mundy is also represented, and 1570–80 must be the earliest possible date. Most of the composers are more or less known, and are of the middle of the century. The contents are mainly motets;

and there are some Masses and Magnificats, in all ninety-six pieces. The composers mentioned are Philip van Wilder, Hyett, Taverner, Tye, W. and J. Mundy, Hake, Okeland, Knight, Tallis, Sheppard, Appleby, Cooper, Blithman, White, Redford, Barber, Ensdall, Byrd, Whitbroke, Johnson, Stonings, Bramston, R. Johnson (priest), Alcoke, Hoskins, and Wright. The music is for four voices throughout, and most of the pieces display the highest style of ecclesiastical art. Among the most remarkable are a Mass by Tallis, and the three Masses on a secular song—'Western Wind, why dost thou blow?' Dr. Terry has availed himself of the treasures contained in these part-books, and has performed the Masses and several motets at Westminster Cathedral.

Additional MS. 30,480–4.

Although on the flyleaf is the signature 'Hammond,' and the date 1615, the music is of the earlier period, and the books were probably written about 1560–70, possibly even in Edward VI's reign. There is a singular resemblance between them and an eighteenth-century score— Addit. MSS. 31,226; the works are nearly the same, but the modern score is more perfect than the older part-books, and must have been made from a fuller original than Hammond's. There is a Passion according to John, ascribed to Tye; it is really Byrd's. A Kyrie by Shepherd is superscribed 'The best song in England.' There is also a 'Service' (the wording being not the same as the authorised version) by Robert Adams, Parsley, Causton, Tye, etc.; and anthems, some by J. Franctyne, Ferynge, Baruch Bullman, and William More.

The Christ Church Part-Books.

There are two sets of part-books at Christ Church, Oxford; one is useless through the absence of the tenor volume. The other (dated 1581) consists of five volumes containing more than 100 pieces, of which fifty-five are by Byrd, and twenty by Robert Whyte; some of these were scored by Burney. There are also eight by Persons, six by Tye, and five by Tallis; and among the other composers may be named John Bawdwine (Baldwin), who has included not only motets, but also an instrumental piece, a Fancy à 3, on the cuckoo's cry, which he gives as g^{ll} e^{ll}. Specially curious is 'Hugh Aston's Maske' for four instruments; it is a long piece, mainly in scale-passages, and at the end of the medius part is the name 'Whitbroke,' probably the arranger of a theme by the venerable inventor of instrumental composition. Bruster, Farrant, Mallorie, Shepherd, Tailer, and Woodcock are represented here; with Bull, Giles, and Strogers, who were all young at the time, and belong to the next generation. These fine part-books (I believe, in Baldwin's writing) are bound with the 'Cantiones Sacræ' of Tallis and Byrd.

Sadler's Part-Books.

John Sadler probably wrote these five books himself; they are dated 1585, and just three centuries later were bought by the Bodleian Library. They contain forty motets and Masses, and three secular pieces. One is by Sadler himself. The selection is curious; half the pieces are by Tallis, Whyte, and Byrd, and the still younger composers Morley and Phillips; but others are of a much older period, including a motet by Merbecke, four by Taverner, and his Mass on 'Western Wind,' and even two motets by Fayrfax, and two others by Hugh Aston. This must have been the last case of the pre-Reformation composers finding a place in part-books; and Sadler must have had old-fashioned tastes, as he lived just at the perfection of the polyphonic style.

The student should remember that Forrest's collection, though begun in the former period, was completed after 1545; and the Peterhouse part-books also belong to the beginning of the Reformation period. According to the composers represented, they belong to the previous chapter, in which they were described.

Addit. MSS. 22,597 and 32,377 are single part-books of anthems and motets. Addit. MSS. 29,246–7 and 31,992 contain arrangements for the lute, in Italian tablature; they are in the same handwriting, and are

lettered Edwardus Paston. Fayrfax and Taverner are
well represented in 29,246. Royal MSS., Appendix
74–6, contain a service; some instrumental pieces
have also been inserted, and various compositions in
score.

The very great advance in instrumental music makes
it all the more regrettable that so few of the MSS. contain
any; but the contents of Mulliner's book are a sufficient
proof of the skill of our performers at this time, and at the
very beginning of the next period we shall find splendid
results. The performers had advanced upon Aston's plan
of runs in one hand against chords in the other, and they
could play in independent florid polyphony. A fantasia
on the plain-song 'Miserere,' by Shelbye, has throughout
two notes in the upper part against three in the middle
and nine in the bass. Stafford Smith made a marginal
note that the piece was not intended to be exactly divided,
but I think the various 'proportions' would have been
precisely what sixteenth-century musicians employed
and appreciated. There is, in most of the pieces in the
Mulliner MS., still a certain stiffness resulting from too
strict contrapuntal calculation; from beginning to end
each piece is without variety, having always the same
'proportions,' as in Shelbye's 'Miserere,' in Tallis's
'Natus est nobis' (two-part, with quavers in bass and
minims in melody), and many others. There are some
exceptions, with perfectly free three-part or four-part
writing; among these the pieces of Redford and Sheppard
are the best. Those of Blithman are more distinguished
by executive difficulties. In one of his settings of 'Eterne
verum conditor' occurs the direction *Melos suave*.

It may be questioned whether these ornate pieces were
for solo display or for accompanying the plain-song in
service. I am inclined to think the latter, as all evidence
points to the conclusion that the music of the polyphonic
age was adorned by the performers as much as possible.
Frequently in the Mulliner MS. the word *meane* occurs
apparently in the sense of *intermezzo*; especially in
Redford's pieces, as 'Iste confessor with a meane,'
'Aurora lucis with a meane.'

Some later MSS. contain virginal music of this age, notably Addit. MS. 30,485, and the Fitzwilliam Virginal Book. There is, however, much less than might be expected. Tallis was the greatest composer, and he seems to have paid little attention to instrumental music. Byrd's music was doubtless the staple during the latter portion; most of it must have been produced then, as also much of Philipps's and Bull's. It will be more completely examined in the next chapter.

The Flemish composers and their Italian pupils had throughout the period published a long succession of secular pieces under the title of *Madrigals*. The Earl of Arundel, when visiting Italy in 1568, employed Tarvisio to compose a set for him. The name was not yet used in England, but the thing existed, and the examples from the Mulliner MS., especially ' In going to my lonely bed,' are admirable.

In spite of all this cultivation of the art there was very little printed. After the 'Litany' in 1544, and Coverdale's suppressed *Goostly Psalms*, came the psalters already mentioned, Merbecke's Prayer Book, Tye's 'Acts of the Apostles,' Day's 'Certaine Notes' (1560 and 1565), and harmonised psalter (1563). After Wynkyn de Worde's collection (1530) no secular music appeared for more than forty years; when at last it came it was the work of perhaps the worst composer of the time, apparently an amateur with plenty of belief in his own powers. This was THOMAS WHYTHORNE, *Gent.*, who published a collection of songs (fourteen for three voices, forty-two for four, and twenty for five) in 1571. It is hard to say whether his poems or his music be the worse. The collection is rare; there are copies, more or less perfect, at the British Museum, the Bodleian Library, and Christ Church. Whythorne, who was born in 1528, also published fifty-two pieces for two voices in 1590; they are less barbarous than the songs, and include fifteen canons. This collection has the composer's portrait.

On January 21st, 1575–6, Queen Elizabeth granted a monopoly of music-publishing to Tallis and Byrd for twenty-one years. The composers immediately issued, in part-books, thirty-four of their 'Cantiones Sacræ.' This venture was too ambitious, and in 1577 the unfortunate speculators declared they had lost '200 marks at least.' In 1582 the Company of Stationers in a petition said that Tallis and Byrd had compositions which they would not print even were there no monopoly. After the death of Tallis the patent was sold to East, and from 1587 onwards we shall find a continual succession of secular publications. The moral seems to be that in Elizabethan times sacred music was not in demand, but madrigals were. The 'Cantiones Sacræ' have been partly printed in score by Hawkins and Burney, and some were early adapted to English words, and are still used as anthems. Draudius mentioned the collection in his *Bibliotheca Classica* (Frankfort, 1612), but with a wrong date. There are copies of the 'Cantiones Sacræ' at the British Museum, at Oxford, and in the Fétis Library at Brussels.

No theoretical treatises were published (except translations of Le Roy's Instruction-book for the Lute in 1568 and 1574, and the elementary rules in two of the psalters) until 1584, when a young Irishman, WILLIAM BATHE, born at Dublin, 1564, issued a *Brief Introduction*, subsequently reprinted. It is remarkable in its perception of the octave, instead of the hexachord, as the foundation of the scale, and for its allusions to the use of accidentals. These would require fuller notice in a work on general musical history. Bathe subsequently became head of the Jesuit College at Salamanca, where he died in 1614. There are copies of his book at the British Museum, the Bodleian Library, and Sion College.

John Case, of Woodstock, published two pedantic books at Oxford: *The Praise of Musicke* (1586), and *Apologia Musices* (1588). The latter concludes with a call to universal rejoicing, adapted from the 150th Psalm, upon the defeat of the Armada. One sentence concerning rewards to musicians is worth quoting:

'Periander Rex Corinthiorum Arionem. . . . Angli non ita pridem Tavernerum, Blithmanum, Tallesium, Morum, aliosque insignos musicos magnis premiis affecerunt; et quæ causa nunc est cur hos superstites adhuc viros Birdum, Mundanum, Bullum,

Morleum, Doulandum, Jonsonum, aliosque hodie permultos instrumentorum peritissimos justis suis laudibus non persequamur?'

This passage leads naturally to the consideration of the known biographical details concerning these and other musicians who appear in this chapter, from Taverner to Byrd. Little was known to Anthony à Wood, whose 'Lives of English Musicians' in the Bodleian Library give few particulars beyond what he gathered from their publications, and those few are not always trustworthy. The Lansdowne MSS., some of the Historical MSS. Commission Reports, and the old Cheque-book of the Chapel Royal furnish various facts, but the sum total of our knowledge is not great.

The names after Taverner on Morley's list of 'authorities' are: Redford, Hodges, Selby, Thorne, Oclande, Averie, Dr. Tye, Dr. Cooper, Dr. Newton, Mr. Tallis, Mr. White, Mr. Persons, Mr. Byrd. It must have been by accident that Morley omitted W. Mundy and J. Shepherd, whom he in his works mentions with Fayrfax, Tye, Tallis, and Whyte, as 'not inferior to the best masters on the Continent.' Dr. Cooper has been dealt with in Chapter V; Hodges and Dr. Newton are unknown. Very few of all the other composers of this period are in any way known personally.

JOHN REDFORD was Master of the Children of St. Paul's Cathedral, and (according to Hawkins) organist and almoner. Tusser, in his well-known autobiographical poem, recounts how, after being 'impressed' as a choir-boy (from Wallingford), he got into St. Paul's choir—

> 'With Redford there, the like no where,
> For cunning such, and virtue much;
> By whom some part of musick's art
> So did I gain.'

This must have been about 1535, as Tusser next went to Eton under Udall (who was at Eton 1534–41), and thence to Cambridge in 1543. Redford, as Master of the Children, had also to prepare dramatic entertainments; and he wrote* a Morality entitled 'The Play of Wit and Science.' Some of his poems have merit. Of Redford's

* See p. 121.

compositions, by far the most are in the Mulliner MS., where there are twenty-three of his organ pieces; the last is followed by the beautiful anonymous anthem which Hawkins printed with his name. Addit. MSS. 15,233 and 29,996 have been described. A fine 'Criste resurgens' is in Addit. MSS. 17,802–5, and another motet in the imperfect part-books at Oxford. In 1552 Sebastian Westcott was Master of the Children at St. Paul's; Redford was probably dead.

To judge by his works, Redford was not equal as an executant to Blithman, but was the best instrumental composer of his time. His arrangement of 'Glorificamus' is the most musical of the organ pieces in the Mulliner MS., or, indeed, of all the instrumental works before Byrd, so far as I have examined them.

JOHN HEYWOOD, famous as a writer of interludes, was (as may be seen in Egerton MS. 2604) one of Henry VIII's virginal players in 1526;[*] he was subsequently in the service of Edward VI and Mary, but being a steadfast Romanist he retired in Elizabeth's reign (with Redford?) to Mechlin, where he died about 1575. His only known composition is a song with lute accompaniment in Addit. MS. 4900, 'What heart can think.'

SELBY was doubtless the WILLIAM SHELBYE whose 'Felix Namque' and 'Miserere' are preserved in the Mulliner MS. The former is in four real parts, long and elaborate; the latter has been described on p. 125.

JOHN THORNE was buried in York Minster, December 7th, 1573; he was skilled in poetry and logic, as well as in music. Hawkins printed a good motet by him from a MS. at Buckingham Palace; there is an 'In Nomine' at Oxford, and a piece in Addit. MS. 29,996.

OCLANDE (Okeland, Oakland) appears in Day's Prayer Books with one anthem in two sections; there is a motet in Addit. MSS. 17,802–5. A Christopher Oclande, schoolmaster of Cheltenham, published Latin poems in 1582.

AVERIE was doubtless the AVERY BURTON whose Mass on the Hexachord is second in Forrest's collection.

---

[*] He was paid 50s. a quarter in 1538–41 (Arundel MS. 97).

'Burton' occurs among Henry VIII's musicians. There is a work by 'Avere' in Redford's MS. 'Thomas Avery' was among the old pensioners of the Royal Household at Elizabeth's accession.

The remaining five composers are of a different and higher order than the above, and their work has remained a living possession of the Anglican Church. They were all, let it be remembered, born and bred before or during the Reformation; and even the youngest remained a fervent Romanist. It may easily be believed that they were more at home in contrapuntally setting Latin motets, Masses, and magnificats than in the heavy chord-successions demanded by the Reformers; and though distinguished in all styles, their highest flights are not those produced for the Anglican Service.

CHRISTOPHER TYE was born, according to Wood, in the West of England; much more probably in the East, where the name was common. 'Tye' was a choirboy at King's College, Cambridge, in 1511–2; and in 1527 a lay-clerk. He graduated Mus.Bac. at Cambridge in 1536; in 1545 he proceeded Mus.Doc., and in 1548 was incorporated at Oxford. Since Edward VI and Tye appear as characters in Rowley's chronicle-play on the life of Henry VIII, it has been supposed he was the young King's preceptor; but there is no real ground for the assertion. In 1541 Tye had become organist of Ely Cathedral. In 1553 he dedicated to Edward VI his doggerel versification of the Acts of the Apostles (fourteen chapters only), with music set to the first two verses of each chapter. The verses are laughably bald; but the music is most admirable. In general the eight lines are treated quite simply, in dulcet fa-burden; but every one of the fourteen pieces contains at least a point of imitation, while some are more complicated. Burney's description that the settings consist of 'fugues and canons of the most artificial and complicated kind' only shows that he cannot have examined them, and that he judged them from the one printed by Hawkins, which happens to be the most complex, and is a masterly double canon. They have been adapted to other words in the nineteenth

century, and sung as sacred part-songs. The original
volume, a tiny black-letter, may be seen at the British
Museum and Lambeth Palace.* In the dedication Tye,
apologising for the words, addresses the young King as
follows:—

> ' My callynge is, another way
>   Your grace shall herein fynde;
> By notes set forth, to synge or playe,
>   To recreate the mynde.
>
> And though they be, not curious
>   But for the letter meete:
> Ye shall them fynde harmonious
>   And eke pleasaunt and swete.'

In the dedication of his 'Acts of the Apostles,' Tye
calls himself 'Gentleman of the Chapel Royal'; his name
does not appear in any list. Perhaps he soon resigned,
for he took holy orders in 1560; and received the benefice
of Little Wilbraham, which he resigned in 1567; of
Newton, which he also resigned in 1570; and of
Doddington-cum-March, afterwards divided into seven,
being the wealthiest in England. In 1571 Tye was asked
to translate some verses by the Bishop of Moray. Tye
died about the end of 1572, for the diocesan registers of
Ely contain the entry that, on March 15th, 1572–3, the
bishop conferred on H. Bellet 'rectoriam de Donyngton
cum Merche per mortem naturalem venerabilis viri
Christopheri Tye, mus. doct., ultimi incumbentis, ibi
vacantem.'

Tye's anthem, 'I will exalt Thee,' whether originally
written to English words or not, is a masterly work, fully
worthy of the enthusiastic description of Burney. It will
keep his memory green while English cathedral music
lasts. Surely it is no light matter that England can boast
of sacred music older than Palestrina's or Lassus's, and
yet so beautiful that thoughts of its antiquity need not
interfere with our enjoyment of the unfading beauties.
Tye's best time was probably between 1540–60; it is
noticeable that he did not contribute to the Prayer Books
and Psalter published by Day in 1560–5.

* There is also a copy at Cambridge, with only two tunes.

A considerable number of works by Tye are still in existence. There are twenty-one Latin and English motets at Oxford, a Mass on the song 'Western Wind' in Addit. MSS. 17,802–5, and a Mass at Peterhouse. The additions to Forrest's part-books in the Bodleian Library, described on p. 90, contain the Mass *Euge Bone*; this is printed in Mr. Arkwright's *Old English Edition*, with an admirable biography; and it has been repeatedly performed at Westminster Cathedral. All important MSS. of sacred music, through the madrigal period, include specimens of Tye's works; and in the great printed collections—from Barnard to Rimbault—he is well represented. No instrumental music by him is known; a few secular works are in Addit. MS. 31,390.

Tye and his pupil Whyte were the last composers, so far as I know, who used a *Gymel*. Tye thus closes the old English school of sacred music, and opens the new in being the first whose works are still performed.* His great merit lay in abandoning needless complications, and writing for beautiful effect only. The imitations and contrivances he uses fall as naturally and musically into their place as do those of Palestrina. Tye was exactly contemporary with Gombert and Morales; but I cannot see that they were his equals.

THOMAS TALLIS was probably only a little younger than Tye. As in 1577 he described himself 'now aged, having served the Queen and her ancestors almost forty years,' he must have been born about 1500–10; he was organist of Waltham Abbey, at the Dissolution in 1540 receiving 20s. wages and 20s. 'reward.' He brought with him from the Abbey the celebrated MS. containing the treatises of Lyonel Power, Chilston, etc., in which his autograph, 'Thomas Tallys,' may still be seen.† In 1528 a certain 'Thomas Talley' graduated B.A. Oxon., and was licensed to proceed M.A. in 1531. Tallis's epitaph tells us that he was married thirty-three years, but had no children. He doubtless entered the Chapel Royal in

---

* But Dr. Terry has introduced even fifteenth-century works at Westminster Cathedral.

† See p. 53.

1540, and was already a celebrated musician. There are motets and a Mass by 'Talys' in the Peterhouse part-books. We hear no more of Tallis till 1557, when Queen Mary granted him, together with Thomas Bower, Master of the Children, a lease for twenty-one years of the Manor of Minster-in-Thanet. The Gentlemen of the Chapel had acted a play before the Queen. Tallis may have written this. At this time his splendid powers were in full culmination; and no doubt the beautiful Mass in Addit. MSS. 17,802–5, the 'Cantiones Sacræ,' and the sublime motet for forty voices had been already produced. The English Cathedral Music, so far as it was not adapted from the Latin, must have followed after the final change under Elizabeth. The monopoly granted in 1575–6 only brought Tallis and Byrd loss, and on June 27th, 1577, they petitioned the Queen for a lease in reversion of crown lands of the yearly value of £40, for twenty-one years, and without fine. In the petition (now in the MSS. at Hatfield) it was stated:

'Tallis is now aged, having served the Queen and her ancestors almost forty years, and never had but one preferment, a lease given him by Queen Mary, and now within a year of expiration, the reversion granted over to another. Bird being called to Her Majesty's service from Lincoln Cathedral, where he was well settled, is now, through great charge of wife and children, fallen into debt and great necessity. By reason of his daily attendance in the Queen's service he is letted from reaping such commodity by teaching as heretofore he did. Her grant two years ago of a license for printing music has fallen out to their loss and hindrance to the value of 200 marks at least.'

The endorsement declares the Queen's pleasure that lands worth £30 a year should accordingly be bestowed on the petitioners. Thenceforward they would neither print music nor permit any one else to do so; the event showed that a collection of madrigals or instrumental music might have repaid their losses. The Cheque-book of the Chapel Royal recorded in 1585:

'Thomas Tallis died the 23rd November, and Henry Eveseed sworne in his place. Childe there.'

The latter clause may refer to either. Tallis was buried in the parish church of Greenwich; the brass plate (in a stone before the altar rails) which preserved his epitaph disappeared when the church was rebuilt in the eighteenth century. A memorial was erected by subscription in 1876.

The only works published by Tallis in his lifetime were the nine tunes in Parker's Psalter, the anthems and canticles in Day's Psalter and Prayer Book, and the sixteen motets in the 'Cantiones Sacræ.' His Preces, Responses, Litany, and Dorian 'Service,' with five anthems (adaptations) were printed by Barnard in 1641, and in score by Boyce. Burney and Hawkins printed three of the unadapted motets; Hawkins giving the wonderful canon, 'Miserere nostri,' and also one of the secular songs from the Mulliner MS. The anthem most frequently sung is 'I call and cry,' an adaptation of 'O sacrum convivium'; Rochlitz included it in his *Auswahl* as 'Verba mea auribus.' But the most wonderful specimen of Tallis's abilities, the forty-voiced motet, 'In spem alium non habui,' was first published by Dr. A. H. Mann in 1888.

To say anything in praise of Tallis, whose Preces are daily heard in the Anglican choral service, and whose 'Evening Hymn' is dear to the whole English-speaking race, may seem needless. Yet it is necessary to point out that he is generally underrated and misunderstood, because his simpler works are so very well known that they have obscured the more ambitious and elaborate. Tallis can only be fairly judged by his great contrapuntal works; the title of 'Father of English Cathedral Music' is not his most honourable title. Let Tallis be ranked as a composer of the highest science, to whom all the difficulties of counterpoint were as child's play, and who produced motets and Masses almost worthy to be ranked with Palestrina's; not as a man fettered by the regulations of the Reformed worship, and forcing himself to write in a succession of solid heavy chords.

In instrumental music Tallis was less at home, and was not equal to some of his contemporaries. A canon of his with running bass was printed in *Musica Antiqua*; the MS. (now in the British Museum as Addit. MS. 30,485) is, unfortunately, imperfect. Other pieces exist in the Mulliner MS. and elsewhere. Besides the three madrigals in the Mulliner MS., and 'As Cæsar wept' in the imperfect part-books, Addit. MSS. 18,936-9, I know of no secular vocal music by Tallis.

He was emphatically a man who rose with his aims, and his biggest work is also his greatest.* The enormous motet for eight five-voiced choirs is perhaps the noblest achievement of the English nation in sacred music. Every earnest student should thoroughly examine this work, noting how the themes are fugued through the choirs, how the various sections of the great body are employed antiphonally, how long-sustained harmonies are occasionally varied by quickly-changing successions of chords, and how imposing an effect is produced by the two rests for all the voices, especially the one before the last clause, when thirteen of the voices stop on the chord of C, and, after a minim rest, all the forty enter on the chord of A. Everything an unaccompanied choir can do is required in this masterpiece of the polyphonic style.

Of Tallis's contemporaries, RICHARD FARRANT claims first mention, being eighth in the list of Edward VI's Chapel Royal. In 1564 he became Master of the Children at Windsor, returned to the Chapel Royal in 1569, and died November 30th, 1580. There are two organ pieces by Farrant in the Mulliner MS.; and services and anthems (still sung) are ascribed to him, but several Farrants are heard of from 1540–1620, and one of the others may have been the author. These anthems, 'Hide not Thy face,' and 'Call to remembrance,' were printed by Barnard, and (with a service) by Boyce; but it was not till 1778 (in the *Cathedral Magazine*) that the work usually associated with Farrant's name was printed. This most exquisite and melodious anthem, 'Lord, for Thy tender mercies' sake,' is, in my opinion, as certainly the culmination of our older sacred music in simple unaffected charm, as Tallis's 'In spem alium non habui' is in

---

* When I wrote this eulogy I had not heard the motet. Dr. A. H. Mann conducted a performance at the London Conference of the Incorporated Society of Musicians in 1898. The highest notes stand out strangely prominent upon the many-parted chords; contrast between various registers is not employed.

sublimity. The part-writing is as graceful, natural, and effective as that of Tye's 'Acts of the Apostles'; and even Burney, with all his eighteenth-century tastes, allowed that the anthem 'has considerable merit with regard to air, as well as of harmony.' Fortunately it is so familiar and so loved that it needs no description; may it ever remain so! But I must not omit that some old copies ascribe it to John Hilton, and its authorship is doubtful. I should have guessed Tye as the author had it been anonymous.

JOHN SHEPHERD (Sheppard), said to have been a choir-boy at St. Paul's, became in 1542 organist of Magdalen College, Oxford, and Fellow 1549–51. About this time he entered the Chapel Royal. In 1554 he supplicated for the degree of Mus.Doc., 'having studied music twenty years,' but it was apparently not granted, as the registers of Magdalen College, the Mulliner MS., and Day's publications never give him the title. In 1555 he was complained against, and very sharply reproved by the Vice-President, after which nothing is known of him. The compositions of Shepherd's still existing are mainly motets, of which there are thirty-nine at Christ Church. In Mulliner's book are short and musical instrumental pieces of his; and the fine anthem, 'O Lord, the Maker of all things' (ascribed by Aldrich and Boyce to Henry VIII), is probably his, or perhaps Mundy's. Burney printed a good 'Esurientes.'

Shepherd, with Taverner and Tye, also composed a mass on the popular song, 'Western Wind, why dost thou blow?' The three are preserved together in Addit. MSS. 17,802–5. It was possibly a friendly emulation which induced the three masters to try their skill on a secular theme. I know no other English instance of this expedient, so great a favourite with the Flemings, and I have met with scarcely any instances of the simultaneous use of different words, justly a sore offence to both Protestant and Romanist zealots The objectionable features of pre-Reformation sacred music, so strongly condemned by the Council of Trent, did not exist in England.

ROBERT JOHNSON has been by some identified with a priest who was chaplain to Anne Boleyn during her short queenship. There was a Scotch priest of this name who was accused of heresy, and fled to England. He composed here a motet; the Psalter of St. Andrews (of which a single part-book is preserved in the British Museum, and others at Edinburgh) contains it. There is a work in Addit. MSS. 17,802–5 by Johnson, and another by 'R. Johnson, priest.' Baldwin's MS. in the Royal Collection has a piece by 'Robert Johnson of Windsor.' They may have been all identical. A madrigal by Johnson, 'Defyled is my name,' was printed by Hawkins from the Mulliner MS.; it is also contained in Hammond's part-books. Burney gives a fine specimen of his treatment (as a motet) of the plain-song, 'Dum transisset Sabbatum,' and contrasts it with Taverner's inferior work on the same *cantus firmus*. Johnson contributed three anthems (see p. 117) to Day's harmonised Prayer Book. In 1575 a Robert Johnson was one of the musicians to Sir T. Kytson, and was lent to the Earl of Leicester for the Kenilworth pageants. We shall meet with others of the name in the next chapter. A Robert Johnson was one of the Proctors of the Arches, and was buried in St. Faith-under-Paul's in 1558.

JOHN MERBECKE, in spite of his long life, has left few works. By far the most important is the Mass *Per arma justitiæ* in Forrest's collection. An anthem was printed by Hawkins. There is an 'Ave dei matris' at Peterhouse, and a 'Domine Jesu Criste' in Sadler's part-books. It is probable that Merbecke was not well inclined to ecclesiastical music. He narrowly escaped martyrdom with Testwood and others in 1544; under Edward VI he published a Concordance to the Bible, in the dedication of which he speaks with regret of the time he had wasted in music and organ-playing. At this time, however, he, according to Wood, graduated Mus.Bac. Oxon.; but this was a period of disorder, and the public scribe (afterwards dismissed for negligence), did not register his name. Merbecke's adaptation of the Latin plain-song to the English Book of Common Prayer appeared in 1550. He

lived till about 1585, and published several theological
works. In a Commonplace Book (1580) he has included
sub 'Musicke' only passages from Calvin and others,
speaking of the superiority of the heart to the voice, etc.
Yet he kept his post at Windsor Castle till his death. He
furnished an account of the proceedings against Testwood
and himself to Fox, who by a slip of the pen put
Merbecke's own name among the martyrs. Fox corrected
the mistake in the flyleaf of 'Errata,' and in the second
edition of his Martyrology, but was warmly attacked for
the error by Romish writers.

RICHARD EDWARDS was born in 1523, in Somersetshire.
In 1541 he entered Corpus Christi College, Oxford, and
graduated M.A. in 1547. A 'George Edwards' stands
twenty-sixth in the list of Edward VI's Chapel Royal.
Richard Edwards appears by one of his poems to have
been early connected with the Royal Household; but
the poem is most likely from a drama. The song in Addit.
MS. 4900, and the 'Terrenum sitiens' at Peterhouse,
were doubtless by George or Richard. Queen Elizabeth
made R. Edwards Master of the Children in 1563; in this
post he particularly distinguished himself as a dramatist.
He wrote plays on the stories of *Palamon and Arcite* and
of *Damon and Pythias*, apparently the first introduction
of classical subjects upon the English stage. He also has
an honourable place in English poetry, having collected
'The Paradyse of Daintie Devyces,' an anthology in
which some of the best pieces are his own; it was published
after his death. On September 3rd, 1566, his *Palamon
and Arcite*, acted at Christ Church, Oxford, so pleased
Queen Elizabeth that she promised Edwards a reward,
but he died on October 31st. His setting of the metricised
Lord's Prayer is included in Day's Psalter, but his chief
musical claim to remembrance is found in the Mulliner
MS. One madrigal therein, 'The Syllye Man,' bears
Edwards's name; in his anthology appears 'By painted
speech the syllye man,' signed Hunnis. The beautiful
poem 'In going to my naked bedde' appears as Edwards's
in 'The Paradyce of Daintie Devyces,' and the still more
beautiful music preserved by Mulliner is doubtless his

also. The setting of Surrey's 'Ye happy dames,' though inferior, has a second part much resembling it, and is probably also by Edwards. At the same time, it should be remembered that 'The Syllye Man' and the piece in Day's Psalter are both much simpler, and not polyphonic, while 'In going to my lonely bedde' and 'Ye happy dames' are both contrapuntal. I believe that the poems in Edwards's anthology, and also those in Addit. MS. 15,233, were written to be sung in interludes.

According to Wood, Edwards was a pupil of GEORGE ETHERIDGE (Etherege, Edrych, Edrycus), an Oxford physician. He was a learned classical scholar, but a stubborn Romanist, and the accuser of Bishop Hooper. Pits speaks of Etheridge as one of the most famous vocal and instrumental musicians in England; it does not appear that any proof remains. Etheridge was still alive in 1585.

ROBERT STONE, who had harmonised Cranmer's Litany, was seventy years in the Chapel Royal, and died in 1613, aged 97. I have seen no other work of Stone's except the motet in Day's Prayer Book.

THOMAS CAUSTON (Cawston, Caustun), whose counterpoint is as pure and musical as Tye's, contributed some, or all, of the canticles to Day's 'Certain Notes,' and also six anthems. Many of the harmonisings in Day's Psalter are by him. Jebb has reprinted a Venite and Communion Service by Causton. The Cheque-book of the Chapel Royal records that Causton died October 28th, 1569. There was a family of the name at Oxted, Surrey.

EDWARD HAKE, who shared in the harmonising of Day's Psalter, was of Windsor Chapel Royal, and is heard of in connection with the proceedings against Testwood and Merbecke. There is an 'In Nomine' of Hake's at Oxford, and a motet in Addit. MSS. 17,802–5. THOMAS APPLEBY also appears in the latter set of part-books; he was organist of Magdalen College, Oxford, in 1539. Wright, of the Chapel Royal, also represented in these part-books, is mentioned in the archives of the town of Rye, to which he sold some choir-books in 1552.

WILLIAM MUNDY, a vicar-choral of St. Paul's, entered the Chapel Royal on February 12th, 1563–4; nothing more is heard of him until his place was filled up on October 12th, 1591, when he was probably dead. His works are still heard in our cathedrals, and the anthem published as Henry VIII's is commonly attributed to Mundy. His son belongs to the next chapter.

Case, in including 'Morum' among the musicians who were highly rewarded, probably alluded to William More, by whom there are anthems and motets in Addit. MSS. 30,480–4 and 31,226. A 'Levavi oculos' in the latter is particularly good. When we remember Tallis's petition, we may fear that the rewards bestowed upon Taverner, Blithman, and More were less munificent than Case's words imply. The name More occurs in the list of the royal musicians.

WILLIAM BLITHMAN (Blytheman) was, according to Tanner, in 1564 choirmaster at Christ Church, Oxford; it does not appear when he entered the Chapel Royal. He graduated Mus.Bac. Cantab. in 1586, and died on Whit-Sunday, 1591. His epitaph in St. Olave's, Queenhithe, mentions his skill as an organist, and that John Bull was his pupil. There are fourteen of his instrumental works in Mulliner's book; one was printed by Hawkins and another by Rimbault. Others may be seen in Addit. MS. 31,403, and in the Fitzwilliam Virginal Book. In Addit. MSS. 17,802–5 there are three motets by him. As the instructor of Bull, Blithman must be regarded as one of the most important pioneers of keyboard music.

WILLIAM HUNNIS, who succeeded Edwards as Master of the Children in the Chapel Royal, and held the post till 1597, is more distinguished as a poet than a composer. The tunes in his three volumes are almost all in what we should now call G minor, and are without harmony.

WILLIAM DAMON (Daman) was apparently one of the Royal Household.* Besides the harmonised Psalter of 1579 and the contrapuntal one of 1591 (in which he is described as 'late one of her Majesties Musitions'), he composed motets and anthems. There are five in the Christ Church part-books, and others in Addit. MSS. 29,372–7 (Myriell's collection), and in Paston's lute-books.

* Query, of Liège ?

Of lesser composers, generally unknown biographically, OSBERT PARSLEY (Persleye) belonged to Norwich Cathedral, where he was buried, aged seventy-one, in 1585. His works are often found in MSS. HENRY STONINGS appears both now and in later MSS.; he must not be confused with William Stonard. RICHARD ALWOODE (Allwood) is called 'priest' in the Masses at Oxford, the last of which is by him. There are also instrumental pieces in Mulliner's book (a complicated 'Voluntary' in the Mixolydian Mode being printed by Hawkins), and others in Addit. MS. 30,485. It seems hardly possible that he was the 'Richard Alyworth' or 'Alsworthe' of the Chapel Royal who died on January 22nd, 1566–7.

An eighteenth-century list of the organists of Ely Cathedral gives 1572–9 as the dates of WILLIAM FOX, whose anthem, 'Teach me Thy way,' was published in the *Parish Choir*. His successor was GEORGE BARCROFT, whose Morning Service in the heavy chord-succession style was published by the Motet Society.

Of all the Anglican music in that style, the service of NATHANIEL PATRICK is the one which may best be compared with Tallis's. Patrick was organist of Worcester Cathedral during this period, as appears from an entry in the Stationers' Registers, October 22nd, 1597. Thomas East had published 'Songs of Sundrye Natures, whereof some are Divine, some are madrigalles, and the rest psalms and hymns in Latin by Nathaniel Patrick, sometyme Master of the Children of the Cathedral Church of Worcester and organist of the same.' No copy of this work is known. Some sacred and secular pieces of Patrick's, probably from it, may be seen in Addit. MSS. 17,786–91 and 18,936–9.

The last three composers on Morley's list still remain to be noticed. ROBERT WHYTE (White, Wight) was a man of great renown in his time, but subsequently forgotten and confused with later composers named White. One anthem of his was printed by Barnard in 1641, otherwise he was forgotten until rediscovered by Burney, who speaks with just enthusiasm of his works, and printed a very fine anthem. Ambros says that if one examines this 'so erstaunt man allerdings ueber den edlen Sinn und reinen Geschmack der sich hier ausspricht.'

This anthem, 'Lord, who shall dwell?' was taken from the Christ Church part-books dated 1581, in which there is a Latin elegy on Whyte. Burney pointed out that this date is anterior to Palestrina's death, and that Whyte could not have learnt from the great works of the Roman school, to which his own bear a remarkable likeness. In the part-books Whyte is described as Bachelor of Arts, Bachelor of Music, organist and Master of the Children at Westminster Abbey. The name appears in the list of Ely organists 1562–7; Whyte had graduated at Cambridge in 1561. In 1570 he went to Westminster Abbey, where he died in the time of plague, November, 1574; he was buried at St. Margaret's Church, November 11th. From his will it appears that his father was living with him; he was therefore not aged, and his children are described as 'minors.' His wife, who died a few days later, bequeathed property to her mother, Katherine Tye. It is therefore probable, from this and an entry in a marriage register at Ely, that Whyte married a daughter of Dr. Tye, his predecessor at Ely, and that he was born about 1540. His works are nearly all sacred, and generally to Latin words; there are thirty motets and anthems, and five Lamentations, in the Christ Church collection. Some fantasias are included in one of Paston's lute-books. The anthem printed by Barnard, 'The Lord bless us and keep us,' seems to me even finer than the one printed by Burney. At every regular choral service these beautiful works should occasionally be heard. I believe that if they had been published as Palestrina's they would have been received without question as genuine. Yet Robert Whyte died, all too early, twenty years before Palestrina and Lassus. Let us revere his memory and treasure his works, and let his name be ever enrolled among England's noblest musicians.

(ROBERT ?) PERSONS, or Parsons, was better remembered than Whyte, though here again later musicians of the same name have been confused with him. He entered the Chapel Royal in 1563, and was drowned at Newark on

January 19th, 1569–70. A madrigal, 'Enforced by love and feare,' may be seen in the Christ Church collection (whence it was copied and printed by Burney), and in Hammond's part-books. A service and a canon-anthem were printed in Barnard's 'Selected Church Music,' and a Burial Service in Lowe's 'Directions' (1661), but whether the Elizabethan composer or another is here meant does not appear. Wood states that he was born at Exeter, was organist to James I, and buried in the cloisters of Westminster Abbey. These statements, on the authority of Dr. Rogers, show how Persons was confused with John Parsons of Westminster Abbey, who was buried in the cloisters in 1623. There was also a later Robert Parsons, a vicar-choral of Exeter in 1634. Secular music by one of them is included in Addit. MSS. 17,786–91.

There were also two Italian composers who came to England, and founded families much heard of in musical records up to the Restoration. In the Peterhouse MSS. there is a Mass and motet by 'Lupus Italus,' and among the Royal Household was 'Ambrose Lupo, de Myllan.' He must have been among the earliest Italian composers. The other was Alfonso Ferrabosco, who came to England in the middle of the century or a little after; his property was seized by the Inquisition, and he remained here. He seems to have been accused of murder, and addressed several petitions to Cecil in consequence. Though Ferrabosco had an annuity of 100 marks from the Queen, his children were maintained after his death by Gomer van Osterwyck of the Chapel Royal, who in 1589 memorialised the Queen on the matter.

Lastly we come to the greatest of the Elizabethan musicians, WILLIAM BYRD (Bird, Berd, Birde). Though in sacred music surpassed by Tallis, as an executant by Bull, as a madrigalist by several, yet Byrd was so distinguished in all styles alike that, on the whole, none of his contemporaries equalled him. He is the central musical figure of the Elizabethan age; celebrated early, and living long; associated with Tallis, associated with Gibbons; born in the early days of the English Reforma-

tion, and living through the culminating time of
ecclesiastical music to see the rise, culmination, decay,
and almost the death of the English madrigal, and the
disuse of vocal counterpoint in favour of dramatic
expression. In all these changes Byrd himself had a
large share, and still more in perfecting the instrumental
forms.

We possess many biographical details concerning this
great composer, yet there are curious difficulties in them.
From his will, published in *The Musician*, June, 1897, it
appears that he was born in 1543. He was a pupil of
Tallis, as we learn from the complimentary poem prefixed
to their 'Cantiones Sacræ'—

> 'Tallisius magno dignus honore senex
> Et Birdus tantum natus decorare magistrum.'

The earliest known fact concerning him is that he was
organist at Lincoln in 1563; whence he was called to
the Chapel Royal (on the death of Persons) in February,
1569–70. His wife, Ellen Birley, was a native of Lincolnshire; and a Henry Byrde was buried in the cathedral in
1512. It has accordingly been suggested that he was a
native of Lincoln. I think it worth mentioning that
beard is (or was) pronounced *berd* in Lincolnshire.
Rimbault asserted that Byrd was the son of a member
of the Chapel Royal, and that he was senior chorister
of St. Paul's in 1554, but these statements rest on no
discoverable authority. Certainly Byrd was a celebrated
man in 1570; and in 1575 he shared with the venerable
Tallis in the monoply of music-printing. Some light is
thrown on his circumstances by their petition of 1577.
As already stated, the Queen granted them lands worth
£30 a year; but Byrd again petitioned Lord Burleigh in
February, 1579–80, through the Earl of Northumberland,
whose daughter he taught. In the letter it is mentioned,
'he can not enjoy that which was his first suit, and granted
unto him.' At this time Byrd was living at Harlington,
near Uxbridge. He composed a three-voiced song for
Lacy's Latin tragedy, *Richardus III*; it is printed in
Musica Antiqua. Now begins a singular period in the
composer's life. He still remained a member of the

Chapel Royal, yet he was repeatedly prosecuted as a Popish recusant, and was sometimes in hiding. True bills were found against his wife and manservant for not attending church several times from 1581–6; and on the last occasion, and in 1592, against Byrd himself. Weston, a Jesuit priest hiding in 1586 (at the house of a certain Mr. Bold), recorded in his autobiography: 'We met there also Mr. Byrd, the most celebrated musician and organist of the English nation, who had been formerly in the Queen's Chapel, and held in the highest estimation; but for his religion he sacrificed everything, both his office and the Court and all those hopes which are nurtured by such persons as pretend to similar places in the dwellings of princes.' No mention of his leaving occurs in the Chapel Royal Cheque-book, and Byrd's immense reputation probably secured him powerful friends, who shielded him from further harm. Tallis was now dead, and Byrd assigned his patent to Thomas East (Este, Est). Three fine Masses, published without title-pages, appeared about this time; a copy of that for five voices, now in the British Museum, was scored and published by the Musical Antiquarian Society. The others were supposed lost till parts interleaved with a later work were discovered by Mr. Barclay Squire in 1888; since then, complete copies of all have been found at Lincoln by Mr. J. E. Matthew; and odd parts by myself in both University Libraries. There are also copies at Christ Church, Oxford.

Byrd's 'Psalms, Songs, and Sonets of Sadness and Pietie,' dedicated to Sir Christopher Hatton, were in print on November 6th, 1587; the known copies are partly undated, partly 1588. 'Songs of Sundry Natures' and contributions to Yonge's and Watson's collections of Italian madrigals quickly followed; and two books of 'Cantiones Sacræ.' These works belong to the next period, as likewise Byrd's subsequent publications: *Medulla Musicke* (1603); 'Gradualia' (1607); 'Psalms, Songs, and Sonetts' (1611); and contributions to *Parthenia* (1611) and Leighton's collection (1614). Besides these, a large number of unpublished works, especially motets, exist; in the British Museum there is a little volume of canons in his autograph, finely written, and each page signed W. B.

Peacham in the *Compleat Gentleman* (1622) begins his account of composers with Byrd's sacred music, saying that he preferred 'before all our *Phœnix* Mr. Byrd, whom in that kind I know not whether any may equall,' and also that some of Byrd's madrigals, such as *La Virginella*, 'cannot be mended by the best Italian of them all.' Morley had in 1597 dedicated his treatise to Byrd, 'never to be named without reverence of musicians.' In Baldwin's MS. in the Royal Collection there is a clumsy poem exalting Byrd above all musicians at home and abroad.

'All that should accompany old age' seems to have been Byrd's, except occasional trouble from persecution. In 1598 he was living at Stondon Place, Essex, on an estate which had been sequestrated from Shelley, a Romanist; yet in that year Byrd was formally excommunicated as a Papist by the Archdiaconal Court of Essex, and was repeatedly 'presented' in later years. Shelley's aged widow attempted to recover Stondon, but Byrd defied and successfully resisted her, King James taking his part. Byrd's name appears in the list of the Chapel Royal in 1604, when an increase of salary was granted. He signed second, next after the venerable Robert Stone. According to Richard Clark, Byrd was present (as one of the organists) when the King went in state to St. Paul's to return thanks for the discovery of the Gunpowder Plot. His recusancy repeatedly brought him further trouble; but apparently not very serious. His will, dated 15th November, 1622, 'now in the eightieth year of myne age,' declares his steadfast Romanism; and his desire to be buried at Stondon with his wife. Then the Cheque-book of the Chapel Royal recorded the death of 'William Byrd, a Father of Musicke,' on 4th July, 1623.

Some services and anthems were included in Barnard's 'Selected Church Music' in 1641. Just 200 years later, the Musical Antiquarian Society published his five-voiced Mass, and afterwards his 'Cantiones Sacræ' with a most inappreciative preface by Horsley. Mr. Arkwright has published the 'Songs of Sundrie Natures' in his *Old English Edition*; and the four-voiced Mass has also appeared. But at present Byrd is mainly known by the favourite canon, 'Non nobis Domine,' first printed in 1651, and traditionally his; and by one of the 'Cantiones,' the beautiful 'Ne irascaris, Domine,' sung as the anthem, 'Bow Thine ear.' According to Wood, Dr. Rogers possessed a piece for forty voices by Byrd; this is now unknown.

It should be noted that twelve of Byrd's 'Psalms, Sonets, and Songs' (1587) were originally composed as solos with instrumental accompaniment, and rearranged for voices only when published. He calls them 'songs of great compasse.' Another technical point is Byrd's use of a free dominant seventh in the final cadence of several of the 'Songs of Sundrie Natures.' The upper voice first takes the supertonic, then skips to the subdominant; 1589 is a very early date for this novelty. The use of a $\frac{6}{3}$ in his 'Preces' is also noteworthy. As a specimen of Byrd's contrapuntal science, the wonderful 'Diliges Dominum' (printed by Hawkins) is sufficient; it is a canon *recte et retro* for eight voices.

Byrd was intimate with Ferrabosco, and they each made in friendly rivalry forty canons on the plain-song 'Miserere.' This was published as *Medulla Musicke*; but no copy is known. Morley pronounced Ferrabosco's share to be superior.

It is not, however, by his sacred or secular vocal music that Byrd deserves remembrance so much as by his compositions for the virginal. We do not know how far his immediate predecessors had advanced upon Hugh Aston's wonderful beginning of keyboard-composition; the loss of their manuscripts prevents our tracing the successive advances. The Mulliner MS. is almost entirely in the contrapuntal style, and is probably organ music; Byrd, though he did not neglect that style, also used popular tunes, and constructed brilliant sets of variations on them. A very valuable and lucid exposition of Byrd's merits as an instrumental composer may be

seen in Ambros's *Geschichte der Musik* III 460, where it
is shown how superior Byrd's artistic creations were to
the clumsy attempts of his Italian contemporaries.
Ambros has written so admirably of those few English
works which he found in Burney's 'History' and in
Parthenia, that we must regret he did not visit England
and examine the great unpublished collections at Cambridge and Eridge Castle. Rubinstein has also described
Byrd as the inventor of artistic instrumental music; and
began his series of 'Historical Recitals' with Byrd and
other Elizabethans. More than one hundred instrumental
works by Byrd are in existence. A beautiful volume
written (by Baldwin of Windsor) for Lady Nevell contains
forty-two pieces, all by 'Byrd, Homo memorabilis'; this
volume contains Byrd's 'Battle-piece,' the first known
attempt to compose instrumental music to a set programme. The yet greater volume in the Fitzwilliam
Museum has sixty-seven pieces by Byrd; and there are
others elsewhere. A MS. written during the Commonwealth (now Addit. MS. 10,337) contains the 'Battle',
with an extra movement. This piece is certainly descriptive, but uninteresting musically.

It is a special honour to Byrd that he was the inventor
of the variation-form, so far as one man is the inventor
of an art. Where Hugh Aston had made a very creditable
attempt,* Byrd perfectly succeeded. His variations on
the 'Carman's Whistle,' and still more those on 'Jhon,
come kisse me now,' may be called masterpieces. The
glory of the conception that a simple tune could be
figurated and repeated in various forms, all woven into
an organic artistic entirety, is the due of William Byrd.

The long life of this greatest of Elizabethan composers has carried us far into the next period; and we
must now return to the Reformation, in order to
mention some particulars of interest concerning music
in Scotland.

A very remarkable proof of Scottish skill in diatonic
harmony, and of artistic enthusiasm, is preserved in the

---

* That is, if ' My Lady Carey's Dompe ' be Aston's. The Hornpipe is
less distinctly on one series of chords.

St. Andrews Psalter, written and illuminated in 1566 by Thomas Wood (Wodde). There are four beautiful part-books, with a supplement; and subsequently Wood made a duplicate copy. David Laing in 1871 described them admirably, as far as they were then known. At Edinburgh there are both the treble copies, both the bassus, and one tenor, while one supplement is at Dublin; the contra-tenor was not known to Laing, but it has since been discovered bound with the supplement, and has (rather unfortunately) drifted into the British Museum. This part-book (Addit. MS. 33,933) is the only one I have seen; it is imperfect, beginning at Psalm xviii, some leaves being also missing later. The work much resembles Day's Psalter, having after the Psalms the metricised Lord's Prayer, Commandments, and Da Pacem, with many annotations, also the Te Deum metricised by Gudman and composed by ANDRO KEMP, both 'sumtyme' of St. Andrews. Kemp was then at Aberdeen. There are also Latin motets. The composers were ANGUS, ANDRO BLACKHALL, DAVID PEEBLES, ROBERT JOHNSON, and Sir JOHN FUTHY. At the end of the part-book in the British Museum there are various instrumental pieces and secular songs, including 'Prince Edward's Paven' and 'The Queene of Inglonds Paven.' In the supplement there is an 'In Nomine' by Tallis. Wood remarks with insight that music changes, 'and if Dr. Farfax were alive in this country he wald be contemnit, and pereish for layk of mentinance'; this shows how Fayrfax was venerated, as Wood evidently selects him as the most renowned of older musicians. Of the composers named, FUTHY (Fethy), 'the first new-fingerit organeist that ever was in Scotland,' had learnt the new execution probably in England, returning home about 1530. In 1544 he was engaged at Aberdeen, and was to teach organ-playing and singing. BLACKHALL, a canon of Holyrood, was in 1567 minister at Ormiston, then at Musselburgh, where he died, 1609. JOHN ANGUS was born about 1515; he was Dean of Dun-fermline, then at Stirling. ROBERT JOHNSON (compare p. 137) was born at Dunse; being accused of heresy he fled to England. DAVID PEEBLES (Peblis), whom Wood calls 'a notable cunning man,' harmonised the Psalms; he was of St. Andrews, and died December, 1579. In 1530 he had set 'Si quis diliget Me' as a motet for five voices, and presented it to James V. Wood evidently feared that music would decay in Scotland.

That the art had been highly cultivated in the North may be seen from Addit. MS. 4911. This was written probably about 1540, and is a very elaborate and valuable treatise in the Scottish dialect, based mainly upon Ornithoparcus. Josquin is quoted. There are many anonymous examples, including a complete Mass in score. This is for four voices, and strangely enough has a plain-song in the tenor with a florid bass nearly always a fifth below at the beginning of each tenor note. There are also examples from Magnificats and motets.

In May and June, 1559, the electric eloquence of Knox suddenly completed the Scottish Reformation. In a few weeks all the Roman worship disappeared from the Lowlands, and the Genevan order was quickly established, all ecclesiastical music being forbidden. Doubtless the compositions of the old Scottish school—from James I onwards—perished largely in the general confusion and devastation. Psalm-singing alone was permitted in worship, and a singular result has been the opposition to any hymn-singing, which has lasted among the 'straiter sort' even to our own day. The Sang Scules, which had been maintained by the monks, naturally suffered; that at Aberdeen, under Futhy and John Black, seems to have held its ground best, but there was no longer a necessity for them. In 1579 an Act of Parliament was passed for their benefit, 'music being almost decayed.' King James VI himself endowed the Sang Scules at Musselburgh and Elgin, and his Queen another at Dunfermline. The King also re-established that at Edinburgh, appointing David Cumming as Maister.

The folk-songs mentioned in the collections of the time are partly English. In the *Complaynte of Scotland* (1549) the shepherds are described singing a number of ballads, among them being Henry VIII's 'Pastance with gude companye.' The 'Gude and Godly Ballates' (printed in

1578) were to be sung to popular tunes, the names of many being thus preserved. It is known to all the world that Mary Stuart, after her return from France, favoured an Italian musician named Rizzio, who was murdered by her husband in 1566; an absurd story has been current that Rizzio invented Scotch music. It first appeared in the eighteenth century, when Italy was supposed to be unquestionably the mother and nurse of all modern arts. Rizzio was only a performer; there is no reason to believe that he ever composed anything.

How far the cultivation of music went among the generality in England and Scotland is by no means clear. Music seems to have been part of the general education of a young lady, as at present, and the allusions* to Byrd's teaching are significant. Whether it was more than a superficial accomplishment or no, and whether the men of the Reformation usually shared in it, do not appear with sufficient distinctness. Such tremendous changes take attention from the arts, though the ordinary daily practice goes on as usual. The word *Lesson*, to express an instrumental composition, occurs in Kendall's *Flowers of Epigrammes*, printed 1577, but mostly written much earlier:

> ' On Saterday I will you send
> Some Lessons for your Lute;
> And for your Citterne eke a few
> Take leaves till time of fruite.'

Queen Elizabeth herself, as is well known, was a skilful performer on the virginals. This name, say some, was given to the instrument in her honour, but it was used before she was born, as I have quoted in Chapter III. She also played on the 'poliphant,' an instrument strung with brass wire. There is a well-known account of her playing in a letter by the Scotch ambassador; and Lyly, in *Euphues and his England*, also alludes to her skill. We do not hear that she composed, but 'two little anthems, or things in metre of hir majestie,' were licensed to be printed in 1578; and ten years later, when she went in state to St. Paul's to return thanks for the destruction

* See pp. 133, 144; and compare p. 79.

of the Spanish Armada, a poem of hers, 'Loke and bowe
downe Thine eare, O Lorde,' was sung before her.
A setting (with Byrd's name) is extant in Paston's lute-
books. She certainly delighted in music, as might be
expected in a child of Henry VIII. A report made in the
following century stated the cost of her musical establishment 'of all kinds' was £1,576 annually.

I must remind my readers that the Chapel Royal had
absorbed all the greatest musical talent of the kingdom.
The number of really fine composers is astonishing, but
all the best were collected in London. This has been,
alas! still more the case since the Civil War. So it has
been in France; there all the leading talents gravitate to
the capital. But so it has not been in Germany or Italy
with manifest advantage musically.

Of all our greatest ecclesiastical composers, one alone,
Orlando Gibbons, lies outside this period; and the names
of Redford, Blithman, Dr. Tye, Shepherd, Mundy,
Causton, Farrant, Tallis, Edwards, Patrick, Whyte,
Persons, and Byrd must ever remain in honour as the
leading composers of this splendid time. Stress must
be laid on the fact that the Golden Age of English music
began already in Henry VIII's reign, lasting for about
eighty years, through the reigns of his three children and
of James I. The Elizabethan period was only the central
portion, not the whole, an assertion which requires
emphasising. At the accession of Elizabeth in 1558,
Tallis and Farrant must have been about fifty years old,
Tye still older; and their great sacred works, especially
the Masses, must have been nearly all produced. We
cannot be too grateful to Thomas Mulliner and those
who have preserved his book, and to the transcriber and
preservers of Addit. MSS. 17,802–5, for giving us so
excellent and undeniable a proof that our English composers were once more, though but for a short time, the
greatest in the world; and that Tye, Edwards, and Tallis
had entered into the perfection of the polyphonic style
some years before the Council of Trent was unmeasured
in denunciation of the Flemish pedantries; and while
Palestrina and Lassus (both younger than Tallis) were

still groping their way through foggy obscurities to the
serene light of the clear style already attained in England.
Lassus visited England during the reign of Queen Mary,
and may have here learned the change from his hard
scientific early style to the perfect beauty of his later
works. I do not assert that Tye and Tallis, even in their
best works, can quite compare with Palestrina; but they
were of an earlier generation. The confusion of tonality
which occasionally produces singular harshness in the
sixteenth-century music is not found in Tye and Farrant;
in others (even in Tallis and Byrd) cases are by no means
uncommon in which the major third and minor third of
a chord clash with very strange effect, suggesting that
we do not quite understand the notation, as Bathe's
treatise (compare p. 127) also suggests.*

* But Continental masters, even Palestrina, and especially Vittoria, often
perpetrated similar crudities. A long discussion, in which Italian, Swiss,
Polish, and German experts took part, was devoted to the question at the
Vienna Congress of the International Musical Society.

CHAPTER V

THE MADRIGALIAN PERIOD
(1588–1630)

Thomas East begins printing music.—List of the Madrigal collections published.—The principal MSS.—The distinction between 'Madrigals' and 'Ayres'—Instrumental Music; Invention of the Fugue.—English performers on the Continent. — The Masques. — Theoretical treatises. — A new school of sacred music.—Rise of the Monodic school of songs. —The Shakespearian age the culminating period of English music.

Representative Composers: Byrd, Philipps, Dowland, Morley, Bull, Wilbye, Gibbons, Coperario, Lanier, Peerson.

THE destruction of the Spanish Armada left England in fullest splendour of power and glory. The very next year Spenser completed and published the first section of his great poem. Then followed the earliest attempt of Bacon to direct the mind of man away from barren words into the path of useful studies. And now a half-educated scapegrace came from a little Midland town, and in a few years showed himself the greatest genius who has ever walked the earth; a dramatist whose works are of all England's glories the most permanent.

But in this wonderful time English music was not quite on a level with English poetry, English heroism, or English philosophy. It was not the first in the world. Palestrina had, about the beginning of Elizabeth's reign, made Italian music superior to all other; and though the English instrumental music was still unrivalled, it had not the immortal beauty of the best polyphonic vocal music. This period, however, produced, on the whole, the greatest results; English music and English poetry were both at their climax. The English instrumental music now began to exercise a marked influence upon the Continent, where it was speedily imitated, and afterwards surpassed. The connection between the earliest German instrumental music and its English models has only recently been traced.

Byrd stood without rival or second among English musicians at the opening of this period. It was probably through the troubles his recusancy brought him that he sold his monopoly to Thomas East (Este, Est), a printer living in Aldersgate Street. We must esteem it fortunate that he did this, as a long succession of secular compositions were published; while (the) previous twelve years, since the heavy loss the 'Cantiones Sacræ' had occasioned, had been quite barren as regards publication.

The events of Byrd's life have been related. Other leading composers, Peter Philipps and Deering, were also Romanists. They all accordingly published Latin sacred music; Philipps and Deering lived on the Continent, and their works appeared there. Other English composers issued secular music almost exclusively. In so earnest a time it may seem strange that ecclesiastical music was scarcely published at all, while so very many madrigals were, and some instrumental music; but the reason may be found, and is well worth finding. The Puritan party had gained great influence both in the Church and the laity; and one of their leaders, George Abbot, became Archbishop of Canterbury in 1611. He was so far opposed to liturgical ceremonies that he removed the organ and choir from the chapel of Lambeth Palace, and some other bishops were of his mind. There was another school of thought in the Church, represented by Hooker and Bancroft, and afterwards by Lancelot Andrewes, but it had little power until the last few years of this period.

With so puritanical an archbishop, and the mass of the nation with similar tendencies, it is not remarkable that secular music was especially cultivated rather than ecclesiastical. I shall show in the next chapter that exactly the same thing happened during the Commonwealth, when the Puritans put down ecclesiastical music altogether, and secular music in consequence flourished exceptionally well. Nobody objected to secular music. The disreputable street minstrels were become a nuisance, and by two Acts of Parliament under Queen Elizabeth they were declared rogues and vagabonds. The Puritan clergymen, such as Gosson, Stubbs, Northbrook, always included the street

minstrels in their attacks upon amusements; careless
readers have supposed that all musicians were meant.
Dr. Bull, a great musician himself, joined in the attacks
on minstrels, just as nowadays we musicians would like
to put down organ-grinders.

The general cultivation of music by all classes has been
frequently enlarged upon. A passage of Morley's treatise
(1597) is the chief ground for the assertion. One of the
interlocutors in the dialogue comes to learn music, telling
how he had been shamed when visiting, as after supper
'music books, as is the custom, were brought,' and upon
expressing his inability to take a part, he was at first
supposed not in earnest, and when he finally convinced
the company, 'every one began to wonder, yea some
whispered to others, demanding how I was brought up.'
The exact literalness of Morley's statement must, of
course, be not too precisely insisted upon; but we may,
at any rate, conclude that it was common to sing during
the evening, and common to find ladies and gentlemen
who could take part in a madrigal fairly correctly. The very
frequent allusions in Shakespeare and his contemporaries
certainly point to general familiarity with the art, and
musical terminology is often used in a way that implies
general comprehension of the technicalities.

At this time an infusion of Italian grace came to refine
our secular music. It might be thought that nothing was
needed to improve upon the songs preserved in the
Mulliner MS., yet their severe beauty would make them
equally suitable for sacred words as for those to which
they were originally written. The renown of Italian vocal
music was now eclipsing all other. Nicholas Yonge, a
Lewes man who had entered St. Paul's choir, obtained
some of the many collections printed on the Continent,
and gave daily performances in his house. Certain
madrigals having been rudely translated, Yonge published
a selection of fifty-seven (under the title *Musica Trans-
alpina*) in 1588, and another set of twenty-four in 1597.
Thomas Watson published some in 1590, and also Morley
in 1598. Yonge and Watson both included specimens
by Byrd; the best Flemish and Italian composers

were drawn upon, and the selections were admirable. No other foreign madrigals appeared in England, until in 1613 Notari (a musician to Prince Henry) published eighteen pieces of florid vocal music under the title *Nuove Musiche*. In 1629 Filmer translated some French part-songs by Guedron and Boisset, and published them as 'Court Aires,' with a dedication to Queen Henrietta Maria. For the sake of completeness, it may here be mentioned that some Latin sacred music by Lassus and Croce was reprinted in England in 1598 and 1606.

A complete list of all the known collections of 'Madrigals,' 'Ayres,' 'Canzonets,' and 'Ballets' published from 1587 to 1630 here follows. The British Museum is remarkably rich in these collections, and almost every one may be found there. All were published in London, except those of Philipps (Phillips) and Deering:

1587	'Psalms, Sonnets, and Songs' (sacred and secular)	Byrd
1588	Two Madrigals in Yonge's 'Musica Transalpina'	Byrd
1589	'Songs of Sundrie Natures'	Byrd
1590	Two Madrigals in Watson's 'Italian Madrigals Englished'	Byrd
1591	'Melodia Olympica' (Madrigals)	Phillips
1593	Canzonets à 3	Morley
1594	Madrigals à 4	Morley
	'Songs and Psalms' (sacred and secular)	J. Mundy
1595	Ballets à 5	Morley
	Ballets with Italian words	Morley
	Canzonets à 2	Morley
1596	Madrigals à 6	Phillips
1597	Ayres	Dowland
	Canzonets à 5 and à 6	Morley
	Six 'Neapolitans' in A. Holborne's 'Cithern-School' (at Cambridge and Royal College)	W. Holborne
	'Songs of Sundry Natures' (lost)	Patrick
	Madrigals	Weelkes
	Madrigals	Kirbye
1598	Canzonets	Farnaby
	Madrigals and Ballets	Weelkes
	Madrigals	Wilbye
	Madrigals à 8	Phillips
	Madrigals and Ayres	Cavendish
1599	Madrigals	Farmer

1599	Madrigals .. .. Bennet
1600	Ayres (a copy was in Halliwell-Phillipps's collection) .. .. Morley
	Ayres .. .. Dowland
	Ayres .. .. Jones
	Madrigals (two sets) .. .. Weelkes
1601	Ayres (for one voice) .. .. Jones
	Ayres (for one voice) .. .. Campion and Rossiter
	Madrigals .. .. Carlton
	'The Triumphs of Oriana' (Madrigals) 23 composers
1603	Ayres .. .. Dowland
	Madrigals à 6 .. .. Phillips
1604	Ayres and Madrigals .. .. Greaves
	Madrigals .. .. Bateson
	Madrigals .. .. East
1605	Ayres .. .. Hume
	Ayres .. .. Pilkington
1606	'An Houres Recreation' (sacred and secular Madrigals) .. .. Allison
	'Funeral Teares' (Ayres) .. .. Coperario
	Ayres .. .. Bartlet
	Ayres .. .. Danyel
	Madrigals .. .. East
1607	Ayres .. .. Ford
	'Poeticall Musicke' (Instrumental pieces and Ayres) Hume
	Madrigals .. .. Jones
	Ayres in a Masque .. Campion, Giles, and Lupo
1608	'Ultimum Vale' (Ayres. Unique at the Royal College of Music) .. .. Jones
	Ayres .. .. Weelkes
	Canzonets .. .. Youll
1609	Ayres .. .. Ferrabosco
	'A Musicall Dreame' (Ayres) .. .. Jones
	Madrigals .. .. Wilbye
1610	Madrigals, etc. .. .. East
	Ayres .. .. Corkine
	R. Dowland's 'Musical Banquet' (Ayres) J. Dowland and others
1611	'The Muses' Garden for Delight' (Ayres, in the Ellesmere Library, now in America) .. Jones
	'Melismata' (Madrigals) .. .. Ravenscroft
	'The XII Wonders of the Worlde' (Ayres) Maynard
	'Psalms, Songs, and Sonetts' (sacred and secular Madrigals) .. .. Byrd
1612	Ayres .. .. Corkine
	'A Pilgrim's Solace' (Ayres) .. .. .. Dowland
	Madrigals .. .. Gibbons

1613	Ayres (two books, sacred and secular) ..	Campion
	Madrigals	Lichfild
	Madrigals	Ward
	'Songs of Mourning for Prince Henry' (Ayres)	Coperario
1614	'Tears and Lamentations of a Sorrowful Soul'	
	(sacred Ayres and Madrigals) ..	Leighton and
		19 other composers
	Madrigals and Pastorals	Pilkington
	Ayres in a 'Maske of Flowers'	John Wilson
	Ayres in a 'Wedding Masque,' Campion, Coperario, Lanier	
	Madrigals in Ravenscroft's *Brief Discourse*	
		Ravenscroft, Pearce, and Bennet
1615	'Sacred Hymns' (Madrigals)	Amner
1617	Ayres (two books)	Campion
1618	Madrigals	Bateson
	Ayres (sung in the Entertainment at Brougham	
	Castle)	Mason and Earsden
1619	Madrigals and Anthems	East
	'Songs of diverse Ayres and Natures' (Madrigals)	Vautor
1620	'Private Musicke' (Ayres and Dialogues for	
	Verse and Chorus)	Peerson
	Canzonets (two books, at Christ Church, Oxford)	Deering
1622	Ayres	Attey
1622-3	'Songs' (Madrigals)	Tomkins
1624	Madrigals and Pastorals	Pilkington
1627	'Ayres or Fa-las' (Madrigals)	Hilton
1630	'Mottects' (Madrigals, with organ)	Peerson

There were several German reprints of Morley's and other publications, described in Eitner's *Quellenlexikon* and J. Bolte's *Singspiele der englischen Komædianten in Deutschland*. A very remarkable and nearly complete collection in the library of King John IV of Portugal disappeared in the earthquake of Lisbon.* Walter Porter's 'Madrigales and Ayres,' published 1632, had an independent instrumental accompaniment which puts them outside the true madrigal; apparently his lost collection, dated 1639, was similar. Martin Peerson's 'Mottects, or Grave Chamber Musique,' also had a two-voiced organ part; but they can be sung as unaccompanied madrigals, and may be reckoned the conclusion of the long series. Dowland's and Morley's works were several times reprinted.

* The catalogue was reprinted by Vasconcellos in 1874; its misunderstandings of English titles are often ludicrous.

Many of the collections consist of twenty-one pieces, the last with extra voices. Morley's ballets seem to have set a fashion in this respect. In Morley's two-voiced canzonets some instrumental pieces are inserted; and this precedent was also much followed.

The various classes of composition were not very accurately distinguished; but there was a definite distinction between madrigals and ayres, which needs explaining. Hawkins was not sufficiently a musician to explain the distinction; and Burney being singularly inappreciative of the style (as may be seen in his History III 131, 326, 347, 385)—in fact, of all our secular music before Purcell —did not think madrigals worth more than a casual glance and contemptuous remark. To this day no writer has set forth the distinctive properties, and consequently some modern reprints are defective. The distinction is nevertheless sufficiently obvious, even to the eye, if the original editions are examined.

By *Madrigals*, contrapuntal works, without independent accompaniment, were intended; *Ayres* had instrumental accompaniment (for the lute, sometimes also the viol-da-gamba), and were not in counterpoint, whether for several voices or solo. There was also a distinction observed between the words employed for each style; the madrigals required a few lines only, each of which had a separate point of imitation; while the ayres were set to the first stanza of a poem, the music being repeated to each stanza. Any doggerel was thought sufficient for a madrigal; while the ayres called forth some of the best lyrical poetry ever produced. In Oliphant's *La Musa Madrigalesca*, and since by Professor Arber, A. H. Bullen, and Mr. Fellowes, very many of the poems have been published. These editors usually regard the music only as the composer's share. It appears to me that, as a rule, the poems and the music were simultaneously conceived; I ground this belief on the detailed parallelism in the metre of the successive stanzas in the Ayres, through which the same music easily fits them all. As good an instance as I can find is No. 7 of Dowland's Ayres (1597), where the fifth line begins 'Dear, sweet, fair, wise,' and the fifth line of the other stanza, 'Earth, heav'n, fire, air,' the music being adapted only for monosyllables. As more explicit proof I may cite the preface to Jones's first book (1600), where he apologizes for his 'cold ayres' and their 'idle ditties.' Campion published other books of verse than his ayres, and has a high place among England's minor poets.* The poems seldom touch upon actual events; the principal exceptions to this rule are in Addit. MSS. 29,401–5, and Egerton MSS. 2009–12, where there are some upon historical subjects. They are probably by Byrd. The others are mainly love-poems, of the style familiar through Ford's 'Since first I saw your face'; some celebrate 'the month of Maying,' and some are of a devotional or meditative cast of thought.

I have not been able to discover the specific properties of *Canzonets*. The *Ballets* had a light dance rhythm, and frequently used Fa-la as a refrain, or even as the title. *Songs* seems to have been used for all styles.

The various styles had various methods of publication. The madrigals were printed in part-books, and unbarred; the ayres in a peculiar form of full-choir-book, the lute accompaniment being placed under the highest voice, and the other parts facing different ways, so that performers might read them sitting round a table. They are always barred in the cantus and lute-part, but not in the other voice-parts. When there is a part for the viol-da-gamba it is unbarred, and sometimes printed with the voice, but facing opposite. The earliest specimen I know is Dowland's first book (1597). Sometimes a collection contains both ayres and madrigals; then the madrigals are printed facing several ways, but all unbarred. The most complicated arrangement is that in Leighton's collection, where there are some 'Consort Songs' for four voices; the cantus is with a treble viol and a lute, the altus with a flute and a cittern, the tenor with a bandora, and the

---

* Very few of the poems set appear elsewhere. A degraded version of Weelkes's 'My flocks feed not' was afterwards inserted in the *Sonnets to Sundry Notes of Music*, printed with *The Passionate Pilgrim*; and Morley's 'It was a lover and his lass' appears in *As You Like It*, though it may yet have been Morley's own.

bass with a viol-da-gamba, all the parts being on the two open pages.

What titles should now be used is a difficult matter to determine. The word *Airs* has a modern meaning which would mislead an audience; and perhaps it is best in programmes to call all these works *Madrigals*. The student—in fact, every professional musician—should carefully remember the distinction between the contrapuntal madrigals and the accompanied part-songs (with two or more stanzas) called *Ayres*. To show the mistakes which ignorance of the distinction has occasioned I may refer to the publications of the Musical Antiquarian Society, in which Dowland's ayres (1597) were printed in score *without* accompaniment; and musicians will be astonished to hear that accompaniments were written by the composers of 'Since first I saw your face,' 'Come again, sweet love,' and 'Rest, sweet nymphs,' all of which are commonly supposed ruined by accompaniment.

In 1847 Dr. Rimbault published *Bibliotheca Madrigaliana*, a bibliography of the above collections; and though it is neither complete nor accurate, it is useful. His list of collections (without the details) was reprinted in Becker's catalogue of sixteenth and seventeenth-century musical publications. The British Museum has a wonderfully fine series, which is almost complete; there are many of the volumes in the library formerly belonging to the Sacred Harmonic Society, and now to the Royal College of Music; and many may be seen at Oxford.

Besides the nearly 2,000 madrigals printed, there are a great number still existing in manuscript. Among those deserving special mention are two by Deering on the 'Cries of London' and the 'Country Cry'; they are very long and elaborate.* 'The Cry of London, with the song,' was entered on the Stationers' Registers in 1599; Deering's piece may have been meant. Four pieces by

---

* Recently edited by Sir F. Bridge. The 'Country Cry' furnished me with an interesting illustration for the Memoir in the *Stratford Town Shakespeare;* the tenor voice monotones the announcement of 'a play made by the Schollers of the Free Schoole.'

Patrick, possibly from the lost 'Songs of Sundry Natures,' are preserved in Addit. MSS. 17,786–91 and 18,936–9; and in the latter MS. are twelve madrigals by William Cobbold, and some by Thomas Wilkinson (who is also represented in Addit. MSS. 29,366–8), and Farrant. Wigthorp appears with Patrick.

The MSS. of this period are too numerous to be all described; the most important are instrumental. The three sets of part-books just mentioned, and another set at Christ Church, Oxford, contain very many madrigals. Comparatively few MSS. are entirely secular.

Baldwin's MS. in the Royal Collection.

This MS. is now deposited in the British Museum. It had been described in Weale's Catalogue of the Albert Hall Loan Exhibition (1885); and Hawkins had printed several pieces from it (by Henry VIII, Dygon, Thorne, and Gyles), with Baldwin's poem in eulogy of Byrd. The MS. was written at various times from 1581 to 1606. Besides the leading composers from Taverner to Byrd and Bevin, several unknown men are represented, including Golder, John Byrchley (of Chester), Moris Gore, John Bedyngham (compare p. 65), and John Wood; and there is a canon à 13 on the Nicene Creed, by Wilkinson (see p. 83). The first part of the volume is written in score; then follow lessons in descant by Gyles, Baldwin, and others; after which compositions have been written in separate parts. They are usually with Latin words; and many of them date from before the Reformation.

Additional MS. 31,390.

This is a remarkably fine full-choir-book, the voice-parts facing different ways. It contains both sacred and secular works, mostly unpublished; and also some In Nomines. Among the composers represented are Mallory, Mudd, Persley, Stonings, Strogers, Picforth, Poynt, and Woodcock, with all the leaders of the period. The date is probably before 1600.

Thomas Myriell's 'Tristitiæ Remedium.'

There was a clergyman of James I's reign named Thomas Myriell; he lived at Barnet, afterwards was vicar of St. Stephen's, Walbrook, where he must have noticed John Dunstable's tomb. He published some sermons. Whether this clergyman wrote Addit. MSS. 29,372–7 it is impossible to say; I think not. This great collection, beautifully written, consists of six big part-books; they each have an engraved title-page, with a classical design, the title, 'Tristitiæ Remedium,' and the date 1616. They contain an immense number of motets, anthems, and madrigals, some by Croce and other Italians; of English composers there are thirty-six, the oldest of whom is Tye. Many anonymous pieces, probably Myriell's own, are included. A large part of the collection is copied from published works, such as Leighton's; but there are many, especially among the anthems, only to be found here. Anthems by Coste, W. Simmes, and Simon Stubbs; and various works by Deering, J. Lugg, Damon, Milton's father, M. Jeffrey, W. White, J. and T. Tomkins, are among the specialities. There are many anthems by Martin Peerson; and the English adaptations (still in use) of some 'Cantiones Sacræ' by Tallis and Byrd. The Latin and English works by Milton are among the most interesting numbers of this most important collection. It should be mentioned that one of Tomkins's 'Songs' (published about 1623) is dedicated to Myriell.

MS. 3095 in the Fétis Library, Brussels.

This collection belonged to Myriell; it contains a great number of pieces from the published collections, including six of Jones's madrigals, concerning birds.

The Hopkinson MS. at Philadelphia.

This consists of sacred and secular music by Giles Farnaby. It belonged to Francis Hopkinson, a signatory of the Declaration of Independence; and remains in possession of his descendants.

The Oxford In Nomines.

At the Music School, Oxford, there is a set of vellum-bound part-books, containing forty In Nomines by John Eglestone, N. Strogers, Leonard Woodson, J. and W. Mundy, Byrd, Elway Bevin, Ferrabosco, Edw. and O. Gibbons, T. Merricocke, H. Stonings, John Gibbs, W. Randall, Bull, R. Parsons, W. Strammar, Tye, Arthur Cocke, Hake, Whyte, Bruster, Weelkes, Clement Woodcock, Persley, and Richard Allison. Another hand has added a few anthems by Hilton and others.

Egerton MSS. 2009–12.

This set is most unfortunately incomplete. It contained sacred and secular madrigals, some of which are among Byrd's published works; it is accordingly probable that all are Byrd's. The tenor part-book is missing, and the altus does not belong to the set, though it contains nearly the same works. The madrigals are interesting in being set to good short poems, some of which are upon historical events. Scarcely any of the imperfect sets are as interesting as this one; it belonged in 1669 to Stephen Aldhouse.

Before leaving the subject of vocal music it is necessary to point out that the declamatory style, more especially characteristic of the following period, had already appeared in James I's reign; as had also the *Dialogues* so much in favour subsequently. The last of Morley's ballets (1595) is in dialogue between the lower and upper voices of the chorus; but there are seven voices, and the incongruity must have been felt. The earliest case of the true Dialogue is the last piece of Dowland's 'Third Book of Ayres' (1603), which is written for two voices and two lutes, with a chorus for five voices. In Coperario's 'Funeral Tears for the Earl of Devonshire' (1606) there is a Dialogue; and there are others by Nicholson and Wigthorp in Addit. MSS. 17,786–91.

Solo Songs, with instrumental accompaniment, had been composed by Byrd; but were rearranged for several voices when he published them in 1587. The first collection of songs published as solos was that of Campion and Rosseter, which was in print on 15th May, 1601;

Jones's 'Second Book of Ayres' is also dated 1601, and claims to be the earliest, but the Campion-Rosseter collection can hardly be later, and is more typical of the new school. Solo songs were beginning to appear in print, as in Barley's *New Book of Tabliture*. Caccini's *Nuove Musiche* appeared in 1602. The ayres of Ferrabosco and Lanier, and afterwards of Lawes, show a leaning to the dramatic declamatory style; at a Masque of Ben Jonson's, performed February 22nd, 1617, Lanier introduced *Recitative*, but this was apparently the only instance before the Commonwealth. Campion's ayres, on the contrary, are tuneful, though simple; when in triple time they anticipate Purcell's best melodies.

The folk-music of the age was in great favour, and its practice thoroughly disseminated. Chappell has well put it:

> 'Tinkers sang catches; milkmaids sang ballads; carters whistled; each trade, and even the beggars, had their special songs; the base-viol hung in the drawing-room for the amusement of waiting visitors; and the lute, cittern, and virginals, for the amusement of waiting customers, were the necessary furniture of the barber's shop. They had music at dinner; music at supper; music at weddings; music at funerals; music at night; music at dawn; music at work; and music at play.'

Chappell has supported this statement by a great number of allusions, especially from the Elizabethan dramatists concerning the barbers. The folk-tunes of the period are very numerous; and some are still quite familiar, notably 'The Bailiff's Daughter of Islington' and 'The Three Ravens.' Still more in the hearts of the English people is the lovely melody sung to Ben Jonson's poem, 'Drink to me only with thine eyes'; whether the tune was written to the poem, or the poem to the tune, is not known.* This is the only case in which a really beautiful poem and a really beautiful folk-tune have been joined in English literature; the Scotch and Irish are much more fortunate in this respect, as we shall see in later chapters. The excessive complication of English metres has had much to do with this deficiency; it is practically impossible to set simple tunes to the very

* But see chap. viii.

uneven lengths of line which our poets delight in. This applies less to the Elizabethan and early Stuart period than to the nineteenth century; but there was far too much of the irregularity in the older time.

Some collections of poetry were written for popular tunes. Clement Robinson's *Handefull of Pleasant Delites* appeared in 1584; Anthony Munday's *Banquet of Dainty Conceits* in 1588. In the former several tunes are written-to, which are mentioned by Shakespeare; among them is a phrase, 'Calen o custure me,' which long puzzled Shakespearian commentators. It is the name of an Irish tune.

The literature of the Elizabethan period also often alludes to the singing of *Catches* by men of various trades. Ordinary canons and rounds are intended, not punning pieces. None were printed until 1609, when Thomas Ravenscroft issued *Pammelia* and *Deuteromelia*, two books which have preserved a vast amount of quaint old music. Among the pieces is the nursery ditty, 'Three blind mice,' but in the minor mode; and the real catch, 'Hold thy peace, thou knave,' sung in Shakespeare's *Twelfth Night*.

We find references to the singing of carols by country folk; and the joyousness of country life is a common theme with the poets, as in Marlowe's 'Come, live with me and be my love,' and Chalkhill's 'O the sweet contentment.' Perhaps as suggestive a passage as any is the following, from *The Devills Banket*, a series of sermons preached and published by Thomas Adams in 1613:

'*Pride* and good husbandrie are neither Kith nor Kin; but *Jaball* and *Juball* are brethren: *Jaball* that dwelt in tents and tended the Heards, had *Juball* to his brother, who was the father of Musicke; to show that *Jaball* and *Juball*, frugalite and Musicke, good Husbandry and Content, are brothers, and dwell together.'

Compare also Kyffin's 'The Blessedness of Brytaine,' written in 1588 to eulogise Queen Elizabeth; and various passages cited by Chappell.

Still greater historically than the madrigals was the English instrumental music during the reigns of Elizabeth and James I; the music for the keyboard then reached its first culminating period. After 1600 the viols came into general favour; nearly all the madrigal collections are

described on the title-page as 'apt for viols and voices.'
A gentleman's house usually contained a chest of viols,
holding six of different sizes; six-parted music was
commonly composed accordingly. The viols being fretted,
a guest was expected to take a part at sight. This style
of music reached its climax during the next period.

Not much instrumental music was published; as
aforesaid, the madrigals were considered suitable to be
either played or sung, and many of the collections of
ayres had a few instrumental pieces inserted. The
following is the list of specially instrumental collections:

1597   'The Cittharn-Schoole.' Instruction-book and
            compositions (Cambridge, and R.C.M.)   Holborne
1599   'Consort Lessons' for 'the Treble Lute, the Pan-
            dora, the Citterne, the Base-Violl, the Flute,
            and the Treble Violl.' (23 pieces) ..   Morley
        ('Pandora' was in the Britwell collection. In 1611
            appeared a second edition; the Flute part is in
            the British Museum, and the Treble-Violl at
            the Royal College.)
1599   'Pavans, Galliards, Allmains, and other short Æirs
            both grave and light,' for five 'Viols, Violins,
            or other Musicall Wind Instruments.' (65
            dance-tunes) .. ..   A. Holborne
        (At the British Museum, and Christ Church,
            Oxford.)
1603   'The Schoole of Musicke.' Instruction-book; and
            music for the Lute, etc. .. .. .. T. Robinson
1605   The First Booke of Ayres (mainly instrumental)
                                                    Tobias Hume
        'Lacrymæ' for the Lute, Viols, or Violins   J. Dowland
1607   'Poeticall Musicke' (almost entirely instrumental)
                                                    T. Hume
1609   'New Citharen Lessons' .. .. T. Robinson
        Lessons for one, two, or three viols tuned lyra-way
                                                    Ferrabosco
        'Lessons for Consort' (arranged like Morley's; the
            Citharn part is at the Royal College of Music)
                                                    P. Rossetor
1610   'Varietie of Lute Lessons'   .. .. .. R. Dowland
1611 (about) *Parthenia,* for the Virginals (reprinted in
            1613 and later) ..   Byrd, Bull, and Gibbons
1621   'Courtly Masquing Aires' for five or six instru-
            ments .. .. J. Adson

Undated. *Parthenia inviolata* for virginals and bass-viol
(Public Library, New York).
'Fantasias' for three Viols .. .. Gibbons
(All unspecified among these are at the British
Museum; almost all appear in King John IV's
catalogue.)

To this list I may add the works published by Englishmen on the Continent, with some of the miscellaneous
collections:

1607 Auserlesene Paduanen und Galliarden. 1ter Theil.
Hamburg. (24 pieces are by W. Brade and
other Englishmen, according to Eitner's
'Bibliographie.')

1609 *Ib.* 2ter Theil. (Four pieces are by Brade and
Bateman.)
Nineteen pieces for five instruments. Hamburg.
(A copy at Breslau) .. .. W. Brade

1611 'Opus neurer Paduanen, Gagliarden, Intraden,
Canzonen, Ricercare, Fantasien, Balletten,
Allemanden, Couranten, Volten und Passa-
mezen lieblich zu gebrauchen mit 5 Stimmen
gesetzt.' Frankfort. (At Berlin, Hamburg,
Nuremburg) .. .. T. Simpson

1612 'Delitiæ Musicæ.' Utrecht. (Eight pieces are by
Dowland. A copy at Breslau.)

1615 'Recreationes Musicæ.' Nuremburg. (Contains
pieces by Aloyson, *Anglus*; J. and R. Dowland.
At Breslau.)

1617 A reprint at Hamburg of Simpson's 'Opus neuer
Paduanen,' etc. (Cassel, Berlin, Hamburg,
Wolfenbüttel.)
Neue auserlesene liebliche Branden Intraden, etc.
Hamburg, 1617. (Complete at Hamburg) W. Brade

1619 Melodiensis Paduanis, Chansons, Galliardis, à 5
Antwerp (at Hamburg) .. .. .. W. Brade

1621 'Tafel-Consort: allerhand lustige Lieder von 4
Instr. und einem G. B. theils seine eigenen,
theils anderer als .. .. .. P. Phillippi,
J. Dowland, Maurice Webster, R. and E.
Johnson,' etc. Hamburg. (G. Bassus at the
British Museum; part-books at Wolfenbüttel.)
T. Simpson

1648 'XX Konincklyche Fantasien om op. 3 Fiolen de
Gamba.' Amsterdam, 1648. (At Wolfen-
büttel and Danzig) .. Lupo, Coprario, Damian
With a reprint of Gibbons's Fantasias.

The English at this time had a great repute for skill
in instrumental music. As far back as 1555 a publication
(at Breslau) of 322 dance-pieces had, according to the
title, included English tunes. Besardus, in the preface to
Thesaurus Harmonicus (an instruction-book for the lute,
published at Cologne in 1603), wrote 'Prout sunt illi
Anglicani concentus suavissimi quidem, ac elegantes.'
At the London Conference of the International Musical
Society a paper on this subject was read by Amalie
Arnheim; and pieces by Brade and Simpson were played.
It should be remembered that this period saw the cul-
mination of the English drama; and wandering parties of
English actors are known to have visited Germany. Jacob
Ayrer (see Henry Morley's edition of Shakespeare's
Tempest) produced a 'Singspiel' in 1618, to be sung
by five persons 'entirely on the melody of the Eng-
lish Roland'; the melody is repeated fifty-four times.
The connection between all kinds of entertainers was
still very close, though the classes were now more
specialised.

Reissmann, in his *Illustrirte Geschichte der deutschen
Musik* (1881), says only that, at the different German Courts
the instrumentalists were, in the latter half of the sixteenth
century, generally English; but the German antiquaries
have since well worked out the connection between the
English dramatists and musicians and Continental princes.
The influence which English instrumental music had in
forming the German school was admirably shown by
Max Seiffert in the *Vierteljahrsschrift für Musikwissen-
schaft* for 1891. It is there pointed out that the first
important German instrumental composer was Samuel
Scheidt, who, in 1624, issued his 'Tabulatura nova.'
Scheidt lived at Halle, and in that central position
received at once the Italian forms from southward, and
English execution from northward; from their union
Scheidt originated the German instrumental music.
Seiffert also mentions that at the Courts—for instance, at
Dresden, Stuttgart, Wolfenbüttel, in towns such as Ham-
burg—English instrumentalists were in high positions.
Michael Prætorius, V. Hausmann, and others reprinted

English compositions. At Danzig there were two English violists in the pay of the city in 1637. Walter Rowe, father and son, were in the service of the Elector of Brandenburg; Valentine Flood also, 1627. John and Clement Dixon were at the Saxon Court, 1632–6. 'Jan Jorden,' an Englishman, lived at Leyden, 1608; a 'Hans Jordon' at Berlin.

English musicians were also supreme in Denmark. Christian IV, a great patron of music and the drama, during his long reign engaged very many English musicians, including Dowland; the gambist, John Norcome; T. Cuttings, lutenist; John Stanley, violist; Darby Scott, harpist; the composers Brade and Simpson; and John Price, piper. Daniel Norcome and Meinert (probably Maynard) were appointed in 1599, but soon fled.

Specially remarkable is the statement in the *Syntagma Musicum* of Prætorius (1615) that the English have invented a peculiar and beautiful style of *Consort*, using both stringed and wind instruments at once!

Of the published collections, *Parthenia* and Gibbons's 'Fantasies' are the most important; but there are MSS. existing—particularly of virginal music—which are far more extensive and remarkable. Keyboard execution had reached an astonishing point; John Bull wrote some most extraordinary difficulties, and some passages by Mundy are little inferior.

The forms adopted were of four kinds—the Dance, each section being repeated with a florid variation; the Fancy, a contrapuntal piece like the madrigals; the descriptive piece, programme-music; and the Variations on a popular air. One Fancy, by Peter Phillips, is a fugue in the modern sense of the word, and was the earliest fugue known to Burney; I have discovered two others by Bull. Of descriptive pieces I can only cite Byrd's 'Battle-piece,' another (for two lutes), and Mundy's 'Storm'; there are some singular attempts at descriptive accompaniments (by the lute!) in Hume's 'Ayres.'

Mr. W. Barclay Squire catalogued the principal MSS. of virginal music (except those in the British Museum) in 'Grove,' art. Virginal Music.

Lady Nevells Booke.

This beautiful volume, yet another of the collections transcribed by John Baldwin of Windsor, was finished in 1591. It is preserved at Eridge Castle, Sussex, and contains forty-two pieces of Byrd's music, including the 'Battle.' No. 35 is called 'Hugh Aston's Grownde.'

Additional MS. 30,485.

This volume may perhaps have been originally two; something is lacking in the middle. Some of the pieces occur in Lady Nevells Booke; there are also works by Blithman, Alwood, Harding, Johnson, Weelkes, Ferdinando (Richardson), Bickrell, Kinlough, Alfonso (Ferrabosco), Bull, and Tallis. Stafford Smith has printed several pieces in *Musica Antiqua*. The date is about 1600.

Additional MS. 30,486.

A smaller volume, about the same date. The music, mainly by Byrd, is interesting through the occasionally marked fingering.* The thumb is freely used, but in the left hand is marked 5, the 1 standing for the little finger; this peculiar fingering remained in favour in England even to the time of Purcell.

A similar MS. dated 1599, and now Addit. MS. 29,485, is mainly English music; the first two bars for the right hand are (very clumsily) fingered, as may be seen in *Musica Antiqua*, p. 71. This MS. is probably English writing, though the titles are Dutch; there is a table of proportions in English.

The Fitzwilliam Virginal Book.

This extraordinary collection is by far the largest of our MSS. of instrumental music. It contains no less than 291 pieces, occupying 418 closely-written pages. Hawkins gave it the name of Queen Elizabeth's Virginal Book, which has caught the popular ear, but is an obvious mistake, as the pieces are sometimes dated at the end of her life, or even after her death. The volume belonged

* But the fingering seems later than the music.

in 1740 to Pepusch, afterwards to Lord Fitzwilliam, who included it in his magnificent bequest to Cambridge University. Chappell, from internal evidence, argued that it was originally written by, or for, some one named Tregian, and referred it to the Cornish family of that name, who were steadfast Romanists and suffered much persecution during this period. Mr. Barclay Squire has strengthened the arguments, and concludes that the volume was written either by Francis Tregian, who died a prisoner in 1619, or possibly by one of his sisters. I agree with this, though the evidence seems inconclusive.

The composers represented are Tallis, Byrd, Phillips, Persons, Hooper, Strogers, Harding, Mundy, E. Johnson, Peerson, Tomkins, Farnaby, Morley, and Bull, with the more obscure Ferdinando Richardson, T. Warrock, Tisdall, T. Oldfield, and W. Inglott; and a few pieces by Sweelinck and other foreigners. Many are, however, arrangements of madrigals by Marenzio, Dowland, and others. The dated pieces are mainly those of Phillips. Among the most interesting are the fugue by Phillips, the amazingly difficult Variations on the Hexachord and Quadran Paven by Bull, and Mundy's attempt to depict 'Faire Wether,' a thunderstorm, and 'a Cleare Day.' Dr. E. W. Naylor has issued an interesting volume on the MS.

Mr. Barclay Squire's catalogue is very complete. As the whole is now published and generally accessible, it needs little description. We may regret that the editors did not keep to the original notation with the part of each hand in its own stave; and that no native publisher was chosen. But English musicians may esteem themselves highly fortunate in having so splendid and splendidly-preserved a proof of their skill as performers and composers at a time when no other nation could produce anything of high importance.

Additional MS. 31,392.

This is a beautifully-bound volume stamped 'Philip' and 'Marie'; thirty-two leaves have been cut out, and the rest contains virginal and lute music by Byrd, Allison,

Pilkington, and others. Valuable as the contents are, one would have preferred to see the earlier leaves rather than these, as they doubtless contained something similar to the music of Thomas Mulliner's Book, but even older.

Additional MS. 23,623.

Although this was written in Belgium, it must be noticed here, as it consists almost entirely of Bull's organ and virginal compositions or arrangements, and is extremely important. It is dated 1628. There are over sixty pieces, on six-lined staves. The most remarkable works are two fugues; in each case the theme is rubricated throughout. One is the first piece in the volume, but reappears with a prelude on fol. 112; it has a double stretto, also augmentation and double diminution. The other is on the ascending hexachord; it is of great length, inversion being much employed. There are several very elaborate arrangements of plain-songs. These were doubtless intended for the organ; but there are also some lighter works, suitable for the virginal, some of which appear in the Fitzwilliam Virginal Book. Whether the two fugues in this volume be earlier or later than the one by Philipps in the Fitzwilliam MS., there is no evidence to show. All three are works of great elaboration.

Jane Pickering's Lute-book.

This is dated 1616, and is in the British Museum as Egerton MSS. 2046. It contains compositions and arrangements by Johnson, Strogers, Drewry, Dowland, Cutting, Bachelor, Collard, Holborne, and Whitfield; then some later pieces in another handwriting; and at the end a battle-piece for two lutes (!) in the older writing.

Additional MSS. 18,940–4.

As the oldest collection of purely viol music I have seen, these part-books must not be omitted. They contain pieces by Deering, Maurice Webster, T. Mudd, and several composers prominent during the next period, and must have been written about the end of the madrigalian period, towards 1630.

Additional MS. 31,416.

These Fantasies for Viols, with a figured bass for the organ, are in the autograph of Coperario, who died 1626. Another such volume, which once belonged to Charles I, is in the Royal Collection.

The Gordon Lute-book.

The original MS. was written 1627, and belonged to Robert Gordon of Straloch. It was lent in 1839 to David Laing, and was transcribed by G. F. Graham. The Lute-book is at present undiscoverable; Graham's transcript belonged to Mr. Taphouse, of Oxford. There is also a copy at Edinburgh. The book contains thirty-one tunes arranged in tablature.

The Skene MS.

Miss Elizabeth Skene, the last representative of an ancient Midlothian family, bequeathed this and other documents to the Faculty of Advocates in 1818. Her great-great-grandfather, John Skene of Hallyards, owned it in Charles I's reign. There are seven different parts (now bound together), containing 115 airs and dance tunes, in tablature. G. F. Graham made a copy in modern notation, published in 1838 by Dauney, a Scotch antiquary. About forty-five seem to be ancient Scotch melodies; the rest are old English folk-songs and French dances.

There are also several collections of lute music in the Cambridge University Library; and two for recorder and viol-da-gamba. In the Royal Collection (now in the British Museum) there are two fine virginal-books. Will. Forster's (principally of Byrd's music) is dated 1624; B. Cosyn's (largely from Bull and Gibbons) is not earlier. Both are catalogued in 'Grove.' Some of the pieces in Addit. MSS. 17,786–91 are for viols; especially two Pavans and seven Fantasies by Okeover, who became organist of Wells Cathedral in 1619, deserve mention, with Fancies by Ward and Peerson. At Trinity College, Dublin, are some important lute-books by Ballet, Dallis, and others.

From this list of published and MS. compositions it will be seen what a height English musicians had reached in instrumental music. 'Lady Nevells Booke' was completed at the very beginning of this period, and has specimens of all the styles known, if we except* the fugue throughout on one subject. The English young ladies of that age, young ladies from whose pattern Shakespeare created Imogen, Rosalind, Beatrice, Portia, Viola, and Miranda, knew neither Chopin nor Beethoven; but they were expected to play upon the virginals, lute, and cittern, and to sing at sight, nor was their repertory at all deficient either in quantity or quality. But then, as now, feminine accomplishments were commonly neglected after marriage. In Burton's 'Anatomy of Melancholy' we are told that—

'Our young women and wives, they that being maids took so much pains to sing, play, and dance, with such cost and charge to their parents to get these graceful qualities, now being married will scarce touch an instrument, they care not for it.'

All the published collections are rare. Gibbons's 'Fantasies' were reprinted in score by the Musical Antiquarian Society. *Parthenia* had been reprinted several times in the seventeenth century; it was also among the Musical Antiquarian Society's publications, and has since been included in Farrenc's 'Trésor des Pianistes' and Litolff's cheap editions, besides reprints in England. The publication of the Fitzwilliam MS. is now completed. For the honour of English music, 'Lady Nevells Booke,' and, above all, the Mulliner MS., also deserve general circulation.

As a point of interest to practical musicians, I may mention that all the MSS. I have seen show thorough appreciation of the importance of convenient notation. The part of each hand is carefully put in its own stave, time-divisions are shown exactly, etc.

Towards the end of this period, Scheidt in Germany, and Frescobaldi in Italy, began to rival the English composers. Frescobaldi in particular had occasional glimpses of the latent grandeur of instrumental music. As yet the

---

* Since I have found that Bull, as well as Phillips, composed fugues, I suspect that the real inventor of the fugue-form was Byrd.

English music for viols was without equal; the violin was unfortunately looked down upon as a vulgar instrument, and the English had no share in its development.

The nascent Opera, which at the end of the sixteenth century appeared in Italy, had its English counterpart in the Masque; and both entertainments originally used mythological materials, and were an amusement for the cultivated aristocracy. The masque never advanced much beyond this limited sphere; and the stage failure of Fletcher's splendid *Faithful Shepherdess* is sufficient proof that the form was not a growth of popular life. Shakespeare, the national poet, with his unrivalled capacity for satisfying all demands, introduced a masque into *The Tempest*, though he did not write an independent one; Ben Jonson, the Court poet, wrote many. Much music was employed in the masques; among the composers were Campion, Coperario, Ferrabosco, and Lanier. The songs were occasionally published; I included the list among the madrigals. Stafford Smith reprinted Mason and Earsden's 'Ayres' (1618); and Mr. Arkwright (as No. 1 of his *Old English Edition*) the masque for Lord Hay's wedding (1607). It should be observed that the composers in this style were not among the leading scientific musicians, and were men of general culture; the same rule prevailed in Italy. But the Italian opera, restricted in its beginnings, ever expanded, while the masque, though flourishing in the reigns of James I and Charles I, became contracted into an excrescence upon a drama. Probably Shakespeare saw its true function; and it has had a fitful existence down even to the present day, in the way which Shakespeare followed. I shall have occasion to return to this topic, as it is very obvious that the weak side of English music has been the dramatic side. English Opera—for such the Jacobean Masque really was—made what seemed a most promising start; but its lack of vital power has made it always a fancy of the hothouse rather than a robust natural growth. At the same time it should be remembered that the English Drama has, during the eighteenth and nineteenth centuries, been no more elevated than the English Opera.

We hear little of James I in connection with music, except during his youth in Scotland. He gave a fresh charter to the Musicians' Company in 1604, giving them a virtual monopoly of performances in and around London; this was further restricted to the City of London by Charles I, and the Fraternity and Sisterhood of Minstrels has since been one of the London Companies.

In theoretical science there are several important works to chronicle. Bathe's treatise was mentioned in the last chapter. In 1596 appeared two anonymous books published by William Barley—'A Pathway to Musicke,' and 'A New Booke of Tabliture.' The former is an ordinary elementary work of no value, in catechism form; the word *sight* is used therein as in Lyonel Power's work, to denote interval from the plain-song. The other work contains an explanation of lute-tablature, with various popular airs arranged.

Another instruction-book, the 'Cittharne-Schoole' of Anthony Holborne, appeared the next year. As it contains both vocal and instrumental compositions, it has already been mentioned. There is a complete copy at Cambridge; Evelyn, and afterwards Rimbault, possessed another, now at the Royal College of Music. It wants one leaf.

It was perhaps the shallowness of the anonymous 'Pathway to Musicke' that induced Thomas Morley to issue in 1597 'A Plaine and Easie Introduction to Practicall Musicke,' the most important of all the English treatises. A second edition appeared in 1608, and another even in 1771; and it was translated into German by J. Caspar Trost, of Halberstadt, but apparently not printed.* Morley dedicated the book to his master, Byrd. It is written in conversation between the pupils Philomathes and Polymathes and their master, Gnorimus. The first part contains the rules of notation, with instructions for learning to sing written music; the second part proceeds to explain the practice of extemporising descant upon a plain-song, or a ground; and the third part gives

---

* Walther's words upon the non-publishing of Trost's translations are ambiguous. Trost's own copy is at Wolfenbüttel.

instructions in composition. Would that Morley had only included a historical section, however short! But on the last page he gives a list of 'Authorities,' first naming the theorists, ancient and mediæval; then the 'Practicioners,' beginning with Josquin and Okeghem, and placing the Englishmen separately. This list has been already given on p. 94. The work abounds in illustrations and remarks which throw light on the state of the art in the sixteenth century; there is a very clear explanation of the rules for ligatures. All who purpose studying mediæval music should begin by thoroughly mastering this work; and it gives Morley right to a place with Ornithoparcus, Glareanus, Zacconi, and Zarlino, as the best of the sixteenth-century theoretical writers.

Thomas Robinson's two instrumental collections both contain some theoretical instruction; 'The Schoole of Musicke' is in dialogue 'betwixt a Knight (who hath children to be taught), and Timotheus that should teach them,' while the 'New Citharen Lessons' have some dialogue between 'Scholler and Master.'

In 1609 Dowland translated Ornithoparcus's *Micrologus*. Useful as this may have been, Dowland would have done better to write a work of his own. In 1610 Robert Dowland's 'Varietie of Lute Lessons' contained some 'Practical Hints' by his father, and also a translation of Besardus; the 'Practical Hints' were translated for the *Monatshefte für Musikgeschichte* of 1891.

Thomas Ravenscroft's interesting *Brief Discourse of . . . Mensurable Musicke* appeared in 1614, and was probably the only attempt to reintroduce the mysteries of proportion. Ravenscroft repeatedly quotes Dunstable's treatise; as already mentioned, I believe he intended the one known as Tunsted's. The most valuable part is the collection of examples, which are four-voiced madrigals 'Concerning the Pleasure of five usuall Recreations. 1. Hunting. 2. Hawking. 3. Dancing. 4. Drinking. 5. Enamouring.' The first two Recreations are illustrated by madrigals containing many technical terms and descriptive passages. 'Enamouring' is elaborately portrayed by two distinct series of madrigals, one dealing

with the romantic courtships of that age, the other series
with Hodge's rough wooing of his 'Zwetehort Malkin.'
The dialect is interesting on philological grounds, and
is exactly similar to the dialect used in Shakespeare's
King Lear, when Edgar, disguised as a peasant, challenges
Oswald. Some of these madrigals were composed by
Ravenscroft himself; five were by John Bennet, and three
by Edward Pearce, organist of St. Paul's Cathedral.

The Rosicrucian, Dr. Robert Flud (1574–1637), published at Oppenheim in 1617 a work on physics and
metaphysics, in which music is treated in the transcen-
dental style of Boethius.

The next writer was Thomas Campion, the many-sided.
In or about 1618 he issued a treatise on *Counterpoint*,
a very remarkable book, showing the change then coming
over the art. Campion distinctly leans towards the modern
system. He advocates the disuse of *ut* and *re*; and this,
though apparently a return to the Greek tetrachords, was
really a great step towards the conception of the modern
scale, of which there is a glimmering in Bathe's *Briefe
Discourse*. Campion still uses *sight* to signify interval, but
makes a most important innovation when he says (p. 2),
'I assume that the true sight and judgment of the upper
three [voices] must proceed from the lowest, which is the
Base,' explaining that ancient musicians took their 'sight'
from the tenor, because their theme lay in that part.
Campion also shows a perception of the root-note to a
chord, calling it 'the place of perfection,' and forbids
false relations, which are common down to a much later
period, even in Bach. A chapter 'Of the Tones of
Musicke' shows a feeling for the key-system; and the
almost invariable use of four-voiced note-against-note
counterpoint shows the transition from horizontal writing
to the vertical music of modern times. Calvisius is
frequently referred to as an authority; but Campion
inexplicably forbids the succession of an octave and a
sixth if the bass falls, as for instance—

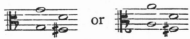

Though of less practical value than Morley's treatise, Campion's is throughout of the highest interest historically; and it was reprinted (with annotations by Christopher Sympson) in 1655 and later. No other, not even Morley's, was then in sufficient request to justify another edition: the value of Campion's was immediate; that of Morley's had already become antiquarian.

This is a convenient moment to allude to the contrapuntal music produced. In 1591 John Farmer published a small work consisting of forty canons accompanying the plain-song 'Miserere.' The only copy I have seen belonged to Rogers, and is now in the Bodleian Library; it wants the title-page and last leaf. The last canon (38th) is to be sung both forwards and backwards, as is also the plain-song, there in triple time. Byrd and the elder Ferrabosco had already exercised their skill in the same task; and their two sets were entered on the Stationers' Registers in 1603, under the title of *Medulla Musicke*, but no copy is known. George Waterhouse made more than 1,000 canons upon the same plain-song; preserved in the Cambridge MSS. A complication of thirty-eight Proportions, by Nathaniel Gyles, is printed in Hawkins's 'History'; and a six-part *Cantus mensurabilis*, by Robert Stevenson, is partly preserved in Addit. MSS. 18,936–9. The younger men of this period, led by Campion, thought more of vocal expression than of scientific complication. A few remained true to the older contrapuntal complexities; and their mention leads naturally to the consideration of the new school of Anglican sacred music.

The Services composed in James I's reign are essentially different from the Elizabethan Services. As I have said, I believe that the anthems also had been fettered by the cry of the Reformers for distinct enunciation; but it is often difficult to tell whether the anthems were adapted from the older Latin motets. Myriell's collection shows that the practice had begun in 1616. The nation was now entirely Protestant, and the English Service was perfectly familiar. There was a party in the Church, small as yet, which followed the lead of Hooker in reverence for externals. The distinct utterance of the words, now less necessary than previously, was neglected in their music; and a taste for 'curious singing' reappeared. How far it was practised outside the Chapel Royal and some of the cathedrals we have no means of knowing. Dallam and his men went down to Cambridge in 1605, and built an organ in King's College; and in 1613, at Worcester Cathedral. Arrangements were made in 1615 for the Gentlemen of the Chapel Royal to attend by rotation. James I, visiting Scotland in 1617, set up an organ at Holyrood. All these doings were no doubt small in comparison with Archbishop Abbot's influence on the Puritan side; but they affected the central point of English sacred music. Especially after Laud was made Bishop of London, in 1628, sacerdotalism became prominent.

This, I believe, is the true explanation of the difference between the simple succession of heavy chords which forms the 'Dorian Service' of Tallis, and the contrapuntal 'Service in F' of Orlando Gibbons. The Jacobean school produced a small amount of work, but of the very highest quality; and its style is, in the very nature of things, superior to that of Tallis's Service. Morley had already given them an example of what might be done.

The Puritan party in the Church were content with the Psalter of Sternhold and Hopkins, of which new editions were continually printed. Daman's harmonised Psalter in the motet style appeared in 1591. East, in 1592, issued 'The Whole Booke of Psalmes,' employing Farmer, Kirbye, Cobbold, Cavendish, Johnson, Blancks, Dowland, Hooper, Allison, and Farnaby, to harmonise the tunes. This fine specimen of diatonic writing was reprinted in score by the Musical Antiquarian Society. Another very fine Psalter, with all the metricised Canticles and Commandments, was published by Allison in 1599; it has lute-accompaniment, being printed in the style of Dowland's Ayres; and it might claim to a place in the list of madrigals. The same may be said of Robert Tailour's Psalter (1615), which contains fifty tunes set like Allison's; it was carelessly printed, and the voice-parts are on the same leaf instead of on opposite pages.

Barley's Psalter, published in 1604, had similar imperfections, possibly owing to the illness and death of the editor, Morley; it contains some admirable settings by Morley, Blancks, Bennet, and Farnaby. All these publications were, however, superseded by Ravenscroft's Psalter, published in 1621, and reprinted in 1633 and subsequently. It preserves some of the older settings, with forty-eight new ones by Ravenscroft, and a few by R. Palmer, Milton, W. Harrison, J. and T. Tomkins, W. Cranford, Warde, and Simon Stubbs, in all 100 pieces.

In all the Psalters, except those of Allison and Tailour, and partly that of Daman, the tune is given to the tenor; and the exceptions show that they were intended for domestic use. The tunes were first called after the names of places in East's 'Whole Booke of Psalmes'; and there can be no reasonable doubt that they were originally named after the places whence they came, not in the meaningless way used since.

A work in a different style appeared in 1623; it was written by George Wither, and consisted of the metricised Canticles and Creeds, etc., to which sixteen tunes were set by Orlando Gibbons. These were in two parts only.

An organ-book of this period, which belonged to Adrian Batten, clearly shows the continuance of florid accompaniments to the Services, and we must not think that Elizabethan and Jacobean ecclesiastical music was performed exactly as it was written. Viols were used in the accompaniments of some anthems. 'Verse-anthems' are not uncommon; there are twelve known by Gibbons.

I incline to the belief that Anglican ecclesiastical music was not generally cultivated during this period. A work quoted in the previous chapter—'The Praise of Musicke' (Royal MSS. 18 *b* 19)—deplores the misuse of the cathedral funds, and the low state of the choral services. Sacred works are common in the madrigals published; Amner's collection is almost entirely devotional, and Leighton's is quite so, but no strictly ecclesiastical music was published, excepting the anthems of Michael East, in 1624. Whether any of the sacred madrigals were used as anthems does not appear.

The Roman Catholic composers, Byrd, Phillips, and Deering, issued much Latin church music. For Byrd's, see p. 145. Phillips's consisted of 'Cantiones Sacræ' à 5, published 1612, and others à 8, in 1613; in which year Phillips also attempted the new monodic style in 'Gemmulæ Sacræ' for two or three voices with *basso continuo*. A singular little book of Catholic devotional poetry, with music by Phillips, appeared at Valenciennes in 1616 and 1621; it is called 'Les Rossignols Spirituels,' and reminds one of Tye's 'Acts of the Apostles,' but the music is only for two voices. 'Deliciæ Sacræ' with *basso continuo* appeared 1622; this was a reprint. Phillips also published Litanies of the B.V.M. in 1623; and 'Paradisus Sacris Cantionibus consitu' with *basso continuo* in 1628 and 1633. Some Masses, etc., appeared after his death; they are mentioned in the catalogue of King John IV's Library. Some of the carols in Phalèse's collection (1629) were by Phillips and 'Jean Buol,' who had also joined the Catholic refugees. Deering (according to Hawkins) issued 'Cantiones Sacræ' à 5 'cum Basso-continuo ad organum' in 1597; this, if true, would show an earlier use of figured bass than even Viadana's. In 1618 appeared Deering's 'Cantica Sacra ad Melodium Madrigalium elaborata 6 vocibus,' and in 1634 his Cantiones Sacræ à 5. His other works, in the monodic style, were printed at a later period, in 1662 and 1675. All these, except Phillips's posthumous volume, are in the British Museum.*

Having thus detailed the madrigals and ayres, etc., the instrumental collections, the dramatic attempts in the masques, the theorists, and the sacred music (Anglican and Latin), I proceed to give a few biographical details concerning the men who created these noble art-works. Byrd, the greatest of all, has been fully dealt with in the preceding chapter; his finest sacred music was published in 1575, and his instrumental music had already been produced at the beginning of this period, as 'Lady Nevells Booke' shows. But he lived almost through this

* For a bibliographical account of these Roman Catholic publications, see the *Kirchenmusikalisches Jahrbuch*, Ratisbon, 1899.

period, till 1623. In his will he directed that he should be buried at Stondon.

An interesting passage occurs in Meres's *Palladis Tamia* (1598), the work which gives us so much information concerning the dates of Shakespeare's plays. There is a section on 'Musicke,' in which this comparison is made (fol. 288*b*):

> 'As Greece had these excellent Musitians: Arion, Orpheus . . . so England hath these: Maister Cooper, Maister Fairfax, Maister Tallis, Maister Taverner, Maister Blithman, Maister Bird, Doctor Tie, Doctor Dallis, Doctor Bull, M. Thomas Mud, sometimes fellow of Pembrook hal in Cambridge, M. Edward Johnson, Maister Blankes, Maister Randall, Maister Philips, Maister Dowland, and M. Morley.'

Another contemporary mention of value is from the chapter 'Of Musicke' in Peacham's *Compleat Gentleman* (1622). After the passage already quoted (p. 146) referring to Byrd, and an account of Vittoria, Lassus, etc., he speaks very appreciatively of Peter Phillips, and concludes:

> 'I willingly, to avoide tediousnesse, forbeare to speak of the worth and excellency of the rest of our English composers, Master Doctor Douland, Tho. Morley, M. Alphonso, M. Wilbie, M. Kirbie, M. Wilkes, Michael East, M. Bateson, M. Deering, with sundry others, inferior to none in the world (how much soever the Italian attributes to himselfe) for depth of skill and richnesse of conceipt.'

The two lists contain most, though not all, of the greatest English musicians up to their time. It is remarkable that Peacham omitted Gibbons. The first seven names on Meres's list have been previously dealt with, and are the greatest of the sixteenth century; but some of the others are less known, and it is not very clear why he included them, unless they were celebrated as performers.

Doctor DALLIS is only known by a volume of lute lessons in the library of Dublin University; he is there styled 'Dr. Dallis of Cambridge.'

THOMAS MUDD was of St. Paul's school, and was born about 1560; he went to Cambridge in 1578 with one of the sizarships for the sons of London mercers. He was

still a Fellow of Pembroke Hall in 1590; and may have
been afterwards organist of Peterborough Cathedral, but
there were several other musicians named Mudd during
the seventeenth century. By Mudd there are Fancies in
Addit. MSS. 18,940–4; an In Nomine in Addit. MS.
31,390; a service and four anthems at Ely; and two
others at Peterhouse. None, so far as I am aware, have
ever been printed.

WILLIAM RANDALL, of Exeter, entered the Chapel Royal
in 1584, and remained there till 1603. There is an
anthem of his, 'Give sentence with me,' in Addit. MSS.
17,792–6, and an In Nomine at Oxford. The words of
two other anthems are in Harl. MS. 6346. Otherwise
he is unknown.

EDWARD BLANCKS is another shadowy figure. He contributed to East's and Barley's Psalters, and there are
two pieces by him in Addit. MS. 31,390. At Peterhouse
there is an Evening Service by 'Blanke,' doubtless the
same man.

EDWARD JOHNSON may have been a relative of the various
musicians named Robert Johnson. He graduated
Mus.Bac. Cantab. in 1594. His known works are very
few; he contributed to East's Psalter, to 'The Triumphs
of Oriana,' and the Hamburg collections. There are
others in Addit. MSS. 30,480–4, and the virginal-books.

Probably Dallis, Mudd, Randall, Blancks, and E.
Johnson produced many other works now lost. A few
other composers may here be mentioned who apparently
have quite an equal right to be reckoned among England's
'excellent Musitions.'

NATHANAEL GYLES was born at Worcester about 1550,
and was a choir-boy at Magdalen College, Oxford,
1559–61. He graduated Mus.Bac. in 1585; Mus.Doc.
not till 1622. In 1597 he succeeded Hunnis as Master
of the Children in the Chapel Royal, having previously
filled the same office at Windsor; and he held both posts
till his death, January 24th, 1633–4. Gyles composed
little; he contributed to Leighton's collection in 1614,
and a good complete service and full anthem were printed
in Barnard's 'Selected Church Music' (1641). Hawkins,

in the Appendix to his History, inserted a mathematical exercise of Gyles's from Baldwin's MS.

ROBERT STEVENSON, organist of Chester Cathedral, who 'had studied music 33 years,' graduated Mus.Bac. Oxon. in 1587, and was licensed to proceed Mus.Doc. in 1596. There is an anthem by Dr. Stevenson at Peterhouse, and a six-voiced contrapuntal exercise in Addit. MSS. 18,936–9. ARTHUR COCK graduated in 1593, and died 1604; he was organist of the Chapel Royal, but I have seen no compositions of his except an In Nomine at Oxford. Anthony Wood states that Cock was of Exeter. THOMAS BOYES (Boice) graduated in 1603; 'he hath composed certain Church Services,' says Wood. Two are preserved at Peterhouse, and one in the Dorian mode at Ely.

JOHN BALDWIN of Windsor, whose copying has been repeatedly mentioned, must not be forgotten. In the Christ Church part-books, and the MS. in the Royal Collection, there are compositions of his. He entered the Chapel Royal in 1594, and died on August 28th, 1615.

EDMUND HOOPER was born at Halberton, Devon; he became Master of the Children at Westminster Abbey in 1588, afterwards organist; and also was a Gentleman of the Chapel Royal. He contributed to East's Psalter and Leighton's sacred madrigals; and there are three anthems in Barnard's collection. One of the anthems was included in the Motet Society's publications. Hooper died July 14th, 1621. The Motet Society also printed an Evening Service by WILLIAM STONARD, organist of Christ Church, Oxford; he graduated Mus.Bac. in 1608, and died 1630. NICHOLAS STROGERS composed a complete Service, printed by Barnard; it has a little movement, but no figuration except in the Amens. Strogers is also represented in the Christ Church part-books, in the lute-books of Paston and Jane Pickering, and other MSS. at the British Museum and Peterhouse. The Preces and Responses composed by WILLIAM SMYTH (organist of Durham Cathedral 1588–98) and his son Edward (organist 1609–11) were printed in Jebb's collection (1846), and are still sung at Durham. MATTHEW JEFFREY, who graduated

Mus.Bac. in 1593, was a vicar-choral at Wells; six-voiced anthems of his are preserved in Myriell's part-books. THOMAS WILKINSON appears in Myriell's and the Peterhouse part-books as a composer of anthems; at Ely there are Kyries and a Burial Service, and, in the British Museum, some madrigals by this unknown musician. Two anthems are scored in Tudway's collection. JOHN PARSONS, perhaps a son of the older Persons or Parsons, was organist of St. Margaret's, Westminster, and, after Hooper's death, of Westminster Abbey. He died 1623.

ELWAY BEVIN entered the Chapel Royal in 1605; according to Wood he was a pupil of Tallis, and became organist of Bristol Cathedral in 1589. There he remained till 1637, when he lost both appointments upon the accusation of Romanism. It is impossible to verify these statements, as the chapter books of Bristol were burnt in the Reform riots of 1831. But in Laud's Visitations (1634) the Bristol organist is described as a 'verie old man,' past work. Bevin's Service was printed by Barnard, and in score by Boyce; it is still occasionally sung. His most important work was published in 1631; it was intended as a treatise upon composition, but is almost entirely occupied by canons. In the Royal Collection are canons in his autograph.

JOHN HOLMES was organist of Winchester Cathedral; and then of Salisbury, 1602–10. He composed a little sacred and secular music; but was more influential as the teacher of ADRIAN BATTEN, a vicar-choral of Westminster Abbey in 1614, and of St. Paul's in 1624. Batten died about 1637. An organ-book of his (preserved at Tenbury College) has been useful in showing the style of florid accompaniment then employed, and in completing the score of Barnard's 'Selected Church Music.' Many of Batten's anthems are preserved; thirty-four were mentioned by Clifford in 1663, and several have been printed by Barnard and Boyce, and in the *Parish Choir*, some being still sung.

All these musicians, even Batten, were probably church officials rather than regular composers; but the period was one of culmination, when the strict diatonic style had reached its perfection, and even second-rate men could produce works which are models of purity, though not of invention. The general character of their works, so far as I am acquainted with them, bears out the explanation previously given concerning the restrictions which the care to make the words intelligible imposed upon Tallis. The works of Bevin and Batten are exceptions, being often contrapuntal, and the latter's 'Deliver me, O Lord,' and 'Hear my prayer,' are admirable specimens of sacred art. We have now to discuss men of higher note—composers who distinguished themselves in all styles, sacred and secular, worthy successors of William Byrd—the great madrigalists.

PETER PHILIPPS (Phillips, Phillippi, Filippi) was probably related to the Robert Philips who was one of Cornysshe's boys, and afterwards in the Chapel Royal, and was proud of his extraordinary lungs, always selecting the *longest* pieces for performance. The Phelyppes of the Fayrfax MS. may have been of the same family. A 'Sancte Deus' and a 'Paternoster' in Addit. MSS. 17,802–5, and an 'Aspice Domine' in Sadler's part-books, may be by Robert, or youthful essays of Peter; probably the latter, as in the Fitzwilliam Virginal Book an arrangement of a madrigal is dated 1580, 'the first one Philipps made.' Philipps, who remained a Romanist, took holy orders and left England; he became Canon of Bethune, and afterwards lived at Rome, then was appointed one of the three organists to the Viceroy of the Netherlands, and in 1610 Canon of Soignies, where he still lived 1633.

Philipps was one of the greatest Elizabethan composers both in sacred music and madrigals; he belonged to the Palestrina school in both styles. He first appeared in print in 1591 with *Melodia Olympica*, sixty-seven madrigals by himself and others (twice reprinted); six-voiced madrigals followed in 1596 (reprinted 1603); eight-voiced in 1598. The rest of his publications were sacred: five-voiced 'Cantiones Sacræ' in 1612, and eight-voiced in 1613; 'Gemmulæ Sacræ' with *basso continuo* in 1613 (reprinted); 'Les Rossignols Spirituels' in 1616 (reprinted); Delicæ Sacræ (reprinted 1622); Litanies in 1623;

'Paradisus Sacris Cantionibus consitu' in 1628-33. Besides these extensive collections, Fullsack included an instrumental piece in 1607, and Phalèse some carols in 1629. In the Fitzwilliam Virginal Book there are nineteen pieces by Philipps, original or arrangements; the most remarkable by far is the 'Fantasia' on fol. 158*b*. This is a complete four-voiced *fugue*, throughout on one simple theme, which occurs thirty-nine times; the entries are all numbered in the MS., and are sometimes direct, sometimes inverted, sometimes in diminution, and about the middle of the piece in double augmentation with great effect. The piece requires considerable power in polyphonic playing. It is the oldest fugue I know, except those of Bull. In King John IV's library was a posthumous volume, including Masses. These we shall hope will some day be discovered. An organ fantasia was printed by Ritter from a MS. at Liège. A few vocal works are accessible in modern score.

THOMAS MORLEY was born in 1557 or 1558, according to Sadler's part-books, where there is a 'Domine non est' marked 'T. Morley, ætatis suæ 19, anno domini 1576.' Morley was a pupil of Byrd; he graduated Mus.Bac. Oxon. in 1588, and entered the Chapel Royal in 1592. He had previously been organist of St. Paul's. The monopoly granted to Tallis and Byrd having expired, Morley obtained another in 1598. On October 7th, 1602, his place at the Chapel Royal was filled up; he was doubtless then dead, as Bateson in 1608, and Ravenscroft in 1614, allude to him as long since deceased. Morley had spoken of his weak health in his treatise.

The publications of Morley's works were: Three-voiced canzonets in 1593 (twice reprinted); four-voiced madrigals in 1594 (reprinted, also twice in Germany); five-voiced ballets in 1595 (reprinted, also with Italian words, and in 1609 with German words); two-voiced canzonets, with seven instrumental pieces, in 1595; five- and six-voiced canzonets in 1597; and 'The First Booke of Ayres, or Little Short Songes to sing and play to the Lute with the Bass-Viol,' in 1600. Besides these six volumes, some of which were enlarged when reprinted,

Morley edited two volumes of Italian madrigals; and the celebrated collection, 'The Triumphs of Oriana,' which is dated 1601, though not entered on the Stationers' Registers till 1603. His 'Consort Lessons' for six instruments, containing twenty-three pieces, were published in 1599; and with two extra pieces in 1611. His invaluable treatise (1597) has been mentioned.

In sacred music Morley was less prolific. Barnard, however, included an Evening Service, an anthem, and a complete service 'to the organs' (that is, with independent organ accompaniment); and motets are preserved in Myriell's and other MSS. A Burial Service, published by Boyce, is still finer, and fully deserves the enthusiastic praises of Burney. There are seven pieces by Morley in the Fitzwilliam Virginal Book.

The charming 'Ballets' of Morley have a dance-rhythm which adds an enlivening interest not found in the contrapuntal madrigals; and they are peculiarly popular at the present day. The German reprints made his name familiar there; and he was mentioned by Walther, and in Jœchers's 'Gelehrten-Lexicon.' Some ballets have been recently republished in Germany, with other Elizabethan madrigals, and are great favourites there. Morley has, however, been accused of plagiarism; possibly the Italian works he edited have been confused with his own works. I only know that a lovelier passage than the setting of 'Suffer us not,' in Morley's Burial Service, can hardly be found in the old sacred music; and that 'The fields above with spangled flowers' (No. 10 in Morley's four-voiced madrigals) is to me as beautiful a madrigal as any ever composed, while his ballet, 'Now is the month of Maying,' is the most popular of all the ballets. When to these diverse achievements we add Morley's treatise—the best produced here—we must all agree that Morley to this day has a place among England's most 'excellent Musitions'; capable of ascending to the solemnest heights of ecclesiastical art, and of charming the most uncultivated ear by tuneful grace. Morley was not long-lived; but his name is writ large on the roll of the world's composers.

Next must be mentioned JOHN DOWLAND, born in 1562; Fuller says he was a native of Westminster. Dowland is in one respect radically different from any composer hitherto mentioned. From the days of Dunstable all musicians have been primarily ecclesiastical, with an occasional excursion into secular music. The first who showed an especial leaning to the secular style was Morley. But in Dowland we meet with a musician who scarcely ever composed sacred music, who was not a member of the Chapel Royal, who cultivated expressive tenderness both in composition and performance. Some of his ayres resemble modern part-songs, and are in no way strange to a modern audience. Dowland was highly celebrated as a lutenist, and made a tour through France, Germany, and Italy about 1585. He graduated with Morley in 1588. A sonnet by Richard Barnfield, reprinted in 1599 in *The Passionate Pilgrim*, contains the famous and often-quoted lines—

> ' Dowland to thee is dear, whose heavenly touch
> Upon the lute doth ravish human sense;
> Spenser to me, whose deep conceit is such
> As passing all conceit, needs no defence.'

This sonnet, though it has not the Shakespearian cadence, has secured immortality for Dowland. Dowland in 1598 became lutenist to the King of Denmark, at the then unprecedented salary of 500 thalers. A gratuity of 600 extra was given him in 1600. To purchase instruments he revisited England in 1605. He was hopelessly careless and extravagant, and was discharged in 1606, returning to England. In 1612 he styles himself 'Lutenist to the Lord Walden,' and boasts that his compositions had been printed at Paris, Antwerp, Cologne, Nuremburg, Frankfort, Leipzig, Amsterdam, and Hamburg. To this list he might have added Heidelberg (where in 1600 one of Dowland's pieces had been included in J. Rude's 'Flores Musicæ'), and Utrecht (where, in 1612, J. Vanden Hove inserted eight of Dowland's in his 'Delitiæ Musicæ'); another was printed at Nuremburg in 1615. In spite of celebrity and popularity, Dowland complained of neglect; and Peacham addressed him a sympathizing sonnet.

Sometimes he is styled **Dr. Dowland**; but it does not appear that he ever took the degree. A Royal Warrant (now Addit. MS. 5750) shows that Dowland died early in 1626.

Dowland published four books of ayres, but no madrigals, in spite of his university degree. The first 'Booke of Songes or Ayres' appeared in 1597, and was four times reprinted. It contains twenty-one pieces for four voices, accompanied by the lute and viol-da-gamba; with a Galliard for two players on one lute. The title-page design was subsequently used for other ayres and Morley's treatise. In Dowland's preface he alludes to his travels, and the patronage he received from the German princes, and in Italy; and gives a letter from Marenzio. He also complains of a recent incorrect and unauthorized publication of some of his lute pieces. His second book followed in 1600; it has twenty-one ayres for two, four, or five voices, the twenty-first being a dialogue with 'chorus.' The lute and bass-viol are mentioned in the title; but there is no part for the latter, except in an instrumental piece at the end. Dowland's third book (1603) is like the first; the last piece is a dialogue for two voices and two lutes, with 'chorus.' In 1612 appeared 'A Pilgrim's Solace,' ayres with lute and viols; No. 19 is a nautical dialogue for two voices and two lutes, with a four-voiced chorus.

Dowland also contributed to East's Psalter and to Leighton's collection; and there are three ayres in his son's 'Musical Banquet,' besides Fantasies and Galliards in the 'Varietie of Lute Lessons.' One of the Pavins in the latter is superscribed 'Mauritius Landgravius Hessiæ fecit in honorem Joanni Doulandi Anglorum Orphei.' The 'Practical Hints' in the same collection and the translation of Ornithoparcus have been previously mentioned.

Dowland's instrumental collection, published in 1605, was entitled 'Lacrymæ, or Seven Teares, figured in seven passionate Pavans,' etc., for five viols, violins, or lute. This was very famous, and is continually alluded to in early Stuart literature; but the publication is now most rare; the Museum has a copy.

The typical work of Dowland's was the first book of ayres; and those by which he is now remembered are all taken thence. It was the model for the subsequent collections; but none, either by Dowland or others, quite reached it. Contrapuntal artifices are seldom employed, and in some pieces there is little independence in the part-writing, the style approaching the part-song with an expressive tune in the upper part. 'Come again, sweet love,' 'Now, O now, I needs must part,' and 'Awake, sweet love,' require no praise, and they are fortunately still familiar, as they will probably always remain. This book was printed in score, but without the accompaniments, by the Musical Antiquarian Society.

Dowland has many points of similarity with the pianist, John Field. Both had infinite capacity for expression in composition and performance. Both were trained scientifically, but invented new forms in which expressive tenderness took the place of contrapuntal learning, and in each case the forms have been preserved in popular favour. Both enjoyed a European celebrity, and had greater success on the Continent than at home. There is even some reason to believe (in spite of the evidence of Meres and Fuller) that Dowland, like Field, came from Dublin; and the grace, tenderness, and frankness of the best Irish character are all present in Dowland's works as in Field's. Dowland's autograph may be seen in Addit. MS. 27,579.*

His son ROBERT, who published 'A Musical Banquet' and 'Varietie of Lute Lessons' in 1610, succeeded his father in the Royal Household; and was still living in 1641, according to Rimbault. The former book contains ayres by John Dowland, Robert Martin, Robert Hales, and Daniel Bachelor, with some foreign composers. The Lute Lessons consist of seven Fantasies, seven Pavins, seven Almaines, and seven Volts, some by John and Robert Dowland and others, but mostly anonymous; the book also contains a translation of Besardus and J. Dowland's 'Practical Hints.' Both works may be seen at the British Museum and the Bodleian Library. There

* Mr. Flood asserts that Dowland studied at Trinity College, Dublin.

is a piece by Robert Dowland in Fuhrmann's 'Recreationes Musicæ.'

JOHN BULL, like John Dowland, was a touring virtuoso, and must have been the greatest executant of his time. He was born in 1563, and according to Anthony Wood may have been connected with a Somersetshire family; he was a pupil of Blithman, and the fact is mentioned in Blithman's epitaph. Bull began to compose early, for an anthem of his is included in the Christ Church part-books; in 1582 he became organist of Hereford Cathedral. He entered the Chapel Royal in 1585, and before 1589 had received a grant of lands from the Queen. In 1586 Bull graduated Mus.Bac. Oxon.; but took the higher degree first at Cambridge, and was incorporated at Oxford in 1592. Upon the opening of Gresham College in 1596, Dr. Bull was appointed the Professor of Music on the Queen's recommendation, and was specially permitted to lecture in English. His first lecture was printed, but is now unknown.* In 1601 he travelled; and at St. Omer is said to have, in a few hours, added forty new voice-parts to a forty-voiced composition. The story, told by Anthony Wood, has been ridiculed by Burney, Ouseley, and Ambros, but is in no way unreasonable. There would be no special difficulty in adding forty new voice-parts to Tallis's forty-voiced motet.

In James I's reign Bull was one of the musicians to Prince Henry, and is frequently mentioned; he resigned the professorship on his marriage in 1607. In 1613 he left England, and became one of the organists to the Viceroy of Flanders; James I's ambassador made a formal complaint that Bull had fled to escape punishment for loose life, but the composer was not surrendered, and no doubt turned Romanist. In 1617 he became organist at Antwerp; he died March, 1628, and was buried in the Cathedral on the 15th.

There is a piece by Bull in Leighton's sacred madrigals, an anthem in Barnard's collection, and another in Boyce's. In 1629 some carols by 'Jean Buol' were included in Phalèse's collection. Otherwise Bull's compositions are

* The title-page is in Bagford's cuttings.

almost entirely instrumental, and show him to have possessed most extraordinary execution. There are seven pieces of his in *Parthenia* (1611); the Fitzwilliam Virginal Book contains forty-three; and there are others in various MSS., the most important of all being the fugues and other works in Addit. MS. 23,623. Ambros mentions a lute-book of Bull's at Vienna. Burney printed extraordinary specimens of Bull's executive complications, taken from some compositions in the Fitzwilliam MS. In contrapuntal invention Bull does not rank high, but in the discovery of novel passages and difficulties he must be ranked among the greatest players who have ever lived.

Whatever may have been the merits of some in Meres's list of 'excellente Musitions,' there can be no doubt of the right of Philipps, Morley, Dowland, and Bull to a place in the glorious company. Each of the four has his own distinct individuality, and is unlike the other three. Philipps, as a Romish ecclesiastic, followed the Palestrina school; 'he affecteth altogether the Italian vein,' said Peacham. Morley excelled as a theorist, a madrigalist, and (when he chose) in sacred music. Dowland, sooner than any other musician, found the means to touch the heart by exquisite performance of tastefully-chosen simplicity. Bull, less distinguished as a composer, was an amazing executant, astonishing the world by unprecedented brilliancy. England may well be proud of these four composers, all worthy successors of Tye, Edwards, Tallis, and Whyte. They had the advantages and the disadvantages of coming into the world a little later than Byrd, and they could produce lighter works than their predecessors; for this reason some pieces by Morley and Dowland are still quite familiar. As we have seen, their music was much reprinted on the Continent even in their own time, and the nineteenth century saw fresh attention directed to these charming works. Professor Maier, of Munich, translated and published a selection which has won great favour in Germany. Ambros describes their great and lasting success at Prague, adding—

'Es giebt nichts Anmuthigeres als gewisse Stücke von Dowland, von Morley. Sie sind zugleich naiv-volksthümlich und adelig-vornehm.'

Ambros's judgment that the English madrigals are essentially different from those of the Flemish and Italian composers is true as regards the 'ayres' of Dowland and others; but I question if Ambros would have said it had he enjoyed a wider acquaintance with the English contrapuntal madrigalists. Besides Edwards, R. Johnson, Tallis, Byrd, Philipps, Morley, and Dowland, there are nearly fifty composers who have left beautiful secular pieces, occasionally rising equal to their predecessors.

The most celebrated collection, 'The Triumphs of Oriana,' may be mentioned here. This series was produced in honour of Queen Elizabeth, though probably suggested by a set of madrigals entitled *Il trionfo di Dori*, and published at Antwerp. Why the English collection, though dated 1601, was not entered on the Stationers' Registers till October 15th, 1603, has not been explained. The Earl of Devonshire bought a copy, December, 1601. There were originally twenty-five madrigals by twenty-three composers. In Hawes's reprint in score (1814) there are twenty-nine, the additions being two which arrived too late, one arranged from G. Croce, and Bateson's 'Oriana's Farewell.' Even yet this is not absolutely complete, and any future edition should include 'Oriana's Farewell' by Vautor, and a kind of supplement by Peacham in Harl. MS. 6855. As the entire collection consists of madrigals, the words are always short and unimportant.

The absentees from the band of composers who joined in this homage to Queen Elizabeth are noteworthy. Neither Byrd, Philipps, nor Deering, all Romanists, are represented. Dowland was in Denmark; Bull was travelling.

Taking the complete work as given by Hawes, the composers are: Morley, the editor, who contributed two pieces, Michael East, Daniel Norcome, John Mundy, Mus.Bac., John Benet, John Hilton, Mus.Bac., George Marson, Mus.Bac., Rev. Richard Carlton, Mus.Bac.,

John Holmes, Richard Nicholson, Mus.Bac., Thomas
Tomkins, Michael Cavendish, William Cobbold, John
Farmer, John Wilbye, Thomas Hunt, Mus.Bac., Thomas
Weelkes, John Milton, George Kirbye, Robert Jones,
John Lisley, Edward Johnson, Mus.Bac., Ellis Gibbons
(two pieces), Thomas Bateson (two numbers printed
subsequently), and Francis Pilkington (printed subsequently). These include almost all the best contrapuntal
madrigalists. The finest numbers are, in my opinion,
those by Morley, Benet, Wilbye, and Bateson.

These composers, so far as is known, were mostly
connected with the cathedrals and collegiate establishments. Some issued individual publications, described
in due course. DANIEL NORCOME was probably, though
not quite certainly, the lay-clerk of Windsor who was
a distinguished violist, and is dealt with in Chapter VI.
THOMAS HUNT and JOHN LISLEY are unknown. GEORGE
MARSON was organist of Canterbury; he was married
there 1599, and buried 5th February, 1631-2. JOHN
HILTON was organist of Trinity College, Cambridge; in
some part-books at Oxford appears the name John
Hilton, senr. The John Hilton who published Fa-las in
1627 may have been his son; the elder was quite possibly
the composer of 'Lord, for Thy tender mercies' sake.'
ELLIS GIBBONS was organist of Salisbury; and JOHN
HOLMES (see p.188) of Winchester. THOMAS TOMKINS was
precentor of Gloucester Cathedral and father of a whole
family of musicians. WILLIAM COBBOLD (1560-1639),
born at Norwich, was cathedral organist 1599-1608,
then choirman; he died and was buried at Beccles.
Cobbold, who had shared in East's Psalter, has left twelve
madrigals and a motet (all imperfect) in Addit. MSS.
18,936-9. RICHARD NICHOLSON, organist of Magdalen
College, Oxford, graduated 1595, and was the first
Oxford Professor of Music; he died 1639. There are
sacred and secular pieces by him in Addit. MSS.
17,786-91 and 17,797. No other composition by these
nine musicians has been printed; but each of their
contributions is quite worthy to stand in the collection,
and shows the hand of an accomplished composer.

JOHN MILTON, father of the great poet, had turned, scrivener, having been disinherited by his father, a rigid Romanist. He was born in 1563 or earlier. In music he was admirably skilled; his great-nephew, Edward Phillips, mentions that he composed a forty-voiced In Nomine for a Polish prince, who rewarded him with a gold chain and medal. Milton contributed four pieces to Leighton's collection, and two harmonisings to Ravenscroft's Psalter. I do not suppose the psalm-tunes were his own. He lived till 1647, and his son's Latin epistle, *Ad Patrem*, testifies to his goodness of heart and musical skill; as does also, according to Professor Morley, the little elegy he discovered in 1868, and printed as Milton's. The most remarkable compositions of the Puritan scrivener are an English setting of the Lamentations, and some Latin motets, preserved by Myriell. The Lamentations and a 'Precamur sancte Domine' are for six voices; the others for five. Mr. Arkwright has published six of Milton's works.

Besides Morley and E. Johnson, already discussed, there yet remain twelve others of the contributors, each of whom published one or more independent collections of madrigals. I discuss them in the order in which their works were issued.

JOHN MUNDY, a son of William Mundy, was born probably before 1560, as there is a work by him in the part-books Addit. MSS. 17,802–5, and Wood states he had been organist of Eton College before succeeding Merbecke at Windsor Castle. In 1586 he graduated Mus.Bac. Oxon., but did not proceed Mus.Doc. till 1624. In 1594 he published 'Songs and Psalms,' a collection of thirty sacred and secular contrapuntal madrigals. Burney printed one with disparaging remarks. More remarkable are the keyboard pieces of John Mundy in the Fitzwilliam Virginal Book; they are the most difficult there except those of Bull, and one is the earliest known attempt to depict a storm. An anthem of his was printed by Barnard. Dr. Mundy was buried at Windsor in 1630.

GEORGE KIRBYE was probably born about 1570 at Bury St. Edmunds. He contributed to East's Psalter.

In 1597 he published twenty-four very fine madrigals;
they were reprinted in score in Mr. Arkwright's *Old
English Edition* in 1891. Mr. Arkwright has discovered
the composer's biography, showing that he married in
1598, and died at Bury in October, 1634. An anthem by
Kirbye in Myriell's collection, dances for viols in Addit.
MSS. 30,826–8, and a few other works, mostly imperfect,
exist. It is singular that so able a composer produced
(or at least published) nothing more. A copy of the
Orianas at Oxford contains an extra madrigal of Kirbye's,
not found in other copies; but only the words differ.

THOMAS WEELKES also published a set of madrigals in
1597; this was reprinted by the Musical Antiquarian
Society in 1846. Next followed some 'Ballets and Madrigals' in 1598 (reprinted 1608); in both works Weelkes
speaks of his youth. In 1600, being organist of Winchester College, he published two more sets of madrigals,
and a fifth set followed in 1608, when he was organist
of Chichester Cathedral. He had graduated Mus.Bac.
Oxon. in 1602. Sacred music of Weelkes's was published by Leighton and Barnard, and in score by the
Musical Antiquarian Society. Perhaps his best work is
his contribution to the Orianas, 'As Vesta was from
Latmos hill descending'; others are still popular. 'To
shorten winter's sadness,' 'The Nightingale,' 'Lady,
your eye my love enforced,' are gems of unfading beauty;
and 'Cease sorrows now,' a very remarkable chromatic
conception, has been called 'perhaps the finest three-part
madrigal in existence.' Weelkes died when on a visit
to London, and was buried in St. Bride's churchyard,
December, 1623.

JOHN WILBYE was a yet greater composer, and has been
justly esteemed 'the chief of English madrigal writers';
his works are equal to any produced in Italy or the
Netherlands in this culminating period. Till recently
his personality was unknown. I wrote in the original
edition: 'One would gladly know something concerning
so great a composer; but, after all, we shall do him more
honour by cherishing and performing his works than by
ferreting out details of his biography.' The Rev. E. H.

Fellowes, having found Wilbye's will, started on the track of his life story and has been able to construct a fairly complete biography. The composer, third son of a tanner, was baptized at Diss, 7th March, 1573–4. Of his education nothing is recorded. About 1592 he came into the household of Sir Thomas Kytson, of Hengrave Hall, Suffolk; there he remained till 1628, when Lady Kytson died, not forgetting Wilbye in her testament. The rest of his life he spent with her daughter, Lady Rivers, at Colchester; he died in 1638, making his will on 10th September; he was probably buried in Trinity Church. He was apparently unmarried; to his relatives and friends he bequeathed houses, lands, and £400 in cash; the principal and residuary legatee was his nephew John, who may be surmised his godson.*

Wilbye's compositions, which most concern us, include a volume of thirty madrigals; another of thirty-four; three contributions to the Oriana and Leighton collections; and a few smaller works and fragments. So gifted a man, in such favourable conditions, might and should have left the world richer by a far greater amount of gems. Perhaps his lines had fallen in places too pleasant for steady industry; and he let the world slide, while fulfilling his routine duties as an honoured and trusted official in a great country family, varied only by a rare visit to their London house in the Austin Friars. A post in the Chapel Royal or a cathedral might have called up and nourished his talents till he was as eminent for sacred music as for madrigals, and the equal of Orlando Gibbons. It was not to be; we must content ourselves with the glorious relics we possess. Wilbye's life of sixty-five years has left for the world's profit: 'Flora gave me fairest flowers,' 'Down in a valley.' 'Sweet honey-sucking bees,' 'Lady, when I behold,' 'Happy, oh happy,' 'The Lady Oriana,' and sixty other such masterpieces; compare this result with the deeds of Palestrina or Lassus. But as regards quality, Wilbye's madrigals will bear comparison with any in existence. Technically, he looks forward, as Lassus did, to the new world of harmonic

---

* Mr. Fellowes has printed the will and other interesting documents.

daring; he often uses long-sustained notes in the bass
with grand result. The variety of mood and treatment
displayed through the collections is beyond all praise;
here England had a composer equal to any of his period,
and it was a culminating period.

MICHAEL CAVENDISH, who had contributed to East's
Psalter, 'was one of the ancient family of the Cavendishes,'
according to Wood. Cavendish's volume of Ayres and
Madrigals, discovered in 1918, was secured by the British
Museum. It contains twenty accompanied Ayres and
eight Madrigals. One spirited and enlivening number,
'Ev'ry bush by springing tree,' had been included in
E. T. Warren's *Vocal Harmony*.

JOHN BENNET (Benet, Bennett) is another of England's
really great composers, and his beautiful madrigals have
not been dulled by the passage of three centuries. He
published them in 1599, calling them his 'first works.'
But he published no more, except contributions to
Barley's Psalter and the Orianas, and five madrigals in
Ravenscroft's 'Brief Discourse.' These latter contain
attempts at programme-music, interesting historically.
The earlier set, published by the Musical Antiquarian
Society, contains some exquisite music; several have been
included in various popular collections of the eighteenth
and nineteenth centuries. Other madrigals, with anthems
and organ music, exist in MS. John Bennet's compositions are still fresh, still beloved, still performed, while
his biography is an absolute blank. Hawes selects
Bennet's 'All creatures now are merry-minded' as the
very best of the Orianas, and it is certainly the oftenest
performed. The singularly picturesque passage, 'Birds
over her do hover,' shows a true master hand, as does in
an equal degree the pathetic madrigal, 'Flow, O my
tears,' music which cannot die.

In the same year (1599) appeared also the madrigals
of JOHN FARMER, whose contrapuntal work, published in
1591, has been mentioned on p. 181. He had also contributed to East's Psalter. In his madrigals he claimed
to have especially studied the prosody of the words,
though he does not satisfy modern requirements in this

respect. Bennet's and Farmer's sets each contain seventeen madrigals, the last with extra voices. Nothing is known of Farmer; he published nothing more except his contribution to the Orianas, good sterling music.

ROBERT JONES was a prolific composer, but his works are rare. His first publication was a book of 'Ayres'; the British Museum copy has no title-page, but one which belonged to Halliwell-Phillipps was dated 1600. In the preface, Jones apologises for his 'cold ayres' and 'idle ditties,' promising in future to use 'more points,' as his chief care had been 'to fit the note to the word.' In 1601 appeared his second book of 'Ayres' for one voice; he claims that there had previously 'not been anie extant of this fashion.' They are accompanied by the lute and the viol-da-gamba in both tablature and ordinary notation. Next, Jones issued his 'First Booke of Madrigals' in 1607. Three more books of Ayres followed, entitled 'Ultimum Vale' (1608), 'A Musicall Dreame' (1609), and 'The Muses' Garden for Delights' (1610). The British Museum has four of the six volumes; 'Ultimum Vale' is at the Royal College of Music; 'The Muses' Garden for Delights' was in the Stafford collection, and quoted by Beloe, but it has been sold to America. Evidently ayres were more in demand than madrigals, as Jones published no others except three contributions to Leighton's collection, and the one he had sent to the Orianas. Jones graduated Mus.Bac. Oxon. in 1597. He was a lutenist and lived in Blackfriars; an attempt was made in 1615 to turn his house into a theatre, but it was opposed and defeated by the Corporation of London. Only two part-books of the Madrigals remain; but six numbers are complete in Myriell's MS. at Brussels. None have been reprinted in score, except two ayres (one of which was quoted by Shakespeare) in *Musica Antiqua*, and the madrigal in the Orianas. Jones's name appears as an anthem composer in Clifford's collection (1663). Robert Jones must not be confused with the older Robert Jones of the Peterhouse part-books (see p. 90); and John Bennet the madrigalist must not be confounded with the John Benet of the fifteenth century.

RICHARD CARLTON (perhaps the son of the Nicholas Carlton of the Mulliner Book) graduated B.A. Cantab. in 1577, and Mus.Bac. soon after. He took holy orders, and belonged to Norwich Cathedral; in 1612 he became vicar of Bawsey and Glosthorp, near Lynn. He apparently died in 1638. In 1601 he contributed to the Orianas, and also published twenty-one madrigals for five voices, which are quite neglected, though bright and tuneful. There is dance music by Carlton in MS., and Tomkins dedicated a song to him.

THOMAS BATESON, another of the best madrigalists, became organist of Chester Cathedral in 1602; in March, 1609, he was vicar-choral of Dublin Cathedral, and also became organist there. As Bateson in 1618 calls himself Mus.Bac., he is supposed to have been the first musical graduate of Dublin University. Bateson's contribution to the Orianas arrived too late, and was printed with 'Oriana's Farewell' in his 'First Set of Madrigals' published in 1604. The Musical Antiquarian Society published these madrigals in score, and also some anthems by Bateson. They are all contrapuntal and elaborate, and rank high among the productions of this glorious period; and the Second Set, published in 1618, is in no way inferior. Nothing more is known of Bateson, except that he died March, 1630.

MICHAEL EAST (Este) was probably a son or other relation of the printer. Like Bateson, he sent his contribution to the Orianas too late; but Morley printed it on the back of the dedication. East issued seven collections of various kinds; there are complete sets at the British Museum and the Royal College. The first, consisting of twenty-four madrigals, appeared in 1604; another set of twenty-two followed in 1606; the preface dated from Ely House, where Sir Christopher Hatton's widow was living. In 1610 East published a collection, including madrigals, anthems, and eight Fancies for five instruments. The Fancies are entitled Desperavi, Peccavi, Vidi, Penitet, Credidi, Vixi, Triumphavi, and Amavi. In 1619 he published two works, in which he calls himself Mus.Bac. and Master of the Choristers at Lichfield

Cathedral; one of these works contains madrigals and anthems, while the other consists of madrigals for three voices, the parts (in the British Museum copy) being entitled Cantus, Quintus, Bassus. The Bishop of Lincoln bestowed an annuity upon East after hearing one of his works, in return for which East dedicated a collection of anthems to the Bishop in 1624. He published no more, except a set of instrumental pieces in 1638 containing eight duets for bass-viols, nine three-part Fancies named after the Muses, and twelve four-part. This collection was reprinted by Playford during the Commonwealth. What became of East after 1638 is not known; Pepys in 1660 repeatedly mentions an 'old East,' 'Gammer East,' not in connection with music. Many of East's pieces are bright and enlivening; 'How merrily we live that shepherds be' has always remained a favourite. Some of his anthems were published by the Musical Antiquarian Society.

FRANCIS PILKINGTON, of Chester Cathedral, graduated Mus.Bac. Oxon. in 1595. He published a 'Book of Ayres' in 1605; they have the usual lute-tablature, but no part for the gamba, though it is mentioned in the title. One of these ayres, 'Rest, sweet nymphs,' was printed by Stafford Smith, afterwards by Hullah, and the whole set by Mr. Arkwright. They are beautiful music to good poetry. At the end is a Pavin for the lute and gamba. In 1613 Pilkington issued 'The First Set of Madrigals and Pastorals,' tuneful and attractive pieces; a Second Set followed in 1624. The First Set contains a piece suggested by the Orianas, and included in Hawes's reprint. The Second Set is partly sacred, and there is one Fancy. The last piece is a Dialogue with lute accompaniment and chorus. A Pavin by the Earl of Derby is added in the Altus part-book. Of all the less-known volumes of ayres, that by Pilkington seems to be the one most deserving performance. There is some lute music by him in Addit. MS. 31,392; and two pieces in Leighton. He died 1638.

The composers who contributed to 'The Triumphs of Oriana' (with Bateson and Pilkington, both included in Hawes's reprint) have now been all dealt with; for the sake of completeness, I will here place two other composers. THOMAS VAUTOR graduated Mus.Bac. Oxon. in 1616; in 1619 he published a set of twenty-two madrigals, calling them 'Songs of Divers Ayres and Natures.' The first two are Fa-las. Another is to Latin words, and there are two elegies. The last is a 'Farewell to Oriana.' Vautor dedicated them to the Duke of Buckingham, then in full power; and mentioned that some had been composed in the house of the Duke's parents.

In Harl. MS. 6855 is a madrigal by HENRY PEACHAM, written in honour of James I, and supplementary to the Orianas. Peacham, author of *The Compleat Gentleman*, does not elsewhere appear as a composer; he was a pupil of Orazio Vecchi. He requires of a 'Compleat Gentleman' musical skill as follows:

'I desire no more in you than to sing your part sure and at the first sight; withal to play the same upon your Viol, or the exercise of the Lute, privately to yourself.'

Such skill, and 'no more,' would be very welcome in a gentleman of the present day;* it is, however, to be remembered that there was no *art* of singing in those days otherwise than the production of the right notes. Morley's treatise, for instance, makes no mention of voice-production or expression. In the concerted singing of that time these were of less importance than in solo-singing. We cannot doubt that in the ayres careful pronunciation was attended to; in the madrigals the words were of no importance. The In Nomines may have been sol-fa'd, or sung without words. The madrigals of James I's reign are usually described as 'Apt for viols and voices.'

Some important composers remain to be described; their works are mainly ayres, and it is probable that several were amateurs having the ordinary practical knowledge of that day, and that they were not asked to contribute to the Orianas because they were not contrapuntists. There are others of a more scientific turn.

RICHARD DEERING (Dering, Diringus) was of the ancient

* *Cf.* Lord Herbert of Cherbury's *Autobiography.*

Kentish family; or, according to another account, the son of Lady Grey, by Deering of Liss, near Petersfield. Like Peter Philipps, he was a Romanist refugee in the Netherlands. He published at Antwerp in 1597 a set of motets entitled *Cantiones Sacræ cum basso continuo ad organum*, according to Hawkins; but the date at least was a mistake, and should have been 1634. Deering was in England, and graduated Mus.Bac. Oxon. in 1610; in 1617 he was organist to the English nuns at Brussels. 'Cantica Sacra' for six voices appeared in 1618. In 1620 some canzonets followed. After the marriage of Charles I Deering became organist to Henrietta Maria; he died in 1630. Deering had composed two long madrigals on popular 'cries,' preserved in Myriell's collection; some music for viols (in Addit. MSS. 18,940–4), and other pieces in MS. His works had a high reputation; the 'Cantiones Sacræ' were mentioned by Draudius. In the monodic style he composed some Latin pieces, very long in favour. Oliver Cromwell 'greatly delighted in them, and used to have them sung before him when Protector. They were published after the Restoration, in 1662; others, not certainly Deering's, followed in 1674.*

GILES FARNABY, of Truro, graduated Mus.Bac. Oxon. in 1592, 'having studied music twelve years.' He contributed to East's and Barley's Psalters, and in 1598 published twenty-one canzonets; one of them, on a descending chromatic passage, has been printed in score. Farnaby was principally an instrumental composer. More than fifty compositions and arrangements in the Fitzwilliam Virginal Book are by Giles Farnaby, among them a little piece for two virginals, one part being simple, the other florid; and there are some by his son, Richard Farnaby. Selections have been issued in popular form.

RICHARD ALLISON (Alison) was a master of pure diatonic polyphony. He published a Psalter in 1599, with the metricised canticles and Ten Commandments, all for four voices with lute accompaniment. In 1606 appeared his 'An Houres Recreation in Musicke,' containing twenty-four sacred and secular madrigals, the last one

* Was there more than one composer named Deering ?

being a thanksgiving for the discovery of the Gunpowder Plot. There are Pavyns for the lute in Addit. MS. 31,392, and an In Nomine at Oxford, by this able musician.

THOMAS CAMPION, born 1575, was a typical Elizabethan amateur of the finest class. A. H. Bullen has brought his poetry into celebrity. He was a physician by profession. In conjunction with Philip Rossetor, Campion published two books of ayres for one voice, lute, and bass-viol, the poetry and half the music being his own. Since these ayres were entered on the Stationers' Registers on May 8th, 1601, they can hardly be later than Jones's Second Book, which claims to be the first published for one voice. Campion also published two books of ayres entirely by himself about 1613: the first, to sacred words, is for four voices and lute; the other, amatory, is for two or three voices and lute; the last number of each being like the ayres of 1601. Two more books appeared in 1617, judging by the dedication; they are for one voice, with lute and bass-viol. The words of all the ayres may be seen in Arber's 'English Garner,' Vol. III; and Bullen has republished the whole of Campion's poetry. Rimbault included a specimen of the fourth book of ayres (he calls it the third) in one of his publications, but it is much unlike Campion's original, having a chorus added. As a technical point of some historical interest I may mention that Campion, in his second and fourth books, used a signature with three flats; the keys of the pieces in question are C minor and F minor.

Campion was also much employed in writing masques, occasionally composing some of the music. One produced at Lord Hay's wedding (in 1607) was published; the songs were by Campion, T. Giles, and T. Lupo, and they have been reprinted by Mr. Arkwright in his *Old English Edition*. Another song in a masque of Campion's was printed with others in 1614. His last publication, a treatise on counterpoint, has been previously described. Campion was buried in St. Dunstan's, Fleet Street, on March 1st, 1620.

A man of many-sided culture, rather than a specialist, is exactly fitted to introduce a novel style; we see this also in Campion's Florentine contemporaries. The prefaces to the ayres of 1601 and 1613 exactly express the feelings of a reflecting cultivated man towards music, and this passage is worth quoting:

'There are some who, to appear the more deep and singular in their judgment, will admit no music but that which is long, intricate, bated with fugue, chained with syncopation, and where the nature of every word is precisely expressed in the note: like the old exploded action in Comedies, when if they did pronounce *Memini*, they would point to the hinder part of their heads; if *Video*, put their finger in their eye. But such childish observing of words is altogether ridiculous; and we ought to maintain, as well in notes as in action, a manly carriage; gracing no word but that which is eminent and emphatical. Nevertheless, as in Poesy we give the pre-eminence to the Heroical Poem; so in Music we yield the chief place to the grave and well-invented Motet: but not to every harsh and dull confused Fantasy, where, in a multitude of Points, the harmony is quite drowned.'

It must not, however, be thought that Campion's compositions are inferior to the generality of the ayres. They more nearly approach the folk-songs than most others, especially when in triple time; but richer harmony is occasionally employed. A chromatic passage at 'mists and darkness' (in No. 1 of the sacred set), and another in No. 4 of the first set, may be instanced. Campion does not appear to have composed madrigals.

PHILIP ROSSETOR (Rossiter), his coadjutor in the ayres of 1601, was a lutenist. He also published a collection of 'Consort Lessons' for six instruments in 1609; the cithern part is at the Royal College of Music. He became one of the Masters of the Children to the Queen's Revels in 1610, and gave dramatic performances at Whitefriars. Rossetor lived in Fetter Lane; he joined in Jones's unsuccessful dramatic enterprise. Campion bequeathed his whole estate to Rossitor, who died 5th May, 1623.

THOMAS GREAVES, who calls himself 'lutenist to Sir Henry Pierrepoint,' but is otherwise unknown, published in 1604 'Songs of Sundrie Kindes,' containing nine ayres and twelve madrigals, of which the last two are Fa-las. Three have been reprinted in score.

TOBIAS HUME, who calls himself Captain, published

his 'First Booke of Ayres' in 1605, and 'Poeticall Musicke' in 1607; both collections are mainly instrumental. Hume, in a soldier's song, requires the lute to imitate trumpets, drums, and 'greate ordnance'; and in another of the ayres it has to represent 'the organes.' Both works have a quaint passage in praise of 'the stateful' Instrument Gambo-Violl,' Hume declaring 'The Trinitie of Musicke, *Parts*, *Passion*, and *Devision*, to be as gracefully united in the Gamba as in the most received instrument that is.' Dowland attacked the assertion. In the 'Poeticall Musicke' there is a hunting song 'sung before two kings, to the admiring of all brave huntsmen.' Hume was in the Charterhouse in 1642, when he published an eccentric tract; he died there insane, 1647.

JOHN DANYEL, who had graduated Mus.Bac. Oxon. in 1604, and was probably brother to the famous sonneteer, published a collection of 'Songs' in 1606; eighteen are ayres for one voice with lute and bass-viol, two are madrigals, and there is one lute solo. He had in 1613 a royal warrant to educate children for the drama, renewed in 1618.

JOHN BARTLETT also published a 'Book of Ayres' in 1606. Fourteen are for four voices, and four for two trebles (with lute); three are for one voice with lute and bass-viol. Bartlett graduated Mus.Bac. Oxon. in 1610.

Bartlett, Danyel, Hume, and Greaves are only names to the immense majority of musicians; even Farnaby, Allison, and Campion are little more. But the case is widely different with THOMAS FORD, whose 'Musicke of Sundrie Kindes' (1607) contains a lovely piece, 'Since first I saw your face,' of which both poetry and music are familiar, are sung everywhere, are loved by all, are the delight of performers and listeners in every town and village in England. Unfortunately, only two verses are usually printed in modern editions; and the harmonies usually sung have been slightly modernised. Ford's only publication consists of ten ayres, a dialogue for two voices and two lutes, and a selection of eighteen dances in tablature for the lyra-viol. Besides the popular 'Since first I saw your face,' the book contains a very beautiful

piece, 'There is a ladie, sweet and kind.' Two 'Songs'
in Leighton's collection are by Ford; also some sacred
canons in Hilton's 'Catch that catch can' (1652). Ford
composed some sacred music; there are twenty anthems
at Oxford. In Clifford's collection of words (1663) is a
dialogue-anthem, 'Look, shepherds, look'; and another
of Ford's anthems was printed by the Musical Antiquarian Society. Ford was one of the musicians to Prince
Henry Stuart, and subsequently to Charles I. He was
buried at St. Margaret's, Westminster, November 17th,
1648. Porter, in 1657, spoke of him as a great musical
authority. Three centuries and more have passed away;
but 'Since first I saw your face' is sung probably every
day in the year, and such immortality as the continual
performance of his music can give is the lot of the
venerable Thomas Ford.

On the contrary, HENRY YOULL, whose three-voiced
canzonets appeared in 1608, is the very least known of
all English madrigalists.

THOMAS RAVENSCROFT holds an important position in
the history of English music. He was born in 1593,
educated in St. Paul's choir, and graduated Mus.Bac.
Cantab. at the age of fourteen. In 1609 he published
'Pammelia' and 'Deuteromelia,' the volumes of canons
and catches already mentioned. A collection of madrigals
entitled *Melismata* followed in 1611. His attempt to
reintroduce Mensurable Music, with the madrigals composed by his master Edward Pearce, himself, and John
Bennet, has been mentioned among the treatises. Another
treatise, of an elementary character, was written by
Ravenscroft, and may be seen in Addit. MS. 19,758. His
only other published work was his celebrated Psalter,
which first appeared in 1621, and contained one hundred
harmonisings, forty-eight by himself. Other madrigals
and motets by Ravenscroft exist in MS. It is not known
when he died. Ravenscroft was possibly an 'infant
prodigy' who remained something of a pedant; but he
deserves honour as the only English musician during the
seventeenth century who asserted Dunstable's right to be
'the first that invented composition.'

ALFONSO FERRABOSCO, son of Byrd's friend and competitor (see p. 181), was in high esteem as a musician. He was born at Greenwich. Two collections, dedicated to his pupil, Prince Henry, appeared in 1609; one is a volume of twenty-eight declamatory ayres, the other a set of lessons for one, two, and three viols tuned lyra-way. They are in tablature, and are mainly Almains and Corantos. The ayres are similar to those of Caccini; several were printed by Burney. Ferrabosco contributed to Leighton's collection but published nothing more. He died in 1627-8, and was succeeded as Court musician by a third Alfonso Ferrabosco. Others of the surname occur during the seventeenth century.

GIOVANNI COPERARIO (Cooper), an Italianised Englishman, also followed the monodic style. In 1606 appeared his 'Funeral Tears for the Earl of Devonshire, which contain six elegies for one voice (and altus ad libitum); the seventh is in dialogue, question and answer, with a 'chorus' of both voices. In 1613 Coperario published another set of elegies (to poems by Campion) on the death of Prince Henry, for one voice. He set part of the songs in the Somerset Wedding Masque (1614); a production at any rate good enough for that occasion. He contributed two pieces to Leighton's collection. Much instrumental music by him exists in Addit. MSS. 23,779 and 31,416 (autograph), and in a volume which belonged to his pupil, Charles I. Coperario, who taught the brothers Lawes, died in 1626.

With them may be mentioned another musician who helped to popularise the dramatic style, NICHOLAS LANIER, who was of mixed French and Italian descent, and was born at Greenwich, September, 1588. Lanier, like Campion, was a gifted man of various culture. He was twice sent by Charles I to Italy to select pictures; and himself was distinguished as a painter and engraver. He shared with Coperario in composing the masque music for the Somerset wedding; in the publication a masque-ayre of Campion's was also inserted. For a masque of Ben Jonson's, performed February 22nd, 1617, Lanier painted the scenery, composed the music, and sang in the performance; on this occasion he introduced *recitative* into England. Many of his ayres were included in publications during the Commonwealth and later. Charles I held Lanier in high regard, appointing him 'Master of the King's Musicke' in 1626, and Marshal of the Corporation of Musicians, established in 1636. Lanier is not heard of during the Civil War and the Commonwealth; three others of the family were paid their arrears of salary in 1645 and 1649, by order of Parliament. At the Restoration, Lanier was reappointed Marshal; he lived at Greenwich, but was buried elsewhere in February, 1666. Being of a later school than the musicians previously mentioned, and also from natural proclivities, he is more distinctly one of the declamatory composers.

THOMAS LUPO, one of the many musicians sprung from the 'Lupus Italus' of the Peterhouse part-books, was one of the musicians to Prince Henry, and afterwards to Charles I; at Oxford there are anthems, fancies, and madrigals of Lupo's, but he published only his share in the masque for Lord Hay's wedding. THOMAS GILES, who collaborated in the masque with Lupo and Campion, was brother to the Master of the Children in the Chapel Royal, but otherwise undistinguished. Lupo contributed to Leighton's collection; and another of these pieces is by 'Timolphus Thopull,' probably Lupo.

WILLIAM CORKINE, personally unknown, published Ayres in 1610 and 1612. Both volumes contain some pieces for the lyra-viol. The tenth in the first volume is in country dialect.

DANIEL BACHELOR, one of the Queen's household, contributed one of the ayres in Dowland's 'Musical Banquet,' and is represented in many of the manuscript lute-books. Dowland also included specimens by ROBERT HALES and ROBERT MARTIN, both unknown.

JOHN MAYNARD, doubtless a lutenist, published in 1611 'The XII Wonders of the World,' twelve poems on 'The Performing Courtier,' 'The Honest Merchant,' etc., set for voice, lute, and gamba. The book also contains instrumental music and a ten-voiced canon. Maynard was perhaps the 'Meinert' at Copenhagen in 1599.

HENRY LICHFILD, another unknown musician, published twenty good five-voiced madrigals in 1613 and 1614. There was an Oxford publisher named Lichfild.

ROBERT TAILOUR, a Court musician, published fifty psalms as five-voiced ayres, with lute accompaniment, in 1615; the parts do not turn the leaf together. There are copies at the British Museum, Lambeth, and Chichester.

JOHN ATTEY, 'Gentleman, and Practicioner of Musicke,' appears only as the composer of a book of four-voiced ayres, issued 1622. Attey dedicated the collection to the Earl and Countess of Bridgwater, saying most were composed under their roof while he was teaching their daughters.

When James I was in Westmorland in 1617 he was magnificently entertained at Brougham Castle by the Earl of Cumberland; the ayres composed for the occasion were printed. They were the work of GEORGE MASON and JOHN EARSDEN, probably the Earl's lutenists. The whole collection was reprinted in *Musica Antiqua*.

Patrick Hannay, a Scotch poet, published 'Philomela, or The Nightingale,' consisting of about one hundred sixteen-lined stanzas, in 1622. On the frontispiece is a border containing music for the first stanza; in one copy this music is given in the body of the work with a bass, and irregularly barred. Apparently the whole poem was to be sung to this strain. The music was reprinted with Hannay's complete works in 1875.

Leighton's 'Teares and Lamentacions of a Sorrowful Soule,' already frequently cited, is divided into three sections: seventeen 'Consort Songs' for four voices and six instruments; twelve Songs (unaccompanied madrigals) for four voices; and twenty-four Songs for five voices. There are eight Consort Songs by Sir WILLIAM LEIGHTON, the editor; and two pieces by KINDERSLEY, besides better-known composers.

There still remain a few of the greater composers to be mentioned, besides some who did not publish. WILLIAM WIGTHORPE, who had studied ten years, graduated Mus.Bac. Oxon. in 1605; there are six secular pieces of his in Addit. MSS. 17,786–91 (including some dialogues), and Clifford quoted his anthems. MATTHEW WHITE, from Wells, in 1613 succeeded the venerable Robert Stone at the Chapel Royal, but resigned next year; he accumulated the musical degrees at Oxford in 1629. Frequently the works of the great Robert Whyte are ascribed in old MSS. to Matthew; and sometimes to WILLIAM WHITE, by whom there is a six-voiced anthem in Myriell, another at Peterhouse, and some instrumental music in Addit. MSS. 17,792–6, and at Oxford. Tomkins dedicated a piece to William White. DANIEL FARRANT is described by Playford as a man of great mechanical ingenuity, having invented several instruments; he, Ferrabosco, and Coperario were the first to use the lyra-viol; that is, to apply the lute-tablature to the fretted viols. Whether Richard Farrant of Windsor (see p. 148), or John Farrant (organist of Ely), or Daniel Farrant composed the madrigals ascribed to 'Farrant' does not appear. John Lake supplicated Mus.Bac. Oxon. in 1616, but was not admitted. There is an anthem in Myriell, several anthems and services at Peterhouse, by JOHN LUGG, and canons in 'Catch that catch can.' I suspect these men were both identical with the John Lugg who was a vicar-choral of Exeter in 1634, and related to the Robert Lugg (of St. John's, Oxford) who graduated 1638. ROBERT RAMSEY graduated Mus.Bac. Cantab. in 1616; there are many anthems and services by this composer at Ely and Peterhouse, and some in his autograph at Anderson's College, Glasgow. Herrick's translation of Horace's 'Donec gratus' (1627) was set by Ramsey; and other secular pieces are in Addit. MSS. 11,608 and 17,786–91. In 1631 Ramsey was Master of the Children of Trinity College, Cambridge. A complete service and a canon by Ramsey are in Tudway's collections, and an anthem is mentioned in Clifford (1664). The brothers Lawes, prominent towards the end of this period, belong more properly to the next.

Of the instrumentalists, ANTHONY HOLBORNE, who published the 'Cittharn Schoole' in 1597, was a Court musician; the book contains six 'Napolitains' by his brother. There are four pieces of A. Holborne's in

Fullsack's collection (Hamburg, 1607), and another in R. Dowland's 'Musical Banquet.' THOMAS ROBINSON was also probably a Court musician; in his 'Schoole of Musicke' there are 'Toys' (a word apparently used at the time for light music), and some pieces for two lutes with psalms in tablature. His 'New Citharen Lessons' include a piece for two citterns, two for voice with cittern and gamba (wrongly printed, like Tailour's Psalter), and some lessons for a cittern with fourteen 'course' of strings.

WILLIAM BRADE was a violist and composer who led a wandering life. He was appointed at the Danish Court, 1594-6, and again later; and was also at Hamburg, at Gottorp, and at Berlin. In 1622 he was again at Gottorp. His publications are detailed on p. 169.

The Thomas Tomkins who had contributed to the Orianas had six sons, all probably musicians. JOHN TOMKINS was born in 1586, was organist of King's College in 1606, and graduated Mus.Bac. in 1608. He belonged to the Chapel Royal, and in 1622 was organist of St. Paul's. He died September 27th, 1638, and was buried in the Cathedral. Anthems by him are in Myriell's part-books, and elsewhere. GILES TOMKINS was organist at King's College after his brother, and in 1630 succeeded Deering in the Royal Household; he was soon after at Salisbury Cathedral as Master of the Children. In 1634 Laud was informed that Tomkins was called to the Chapel Royal occasionally, and left the choir-boys uncared for. Tomkins was still at Salisbury when he died in 1668.

THOMAS TOMKINS, the most prominent of the brothers, was born in Pembrokeshire, probably about 1585–90, and graduated Mus.Bac. Oxon. in 1607. He then became organist of Worcester Cathedral, and also of the Chapel Royal in 1621. He was nominated composer for voices and wind in 1628, but King Charles revoked the warrant. He had issued a collection of 'Songs' (sacred and secular madrigals) in 1622–3. They are dedicated to the Earl of Pembroke; and each has also a separate dedication to a musician. 'My ancient and much reverenced master, Mr. Byrd,' Tomkins's father, his five brothers, his son,

Dr. Dowland, Myriell, Carlton, Coperario, Will. White, O. Gibbons, Danyel, H. Molle, Dr. Heather, and Dr. Gyles are among the dedicatees. Tomkins sided with Manwaring, the Laudian dean of Worcester, against the bishop and townsmen; he is not heard of during the troubles. He died, and was buried in a Worcestershire village, June, 1656. A great collection of his sacred music, published 1668, is entitled *Musica Deo Sacra et Ecclesiæ Anglicanæ*. It contains five Services and ninety-eight anthems, in four part-books, with separate organ part of 337 pages. One anthem, 'O praise the Lord all ye heathen,' is twelve-voiced. The important MS. 29,996 (see Chapter IV) was completed by Tomkins.

JOHN WARD in 1613 published twenty-eight good madrigals; one of these, 'Die not, fond man, before thy day,' is still much sung. Since Barnard printed an Evening Service and two verse-anthems of Warde's, the latter must have been dead before 1641. One of the anthems, 'Let God arise,' has a very elaborate organ part. Ward assisted in Ravenscroft's Psalter.

MARTIN PEERSON (Pearson, Pierson) was 'born, as it seems, at Ely,' according to A. Wood. He graduated Mus.Bac. Oxon. in 1613. Many of his anthems are preserved in Myriell; and he contributed to Leighton's collection. His publications both incline to the accompanied school rather than the pure polyphony of the madrigals. The first appeared in 1620, and is entitled *Private Musicke*; it is complete at Oxford, incomplete at the British Museum; a full-choir-book, facing different ways, with a bass part under the cantus. This is explained by the title, which asserts that the work 'being Verse and Chorus is fit for Voyces and Viols, and for want of Viols they may be performed to either the Virginall or Lute, where the proficient can play upon the Ground, or for a shift to the Base Viol alone.' It is evident Peerson did not anticipate unaccompanied singing. One of the pieces was composed in 1604 for the 'King and Queen's Maying at Highgate.' In 1630 followed 'Mottects, or Grave Chamber Musique'; these are twenty-three madrigals, and an elegy on Sir Fulke Grevil, Lord Brooke.

Besides five part-books, this work includes a separate
organ part, consisting of a figured bass and a melody.
This publication may be considered the last of the madrigal collections, and the bridge to the style of the next
period. Peerson was at this time Master of the Children
at St. Paul's. It appears, by Laud's visitation in 1636,
that Peerson had sustained some loss which Laud had
repaired; and though Peerson's duties were at an end
in 1642, he was able to bequeath £100 to the poor of
Doddington-cum-March, near Ely, when he died in 1650.
He was buried in the chapel of St. Faith, under the Cathedral. Some of his Fancies for viols are remarkably good.

JOHN HILTON, who published a collection of madrigals
in 1627, issued a more important work under the
Commonwealth, and is therefore left to the next chapter.

JOHN AMNER became organist of Ely in 1610. He
graduated Mus.Bac. Oxon. in 1613, and was incorporated
at Cambridge in 1640, dying in 1641. Much Church
music of his, both Services and anthems, is preserved at
Ely, Peterhouse, and Christ Church. His only publication, 'Sacred Hymnes,' appeared in 1615; it consists of
twenty-five madrigals (some marked 'A Mottect,' others
'An Alleluia'), with an elegy on Thomas Hynson.
There is a Latin text at the foot of nearly every page.

William Gibbons, one of the Waits of Cambridge, had
three sons who were all choir-boys at King's College,
and became leading musicians, the youngest being among
the most gifted composers England has ever produced.
The eldest, EDWARD GIBBONS, born about 1565, was
organist of King's College; he graduated Mus.Bac.
Cantab., being incorporated at Oxford in 1592, and soon
after was organist at Bristol Cathedral. In 1611 he
became one of the priest-vicars, though he was a layman,
of Exeter Cathedral, where he remained till the Puritan
army took Exeter in 1645. In Walker's *Sufferings of
the Clergy* it is asserted that Gibbons had made two rich
marriages, and advanced £1,000 to Charles I, but was
turned out of his home when over eighty years old. An
anthem by E. Gibbons is at Ely, and in score in Tudway's
collection, and an In Nomine at Oxford.

ELLIS GIBBONS, the second brother, has been mentioned as a contributor to the Orianas, when he was organist of Salisbury Cathedral.

ORLANDO GIBBONS, the youngest brother, was, on the whole, the greatest musician who appeared after Byrd in this period, and remains one of the greatest in our history. He was born in 1583; in 1596 he was at King's College under his brother Edward, but already in 1604 he succeeded Arthur Cock as organist to the Chapel Royal. About 1609, or later, he published a set of nine Fancies for three viols; these were reprinted in score by the Musical Antiquarian Society, and are remarkably fine specimens of contrapuntal music, No. 1 especially so. In 1611 Gibbons joined Byrd and Bull in publishing *Parthenia*; it should be remembered that the 'ancient and much reverenced' Byrd and the astonishing performer Dr. Bull were much the seniors of young Gibbons, and it is an interesting fact in the publication of 'the first music ever printed for the virginals,' that one of the three composers was about seventy years old, another about fifty, while their associate was only twenty-eight. In Gibbons's share there is a very fine fantasia. In 1612 appeared Gibbons's glorious five-voiced madrigals, which are represented in the popular mind by one only, 'The silver swan,' but that one is among the most familiar of all madrigals; 'Dainty fine bird' is another splendid work often sung. The whole collection was printed by the Musical Antiquarian Society. Gibbons published no more except a contribution to Leighton and the tunes to Wither's Psalter. In May, 1622, he supplicated for a degree at Oxford, and was created Mus.Doc. with Heather (see p. 222). The correspondence is given in Hawkins's *History of Music*. In 1623 Gibbons became organist at Westminster Abbey; but he died two years later.* He had gone with the Court to Canterbury for the marriage of Charles I; while there he died of apoplexy, on Whit Sunday, June 5th, 1625. A drunken Groom of the Vestry had badly hurt him in 1620. He was buried in the Cathedral, leaving several children; the two sons became

* For biographical details see *Musical Herald*, Dec., 1919.

musicians, and one will be heard of again. The other, called after his father, seems to have made no mark.

Orlando Gibbons, in spite of his distinction as a madrigalist and instrumental composer, is most celebrated for his immortal ecclesiastical music. Barnard, in 1641, printed two Services, Preces, and four anthems; Ouseley's complete edition in score appeared in 1873. The Service in F, and the wonderful anthems, 'O clap your hands,' 'Almighty and everlasting God,' and especially 'Hosanna to the Son of David,' are above all praise, and are fortunately so familiar in our cathedrals that they need description as little as does 'The silver swan.' In them we may see the return to contrapuntal writing in its noblest form, and the superiority to the heavy style of Tallis's Dorian Service is obvious. The difficulty of performance is, of course, increased, and the words, upon the clear enunciation of which the Reformers had laid such stress, are less intelligible; but the Anglican Service was now perfectly familiar to the nation. The anthems, still finer than the Service in F, are among the most beautiful specimens of polyphonic writing ever produced. In the complete edition there are eleven full anthems, and twelve with verses, two of which have an accompaniment for viols. Confusion of tonality is not quite absent.

Gibbons was not a man of his age as regards the monodic style, which he apparently did not even attempt. His improvements lay in another direction; and as the creator of the contrapuntal Anglican ecclesiastical music he is best entitled to remembrance. In this he was musically the representative of that party in the Church which followed Hooker, Bancroft, and Andrewes, in reverencing externals, and turning away from the Genevan theology. Musically, this school was probably limited to the Chapel Royal; and Gibbons did not live to see the short triumph of sacerdotalism which brought on the Civil War. He was much more fortunate than his predecessors, in being unrestrained in his ecclesiastical music by the fetters which had been too ponderous even for Tallis; and when we remember his Service in F, his anthem, 'Hosanna to the Son of David,' his madrigal,

'The silver swan,' and the assistance he gave to the creation of structural formative music by his Fantasies, we must agree that he was the ablest musician of his time in Europe, except as regards the dramatic style.

A few words are necessary concerning the introduction of music into the Elizabethan and early Stuart dramas. There were instrumental performances between the acts, the players being probably stationed in a box at the side. In *Gorboduc* (1562), the very beginning of Elizabethan drama, there is a dumb show before each act, accompanied by instruments. Violins play before the first act; cornets before the second; flutes before the third; hautboys, for the appearance of Furies, before the fourth; drums and flutes before the last. Similarly in Hughes's *Misfortunes of Arthur* (1587), and *Jocasta*. Evidently the 'Consort' of various instruments, so much admired by Prætorius, had not then been invented. In *Fedele and Fortunio* (1584) a dance is prescribed to be played in each interval. Marston's *Sophonisba* (1606) directs 'infernal music' during an incantation; also 'a bass lute and treble violl for the act.' In Beaumont and Fletcher's *Knight of the Burning Pestle*, Dowland's 'Lachrymæ' is played. Much singing is employed in the later Elizabethan comedies; and even many tragedies have a 'singing part' (as, for instance, Valerius in T. Heywood's *Lucrece*). The unpublished plays collected by Warburton, or rather the sorry remnant now in Lansdowne MS. 807, have preserved three songs. Morley's setting of 'It was a lover and his lass' was included in his Ayres (1600). The incantation scene in Middleton's *Witch*, interpolated in Davenant's arrangement of *Macbeth*, had music composed by ROBERT JOHNSON, probably a relative of the various Johnsons mentioned on pp. 137 and 186; it is published in *Musica Antiqua*. Robert Johnson, who was one of Prince Henry's lutenists, also composed the music for Shakespeare's *Tempest*; and afterwards songs for Fletcher's *Valentinian* and *Mad Lover*, and Ben Jonson's (his relative?) *Masque of the Gipsies*. These are in part preserved. One of the 'Consort Songs' in Leighton's collection, and pieces in later publications, are by

Johnson. It was in the Masques (see p. 177) that dramatic music was most employed.

Until Byrd's patent expired, all the music published in London was issued by Thomas East; then William Barley entered the field, and obtained an assignment of Morley's patent. East also continued to publish till his death in 1609, when Thomas Snodham succeeded him; and John Windet issued some works. Their type-printing was very rough; Adson's collection (1621) is scarcely legible. Engraving was introduced; and W. Hole executed the plates of Gibbons's 'Fantasies,' of *Parthenia*, and Notari's *Nuove Musiche* in a neat and finished manner.

Of miscellaneous musical events the most important were the creations of a Gresham Professor of Music in 1596, and of an Oxford Professor in 1627. The appointment of a Professor of Music had been specially desired in Sir Thomas Gresham's will; and Dr. Bull was selected on the recommendation of Queen Elizabeth. Byrd's son acted as his deputy in 1601. Upon Bull's resignation in 1607 a physician named Clayton succeeded him, then Taverner, a clergyman, followed in 1610, and actually not one single musician was appointed for a century and a half! The intentions of the munificent founder were most grossly disregarded, and only one distinguished man in any class was ever selected—Sir William Petty, the scientist, who was appointed during the Commonwealth. The lectures of Taverner, remarkable only for classical pedantry, may be seen in Sloane MS. 2329.

The Oxford Professorship was endowed by Dr. William Heather (Heyther). He was a lay vicar of Westminster Abbey, a Gentleman of the Chapel Royal, and a friend of Camden, whose endowment of a Professorship of History he bore to the University, for which he was made Mus.Doc. in 1622. Gibbons's 'O clap your hands' was sung, according to tradition, at the admission of Heather and Gibbons. On February 2nd, 1626–7, Heather founded the 'Musicke Lecture,' endowing it with £3 a year; and a Choragus, who was to maintain weekly practices in the Music School, and to take charge of the books and instruments given by Heather, received £13 6s. 8d. The lectures were hardly ever given; and the Choragus was soon called Professor of Music. In 1848 the offices were separated, and in 1856 a Coryphœus (or Precentor) was instituted. The duties of all three officials were then distinctly defined; and the ability and zeal of the Professors has much advanced musical culture in Oxford.

Heather selected, as the Choragus, Richard Nicholson, Mus.Bac., organist of Magdalen College, and a contributor to 'The Triumphs of Oriana.' The instruments bequeathed disappeared during the turmoil of the Civil War; as did also the volumes of music, but most of these were returned after the Restoration, and are still in the Music School. They include Forrest's collection of Masses, many volumes of madrigals, and Adson's 'Courtly Masquing Ayres.' A fresh collection of instruments and some new works were obtained after the Restoration; a great amount of instrumental music was presented at this time. The latter still remains; the instruments were destroyed or sold about 1850.

We may now sum up the results of the Madrigalian Period. It must have begun even in Henry VIII's time, if Surrey composed his own music to 'Ye dainty dames'; certainly a few years later, when the Mulliner Book was written, and so fortunately for us preserved 'In going to my naked bed' and the other secular music of Edwards, Robert Johnson, and Tallis. In 1588 began the culminating period of English music, the central time. The preceding period had, on the whole, been greater in ecclesiastical music; the next period was greater in concerted instrumental music; the later seventeenth century was greater in dramatic music, and produced the rarest individual genius England can boast. But the Shakespearian age saw the climax of English music as a whole, the madrigals, the ayres, the keyboard music, the contrapuntal Anglican sacred music. The entire result is a magnificent monument of the nation's genius. Thousands of motets, anthems, madrigals, ayres, and ballets, hundreds of fancies, variations, dances, and programme - pieces still exist; unchanged by time, unaffected by fashion, undisturbed by non-appreciation, these beautiful conceptions have remained immortal in their loveliness. And what is specially to be remembered, as Ambros noticed, is the fact that the school has never been forgotten or neglected. During the Commonwealth Playford was selling the madrigals of Wilbye, the ballets of Morley, the ayres of Campion. In the eighteenth century the Academy of Ancient Music was performing the madrigals of Byrd, Morley, Wilbye, Farmer, Weelkes, and Bennet. The foundation of the Madrigal Society in 1741, and its continuance to this day; the issue of hundreds of works in score, their inclusion in the cheapest publications, all point to a delight in our great old composers such as no other nation shows. The Netherlanders (except a few enthusiasts such as Dr. Lange) do little for their fine ancient secular music; the Italians care still less for theirs; France and Germany had scarcely any. Of the music composed between 1550 and 1630 it is only the English which has secured a permanent hold, which is more than a research and study for antiquaries, and which has been performed without intermission through the three centuries. It may be admitted that ordinary knowledge is limited to a comparatively few specimens, though our choral societies perform a fair number; a collection containing one representative example from each composer would be a boon. The popular editions generally omit one or more verses of the ayres. It may also be freely admitted that our professional musicians do not, as a rule, realise how fine and important these immortal masterpieces are, and do not sufficiently display them to the rest of the world. By the irony of fate our principal musical historian was quite insensible to the merits of the style, and has written in a most contemptuous tone of madrigals generally; and though he has been quite alone in his opinion, yet there has generally been too strong a propensity to look upon the Elizabethan madrigals, and the sacred music also, as household possessions which we ourselves may duly prize, but which are not sufficiently important to be spoken of before the world. Let any who have this feeling read the chapter on English music in the third volume of Ambros's History, and learn how admirably one of the very greatest authorities has spoken of those few works, sacred and secular, with which he had made acquaintance.* The best Elizabethan madrigals are, like Shakespeare's sonnets, priceless gems, imperishable, flawless art-works. To know something of the poetry, something of the music, ought to be a part of every Englishman's and English-woman's education. Let us hope that so it may be in the future; then, as the English language more and more overspreads the globe, these beautiful poems and beautiful sounds will never be silent, and the air will continually vibrate with their music, even as it now probably never for one moment ceases to reverberate the words of Shakespeare.

* The Imperial Library at Vienna subscribed to the Musical Antiquarian Society. If Ambros had known this we should have had his judgment on the madrigals of Wilbye, Gibbons, Weelkes, Bateson, and Bennet. ' Since first I saw your face' has been much sung in Germany.

CHAPTER VI

THE AGE OF THE DECLAMATORY SONGS, OF THE FANCIES FOR VIOLS, AND OF THE SUPPRESSION OF ECCLESIASTICAL MUSIC (1630-1660)

Disappearance of polyphonic vocal writing.—The connection of the monodic school with the song-poets.—The Puritan Archbishop Abbot succeeded by Laud.—The Laudian Sacerdotalism.—Barnard's 'Selected Church Musick.'—Outbreak of the Civil War and suppression of organs and choirs.—The exaggerated accusations of later musical historians.—Refutation of these slanders upon the Puritans.—Brilliant period of secular music during the Commonwealth. —Playford sets up as music-publisher.—Cromwell's patronage of the art.—The instrumental 'Fancies.'—Introduction of opera and of violin-execution.—List of the collections published during the Commonwealth.—Pride of the English at this time in their instrumental music.—The Quakers abjure all music.—Eccles's testimony.—A challenge to objectors.

DURING this period the connection of musical history with general English history was more prominent and essential than at any other time; and since it has been more misrepresented than any other, I shall have to discuss the matter somewhat in detail.

In the year 1630 the change which had demolished the Palestrina school in Italy had also been completed in England. In each country secular composition was more cultivated than ecclesiastical, though for different reasons. Opera and the violin absorbed most of the energy of Italian musicians; and Frescobaldi was advancing the organ style. In England attention was mainly occupied by the declamatory Ayres and Dialogues, and the Fancies for viols. There was a temporary recrudescence of ecclesiastical music, which was speedily put down altogether. There was a great decline in music-publishing; but during the Commonwealth it was resumed. The keyboard-execution appears to have somewhat declined from the Elizabethan standard, and before the end

of the period both Italy and Germany were superior to
England in this respect, though the English did not yet
believe it.

The sonnet which Milton addressed to Henry Lawes
exactly expresses the merits of the Ayres and Dialogues,
which form the principal portion of the vocal music
during this period and part of the next. Large collections were published during the Commonwealth and
afterwards, showing that they must have been in general
favour. Their character cannot be fully appreciated
without some knowledge of the contemporary poetry.
Poetry and music were at this time most intimately
connected, though no longer produced by the same man.
The leading musicians and the leading poets were on
intimate terms, and the poets continually proclaimed their
appreciation. The music acted on the songs; the songs
again on the music. This was the flower-time of song-
writing, the age which produced Suckling, Lovelace,
Wither, Carew, Brome, Waller, and, above all, Herrick.
They have remained to this day the most popular of our
song-writers, though Herrick was forgotten during the
eighteenth century. There is in most of their works a
somewhat artificial sentiment, which prevents them being
in the hearts and minds of Englishmen so entirely and
universally as the songs of Burns and Moore are in the
hearts, minds, and tongues of Scotchmen and Irishmen;
yet many phrases from their songs have passed into the
language. Most of them were Court poets, and wrote for
cultivated society rather than for the nation; but they
enjoyed immense appreciation. Herrick in his remote
vicarage wrote with truer taste; and his works have
proved the most enduring.

The delight of the educated public in this style of
poetry was still further increased by a species of composition admirably calculated to display and illustrate the
words, though in itself uninteresting. The poems were
set to a succession of notes, the relative lengths of which
were chosen so as to make prominent those syllables
which were required to be prominent by the sense of the
words and the prosody of the metres, the latter frequently

of great complication. Such a style—the *arioso parlante*—
is, strictly speaking, not musical but literary; if the best
specimens are played on an instrument instead of being
sung, then they sound poor, almost absurd. The audience
at a performance of any such should think only of following the words; then the declamatory music will be
appreciated. As in Campion's ayres, the settings in triple
time were those which approached tunes nearer than the
others did.

We now read of solo-singing in a manner which
implies an entirely different method and much higher
style of performance than had been practised by the older
musicians. Singing, as it was taught in the treatises of
Bathe and Morley, signifies only a knowledge of notation;
of voice-production or expression there is no mention.
The same had been the case in Italy, as we know from the
exact description of Delle Valle; dramatic expression was
first introduced by the Florentine monodic school. We
must suppose that Lawes and the other musicians of this
period were distinguished as declamatory singers. The
highly cultivated aristocracy must have thoroughly appreciated the intellectual union of good poetry and expressive declamation. Especially the Dialogues, usually
to amatory words, were doubtless great favourites with
the courtly lovers of the time. The question-and-answer
form (used by Coperario in the last of the 'Funeral
Teares') was a favourite method; but a persuasive form,
the lady first rejecting, then yielding, was naturally a
popular form of the love-poems. At the last verse the
two voices usually joined, the union being called *Chorus*.
George Herbert wrote an anthem in dialogue between a
Christian and Death; and another (for Christmas) was
set by Ford. The form was repeatedly used in Herrick's
poetry.

The higher cultivation of singing caused a predominance of solo works, and polyphonic vocal music
was neglected. After Peerson's 'Mottects' (1630) no
more madrigals are known, unless the two collections of
Porter's be counted; the poetry shows these to have been
ayres rather than madrigals, and they had independent

accompaniments. But from 1630–50 little music of any kind was published; and what appeared was of little importance, excepting Barnard's collection.

Polyphony, abandoned in secular vocal music, was more than ever cultivated in the Fancies; and immense numbers of works for viols were composed at this time.* If the keyboard music had been of equal importance, then the reign of Charles I and the Commonwealth would have been the greatest English period as regards instrumental music; but no advance seems to have been made upon the Elizabethan virginalists and organists. *Parthenia* was reprinted in 1635, also twice during the Commonwealth; no fresh collection was issued until 1657. In 1638 Michael East published his last work, a set of twenty-nine pieces for viols; it was reprinted during the Commonwealth, when much other music of the same kind also appeared. The Fancies for viols frequently had figured-bass accompaniments.

Besides the contrapuntal Fancies, lighter works founded upon dance forms were composed; and these were frequently for two parts only, and seem inexplicably thin. Very many were published by Playford in 1651 and 1655; and some appeared in 1678. That such slight and short pieces should have been the work of composers who also produced the elaborate contrapuntal Fancies seems puzzling.

Turning to dramatic music we find several events of the highest importance. Masques were still cultivated during the reign of Charles I; when Shirley's *Triumph of Peace* was acted at the Inns of Court in 1633, £100 each was paid to W. Lawes and Simon Ives for the music. In the following year the most celebrated of all masques, Milton's *Comus* was written and performed. It is a point of some interest, as will be shown, that *Comus* was written for Ludlow Castle, not for London or the Court. The theatres were closed during the Civil War; and though an attempt was made to re-open them in 1647, it was suppressed. After the King's

* A MS. written at Stockholm, with the date 1641, includes pieces by Byrd, Bull, Phillips, and Tomkins.

execution, the actors petitioned that they might be allowed to perform for a time upon trial of good behaviour; but it does not appear that their request was granted. Shirley's masque, *Cupid and Death*, was acted before the Portuguese ambassador in 1653; the music, by Lock and Christopher Gibbons, is still preserved. Plays, though still illegal, were occasionally acted in a quasi-surreptitious manner during the Commonwealth. In 1656 a serious attempt was made by Davenant to evade the law against plays, by the introduction of *opera*. This was accomplished by a mixed entertainment performed at Rutland House, Aldersgate Street, on May 23rd; and speedily followed by true operatic performances, though on a small scale. These seem to have been tolerated, and thenceforward they went on without interruption till the Restoration. A question was raised, concerning their legality, in Richard Cromwell's parliament; but apparently they were not meddled with, and still continued. They will be further described later in this chapter.

But the most prominent musical matter during this age was the suppression of ecclesiastical music for nearly twenty years. The great bulk of the nation inclined more or less towards Puritanism, but in 1630 the sacerdotal and anti-Genevan school of theologians was acquiring power in the Church. Ceremonies instead of preaching, and reverence for externals, were studied and inculcated. The symbolism dear to contemplative men was revived. George Herbert became vicar of Bemerton. Nicholas Ferrar had established an Anglican monastic establishment at Little Gidding. Cosin was at Durham. More important still, the most conscientious, thorough-going, and uncompromising man of the whole party was Bishop of London, and had been promised the Archbishopric of Canterbury.

Good evidence that reverence in externals had not always been cultivated in the Chapel Royal itself may be seen in the statutes issued by Laud in 1632. The Gentlemen were required 'to come in decent manner in their gowns and surplices, and not in cloaks and surplices, nor with boots and spurs.' In the following year Abbot

died, and on August 6th King Charles addressed Laud as
'My Lord's Grace of Canterbury.'

Never had the nation seemed further from civil war
than then. England had been sixty years without even
a serious riot. There were no dynastic questions; no
dangers from abroad; no warlike barons with crowds of
retainers at home. But the appointment of Laud, and
his influence with the King, made an outbreak certain.
He was personally unpopular; and the whole body of
the nobility was further disgusted when the King made
Juxon the Lord High Treasurer. The clergy of that age
were not of gentle birth or socially respected; and rank
was a very important thing, in every Englishman's opinion.
The Puritan Lord Brooke no doubt spoke the mind of
the whole nation when he attacked bishops as low-born
upstarts who presumed to thrust themselves among the
nobility, and even into the King's Council. Every London
apprentice, every country farmer was offended as truly
as the nobility, when Churchmen were put into high
places. Laud cared to conciliate nobody, and for seven
years exercised unbounded authority in matters ecclesiastical, with great severity upon offenders of every description, both in doctrine and morals. In Scotland the yoke
was thrown off in 1637.

The Anglican Church was sadly in need of an
organising head; and the Laudian principles were finally
adopted, and rule at the present day, though only the
abandonment of Laud's methods made them possible.
In Abbot's long rule theology had been thought of more
consequence than discipline. Laud, on removing to
Lambeth Palace, immediately restored the ornate services,
and re-erected the organ. Elaborate ritual was encouraged
everywhere. Fuller states that many organs were built
at Cambridge in 1633–4; Cosin was made Master of
Peterhouse, and to this we owe the later sets of MSS.
there. These contain a great number of services and
anthems, mostly by musicians of this time, with a few
by Tallis, Byrd, and other Elizabethans, in all sixty-two
composers. Some volumes written at Durham after the
Restoration have similar contents.

At the same time Robert Dallam built a new organ for York Cathedral; one at Canterbury followed in 1635; Harris built one at Magdalen College, Oxford, in 1637.

Laud in 1634 held a visitation of the Province of Canterbury. Some of the replies to his questions exist among the MSS. of the House of Lords; occasionally there are matters of interest concerning the organists and choirs. In several cases there are allusions to frequent absences due to attendance at the Chapel Royal. At Canterbury it was stated:

'In lieu of a deacon and subdeacon, whose office it was to read the Epistle and Gospel (supplied now by the Dean, prebendaries, and petticanons), are substituted two corniters and two sackbutters, whom we most willingly maintain for the decorum of our quire, though with greater charge than we might have done the other.'

The allusions to Giles Tomkins, Edward Gibbons, Elway Bevin, and Martin Peerson have been mentioned in the preceding chapter. At Exeter the vicars-choral, G. Randall, John Lugg, and Robert Parsons, reported that they had 'a most skilful organist,' but do not name him. Laud ordered the Chapter of Lichfield Cathedral to improve 'the organes,' recommending 'that you putt them both into one, and make a chayre organ of them.'

Laud was apparently himself musical. In his will he bequeathed the organ at Lambeth to the see; the organ at Croydon, his harp, chest of viols, and harpsichord, with £50, to John Cob, probably his household musician. In the Peterhouse part-books, and in Tudway's scores, there is another anthem composed by 'Laud'; and at Peterhouse and Durham there is also an 'Easter Anthem' by 'Juxon.' I take these to have been the archbishop and his successor.

In Scotland the only musical result of the attempt to establish Episcopacy was the harmonised Psalter published by Edward Miller, of Holyrood Chapel, in 1635; Miller says the harmonisings were by 'the primest musicians that ever this kingdom had, as John Deane Angus, Blackhall, Smith, Peebles, Sharp, Black, Buchan, and others, famous for their skill in this kind.' It was reprinted in 1864. At the outbreak against the Liturgy in 1637 the organ which James I had set up at Holyrood was destroyed, the choir turned away, and all the Scotch ecclesiastical music stopped.

The English ecclesiastical music had only five years more to prosper before the storm burst. The ill-success of the King's expeditions against the Scots brought the calling of the Long Parliament. All the pent-up anger of the nation broke out. Laud and other bishops were sent to the Tower. Both Houses joined in an irresistible attack on the remains of feudalism. One of the earliest Churchmen attacked was Dr. Cosin, who, in answer to a charge of worshipping saints, protested that he had cut out of the Durham choir-books an 'Anthem of the Three Kings of Colen.'

Just at this time, and not a day too soon, came the principal publication in the reign of Charles I, to whom it was dedicated. This was a great collection of church music, both services and anthems, edited by John Barnard, minor canon of St. Paul's. Barnard stated in his preface that he had included only works by deceased masters, and that a collection of living composers' works would follow. This promise he did not fulfil, doubtless owing to the war. The title was 'The First Book of Selected Church Musick.' Unfortunately it was issued in ten part-books, and was never reprinted. An organ part is absolutely necessary, but none has ever been discovered. Some copies were doubtless destroyed during the Civil War; others were worn out by long use, until in the middle of the eighteenth century it was found that no complete set remained, though there were eight of the ten at Hereford Cathedral. In 1862 another set of eight was bought by the Sacred Harmonic Society; this set contained the two missing (one being duplicate) from the Hereford set, which was accordingly completed by the duplicate and a transcript of the other (the medius cantoris).* Several of both sets were imperfect; but by the aid of other copies at Lichfield, and Batten's organ-book, a complete score was made by John Bishop of Cheltenham. It is now in the British Museum as Addit.

* This set has been sold to Christ Church, Oxford.

MSS. 30,085–7. I think it probable that not many copies of Barnard's work were issued. The printing is fairly good; the words are in a very singular and quaint character, which should not be overlooked by students of ecclesiastical art under the Stuarts. The contents of Barnard's collection were:

Complete Services by Tallis, Strogers, Bevin, Byrd, W. Mundy, Parsons, Morley, and Dr. Gyles, and two by O. Gibbons; *Evening Services* by Ward and Morley, and two by Byrd; a *Te Deum* by L. Woodson; *Preces* and *Psalms* by Tallis, Byrd, and Gibbons; *Responses* and *Litany* by Tallis; forty-two *Full Anthems*—by Tallis (5), Tye (6), Byrd (6), Hooper (3), Farrant (2), Shepherd (2), W. Mundy (3), O. Gibbons (5), Batten (6), R. Whyte, Gyles, Persons, and Weelkes; twelve *Anthems with Verses*—by Byrd (5), Ward (2), W. Mundy, Morley, Gibbons, Batten, and Dr. Bull.

Most of these are still sung, and nearly all the best works of the English polyphonists are to be found here. Causton is unrepresented, and Whyte has but one piece; the task of selection must have been most difficult, as an enormous amount of ecclesiastical music had been left by the Elizabethan and Jacobean composers, of whom nearly 200 are mentioned in the previous chapters. Among the MSS. at the Royal College are seven part-books of 130 services and anthems, apparently collected by Barnard when preparing his work.

The Verse-Anthems all require an organ part; without Batten's MS. this could not have been supplied. Byrd's 'O Lord, rebuke me not,' begins with an unaccompanied solo; but otherwise all the verse-passages have a polyphonic accompaniment, the most elaborate being that to Ward's 'Let God arise.'

Another publication which has hitherto * escaped attention and is not in Bullen's catalogue is known by a single copy in the British Museum. This is a reprint of the *Siren cœlestis* published at Munich by G. Victorinus in 1616. The English reprint, dated 1638, contains the two-voiced pieces only; they are written in a figure notation on Tonic Sol-fa principles, thus resembling the Galin-Paris-Chevé method. Time-divisions are expressed by dots. There are twenty-seven pieces, by Agazzari,

* Except in Eitner's *Bibliographie*, whence I became aware of it.

Cifra, etc. This was the only instance since the publications of Lassus and Croce (1606) of an English reprint of foreign sacred music; and (with Filmer's translation of French part-songs in 1629) was an indication of the slight Romanist element due to the Queen, Henrietta Maria.

Church music was an early object of attack in the Long Parliament. On March 12th, 1641, the House of Lords appointed a committee, including ten bishops, to report upon ecclesiastical matters; a sub-committee (with four bishops) conferred with divines of various parties, and prepared a report, in which one of the Memoranda for Reformation was:

'That the music used in cathedral and collegiate churches be framed with less curiosity; and that no hymns or anthems be used where ditties are framed by private men, but such as are contained in the Holy Scriptures, or in our liturgy or prayers, or have public allowance.'

Among the recent 'Innovations' reported were the use of Latin in the service, at Oxford and Cambridge; and singing the Te Deum in prose in parish churches. The former allegation was in part directed at Cosin.

If matters had gone no farther, little or no harm would have ensued; but the Genevan theology was prominent in the House of Commons, and an attack upon cathedrals began soon after. Hacket, prebendary of St. Paul's, was selected to defend them, and was heard at the bar of the House on May 12th. He apparently referred little to music, beyond recommending that it should be made simpler, thus, in substance, advocating a return to the harmonic style. Afterwards, Dr. Cornelius Burges spoke on the other side; and especially attacked cathedral choirs. He pointed out (as Bishop Earle had done in his *Microcosmography*) the drunken habits of the choirmen, who when leaving the cathedrals went to the alehouses; and he denounced music in churches as 'useless and hurtful.' Nothing was resolved on at this time.

The Puritans in the House of Commons continually raised their demands; and after the summer recess the Irish Rebellion embittered them more than ever. A year earlier all the nation, though it was a period of singular prosperity, was burning with indignation against the Government; now there were two parties in Parliament as in the country. London was strongly Puritan; a letter in the Coke MSS., dated September 20th, 1641, says: 'Upon Sunday last I hear an assembly of them would have come into the Church in Paul's to have overthrowne the organs and defaced divers other ornaments.' A mob kept the bishops out of the House of Lords. The breach grew ever wider; Falkland and other Episcopalians joined the Royalist party, the King tried to seize the leading Puritan members, and in the summer of 1642 war was declared.

The hatred of the Puritans to bishops, cathedrals, and ornate services now had full play. Almost on the very day the King set up his standard the soldiery ruined the organ at Canterbury Cathedral and 'mangled the service-books, bestrewing the pavement with the leaves.' The organ at Rochester, having been threatened by the same army, was taken down and set up in a tavern at Greenwich. Soon afterwards the Earl of Essex's army destroyed the organ at Worcester. At Westminster Abbey the soldiers carried off the organ pipes and bartered them at the alehouses. When Sir William Waller's army took Chichester the organ was hewn down with pole-axes and the choir-books thrown about in derision; and at Exeter some of the soldiers marched along the streets blowing the pipes of the organ they had pulled down. The poet Wild, a Puritan soldier, described similar mischief at Winchester, where a bonfire was made of the choir-books; similarly at Norwich by the townsmen under Alderman Lindsay and the sheriff. The library of Lichfield was burnt in the siege; it is worth recording that its special treasure, the Gospels of St. Chad, was saved by Higgins, the precentor, and there are still seven volumes of Barnard's collection there. At Peterborough, Cromwell's own regiment destroyed the organ and library, and Cromwell himself wrote to Ely requiring a cessation of the 'choir service, so unedifying and offensive,' and as this command was ignored, visited Ely himself and stopped the service in the middle. *Mercurius*

Rusticus (published at Oxford), by Ryves, Dean of Chichester, gives some account of these outrages; but in most cases he writes avowedly upon hearsay, and the book was subsequently reprinted without further information.*

The organs of that age were but small and easily replaced. After the early fights the Royalist cause prospered in the West; and cathedral services were doubtless resumed at Exeter and Worcester for two or three years more. There was an organ at Exeter which, after the final surrender, was taken out into the churchyard till it was sold in 1657. The last city to hold out was Worcester; on the morning of the surrender to Fairfax and Cromwell, 22nd July, 1646, many Royalist officers attended the cathedral service, the last in England.

In the meantime the Lords and Commons at Westminster were proceeding in the same path with legal steps. On January 26th, 1643, a Bill for the total abolition of Episcopacy was passed. On May 9th, 1644, organs were included with 'superstitious monuments' in an Act which enjoined their complete removal from all churches and colleges. This was soon effected in most cases, though there were some striking exceptions; among the organs untouched being those of Old St. Paul's, York, Durham, and Lincoln Cathedrals; St. John's and Magdalen Colleges, Oxford; and Christ's College, Cambridge. When the war closed in 1646 a great and fundamental change had come over English music. There were no more cathedral services maintaining organists and singers and training choir-boys. The Chapel Royal itself had been disbanded. The interruption lasted fourteen years more.

Thus a distinct break in the history of English ecclesiastical music occurred; and though not a long one, it was further widened by the new style introduced by Charles II.

* At our cathedrals all destruction, whether the work of the early Reformers or the Puritans, is commonly ascribed to ' Cromwell's soldiers '; justly so as regards Peterborough, but Peterborough only. The other Puritan mischief was done in the early months of the war, when Cromwell was only a troop-captain stationed at Cambridge. It is strange that neither Gardiner in ' The Great Civil War,' nor Firth in the ' Dictionary of National Biography,' alludes to Cromwell's march into Peterborough; Gunton gave full details.

Notices of a few composers of services and anthems before the war may here be inserted.

WILLIAM CRANFORD (according to Wood, a member of St. Paul's choir) assisted in Ravenscroft's Psalter; there are anthems by him in the Peterhouse and Durham part-books. Burney mentions some fancies by Cranford, and Hilton included some catches of Cranford's in his 'Catch that catch can' (1652).

JOHN HILTON has been already alluded to, as he published madrigals for three voices, calling them 'Ayres or Fa-las,' in 1627. He had graduated Mus.Bac. Cantab. in the previous year. The Fa-las are dedicated to Dr. Heather in language suggesting that he had been Hilton's teacher. In 1628 Hilton became organist and parish-clerk of St. Margaret's, Westminster. He composed an 'Evening Service,' printed by Rimbault. A portrait of Hilton at Oxford is dated 1649, ætat. 50; he was accordingly born in 1599, and in the dedication of his Fa-las he speaks of his youth. The contributor to the Orianas must, therefore, have been the elder John Hilton. The attribution to Hilton of 'Lord, for Thy tender mercies' sake,' has also been mentioned; its non-appearance in Barnard's 'Selected Church Musick' is certainly in favour of this theory. In 1652 Hilton edited for Playford a great collection of catches and canons, entitled 'Catch that catch can'; the first thirty-two and some others are by himself. One is quite familiar to every child to this day—the round, 'Come, follow, follow me.' Hilton's ayres or fa-las were reprinted in score by the Musical Antiquarian Society, and several are in Hullah's collections. Hilton was buried at St. Margaret's on March 21st, 1657; ecclesiastical music being then forbidden, the Fraternity of Musicians sang, as Wood relates, 'in the house over his corpse before it went to the grave, and kept time on the coffin.' There are anthems by Hilton at Peterhouse; and he composed one of the elegies on W. Lawes.*

JOHN (or Richard) HUTCHINSON, of York, was organist

* A fine dialogue, *Job*, was printed by Dr. Nagel in Eitner's 'Monatshefte,' 1897.

of Durham Cathedral from 1614; he died 1646. There are six anthems of his in the Peterhouse and Ely collections.

GEORGE JEFFREY (Jeffries) was steward to Lord Hatton. During the war he was with King Charles, to whom he was organist at Oxford. Many of his sacred pieces are preserved; at the Royal College there are eighty Latin and English motets in his autograph.

HENRY LOOSEMORE, born in Devonshire about 1600, was a choir-boy at Cambridge, and afterwards organist of King's College. He graduated Mus.Bac. in 1640. During the interregnum he taught music to the North family at Kirtling. At the Restoration he returned to King's College, using his private organ. Soon afterwards he turned Romanist, entering a priory abroad, where he died in 1670. Services, litanies, and eleven anthems by H. Loosemore are at Peterhouse, one of them probably autograph. There were other musicians of the family. John Loosemore was also an organ-builder, and was paid in 1634 by the town of Hartland 'for setting upp six Sentences in the church, and on the porch, and for playing the organs, £1. For a dial for the church 12s.' George Loosemore graduated Mus.Doc. Cantab., and became organist of Trinity College after the Restoration. One of the family composed instrumental music, mentioned in the sale-catalogue of Thomas Britton (1715).

HENRY MOLLE, to whom a song of Tomkins's collection is dedicated, is represented in the Peterhouse part-books by two Evening Services, a Latin Te Deum and Litany (composed for Cosin), and an English anthem and Litany.

JOHN MUDD, organist of Peterborough, and (after the Restoration) perhaps at Lincoln, is also represented at Peterhouse, Durham, and Ely; as also are HENRY PALMER (who had contributed to Ravenscroft's Psalter), and several other unknown musicians.

ROBERT PARSONS, the vicar-choral of Exeter mentioned in Laud's Visitation, I suspect to be the composer of many pieces attributed to the Persons drowned at Newark in

1570. Wood states that he was organist of Westminster Abbey ('to King James I—so Dr. Rogers'), thus confusing him with John Parsons.

RICHARD PORTMAN, a pupil of Orlando Gibbons, became organist of Westminster Abbey in 1633, and entered the Chapel Royal in 1638. Dean Williams took him on a visit to France. Services and anthems by Portman are preserved in the Peterhouse and several other collections. After the suppression of ecclesiastical music Portman was a teacher; and he had a share in the 'Monument Money' (or fees for showing the royal monuments at the Abbey). Playford, in his list of the principal London teachers during the Commonwealth, puts Portman first among those 'for Organ or Virginall.' A petition to Cromwell's Council of State on February 29th, 1656, spoke of Portman as 'recently deceased.' Wood says (on the authority of Rogers) that he was buried in the Abbey cloisters.

THOMAS WILSON, organist of Peterhouse, is represented in the part-books by seven services and nine anthems.

LEONARD WOODSON, three of whose family were in the Chapel Royal in 1604, was born at Winchester. He was organist of Eton, and in the choir at Windsor Castle. Since Barnard included a Te Deum of Woodson's, he must have been dead in 1641. Anthems by him are at Peterhouse and elsewhere, and are mentioned by Clifford.

Other church composers before the war, but more prominent afterwards, were Dr. William Child, Christopher Gibbons, Albertus Bryne, Randolph Jewit, Thomas Mace, Dr. Benjamin Rogers, to whom may be added the brothers Lawes, more distinguished in secular music. We hear also in Clifford's collection, Wood's MS. Lives, and the Peterhouse and Durham MSS., of John Cob, R. Gibbs (of Norwich), Peter Stringer (of Chester), R. Hinde, R. Carr, J. Frith, J. Heath (of Rochester), etc.

What became of the organists and choirmen after the suppression of choral services we do not hear, with a few exceptions. The best were teachers in London; many lived at Oxford, and made a very vigorous musical life there for some years. Some had taken active part in the war; and it is probable that comparatively few claimed their old posts after the Restoration.

Of secular composers, WALTER PORTER deserves special mention. He had been a pupil of Monteverdi. His collection of madrigals with *continuo* and instrumental interludes was long concealed in the library at Britwell till the sale, 1919. A publication of accompanied madrigals, advertised by Playford with the date 1639, is perhaps only the same. Porter (according to Wood) was son of Henry Porter, who graduated Mus.Bac. Oxon. in 1600. The son entered the Chapel Royal in 1617, and was Master of the Children at Westminster Abbey in 1639. Afterwards he was patronised by Sir Edward Spencer. In 1657 he published his last work, seventeen 'Mottets' for two voices and bass. They are usually to psalms from Sandys's version; each has a separate dedication, the seventeenth to Hilton. In the preface Porter speaks of his growing infirmity, and refers to Ford and R. Johnson as great masters. The copies at the Bodleian Library and the British Museum are incomplete; there are others at Christ Church and the Royal College. Porter was buried at St. Margaret's, Westminster, November 30th, 1659. It is to be hoped his accompanied madrigals will be discovered; as specimens of the transition style they will be valuable. Porter's anthems appear in word-books of the period.

No other secular music was published until the Commonwealth; nor any instrumental music except the third edition of *Parthenia*, and Michael East's collection. In psalters some work of interest was done. Sandys's translation (with a paraphrase upon other parts of the Bible) appeared in 1637, and had some tunes for voice and bass by Henry Lawes. Child issued a selection of 'Choice Psalms' as three-voiced motets in 1639; this was twice reprinted during the Commonwealth. After the war Henry Lawes published another similar collection by himself and his brother William, with elegies on the latter by nine composers, and some canons and an elegy on John Tomkins by William Lawes. A reprint of Ravenscroft's Psalter in 1631, Lichfild's Latin Psalter in

1638, and Burton's in 1644, may be mentioned. Apart from these psalters, and the treatises of Bevin (see p. 242) and Charles Butler, the music published in Charles I's reign was:

1627   Hilton's Ayres or Fa-las.
1629   Filmer's translation of French part-songs.
1630   Peerson's 'Mottects.'
1632   Porter's accompanied Madrigals.
1635   A reprint of *Parthenia*.
1638   East's pieces for Viols.
       An edition of 'Siren cœlestis.'
1639   Porter's Madrigals with *basso continuo*.   (Lost.)
       Child's 'Choice Psalms' (twenty Motets).
1641   Barnard's 'Selected Church Musick.'
1648   'Choice Psalms,' etc., by the brothers Lawes.

By far the most important of these was Barnard's 'Church Musick.' The entire list is small and unimportant compared with the splendid productions of the previous forty years, while the list of publications during the Commonwealth is far longer. The age was everywhere one of transition in musical matters; but why so little music was published in England is not clear. The British Museum contains all the eleven collections except Porter's second set; several, however, being imperfect. A voice-part of Child's motets is at the Bodleian; fragments of Barnard's 'Church Musick' are at the British Museum in Addit. MS. 30,478, and larger portions are at Christ Church, Lichfield, Canterbury, and the Royal College.

All this chapter hitherto has contained nothing controversial, being simply a record of facts, all of which may be found in some form elsewhere; and except a description of the ayres and dialogues, and the poetry connected with them, I have added little of my own discovering or excogitation. But I have now to enter on the part of this book which will, I fear, excite more contention than anything else in my History, in which I have to run counter to popular ideas, and to deny assertions by historians of received authority, who have unquestioningly been believed because in this matter they have made themselves the utterance of the ordinary conception of what an English Puritan was like.

It will be found, upon close examination, that Burney, Chappell, Ouseley, Hullah, and others who have followed them, all contradict themselves most strangely in what they have said concerning the Puritans. While asserting that the Puritans suppressed all music, and persecuted musicians, they yet mention facts which are perfectly incompatible with such a statement. They have spoken of the revived activity in music-publishing during the Commonwealth, of the operatic performances, the meetings at Oxford, the violin-playing; of the musical tastes of Cromwell and Milton. The self-contradiction of these historians makes the task of refuting them easier; but I do not dream of uprooting popular prejudice in the matter.

Why the Puritans, like the early Reformers (see pp. 107–110), objected to organs, prose chanting, and church music generally is not very clear; personal dislike to Laud and the bishops was a very strong factor in embittering the attack upon cathedral services. Even Milton, proclaiming to the world in 1641 that he one day hoped to do what 'the greatest and choicest wits of Athens, Rome, or modern Italy, and those old Hebrews' had done, yet thought it impossible until 'the land had once freed herself from the impertinent yoke of Prelaty, under whose inquisitorious and tyrannical duncery no free and splendid wit can flourish.' Among the bishops themselves there were some who disliked organs, notably Potter of Carlisle; and Jeremy Taylor was very half-hearted in approving them (Ductor Dubitantium III, 4). I think it probable that the florid accompaniments were carried to a great extent, and considered a part of the ornate ritual. The specimens of organ accompaniments still remaining would be as much objected to in our days as they were then.*

But the result, whatever the cause, was a violent dislike to church music, and its complete suppression by

---

* It appears, from the preface to Richard Baxter's *Poetical Fragments*, that some precisians objected to the last two Psalms !

the Puritans. The mistake which some musical historians have made is to suppose that all music was suppressed because ecclesiastical music was. This is just as untrue and as unreasonable as it would be for a future historian to say that in the twentieth century no tobacco-smoking was allowed in England; it is true that the Puritans did not permit music in church, and it is true that at present tobacco-smoking would not be allowed in a church. Outside a church, music was as much unquestioned then as smoking is unquestioned now; and the great Puritan leaders, whatever some obscure fanatics may have thought, were distinguished by quite unusual appreciation of the art. As typical Puritans, one may select Cromwell, Milton, and Bunyan; the first a man of the highest practical genius, the second a man of highest literary cultivated genius, the third a man of literary uncultivated genius. All three alike were enthusiastic amateurs in different ways.

In the Puritan attacks upon theatres there is not a single case of an attack upon music as such. The references to music in them show in what honour the Puritans held it. For instance, in an anonymous *Short Treatise against Stage-Plays* (1625), reprinted in the 'Roxburgh Library' for 1869, there is a list of 'natural recreations,' such as change of occupation, sleep, etc., concluding—

'Musicke is a chearefull recreation to the minde that hath been blunted with serious meditations. These and such like are holy and good recreations both comfortable and profitable.'

William Perkins, in his elaborate *Cases of Conscience*, 1631, discusses 'Recreations' at length; he pronounces theatrical representations, mixed dancing, and games of chance to be unlawful; but approves 'games of wit or industry.' Athletics, fencing, music, chess, 'and all of this kind, wherein the industry of the mind and body hath the chiefest stroke, are very commendable, and not to be disliked.'

Prynne's celebrated attack upon all light amusements— the *Histriomastix*—has a special section attacking light music; but this begins (p. 274) with the words—

'That Musicke of itselfe is lawfull, usefull, and commendable; no man, no Christian dares denie, since the Scriptures, Fathers, and generally all Christian, all Pagan Authors extant, do with one consent averre it.'

The Puritans objected to certain things, among them being ecclesiastical music, Sunday amusements of all kinds, and theatres; but they did not object to everything pleasant. It is very much easier to apprehend the false idea that they objected to everything, than to carefully distinguish what they disliked, what they thought indifferent, and what they encouraged. Some historians, even Macaulay, have depicted them as averse to all kinds of art and science; and as regards music in particular, the common belief has been fairly represented by the statement of Hullah:

'Music, when enjoyed at all in England, was a stolen pleasure, and the only vocal exercise recognised by the law of the land was the practice of unisonous metrical psalmody.'*

These slanders have mainly arisen from the flippant accusations of Burney, who has been blindly copied by Ouseley, Hullah, and others, even Chappell; and no one except Sir G. A. Macfarren, and afterwards Sir Hubert Parry, has denied them. It may be confessed that they consort well with what may be called the 'stage Puritan,' who is about as much like a seventeenth-century Puritan as a stage Scotchman (with a kilt) is like an Edinburgh or Glasgow gentleman. But the only ground whatever for the assertion that the Puritans objected to music occurs in a sentence in Anthony à Wood's autobiography. Describing the great musical gatherings at Oxford during the Commonwealth, he says that vocal music was the more used, as 'being discountenanced by the Presbyterians and Independents.' Even in this there is at the same time a proof that music was not 'a stolen pleasure.' And this chance utterance of an adversary is of no importance compared with the writings of the Puritans themselves, and they are so unmistakable and frequent that one would almost imagine the Puritans foresaw what slanders would be invented concerning them, and

* Hullah does indeed add: 'The musical art appears to have been a good deal culivated in private.'

determined to give the very strongest unequivocal testimony of their opinions, both by words and deeds.

They followed Archbishop Abbot in removing organs
and choirs from churches, sometimes doing it roughly.
When their power was fully established they forbade
'profane singing and dancing' on the Sabbath. *On the
Sabbath* expresses the real offence. Lady Hutchison was
convicted at Nottingham in 1656 of having a concert in
her house *on the Sabbath*. Even Macaulay's often-quoted
assertion that the Puritans, objecting to bear-baiting,
tormented both spectators and bear, is supported only by
an instance of bear-baiting *on the Sabbath*, when some of
Cromwell's regiments topped the 'sport' and shot the
bears. The roving country fiddlers or crowders were
treated as rogues and vagabonds, just as Queen Elizabeth
had enacted, which injured music no more than putting
down organ-grinders would do now. This is *all* the
harm the Puritans did to the divine art. A few of their
opinions concerning it may now be given.

To begin with a book which is in every house, and
was written by a Puritan soldier and preacher when under
persecution, Bunyan's *Pilgrim's Progress*. There we read
(in the second part) that the Interpreter entertained his
guests with music during meals; that in the dining-room
of the House Beautiful there was a pair of virginals, and
personified Prudence 'kindly obliged' with a solo and a
song; that Christiana herself 'could play if need was on
the viol, and her daughter Mercy on the lute, so she
played them a lesson,' while Giant Despair's released
prisoners danced. In Bunyan's *Holy War* we read how
Prince Emanuel, during his triumph through Mansoul,
' was entertained with the song, by them that had the best
skill in musick.' One of Bunyan's *Divine Emblems* compares a 'skilful player on an instrument' to a gospel
minister. There was a story that Bunyan cut a flute out
of a leg of his prison chair, his jailor never being able to
discover it. He is an unanswerable example of lower-
class Puritan taste.

Next let us take the evidence of the best Puritan
history, the Memoirs of the stern, lofty-spirited Lucy

Hutchinson, who looked upon Cromwell as a traitor to the Republican cause. She thus describes her husband, one of the regicides:

'He could dance admirably well, but neither in youth nor riper years made any practice of it, he had skill in fencing such as became a gentleman, he had a great love to music, and often diverted himself with a viol on which he play'd masterly, he had an exact ear and judgment in other music, he shott excellently.'

She also speaks of Colonel Hutchinson's musical studies when he was at Peterhouse and Lincoln's Inn; afterwards he boarded with Colman. During the Protectorate he refused to acknowledge Cromwell, and retired to his country house, where he had built a ballroom; there he occupied himself with music, and teaching his children music and dancing, and other accomplishments. Such was the life of one of the leaders among the military saints who sat in judgment upon their king.

In 1653 Cromwell sent Bulstrode Whitelocke on an embassy to Queen Christina of Sweden, of which a detailed account was afterwards published. In the list of the retinue occur two names 'chiefly for music,' besides two trumpeters. Whitelocke's chaplain was Dr. Ingelo (the friend of Benjamin Rogers); during the winter nights the ambassador's retinue, under Ingelo's direction, used to regularly occupy themselves with concerted music, in which Whitelocke himself sometimes took part, 'having been in his younger days a master and composer of music.' There are many interesting references to Swedish music and dancing. Whitelocke's party repeatedly played to Queen Christina; and on April 17th 'some of her musicians (Italians and Germans)' returned the compliment, 'and they played many lessons of English composition,' which were shown them. On March 7th, Queen Christina had said 'she never heard so good a concert of music, and of English songs; and desired Whitelocke, at his return to England, to procure her some.' The church musicians had also visited the Puritan ambassador, 'and wondered when they saw him and divers of his people to understand their art and to sing with them, which they thought had been generally

abhorred in England.' Whitelocke thought it his duty to
strongly express his opinion upon the lax un-Puritanical
observance of the Sabbath in Sweden; but when the
Queen asked him concerning dancing in England, he
replied: 'Some there do not approve it, but it is not
prohibited by any law, and many there do use it.'

Whitelocke's *Memorials*, however, give little information
concerning music, though he alludes to his compositions
and his connection with Simon Ives.

It is remarkable that Whitelocke never names the
English composers whose works he took to Sweden. We
learn from Wood's 'Lives' that they were by Rogers,
with perhaps some of the 'Divisions upon Grounds' by
Butler and Norcome, so extolled by Sympson. In the
same year (1653) the Archduke, afterwards the Emperor
Leopold I, visited England; and a collection of Fancies
by Rogers was formally presented to him, as it was
supposed 'they were the best that *could* be made.'

Milton, as the son of a composer, was naturally
educated in music, and some of the most familiar passages
in English poetry were inspired by his taste and knowledge. His connection with Lawes has been already
mentioned; this friendship and his classical sympathies
caused him to thoroughly appreciate the change to the
declamatory style, and though he speaks of the 'service
high and anthem clear,' he does not allude to the contrapuntal madrigals popular in his youth. No one will
count him as opposed to music; yet, since it may be
alleged that he was not a typical Puritan, it may be well
to quote, not familiar or unfamiliar passages from his
poems, but some words from his prose. In November,
1644 (at the very height of the war, between Cromwell's
victories at Marston Moor and Naseby), Milton published
Areopagitica, an argument for liberty of the Press. He
argues that if it be right to enslave the Press, then it
would be also logically necessary to fetter music and
dancing with regulations, which would be impossible:

'If we think to regulate printing, thereby to rectify manners, we
must regulate all recreations and pastimes, all that is delightful to
man. No music must be heard. no song be set or sung, but what is

grave and Doric. There must be licensing dancers, that no gesture, motion, or deportment be taught our youth, but what by their allowance shall be thought honest; for such Plato was provided of. It will ask more than the work of twenty licensers, to examine all the lutes, violins, and the ghitarrs in every house; they must not be suffered to prattle as they do, but must be licensed what they may say. And who shall silence all the airs and madrigals, that whisper softness in chambers? . . . The villages also must have their visitors to enquire what lectures the bagpipe and the rebeck reads, even to the ballatry and the gammuth of every municipal fiddler, for these are the countryman's Arcadias and his Monte Mayors' [i.e. the countryman's popular novels].

To add to the force of this passage, let it be remembered that Milton was living in London, the Puritan stronghold; yet he could speak of musical instruments as a possession of 'every house,' music being so universal that it would be impossible to meddle with it, which those who wished to enslave the Press ought logically to do also.

The *Areopagitica* was a political pamphlet; in an earlier attack upon Episcopacy,* Milton had used the beauty of music as an argument against set forms of prayer, pointing out that 'Variety (as both music and rhetoric teacheth us) erects and rouses an auditory, like the masterful running over many chords and divisions; whereas if men should ever be thumbing the drone of one plain-song, it would be a dull opiate to the most wakeful attention.' Could Milton have used such an illustration if his own party, or even a section of his own party, had looked upon music as sinful? Milton also included music in his scheme of education, published just before the *Areopagitica*.

But, the reader may ask, is there no evidence on the other side? Cannot there be found passages written by Royalists, complaining of the 'persecution of music,' such as recent musical historians have related? All I can reply is, that I have never in the whole course of my reading met with any such; nor have I found any evidence of Puritan aversion to art excepting the one sentence I have quoted from Anthony à Wood. There had been musicians on the *Mayflower* in 1620. Still further, I challenge any

* *Animadversions on the Remonstrant II.*

writer to point out any enactment by the Puritans against music or dancing *on week-days*.   But after the war there were indeed some outbursts of wildest fanaticism by individual zealots here and there; and an utterance by one of these (quoted later) fortunately gives even more distinct and explicit evidence for my statements than any other yet mentioned.

The diarists also in no way suggest any restrictions upon music, which is the more important as both Evelyn and Pepys were enthusiastic amateurs. The latter, most unfortunately for posterity, did not begin his diary until the anarchical time, which speedily brought back the exiled Stuarts; but those few months are full of allusions to music, beginning on January 2nd, 1659–60, and never hinting that any restraint lay upon it. Evelyn's Diary covers the entire period; but he was out of England 1643–7, and again 1650–2. He does not often allude to music; when he does, it is always to record something interesting. During this period he notes matters on June 13th, 1649; February 6th, 1650; August 1st, 1652; January 20th, July 11–12th, October 1st, November 28th, 1654; March 4th, October 2nd, 1656; September 15th, 1657; and May 5th, 1659. His tour through England with his French-educated wife in 1654 is especially noteworthy, showing that ordinary social life went on just as usual. Evelyn was a zealous Royalist, and would have told us if the ruling Puritans had attacked music. Fuller, in *Worthies of England*, mentions how music, expelled from the Church, was welcomed and cherished by the nobility and gentry.

Anthony à Wood, of similar tastes, though he has furnished the one sentence which bears against my defence of the Puritans, yet gives an elaborate account of the Oxford meetings, with not the slightest hint that they were illegal. Richard Flecknoe, in his *Enigmatical Characters* (published in 1658), describes 'A School of Young Gentlewomen' much as a cynical musician would do now; saying that they have cheap and bad masters, 'learning to quaver instead of singing, hop instead of dancing, and rake the Ghitar, rumble the Virginals, and scratch and thrumb the Lute, instead of playing neatly and handsomely.' Flecknoe sneers at the French dancing-masters and lutenists, who seem to have enjoyed plenty of success in England; warning the dancing-master to hide his kit, lest the saints should take him for a vagrant crowder and break it over his head; and satirising the lutenist for his captious fault-finding with English lutes and lute-playing. Not a word of lute-playing or dancing being illegal.

A remarkable and very interesting biography entitled *The Virgin's Pattern* was published in 1661 by Daniel Batchiler. The heroine, described as a model of all graces and perfections, was Susannah Perwich, the daughter of a London schoolmaster. She lived from 1636 to 1661, exactly through the troubled time. From early years she had extraordinary skill in music, and was also 'an incomparable dancer.' Batchiler asserts that she was even celebrated on the Continent, and foreign visitors to England would go to see her as one of the London rarities. In 1657 her lover died, and she spent the rest of her short life in piety and devotion, studying Baxter, Spurstow, and other Puritan divines; visiting prisoners, and entertaining them with her performances; and though she would have preferred to give her spare time to religion rather than music, she would say that she now understood and enjoyed better than ever the very best music. So lived and died an accomplished Puritan young lady. Among her masters were Rogers and E. Colman; her sister was a pupil of Albertus Bryne. In a poem to her memory, Batchiler mentions thirteen leading musicians of the time; he was evidently a Puritan, and writes as though in expectation of persecution.

As it happens, the one taste which Hullah and Ouseley have conceded to the Puritans, that of psalm-singing, was far from universal among them. Many doubted whether it was right to sing psalms in congregations, where unbelievers might join their voices; and the Baptists actually altogether gave up singing in public worship. A Psalter (containing twenty-five tunes, with quaint remarks) was published by W. Burton in 1644;

in the preface he says, 'Lest any man (in this stumbling age) should stumble at the lawfulness of singing David's Psalms, as not proper to our occasions,' let such a one read 2 Chron. xxix. 30.   The New England Puritans retained psalm-singing, and their example prevailed.*

John Cotton (1584–1652), one of the most influential Puritans in New England, published a tract in favour of public psalm-singing, adding that a private Christian may write a spiritual song and sing it privately—

'. . . nor doe we forbid the private use of an Instrument of Musick therewithall; so that attention to the Instrument doe not divert the heart from attention to the matter of the Song.'

'T. F. Minister of Exon,' in *Six Sermons*, 1653, argued that hymns ought not to be used even privately; but had no objection to secular songs—

'. . . even as a man may play a Lesson on a Lute or other instrument to refresh his spirits.'

Richard Baxter, in *A Christian Directory*, 1673, mentions that he had known precisians who objected to music either 'privately or publicly with a Psalm, that scrupled not using it in common mirth.'

Having now, I trust, completely satisfied every reader that the accusations of Burney, Hullah, Ouseley (and others) are utterly groundless and unqualified libels upon the Puritans (except only as regards ecclesiastical music, and the disreputable street minstrels), I proceed to give some account of music as it really was during the eighteen years which elapsed from the outbreak of civil war to the Restoration.   During the first five years nothing was published, except Burton's Psalter and reprints; in 1648 appeared the 'Choice Psalms' of the brothers Lawes, described on p. 265.   Nor is there any record of musical doings; the mischief in some cathedrals and the general removal of organs are alone heard of.   Some of these organs were set up in taverns, according to a French traveller.

At the Puritan visitation of the universities, Arthur Phillipps, the Oxford Professor of Music, submitted,

* The Westminster Assembly formally sanctioned psalm-singing, recommending lining-out by the minister where many could not read.

but afterwards was removed as a Papist. Among the recommendations of the Cambridge Visitors was that Charles Colman be made Mus.Doc., which was acted upon.

In 1650, England being now sullenly tranquil and prosperous, began the long series of publications which forms one of the special features of music under the Commonwealth. JOHN PLAYFORD (afterwards Clerk of the Temple Church), a bookseller, issued the *English Dancing Master*, a quarto volume containing rules for country dancing, and 104 tunes for the 'Treble Violin.' He also issued some Cithern pieces, and reprinted Child's Psalms. In the next year Playford tried a collection, which was so well received that he determined to persevere in this new venture, and became the first regular music publisher. From this time a continual stream of publications issued from the press, and has never since ceased. The complete list during the Commonwealth is—

1650　*The English Dancing Master* . . . with the tune to each dance (104 folk-tunes; British Museum).
'A New Book for Cithern' (advertised in *A Musical Banquet*).
A reprint of Child's 'Choice Psalms' (a copy at the Bodleian Library).

1651　*A Musical Banquet*, in three books, consisting of twenty-seven lessons for the Lyra-Viol; 'Musica Harmonia' for Treble and Bass Viol; and 'Musick and Mirth,' twenty Rounds and Catches (at the Bodleian Library).

1652　Playford's 'Choice Ayres and Dialogues' (British Museum).
'Catch that Catch can,' 100 Rounds and 42 Sacred Canons (British Museum).
'A Book of New Lessons for the Cythern and Gittern' (Euing Library, Glasgow).
'Musick's Recreation on the Lyra-Viol,' 117 pieces (British Museum).
A reprint of *The English Dancing Master*, 112 tunes (*Ib.*).

1653　Henry Lawes's 'Ayres and Dialogues' (*Ib.*).
Lord Brouncker's 'Excellent Compendium of Music'; an annotated translation of Descartes (*Ib.*).
'Select Musicall Ayres and Dialogues' (*Ib.*).
A reprint of Michael East's 'Fantasies for Viols' (Royal College).

1654　'Breefe Introduction to the Skill of Music for Song or Violl' (British Museum).

History of English Music

1655 An enlarged edition of the 'Breefe Introduction,' with Sympson's annotated edition of Campion's 'Counterpoint' (*Ib.*).

Lawes's 'Second Book of Ayres and Dialogues' (*Ib.*).

A reprint of *Parthenia* (*Ib.*).

A reprint of 'Musick's Recreation on the Lyra-Violl' (*Ib.*).

'Court Ayres,' an enlarged reprint of 'Musica Harmonia'; 245 dance-pieces (*Ib.*, also Bodleian Library).

An independent issue of Sympson's Campion (British Museum).

1656 Lock's 'Little Consort,' forty pieces for viols (British Museum, Bodleian Library, Royal College).

Child's 'Choise Musick' (Royal College).

Gamble's 'Ayres and Dialogues' (British Museum).

1657 'A collection of Virginal Music' (according to Burney and others).

Wilson's 'Psalterium Carolinum' (British Museum).

Porter's 'Mottets' (Bodleian, Christ Church, Royal College).

A reprint of *The English Dancing Master*, 132 tunes (British Museum).

1658 Lawes's 'Third Book of Ayres and Dialogues' (*Ib.*).

A reprint of 'Catch that Catch can,' 131 Catches and Rounds, 31 Sacred Canons (*Ib.*).

A reprint of the 'Breefe Introduction' (*Ib.*).

1659 'Select Ayres and Dialogues' (*Ib.*).

A reprint of *Parthenia*.

Gamble's 'Second Book of Ayres and Dialogues' (Royal College; Fétis Library).

Sympson's 'Division-Viol' (British Museum).

Dr. Wilson's Cheerful Ayres and Ballads (*Ib.*).

To this list may fairly be added the libretti of Davenant's 'First Day's Entertainment,' and three operas; 1656–9. A complete set of these may be seen at the British Museum; and also at the Bodleian Library.

All this great amount of music-publication took place at a time when music was 'a stolen pleasure,' according to Hullah; when Burney says that 'Ten years of gloomy silence seem to have elapsed before a string was suffered to vibrate, or a pipe to breathe aloud in the kingdom'; when, according to Ouseley, 'no public performance of any sort of music was permitted.'

Another slander upon the Puritans must also be denied. Several writers have spoken of an order to destroy all the choir-books. No such order was ever issued by any one. Some choir-books were, however, destroyed, as I have related; but there is no evidence that this was usual, and hundreds of anthems and services remain to this day.

In some 'Directions' prefixed to Playford's *Musical Banquet*, Playford declares London to be 'at present furnished with many excellent and able Masters in this Art and Science, some of whose names for information of such as desire to become Practitioners therein, I have here inserted.' For the 'Voyce or Viol' he names H. Lawes, C. and E. Colman, W. Webb, J. Birkenshaw, G. Hudson, D. Mell, T. Bates, S. Bing, T. Mayland, Capt. Cooke, H. Ferrabosco, J. Harding, Jer. Savile, G. Goodgroome, John Este, W. Paget, Gregory, *cum multis aliis*; and for the 'Organ or Virginall,' R. Portman, Chr. Gibbons, Rand. Jewitt, J. Cobb, J. Hinkston, Parmelow, Brian, B. Sandley, Benj. Rogers, *cum multis aliis*. This work was published in 1651, the year of the final defeat of the Royalists by Cromwell's 'crowning mercy' at Worcester. It is obvious that Playford, at any rate, was not aware that music was then 'a stolen pleasure.' He tells us in a later preface (to 'Court Ayres') that he had printed only a small number of *A Musical Banquet*; but it was so well received that he resolved to issue the sections separately and in an enlarged form. There was evidently a very extensive demand for music, both vocal and instrumental.

As so much was printed, the MSS. are of less importance. There are some autographs of the brothers Lawes in Addit. MSS. 31,432-4; and others by Lock, Hingston, and Sympson, mainly instrumental. Elizabeth Rogers's 'Virginal Book' is Addit. MS. 10,337; it is dated 1656, and the influence of the period is shown by the inclusion of a number of Marches and Byrd's 'Battle-piece,' from 'The Soldier's Summons' to 'The Burial of the Dead,' which is an extra movement only found in this MS. But the Fancies, Consorts, etc., in the Music School, Oxford; at Christ Church; at Dublin (Marsh's Library), and elsewhere, may be counted by *thousands*. They were mainly composed at this time; Charles II disliked Fancies, and they quickly fell out of favour after the

Restoration. Little or nothing has been done in recent times with these remains of our ancestors' taste.

Of the vocal music, two fine volumes in the British Museum, Addit. MSS. 10,338 and 11,608, deserve mention; with Egerton MS. 2013.

It is now necessary to resume the historical summary of events interrupted at p. 237.

Soon after the Parliament had conquered, the Presbyterians found that the army would not suffer them to replace the Laudian tyranny by the Genevan yoke. The Independents were not numerous in the country, but they constituted the great body of the army, and were organised and directed by a great practical genius. The Parliament was forced to submit, and a fresh outbreak by Presbyterians and Royalists combined was easily put down. The Presbyterian members were excluded from Parliament, and the King was beheaded. Ireland and Scotland were reduced to obedience; and finally the general of the army expelled the remaining Independent members, declared himself Protector, and assumed regal state at Whitehall.

Cromwell had always loved music, and during his short reign did a very great deal for the art. We now, for the first time in our history, read of regular State concerts. These seem to have been the origin of concerts in England. To invite an audience specially to hear formal performances by skilled musicians is unheard of previously and was apparently the invention of Oliver Cromwell. It was speedily imitated elsewhere. Roger North's account of the meetings in London taverns has been supposed to refer only to the reign of Charles II, but the supposition is in no way countenanced by North's words; and Pepys mentions hearing a concert at 'The Mitre,' Fleet Street, on February 18th, 1659–60 (before the Restoration was even thought possible), and with no hint that a concert was at all a novelty.

All Cromwell's biographers have alluded to his enthusiasm for music. Thurloe describes the banquet to the Dutch ambassadors, when, after the music (vocal and instrumental), the Protector called for a psalm, which he afterwards presented to the visitors. Masson's monumental work on 'Milton and his Times,' vols. IV, 572–3, and V, 257, 298, is worthy of consultation in this connection; as are also Fletcher's 'Perfect Politician,' and even the libellous abuse of Heath—Carlyle's 'Carrion Heath'—who compares Cromwell to 'wicked Saul' in desiring peace to his conscience from 'those harmonious charms.' Carlyle, however, has never alluded to his hero's tastes but once; when, after describing the meeting of the Protector's second Parliament, he tells how the members were taken to hear a concert, 'the Protector being very fond of music.'

The Master of Cromwell's Private Music, and instructor to his daughters, was John Hingston, who was rewarded with a pension of £100. Hingston, with two boys, his pupils, was accustomed to sing to Cromwell the Latin motets of Deering, 'which Oliver was most taken with.' The account is in Rogers's writing among Wood's MS. Lives of Musicians. Hingston, Mell, the six other musicians, and the two boys, walked in Cromwell's funeral procession.

In 1654 Evelyn heard 'Mr. Gibbon' play on the organ at Magdalen College, Oxford; in the same year it was taken down and removed to Hampton Court Palace. Cromwell also had an organ at the Cockpit in Whitehall. His love of music was used to obtain favours from him; as in the case of James Quin, who had been ejected from Christ Church, but was a fine singer, and at once obtained his place again after he had sung before Cromwell. In 1656 the Professorship of Music was revived at Oxford, and Dr. Wilson was appointed; and afterwards Cromwell issued a mandate to the University of Cambridge, commanding them to dispense with their regulations and create Rogers a Mus.Bac.

In spite of Cromwell's patronage, and that of the nobility and gentry, we may readily believe that the suppression of cathedral choirs was severely felt; and on February 19th, 1657, Hingston, Mell, Howes, Gregory, and Hudson petitioned that the loss might be repaired by the establishment of a 'Corporation or College,' which

should have 'reasonable powers to read and practise
publiquely all sorts of Musick, to suppresse the singing
of obscene, scandalous, and defamatory Songs and Ballads,
and to reform the abuses in making all sorts of instruments of Musick, and in all things to regulate the profession of Musick.' The petition is endorsed, 'Mr.
Hinkston and others, Gentlemen of His Highness'
Musique.' The Council of State nominated a committee
to confer with them; it does not appear that any action
was taken.

Apart from London and Cromwell's Court, we hear
little of music except at Oxford. We may suppose that
the enthusiastic amateur Dr. Ingelo kept up some musical
life at Cambridge and Eton; a note in the Baker MSS.
mentions that there was to be a 'Music Act' in 1658.
But Anthony Wood has given us a full account of the
brilliant musical life at Oxford, which was more remarkable during the Commonwealth than it has ever been
before or since. Wood says that his life was then 'a
perfect Elysium.' Regular weekly meetings took place
at Magdalen, Oriel, Wadham, New, Queen's, and Exeter
Colleges; but the most important were those held in the
house of William Ellis, Mus.Bac. Viols, with the harpsichord and organ, were used; the violin was only beginning
to be esteemed. Several ex-choirmen took part till the
Restoration.

The London operatic performances took place at
Rutland House; afterwards in Drury Lane. 'The First
Day's Entertainment,' on May 23rd, 1656, was probably
intended as a feeler to test whether operatic performances
would be permitted. It began with a flourish, after which
was a prologue in which occurs the significant couplet:

> ' Think this your passage, and the narrow way
>   To our Elysian field, the Opera.'

Then a selection of 'Sullen Musick' introduced a speech
by Diogenes; answered by 'Lively Musick' and a speech
by Aristophanes, advocating amusements. Next followed
two songs. The second part of the Entertainment began
with music 'after the French composition,' and a speech

extolling Paris, answered by music imitating the London
Waits, and a speech in praise of London; after which
came a song and the epilogue, the whole concluding
with a 'Flourish of Loud Musick.' The composers employed were H. Lawes, Dr. Colman, Cook, and Hudson.

Four hundred places at this entertainment had been
provided, but only 150 attended. As no objection was
made, Davenant next proceeded to perform an opera,
The Siege of Rhodes. The libretto is dated August 17th,
1656, and apologises for shortcomings, the room being
only eleven feet high, and the stage fifteen feet deep,
'including the places of passage reserved for the Musick.'
The composers and performers are claimed to be 'the
most transcendent of England in that art, and perhaps
not unequal to the best masters abroad'; at the same time
the audience are warned that the music is in 'Recitative,
and therefore unpractised here, though of great reputation amongst other nations,' and are further informed
that 'frequent alterations of measure are necessary to
recitative musick for variation of Ayres,' the metres
having been written accordingly. There were five changes
of scenery. Twelve vocalists took part, though there were
but seven characters; the principal were *Solyman*, sung
by Captain Cooke, and *Ianthe*, sung by Mrs. Colman,
who is therefore reckoned the actress who first appeared
in public. Among the other performers were Matthew
Lock and Purcell's father. The band numbered six, and
included Christopher Gibbons, Baltzar, and Banister.
The composers employed were five: Henry Lawes, who
set the first and last acts; Cook, who undertook the second
and third; while Lock took the fourth, and Dr. Colman
and Hudson composed the instrumental entr'actes.

Another opera, *The Cruelty of the Spaniards in Peru*,
followed in 1658. The libretto states that it was 'Represented daily at the Cockpit in Drury Lane at three after
noone punctually,' and in spite of all the expenses 'there
is a good provision of places for a shilling.' In the next
year followed *The History of Sir Francis Drake*, connected
with the preceding opera; and Flecknoe's *Marriage of
Ocean and Britannia*. Some have asserted that Cromwell

was in 1658 contemplating a war with Spain, and secretly
encouraged the production of an opera which displayed
Spanish crimes; but in that year he died.

As ordinary plays were then really 'a stolen pleasure,'
it is probable that these operatic performances were
extensively patronised. We hear little of them; Evelyn
was present on May 5th, 1659, but thought the music,
singing, and scenery alike were far inferior to the Italian,
and that the performances ought not be to permitted in
such a troublous time. Evelyn, however, was a Cavalier.
His verdict was more uncomplimentary than Coryat's had
been early in the century; that quaint writer said the
Venetian actors could 'not compare with ours for music.'
The music of these operas has not been preserved; but
we may suppose the songs to have been similar to Lawes's
songs in *Comus* and the music written by Lock and
Gibbons for *Cupid and Death* in 1653, while the recitative-
dialogue was probably not far removed in style. The
dramas were published separately, and also among
Davenant's 'Collected Works,' in 1672; an examination
of the original editions will show the curious that there
was actually a *daily* opera in London under the Puritan
rule.

The ancient pride of the English in the superiority of
their music had now melted, as far as vocal music was
concerned, before the splendour of the Italian achievements since 1560; but it was still maintained as regards
instrumental music. The presentation of Rogers's
'Fancies' to the Archduke, and to the Queen of Sweden,
is a significant proof of this feeling; one may easily
believe that Cromwell, intensely patriotic as well as
thoroughly musical, fully shared in this pride. As regards
execution, it was certainly unjustified. In 1656 Thomas
Baltzar of Lübeck came to England, and for the first time
showed the English musicians some capabilities of the
violin they had so despised. Evelyn heard him on
March 4th; in the following year he went to Oxford,
and Anthony Wood describes the amazement of all the
Oxford society when they heard Baltzar's mastery of the
shift and double-stopping. But this check seems not to

have daunted the pride of the English in their compositions. Matthew Lock in 1656 wrote: 'I never saw any
foreign instrumental music (a few French corantos ex-
cepted) worthy an Englishman's transcribing.' Christopher Sympson in 1659 followed in the same strain; and
in his 'Compendium of Practical Music' (1665) gave
it as his opinion that no nation was 'equal to the
English in that way.' John Birchensha also wrote in
1663: 'I am persuaded that there is as much excellency
in the Musick that hath been, and is now composed in
England, as in any part of the world, for ayre, variety,
and substance.' But this pride scarcely survived the
Restoration, when light music was at first in exclusive
favour at Court, and afterwards Purcell proclaimed the
superiority of Italian music; the Sonata then quickly
destroyed the Fancie and the Consort.

So little opportunity exists at present for duly testing
these works, so highly valued in their own day, that I
am diffident of expressing any opinion upon their merits.
I think the 'Consorts' of light music (generally for only
two or three instruments) weak and empty, though
graceful and melodious; but the 'Fancies' are often
remarkably good contrapuntal music. Among the best
I have seen are some contained in six fine volumes
presented by Hingston to the Music School, Oxford.

With operas and concerts established, execution improved, composition and publication in full activity, the
Commonwealth may be described as one of our most
brilliant musical periods. Playford's collections require
some description; on the covers he advertises Elizabethan
madrigals.

The English Dancing Master (an oblong quarto volume)
contains descriptions of the figures of Country Dances,
with 104 tunes for the 'Treble Violin.' It was entered
at Stationers' Hall, November 7th, 1650. An edition in
duodecimo, with 112 tunes, appeared in 1652; Playford
says he reissued the work because it was being pirated.
The next, in 1657, has 132 tunes, and also some French
dances and other old melodies for the violin. Altogether
eighteen editions are known, the last being dated 1728;

the later are much larger. Many beautiful old folk-tunes have been preserved by inclusion in this work; Chappell says it is widely diffused in Italy.

A Musical Banquet was Playford's next attempt; he printed only a few copies, of which two are preserved, one in the Douce Collection; the other, from Britwell, was absorbed by the American collector. It contains some 'Directions' already quoted; twenty-seven lessons for the Lyra-Viol, some by Jenkins; thirty-one pieces for two viols (generally Almains, Corantos, and Sarabands), by W. Lawes, Jenkins, C. Colman, R. Cooke, and Sympson; and twenty rounds and catches, including Byrd's 'Non nobis,' and 'A boat, a boat,' ascribed to Holmes. The separate sections, when reprinted, were developed into the 'Breefe Introduction,' and the following three collections.

Musick's Recreation on the Lyra-Violl, published in 1652, and reprinted in 1655 and 1661, has 117 pieces in tablature, with a short introduction by Playford.

Catch that catch can, edited by Hilton, contains 100 rounds, etc., and forty-two 'Sacred hymns and canons.' The composers were Hilton, W. and H. Lawes, E. Nelham, T. Holmes, Cranford, Ellis, T. Brewer, W. Webb, Jenkins, J. Cobb, Child, W. Howes, Ives, Wilson, and T. Pierce. By far the best-known pieces are 'A boat, a boat,' here ascribed to Jenkins, and Hilton's 'Come follow, follow me'; but many others are still sung. Playford's reprint in 1658 contains thirty-one more rounds (including 'Three blind mice' and others from *Pammelia*), but fewer sacred pieces; he prefixed a few rules, saying that rounds should be sung four or five times. Subsequent editions had other music, and were called *The Musical Companion*; at the end of these appears Jeremiah Savile's 'The Waits.'

Court Ayres, which completed the enlarged reprinting of *A Musical Banquet*, contains 245 'Pavins, Almaines, Corants, and Sarabands, Treble and Basse, for Viols or Violins.' The pieces are grouped as Suites. The composers were W. Lawes, Dr. Colman, Jenkins, Rogers, Mell, Banister, Gregory, Captain Silas Taylor, Lock, and

T. Gibbes. This collection was so much in demand that it was reprinted 'beyond the seas' to Playford's great loss; and he consequently printed no more till 1662, when he issued an enlarged edition called *Courtly Masquing Ayres*, of which there is a copy at the Royal College.

Playford's *Select Musicall Ayres and Dialogues*, issued in 1652, was the first publication of this favourite style of composition; and its success was evident from the fact that another set was issued the very next year, a third in 1659, and two others after the Restoration, besides the independent publications of H. Lawes and Gamble. The first collection contained declamatory works by Wilson, Dr. Colman, W. and H. Lawes, Lanier, Webb, Smegergill (*alias* Cæsar), R. Johnson, and J. Taylor. Their character may be gathered from my remarks on pp. 227–8.

John Playford in this, as in his other ventures, had exactly discovered the secret of satisfying public taste; and as the first Englishman who appeared in the capacity of a music-publisher, he is an important figure in our history. He was born in 1623, became clerk of the Temple Church in 1653, and continued to publish throughout the reign of Charles II. His printer was W. Godbid.

Several foreign collections of light music still included English tunes; but the only important publication abroad was a collection of works which appeared at Innspruck in 1653, and were composed by WILLIAM YOUNG. Walter calls them sonatas, and informs us that they were in three, four, and five parts, and were dedicated to the Archduke Ferdinand Charles. There is a copy at Upsala. Eitner mentions another formerly at Groningen. Young ('Joungh') was apparently in the service of the Archduke when he was Governor of the Netherlands. The Music School, Oxford, contains MSS. of Young's works. Young also published Fancies in 1669; they were mentioned by Wood and advertised by Playford. Specimens of the sonatas were played at a Gresham lecture in 1912. I have seen neither collection.

Proceeding now to biographical notices, I must

premise that all English musicians in the middle of the
seventeenth century may be counted as composers of
'Ayres and Dialogues,' just as 150 years later every
English musician as a matter of course was a glee-
composer. Not many have been included in modern
reprints; and the specimens selected are naturally those
most acceptable to modern taste, and are hardly representative. 'Sweet Echo' (from *Comus*) and the 'Ariadne,'
which opens H. Lawes's first book, may be named as
good typical examples.

WILLIAM LAWES was born at Dinton, Wiltshire,
probably about 1580–5; and after singing in the choir
of Chichester Cathedral, entered the Chapel Royal in
1603. He was patronised by the Earl of Hertford, who
enabled him to take lessons of Coperario. Lawes was a
fertile composer in all styles, especially instrumental; his
brother wrote of him:

'Besides his Fancies of 3, 4, 5, and 6 parts to the Viols and Organ,
he hath made above 30 severall sorts of Musick for Voices and
Instruments: Neither was there any Instrument then in use, but he
compos'd to it so aptly, as if he had only studied that.'

Nothing of W. Lawes's was published during his life.
On the breaking out of the war he joined the Royalist
army; as he was held in the highest esteem, Lord Gerrard
made him a commissary to protect him from danger, but
he was nevertheless killed at the siege of Chester in 1645.
The King wore a special mourning for him; elegies were
written by Herrick and others, and set by several
musicians. Eight are printed in the 'Choice Psalms'
published by Henry Lawes in 1648, which contain some
pieces of William's. Vocal and instrumental pieces are
included in Playford's *Musical Banquet* and several other
collections, and much more exists in MS. A work called
the 'Royal Consort' was especially famous.

HENRY LAWES, the representative composer of the
declamatory school, was born at Dinton in December,
1595. He also was taught by Coperario; and entered the
Chapel Royal in 1626. At this time he was celebrated as
a performer, and had taken part with Lanier in a 'Court
Masque' preserved in the Cholmondely MSS. The

enthusiastic eulogies from Milton, Waller, and Herrick have immortalised Henry Lawes; it is probable that Milton was his pupil, and they were certainly on intimate terms. Among Lawes's pupils was Lady Alice Egerton, daughter of the Earl of Bridgewater; when the latter was appointed Lord-President of Wales and the Marches (an office filled in semi-regal state at Ludlow Castle), Milton wrote *Comus* for the festivities, at the invitation of Lawes, who set the songs, himself taking the part of the Attendant Spirit. The 'Lady's Song' has been printed both by Hawkins and Burney; Lawes must have had full confidence in the powers of his pupil, then scarcely in her teens. The friendship between the poet and the composer was again of use in 1638, when Lawes obtained Milton's passport for Continental travel. Lawes did not publish the music to *Comus*.

Sandys's Psalter contained tunes by Henry Lawes for voice and bass only, barred. Lawes may have fought in the war; nothing is heard of him till 1648, when he issued four part-books containing the 'Choice Psalms for three voices and thorowbase' by himself and his brother, with other pieces. He is next mentioned in Playford's list of London teachers. As Playford had included some of Lawes's works in his 'Choice Ayres and Dialogues,' Lawes himself issued a large volume in 1653; in the dedication the composer says, 'Since my Attendance on his late Majesty (my most Gracious Master), I have neglected the exercise of my Profession.' The preface is good evidence of the repute which Italian music had attained, and of the ignorance of early musical history, which was already complete; Lawes having alluded to the Druids and Bards, and their musical skill, continues—

'How their Successors held it up I know not; but K. Henry VIII did much advance it, especially in the former part of his reign, when his minde was more intent upon Arts and Sciences, at which time he invited all the greatest masters out of Italy and other countries, and himself gave example.'

Lawes would doubtless have been amazed to hear that in Henry VIII's youth there were no Italian composers at all, and would probably not have credited

the fact that a century before Henry VIII's time Italy
imported musicians from England. Yet Lawes himself
complained of the undue appreciation of Italian music;
and had set a list of Italian songs, which had been much
applauded as real Italian poetry and music. This *jeu
d'esprit* he has included in the volume.

In 1655 another collection appeared; three pieces in
it were the composition of his pupil Lady Dering, to
whom the volume is dedicated. A third set followed
in 1658. All are written for voice and unfigured bass.
Lawes's share in Davenant's opera has been mentioned.
At the Restoration Lawes was reinstated in the Chapel
Royal as 'Clerk of the Cheque'; he composed one of
the coronation anthems, but was in failing health (as
Pepys noted) and died October 21st, 1662. He was
buried in the cloisters of Westminster Abbey.

Whatever may be thought of Lawes's abilities, there
is no question of the extraordinary popularity and esteem
which his works attained. His music soon passed into
oblivion, but Milton, Herrick, and Waller had preserved
his name. When Hawkins and Burney examined his songs
they found them wanting in all the qualities prized in the
eighteenth century. Subsequent writers have done him
more justice, but his music is not at all known except
by the three specimens in Hullah's *English Songs*. The
first of these, 'While I listen to thy voice,' is a good
example of the declamatory 'Ayres'; the others are
more tuneful.

CHARLES COLMAN (Coleman) was another of Charles I's
musicians; he lived at Richmond, where Hutchinson, the
future regicide, boarded with him. He afterwards sub-
sisted by teaching. Works of Colman's (both vocal and
instrumental) are included in Playford's collections; and
he shared in the operatic compositions. Colman died
July, 1664. His son, EDWARD COLMAN, also a composer
and a member of the Chapel Royal, was one of the
performers in Davenant's opera, and his wife took the
heroines. He died 1669.

Should any man attempt to explain away my proofs
that the Puritans did not suppress music, he will find

one fact connected with the elder Colman a particularly hard nut to crack. The committee for the reformation of the University of Cambridge recommended that Charles Colman should be made Doctor of Music; and he was accordingly created Mus.Doc. on July 2nd, 1651. It is probable that this was done by the influence of Colman's old friend Hutchinson; unless, which I think more likely, several leading musicians were recommended for the honour, and only Colman accepted it. At any rate, Colman was recommended by the Puritan committee, and created by the Puritanised University; and should any one attempt to reassert the old slanders of Burney, Ouseley, and Hullah, I think he will have to avoid mentioning this fact.

ARTHUR PHILLIPPS had succeeded Nicholson as the Oxford Professor in 1639. Wood says he was related to Peter Philipps, and had become organist of Bristol Cathedral in 1638. Phillipps next took Nicholson's organistship at Magdalen College, and the Professorship. He was still at Oxford when the Puritan Visitors came; afterwards he turned Romanist, went to France, and subsequently was organist to Mr. Caryl, a Sussex Romanist. The Carylls of Harting are no doubt intended; 'Mr. Phillipps's room' is mentioned in their correspondence, Addit. MS. 28,226. He seems to have been a good composer; but none of his works were printed. Wood says that Phillipps set Stanley's 'Requiem, or Liberty of an Imprisoned Loyalist,' and Pierce's 'Resurrection.' Phillipps was born at Winchester in 1605; it is not known when he died. A set of variations on a Ground by him may be seen in Addit. MS. 29,996.

JOHN WILSON, who succeeded Phillipps as Oxford Professor, was born at Faversham, April 5th, 1594; Wood says he was a kinsman of Walter Porter. Rimbault tried to identify him with the 'Jacke Wilson' who sang in Shakespeare's plays. Wilson was certainly celebrated as a singer and lutenist, and is termed 'curious Wilson' in some lines of Herrick's to H. Lawes. During the war, Wilson was with the King at Oxford, and in 1644 obtained the degree of Mus.Doc.; on the surrender in

1646 he settled at Sarsden with Sir William and Lady Walter, who were great patrons of music. In 1656 Cromwell made him Professor of Music at Oxford, with apartments at Balliol College; which favour Wilson repaid by publishing in 1657, at Oxford, a setting for three voices and thorough-bass of a number of poems by Stanley, in which twenty-seven of the Psalms are adapted to events in the late war and the words of David are put into the mouth of Charles I. Wilson has taken the first three verses of each Psalm and set them as one long stanza. The title (evidently adapted from *Eikon Basilike*) is *Psalterium Carolinum : The Devotions of His Sacred Majestie in his Solitudes and Sufferings*; and it is very remarkable that such a work was published by Cromwell's own Professor of Music in 1657, when the Protector was absolute monarch over the British Islands, and foreign rulers trembled before the English ambassadors. Probably Wilson wished to show the world his steady Royalism.

In 1660 Wilson published 'Cheerful Ayres and Ballads,' also at Oxford, where it was printed, being 'the first essay of musick-printing' there. The volume contains about seventy pieces, of which three are by R. Johnson and one by Lanier. They are in the main tuneful rather than declamatory; the words are taken from fine poetry, including many familiar pieces by Shakespeare, Fletcher, Lovelace, etc. Most collections of the time include pieces by Wilson, who remained at Oxford until he succeeded Lawes in the Chapel Royal, when he settled at Westminster. He died February 22nd, 1673, and was buried in the Abbey cloisters.

With these graduated musicians William Child (whose Service in D had been a favourite of Charles I) and Benjamin Rogers might be included; both lived almost through the century, and the former is not heard of during the interregnum. Rogers was in the highest estimation as an instrumental composer, and his works were presented to foreign rulers as 'the best that *could* be made' anywhere. Both composers will be more fully mentioned in the next chapter, as their work during the Commonwealth has not endured. Matthew Lock, a shorter-lived man, may also be left to the Restoration period, though prominent during the Commonwealth as a composer and singer, and loud in his asseverations that English instrumental music was the best in the world. Captain Cooke and Christopher Gibbons are also left till the next chapter.

JOHN GAMBLE, who had been a cornet-player in the Chapel Royal, published in 1656 a collection of eighty-five Ayres and two Dialogues, to words by T. Stanley. The style is the declamatory prosodic recitation used by Lanier and Lawes; but Gamble's are distinctly inferior, and show the dullness of the music at its dullest. They were, however, received with delight; and Gamble was fêted at Oxford in 1658, as Mell had been. Another collection appeared in 1659, several poets of the time furnishing the words. One piece is in F minor. His Commonplace-book is now in America. After the Restoration Gamble was again at Court, was impoverished by the Great Fire, and lived till 1687.

JOHN HINGSTON (Hingestone, Hinkson), as the Court organist to Cromwell, naturally calls for special notice. It is not known when he was born; probably before 1610, as he was a pupil of Orlando Gibbons, and then became one of Charles I's musicians. Playford mentions him among the leading London teachers of keyed instruments in 1651. Afterwards, becoming organist to Cromwell, and teacher of music to the Protector's daughters, he was in flourishing circumstances. His performance with his pupils of Deering's motets has been mentioned. It is somewhat strange that none of Hingston's music was printed. There are some pieces of his for two gambas in Addit. MS. 31,436; but by far the most important of his works are in six volumes, which he presented to the Music School, Oxford, containing a great number of Fancies, some of which are remarkably good. They are for various combinations of instruments; one is for two cornets and one 'sagbutt,' with organ. Hingston gave concerts in his house; and Sir Roger Lestrange told how he was once taking part when Cromwell came in. After the Restoration Hingston was again in the Chapel Royal, as 'keeper of ye organes'; two of his anthems are mentioned by Clifford. When Evans, the unrivalled harpist, died 'from mere want' (not having for years received any money from Charles II), Pepys recorded that Hingston happened to meet the parish funeral, which was 'in the dark at night without one link,' and gave '12d. to buy two or three links.' Hingston, whatever his personal predilections were, must surely have then contrasted the prosperity of Cromwell's musicians against the wretched fate of those who served Charles II. Beyond Hingston's presentation of his compositions and his portrait to the Music School, Oxford, and his attendance at the revived Corporation of Music (where he signs Jo. Hingeston), we hear nothing more of him until the entry of his burial at St. Margaret's Church, Westminster, December 17th, 1683. There, with Robert Whyte, Thomas Ford, John Hilton, and Walter Porter, sleeps the musician who was selected to be organist to Oliver Cromwell.

SIMON IVES was born at Ware, July, 1600, and became a vicar-choral of St. Paul's. He shared with W. Lawes in composing music for the masque performed by the Inns of Court in 1633; and became a singing-master on the suppression of cathedral choirs, but is not mentioned in Playford's list. Of the elegies upon W. Lawes, Ives's is among the best; it was printed in score in *Musica Antiqua*. One of Ives's rounds, 'Come, honest friends and jovial boys,' is still sung. Ives died July, 1662, bequeathing to the Petty Canons of St. Paul's a set of Fancies and In Nomines and a chest of viols. He had a son of the same name (at Cambridge about 1644) who apparently died young. Compositions by both are in *Music's Recreation on the Lyra-Viol*.

JOHN JENKINS, called by Anthony Wood 'a little man with a great soul,' is the typical instrumental composer of the period, as Henry Lawes is the typical song-writer. Jenkins was born at Maidstone in 1592; he became a fine performer on the lute and viol, and was one of the musicians to Charles I. His Fancies and dance-pieces were eagerly sought after; he was a most prolific composer, and attained almost a European reputation. There are

Fancies in his autograph in Addit. MSS. 29,290 and
31,423. Roger North (born 1650) has in his *Memoirs of
Musick* described the immense popularity and celebrity
of Jenkins's works, and their complete oblivion soon
after; Jenkins had composed 'horseloads,' according to
North, and had completely lost count of them. Wood
relates that Jenkins was fond of composing vocal music,
in which he was less skilled; he was one of the elegists
upon W. Lawes, and occasionally appears in other collections. He composed music to *Theophila*, a tedious
pedantic poem by Benlowe; this setting, probably of the
first stanza, was apparently not published. He is well
represented in the instrumental collections, from *A
Musical Banquet* down to the time of his death in 1678.
Hawkins, copied by every subsequent writer, has stated
that Jenkins published in 1660 'Twelve Sonatas for two
Violins and a Base, with a Thorough Base for the Organ
or Theorbo,' reprinted at Amsterdam in 1664.* I have
been unable to verify this statement; Wood does not
mention the collection, and it does not appear in Goo-
vaerts's 'Bibliographie de la Typographie Musicale dans
les Pays-Bas.' Among the works of Jenkins in especial
favour were 'The Five Bells Consort' and 'The Mitter
Rant'; a 'Sute in D-sol-re,' for treble and bass, was
printed in 'New Ayres and Dialogues' (1678). These
may be seen in *Musica Antiqua*. The only one of Jenkins's
'Fancies' I have ever seen in print is in Hullah's *History
of the Transitional Period*; great numbers exist in the
British Museum, at Oxford, and in the Hamburg Library.
Anthems and canzonets are also preserved.

Jenkins lived much in Norfolk, especially with Sir
Hamon Lestrange, the Royalist antiquary; afterwards
with Sir Philip Wodehouse at Kimberley. Blomfield's
'History of Norfolk' has preserved Jenkins's epitaph
in Kimberley Church; the composer died October 27th,
1678, aged eighty-six. Even in 1690 Playford printed two
of Jenkins's 'Rants'; then he was already become antiquated, and his very name had passed out of general

---

* Eitner mentions a collection of 200 pieces by eleven leading English
violists; Amsterdam, 1664, edited by Jenkins, with 67 Arias of his own.

remembrance when North wrote in 1728. All Jenkins's 'horseloads' of Fancies and Court Ayres and Sutes and Jiggs and Rants are but curiosities scarcely looked at even by the antiquary, while his anthems and canzonets are still less remembered; but one little trifle (anonymous in *A Musical Banquet*, but ascribed to Jenkins in *Catch that Catch can*) has remained perfectly familiar even to our own day, for it is scarcely an exaggeration to say that every man, woman, and child in England has heard the round, 'A boat, a boat, haste to the ferry.'

DAVIS MELL, who was born at Wilton, November 15th, 1604, was counted the best violinist in England. Mell was one of Cromwell's musicians, and signed next after Hingston in the petition to Cromwell for the establishment of a national College of Music. He visited Oxford in 1657, Wood and others giving him a grand reception. Even Baltzar, though he amazed every one by his execution, was not reckoned the equal of Mell as regards tone and expression. Mell seems to have composed little; there are pieces of his in Playford's *Court Ayres* and subsequently in the *Division Violin* (1685). Wood says that Mell had singular cleverness in making watches. He probably died soon after the Restoration.

Evelyn mentions 'Paul Wheeler' with Mell as the best violinists known until Baltzar came. The name 'Paulwheel' is attached to two pieces in the *Division Violin*; in *The Virgin's Pattern* appears 'Polewheel,' and the musician probably bore that Cornish name.

CHRISTOPHER SYMPSON (Simpson) may have been related to the Thomas Simpson who published much instrumental music in Germany in 1611 and 1621. He was probably born about 1600, and served in the Royalist army under the Marquis of Newcastle; afterwards settling in Leicestershire with Sir Robert Bolles. He annotated Campion's treatise for Playford in 1655; this was reprinted in 1664, and also included in some editions of Playford's 'Breefe Introduction.' In 1659 Sympson published an important treatise, '*The Division Violist*; or, An Introduction to the Playing upon a Ground.' It is dedicated to Bolles; Dr. Colman, Jenkins, Lock, and others sent commendatory verses. The superiority of English instrumental music is here asserted, both at the close and in this interesting passage:

'I would have you peruse the Divisions which other men have made upon Grounds; as those of Mr. Hy. Butler, Mr. Daniel Norcome, and divers other excellent men of this our nation who (hitherto) have had the preheminence for this particular Instrument.'

The work had been prepared for Sir Robert's son, who had succeeded him when the second edition was published in 1667; this edition had a Latin translation, and the title *Chelys Minuritionum Artificio Exornata*. A third followed in 1712, containing two additional pieces styled 'Sonatas.' Copies of Sympson's *Division-Violist* at Oxford and the Royal College are bound up with many pieces for viols, some of which are by Butler and Norcome.

Sympson also published a useful treatise, *Principles of Practical Musick*, in 1665; reprinted (as *Compendium of Practical Music*) in 1667, 1678, and at least six times more, one edition being dated 1732. It contains instructions in counterpoint and canon. Both the *Division-Viol* and the *Compendium* contained Sympson's portrait. He lived latterly at Turnstile, Holborn, and was a Romanist, according to Wood; he died in the summer of 1669. In the Music School, Oxford, there are Fancies, Airs, and Galliards of his inscribed with the names of the months and seasons; also at the British Museum (wrongly catalogued) in Addit. MS. 31,436.

HENRY BUTLER was a Romanist, and taught the King of Spain; according to Wadsworth's report he was the only English refugee at Madrid whose pension was regularly paid. An unknown JOSEPH BUTLER composed part of a collection published at Amsterdam in 1652.

DANIEL NORCOME, supposing him the madrigalist who contributed to the *Triumphs of Oriana*, had been a lay-clerk of Windsor. He figures among the English musicians at the Danish court, where he received a high salary, 350 Daler. He remained there 1599–1601, when he fled with John Meinert (? Maynard), a bass-singer. After a year's search in Germany, Hungary, and Italy, they were traced to Venice. Norcome turned Romanist, and became Court musician at Brussels; he died 1647.

WILLIAM HOWE (Howes) was one of the Worcester Waytes, then a petty canon of Windsor Castle, going to Oxford during the war, subsequently living at Windsor. Howe joined in the petition for a College of Music. After the Restoration he was a corneteer in the Chapel Royal. Howes, with Stephen Bing, William Gregory, and Stifkins (a lutenist), are among the musicians called upon by Batchiler to lament for Susanna Perwich.

THOMAS BREWER, born 1611, educated at Christ's Hospital, and taught music there that he might more easily be apprenticed, appears in several collections (1652-63); and his 'Turn, Amaryllis,' in Playford's third book of 'Ayres and Dialogues' (1659), is there called a *Glee*. This is the earliest instance of the old Anglo-Saxon word being used to denote vocal concerted music.

Most of the other leading musicians of this period are included in Playford's list of London teachers. Alphonso Marsh (1627–81), Richard Cook (who had lived at Sir Robert Bolles's with Sympson), John Carwarden, and John Este (who had been a barber) must not be omitted from the roll of musicians prominent during the Commonwealth. Before taking the regular amateurs who deserve notice, EDMUND CHILMEAD should be mentioned; he was an able mathematician and linguist, but being expelled from Oxford University by the Puritans, came to London and held a weekly music-meeting at the 'Black Horse' in Aldersgate Street till his death, 1653–4. A few compositions by Chilmead remain. Among enthusiastic amateurs, Sympson's patron, Sir Robert Bolles, was prominent. In the dedication to him of the *New World of Words* (1662) by Edward Phillips (Milton's nephew) his skill is thus alluded to: 'Your whole retinue, following your example, are able performers in Musick, and may as truly be called your Quire as your family.' Bolles had fought on the Parliamentary side in the war. Another able amateur, Sir Peter Leycester, was a Royalist and antiquary, and has left a treatise on music (in the Tabley MSS.) which appears remarkably good. Anthony Wood

Pepys, and Evelyn have all left invaluable accounts of the music at Oxford and elsewhere. Nathaniel Ingelo, a Puritan clergyman (1620–83), had great enthusiasm for the art; he preached at Bristol to a congregation which thought him too much given to music, went to Sweden as chaplain to Whitelocke's embassy, taking with him Rogers's works (which he presented to Queen Christina) and directing the musical performances of Whitelocke's retinue. After the Restoration he conformed to the Episcopal Church, and kept his Fellowship of Eton College, but was always disliked there as Puritanically inclined, and was in danger towards the close of his life.

An amateur who had real and enduring influence on the progress of music in England was Colonel John Humfrey, 'a great Oliverian,' says Anthony Wood, who has further informed us that Colonel Humfrey was 'given much to music' and 'was swordbearer to W. Bradshaw.' But the stout old Ironside is interesting here through another statement of Wood's, which was misread by Hawkins, and has been misstated ever since by everybody. Wood, in writing of Pelham Humfrey, says 'Colonel John Humphrey, a great Oliverian, was his master.' The last word was taken by Hawkins to be *uncle*; and all books since have said that Pelham was the nephew instead of the pupil of Colonel Humfrey, who was no doubt a very near relative. Pelham was so epoch-making in English musical history that Colonel John Humfrey, as his master, must be reckoned an amateur of the very first importance. Any historian who attempts to revive the old slanders on the Puritans will have to avoid the fact that at the trial of Charles I a musical amateur was the President's swordbearer.

A man of extraordinary gifts, but who did little with them, was SILAS TAYLOR (*alias* Domvill), distinguished both as a musician and an antiquary and in many branches of learning. Anthony Wood has given his full biography (in *Athenæ Oxonienses*, II 464–5). He was the son of Sylvanus Taylor, who, according to Wood, was a 'grand Oliverian,' and a member of the High Court of Justice; but his name does not appear among the regicides. Silas Taylor was born at Harley, Shropshire, in 1624; he was at Oxford when the war broke out, then entered the Puritan army and became a captain in Massey's regiment of Ironsides. He was appointed sequestrator of the Royalists in Herefordshire, was granted the Bishop's Palace, and carried off the cathedral MSS.; during the Protectorate he made antiquarian collections of the county, occasionally visiting Oxford and taking part in the music-meetings, at which his brother Sylvanus was a regular assistant. Both were good musicians; some pieces by the elder were included in Playford's *Court Ayres*, and there are Fancies by Sylvanus Taylor at Oxford. Silas, having been cashiered at the Restoration, found employment in the Custom-house at Dunkirk, and subsequently (probably with Pepys's help) at Harwich, where he died in 1678. His principal work was a 'History of Gavelkind.' After the Restoration he composed both Latin and English sacred music, which was performed in the Chapel Royal and in the Queen's private chapel. There are anthems of his at Tenbury and Ely, and twenty-nine psalms and motets for two voices and figured bass at the Fitzwilliam Museum; collections in his autograph are in Addit. MS. 4910. Taylor was friendly with Pepys, who repeatedly mentions him; and Wood says he was a man of great abilities, which were lost by his living a military life. I have given him more attention than is strictly his due, because he was an officer of the Puritan army, and yet he published dance-music during the Commonwealth; which would be impossible if the stories of Burney, Ouseley, Hullah, and Chappell were literally true.

Colonel Hutchinson, the regicide, was another excellent amateur; his wife's account of him has been quoted. Humfrey, Taylor, Hutchinson were men among the leading Puritan officers who were distinguished by their musical tastes; and not one of their contemporaries in mentioning them has in any way recorded his surprise at Cromwell's Ironsides being musical, or spoken as if they were in any way exceptions among the Puritan army. Bunyan, an obscure private soldier, was like-minded with them; so was their wonderful general; so was their greatest defender with the pen.

My readers may now judge whether or not music was prohibited under the Puritan rule. That the organs were removed from the churches is true; that the choirs were disbanded is true; that the choir-books of at least four cathedrals were destroyed is true; that the theatres were closed is true. But that music was forbidden, or even discouraged, is not true. All through the clash of warring sects the national love and cultivation of the art continued in vigour; and the suppression of ecclesiastical music only caused a greater cultivation of secular music. The Puritans refused the assistance of art in Divine worship; and a few even rejected psalm-singing, lest some of the unregenerate should mingle their voices with the elect. There were probably zealots here and there who thought it well to abstain from amusement altogether, even on week days. But the great body of the Puritans rejected music no more than good eating and drinking. The daily life of the ordinary citizen went on much as usual, while on Marston Moor the Ironsides were breaking down Newcastle's Whitecoats, or Colonel Pride stood at the door of Parliament to exclude the Presbyterian members, or even on that cold winter day when the great groan arose from the thousands who saw the masked headsman's axe descend on the neck of the Lord's Anointed. Then in the quieter years which followed the country was governed by a man who not only sought out and encouraged 'all ingenious or eximious persons in any arts,' but was in particular passionately fond of music, and did all he could for it. His reign was short; in the fullness of power and fame he went to his grave among the ancient kings of England; his son could not maintain the new fabric of government, and out of the general anarchy the old monarchy rose again to life. But the seed sown by the great Protector's enthusiastic love and discerning patronage of music broke forth into full flower in the next generation; and we musicians have especial cause to honour the memory of Oliver Cromwell.

A specially disgraceful slander has been founded on a

manipulation of the resolution passed at a Baptist conference held at Bridgewater in 1655. Playing on musical
instruments was pronounced not unlawful, but to be
used with caution, and not to give offence to 'tender
brethren.' This is garbled in Rimbault and Hopkins's
History of the Organ by quoting the first sentence *only*
and carefully suppressing the rest. The entire resolution
is given in G. Roberts's *History of the Southern Counties*,
p. 235. The question had been propounded: 'Whether
it is lawful for a believer to keep an instrument or instruments of music in his house, playing or admitting others
to play thereon?' The answer was:

> 'It is the duty of the saintes to abstaine from all appearance of evil,
> and not to make pensioners for the flesh, to fulfil ye lusts thereof, to
> redeem the time, and to do all they do to the glory of God; and though
> we cannot conclude the use of such instruments to be unlawful, yet
> we desire the saints to be very cautious lest they trangress the
> aforesaid rules in the use of it, and do what may not be of good
> report, and so give offence to their tender brethren.'

Rimbault and Hopkins quoted only the opening words
as far as *thereof*, with no indication that the resolution
declares *we cannot conclude the use of such instruments to
be unlawful*. In place of the suppressed qualification
appeared the falsity, 'Every effort was made to discourage
their use, even in private houses.'

This whole slander was literally reprinted in Grove's
Dictionary, art. 'Organ'; I exposed it, but it is literally
reprinted in the second edition of the *Dictionary*.

Even yet, notwithstanding all I have adduced to show
that music was not persecuted but was brilliantly
flourishing under the Puritan rule; notwithstanding the
passages from Bunyan, Mrs. Hutchinson, Whitelocke, and
Milton; notwithstanding the doings of Cromwell and
some of his officers; notwithstanding the introduction and
establishment of concerts and daily operas; notwithstanding the unprecedented series of publications of all
kinds—even yet I have not unmasked my heaviest
artillery. I have now to show that the opinions of the
leading Puritans were shared by their humbler followers.
I do not wish to prove too much; and I may readily grant

that the austerity advocated by the Puritans was in itself unfavourable to amusements, even those which were less objected to. Dr. Ingelo's congregation at Bristol thought him overfond of the art. What I have endeavoured to prove is the utter falsity of the libels of Burney, Hullah, Ouseley, etc., to the effect that all music was put down and persecuted, that the Puritans made it illegal, that the art was ruined for the time. I believe I have irrefragably shown that the exact contrary was the case, and I distinctly challenge any one to disprove my facts, which are taken from quite familiar works.

But in the turmoil the seething brains of some enthusiasts broke forth into wildest insanity. During the Commonwealth George Fox founded the Quakers; and the Puritans severely persecuted this new sect, which gave up ceremonies of every kind, and forbade its members the practice of every art. Singing was not unknown in their early years, but was soon formally prohibited by the leaders. One of the Quakers, Humphrey Sharp, published a wild tract addressed 'To the musicioners, the pipers, the players,' etc. in 1658. The Quakers also obtained the adhesion of a good professional musician named SOLOMON ECCLES, who had already tried several religions, having been an Episcopalian, a Presbyterian, an Independent, a Baptist, and an Antinomian; upon turning Quaker he publicly burnt his instruments on Tower Hill, and broke them when the mob put out the fire. He tells us this in a tract he put forth in 1667; and this tract is the very best evidence of all, that the Puritans, as a body, in no way objected to music. It is in the form of a dialogue between 'a Church musician who calls music the gift of God,' a Baptist calling it 'a harmless and decent practice,' and himself, the Quaker, who disallows it. Here is a passage, where Eccles describes his experiences as a professional musician among the Presbyterians, Independents, Baptists, and Antinomians.

MUSITIAN.—Pray let me know why you forsook so good a calling? QUAKER.—While I was taught of men, I could follow it: (viz.) When the Church of England was governed by Episcopal Order, I could follow it. and call'd it *the gift of God*; and when I became

more strict, a *Presbyter*, I made a trade of it, and never questioned it
at all; and after that I became an *Independent*, I could follow it; and
when I came further, and was *baptized with water*, and eat *Bread and
Wine* with them about the year 1642, they encouraged me in it, and
some of them had their Children taught on the *Virginals*; but I
went further, and was an *Antinomian* (so called) and then I could
teach mens Sons and Daughters on the Virginals and on the Viol,
and I got the last two years more than £130 a year with my own
hands, and lived very high, and perceived that the longer I followed
it, the greater income I had; but when Truth came, I was not able
to stand before it. . . .

MUSITIAN.—But, Friend, you undervalue Music too much; 'tis
true that in case you had been a Fidler, it had been no great matter
if you had cast it off, but to teach mens sons and daughters on the
Virginals and Viol, it is as harmless a calling as any man can follow.
How say you, sir?

BAPTIST.—It is a very harmless calling: there is sufficient proof
of Scripture for the lawfulness.

I doubt whether any man who reads this will venture
in cold blood to revive the assertion that the Puritans
prohibited music and persecuted musicians. Eccles was a
professional musician (as were his sons after him); he
had been a Presbyterian, and 'never questioned' it, an
Independent, a Baptist, and an Antinomian, all the while
remaining a successful professor of the art. Yet Hullah
would have us believe music was 'a stolen pleasure' at
that very time. All the evidence I have previously adduced,
even Milton's, seems to me less important and convincing
than Eccles's, as he had been through all the Puritan
sects, and gives us some view of their inner life, receiving
welcome and patronage in his art from the Baptists, and
continually prospering as a professional musician until he
turned Quaker. His evidence proves that the rank and
file of the Puritans objected to music no more than did
the practical genius who led them to victory, or the literary
genius who defended them before Europe.

Why have the Puritans been so foully belied? Mainly
because the popular imagination takes a salient point, and
is apt to look at that distinguishing mark *only*. In this
case, because the Puritans objected to music for one
particular object, and forbade it for that object, careless
people have supposed that they necessarily objected to

music at all times and places. So also there are millions of people who, having heard that it is sometimes very foggy in London, suppose that it is always foggy there, and that the sun is never seen at all. In the popular imagination all Puritans are exactly alike; and it is forgotten that some of the greatest nobles of the land were among them, as well as sturdy yeomen and small shopkeepers. In all branches of thought, whether dealing with palpable facts of the present, or recorded facts of the past, the attentive observer may see how the world generalises from one fact only, and quite overlooks light and shade, modifications and details. And when an exaggeration or mistake has once been stated, it is almost impossible to get it corrected. Some careless reader once stated that Milton reproached Charles I for reading Shakespeare; Milton did nothing of the kind, yet the mistake, though pointed out, was repeated by Scott; and though again pointed out, has been once more repeated,* or at least implied, by Swinburne. Possibly the exaggerations and slanders of Burney will be once more repeated; but I doubt if any musical historian will seriously attempt to explain away my version of the matter. I distinctly, and in the most unequivocal words, challenge any one to answer me.

---

* ' Milton also lived to make oblique recantation of his early praise of Shakespeare ' (Swinburne's *Essays and Studies*, p. 15). What Milton really said was that King Charles, knowing Shakespeare's works, ought to have profited by them, and applied Richard the Third's hypocritical speeches to himself.

CHAPTER VII

THE PERIOD OF FOREIGN INFLUENCE AND OF DRAMATIC MUSIC (1660-1700)

Restoration of ecclesiastical music.—The organ-builders.— Organist-composers of the older generation.—Charles II changes the character of both sacred and secular music.— Fancies and contrapuntal anthems disused.—French models followed.—Concerts.—Celebrations of St. Cecilia's Day.— Sacred music.—Catches.—The dramas with music, or English operas.—Purcell follows Italian models, and unites contrapuntal writing with intellectual declamation and melodic beauty, thus becoming the greatest English composer. —The age of the Restoration especially the greatest in English dramatic music.

Representative Composers : Child, Rogers, Lock, Humfrey and Purcell.

CHARLES II entered London on May 29th, 1660; and on the third Sunday after, June 17th, Pepys noted in his diary, 'This day the organs did begin to play at Whitehall before the King.' Three Sundays later, Pepys himself attended, and for the first time in his life heard a service with the organ and surpliced choir. On November 4th he heard the organ in West-minster Abbey. There was a rush to erect instruments in ~~~~~~ Magdalen College received back the organ ~~~~~~~~~~~~ and which was at a ~~~~~~~~~~~ ey, where some of ~~~~~~~~~~ e organ was lent to ~~~~~~~~~~ rection. Rochester ~~~~~~~~~ Greenwich. John ~~~~~~~~~ athedral service' at ~~~~~~~~ n Loosemore built ~~~~~~~~ eting the permanent ~~~~~~~~ f Peterborough, and ~~~~~~~~ upied; John Taunton ~~~~~~~~ Wells; Harris, an old ~~~~~~~ e Continent, returned, ~~~~~~~ d a German, Bernhard

Schmidt (Father Smith), was already in England. Renatus Harris and Father Smith were subsequently bitter rivals. The cathedral and collegiate churches were soon provided with instruments, which, however, were, like the older English organs, small and without pedals. Parish churches in general remained organless; even in Queen Anne's time the existence of an organ was considered to denote a leaning to the High Church party, and not till the Oxford Movement of the nineteenth century was one usually seen in a village church.

The replacing of choral services at first gave some trouble. From fourteen to eighteen years had elapsed since the venerable arches of our cathedrals had echoed prose chanting and anthems; for some time after the suppression, attempts had been made to carry on the services privately (for instance, by Weaver, of Windsor Castle), but these must have died out. Choir-boys could not be selected and trained in a day, and the Anglican choral traditions were growing faint. Edward Lowe, who had been organist of Christ Church, Oxford, published in 1661 a tract entitled 'Short Directions for the Performance of Cathedral Service,' containing Preces, Responses, Litany, etc., and reprinted it with additions in 1664. Apparently as a proof that anthems contained nothing Popish, a collection of the words of those used at York Cathedral was published by S. Bulkley in 1662; and of those used at St. Paul's, by James Clifford (a minor canon) in 1663 and 1664. In two or three years all the difficulties of reconstruction had been fully surmounted, and trained choir-boys had taken the place of the cornets and falsetto-singing which at first were used as substitutes for trebles.

Clifford's collection is a landmark in the history of English ecclesiastical music; and since Ouseley and others have asserted that scarcely any choir-books remained at the Restoration, it may be well to mention that in the second edition (the only one I have seen) Clifford gives the words of 393 anthems, many of them set by two or three composers; some were, however, then new. Among the composers were Tallis, Tye, Whyte, Byrd, Gibbons, and the other Elizabethans whose anthems are in Barnard's collection; Hilton, Ford, R. Price, Bryne, M. East, H. and W. Lawes, H. and E. Smith, Cobb, Molle, R. Johnson, T., J., and G. Tomkins, C. Gibbons, L. Fisher, Stonard, H. Loosemore, Jeffries, R. Jewett, Benet, Wilkinson, Gibbs, Amner, Holmes, Coste, Cranford, Dr. Wilson, R. Gibbs (of Norwich), Wigthorpe, L. Woodson, R. Hutchinson, Rogers, Peerson, Mudd, J. Heath, Child, P. Stringer (of Chester), R. Hinde, Portman, G. Mason, Hingston, R. Carr, E. Lowe, Captain Cooke, Lock, Leighton, R. Jones, A. Ferrabosco, Ramsey, W. Tucker, P. Warner, Mr. (Arthur?) Phillips, R. Browne (of Worcester), N. S., and C. J. There are more than twenty by Captain Cooke, and fourteen by his pupils, Pelham Humfrey, Blow, and R. Smith, then Children of the Chapel Royal.

Cosin was now made Bishop of Durham. In 1664 and 1670 some magnificent choir-books were written there, two of which have somehow drifted into the British Museum as Addit. MSS. 30,478–9. They consist entirely of anthems, of which there are nearly 300; many are also in the Peterhouse choir-books (*see* pp. 91, 231). Among the lesser-known composers' names are Foster, Yarrow, Rutter, Read, Hirdson, Warwick, Palmer, Nichols, Geeres, D. Taylor, Stephenson, Sol. Tozer, Cutts, Gale, Juxon, and Greggs. The anthem part of Barnard's collection has been inserted in MS. 30,478.

In re-establishing the Chapel Royal, the selection of Captain Cooke as Master of the Children seems to have been abundantly justified. Lawes was made 'Clarke of the Checke.' A list of the thirty others (eight clergymen) who attended the coronation of Charles II appears in the Cheque-Book; Edward Lowe, Child, and Gibbons are there distinguished as the organists. Hingston was not among them, but he is mentioned subsequently. The anthem, 'Zadock the priest,' was composed by Lawes; and another anthem by Cooke. The music for the procession through the City had been entrusted to Lock.

At the Restoration the principal musicians were H. Lawes, Dr. Wilson, Jenkins, Hingston, Sympson, with the still older Lanier. These have been already spoken of; and some who have been left for the present chapter were, nevertheless, previously famous. Henry Lawes and Simon Ives only lived till 1662; Dr. Colman died in 1664, and his son Edward in 1669; Sympson also in 1669; Lanier in 1666. Wilson, Jenkins, and Silas Taylor lived till 1678; Hingston and Gamble a few years longer. Some remaining musicians of the older period must be dealt with before the 'School of the Restoration' is described.

WILLIAM CHILD was born at Bristol in 1606, and taught there by Elway Bevin. He succeeded Mundy in 1630 at Windsor Castle; on the death of Gyles he took the entire duty, and ever since there has been but one organist. In 1631 he graduated Mus.Bac. Oxon., but did not proceed Mus.Doc. till 1663. He composed much church music, some of which, being simple in structure, was ridiculed; upon which he produced his masterly Service in D major (called his 'Sharp Service'), which Playford says was a favourite with Charles I. In 1639 Child issued a work with the significant title, 'The first set of Psalms of III voyces, fitt for private chapels or other private meetings, with a continual basse either for the Organ or Theorbo, newly composed after the Italian way.' It contains the first sixteen Psalms and four others, set as anthems. This work was reprinted in 1650 by Playford, but he used the original title and plates, and Child is still called 'Organist of his Majesties free chapel of Windsor!' A third edition appeared in 1656, with a new title, 'Choise Musick to the Psalms of David.' At this time Child, it is said, had retired to a small farm. Some of Playford's collections contain pieces of his; but we hear nothing of him till the Restoration, when he became composer to the King. Under the lax government of Charles II, Dr. Child's salary fell into arrears, which amounted to about £500; one day he carelessly said he would take £5 and some bottles of wine for his chance of getting the money, and the canons of Windsor took him at his word. But afterwards James II paid arrears; Child now repented his hasty bargain, and the canons generously repaid him on condition that he would repave the choir of St. George's Chapel with marble. Child lived on till March 23rd, 1696–7, and was buried in the Chapel

CHRISTOPHER GIBBONS, second son of the great Orlando, was born August, 1615, and after his father's death was choir-boy at Exeter. About 1638 he became organist of Winchester Cathedral, afterwards joining the Royalist army. He was one of the leading London teachers in 1651, and composed part of the music for Shirley's *Cupid and Death* in 1653; in 1654 he played on Magdalen College organ to Evelyn. In Davenant's operatic performances he took part in the accompaniments; and, in general, performance rather than composition was his pursuit. He was made organist of Westminster Abbey after the Restoration, and of the Chapel Royal; and in 1664 obtained a royal warrant to be made Mus.Doc. Oxon. Dr. Gibbons died October 20th, 1676, and was buried in the Abbey cloisters. A few of his compositions exist, some being printed in Playford's *Cantica Sacra* (1674).

BENJAMIN ROGERS, another long-lived organist and composer, was born at Windsor in 1614; and after serving in the choir, was organist at Dublin. He returned to Windsor Castle at the breaking out of the Irish rebellion in 1641; and though the choir was soon after silenced, Rogers was pensioned. He taught music in Windsor and London during the Commonwealth; and came into the highest repute as a composer of instrumental music. His twelve Fancies for viols and organ were presented to the Archduke of Austria, as it was supposed they were the best music that *could* be made. A letter from Rogers (in Wood's MS. 'Lives') gives further account of the honours paid him in Sweden, where Dr. Ingelo presented to Queen Christina 'two sets of musique which I had newly made, being four parts, viz. two treble violins, tenor, bass in E lamy, which were often played by the Queen's Italian musicians.' A Suite is preserved at Upsala, and many Consorts in the Hamburg Library. In Holland too he was equally honoured; Playford having sent some of his works to Holland which were 'played by able masters to the States-General, at the peace festivities, they were so liked that the Noblemen and others at the playing thereof did drink the great rummer of wine to Minehere Rogers of England.' Cromwell, at the request of Ingelo, sent a mandate (May 28th, 1658) to Cambridge commanding the University statutes to be dispensed with, and Rogers to be created Mus.Bac. without residence; the mandate concludes Carlyle's work. We are not informed that the Puritanised University replied that music was 'against the law of the land,' or 'a foolish vanitie,' or any other of the abusive terms which some writers would have us believe were applied to music by the Puritans; the sober-garbed, Scripture-quoting scholars who then ruled the University seem to have been as ready to honour Rogers as they had been to honour Colman a few years before, and they signalised the reception of the renowned English composer by a grand concert at the Commencement. At the Restoration, Ingelo brought Rogers to Eton; they had written and set the 'Hymnus Eucharisticus,' sung at the London banquet to Charles II. Rogers also assisted at Windsor Castle until in 1664 the enthusiastic amateur, Thomas Pierce, called him to Magdalen College, persuading the foundation to raise the salary to £60 a year. He had not proceeded Mus.Doc. at Cambridge, but graduated instead at Oxford in 1669. During his long life the style in which he had obtained such success was quite superseded by the instrumental style of France, then of Italy; and he actually outlived Purcell, who had combined all the various elements into a new style. In the meantime, Rogers had produced some ecclesiastical works (both services and anthems), which have always remained in favour; while his 'Hymnus Eucharisticus' is still sung every May morning from Magdalen Tower, the first stanza being daily used as Grace before the College dinner. In 1685 Dr. Rogers was pensioned off on charges of loose conduct, but he lived till June, 1698. Many of the statements in Wood's 'Lives' are given on the authority of Dr. Rogers; and some rare works that belonged to him have found their way into the Bodleian Library.

Both Dr. Child and Dr. Rogers cultivated melody in

their ecclesiastical music; yet succeeded in preserving most of the merits of the older school. Their works have remained in deserved respect and regular use; and there is none of the confusion of tonality which occasionally offends modern ears in Tallis and Byrd, though there is also less contrapuntal grandeur. Two others of the older Restoration school deserve mention.

ALBERTUS BRYNE (Brian), born about 1621, was a pupil of John Tomkins, and on the death of his master obtained, at the age of seventeen, the organistship of St. Paul's. In the Commonwealth he was a leading teacher; and is called 'that famously velvet-fingered organist' in *The Virgin's Pattern*. At the Restoration he returned to his old post, and after the Great Fire was organist of Westminster Abbey. There are good anthems, a Service, and some instrumental music by Bryne in existence. His son, of the same name, was organist at Dulwich College.

RANDAL JEWETT, born 1603, was organist of both Dublin Cathedrals, 1631–9; in 1643 of Chester Cathedral, and again of Dublin 1646. Then he came to London, as he is in Playford's list in 1651; after the Restoration he was organist of Winchester, where he died July 1675. There are anthems by Jewett in Tudway's collection.

The older musicians no doubt for a time maintained their strenuous belief in the superiority of English instrumental music; and in 1667 Sympson re-issued his *Division-Violist* with a Latin translation for the benefit of foreigners, while Birchensha (Berkenshaw), translating Alstedius's 'Templum Musicum' in 1663, gave utterance to the belief in words previously quoted. But we hear no more of this boasting.

Playford continued to publish, though his collections were less numerous for some years after the Restoration. His *Courtly Masquing Airs* (1662) was an enlarged reprint of the *Court Ayres* of 1655. Two more sets of *Ayres and Dialogues* appeared in 1669 and 1685; the former contains a reprint of Lawes's first two sets, and is recommended to be bound with Lawes's third set, as the whole would then include the best vocal music composed during the past twenty years. Some of the *Ayres* are of Playford's own composition; and some are Italian, the rest being by Wilson, the Colmans, Lanier, etc. The other book is similar. *Catch that Catch Can*, with additions and a miscellaneous second part, was reprinted in 1667; and (as *The Musical Companion*) in 1673.

Deering's *Cantica Sacra*, with a dedication to the Queen Dowager, appeared in 1662; a larger collection, with forty pieces by various authors, followed in 1674. These were published in three part-books, and are for a treble and a bass voice generally (sometimes two trebles or tenors) and a thorowbase. The first eight are doubtfully by Deering; then follow one each by Lawes, G. Jeffries, and Chr. Gibbons, four by Dr. Rogers, six by Lock, and one by Playford himself, all these being to Latin words. The others, to English words, are three each by Gibbons, Rogers, and Isaac Blackwell, one by Wise, two each by Lock and John Jackson, and four by Playford.

Another fresh attempt of Playford's was *Musick's Delight on the Cithren*, dated 1666, and preserved at the British Museum and Bodleian Libraries. The work contains a diagram of the Cithern, which was fretted, and strung with eight wire strings, 'divided into four course, two in a course'; some instructions for tuning and performance; and eighty-four lessons in tablature, some by Lock, Ives, W. Lawes, and Dr. Colman. There are also seventeen songs to good poetry, accompanied by the cithern.

Musick's Handmaid, a collection of (not very remarkable) virginal music, was published in 1663 and reprinted 1678. It contains a number of short pieces on six-lined staves; it was beautifully engraved, and the superiority over the rugged type-printing was obvious. In the preface Playford said, 'The Virginal is strung with one single course of strings; the Harpsichord with two or more, and is fuller and louder'; and he gives a few instructions. Much of the work was reprinted in *Musica Antiqua*.

The Division-Violin was probably published not long

after the Restoration; I only know the second edition, dated 1685, a copy of which is preserved at the Bodleian Library. There are thirty pieces in the index, by Reading, Polwhele, Sympson, Mell, Becket, Tollet, Baltzar, etc.; the book contains thirty-six, two of which are by Solomon 'Eagles.' One by P. Becket has double-notes and chords.

The Pleasant Companion (1682) was an instruction-book by THOMAS GREETING, *Gent.*, for the flageolet; a peculiar notation is used, consisting of dots corresponding to the holes to be stopped, with a cross for the higher octave. Seventy-nine tunes are given in this flageolet-tablature; they were mostly by John Banister, with some by Lock, Jeffry, Banister, Humfrey, and R. Smith.

The Genteel Companion, by HUMPHREY SALTER, *Gent.*, was a similar work for the Recorder; in the frontis-piece a larger instrument than the flageolet is shown. There are some instructions, with twelve tunes, both in gamut and the dot-tablature, besides about fifty in the gamut only. *The Delightful Companion*, also for the Recorder, was published by Carr. *A Vade Mecum* for the Recorder is preserved in the Douce Collection.

In the preface to *The Division-Violin* Playford referred to his increasing age and sickness; he soon after retired, leaving his business to his son Henry and to R. Carr. At this time his son John was in partnership with Godbid's widow, printing; but he died in 1686, Purcell setting an elegy. The father lived some years longer; his will was proved in August, 1694. His auction-catalogue is repeatedly mentioned in Wood's MS. 'Lives.' For many years his *Breefe Introduction to the Skill of Musick* and his three-voiced Psalter were reprinted; the British Museum has twenty-four editions of the former. As a good musician, and the first Englishman who made a special business of music-publishing, Honest John Playford deserves remembrance.

Other collections, such as *Apollo's Banquet*, *The Treasury of Musick*, *The Vade Mecum or Necessary Companion*, *Youth's Delight on the Flageolet*, must not be omitted; in particular, a singular volume edited by 'Cl. J.,' and published by Brome, deserves notice. It is

called *New Ayres and Dialogues*, and appeared in 1678;
a good poem in praise of music, signed J. D. (Denham?),
is prefixed. There are sixty-one songs, several Dialogues, and a Trialogue, by seventeen leading composers
of the preceding and contemporary reigns, from W. Lawes
to Purcell and Wise; then follow Lessons (some grouped
in 'Sutes') by Banister, T. Low, T. Farmer, Jenkins,
and others, for two viols or violins, the parts facing
different ways.

Whether the term 'Suite' arose in England is not
clear; but it seems probable. The succession of Almain,
Courante, and Saraband had been distinctly the ruling
principle in the *Musica Harmonia* of W. Lawes and
others, published in 1651; and the name 'Suite,' 'Sute,'
or 'Sett of Lessons' was commonly used in England,
while the French composers called a succession of pieces
'Ordres,' and the Germans used the word 'Partita.'

I may here mention an extremely quaint and interesting
instruction-book for the lute, entitled *Musick's Monument*,
published in 1676 by THOMAS MACE, a chorister of Trinity
College, Cambridge. Mace was born in 1613; and since
there is an anthem by him in the Peterhouse books, he
was doubtless at Cambridge before the war. From his
book we learn that he was in York during the siege in
1644; he speaks of congregational singing with organ accompaniment as a usage peculiar to York Minster. He
complained of growing deafness; in 1690 he came to London and advertised the sale of his instruments and music.
Musick's Monument is highly amusing from its quaint
conceits and singular style; the use of many adjectives
hyphened together gives the letterpress a peculiar appearance, but is advantageous for its clearness. Mace treated
principally of the lute, but partly also of sacred music
and concert-giving. He shows himself an adherent of the
old school, sneering at the 'scolding violins,' complaining
that art was 'going to the dogs,' and that self-sufficient
young students despised the noble works of the style
prevalent in his youth.

But while Child, Rogers, and Mace were still in full
vigour the influence of a man whom they all outlived had

completely brought their works into discredit, and they lived to find only their ecclesiastical music remembered, and all their contemporaries superseded and forgotten. It was Charles II who killed the older English school, vocal and instrumental alike; and who finally killed the pride of the English in their music. He cared for no music unless he could beat time to it; and the contrapuntal Fancies he abhorred, meeting every argument with 'Have I not ears?' Not long after the Restoration he formed a band of twenty-four violins (of course including the larger-sized instruments), in imitation of the 'Vingt-quatre Violons du Roy' organised by Louis XIII. This institution finally ousted the viol, whose supremacy had already been shaken during the Commonwealth, as the capabilities of the despised violin became evident. Baltzar, the great Lübeck violinist, who had come to England in 1656, was appointed the Master of Charles II's Violins; he died July, 1663, when John Banister succeeded him and was commanded to select twelve of the twenty-four to follow the King everywhere. Banister was sent for further study to France, but was dismissed after his return for expressing his opinion that the English violinists were superior to the French. This band of twenty-four violins played while the Court was dining, and on December 21st, 1662, Evelyn records that they were introduced into the Chapel Royal to play symphonies and ritornellos between each section of the anthems. Tudway says this was only to be done when the King himself was present; but it was a fundamental change, and Evelyn records his opinion with some warmth:

'Instead of the ancient, grave, and solemn wind musique accompanying the organ, was introduced a concert of twenty-four violins between every pause, after the French fantastical light way, better suiting a tavern or playhouse than a church. This was the first time of change, and now we no more heard the cornet, which gave life to the organ; that instrument quite left off in which the English were so skilful!'

The point especially to be apprehended is the introduction of the ritornellos 'between every pause.' Previously all sacred music had been vocal from beginning to end, the instruments playing with the voices, though (as I believe) with as much embellishment as possible; now there were to be ritornellos, and Charles II wished them to be such as he could beat time to. After his death the violins were not used in the Chapel Royal, but the ritornellos and symphonies were still played on the organ.

It must not be thought that Charles II's influence in all this inroad upon English music was entirely harmful. Since 1600 the *expressive* capabilities of music had been enormously developed in Italy; and the French musicians had refined the lighter branches of the art, which the English composers had thought beneath their notice. The contrapuntal Fancies had been worked out in the preceding period; new material was required, and an acquaintance with foreign discoveries.

The popular cultivation of music was declining. As greater skill and refinement in singing, and greater instrumental execution were introduced, ordinary performances were less and less in favour; and we hear less of every one being expected to take part, or of mechanics singing together. We, however, find mention of the musical skill of domestic servants, especially by Pepys, though he refers to the better kind; he would hear a waiting-maid play and sing before engaging her. Music seems to have been carefully taught in charity schools as a qualification for the children to become apprentices and servant-maids; Thomas Brewer had been originally trained for this reason. The barbers began to neglect music, especially after periwigs were introduced. In country places we may suppose that little change took place; Mace speaks of stretched strings being found in the cupboards of country houses. Pepys, on his visit to Huntingdonshire (October, 1662), recorded that the milkmaids 'come all home together in pomp with their milk, and sometimes they have musique go before them.' This 'musique' was probably a pipe and tabor; in Bunyan's allegory, *The Holy War*, a pipe and tabor precede the released prisoners' joyful entry into Mansoul. Chamberlayne's *Angliæ Notitia* (1669) mentions (among the recreations of the commonalty) bell-ringing, 'a Recreation used in no other Country of the World'; Hentzner, in Queen Elizabeth's reign, had been struck with the same feature.

The Restoration was unfavourable to the opera, as the ordinary theatres were re-opened, and the nascent opera was superseded by the play. In Davenant's *Playhouse to Let* (a comedy introducing excerpts from several works, connected by a dialogue between the Housekeeper, a Player, and a Musician) the Musician defends recitative against the arguments of the Player; the third and fourth acts of the comedy are then occupied by *The History of Sir Francis Drake* and *The Cruelty of the Spaniards in Peru.* But no other opera was produced after the Restoration. Stilted rhyming tragedies and amazingly immoral comedies were the chief features of the Restoration drama. The works of Shakespeare and other Elizabethan writers were revived with extensive additions introducing music and spectacle; the opera was replaced by the play with music. Dryden turned *Paradise Lost* into a rhyming opera, but it was apparently not set; E. Eccleston wrote a most absurd imitation, *Noah's Flood.* There is little doubt that the English public failed to appreciate the singing of ordinary dialogue in recitative; and Dryden advocated the entrusting of the musical portions to super-natural or maniacal characters only, from whom the speech-in-song would sound less unnatural than from ordinary persons. This theory seems to have been generally accepted, and partly explains the interpolations thought necessary whenever an Elizabethan drama was revived. It was customary to compose special music for the entr'actes; these pieces were called 'Curtain Tunes.' Magalotti's interesting account of the Grand Duke Cosmo's visit to England in 1669 mentions that 'the most delightful symphonies' were played before the dramas; on which account many came early.

The State Concerts which Cromwell had introduced at Whitehall were not imitated by Charles II; but the idea of an audience assembling to *listen* to music, not to take part, had been followed up before the Restoration. It became the custom to hold concerts in taverns. Roger North tells us that a weekly meeting was held in a tavern near St. Paul's, 'where there was a chamber organ that one Phillips played upon, and some shopkeepers and foremen came weekly to sing in concert, and to hear, and enjoy ale and tobacco, and after some time the audience grew strong.' They chiefly used *Catch that Catch Can*, of which the third edition (1667) is dedicated by Playford to his 'endeared friends of the late Musick Society and meeting in the Old Jury.' These meetings must have been temporarily stopped by the Great Fire. The tavern near St. Paul's exhibited the sign of the 'Swan and Lyre'; and was long known by the name of the 'Goose and Gridiron,' into which the sign was degraded. It has now been destroyed. Another club met at the 'Hole in the Wall,' Baldwin's Gardens. North further tells us that the 'inclination of the citizens to follow musick,' shown by these meetings, 'was confirmed by many little entertainments the masters voluntarily made for their scollers, for being knowne they were alwaies crowded.'

John Banister, having lost his place at Court, hired a large room in Whitefriars, close to the Temple gate, furnished it with a raised box for the performers, and seats at small tables for the audience; in the *London Gazette*, December 30th, 1672, he advertised:

'These are to give notice that at Mr. Banister's house, now called the Music-school, over against the George Tavern in White Friars, this present Monday, will be musick performed by excellent masters, beginning precisely at four of the clocke in the afternoon, and every afternoon for the future, precisely at the same hour.'

These concerts were, nevertheless, as North says, 'ale-house fashion' in their seats at small tables. They must have resembled the better class of smoking concerts in our own day; one shilling was charged. North declares:

'There was very good music, for Banister found means to procure the best hands in town and some voices to come and perform there; and there wanted no variety of humour, for Banister himself among other things did wonders upon a flageolet, to a thorough-base, and the several masters had their solos.'

This was the first establishment of regular concerts

outside a tavern; they are repeatedly advertised later. In 1678 Thomas Britton's concerts were established in Clerkenwell, and lasted till 1714. Another concert-room independent of ale and tobacco, was opened about 1680 in Villiers Street, and became very fashionable.

These performances led to a culmination in the celebrations of St. Cecilia's Day (November 22nd) which are first definitely mentioned in 1683, and were repeated in 1684, 1685, 1687, 1690–1703. Why they were discontinued is not known. An excellent account of these celebrations, and of other similar attempts, was published by W. H. Husk in 1857. They were apparently managed, as Husk says, by—

'A body of persons associated together (whether for any other purpose than these celebrations cannot be traced) under the name of "The Musical Society." The members of this Society annually appointed certain of their body (some of them professors of music and others amateurs) as stewards of the festival, to whom appears to have been committed the task of making the requisite arrangements. On the 22nd day of November, the members of the Society attended Divine Service at St. Bride's Church, where a choral service and an anthem, occasionally composed for the festival, were performed, and a sermon, usually in defence of church music, was preached. They afterwards repaired to another place, where an ode in praise of music, written and composed expressly for the festival, was performed; after which they sat down to an entertainment.'

Among the poets employed were Oldham, Brady, Tate, Durfey, Shadwell, Addison, Congreve, and, above all, Dryden, whose Odes for the celebrations in 1687 and 1697 are the most spirited and spirit-stirring in the English language. The first performance was held at the concert-room in Villiers Street, the others in Stationers' Hall. The church service is not heard of before 1693. The composers of the Odes were Purcell (1683 and 1692), Blow, Turner, Draghi, King, Finger, D. Purcell, Jer. Clark, J. Eccles, Norris, and Hart; unfortunately the best poems did not fall to the best composers. There were even celebrations in several other towns, especially Oxford; the information about them is very scanty, but the main features were the same as those of the London performances.

By the time these celebrations had begun the change in the style of English music had been entirely accomplished. Charles II's orders for a livelier style of sacred music could hardly be obeyed by Child and Gibbons; but Captain Cooke probably had better success, being a most distinguished singer. Apparently he composed solo anthems. Some of his pupils quickly showed powers in the same direction, and were encouraged by the King. The most gifted, Pelham Humfrey, was sent to Paris for further study, and on his return inaugurated a style completely unlike the harmonic style of Tallis's Dorian Service, or the contrapuntal style of Orlando Gibbons's Service in F. Declamation was studied as carefully as in the Ayres and Dialogues of the period; but with a richer employment of purely musical resources. The anthems (and even the services to some extent) consisted of a series of short movements, some for a solo voice, some choral. Though using more advanced and richer musical resources than their predecessors, the composers of the Restoration certainly did not attain a high ideal of sacred art; and the separate movements are too short and too slightly developed to be musically satisfying.

The congregational psalmody of this period is not much alluded to, and we cannot form a very definite idea of it. There is one description by Magalotti of psalm-singing at Exeter, 'first by one alone, then by all together'; Mace speaks as if he had never heard of organ accompaniments except at York. When there was an organ, the custom seems to have been to accompany the tune with a bass only; the florid figuration of the melody was still fashionable, and curious specimens of the style may be seen in Daniel Purcell's 'The Psalms set full.' Both Churchmen and Dissenters practised 'lining out'; where there was an organ florid interludes were played. Playford published a folio four-voiced Psalter in 1671; a more portable three-voiced appeared in 1677, and was the favourite Psalter for many years. There was a tendency to limit the number of tunes, and in many places only five or six were used. Tate and Brady's new version of the Psalter appeared in 1696; hymns were not thought of till the eighteenth century. Sermons and tracts upon the question of church music were frequent.

The Parliament called in 1661 was almost entirely Royalist, and urged persecution of the Puritan party, to which the King after some hesitation consented. Uniformity of worship was insisted on, and enforced with injudicious severity. Over two thousand clergymen were deprived; and the Nonconformists became a separate body, at first persecuted, but at the Revolution receiving legal toleration. The Nonconformists were now outside the Established Church, and each congregation became more and more isolated; Presbyterianism weakened in England, the Independents and Baptists soon forming the great majority of the Dissenters. The extremer Separatists were still undecided whether to admit singing in public worship; the Quakers finally rejected it. During the occasional persecutions (1662–88), the secrecy of the services did not always permit singing, and one record in 1682 mentions 'we sang a psalm in a low voice.' A congregation at Bristol used singing as a defence; they curtained off part of the room, placing the preacher and others of the brethren behind the curtain, so that the preacher could not be recognised and informed against; and if officers came to arrest the preacher, a psalm, previously announced, was at once begun, and the curtain drawn back, so that nothing illegal could be alleged. The Baptists were violently divided on the question of singing with possible unbelievers; on the introduction by Keach of a psalm at the Horselydown Chapel (which is the earliest case known) discontent was excited, and in 1693 some of the brethren seceded, and founded a chapel in which there was no singing for forty years. No Dissenters used organs or other instruments.

Musical history, at this time as elsewhen, was a part of general history; and we may see a typical Restoration peculiarity in the words set to music. It was an age of strongest contrasts; of general sneering at piety and decency, and intense appreciation of long sermons; when priests were commonly derided as hypocrites, and the sentinels at the Tower asked a blessing as the Seven

Bishops passed them; of open and impudently boasting immorality, and severe persecution of Dissenters; of Wycherley, Rochester, and Aphra Behn, as of Milton, Bunyan, Baxter, Henry More, Leighton, and Ken. The composers of the Restoration were equally at home in setting the most sacred and the most disgustingly vulgar words. As in a volume of Herrick's poetry, the transition is from one extreme to the other, from high and pure thinking to the lowest ideas and filthiest expressions. The fouler part of their work was accomplished by means of the Catch, which was certainly developed by the attempts to introduce open or veiled obscenity; and it is at this period that the Catch in its modern sense became important, though canons and rounds were still all included under the term Catches.

The Catch is a purely English form of art; and though its beginnings were of the worst, it had a better development later, as finer manners led self-respecting musicians to apply its capabilities to innocent amusement. Music has little intrinsic humour; but the Catch gives splendid facilities for the humorous use of words. It is remarkable that this suggestive form has not been used by foreign composers.

Many of the best English folk-tunes are first heard of in this period; especially the enlivening English country-dances and hornpipes then assumed the character they have since retained. 'Come, lasses and lads,' 'Sir Roger de Coverley,' and the 'College Hornpipe' all date from the late seventeenth century; and the lovely melodies, 'My lodging is on the cold ground' and 'Barbara Allen,' are among the serious strains. Among the collections published by Henry Playford are many with the title *Drollery*, usually connected with some place, as Westminster Drollery, Norfolk Drollery, Berkshire Drollery, etc.; they contained popular songs with tunes (generally unharmonised), and catches.

There was a sufficiency of instruction-books. The Gamba was still used; probably towards 1700 appeared *The Compleat Violist*, by 'the late' Mr. BENJAMIN HELY. It contains a few instructions, the Psalm-tunes 'as they

are sung in churches where there are organs,' and pieces.
There is a copy in the Douce Collection. Nothing is
known of the author. Sympson's *Division-Violist* was reprinted in 1667 with a Latin translation, and again as late as
1712. Besides Thomas Greeting's treatise for the flageolet and Humphrey Salter's for the recorder, there were
books for the flute and hautboy, and several for singing;
among the latter may be mentioned A. B.'s *Synopsis of
Vocal Musick* (dedicated in Latin to Archbishop Sheldon
in 1680). It is a very well-written treatise, and uses the
octave scale instead of the tetrachords recommended by
Campion and at this time general in England. T. Cross's
Nolens Volens Violin Tutor (1695) has an exact diagram
of the fingerboard, with the stops marked, the learner
being directed to mark them on his instrument. The
guitar was for a time fashionable owing to the fine playing
of Francisco Corbeta; Playford wrote in *Musick's Delight
on the Cithren*:

'Not a city-dame, though but a Tap-wife, but is ambitious to
have her daughters taught by *Monsieur la Novo Kickshawibus* on
the gittar.'

In theory the only new work which appeared was Sympson's; one of the editions of Playford's was revised by
Purcell. The Bodleian Library is specially rich in the
instruction-books of this period.

Though the Viol-da-Gamba was still in favour, we
hear little of the treble viols after the Restoration; the
lute also, and its tablature notation, were getting antiquated, and Mace's book was among the latest instances
of tablature. The compositions for the keyed instruments
are all much easier than the compositions of the Elizabethan virginalists; they are also slight and short. The
earlier fingering (5 denoting the thumb in the left hand)
was still employed. Purcell gave fingering for the scale
of C, using the thumb on the first note of two octaves,
but not again. The highest note used for the violin, even
in Purcell's sonatas, was c'''.

The musical history of this and later periods requires
little research, as the great amount of publication renders
acquaintance with the works produced a comparatively

easy task, though several publications are extremely rare. As regards facts, we are fortunate in possessing Roger North's *Memoirs of Musick* (not published till 1846), whence a good general idea of matters may be gained; besides the diaries of Pepys and Evelyn, and the collections of Anthony Wood. The establishment of newspapers and the continually greater diffusion of printing also made personal allusions to musicians more frequent; henceforth documentary proofs are common, and we can generally discover the main events of even obscurer musicians' lives.

The references to music in Evelyn's diary are only occasional; the most important after the Restoration concern the anthems at the coronation, the introduction of the violins into the Chapel Royal, and the opera on January 5th, 1674. Pepys constantly alludes to his own or others' performances; I had begun to make a list of his allusions, but in the first three months alone (January–March, 1659–60) found twenty-nine, of which those on January 16th, February 18th, 20th, 21st, and 22nd are important. There are hundreds more in his immortal record, many of the highest interest.

Before taking the biographical notices, miscellaneous matters must be dismissed. There was evidently an attempt to establish Italian opera in 1660 under Giulio Gentileschi; also in 1674 a visit from a touring company, as appears by Evelyn's note. In 1683 the King, supposing the French *Grand Opéra* suspended during the royal mourning, sent Betterton to Paris to bring over Lulli and his company; but the object was not attained. Cambert and Grabu had previously settled in London; the former came in disappointment at the success of Lulli; and had an opera performed at Court in 1677. Grabu had the honour of setting Dryden's *Albion and Albanius;* the opera was published, and is good spirited work of considerable dramatic power, though rather dull musically. Other foreign musicians prominent in England after the Restoration were Giovanni Baptista Draghi (sometimes confused with Lulli), Nicola Matteis, and Godfrey Finger; while Pietro Reggio, who had been at

Stockholm when Whitelocke was sent there in 1653 (*see* p. 247), settled at Oxford.

Upon the re-establishment of cathedral services the Oxford society, which had made such a brilliant musical life during the Commonwealth, rapidly dispersed, and about 1662 the meetings ceased. In that year the Professor of Music, Dr. Wilson, resigned, and came to London; Edward Lowe, organist of Christ Church, took the post. Lowe died in 1682; and was succeeded by Richard Goodson, his son of the same name succeeding in 1718. In this period the magnificent musical library of Christ Church was accumulated. At Cambridge the University established a Professorship of Music in July, 1684, held first by Staggins (1684–1705), next by Tudway. Great acoustical discoveries were made in this period; Noble and Pigot, two Oxford students, independently made the discovery in 1676 that the successive partial-tones of a fundamental note build up the chord of the dominant seventh; excellent treatises on the relation between harmony and mathematics were written by Sir Francis North in 1677, and by Dr. Holder in 1694; and various memoirs by Turner, Morland, and especially by Wallis, are of great scientific value. The unrivalled genius of Newton, so amazingly employed for thirty years, and so amazingly wasted for thirty years more, was little concerned with acoustics; his principal attempt in this direction was a theoretical calculation of the velocity of sound. Newton had discovered the differential equation of mechanical vibrations, but it has never been solved; by assuming that the vibrations take place in every direction at equal velocities, the equation is simplified, and then easily solved. From the solution Newton calculated the velocity of sound; but experiment proved that his result was too small; and this was never explained until Laplace showed that the resulting heat accelerated the velocity one-sixth.

At the close of the seventeenth century a soldier named John Simcock, of Captain Bell's troop, invented an instrument which he called 'The Bell Harp,' still occasionally heard. It is 'a kind of wire-strung psaltery,' and is swung round in the air as it is played. Another instrument, upon which a treatise was published, was called the 'Psalterer,' and was a large viol (resembling a Tromba Marina), with two strings for the treble and bass of the psalms. A semitonic tablature was proposed for it; and various psalm-tunes and pieces were given in this notation, but nothing more is heard of the instrument, though it might have been advantageously employed where there was no church organ. Mr. Taphouse possessed a MS. of arrangements for the Psalterer.

A number of the aristocracy, justly piqued at the superiority of the Italians, in 1700 subscribed 200 guineas for a prize setting of Congreve's masque, *The Judgment of Paris*. The first prize (£100) was awarded to John Weldon; the second (£50) to John Eccles; the third to Daniel Purcell; and the fourth to Godfrey Finger, who thought himself unfairly treated, and returned to Germany.

Henry Playford, who was born in 1657, Lawes being his godfather, succeeded his father in 1685; and, in partnership with Carr, published *The Theatre of Music*, but after a time published alone. One of his principal collections was *Harmonia Sacra*, published in 1688; it was dedicated to Ken, an apt selection, as this was the year of the Trial of the Seven Bishops, and Ken was musical, having in his youth taken part in the Oxford meetings. The volume contains twenty-nine pieces (either to Biblical or poetical words) for voice and bass; twelve are by Purcell, four by Lock, three by Humfrey, and seven by Blow, with others by Turner and John Jackson, and a Dialogue by Humfrey and Blow in conjunction. In the preface Playford says:

'As for the Musical Part, it was composed by the most Skilful Masters of this Age; and though some of them are now dead, yet their Composures have been review'd by Mr. Henry Purcell, whose tender Regard for the Reputation of those great Men made him careful that nothing should be published which, through the negligence of Transcribers, might reflect upon their Memory.'

A second part of *Harmonia Sacra*, with a dedication to Aldrich, followed in 1693. It contains Latin motets by Carissimi and others, the remainder being English poems. There are seventeen pieces in all, six being by Purcell, one by his brother, two by Clarke, and one each by Blow, R. King, and Barrincloe. By far the most remarkable piece in this collection is Purcell's magnificent *scena*, 'In guilty night.' There are complimentary verses to Blow and Purcell.

About this time Henry Playford had removed his business to Temple Change, Fleet Street, still living, as his father had done, in Arundel Street, Strand. He lived till about 1710, and continued to publish; but rivals had arisen. Some important works were issued by Heptinstall, and others by John Walsh, who began publishing about 1690 in Catherine Street, Strand, and after Playford's death was the leading publisher. Walsh soon omitted the date of publication from everything he issued. John Hare issued some works and then joined Walsh.

A great many of Henry Playford's collections fully shared the grossness of the age. His *Wit and Mirth* (1707) and the later editions of *The Musical Companion* are sadly soiled by vulgarity. That such publications as *Harmonia Sacra*, and also the viler catches and songs, should be issued by the same publisher, and composed by the same musicians, is another of the contrasts familiar to students of the Restoration period.

After the first few years of Charles II's reign we hear no more of the pride of the English in their instrumental music, which had been so singularly strong during the Commonwealth; and ever since, except for a few years as regards Purcell, there has been no general belief that English musicians were equal to foreigners. Neither have they been equal to the best foreign composers and performers at any given moment since 1695; since Purcell's death there has always been at least one composer on the Continent (not to mention performers) producing works far superior to anything England could show. It was Purcell himself who first plainly admitted that English music was inferior to Italian, although he was then beginning to surpass all his Italian contemporaries. At the beginning of Charles II's reign French fashions were dominant in music as in other matters; but they were speedily disused as the compositions of Carissimi, Stradella, and Bassani became known. When Corelli's works first arrived is a moot point, and is of interest in connection with Purcell; they were known before 1693, when Purcell was complimented (in *Harmonia Sacra*) on possessing—

'Corelli's genius to Bassani's join'd.'

Purcell was the first to recognise how very far Frescobaldi, Carissimi, Stradella, and their successors had developed the art in richness of detail, expressive capacity, and structural beauty; and by adopting these improvements he at once shot immeasurably ahead of his contemporaries. In doing this he also succeeded in avoiding a too close copying of the Italian school, and in preserving a national style; and the difficulties of his task stimulated his invention so splendidly that he advanced to be the greatest composer of his age in Europe, and the greatest musician England has ever produced, so eclipsing his immediate predecessors that their secular music was completely forgotten, and nothing more was heard of the brothers Lawes, Dr. Wilson, and Jenkins, until musical historians a century later began to hunt out their works. The ecclesiastical composers and the Elizabethan madrigalists were not forgotten, and certain specimens of their works remained in favour. Large collections of services and anthems were made by James Hawkins, organist of Ely Cathedral, and by Dean Aldrich at Oxford; at the Fitzwilliam Museum, Cambridge, there are very many services and anthems in Blow's handwriting, and a volume of anthems copied by Purcell. The composers of the Restoration were thus familiar with the sterling counterpoint of the Elizabethan composers, and had all models of style at hand from which to form their own.

The Corporation of Music which Charles I had established, and which Cromwell's musicians wished to revive with extended powers, was again set up at the Restoration, N. Lanier resuming his post as Marshal. A room was hired for its meetings, and an attempt was made to enforce a jurisdiction and a monopoly, but this was soon discontinued. Its order-book is now Harleian MS. 1911;

the minutes have preserved the signatures of Lanier, Hingston, Humfrey, Blow, T. Purcell, and others. The orders are soon scanty, the last being dated 1679.

The history of the Chapel Royal is at this period almost the whole of English musical history, as it had been for many years during the Reformation.

The destruction of the remnants of feudalism during the Civil War had once more, and this time finally, concentrated the musical talent of England in London. This may be seen by comparing the dedications of the printed music under Charles II with those under James I. The madrigalists—Dowland, Greaves, East, Attey, Corkine, Bartlett, Vautor, etc.—were members of some nobleman's household establishment, and dedicated their works to their patrons; musicians after the Civil War are fashionable performers and teachers, appealing indeed for patronage in their dedications, but no longer retainers of a particular nobleman. There was no longer a great nobleman keeping semi-regal state at Ludlow Castle for whose court Milton could write a masque and Lawes compose the music. In the drama the influence of the metropolis is still more obvious; and the Restoration comedies constantly lay the entire scene in London and the parks, as if no other part of England was worth mentioning. Sneers at country gentlemen and gentlewomen are frequent enough, showing how polite society looked down upon the provinces. In Oxford alone could the life and social atmosphere compete with London; and the Court and Parliament removed thither during the Great Plague, and during the tumult of the Exclusion agitation. A few volumes of music were published at Oxford. Cambridge, though the greatest of all philosophers lived and taught there, had less social, political, and artistic influence. Similar conditions prevail to the present day, according to the usual rule that the highest general average does not produce the highest genius. Every other town was, and is, 'provincial.' Here is the real reason why the country which invented musical composition and produced Shakespeare has done so little either in music or the drama for 200 years past.

Scotland and Ireland at the Restoration resumed their governments independent of the English Parliament, and their capitals retained a local character. Edinburgh produced no music worth noticing during the late seventeenth century, if we except a certain commemoration of St. Cecilia, said to have taken place at Edinburgh in 1695, and to have consisted of instrumental music, including works by Corelli, Bassani, and Pepusch, played by thirty amateurs and professionals. The story is questionable, especially as Pepusch was not yet in England. The Sang Scules are occasionally mentioned, as at Dundee (during the Commonwealth), and especially at Aberdeen, where the scholars are recorded to have sung at a 'lyik or nicht walk' (funeral) in 1631; in 1666 their master was paid for a similar service. At Aberdeen appeared the only secular music printed in Scotland during this period. This work, published by John Forbes in 1662, is known as the *Aberdeen Cantus*, and contained a number of tunes by English and Italian authors; with an 'Introduction to Music' by THOMAS DAVIDSON. Forbes issued a second edition in 1666; and a third with some three-voiced 'Ayres' in 1682. The latter is entitled 'Songs and Fancies, both apt for Voices and Viols'; it was reprinted in 1879. Probably music was little cultivated in Scotland; it is mentioned in 1669 that there was not one musician in Glasgow. Letters in the Duke of Argyll's MSS., written 1667, mention a song, 'Auld Lang Syne.'

At Dublin the centenary of the establishment of Trinity College was celebrated on January 9th, 1693-4, when an Ode composed by Purcell was performed.

We may now turn to biographical notices. Besides Child, Rogers, and Wilson, the only older musicians who did important work in Charles II's reign were the two now to be mentioned; though prominent musicians during the Commonwealth, their best claim to notice is the work they did after the Restoration.

MATTHEW LOCK (Locke) was a choir-boy at Exeter under Edward Gibbons, and must have been born 1625-30, as his name is cut in the choir screen with the date 1638, and again with the date 1641. The next

thing known of him is that he was in the Netherlands in
1648, as appears by Addit. MS. 31,437; his name again
appears in 1653 as composer (with C. Gibbons, another
Exeter choir-boy) of the music for *Cupid and Death*,
already mentioned. The copy in Addit. MS. 17,799 is
in Lock's autograph. In 1656 Lock published a 'Little
Consort,' a collection of forty 'Pavans, Ayres, Corants,
and Sarabands' for three viols or violins; in the preface
he says they were composed at the request of William
Wake, 'an intimate friend, and great Master in Musick,'
for his pupils. (This has been misread that Wake was
Lock's own master.) Lock had a large share in the operatic
performances. He married, Wood tells us, a Herefordshire lady named Garnons, through whom he became
acquainted with Captain Silas Taylor; Pepys mentions
meeting them and Purcell's father on the day when Monk
declared for a free parliament. Lock composed the
Procession Music for the coronation preparations, and
was subsequently organist to Queen Catherine. On
April 1st, 1666, some new music he had composed for the
Chapel Royal offended the choir, because there appeared
the innovation of a differently composed Kyrie after each
Commandment; the choir spoilt the performance, upon
which Lock published the Responses and Nicene Creed
under the title of 'Modern Church Music . . . Vindicated,' with an acrimonious preface. The music is on
a four-page sheet, unbarred; but is noteworthy from its
being in score. Lock's next work was the instrumental
part of the music to Davenant's version of *The Tempest*.
In 1672 a similar treatment of *Macbeth* was (according
to Downes) set by Lock, and this statement has produced
much debate as to whether this was the accepted and
familiar music to the tragedy. My own opinion is that
the well-known strains are too advanced in style, and require too advanced a technique for any composer of
Lock's generation; and let any one who examines the
question begin by studying the music to *Psyche*, of which
Lock composed the vocal part, publishing the score in
1675 with his contributions for *The Tempest*. The music
to *Macbeth* seems of quite a different school, both in

composition and technical requirements. In the preface to *Psyche*, Lock states that by 'Opera' the Italians signify a written musical piece, in contradistinction from their extempore comedies; he had not set the entire opera, but had relieved the music 'with interlocutions, as more proper to our Genius.' In *Psyche*, which is accompanied only by strings, Lock claims that he had included—

'From Ballad to single Air, Counterpoint, Recitative, Fuge, Canon, and Chromatick Musick; which variety (without vanity be it said) was never in Court or Theatre till now presented in this Nation: though I must confess there has been something done (and more by me than any other) of this kind.'

In 1673 Lock had edited a collection of harpsichord music, *Melothesia*, preceded by some directions for playing from figured bass. The book contains six pages of rules, and eighty-four of music by several composers. The pieces, all short, are principally Preludes, Sarabands, Almains, Corants, Jigs, and Gavots, evidently intended as Suites, though not so entitled; on pp. 59–61 is an unsigned piece headed 'Charity.' At the end are six organ pieces by Lock.

At this time Lock was engaged in a discussion with THOMAS SALMON, a clerical amateur who had published an essay entitled *The Advancement of Music*, proposing to use a six-lined staff invariably, and to write B, M, or T (Bass, Mean, or Treble) instead of the old clefs. This would give the same note for every stave, and was a highly practical suggestion; Lock attacked it in *Observations upon a late Essay*, employing disgusting abuse as well as argument. Salmon replied with natural warmth, but dignity, in a *Vindication*; Lock again appeared in *The Present Practice of Music Vindicated*, with a letter from Playford in support, and a *Duellum Musicum* by John Philips, Milton's nephew. Though Salmon did not go deep enough, as what we require is a semitonic notation, yet his system would have been an enormous improvement, and was sufficient for the compass of music then in use, admitting also of expansion to our seven-octave instruments.

Lock lived only till August, 1677; it is said that he was buried in the Savoy Chapel. Probably his name will always be remembered in connection with the music to *Macbeth*, which was published by Dr. Boyce as Lock's.

Through his friendship with Lock, some anthems were composed by Silas Taylor for the private chapel of Queen Catherine, for which he was complimented by Charles II. Rather a singular ending for the life of an officer in the Ironsides! Some of these may be among the pieces of Taylor's now at Cambridge.

HENRY COOKE, appointed Master of the Children at the Chapel Royal in 1660, had been in Charles I's Chapel, and then a captain in the Royalist army. Playford mentions him among the London teachers during the Commonwealth; and he had a leading part in Davenant's operatic performances. Evelyn records visits from Cooke, calling him the best singer 'after the Italian way' in England. Pepys also repeatedly alludes to his singing, but calls him 'a vain conceited coxcomb'; while Anthony Wood asserts that he died from sheer jealousy of Humfrey. However that may be, Cooke certainly produced a wonderful succession of pupils; for the first set of boys he trained included Humfrey, Wise, Blow, and R. Smith; and in a few years followed Tudway, Turner, and Henry Purcell. Clifford's collection mentions more than twenty anthems by Captain Cooke; but none are now sung. Cooke died July 13th, 1672, and was buried in the cloisters of Westminster Abbey.

Of other musicians still working in the early years of Charles II's reign, Thomas Blagrave (d. 1688), John Goodgroome, John Harding (d. 1684), Roger Hill (d. 1674), John Moss, and William Thatcher may be mentioned before I turn entirely to the new school of composers whose taste was formed in the Chapel Royal of Charles II.

PELHAM HUMFREY (Humphreys) was the most gifted of Captain Cooke's first set of boys. He was born in 1647. I have already explained the mistake arising from Hawkins's misreading of Wood's MSS., where Colonel Humfrey (sword-bearer to Bradshaw at Charles I's trial) is called the composer's *master*, which Hawkins misread *uncle*. Colonel Humfrey was indeed probably his father or uncle; and the name Pelham may have been a subsequent change, as a Puritan child in 1647 would more probably have been named Maher-shalal-hash-baz, or Smite-them-hip-and-thigh-even-unto-the-going-down-of-the-sun. The young musician was thirteen years old at the Restoration, and could not have sung long in the Chapel Royal before his voice broke; he began to compose early, as five anthems of his are mentioned in Clifford's collection; and on November 22nd, 1663, Pepys noted—

'The anthem was good after sermon, being the 51st psalm made for five voices by one of Captain Cooke's boys, a pretty boy, and they say there are four or five of them that can do as much.'

Humfrey's setting of the 51st Psalm for five voices was printed in Boyce's *Cathedral Music*. In 1664 the King sent him to France and Italy for further study. Apparently he stopped at Paris, where Lulli was already *maître de musique* to Louis XIV, and was composing the court ballets, though he had not as yet started on his career as opera manager and composer. In October, 1667, Humfrey returned to London, and was sworn a Gentleman of the Chapel Royal. On November 15th he visited Pepys, who describes him as 'An absolute Monsieur as full of form, confidence, and vanity,' ridiculing all the London performers, and with an overweening opinion of himself. Humfrey certainly possessed extraordinary musical abilities; he at once introduced the declamatory recitative into English ecclesiastical music, and his works in this style—'Hear, O heavens,' and 'O Lord my God'—are of permanent value, and distinguished by fine dramatic feeling quite akin to Lulli's. Many spirited secular songs were set by him (some written as well as set); and in 1670 he assisted in producing music to *The Tempest*. On Cooke's death Humfrey succeeded him as Master of the Children, and was made Composer in Ordinary for the King's violins; but himself died, aged only twenty-seven, on July 14th, 1674, at Windsor. He was buried, with so many other musicians of his time, in the cloisters of Westminster Abbey.

Humfrey's early death was a great loss to English music, though he had left a pupil even more gifted than himself. He had never a fair opportunity of displaying his unquestionable dramatic powers; in declamatory opera he would have been exactly at home, and might have done great work. To be a successful opera-composer requires other gifts besides the purely musical, and Pelham Humfrey apparently had these. In addition he had the King's support; nor were the dramatic circumstances of the age at all unpropitious. But Humfrey has at least left anthems and a Grand Chant which have kept his memory green in the Anglican Church; and some of his songs, notably 'I pass all my hours in a shady cool grove,' have been reprinted and sung even in our own time. Burney, as might be expected, failed to appreciate them.

His fellow-chorister and friend, JOHN BLOW, was a much longer-lived man, though far less gifted. Blow, as Dr. Rogers told Wood, was born in London; North Collingham was also suggested, but Dr. Cummings discovered that Blow was born at Newark, 21st February, 1648–9. Blow began the study of music under Hingston and C. Gibbons; if he had been born a year or two earlier I should have guessed he was one of the two boys who used to sing Deering's motets with Hingston to Cromwell; but he was under ten years old at Cromwell's death. He was one of Cooke's first set of boys, and three anthems of his are mentioned by Clifford. Blow in 1669 became virginalist to the King. In 1669 he succeeded Bryne as organist of Westminster Abbey, returning to the Chapel Royal in 1674 as Master of the Children. He relinquished his appointment at the Abbey in 1680 in favour of his pupil Purcell, after whose death he resumed it. In the meantime he had been (1687–93) Master of the Children and Almoner of St. Paul's Cathedral, resigning both posts to Jeremiah Clarke. Blow composed incidental pieces for many occasions, among them being: Complimentary Odes; the anthem,' I was glad when they said,' for the opening of St. Paul's Cathedral; and a setting of Deborah's Song for the victory of Blenheim. Blow had in early youth shared with Pelham Humfrey and Turner the composition of the

'Club-Anthem'; afterwards he collaborated with Humfrey in a Dialogue; and near the end of his life came another collaboration in the thanksgiving anthem for the Union with Scotland, which was 'Behold, how good and joyful,' set by Blow, Clarke, and Croft in conjunction. Blow died October 1st, 1708, and was buried near Purcell, bequeathing considerable property. He had restricted himself to church music more than his contemporaries did; his one dramatic composition was a masque, *Venus and Adonis*, acted at Court only.* He composed, however, many songs, a few catches, some harpsichord lessons, the odes for St. Cecilia's Day in 1684 and several later years; and in 1700 published a volume of his songs under the title *Amphion Anglicus*. His instrumental music is least valuable, as it displays the crudities of a transitional period. Burney severely attacked Blow's harmony, giving many instances which to modern ears seem innocent enough. The two-voiced secular song, 'Go, perjured man,' written in emulation of Carissimi's 'Dite O cieli,' remained long in favour. But the really enduring work of Blow is his church music; he composed fourteen services and more than one hundred anthems. The words of eighteen anthems are given in John Church's *Divine Harmony* (1712); eleven were printed by Boyce, with three services. Perhaps the very best of Blow's works is the anthem,' I beheld, and lo!' while ' I was in the spirit' is little inferior. The rhythmical feeling in these shows the influence of Charles II, and a comparison between them and the anthems of Farrant and Gibbons will exactly display the difference between the Elizabethan polyphonists and the school created in compliance with the Merry Monarch's taste. Blow's anthems are in triple time, and might almost serve for minuets. Also, as they consist of several movements, they are considerably longer than most Elizabethan anthems; and they have ritornellos for violins which make them quite typical specimens of the Restoration school.

Archbishop Sancroft, according to Wood, made Blow

---

* Mr. Arkwright reprinted the masque; it has been performed in 1920. In editing 'Six Songs' he has discussed Blow's harmonic 'licences.'

a Doctor of Music. There is some question of an exercise, performed at Oxford about 1678; but Wood does not mention it. Blow is an important figure in our musical history after the Restoration, though he had not genius. It is a sad fact that Dr. Blow, though he so long outlived his gifted contemporary Humfrey, and by thirteen years his own pupil Purcell, and by a year even his later pupil Clarke, yet himself only lived to be sixty.

ROBERT SMITH, six of whose anthems appear in Clifford's collection, did not fulfil his early promise, though his name appears in *Melothesia*, Greeting's book, and elsewhere.

GEORGE BOLTON published *Songs of several sorts*; only the title page is preserved.

MICHAEL WISE, another highly-gifted and short-lived member of the first set of Cooke's boys, was born at Salisbury or the neighbourhood about 1648, or probably earlier, as in 1663 he had left the choir for Windsor Castle. In 1668 Wise became organist of Salisbury Cathedral, re-entering the Chapel Royal in 1676. He was expelled in 1685; his appointment at St. Paul's Cathedral in 1687 may, considering the circumstances of the times, have been a protest against his expulsion. He was made Almoner and Master of the Children at St. Paul's, but died the same year. Being apparently of an exceedingly irascible disposition, he, on August 24th, quarrelled with his wife, then went into the street (at Salisbury) and attacked a watchman, who killed him. Wise had composed some really beautiful anthems, displaying the merits of the Restoration school without the faults; and his death was a distinct loss to English music. Six anthems were printed by Boyce.

WILLIAM TURNER, who shared in the 'Club-Anthem,' was born at Oxford in 1652, and was for a time choir-boy at Christ Church before entering the Chapel Royal. According to Tudway, the anthem, 'I will alway give thanks,' was composed in one day, when news of a victory over the Dutch arrived on a Saturday, and none of the older musicians would accept the task of composing an anthem for the morrow. No victory over the Dutch quite fits the story; and perhaps the statement of Hawkins, that the collaboration was simply a memento of the youthful friendship of Humfrey, Blow, and Turner, is the real truth. The middle solo was Turner's share. Turner afterwards was at Lincoln Cathedral, soon returning to the Chapel Royal. He graduated Mus.Doc. Cantab. in 1696. Dr. Turner, unlike his old companions, was exceptionally long-lived; and after a married life of almost seventy years, his wife died on January 9th, himself on January 13th, and they were buried in one grave, on January 16th, 1740. Turner, who was bred in the time of Henry Lawes and John Jenkins, must thus have known Handel's works (probably even some of the oratorios) in his old age. For so long-lived a musician, his compositions are not numerous; his principal effort was the Ode for St. Cecilia's Day, 1685. A MS. at Cambridge contains more than one hundred songs and catches by Turner.

The second set of Cooke's choir-boys had as composers all the advantage which arises from a later start, a very great advantage in a transitional epoch. They entered into the novel style which Humfrey had created, and improved upon the crude beginnings of the declamatory sacred music.

Thomas Tudway is reckoned among them; I must confess to doubts on the matter, as in the case of Wise. Tudway, at any rate, became a tenor at Windsor Castle on April 22nd, 1664, and in 1670 was made organist of King's College, Cambridge, where he remained till his death, 23rd November, 1726. Obscure points in his academic career are discussed in the 'Dictionary of National Biography.' In 1705 he succeeded Staggins as Cambridge Professor; the following January, having given offence by some words which reflected upon Queen Anne, he was suspended. The offence was a pun upon Hertford Burgess and Daniel Burgess, which was apparently taken as an insinuation that Queen Anne favoured Dissent. In March, 1707, he made a public retractation and was reinstated. Queen Anne had been present when Dr. Tudway's degree exercise was performed in King's College Chapel, April 16th, 1705; and had made him Composer and Organist Extraordinary. It was doubtless by Tudway that the words of the anthems sung in King's College Chapel were published in 1706; the only older composers mentioned are Tallis, Byrd, Hooper, W. Mundy, Tomkins, Batten, Bull, and Mudd. By far Tudway's greatest deed was the forming an immense collection of Anglican sacred music, which he copied in score into six bulky volumes, now in the Harleian MSS.* There are useful though not quite trustworthy biographical remarks, and to the last volume is prefixed an attempt at a History of Music; but Tudway, like Lawes, knew nothing before Henry VIII. The collection seems to have been largely founded on the MSS. at Ely; it begins with Tye, Tallis, Farrant, W. Mundy, and Byrd, and continues till Queen Anne's time, the last piece being the Utrecht Te Deum and Jubilate by 'Hendale.' There are altogether seventy complete or incomplete services, and 244 anthems, by eighty-five composers. Nineteen anthems and a service are Tudway's own work. The prefaces are most interesting as affording a view of a cultivated English musician's knowledge and opinions during the early eighteenth century; and in the personal recollections, especially of Purcell. Accuracy was, unfortunately, not Tudway's strong point. His index mentions composers who are not represented in the volumes; he thought scarcely forty anthems of the older school were to be found, yet he himself included over sixty. As 'every one is become a Composer of Church Music,' he reckoned 500 anthems had been composed and performed since the Restoration. The older masters, he stated, did not look upon their madrigals as 'compositions,' a word to be reserved for solid serious music.

HENRY HALL, the son of a captain in the army, was born at Windsor about 1655. After leaving the Chapel Royal he became organist of Exeter Cathedral in 1674; then vicar-choral of Hereford Cathedral in 1679, and organist in 1688, remaining there till his death, March 30th, 1707. Good anthems and services by Hall are

---

* MSS. 7337-42 ; see also the correspondence in 3782.

included in Tudway's collection; and secular pieces in various publications. He had a son of the name, who succeeded him at Hereford, dying in 1713. Both were poets of some merit; the father wrote enthusiastic verses to his fellow choir-boy, Purcell. A Dialogue between Cromwell and Charon, preserved in several collections, is ascribed to Henry Hall. It is not easy to distinguish the productions of the two; the father was the better composer, the son the better poet.

HENRY PURCELL, the greatest of English composers, far outshone his fellows of the Chapel Royal, and as summing up in himself all the merits of this period, will fitly be placed at the end of the chapter. Since, however, he was a known composer in 1676, it must be remembered that others learned from him, and that before the end of the century all English composers had before them models of construction in large forms, of vocal declamation, and of artistic melody. After his admission we hear of no other Chapel Royal boy until Jeremiah Clarke and Vaughan Richardson, who belong rather to the next chapter, with Croft, Church, and Weldon.

Of other composers of sacred music, PICKAVER was organist of New College, Oxford, till 1664, then at Winchester College, dying in 1678. He has left some anthems and other sacred music. BENJAMIN LAMB, organist of Eton; THOMAS HECHT, organist of Lincoln Cathedral, then (1695–1734) of Magdalen College; ALLANSON, his successor at Lincoln (d. 1705); NICHOLAS WOOTTON, organist of Canterbury Cathedral (d. 1700), and others, all produced anthems which Tudway found worthy to be included in his collection. ISAAC BLACKWELL, unknown, is represented in Tudway, and in several printed collections of the time; as is also JOHN JACKSON, organist of Wells.

JOHN READING is a name which occurs frequently in connection with music. A clergyman of that name preached a sermon in defence of church music, and published it in 1663. A John Reading was singer at the theatres about 1690. Another was organist of Chichester

Cathedral from 1674 to 1720; and a still later one belongs to the next period, living till 1764. The most important of all was at Lincoln Cathedral in 1667, then organist of Winchester Cathedral after Jewett's death in 1675; in 1681 he left this post for that at Winchester College, where he died in 1692. He is supposed to be buried in the cloisters. His name is dear to all Wykehamists, as he is traditionally the composer of 'Dulce Domum' and the Election graces. They were first printed in Hayes's *Harmonia Wiccamica;* and Walker published (on a four-page sheet) 'Benedic nobis.' An anthem by him is mentioned in *Divine Harmony*; and Jebb has printed liturgical music of Reading's.

WILLIAM KING, though of an older generation, is not heard of in connection with music until 1664, when he succeeded Pickaver at New College. He was born at Winchester in 1624, being son of the organist; and during the Commonwealth was at Oxford. Though he composed a service and some anthems, he is more remarkable as the composer of a very rare collection of secular songs by Cowley and others, for one, two, or three voices and a figured bass, published at Oxford in 1668. At the end is a *Gloria Patri* for three voices. W. King died November 17th, 1680.

Among the Ely collections are several anthems and services by JOHN FERRABOSCO, probably the last representative of this gifted family; he was organist of Ely, 1662–82. One service was scored by Tudway. For six months after his death the post was temporarily filled by THOMAS BULLIS, whose father was also in the choir; both have left services and anthems still preserved there.

There were several clerical dignitaries during this period who did some very useful work. The oldest was WILLIAM HOLDER, who was born about 1614 in Nottinghamshire, and educated at Cambridge. After the Restoration he became Canon of St. Paul's, and in 1674 Sub-dean of the Chapel Royal, living till January 24th, 1697. Holder's most valuable work was a capital treatise on acoustics, published in 1694 and reprinted in 1700; there are also good compositions by him in Tudway's collection.

WILLIAM TUCKER, precentor of Westminster Abbey, has left some fine services and anthems (at Ely and elsewhere); one anthem was printed by Page. Tucker died February 28th, 1678-9, and was buried in the Abbey cloisters. ROBERT CREYGHTON was son of a Scotchman, a divine of the Laudian school, who went into exile, and was subsequently Bishop of Bath and Wells. The composer, born in 1639, was made Greek Professor at Cambridge in 1662, and in 1674 Canon of Wells, where he spent the remaining sixty years of his life. Creyghton composed services, anthems, and chants, which are still sung; his anthem in canon, 'I will arise,' has been a general favourite, and his Service in E flat has real ecclesiastical dignity. He died at Wells, aged 94, on February 13th, 1733-4.

HENRY ALDRICH, born in 1647 and educated at Oxford, became Dean of Christ Church after the expulsion of Massey in 1689; he was equally distinguished in learning, architecture, and music. He formed a splendid musical library, which he bequeathed to his college; it consists almost entirely of English and Italian music. Other bequests and additions have made this library the finest in England, except those at the British Museum and Royal College. Havergal wrote a beautifully illuminated catalogue of the Christ Church collection, whence it appears that 'the printed works contain compositions by more than 180 composers; while the MSS. contain 1,075 anonymous pieces and 2,417 pieces by known composers, of whom 182 are English, eighty Italian, and fourteen composers of other nations.' In addition to this list there are separate movements of operas, services, etc., and instrumental Fancies, to the number of several thousands. The part-books dated 1581 have been described on p. 123. Among the printed rarities are Whythorne's 'Songs' (1571), Holborne's 'Consort Lessons' (1599), Deering's Canzonets (1620), Adson's 'Courtly Masquing Aires' (1621), Filmer's 'Court Aires' (1629), Porter's 'Mottets' (1657), Tomkins's *Musica Deo Sacra* (1668), Bowman's 'Songs' (1677), F. Smith's *Musica Oxoniensis* (1698), and Croft's Sonatas for two flutes, with

many of the Elizabethan collections of Madrigals and
Ayres.* Barnard's *Selected Church Musick* has been
bought from Hereford. Aldrich adapted motets from
Palestrina and others to English words; and himself composed two complete Services (printed by Boyce and Arnold)
and some anthems. They are still in use. The popular
practice of catch-singing was encouraged by Aldrich, who
composed two yet sung, being the only two catches of the
Restoration period endurable at the present day. One is
written to be sung by four smokers; another is upon
the bells of Christ Church. Aldrich, who bestowed the
greatest pains upon the choral service of his cathedral,
died December 14th, 1710.

Leaving many organist-composers to the next period,
we turn now to those musicians who were more especially
occupied with secular music; reminding the reader that
the theatres were closely connected with musical matters.
Most dramas of the Restoration period, whether the stilted
tragedies or the gross comedies, introduced a considerable
amount of music, and any revival of Elizabethan drama
was always rearranged to suit the altered conditions.
Generally two or three composers were engaged for a
drama in which there was much music, as had been done
by Davenant during the Commonwealth. Most of the
organist-composers already mentioned had produced some
secular music.

HENRY BOWMAN, although he was organist of Trinity
College, Cambridge, has left only one anthem, but several
collections of secular music. One of them was published
in 1677, and bears the imprimatur of the Vice-Chancellor
of Oxford. It is printed in a peculiar way; there are
Ritornelli for Viol and Bass, each Ritornello apparently
intended for several songs. There are twenty-eight pieces
for one, two, and three voices. Other works of Bowman's in MS. are preserved at Oxford.

JOHN BANISTER, already frequently mentioned, was
born in 1630, and was son and pupil of one of the Waits
of St. Giles's. He was one of the orchestra in Davenant's
operas. After the Restoration he was in the King's Band;

* Mr. A. Hiff has published the catalogue.

I have told (p. 292) how he succeeded Baltzar as Master of the Twenty-four Violins, and was dismissed for preferring the English players to the French. The story is given in Wood's MS. Lives. Setting up a concert-room in his house, and giving daily concerts from 1672 onwards, was Banister's principal deed; North's account is quoted on p. 295. There are pieces by Banister for two viols or violins (treble and bass) in 'New Ayres and Dialogues' (1678); and many tunes in Greeting's *Pleasant Companion* and Playford's *Division Violin*. He also collaborated with Humfrey in the *Tempest* music, and published some music to *Circe*. John Banister died October 3rd, 1679. His son of the same name, a fine violinist, lived till 1735.

THOMAS FARMER had been one of the Waits of London, but acquired sufficient skill to be made Mus.Bac. Cantab. in 1684. Some of his Lessons for Viols or Violins were printed in 'New Ayres and Dialogues' (1678). He died still young in 1693, and Purcell set an elegy on him written by Tate. Farmer had composed tuneful music for the stage, and was evidently a musician of considerable natural powers; Playford advertised a Consort of his in two and four parts, and another in three parts, which I have not seen.

NICHOLAS STAGGINS was the son of a 'common musician,' probably one of the roving fiddlers or minstrels so much looked down upon by the educated artists. Staggins himself had received small tuition, but became Master of the King's Band in 1682; and Charles II then ordered the University of Cambridge to create him Mus.Doc. The King was obeyed, amidst much ridicule and dissatisfaction; but Staggins sent an exercise, the performance of which silenced all objection, and in July, 1684, the University created for him the office of Professor of Music. He died in 1705. Staggins, in company with many others of the Royal musicians, obtained *several years' arrears* of salary in 1677.

RAPHAEL COURTEVILLE, like Henry Hall and John Banister, and possibly John Reading, had a father and a son of the same name, all musicians. A Raphael Courteville, who had been in Charles I's Chapel Royal, died in 1675; his son, one of the Children there, composed many songs found in various collections, and published some instrumental music, including a 'Sute of Ayres' in Cross's 'Violin Tutor' (1685), six sonatas for two violins, and others for two flutes. He is better remembered by his psalm-tune 'St. James's,' named after the church in Piccadilly, of which he was the first organist. Courteville had the honour of being associated with Purcell in composing music for *Don Quixote* (1695). He seems to have lived long, while his son (who succeeded him at St. James's, and was a political writer nicknamed Court-Evil) lived till 1771. A JOHN CCURTEVILLE appears in some of Playford's publications.

THOMAS BRITTON, though he was not a composer, deserves full notice in any account of English music. This celebrated 'musical small-coal man' had an extraordinary natural taste for music, antiquities, and learning of all kinds; he lived in intimacy with some of the greatest noblemen. He was born about 1650 at Higham Ferrers, and was apprenticed in London; he had a shop in Aylesbury Street, Clerkenwell, and cried 'small-coal' through the streets every morning. In 1678 he established concerts in a long low room over his shop; and there every Thursday the leaders of rank and fashion were to be met during nearly forty years, and the finest performers might be heard. Handel directed at these concerts when he first came to England. The brilliant company which assembled, and the respect in which Britton was held, caused a very general belief that he was really a political agent, and that his concerts were a blind for conspirators' meetings. The subscription to his club was ten shillings; nor would he receive any further assistance from his wealthy patrons. A member of the club played a trick upon him by means of a celebrated ventriloquist, who so frightened Britton that he died a week later, September 27th, 1714. His friends and supporters attended his funeral in St. James's Church, Clerkenwell; and his valuable library was sold by auction. The catalogue, given *in extenso* by Hawkins, is interesting as showing what music was then in use.

Doubtless all cultivated men of that age were more or less musical, just as they were also poetasters. In Ravenscroft's *The Citizen turned Gentleman* (1672) the would-be aristocrat is told that a weekly music-club at his house would be necessary for his attempted grandeur. The North family were distinguished amateurs; Sir Francis North's *Philosophical Treatise of Music* and his brother Roger's *Memoirs of Musick* are admirable. Sir Samuel Morland, who had been an ambassador from Cromwell to the Vaudois, invented the speaking-trumpet; but just before his death (as Evelyn records) he 'buried £200 worth of music-books six feet under ground, being, as he said, love-songs and vanity,' and restricted himself to sacred music. He must have had an extensive musical library, as the ordinary price of the smaller collections was half a crown. The cultivation of music was general; Pepys noted that in the flight of the citizens at the Great Fire, of the lighters and boats which crowded the Thames hardly one in three 'that had the goods of a house in but there was a pair of virginals in it.'

One question still remains to be just touched upon. Was *God save the King* composed in 1688? It certainly was not generally known until 1745; but there is some reason to believe that it was composed to Latin words, and sung in James II's Chapel Royal when the news of the Prince of Orange's landing arrived. This points to Purcell as the composer; a claim has been set up for Anthony Young, at that time organist of Allhallows, Barking. Nothing can be considered definitely settled hitherto, as regards either the composer or the date of composition, except that the National Anthem existed in 1742. (See pp. 367–9).

We may now conclude this chapter with an account of the Purcell family, in one of whom the musical genius of England finally culminated before it died. Whence the family came we do not know. There were two brothers, Henry and Thomas, who were appointed Gentlemen of the Chapel Royal at the Restoration; one of these was doubtless the 'Purcell, master of musique,' whom Pepys met with Lock and Silas Taylor at the 'Coffee House' on February 21st, 1659–60. Henry had taken part in Davenant's operas. Thomas Purcell was made Master of the King's Band of Violins in conjunction with Pelham Humfrey; he lived till July 31st, 1682. His brother Henry was father of England's greatest musician, and of two other distinguished men; this Henry Purcell died comparatively young, August 11th, 1664. In *The Musical Companion* (1667) is a song, 'Sweet Tyranness,' composed by him. Of his sons, the eldest (1653–1717) had a share in the capture of Gibraltar and Barcelona. The youngest, a musician of considerable ability, will be left to the next chapter.

HENRY PURCELL, second son of the elder musician of that name, was the man who more than any other English musician deserves the appellation *genius*. He was born, according to tradition, in a house, the remains of which are still standing, at the end of St. Ann's Lane, Old Pye Street, Westminster. The date is not precisely known; by the inscription on his tombstone it must have been either at the end of 1658 or in 1659, more probably the latter, though the earlier has been commonly adopted. Not long after his father's death in 1664 he became a choir-boy of the Chapel Royal. Under Captain Cooke, afterwards under Humfrey, and lastly under Blow, he studied and advanced, acquired practical experience and doubtless theoretical guidance. There is no mention of his travelling. Morley's treatise, Campion's, and Butler's he probably studied; Sympson's certainly; but there was a yet better school available, and he fully used it. He copied out existing masterpieces in score; a volume in his writing dated 1673 (now in the Fitzwilliam Museum) contains eleven anthems of his own composition—showing that while still a choir-boy he had been a diligent and inventive composer—besides thirty-two by other composers. Even the song 'Sweet Tyranness,' which Playford had published in 1667, has sometimes been supposed the child's own composition; but it was more probably his father's, though not necessarily. Only three years later, an Ode which the boys sang on the King's birthday, May 29th, 1670, had been entrusted to Purcell to set, though he was but eleven years old. This Ode I have not seen; it is said that Dr. Rimbault had a copy.

In the volume of anthems now at Cambridge, and written in Purcell's fifteenth year, his teachers are well represented, Blow by ten anthems, Humfrey by five; and there are six by Lock and one by Child; the remainder are by Elizabethan or Jacobean composers. Tallis's ' I call and cry,' Byrd's 'Bow Thine ear,' and Gibbons's 'Hosanna' are there; with others by W. Mundy, T. Tomkins, Giles, and Batten. The young genius had thus full opportunity of acquiring the contrapuntal style of sacred music, while all around him he daily heard the declamatory style which had developed from Campion, Lanier, and Lawes, with assistance from Italy and France. How to unite the merits of these conflicting elements into a new style was the task that lay before Purcell. It was a task of immense difficulty, and he did not solve the problem immediately.

The question here arises, did Purcell compose the music to *Macbeth*, which so long passed as Lock's? I have already declared my opinion that 1672 is too early a date for it, whoever the composer was. It was ascribed to Purcell by the Academy of Ancient Music in the next century. Dr. W. H. Cummings had an ancient copy,* which he believed to be the original score and in Purcell's youthful handwriting. The music has quite the delightful freshness appropriate to the early work of a genius; and if there had been such a one about the time of Purcell's death, I should unhesitatingly ascribe it to him. Our knowledge on the subject does not warrant my forming a positive opinion as to the real composer; but let us not forget that these beautiful pieces have been performed on the stage and in concert-rooms for over two centuries, that they are far older than any dramatic music now performed in any other country. The next in point of date which is really on the repertory is Gluck's *Orfeo*, produced 1762.

In 1676 Purcell became copyist at Westminster Abbey, and entered into a regular connection with the stage, being engaged as composer at Dorset Garden Theatre. In

* It was sold after his death.

this year he contributed music to three plays, Dryden's tragedy *Aurungzebe*, Shadwell's comedy *Epsom Wells*, and his tragedy *The Libertine*. The last (on the Spanish legend so inspiring to Mozart) contains two pieces still familiar, the song 'Nymphs and Shepherds' and the chorus 'In these delightful pleasant groves.' Thus at the age of seventeen or eighteen Purcell had made permanent additions to the stock of English music. In the same year a piece by him was published in Playford's 'Ayres and Dialogues.' In 1677 he wrote an overture and eight other pieces for Aphra Behn's *Abdelazor*; and in 1678 followed a still greater work, the masque introduced by Shadwell into his version of Shakespeare's *Timon of Athens*, for which Purcell composed a series of masterly movements far in advance of anything his contemporaries could attain. The 'New Airs and Dialogues' published by Broome contained several pieces of his, including an improved version of the 'Sweet Tyranness' of 1667, and a Trialogue. He now resigned his post as copyist, but resumed it in 1688. Another collection of Playford's in 1679 contained several of Purcell's pieces, among them an elegy on the death of Matthew Lock. In the next year Dr. Blow resigned the organistship of Westminster Abbey to make way for his wonderful pupil. Plays by Lee and Durfey (*Œdipus*, *Theodosius*, and *The Virtuous Wife*) were enriched with Purcell's music, but he then relinquished his connection with the theatre till 1686. It must be remembered that Dorset Garden Theatre (the Duke's company) was declining, and joined forces with the King's company at Drury Lane soon after. A class of composition peculiarly Purcellian—the complimentary Ode—was first essayed at this time.

We now reach a composition of the greatest importance; its date, in spite of close investigation, remains doubtful. The wife of a certain Josias Priest (who was a dancing-master connected with the theatres and celebrated as a grotesque dancer) kept a fashionable boarding-school in Leicester Fields, which in 1680 removed to Chelsea. Purcell probably taught in this school, as he was engaged to set an opera performed there. This was written by

Nahum Tate on the story of Dido and Æneas (as told by Virgil), with malevolent witches substituted for Olympian councils separating the lovers. The diction is poor enough, but the drama is fairly well devised, and gave Purcell full opportunity. He set it throughout, without spoken dialogue. There was also a prologue for music, which he apparently did not set; and an epilogue spoken by Lady Dorothy Burke, which was doubtless intended to comfort the minds of the aristocratic parents of the performers, though in these days it would be thought too impudent for any girl to recite. Lady Dorothy had probably been the heroine; there is a tradition that Purcell himself sang the alto part, 'Anna.' At drawing-room performances ' Belinda ' was substituted. Since the sorceress is given to a bass voice, and the choruses are for the usual S.A.T.B., it is probable that Purcell took some of the Abbey choir to assist. The music is always admirable, as dramatically expressive as that of Lanier, Lawes, or Humfrey, combined with constructive power and contrapuntal mastery such as they never attempted. In particular the combination of pathetic declamation with a ground-bass was a triumph of novelty and invention; these exactly opposite resources were fused into a death-song of surpassing beauty. A most spirited chorus, 'To the hills and the vales,' and a trio, 'Fear no danger to ensue,' must be mentioned. Some echo-effects recall the *Macbeth* music.

Yet *Dido and Æneas*, in spite of its splendid merits, does not always display the mature Purcell. He had not completely mastered the task before him. The music has still an overbalance of the declamatory style, though it was melody which Purcell was attempting. He reached it in 'Fear no danger,' but much of the opera is Lully *arioso*. It was probably at this time that Purcell became acquainted with his especial favourites, the works of Stradella, the sweetness of which added the one ingredient still necessary to Purcell's full perfection.

After 1680 came the great Tory reaction, and during the next few years Purcell's complimentary Odes were frequent. On July 14th, 1682, he was appointed organist at the Chapel Royal in succession to Professor Edward

Lowe, and was sworn in on September 16th. Some of his best anthems are known to have been composed at this time.

In 1683 he made two very important steps forward. Subscriptions had been invited for a set of twelve sonatas for two violins and a bass with keyboard accompaniment, which were issued in June.* This collection, now extremely rare, has a very interesting preface, in which Purcell proclaims his preference of Italian music to French, asserting that in the sonatas he had ' faithfully endeavoured a just imitation of the most famed Italian masters, principally to bring the seriousness and gravity of that sort of music into vogue and reputation among our countrymen, whose humour, 'tis time now, should begin to loathe the levity and balladry of our neighbours.' Purcell not only saw the superiority of Italian music, but also of the specially Italian instrument, the violin; he disliked the viol, composed a satirical catch on it, and his influence doubtless hastened the disuse of the viol. Italian terms (*Adagio, Presto, Piano*, etc.) are used in these sonatas and explained in the preface. In the year 1683 the celebrations of St. Cecilia's Day assumed importance. Purcell composed three Odes; the finest was performed and published in score; the others have now also appeared in the Complete Edition. A fine Sonata, for solo violin with continuo, was also probably composed at this time.

These Sonatas and Odes, though they were quickly surpassed by the ever-improving composer, nevertheless show the mature Purcell; upon the declamatory merits of the Lawes-Humfrey style, and the severer beauty of Elizabethan counterpoint, which had been united in so masterly a fashion in *Dido and Æneas*, Purcell had now succeeded in superadding the entrancing sweetness of Italian melody. The task which Purcell had accomplished was again presented a century later, and was solved by Mozart; but owing to their varying circumstances, the two geniuses set about it in a precisely opposite way. Mozart began with the Italian melody around him in his

---

* The earliest English use of the term *Sonata*.

childhood, subsequently became acquainted with the declamatory style of Gluck, and last of all with Bach's polyphony.

For the coronation of James II (April 23rd, 1685) Purcell composed two magnificent anthems—'I was glad,' and 'My heart is inditing.' Then he returned to the drama, producing music for *Circe*, and in 1686 for the revival of Dryden's *Tyrannic Love*. This contains a fine duet, 'Hark, my Damilcar' (misprinted 'Doridcar' to this day). Complimentary odes were frequent during the short reign of James II, and some splendid Latin motets for the Chapel Royal exist. Pre-eminent is the setting of 'Jehova, quam multi.' One of the odes contained a duet for altos, 'Let Cæsar and Urania live,' which was introduced by the Court composers into official compositions for a century after.

From this time trumpet solos become a special feature of Purcell's works. They were written for John Shore (or Showers), son of Mathias Shore, from 1685–1700 Sergeant-Trumpeter, who was succeeded by his son William, followed by John, whose successor was Handel's trumpeter, Valentine Snow.

But Purcell's complimentary odes to James II were far less politically effective than a Quickstep which he had composed, and which was adapted by somebody, probably Lord Wharton, to the doggerel words of 'Lillibullero.' Wharton boasted that this song 'had sung a deluded Prince out of three kingdoms,' but it was too absurd to have had the slightest effect had it not been set to a catching tune. Purcell transferred his services to William III and Mary, though they cared little for music, especially ecclesiastical music; and the Twenty-four Violins were by them excluded from the Chapel Royal, though interludes were still given on the organ. Their coronation produced a difficulty between Purcell and the Chapter of Westminster Abbey; he had taken money for admission of spectators to the organ-loft, and was threatened with suspension and loss of salary if he did not refund it. The matter was in some way accommodated.

The odes composed for James II were decidedly

surpassed by the 'Yorkshire Feast Song' in praise of
King William, performed March 27th, 1690; this splendid
work began the publications of the Purcell Society. Other
official works for the Royal family were produced during
the few remaining years of Purcell's life; the last was
a beautiful Birthday Ode for the Duke of Gloucester.
Especially celebrated is the anthem,'Blessed is the man,'
composed for Queen Mary's funeral in March, 1695.
Tudway in the preface to one of his MS. volumes thus
speaks of this anthem:

> 'I appeal to all that were present, as well such as understood music,
> as those that did not, whether they ever heard anything so rapturously
> fine and solemn, and so heavenly in the operation, which drew tears
> from us all.'

Macaulay mentions the 'few flakes of snow on the black
plumes of the funeral car,' but not this immortal composition. In the Burial Service, the passage, 'Thou
knowest, Lord, the secret of our hearts,' was so exquisitely
set by Purcell that it has been since used at every choral
funeral in Westminster Abbey and St. Paul's; Croft
incorporated this movement into his setting of the whole
Burial Service. Purcell also set two Latin elegies on the
Queen.

In this last period of Purcell's life he produced other
very important sacred music. In 1688 the first volume
of *Harmonia Sacra* contained twelve pieces of his;
Playford stated in the preface that Purcell had edited the
whole. Six pieces were published in the second volume
(1693), including the magnificent *scena*,'In guiltie night.'
This volume is preceded by a poem of Tom Brown's,
contrasting the old psalter and composers with the new,
and exalting Purcell. (See p. 305).

Greatest of all his sacred music are the magnificent Te
Deum and Jubilate composed and performed in 1694.
Trumpets and drums have independent accompaniments in these movements, and the alternate dissonances
of the trumpets and violins against an ascending scale
of the basses formed a harmonic succession and orchestral
effect of unprecedented originality. This passage shows
more than any other how genius can revivify the deadest

formulæ. Every musician who for the first time heard that familiar succession made strikingly novel by Purcell must have felt it as a revelation; a dry formula had been vivified into living emotion, and the daring effect of the dissonances on one part of the orchestra resolved by another part must have thrilled the auditors. Purcell also, like a true English musician, loved choral effects; and his own, in this composition, are finer than any produced before the oratorio-choruses of Handel.

In the meantime Purcell had since 1686 been active in dramatic music. Dramas or arrangements by Durfey, Shadwell, Settle, Crowne, Southerne, Lee, Congreve, and Dryden were supplied with songs or instrumental music; unfortunately nothing larger was required, except in one case. Several of his contributions, notably those to Shadwell's version of *The Tempest*, and to Dryden's *Indian Queen*, are remarkably fine; but they are in the main simply incidental songs, quite as effective when sung apart from the drama as they are in their context. *Dioclesian*, composed in 1690, was published in score.

The one exception was a drama on the subject of *King Arthur*, written by Dryden in 1691. The poet here collaborated with the musician, and wrote what is really an opera libretto. Purcell, having in this a much higher task than in his other dramatic essays, rose to the occasion with all the power of genius, and his greatest secular music was inspired by this collaboration. Every number is a masterpiece, while 'Come, if you dare,' the Frost-Spirit's Chorus, and 'Fairest Isle, all isles excelling,' are beyond all praise. In this work the model of ENGLISH OPERA was established; and most admirable work can be achieved after that model, even without the aid of such genius as Purcell's and Dryden's. Let only a practised dramatist-poet ally himself and collaborate with a practised composer with some stage experience, and success can scarcely be wanting. We have seen this in our own time.

So fertile a genius had naturally displayed itself in all ways; songs, catches, harpsichord pieces, concerted music of all kinds, had poured in great numbers from

Purcell's fluent pen. As the world knows, the end came too soon; Purcell composed 'In rosy bowers,' and then died, November 21st, 1695, in his thirty-seventh year. The tradition which ascribes his death to the cold caught through his wife's locking him out all night is very ancient, and I see no reason to disbelieve it. Some words by Humphrey Wanley in his catalogue of the Harleian MSS. certainly support it. Purcell, like Mozart, had to pay with his life for his weaknesses of character.

Only in Westminster Abbey was a fitting grave for the greatest of English musicians. There he was laid to rest beneath the organ on November 26th. The epitaph shows that his contemporaries felt how irreparable was their loss.

Has England done its duty towards Purcell, whom it has always recognised as its greatest musician? It has not. A few of his anthems and a few of his songs are very frequently performed; he has been remembered and extolled, but his works have not all been published even yet.[*] As always in artistic matters, the artists themselves are to blame; we have thousands of professional musicians, and probably the majority of them do not own a single work of Purcell's, nor could quote one of his themes except, perhaps, 'Come, if you dare.' Purcell never had a libretto suitable for an extended concert-work. Had he set such a poem as *Acis and Galatea*, he would be far better known. The last Ode for St. Cecilia's Day 1692, the *Te Deum and Jubilate*, the Masques in *King Arthur* and *Timon of Athens*, most nearly fulfil modern concert requirements. Unluckily Dryden's great Ode was entrusted to Draghi, not to Purcell, who was dead before the yet greater *Alexander's Feast* was written. Let those who really know his works and their importance still continue unremittingly to push them forward, to publish and perform them, to keep England and the world in remembrance that there was one composer during the late seventeenth century who possessed genius, and who (unlike his English, French, and German contemporaries, or even the Italians he so much

---

[*] This neglect has been largely remedied in the twentieth century.

admired) produced music unaffected by the lapse of time and the changes of fashion, being entirely original, entirely beautiful, immortal.

Burney, so inappreciative of the older English secular music, has written admirably on the merits of Purcell, and it may be thought that little need be added to his laudation and to the biography written by Cummings. I must, however, touch upon one point, in my opinion of high importance, and which is ignored by these writers.

The best of Purcell's tunes, 'Come, if you dare,' 'Britons, strike home,' 'Fairest isle, all isles excelling,' with others, are all in triple measure, and consist principally of minims and crotchets. They are thus connected with, and developed from, the older style of tune occasionally used by H. Lawes, and still earlier by T. Campion; Purcell's tunes are far finer, yet the relationship is evident. This side of Purcell's genius is the most specifically English; and he seems to have crowned in it the ancient English pattern of melody. Now, 'God save the King' is also in triple measure, and opens like 'Britons, strike home'; this seems an additional argument in favour of Purcell's authorship, but otherwise the family likeness is not strong. The consummation of the older style of melody should be remembered as one of Purcell's merits; it can, of course, be appreciated only by those who know the older attempts, even as far back as 'Sumer is icumen in' and the two tunes (see p. 26) in MS. Vespasian *a* 18.

While adding this national element to the structural beauty and expressive power of the Italians, Purcell preserved the declamatory merits of Lawes and Humfrey; and as Burney rightly judged, Purcell was superior to Handel in his treatment of English words. Nor is the superiority entirely due to Handel's foreign origin and education, but in part to Purcell's early surroundings, when declamatory Ayres and Dialogues were still in favour, and when he must have continually heard music whose only merit now seems its exact correspondence with the words. This merit he preserved in his own music, but he added other qualities which enormously enriched his style; and these other qualities appealed more to the

public than did the intellectual union of tone and word.*
This intellectual quality, which the older compositions
had, was speedily lost altogether. Handel and the Italian
Opera completed the separation of music from English
poetry, and the arts have been sundered ever since. One
result of this is an ignoring of our music among literary
men; even students of early poetic and dramatic literature,
though they perfectly well know that the early poets and
dramatists were musicians, yet do not make themselves
acquainted with music and musical antiquities, and
consequently perpetuate gross mistakes when writing of
sixteenth and seventeenth-century literature. The omissions are often yet worse. Many serious faults in otherwise admirable work have arisen solely through this
defect. Macaulay's entire omission of music from his
famous chapter on the State of England in 1685 is a
striking instance enough; indeed typical. Again, our poets
in general do not write with the intention that their lyrics
shall be set and sung; and by this isolation they do not
penetrate into the hearts of the nation as they should
do. I am here, of course, speaking of England only, in the
restricted sense of the word; Scotland and Ireland are
more fortunate.

With Purcell's early death ends the important period
of English music. The centralising of the whole country
in London then completed its mischief; and ever since the
music of England has been important only to ourselves.
The creative men have studied and developed in some
small German, Italian, or Polish town, and when they
have matured have come to London or Paris to use their
powers. In London or Paris individuality has no opportunity to develop, and originality is smoothed into routine,
or else becomes eccentricity. It is interesting to notice
also that Bach and Beethoven, the two great geniuses who
did not travel, were both just a little deficient in those
practical qualities which the cosmopolitanism of London
or Paris would have given them; and they address a
narrower circle than, for instance, Handel or Mozart.

* See Sir Hubert Parry's admirable remarks on Purcell's scenas for a solo
voice, *Oxford History of Music*, vol. iii.

London is even more handicapped than Paris; for Paris at least has state-supported Grand Opera houses, and Frenchmen have distinguished themselves in the applied music of the stage, though creating no pure music of the first rank. In England we have done almost nothing, either in opera or in the spoken drama, since the time of Purcell. The average Englishman is no doubt more deficient in the dramatic sense than in any other artistic gift; and many of our theatrical performances are an absolute disgrace to our intelligence. No theatrical manager would now expect to attract popular audiences with the poetry of Dryden set by Purcell. It was on the dramatic side, above all, that Purcell made his per od the greatest in English music; his early training in the declamatory style prevented his melodic invention and contrapuntal science from overbalancing the interest in the words.

I may just mention further that Purcell was particularly successful in his use of a *basso ostinato*, or *quasi ostinato*. A masterly use of the latter may be seen in his Ode for St. Cecilia's Day, 1692. This Ode, one of his finest works, contains also other technical points worth noting—an unprepared diminished seventh (a very early instance), a charmingly natural passage of imitation in contrary motion, and a double fugue, the theme once appearing in augmentation with splendid effect. This Ode must have sounded wonderfully original and rich when first produced.

CHAPTER VIII

THE PERIOD OF PATRIOTIC SONGS
(1701-1800)

After Purcell.—Ruinous effects of centralisation.—Ecclesiastical composers of Queen Anne's reign.—Establishment of Italian opera.—Arrival of Handel; his English life, and invention of the concert-oratorio.—The Academy of Ancient Music, and the Madrigal Society.—The ballad operas.— Handel's successors.—Arne and his contemporaries.—Evolution of the glee.—Historians, and editors of old music.— The Handel Commemoration.—Folk-tunes written-for by the Scotch and Irish poets.—The only enduring eighteenth-century secular music an outcome of the patriotic enthusiasm.

WE have now reached the prosaic period, when England, for 300 years distinguished by its musical skill, sank so far from its old repute as to acquire the name of an unmusical country, a disrepute which it still retains so far that many read with astonishment and even incredulity of its glorious achievements in the past.

What could have been the reason or reasons for so extraordinary a change? The principal reason undoubtedly was and is the centralisation of England in London, which gives no chance to performers or composers elsewhere. London itself has too huge, heterogeneous, and changing a population to be an artistic centre at all commensurable with its importance in the kingdom, while at the same time it prevents any other town from becoming one, as all first-rate talent of every description gravitates there; London musicians themselves have to contend with the very greatest performers of the whole world. No other town in the British Islands offers any career to a musician except as an organist or teacher. We have no small governments or local princes requiring local orchestras, if we except the Viceroy of Ireland; and our cathedrals, which might partially replace this want, are generally in small towns which have been very far outstripped by others, and now have little importance even in their own province. Consequently our best musicians avoid them and come to London.

This centralising had already begun under James I, when complaints were made that the northern castles were neglected and falling into ruin; it was enormously accelerated by the Civil War, when the castles of the Royalist nobility were all dismantled. Still, the comparative slowness of communication caused the county towns to remain centres of local life all through the eighteenth century, and there the county families usually made some society during the winter. Since the eighteenth century even this feature has disappeared, and, in addition, the leading citizens of every large town live away from their businesses, in a remote suburb, or even in the country. All these matters result in a lack of artistic life, which seems to flourish most in a comparatively small, restricted, self-centred community, such as the capitals of small German states in the eighteenth century, the cities of Italy in the Middle Ages, and of Greece in antiquity. The conditions of English life are fundamentally opposed to these, and for that reason we have produced no great school of tone-art since the short-lived burst of talent which culminated in Purcell.

To all this has been superadded a timidity, bringing a lack of invention, in English performers. In all the development of technical skill since 1700 they have taken no part. When Corelli's compositions arrived, our English violinists thought them incredibly difficult; presently they learnt to play them. Geminiani and Veracini showed greater difficulties; the English violinists studied them, and in time mastered them. Much greater execution was shown by Giardini; our violinists duly acquired it. A yet farther advance was made by Viotti; and again it was reached. Last of all, Paganini showed the world the limits of possibility; and English violinists practised away until they could play his harmonics and effects of *pizzicato* and springing bow. But not one English violinist discovered anything by himself. And so it was with the pianoforte; but here there was one exception, John Field. From Purcell to the present day not a single effect has been discovered by any native of the British Islands (except John Field) either upon the keyed, the bowed, or the wind instruments. The modern harp execution was invented here. Otherwise our musicians have patiently studied up the inventions of others; and our composers and performers have alike been behind the age, and their works have made no lasting impression.

Admitting all these defects, the worst result of which has been the complete lack of native opera, it does not necessarily follow that the English nation is unmusical because its composers and performers are not of the greatest; but in the popular mind the extremes stand for the whole mass. Where the very greatest composers and performers appear, there the world supposes the average of mankind must also be musical without exception. It is also to be noticed that the English drama, once the grandest in the world, fell from its high estate at precisely the same moment as did English music. The Restoration drama had still some high literary qualities; but since Congreve abandoned dramatic writing in 1700, our literature and the stage have been but slightly connected. Neither has our lyric poetry, still less our narrative poetry, been at all connected with music; and while the student of literature must not overlook the Elizabethan and Stuart collections of vocal music, he need hardly examine the words of later songs.

There was, however, a number of short pieces, or more strictly of tunes, produced in the eighteenth century which have become a part of the nation's artistic possession. Every leading musician composed tunes which are interwoven with the national life, as familiar as household words. Otherwise nothing was produced of importance during the whole eighteenth century except by foreigners; the Anglican Church, indeed, somewhat added to its store of enduringly valuable services and anthems, but everything else is forgotten except the tunes to popular ballads and hymns, a few catches, and some glees.

In the early period of decline there was still 'the warmth of western sun.' Even before the eighteenth century began, a school of young composers, several of considerable talent, had followed Purcell's guidance. Of older musicians, Blow, Turner, and Tudway were still

actively working. The pre-Restoration style was entirely
dead and even forgotten except by a few survivors who
could remember the Commonwealth. Tudway, writing
to his son, gave an exact description of a 'chest of viols'
as an ancient curiosity no longer to be found. It must,
however, be recorded that the Viol-da-Gamba still held
its ground, both in Germany and England; and here it
has never been quite forgotten, and a school of amateurs
have always kept it in use. We read very little of the lute,
except that a lutenist's place was created at the Chapel
Royal in 1715; I know no more publications for the
instrument, but the word *lute* has acquired a conventional
meaning in poetry. About 1700 the flute seems to have
been considerably cultivated; and several composers
published sonatas for two flutes. Walsh issued a volume
called *The Division Flute*; pieces by Solomon Eccles,
probably the Quaker's son, occur in it.

The composers who flourished between Purcell's death
and Handel's settlement in England contributed some
interesting additions to the cathedral repertory; and Queen
Anne's reign, when the Church had enormous influence
and was at the height of popular favour, was by no means
undistinguished in the production of sacred music. A
collection of the words of anthems used in the Chapel
Royal was published in 1712 by Dr. Dolben (the Dean)
and John Church, under the title of *Divine Harmony*;
it includes 235 anthems, mainly of the Restoration school,
though Tallis, Byrd, Farrant, Gibbons, Batten, and Child
are represented. Thanksgiving anthems for Blenheim,
Ramillies, and Oudenarde, and for the Union with Scotland, are interesting historically. The preface shows once
more the ignorance of early musical history, and has one
little last spark of the old English pride in English music:

'In the beginning of the Reign of King Henry 8, and sometime
before, many excellent arts and inventions had either a Birth or
Resurrection; . . . Musick (among others) arose from the obscurity
under which it had been buried for many Ages, and was then improved
and has since flourished to such a degree that we have no reason to
envy any foreign Compositions.'

Creyghton and Aldrich were still working; two other

clerical amateur composers must be mentioned, the Hon. and Rev. EDWARD FINCH (1664–1738), prebendary of York, and Dr. PHILIP FALLE, of Durham. The satirist ARBUTHNOT was a good musician, and one of his anthems was included in *Divine Harmony*. A clergyman named Arthur Bedford published *The Great Abuse of Musick*, in which he called the deaths of Purcell and Blow evident judgments sent upon the nation for the degradation of the art by objectionable words.

Of the ecclesiastical composers who flourished under Anne, and were all born in Charles II's reign, the oldest was DANIEL PURCELL, who, though his fame burns dim beside his gifted brother's, yet had considerable talent as a musician. He was born probably about 1660; the first thing known of him is his appointment as organist of Magdalen College, Oxford, where he remained from 1688–95. Anthems by him still exist there. Returning to London, he composed music for various dramas, besides setting Odes which were performed on St. Cecilia's Day—at Oxford in 1693, 1699, and 1707, and at the London celebration of 1698. From 1713–17 Daniel Purcell was organist (without regular pay) of Sacheverell's Church, St. Andrew's, Holborn; in 1718 appeared a work of much historical interest, entitled 'The Psalms set full for Organ or Harpsichord, as they are plaid in Churches and Chappels in the manner given out, as also with their Interludes of great Variety,' by Mr. Daniel Purcell. Each psalm-tune is treated in the two ways; once 'as given out' with plenty of figuration and embellishment, and once with interludes between each line. The treatment is somewhat primitive; and a specimen would probably convince a modern congregation that organ-playing was indeed 'a foolishe vanitie.' D. Purcell had published three sonatas for two flutes and a figured bass; they are all in four movements—*Adagio, Allegro, Largo, Giga*. He died in 1717, having produced a large amount of compositions of nearly every kind; J. Stafford Smith reprinted some. D. Purcell, like Tudway, was an inveterate punster.

JEREMIAH CLARKE was born in 1669, or earlier. He

was one of Blow's choir-boys; in 1693 he was made organist of Winchester College. Blow then resigned his appointments at St. Paul's Cathedral in favour of Clarke, who also became organist when the services began. Afterwards Clarke fell in love with a lady of rank, in despair lost his reason, and shot himself, December 1st, 1707. After his death a volume of 'Lessons for the Harpsichord or Spinnet' was published, the best English instrumental music of Queen Anne's reign I have seen; they consist of seven Suites (though not so entitled), containing twenty-five pieces. The keys are G major, A major, B minor, C minor, C major (two Suites), and D major; nearly every Suite has an Allemand, Corant, and Minuet, and there are also Marches, a Saraband, an Entry, an Aire, and Jiggs. The second Suite contains a 'Round O,' which is in the primitive rondo-form consisting of three sections, of which the first is literally repeated after the second, and again after the third. The writing is melodious, graceful, and though not brilliant is well adapted to the instrument. There are copies at Sion College and the Fitzwilliam Museum. Clarke had in 1696 published 'Auto-Melodia, or the Art of Playing the Flute'; and he attempted dramatic music. More important than this must have been his setting of Dryden's *Alexander's Feast* for St. Cecilia's Day, 1697. The music is lost; but to adequately set so grand a poem must have been a task beyond Clarke's powers. It was, however, again performed on December 9th and 16th; at the last a Pastoral of Clarke's on the Peace of Ryswick was added. This, also lost, was a task probably more adapted to his tender expressive style than setting the spirit-stirring Ode had been.

These gentle powers of Clarke's found full scope in his pathetic anthems, which, besides two hymn-tunes, are still in favour; and on the whole I am inclined to look upon Jeremiah Clarke as the most gifted composer among Purcell's immediate successors.

JOHN GOLDWIN, a pupil of Dr. Child, succeeded his master at Windsor Castle. His church music is still in favour; Boyce, Arnold, and Page all printed specimens.

His anthem, 'I have set God alway before me,' is admirable. In Aldrich's library at Christ Church there are twenty-one anthems composed by Goldwin, who died November 7th, 1719.

JOHN WELDON, born at Chichester, January 19th, 1676, was educated at Eton under J. Walter, afterwards under Purcell. In 1694 he became organist of New College, Oxford; some of his music was published there by Francis Smith in 1698, and in 1700 he won the prize for setting Congreve's *Judgment of Paris*. Weldon's setting was not published, and only one song has survived. Next year he entered the Chapel Royal, succeeded Dr. Blow as organist in 1708, and was made Second Composer in 1715; he was also organist of St. Bride's, Fleet Street, and in 1726 of St. Martin's-in-the-Fields. He died May 7th, 1736. Weldon is only remembered by two beautiful anthems, 'In Thee, O Lord,' and 'Hear my crying'; but many others exist, among them six solo anthems written for a favourite counter-tenor, Richard Elford, and published in 1710. Weldon also published three books of songs.

WILLIAM CROFT was born at Nether Eatington, Warwickshire, December, 1678. He was a Chapel Royal choir-boy under Blow; and subsequently the first organist of St. Anne's, Soho, a church to this day distinguished by the excellence of its musical service. In 1700 he re-entered the Chapel Royal, with the reversion (jointly with Clarke) of the organist's post, which fell to them in 1704, and to Croft entirely in 1707. Next year Croft succeeded Blow as organist of Westminster Abbey, Master of the Children and Composer to the Chapel Royal. He left St. Anne's in 1711; in 1708 a Psalter had appeared (probably edited by him) in which occurs the fine melody called 'St. Anne's Tune,' popular everywhere to this day, and another still finer called 'Hanover.' The former is directly ascribed to Croft by his contemporaries Hart and Church; and 'Hanover' is probably his. These tunes are, in my opinion, of importance historically, as they are the earliest examples of the English psalm-tune as distinguished from the Genevan; they require quicker singing, and the glorious rhythmical impulse of 'Hanover' and its triple measure marked at once a distinct originality. The tunes themselves, not their treatment, offer the whole musical interest; the style is, therefore, especially adapted to congregational singing, nor are its best examples at all unsuited to application in more elaborate forms, as Macfarren showed in his splendid fugue on 'Hanover.' The best and most popular hymn-tunes have ever since had something of a distinct march-rhythm; which 'Hanover' has, though in triple measure. This tune has much in common with 'Rule, Britannia,' and expresses all the best side of English religion, healthy, simple, strong, and sincere; a tune in which all England's great men throughout the centuries might unite, a tune which King Alfred could have enjoyed, a tune for Grosseteste and Wickliffe and Latimer, in which Herbert and Cosin might join with Cromwell and Milton, with Bunyan and Ken, with Wesley and Toplady, with Arnold and Selwyn, with Keble and Spurgeon.

In 1713 Croft graduated Mus.Doc. Oxon., and published his exercise; and in 1724 he issued *Musica Sacra*—thirty anthems and a Burial Service—the first important publication of sacred music in score. This estimable man died August 14th, 1727, and was buried in Westminster Abbey. His sonatas for two flutes, harpsichord music, and songs are of little importance; but his spirited anthems (of which twenty-six are mentioned in *Divine Harmony*) are still favourites, and by the hymn-tunes 'St. Anne's' and 'Hanover' he is in undying remembrance.

JOHN CHURCH was born at Windsor in 1675, and was a pupil of Child and Goldwin there, afterwards singing at St. John's College, Oxford. In 1697 he entered the Chapel Royal, and also became Master of the Abbey choir-boys. In 1712 he edited *Divine Harmony*, already described; it has been sometimes ascribed to Dr. Croft, but Thomas Ford's MS. collections in the Bodleian Library distinctiy assign it to Church, and the preface refers to Croft in a way which shows he was not the writer. The work is scarce; there is a copy at Sion College. Church also

published (about 1723) a treatise on Psalmody, in dialogue
between Theophilus and Philemon. A semibreve is
directed to be as long as 'four strokes of a large Pendulum
Clock.' Besides many psalm-tunes, the volume contains
three anthems of Church's and some of Dr. Croft's.
Tudway also included services and anthems by Church,
who died January 6th, 1741. His cousin Richard Church
(1699–1776), organist of Gloucester, must not be confused
with him.

THOMAS WANLESS became organist of York Cathedral
in 1691, and graduated Mus.Bac. Cantab. in 1698. Three
versions of a remarkably fine Litany by Wanless were
printed in Jebb's 'Choral Responses and Litanies'; a
good full anthem in the Tudway collection is the only
other work of his I have seen. Wanless died in 1721;
he had published in 1703 the words of the anthems sung
at York.

PHILIP HART (probably the son of a York singer who
entered the Chapel Royal in 1670) seems to have lived
to a very great age. He had contributed to several of
Playford's collections, and in 1703 composed the Ode
for St. Cecilia's Day. During his life he was organist at
several London churches. He published a setting of
Milton's Morning Hymn, and a collection of fugues and
suites for organ or harpsichord. In playing he used the
shake to a most exaggerated extent. Tudway's collection
includes anthems by Hart, who died July 17th, 1749.

WILLIAM NORRIS, a Chapel Royal boy in 1685, was
subsequently choirmaster at Lincoln. He had composed
the Ode for St. Cecilia's Day in 1702. Services and
anthems of his are preserved in Tudway and elsewhere.
WILLIAM BRODERIP (1683–1726), organist of Wells
Cathedral, JAMES HAWKINS and his successors at Ely,
THOMAS KEMPTON and RICHARD LANGDON, all left
'Chanting Services,' each verse of the canticles being
set in alternation with a verse in plain-chant. GEORGE
HOLMES, at Lincoln 1705–20, and DANIEL HENSTRIDGE,
at Canterbury Cathedral 1700–30, composed good anthems and Services. Ten anthems by ANTHONY WALKLEY,
of Salisbury Cathedral, are mentioned in *Divine Harmony*.

The organists of Winchester Cathedral and College were at this time important. After Jeremiah Clarke, the College organist was JOHN BISHOP, who was born in 1665, and, according to Ford's MSS., a pupil of Rosingrave at Salisbury, afterwards in the choir of King's College, Cambridge, then at Winchester. Bishop also sang in the Cathedral choir, and in 1729 became Cathedral organist. He composed 'Jam lucis orto sidere,' printed with Reading's pieces in *Harmonia Wiccamica*; and he had composed many tunes for Michael Broom's treatise, *The Divine Music Scholar's Guide*. According to Ford he published *Harmonia lenis* for two flutes. Bishop's Service in D major is highly praised. He died 1737.

VAUGHAN RICHARDSON was a choir-boy in the Chapel Royal in 1685; there were others of the name Richardson there at the time. After Vaughan Richardson's voice broke he became organist of Winchester Cathedral, where he remained till his death in 1729. He set Odes for the Winchester celebrations of St. Cecilia's Day in 1700 and 1703, and published a collection of songs in 1701. His sacred music is valuable; eight anthems are mentioned in *Divine Harmony*; one was printed by Page, and there is an Evening Service in Tudway. ' O, how amiable,' remains a stock-piece. Vaughan Richardson was succeeded at the Cathedral by Bishop. A 'Wm. Richardson' published 'Lessons for the Harpsichord or Spinnet' in 1708; they are more difficult than Clarke's, but less musical.

JOHN READING, the last musician who bore this name, was born in 1667, trained in the Chapel Royal under Blow (as he states in one of his publications), and became organist of Dulwich College in 1700. In 1702 he entered the choir of Lincoln Cathedral, where he held exactly the same posts as the older John Reading had done. In 1707 he returned to London, and was passing the house of his friend Clarke on December 1st when he heard the fatal pistol-shot. Reading published a book of songs, in which he proclaimed himself a worshipper of the Italian school; and also a set of anthems. He held various organ appointments in London, and lived till September 2nd,

1764. He is remembered as the reputed composer of 'Adeste fideles.'*

RICHARD BRIND, who succeeded Clarke at St. Paul's, is little heard of as a composer; but there are five anthems of his mentioned in *Divine Harmony*. He died in 1718.

WILLIAM HINE was born at Brightwell, Oxfordshire, in 1687, and educated in the choir of Magdalen College; also studying under Clarke. In 1712 he became organist of Gloucester Cathedral, where he died August 28th, 1730. His widow published *Harmonia Sacra Glocestriensis*, containing a Te Deum by Henry Hall (see p. 317), with anthems and a florid voluntary by Hine.

THOMAS DEANE is a shadowy figure considering his period. He composed music to a tragedy, and is said, on the authority of Burney, to have performed a solo of Corelli's in 1709 for the first time in England. I understand Burney's words differently, viz. that this was the first special advertisement of a soloist. Nothing more is known of Deane except that he graduated Mus.Doc. Oxon. in 1731, and that Burney states he was organist at Warwick and Coventry. Some ecclesiastical music by Dr. Deane exists.

All these composers may be considered of the Purcell school, and their works, though they were of course less richly musical than his, had the same merits as his. We have now to turn to a man of considerable influence, who founded a new but inferior school of ecclesiastical music. CHARLES KING was born at Bury St. Edmunds in 1687, and was educated in St. Paul's choir under Blow and Clarke; he succeeded the latter as choirmaster, and graduated Mus.Bac. Oxon. in 1707. Hawkins states that King was indolent, but far from untalented; at any rate, he invented a style of his own, perhaps the easiest of all styles for a musician to compose in, and the most wearying for a musician to listen to. He used only commonplace phrases of his time with the plainest harmonies and no counterpoint; his services are consequently easy to perform, and appealed to tastes which could not

---

* See *Musical Antiquary*, April, 1910; *Musical Times*, August, 1912; J. T. Lightwood's *Hymn-Tunes and their Story*.

appreciate the higher attempts of Croft and Clarke. Though King's services inaugurated the worst style of Anglican music, they were certainly practical and taking; and Dr. Greene was never tired of parading his joke that King was a *serviceable* man. Tudway included some in his collection, and several were printed by Arnold and Page, and even in later times. Many organist-composers in the eighteenth century followed this style, and Boyce showed that it could be treated with beautiful results. King died in 1748.

There are also some musicians who were secular composers only, who belong to the pre-Handelian period of English music, though living into the period of his oratorios. The church composers already mentioned contributed a large part of the secular music used in this period, but the following were specially secular.

Solomon Eccles left several sons, all musicians. It appears to me that one was also named Solomon; this has caused some writers to believe that the Quaker returned to his profession. I ground my belief on the occurrence of the name in the King's Band for 1700, and the compositions in the *Division-Violin* and Walsh's *Division-Flute*. This younger Solomon Eccles (also 'Eagles') had composed the music for Otway's *Venice Preserved*; it may be seen in Addit. MSS. 29,283–5.

JOHN ECCLES succeeded Staggins as Master of the King's Band; and since he is described as his father's pupil, was probably born about 1650. He was a prominent figure among London musicians, and from 1685 onwards composed music for many dramas. A large selection of his songs was published about 1710, and many catches and instrumental pieces were included in various collections; Eccles had a good vein of melody, and his music was very popular. The Ode for St. Cecilia's Day, 1701, was set by him. As Master of the King's Band he regularly set the annual Odes written by the wretched poetasters, who then (and long after) disgraced the office of Poet Laureate; otherwise Eccles's later years were passed in retirement at Kingston-upon-Thames, as an angler. He lived till January, 1735. His brother, HENRY

ECCLES, a violinist, thought himself unfairly neglected, and about 1715 left the King's Band and went to Paris; in 1720 he published twelve solos in the style of Corelli. He died 1742. The youngest brother Thomas was perhaps the ablest of all, but was idle and dissipated, and sank into a mere tavern fiddler.*

RICHARD LEVERIDGE, a bass singer, was born in 1670, and lived till 1758. He composed a great many songs, and even music for several dramas; his *Macbeth* music, composed in 1708, may be seen in the Fitzwilliam Museum. Two volumes of his songs were published in 1727. In 1730 he advertised a challenge to sing a bass song against any man in England for a wager of 100 guineas. In his old age he continued to sing, but his style was hopelessly old-fashioned, and his friends supported him. Leveridge's claim to remembrance is the composition of a tune—'The Roast Beef of Old England'—and it is a sufficient claim. 'All in the Downs' is another of his songs.

JOHN RAVENSCROFT had been one of the Waits of the Tower Hamlets, but afterwards rose to a much better position. He published twelve sonatas at Rome in 1695.

WILLIAM CORBETT was much more cultivated than any of the above. He used the arms of the Shropshire family. The date of his birth is not known, but he was a leading violinist and composer at the beginning of the eighteenth century. Afterwards he paid a visit to Italy; then went there again with Government aid, and for a long time collected instruments and music, while he was probably acting as a spy upon the Pretender. He finally left Italy in 1724, on his return publishing a number of Concertos for strings, professing to exhibit the styles of various countries and cities. He died in 1748, bequeathing his collections to Gresham College, which could not conveniently receive them; they were accordingly sold by auction. His concertos, those published before his Italian visits as well as his later creations, have considerable merit; he had also issued sonatas for flutes.

The name JAMES PAISIBLE (Peasable) frequently occurs

* *The Strad*, March and July, 1917.

in collections of flute-music in the previous period and the beginning of this; and some dramas about 1700 had music by this composer, who was perhaps a foreigner. He led the King's Band 1714-9. A Thomas Paisible published much dance music.

JOHN ISHAM deserves mention. He was deputy to Dr. Croft, and succeeded him at St. Anne's, Soho. In 1713 he graduated Mus.Bac. Oxon.; and composed anthems, but was better known as a secular composer. He died in June, 1726.

The sacred and secular composers who have now been mentioned have taken us far into the eighteenth century; yet even the youngest must have been born before the Revolution. There happened to be an unusual proportion of long-lived musicians at this period, beginning with Creyghton, born before the Civil War, and Dr. Turner; besides Dr. Tudway, Philip Hart, John Eccles, Leveridge, Corbett, and finally Reading, who even outlived Handel. It must be remembered that some of these were Purcell's seniors; the others, besides Clarke, Croft, etc., were directly or indirectly Purcell's pupils. None of them, except perhaps Reading, were in any way affected by Handel. I have now to mention a foreigner who had a very considerable and beneficial influence upon English musical history, and who must always be remembered with respect.

JOHANN CHRISTOPH PEPUSCH was born at Berlin in 1667, and came to England about 1700. He graduated Mus.Doc. Oxon. with Croft in 1713. Of his compositions a song, 'Alexis,' was extremely popular in England for more than a century; and it was Pepusch who selected and arranged the tunes for *The Beggars' Opera*. But his singular dislike of the prevalent Italian style, and appreciation of sixteenth-century music, led to his holding a quite unique position in the artistic world, and he most fortunately found some disciples. In the preservation of older English music he did invaluable work. The great Virginal Book was first mentioned in his library, and he had obtained transcripts of some early treatises which would otherwise have been for ever lost in the

fire of 1731.* Dr. Pepusch was certainly the earliest
musician to study mediæval MSS. He cared so little
for contemporary music that he would only admit Handel
to be 'a good practical musician.' In 1737 he became
organist at the Charterhouse, passing the rest of his life
in study there; and in assisting young musicians with his
profound theoretical and general knowledge. His attempts
at acoustical studies and the investigation of Greek music
were nullified by his little classical and no mathematical
learning. He was conductor of the Academy of Ancient
Music till his death, and bequeathed it half his library,
the rest to private persons; through mischance and neglect
it was frittered away, Hawkins fortunately obtaining
much, which he afterwards presented to the British
Museum. Among Pepusch's pupils were Boyce, Travers,
and Cooke; his amanuensis was Immyns; and all these
names are of importance in English music. Pepusch
died in 1752.

JOHN ERNEST GALLIARD, with more invention than
Dr. Pepusch, was another leading London musician. He
was born at Zell, Hanover, in 1687, and came to England
about 1706; much dramatic and other music was contributed by him, including a fine setting of the Morning
Hymn from Milton. Galliard died in 1749.

In these musicians, English and foreign, we have thus
reached a later period; and our authorities are now the
two historians, Sir John Hawkins and Dr. Burney. The
latter, though born and educated elsewhere, was in London 1744–51; while Hawkins was born in London, 1719.
They thus spoke with personal knowledge of all the
longer-lived musicians, and could hear of Clarke and
Croft from the friends of these. Thomas Ford, whose
MSS. collections I have frequently quoted, was a chaplain
of Christ Church, Oxford; his Lives give some particulars
of the Queen Anne musicians besides copying Wood's
MSS. I shall have later to explain my doubts concerning
Hawkins's authority in one matter which he certainly
should have known thoroughly.

The generation which was born about the same time

* See Addit. MS. 4911.

with Handel and Bach was in England sterile musically. Between 1680 and 1710 scarcely any names of interest appear; in 1710 there was a fresh outburst of talent, as Arne, Boyce, Howard, and Avison were all born in that year. Deferring for the present their seniors—Greene, Rosingrave, and Travers—it is now the place to turn to an account of the establishment of Italian opera, and the doings of Handel, the greatest figure in any account of London music in the eighteenth century. Burney wrote a most elaborate description of every Italian opera performed in London; both by taste and interest he was led to give an altogether disproportioned share of attention to this department, and his details are so full as to make the last volume of his history almost unreadable. I shall give a very brief summary of the establishment of opera in Queen Anne's reign, especially as I have no fact to add to Burney's. The earlier performances have been mentioned on p. 301.

At the end of Charles the Second's reign there was only one theatre in London; but through a quarrel another was opened in Lincoln's Inn Fields in 1695, and Vanbrugh built a splendid edifice in the Haymarket, which was opened in 1705, and was the principal home of opera in England for 180 years. Drury Lane, however, preceded it in the formal establishment of opera. This was done by Dieupart, a French violinist and harpsichordist, and Haym, an Italian of German parentage. With them was associated a very poor English musician, Thomas Clayton, who had visited Italy. It was said that the music of his opera *Arsinoe* (1705) was compiled from pieces he had brought thence; but it seems really too poor for any one except Clayton himself. *Arsinoe* was advertised as 'a new opera after the Italian manner all sung.' Various arrangements of A. Scarlatti's and other operas were also given; some of the characters sang in English, others in Italian. William Corbett was the orchestral leader.

Addison now wrote the opera *Rosamond*, which Clayton set, and performed in 1707. The songs are among the very best poetry Addison ever wrote, and if he had collaborated with a real dramatist (Congreve, for instance),

the work might have been a literary masterpiece of
its time. But it has little stage interest; and however
good, would have been ruined by the intolerable badness
of Clayton's music. At this critical moment the cause of
English Opera was taken up by the very weakest possible
champion, with whom defeat was certain; and English
Opera fell to rise no more, except in a lower form, and
then only for brief periods. Addison thenceforward
continually sneered at the lyric drama; if he had tried
again, and with Eccles or Weldon as his composer, he
might have permanently established English Opera.

Only Italian operas, generally by A. Scarlatti, were
afterwards given at Drury Lane, still partly in English.
At last in 1710 *Almahide*, by an unknown author and
composer, was sung entirely in Italian, and entirely by
Italians.

The principal singer in these performances had been
Margherita de L'Epine, an Italian who came to England
(with a German named Greber) in 1692, and sang in
concerts very frequently, especially at York Buildings.
She appears to have been the first great bravura-singer
heard in London, and was also a fine harpsichordist and
dancer. Her principal rival was an Englishwoman named
Tofts, who, however, lost her reason in 1709. Valentini
(a castrato), Nicolini (a tenor), and a German always
known as the Baroness (said by Wanley to have been
the lady who cost Stradella his life) were the principal
other performers. Intrigues and quarrels abounded, as
they have done ever since at the Italian Opera.

So matters stood when *Almahide* was performed, and
Addison wrote that the town was weary of understanding
only half the opera, and resolved to understand none of
it. Then a change came over English art. Some noblemen who had visited the Electress Sophia of Hanover
invited her capellmeister to London. He eagerly accepted,
and at the end of 1710 arrived 'Signor Hendel, a famous
Italian composer.' Everything was ready for him. With
a few occasional visits to the Continent he was a Londoner
for the rest of his life (almost half a century), and beyond
all comparison the greatest figure in the musical world.

Handel was no more an Englishman than Gluck was a Frenchman, but the story of English music cannot omit the account of Handel's works, as they were written for English taste, and all the greatest to English words. He began with *Rinaldo*, produced at the Haymarket Theatre, February 24th, 1711, and an immense success. Addison sneered at the flight of living birds and other accessories.

It should not be forgotten that Handel assisted at Britton's concerts; and one can imagine the delight of the old 'small-coal man' as so tremendous a performer extemporised on the harpsichord or organ, and his thoughts ran back to the modest execution which thirty years earlier had been thought wonderful. The world knows how Handel overstayed his leave of absence, was in disgrace when George I came to the throne, and was forgiven after producing the Water Music, visited Germany in 1716 with the King, and on his final settlement here became chapel-master to the magnificent Duke of Chandos. This was the only post in England analogous to the dozens of such in Germany; and while a chapel of musicians is a dignified appendage to a large or small ruler's princely establishment, yet for a rich nobleman it is only a costly extravagance, and was one of the many ways in which the Duke of Chandos sought to spend his immense fortune. To it, however, we owe the *Chandos Anthems* (which are more akin to the German Church-Cantata than to English cathedral music), *Acis and Galatea*, and even Handel's oratorios.

The performances of Italian Opera continued in the Haymarket at the King's Theatre until 1717, and Handel had composed several new works, one of them being *Amadigi*, in which appeared an extremely fine soprano named Anastatia Robinson, a pupil of Croft and others. Margherita de L'Epine married Dr. Pepusch in 1718, and she sang no more in public.

The loss of so favourite an entertainment was regretted by the King and the nobility, and £50,000 was subscribed as a guarantee fund for a permanent Italian Opera. Handel went to Dresden and engaged singers; the composers Bononcini and Ariosti also came to London.

A governor, a deputy-governor, and twenty directors were chosen from the nobility; the King's Theatre in the Haymarket was taken, under the title of 'Royal Academy of Music.' The first performance took place April 2nd, 1720. This was the year of the South Sea Bubble, and for some time subsequently finance was in an unsettled state; the undertaking did not prosper, and continual calls were made upon the guarantors, until in 1728 all the money subscribed had been spent, and the enterprise was abandoned. Anastatia Robinson was one of the singers; in 1723 she married the Earl of Peterborough and retired. One of Dr. Turner's daughters, who had married the organist John Robinson, also sang at least once; Rosingrave directed an opera by his friend D. Scarlatti; and the famous trumpeter Valentine Snow played in the orchestra. Otherwise no Englishman had anything to do with the performances, which belong rather to general than to English musical history. For the same reason it is unnecessary to describe the performances; the reader need only remember that an opera in those days consisted of a succession of airs and duets only, with a concerted piece and dance at the end.

Attempts have been made by Ouseley, Macfarren, and others to accuse Italian Opera with the crime of preventing English musical genius from developing; they overlooked the fact that up till about 1840 Italian Opera ruled Germany as much as it did England, that its refinements in performance and the structural perfection of the airs were equally necessary to each country's composers. But England was centralised; Germany was not. There is no doubt that the formal beauty of Bach's works was owing to his study of Italian models; but he had no personal Italian rivalry to contend with at Weimar, Cœthen, or Leipzig, neither had Haydn at Esterhaz, as Handel had in London, Gluck in Paris, and Mozart in Vienna. A very great deal is involved in these facts.

The very best of Handel's English contemporaries were immeasurably below him, as may be easily seen if the very best of Weldon's, Croft's, or Greene's anthems be compared with the *Chandos Anthems*. He was a genius; they were only talents, and not even first-class talents. In spite of the personal opposition which Handel roused, it is evident that all felt his superiority as a composer, except Pepusch and his little knot of antiquaries. A satirical poem, *The Session of Musicians*, published in 1724, somewhat roughly expresses the general feeling. The various musicians of the time all appear before Apollo in competition for the laureate's crown, and all are successively rejected till Handel appears. Among the competitors:

' Gr—n, Cr—ts, and some in the Cathedral Taste
Their Compliments in form to Phœbus past;
Whilst the whole Choir sang Anthems in their Praise,
Thinking to cheat the God out of the Bays;
Who far from being pleas'd, stamp'd, fum'd, and swore
Such Musick he had never heard before;
Vowing he'd leave the Laurel in the lurch
Rather than place it in an *English Church*.'

This poem is in other respects interesting. Its account of instrumentalists throws light on the performers and performances of that day:

' Masters of various Instruments flock here,
The Scottish pipe, and British harp appear;
Lutes and Guitars do form a beauteous line
Whilst Dulcimers with Pipe and Tabor join;
From gay Moorfields, Sweet Singers did attend,
Wapping and Redriff did their Fiddlers send;
Of my Lord Mayor's choice Band there came the chief,
Who whet his Lordship's stomach to his Beef;
The Parish-Clerks and Waits form one large Group
And Organists swell up that bright, Psalm-singing Troop;
Each Dancing-Master thought it wondrous fit,
To flourish thither with his little Kit;
The Playhouse Bands in decent Order come
Conducted thither by a Tragick Drum;
The *Op'ra Orchest* them o'erlooked with pride
And showed superior skill—in a superior Stride.'

Among the competing composers is Dieupart, who is recommended not to spoil the singing, but to play his solos 'betwixt the Acts.' Ariosti, Bononcini, and others are all rejected, and Handel is finally crowned. At this

time Handel had produced none of his best works; yet
he, in Burney's apt quotation, 'bestrode our narrow world
like a Colossus.'

Political feelings entered into every phase of life;
and since Handel was the favourite of King George, the
Duchess of Marlborough supported Bononcini, who had
the honour of composing an anthem—'When Saul was
king over us'—for the great duke's funeral in Westminster
Abbey.   Considerable rivalry between the composers
arose, and an epigram was written by the Lancashire poet,
John Byrom:

> ' Some say, compared with Bononcini,
> That Mynheer Handel's but a ninny;
> Others aver that he to Handel
> Is scarcely fit to hold a candle;
> Strange all this difference should be
> 'Twixt Tweedeldum and Tweedeldee!'

This epigram has been frequently attributed to Swift; it
has given two phrases to the English language.

There was, however, a very general feeling that Handel
was the greatest musician, though the nobility disliked his
independent and somewhat rough manners. *The Session
of Musicians* was a fair representative of popular opinion.
Another rivalry arose in 1726 between the great sopranos
Cuzzoni and Faustina Bordoni; the supporters of each
artist hissed everything the other did, and on the night
of Cuzzoni's benefit there was nearly a riot.   At the
beginning of 1728 *The Beggars' Opera* was produced at
Lincoln's Inn Fields, and its success finally ruined the
Italian Opera, which was then abandoned.   Bononcini
was comfortably settled with the Duchess of Marlborough;
but he was accused of palming off a madrigal of Lotti's
as one of his own, and had to leave England.

The proprietor of the King's Theatre, a Swiss named
Heidegger, entered into partnership with Handel; they
continued the operas on their own account for some years
with no great success. The fashionable world had grown
tired of their toy. Handel tried a performance, with
scenery, but without action, of *Acis and Galatea*, 'the performers being disposed after the manner of the coronation

music.' This return to the English language was successful; and the Academy of Ancient Music performed,
also with scenery and dresses, a masque, *Haman and
Mordecai*, which Handel had composed in 1720 for the
Duke of Chandos. Pope, according to the advertisements,
had written the poem. Its success led Handel to perform
it himself, with additions, under the title of *Esther*, on
May 2nd, 1732. The Bishop of London refused per-
mission for the choir-boys of the Chapel Royal to appear
as chorus in a theatrical performance; the decision was
of importance in musical history, and affected libretto-
construction.

The following February Handel composed a similar
work on the story of *Deborah*, which was less successful;
and then, *Athalia*, which he performed at Oxford in
July. This excursion led to some splenetic remarks in
the journal of the antiquary Hearne, who, as a good
Jacobite, detested the Elector of Hanover's chapel-master
and his 'foreign fiddlers.' On this occasion Handel gave
a most extraordinary exhibition of his skill in organ-
playing.

The complete breach between Handel and the nobility
occurred at this time, through his quarrel with the male
alto Senesino, who was a great favourite. Handel left
the King's Theatre, and started as an impresario at
Lincoln's Inn Fields, but he soon removed to the new
theatre at Covent Garden. A number of the nobility
started a rival opera at the King's Theatre, sending to
Dresden for Hasse, who refused to come, upon which
Porpora was secured. They also carried off most of
Handel's singers; but their orchestra, as Burney says,
'was small,' consisting only of Carbonelli, Festing,
Valentine Snow, and a dancing-master named Kewar,
who was a good musician. An orchestra of three violins
and a trumpet would hardly be considered an orchestra
in these days. This theatre was patronised by the Prince
of Wales and the opposition; King George II and Queen
Caroline were true to Handel. There were four other
theatres then open in London, and both operas failed;
but the competition led to all the great singers visiting

England, Farinelli appearing at the King's Theatre, Caffarelli at Covent Garden. Strada and Carestini were Handel's mainstay. When Farinelli first gave forth his renowned power of beginning with a mere point, swelling to a *fortissimo*, and diminishing to a point again, the applause lasted full five minutes, and Lady Cowper called out, 'One God and one Farinelli!' Yet there were so many entertainments at the time that, according to Cibber, Farinelli himself once sang to an audience of £35. In 1736 Handel tried concerts again with a setting of Dryden's *Alexander's Feast*. But next year he became bankrupt, having spent his large savings in the conflict; and the other house also closed. He returned to oratorio, giving *Saul* in 1738, and *Israel in Egypt* in 1739. The latter was a failure. His last attempt at opera was *Deidamia*, composed 1740 and performed 1741; but then, hearing that the Earl of Middlesex was about to enter into competition with him, he resolved to visit Ireland. and finally relinquished opera.

Before starting, he composed *Messiah* and *Samson*. The former he performed April 13th, 1742, at the Music Hall, Fishamble Street, Dublin, for the benefit of the City Prison. His visit to Ireland was one continued triumph. He returned in the autumn and produced *Samson* at Covent Garden Theatre with brilliant success on February 17th. *Messiah* followed on March 23rd. King George and a large audience were deeply impressed throughout, till at the unison passage all with one impulse started to their feet, and the custom of standing during the 'Hallelujah Chorus' has ever since been observed. But all the sublimity of *Messiah* and *Samson* could not ward off the hostility of the upper classes; and not till 1747 did Handel's performances prove profitable. Thenceforward he was uniformly successful. The King and the people actively supported him, and the personal opposition of the aristocracy died down. The oratorios were given in Lent at Covent Garden Theatre.

It is needful to describe, as far as we can, the performances for which Handel devised his great works. An oratorio performance is to us something entirely

different; so much so, that considerable historical knowledge is necessary to bring before the mind Handel's
intentions. Oratorio—the narrative rendering of a story
from the Bible—is to us quite familiar; but to the English
of Handel's time it was quite new; and even in Italy
oratorios were an ecclesiastical function analogous to the
Mystery-Plays of an earlier time. The concert-oratorio
was Handel's invention. There was no popular sale for
such works as now; Handel never saw one of his oratorios
in print, though the successful songs were published. At
this time, and for long after, theatrical performances were
forbidden on Wednesdays and Fridays in Lent.

The proportion of performers for which Handel calculated his effects was quite unlike ours. He wrote for a choir
of perhaps twenty or thirty, and an orchestra about as
numerous, with plenty of powerful oboes and bassoons
intended for military music. We think of a huge amateur
choir painfully practising up the choral numbers; but
Handel had a few competent singers to provide for, and
could have a new oratorio transcribed, rehearsed, and
performed in two or three weeks. It is only reasonable
to suppose that Handel's performances were much
brighter than the lumbering jogtrot now thought necessary
to oratorio. Handel, until his blindness, sat at the harpsichord and accompanied everything; sometime; he played
organ solos during the interval. He had ' trackers,' previously unknown in England, made from his harpsichord
to the organ.

Handel to a very considerable extent controlled English
musical thought during many decades; and an exact
knowledge of his resources is of use to practical musicians.
His invention of concert-oratorio was immediately imitated by Defesch (a Fleming who came to England in
1731), who produced *Judith* in 1733, and by others,
especially Johann Christoph Schmidt, Handel's amanuensis, and the first organist of the Foundling Hospital;
and in 1755 Arne tried his hand. After Handel's death
in 1759 the performances were continued every Lent by
J. C. Schmidt (or Smith) and John Stanley until 1774,
when Smith retired, and Linley joined Stanley, until the

latter died in 1786, when Dr. Arnold joined Linley. Occasional new works were produced, but they were childish compared to Handel's, which were the staple of the performances. In 1795 John Ashley entered into competition with them, and vulgarised the performances, which became a mere unconnected set of show-pieces, and for many years afterwards the two patent theatres replenished their receipts by variety programmes of all kinds every Lent, under the name of 'Oratorios.'

In the meantime Handel's works had been, even during his lifetime, occasionally performed elsewhere, even out of London. The *Messiah*, the words being taken from the Bible, was early looked upon in a different light from the others, which are to rhyme—and generally doggerel rhyme—excepting *Israel in Egypt*, then little known because of its lack of solos; in 1752 the *Messiah* was performed in Salisbury Cathedral at the Musical Festival, and in 1759 at Hereford. When the Wesleyan movement attained force, oratorios were performed in some of the chapels; and in due time oratorios began to be regarded as peculiarly sacred music, as Handel would most certainly have desired. Of late the national love of oratorio has apparently much declined, but it continued in full force for a century and a half, and has partly replaced our want of opera.

Returning now to the story of early eighteenth-century music, certain English composers who were contemporary with Handel, though a little younger, must be mentioned. The most famous is MAURICE GREENE, born 1695, the son of a London clergyman. He was a pupil of Brind, whom he succeeded at St. Paul's in 1718. On Tudway's death he was made Cambridge Professor, accumulating the degrees at the same time; and in 1735 succeeded Eccles as Master of the King's Band. Greene had been friendly with Handel, then with Bononcini, upon which he lost Handel's acquaintance. He was an original member of the Academy of Vocal Musick, but established a meeting of his own in 1731. He composed many anthems (of which forty were printed in 1743) and services still in use. He also composed good spirited secular music;

that he should have set and published Spenser's sonnets in 1738 is a fact of literary interest, as in the age of Pope, Spenser was scarcely mentioned. In 1750 Dr. Greene inherited a large estate, upon which he began to prepare an edition in score of the best English ecclesiastical music of all schools; but died, leaving his materials to Dr. Boyce, on December 1st, 1755. Dr. Greene was buried in his father's church, St. Olave, Jewry; on its demolition his remains were removed to St. Paul's.

CHARLES STROUD (1705–26) in his very short life produced an anthem, 'Hear my prayer,' which is still a favourite; his powers must have been unusual, and he might have attained to higher flights than any of his English contemporaries.

THOMAS ROSINGRAVE was the son of Daniel Rosingrave, one of Humfrey's choir-boys, and organist of Salisbury Cathedral 1693–8, subsequently at Dublin. Thomas Rosingrave, according to his epitaph, was born 1688–9; he showed such talent that the Dean and Chapter of Dublin sent him to Italy in 1710. At Venice he composed an anthem with orchestral accompaniment, preserved in Tudway. There he heard Scarlatti play, to his complete astonishment; and studied with him. In 1720 Rosingrave was in London, and assisted in the operatic performances. He was made the first organist of St. George's, Hanover Square; but he lost his reason through a love affair, and after 1737 his work was done by deputy. At times he recovered sanity; in 1753 he returned to Ireland, where he died, 26th June, 1766. He published some music for the flute, six good fugues for harpsichord, and some cantatas, besides introducing his friend Scarlatti's Leçons.

JOHN TRAVERS (1703–58), a choir-boy at Windsor Castle, was articled to Greene at the expense of Godolphin, Provost of Eton; afterwards he was taught by Pepusch. Sacred and secular music of considerable merit was composed by Travers, and is not forgotten; 'Ascribe unto the Lord' remains a stock piece. In 1737 he became organist of the Chapel Royal. Through Pepusch's training he was enabled to study some historical aspects of music; he composed melodies in the ecclesiastical

Modes, and scored some pieces (see p. 83) from the ancient MS. at Eton.

Of a lower kind, though of considerable influence, were JAMES KENT (1700–76), organist of Winchester Cathedral after John Bishop, and JOHN ROBINSON (1682–1762) at Westminster Abbey after Croft's death. Kent composed commonplace anthems and Services; while Robinson introduced a commonplace style of organ-playing, showing off solo stops with florid runs. Both did much to lower public taste.

It is now the moment to mention certain institutions of very great and lasting importance. The oldest was called The Academy of Ancient Music; and an account of its origin was published in 1770 by Hawkins, a member. He certainly ought to have known the truth of the matter, but I have reasons to suspect most serious inaccuracies in his account. Burney, who might have corrected it, apparently thought a Society that performed madrigals must be beneath his notice. Hawkins stated that the Academy was formed about 1710, met at the 'Crown and Anchor' in the Strand, that Needler was the first leader, that in 1728 Greene took away the choir-boys of St. Paul's, and in 1734 Gates took away the choir-boys of the Chapel Royal. All this is distinct enough; but in the British Museum (Addit. MS. 11,732) is the original minute-book of the Academy of Vocal Musick, which seems to give a different account. The first meeting was held January 7th, 1725–6,* when there were present Rev. S. Estwick, Messrs. Baker, Husband, Carleton, Hughes, Chelsum, Freeman, King, Gates, Weely, Dr. Pepusch, Greene, Galliard, and the Children of St. Paul's. It was agreed to meet every alternate Friday at the 'Crown and Anchor.' In 1727 Steffani was asked to be President. Fresh resolutions were drawn up on May 26th, 1731, among them being:

'By the compositions of the Ancients is meant of such as lived before the end of the 16th century.'

'That Dr. Pepusch be desired to demand of Dr. Greene the Six Motets yᵉ Bishop of Spiga [Steffani] sent the Academy.'

---

* This date appears also in an account-book preserved at the Conservatoire Library, Paris.

After this date we know nothing more of the Academy of Vocal Musick; I therefore suppose its name was changed to the Academy of Ancient Music. After Gates's secession, Pepusch was the director, the Academy advertising that children who would sing at the concerts would be taught by Pepusch gratis. Needler, Accountant-General of the Excise (1685–1760), visited Oxford to consult Aldrich's bequest, from which he scored a great number of old English and Italian works, filling twenty-eight volumes now in the British Museum. Pepusch was succeeded by Cooke. In 1761 the words of the repertory were published, and an enlarged edition followed in 1768; the volume is interesting, showing that the madrigalists, forgotten everywhere else, were still cultivated in England. Motets by Mouton, Lassus, and Vittoria, besides Palestrina and other Italians, are included; also a Lamentation by Tallis; the madrigals were by Marenzio, Lassus, Palestrina; and of English composers, Byrd, Morley, Farmer, Bennet, Wilbye, Weelkes, Gibbons, and East. Later and living composers also are represented. After Cooke's death Arnold conducted; but the Academy ended in 1792, having done noble work.

The annual festival of the Sons of the Clergy had 'music' (that is, orchestral accompaniment) added to the service in 1698; Purcell's 'Te Deum' and 'Jubilate' were performed every year until Handel's 'Utrecht Te Deum and Jubilate' was substituted in 1713, and afterwards the two services were given in alternate years until Handel's for the victory of Dettingen took their place in 1743, and was nearly always given afterwards, with the overture to *Esther* as a prelude to the service.

The provincial Festivals came into existence during the eighteenth century. The earliest recorded Festival of the Three Choirs was held at Gloucester in 1724. These Festivals at first consisted of united services (with orchestra) during two days, and concerts in the evenings. Handel's oratorios were soon given, and in 1759 the *Messiah* was performed in Hereford Cathedral. All other oratorios were restricted to the Shire Hall concerts until 1787, when *Israel in Egypt* was admitted to Gloucester

Cathedral. The Birmingham Festivals began in 1768, with a band of twenty-five and a chorus of forty; the next was in 1778. In 1784 they became triennial. These also included the 'Te Deum' and 'Jubilate' with orchestral accompaniment, sung in St. Philip's Church.

The Royal Society of Musicians, a noble charitable institution, was founded in 1738. Festing and Weide-mann, discovering the children of an old comrade in poverty, relieved them, and originated a Society to which Handel, Arne, Boyce, and others gave warm support. Handel was especially helpful. The Society was chartered in 1789, and has received many munificent donations and bequests. It performs *Messiah* annually.

The next institution founded was one which has lasted in full prosperity down to our own times. The Madrigal Society owes its origin to JOHN IMMYNS, a worthy man like-minded with Pepusch (to whom he was amanuensis) in his complete dislike of the style prevalent in his own day. Immyns had been an unsuccessful attorney; he taught himself the lute from Mace's book, and became lutenist at the Chapel Royal. Upon English music he has made a permanent mark. In 1741* he founded the Madrigal Society, which first met at the 'Twelve Bells' in Bride Lane; we fortunately possess some account of the day of small things from one of the earliest members—Hawkins. Burney, of course, ignored a Society so very vulgar-minded as to devote itself entirely to madrigals. Hawkins tells us that:

'Most of them were mechanics, some weavers from Spitalfields, others of various trades and occupations, who were well versed in the practice of Psalmody, and who, with a little pains and the help of the ordinary solmisation, which many of them were very expert in, became soon able to sing almost at sight a part in an English or even an Italian madrigal. They also sang catches, rounds, and canons, though not elegantly, yet with a degree of correctness that did justice to the harmony; and to vary the entertainment, Immyns would sometimes read, by way of lecture, a chapter from Zarlino, translated by himself. They were men not less distinguished by their love of vocal harmony than by the harmless simplicity of their tempers, and by their friendly disposition towards each other.'

* 1741 is probably a misprint for 1744 in Hawkins's History.

Here was artistic endeavour of the truest, combined with all the pleasures which such cultivation can bring. The Society at times made excursions; on Whit Monday, 1751, the old minute-book records an expedition up the river. These men were unlearned mechanics, working hard all day, meeting at night to perform the beautiful works of past centuries, studying and loving music, and obtaining an exceeding great reward. In such assemblies flourishes genuine artistic enthusiasm, and well would it be for English music if such a one existed now in every town. The honest work of the Madrigal Society did not long remain unnoticed. Good musicians and singers joined, the subscription was raised in 1768, the numbers increased, and occasionally entertainments were given to friends. The original character of the Society was in time quite lost; but it lived on and still lives, though not perhaps nearly so useful as it might be if it were more before the world. As the oldest musical society in England,* specially devoted to that branch of music in which England was specially distinguished, it would seem to many that the Madrigal Society deserves a far more prominent position than it has at present, when scarcely any know of its existence.

Immyns died April 15th, 1764. A score of Tallis's 'Forty-voiced Motet' is among his MSS. in the Madrigal Society's library; and at the Fitzwilliam Museum are two volumes containing a great number of sacred and secular pieces by Byrd, Morley, Wilbye, and others (both English and Italian), in his writing, with some similar pieces by himself. Other MSS. of his are at the British Museum.

SAMUEL HOWARD, of a rather later generation, was apparently like-minded in his indifference to eighteenth-century music, and may accordingly be mentioned here. He was born in 1710, was a Chapel Royal boy under Croft, and a pupil of Pepusch. According to Burney, Howard not only despised the ruling Italian style, but would never even hear any of it. He was organist in

---

* There are existing Dutch and Irish musical societies still older; the Gentlemen's Concerts at Manchester were alive and active political centres in 1745, but are now unfortunately ceasing.

London, graduated Mus.Doc. in 1769, and died 1782.
A good many of his vocal and instrumental compositions
were published, of which only the hymn-tunes 'Howard'
and 'St. Bride's' are remembered.

Pepusch had made himself the centre of a knot of
musicians who were quite unaffected by the current of
Italian influence which had overwhelmed almost all
Europe.   Immyns, Travers, Dr. Howard, and the still
to be mentioned Dr. Cooke, lived in the creations of the
past, and followed them in their own works.

The musical literature of the eighteenth century hardly
requires examination till we reach the great Histories.
A treatise by William Turner, entitled *Sound Anatomised*,
appeared in 1724, and is of some value; it has one fault
(common enough among musicians), the persistence in
clumsy notation.   Some persons in that age had justly
complained against composers for not writing systematic
key-signatures; Turner took the wrong side, and thought
key-signatures were not required at all if people would
only learn where the semitones come.   He mentions that
the natural, or 'Mark of Restoration,' had only been
introduced within the previous twenty years, and was
still not universal.

A new though unimportant form of art came into great
vogue at this time.   The BALLAD OPERA is said to owe its
existence to a remark of Swift's that 'A Newgate Pastoral
might be made a pretty thing.'   From this hint Gay
constructed *The Beggars' Opera*, a drama of moderate
literary merit and objectionable morality; but the music
was entrusted to Dr. Pepusch, who arranged the songs
and overture from favourite folk-tunes, and so effective
was the result that the opera (first played at Lincoln's
Inn Fields, January 29th, 1727-8) was given sixty-two
times during the first season, and remains a stock piece
of the British stage.   Many of the loveliest of our folk-
tunes are introduced, and Pepusch had the delight of
seeing the Italian opera in the Haymarket entirely ruined.

The success of *The Beggars' Opera* naturally led to a
host of imitations; and Ballad Opera furnished a large
portion of theatrical entertainments during the next ten

or twelve years. As usual, the imitations had not the success of the original, and were all quickly forgotten. Ballad Opera, however, heralded a revival of English Opera, at which apparently not even an attempt had been made since Clayton's miserable failure in *Rosamond*. Attempts at a burlesque of Italian Opera were repeatedly made; one called *The Dragon of Wantley*, set by a German named Lampe, was especially successful in 1737.

HENRY CAREY had written this drama, and others set by Lampe. He was born probably about 1690, as he spoke of his youth in a publication dated 1713. He was perhaps a son of Lord Halifax. Carey was one of the semi-geniuses in poetry and music who have splendid capacity for expression, but none for intellectual culti-vation, and consequently never rise to a high rank, though they make occasional wonderfully lucky strokes; he published a vast amount of poetical and dramatic work of all kinds, sometimes with music of his own. In 1739 he issued one hundred ballads written and composed by himself. Among these was 'Sally in our Alley,' a charming poem to a charming tune; but the ballad-singers quickly disused the tune for a still finer melody, an old folk-tune called 'The Country Lass,' now in-separably wedded to Carey's poem.

The most interesting question connected with Carey is, of course, the claim set up for him as the composer of the National Anthem, which was printed in *Harmonia Anglicana* in 1742 or 1743, and came into prominence during the Young Pretender's invasion in 1745, when it was sung at Drury Lane Theatre on September 28th, harmonised by Arne; and directly after, at Covent Garden, harmonised by Burney. It was then printed in its present form; the previous version had begun with the tonic three times; the fourth and fifth bars and the cadence being also considerably different, and quite inferior. In one of Benjamin Victor's letters to Garrick, with the date October, 1745, the performance is alluded to, and the piece is said to be:

'The very words and music, of an old anthem which was sung at St. James's Chapel, when the Prince of Orange landed.'

The National Anthem was now at once established as such, but no further thought seems to have been given to its authorship, and it is not mentioned in the histories of either Hawkins or Burney. Carey had already passed away, having been found dead on October 4th, 1743. The tune was soon adopted as a National Anthem in several other countries; the feeling arose that it was the duty of a country to have a National Anthem, and in one electrical moment the 'Marseillaise' flashed through France, as in a similar crisis seventy-eight years later 'Die Wacht am Rhein' flashed through Germany. The Austrian National Hymn was composed by Haydn specially because he envied the English for their National Anthem; and Beethoven said he must show us what a blessing we have in it, though he hardly succeeded. Lwoff composed the fine Russian Hymn as a substitute for 'God save the King,' which was used in Russia till 1833. In Germany it is universally known as 'Heil dir im Siegerkranz,' to which it was adapted in 1790; and I have personally known a German servant-girl who, being new to England, thought when she heard a military band play it as she came up that it was played in her own honour, though she could not understand how they could know that she was a German!

It was not till 1795 that the authorship began to be discussed. Then Carey's son applied for help to George III on the ground of his father's services in this matter; and the claim was supported by J. C. Smith (Handel's amanuensis), who asserted that Carey had brought the MS. to him to correct the harmony. Another statement soon followed, that in 1740, at a dinner in Cornhill to celebrate the capture of Portobello, 'God save the King' was sung by Carey, and 'the applause he received was very great, especially when he announced it to be his own composition.' But Burney then declared it was a received opinion that the National Anthem was composed for James II and sung in his chapel; and notwithstanding the evidence in favour of Henry Carey, conjecture points to the composer of 'Britons, strike home,' and 'Come if you dare,' as the composer of 'God save the King.'

Fresh light was thrown upon the matter when Mr. W. H. Cummings discovered that in 1743–4 a concert was given by John Travers, when a Latin chorus was sung, of which the words were:

O Deus Optime	Exurgat Dominus
Salvum nunc facito	Rebelles dissipet,
Regem nostrum;	Et reprimat;
Sit læta victoria	Dolos confundito
Comes et gloria	Fraudes depellito
Salvum jam facito	In Te sit sita spec
Tu Dominum.	O salva nos.

It would seem practically certain from this evidence that the National Anthem was really composed for James II about 1688. The Rev. Mr. Henslowe published a pamphlet in 1849 asserting that Dr. Arne's wife had received a pension as the eldest descendant of the composer of the National Anthem—Anthony Young, organist of Allhallows, Barking—and that Mrs. Arne had left a legacy to Mrs. Henslowe. There is no other evidence for this claim (unless the inferiority of the first-published version be taken as such), and the probability is that 'God save the King' is the composition of Henry Purcell, and the words perhaps translated into English by Henry Carey. I cannot refrain from an allusion to the extraordinary ignorance of musical matters shown in the reference to Carey in Macaulay's History, chapter xxi, where Carey's claim to the National Anthem is not even mentioned.

We now arrive at the greatest English musician of the eighteenth century, THOMAS AUGUSTINE ARNE. He was born in King Street, Covent Garden, March 12th, 1710, and was educated at Eton, being intended, like Handel, for the law. He secretly practised on a muffled spinet, took lessons on the violin, and one night his amazed father, who did not suspect these pursuits, saw his son leading an orchestra at a private concert. Arne was, after a short struggle, permitted to follow his own bent. He taught his sister (the famous Mrs. Cibber) and brother to sing, and in 1733 reset Addison's opera *Rosamond*, which was performed with success. His reputation was

made by a setting of Milton's *Comus* in 1738 for Drury
Lane; and was crowned on August 14th, 1740, by the
masque *Alfred,* played in a temporary theatre in the
garden of 'Cliefden's proud alcove,' then the residence
of Frederic, Prince of Wales. The conclusion to this
masque is the song of 'Rule, Britannia,' probably the
finest national air in existence; as Wagner said, the first
eight notes contain the whole character of the English
people.* In the same year Arne composed the songs in
As You Like It for the revival at Drury Lane, and some
of these are almost as well known as 'Rule, Britannia.'
Still more familiar is the exquisite 'Where the bee sucks,'
composed for a revival of *The Tempest* in 1746. A vast
number of other songs were composed by Arne for the
entertainments at Vauxhall, Ranelagh, and Marylebone
Gardens, and for many dramas at Drury Lane. Among
these was an arrangement, with additions, of Purcell's
King Arthur, performed in 1770. Arne also published
much instrumental music of no great importance; as a
contemporary of Emanuel Bach, he wrote in the transition
style before the true binary form was evolved. Still his
harpsichord sonatas and organ concertos will bear an
occasional hearing. Many of his works have been re-
issued in various editions.

The most enduring of his larger attempts was the
opera *Artaxerxes,* translated by himself from Metastasio,
and set 'after the Italian manner'—that is, sung throughout. It was produced at Covent Garden Theatre, February 2nd, 1762, enjoyed great and lasting success, and was
performed as late as 1829. The part of 'Mandane' was
written in a very florid style for Arne's pupil, Miss Brent.

Encouraged by the success of *Artaxerxes,* Arne attacked
the Italian supremacy in its stronghold—the King's
Theatre in the Haymarket. He composed Metastasio's
Olimpiade in the original language, and it was performed
twice in 1765; then it was shelved through intrigues.
This was the only eighteenth-century English attempt at
Italian Opera.

* But how many Britons know the words, even of the second stanza?
And the accepted version of the refrain is weaker than Arne's original. (See
Musical Times, April, 1900.)

Arne also, with less success, attempted oratorio. His *Judith* (1755) and *Abel* (1764) contain melodious and effective solos, with weak choral writing in vain attempt at rivalling Handel. He, however, had influence on the development of choral music by introducing female voices into the choir at a performance of his *Judith* at Covent Garden on February 26th, 1773. Previously choir-boys only had been employed. It must be remembered that Arne had not enjoyed the advantages of a training as a Chapel Royal choir-boy.

Arne was also concerned with others in setting a number of Horace's odes, translated into Italian by Bottarelli. He had some literary pretensions, and composed incidental music for Mason's *Caractacus* (1776).*

In 1759 Arne had graduated Mus.Doc. Oxon. He died March 5th, 1778, and was buried in the church of St. Paul, Covent Garden. He is unforgettable as the composer of 'Rule, Britannia,' and 'Where the bee sucks'; nor is the exquisite air, 'Water parted from the sea,' likely to pass out of remembrance for centuries to come. Whether he reached his full powers is another question. Certainly his principal gift was melody, and in that he did as much as any man need do by composing a genuine patriotic national air of the highest merit and Shakespeare songs which are almost as enduring as the poetry which inspired them.

Contemporary with him was WILLIAM BOYCE, also born in 1710, who, like Arne, is remembered by a patriotic song; but his life was spent in the service of the Church. He was born in Upper Thames Street, and educated under Charles King and Maurice Greene at St. Paul's, and afterwards under Dr. Pepusch. Deafness began to come upon Boyce when he was still young. He held various organ appointments in London, becoming composer to the Chapel Royal on the death of Weldon in 1736. Having been selected to compose the Installation Ode of a new Chancellor to Cambridge University in 1749, he was created Mus.Doc. Dr. Boyce succeeded

* There was also an operatic setting of *Caractacus*. Mr. Sonneck has shown it was a rather later production, and not Arne's.

Travers as organist to the Chapel Royal. Dr. Greene
bequeathed his pupil the task of completing and publishing his collection of English Cathedral Music, which
Boyce finally accomplished in 1778.   This was the
earliest publication of sixteenth and seventeenth-century
ecclesiastical music in score; it contains fourteen Services,
by Tallis, Morley, Farrant, Byrd, Bevin, Child (two),
Gibbons, Rogers, Blow (three), Aldrich, and Purcell;
and seventy-one anthems, by Henry VIII (really by
Mundy or Sheppard), Tallis ('I call and cry'), Tye (two),
Farrant (two), Byrd (three), Gibbons (five), Batten
(three), Child (three), Rogers (two), Blow (ten), Aldrich
(two), Creyghton (one), Purcell (nine), Goldwin (one),
Clarke (three), Croft (four), Weldon (two), W. Lawes
(one), Lock (one), Humfrey (seven), Wise (six), Bull
(one), and Turner (one); with a few chants, etc. It will
be seen that the School of the Restoration preponderates
over the purer Elizabethan, otherwise the selection is
admirable. Boyce's *Cathedral Music* brought him little
reward; but it was reprinted after his death, and again
with additional anthems and services in 1849.   The
importance of this publication was set forth by Chrysander in an article (see p. 115) on the Chapel Royal in
Handel's time, where the historic continuity of the
Anglican Church is well explained; so that even moder-
ately gifted men were enabled to work upon the foundations laid by past generations and carry the edifice
higher, while in the Lutheran Church even the greatest
masters only contributed individual work, which their
successors immediately demolished. In 1778 also appeared
a publication called the *Cathedral Magazine*; this contained anthems only, in score, and filled some omissions
of Boyce's.   Notably 'Lord, for Thy tender mercies'
sake,' ascribed to Farrant, here appeared for the first
time in print.
    Many services and anthems of Boyce's own were
published after his death; and he had published much
vocal and instrumental music.   Some of the latter is
unusually good for its period, and has been recently
republished; while his Service in A shows that the

harmonic style of Charles King could be treated with good results. All else is forgotten except one song; but that song is the glorious tune, 'Heart of Oak,' as familiar as 'Rule, Britannia,' to every Englishman. Dr. Boyce, a worthy man in every way, died February 7th, 1779, and was buried in St. Paul's Cathedral.

JOHN STANLEY, another Londoner, was born in 1714, and blinded in infancy by an accident. He was a pupil of Dr. Greene, and at the age of eleven became a London organist, at sixteen graduating Mus.Bac. Oxon. From 1734 he was organist of the Temple Church. After Handel's death, the Lenten oratorios were continued by J. C. Smith and Stanley, the latter composing several new oratorios with fair success. Stanley was also in great esteem as a performer and teacher, and published many compositions, his organ music being even yet not quite forgotten. Of all recorded powers of musical memory, Stanley's were probably the most wonderful. He died May 19th, 1786.

JOSEPH KELWAY, who succeeded Weldon as organist of St. Martin's, was in the highest repute as an extemporiser; but Burney says his harpsichord Lessons (published 1764) disappointed everybody. They have more character and originality than other works of the time, and are less polished, more difficult, and not so well constructed as usual. Kelway died in 1782.

CHARLES AVISON was born in 1710 (the same year as Arne, Boyce, and Howard) at Newcastle. After a visit to Italy, he settled at his native place as organist of St. Nicholas (now Newcastle Cathedral) till his death in 1770. His son and grandson succeeded him there. He published concertos for strings, and a treatise on 'Musical Expression,' in which his master (Geminiani) is put forward as the great model of composition; Handel being only once mentioned. One of the Avisons composed an air which was adapted to Moore's 'Sound the loud timbrel,' and was long extremely popular in religious circles, both in England and America.

Avison's treatise was answered by Dr. WILLIAM HAYES (1707–77), who had succeeded the younger Goodson as

Oxford Professor. One of his sons, Dr. PHILIP HAYES (1738–97), was the next Professor. The Hayes family may be taken as typical specimens of the eighteenth-century English musicians—good organists, practised singers, thoroughly understanding the voice, and utterly uninventive composers. The father's 'Praise the Lord, O Jerusalem,' remains on the cathedral repertory.

Dr. WORGAN (1724–94) has been remembered because his name was often attached to the grand melody sung to the Easter Hymn, which, however, had been published in 1708. Under the tuition of his brother and Rosingrave he became a very fine organist, and composed much music of all kinds, up to oratorios.

Dr. CHARLES BURNEY, born at Shrewsbury, April 7th, 1726, is now only known by his bulky 'History of Music,' but in his time he was a leading composer and performer. He was a choir-boy at Chester, where he made Handel's acquaintance in 1741; he is the authority for many familiar anecdotes of Handel. Burney came to London in 1744, removed to Lyme Regis in 1751, finally returning to London in 1760. The exercise for his degree in 1769 was frequently performed both in England and Germany. He travelled on the Continent, publishing accounts of the *Present State of Music* in various countries. Some twenty years were devoted to his History; on its completion he became organist of Chelsea College, where he died, April 14th, 1814. His daughter, Frances d'Arblay, the brilliant novelist and diarist, has left full accounts of his life.

The Linley family were of considerable importance in the eighteenth century. THOMAS LINLEY, born at Wells in 1732, composed much graceful vocal music; and his madrigal, 'Let me careless,' has succeeded in maintaining its place on the repertory of choral societies. He joined Stanley in the Lenten oratorios after J. C. Smith's retirement, and composed much very successful music for dramas. All his six children were distinguished; the three daughters were brilliant singers, but died young. The eldest was Sheridan's wife. The eldest son, Thomas, showed perhaps greater musical talent than any

Englishman of his time; he was born at Bath in 1756, played a violin concerto at eight years old, went to Italy and became very intimate with Mozart, returned and composed industriously, but, alas, was drowned on August 6th, 1778, to the severe detriment of English music. The second son was organist of Dulwich. The elder Thomas Linley died in London, November 19th, 1795, but was buried in Wells Cathedral; his youngest son, William Linley, went to India, and returning rich, devoted himself to literature and music till his death in 1835.

The names of Thomas Chilcot (of Bath), the Rev. William Felton (of Hereford Cathedral), Dr. John Alcock (of Lichfield Cathedral), and Dr. Thomas Dupuis, organist of the Chapel Royal after Boyce, just deserve mention. A little higher point as a composer was attained by Dr. JAMES NARES (1715–83), born near London, educated in the Chapel Royal, organist of York Minster 1734–56, then of the Chapel Royal. His ecclesiastical music has been more successful than it deserves, and is still used. He issued some remarkably good harpsichord Lessons; but attacked the 'fashionable passages which, though adopted lately by some of the ablest masters, he cannot help considering as Instances of a false Taste which seems advancing too fast in all sorts of Music.' What Nares objected to was the chromatic scale, or, as he called it, 'wanton and improper successions of half-notes.'

Of a different class, and with decided and considerable merit as a secular composer, was WILLIAM JACKSON, born at Exeter, May, 1730. He was a well-educated and generally cultivated man, studied music under Travers, and finally followed the art, though giving much time to literature and painting. His songs are always tasteful, and some are of unfading beauty; as for his famous service, the familiar 'Jackson in F,' it is one of the works which it is 'vain to blame and useless to praise.' Jackson became organist of Exeter Cathedral in 1777, and died July 12th, 1803. In one of his many essays he severely attacked the disgusting catches which were still sung, and shamed the performers into an observance of decency. Jackson, though he became a musician, was evidently always one of the half-amateurish school of Carey, a school flourishing in every country where any art has attained a certain repute.

We now enter a fresh period, one of considerable interest historically, in which appeared another form quite peculiar to English music—the GLEE. It should be noticed that through the whole Handel-Arne period the school of Pepusch had kept up the interest in pure vocal music; and most of the leading composers, even those not under Pepusch's influence, had contributed works quite unlike the ornamented Italianism prevalent, which was falling everywhere into effete routine. Linley's madrigal is, perhaps, the best of these unaccompanied works. Now came a new art-form. A Glee may be defined as an unaccompanied piece for three or more solo voices; to this may be added that it is 'set throughout,' the music not being repeated to successive stanzas. The Glee differs from the Madrigal mainly in being intended to specially display solo voices; madrigals are best sung by a chorus. The 'Ayres' of the Elizabethan and Jacobean composers are unlike glees in having accompaniment and repeating the same music to several stanzas. Glees were generally written entirely for male voices, and require a male alto; they were in full popularity from about 1780 to 1860, but are now much less heard, partly, indeed, through the neglect of falsetto-singing.

The word glee is derived from the Anglo-Saxon *gligg*, which meant entertainment of every sort, as was explained in Chapter I. In the sense of part-music it occurs first in Playford's third set of 'Ayres and Dialogues,' published 1659, where Brewer's 'Turn, Amaryllis' is headed Glee. The name was occasionally used without any definite meaning for a century after; about 1760 it seems to have been specialised into the form I have defined above. Being written for solo vocalists, in an age when singing was highly cultivated, glees are consequently *vocal* above everything; and they are usually set to fine poetry, and depend very largely on the expressive delivery of the words. Unaccompanied solo pieces

cannot be very long, and consequently glees are *small*
compositions, but the best examples are characterised
by very high qualities, and if real genius had cultivated
their resources, they would be found capable of splendid
development. There was very quickly a tendency to
turn them into simple successions of harmony; in this
style a glee is, perhaps, the feeblest of all compositions,
but the best specimens are of quite a different order, and
have a polyphonic style of their own, giving each voice
plenty of independent work, and fully displaying the
peculiarities of each kind of voice. The best glee-writers
frequently chose picturesque and dramatic words which
suggested many short sections rather than one homo-
geneous movement; and their works accordingly are of
a kind which has been well described as *musical mosaic*.
This is, however, by no means invariably the case; and
some glees exhibit masterly continuity and construction.
Glees, as a special branch of music, should not be forgotten; their performance necessitates finished singing,
and has a highly beneficial effect upon the vocal art.

Several societies were founded for the cultivation of
this and kindred forms of vocal music. The Noblemen's
and Gentlemen's Catch Club, which still exists, was
founded by a number of amateurs in November, 1761;
the Royal Princes subsequently joined, and were all
active members. From 1763 to 1794 the Catch Club
gave annual prizes for catches, canons, and glees; and
occasionally at later periods, especially at the centenary
in 1861. Another institution of the same kind, the
Anacreontic Society, was also highly aristocratic, with
professional musicians as honorary members; but it
dissolved, as the Duchess of Devonshire was present in
a box under the orchestra, and certain pieces were not
allowed to be sung in her hearing, at which restraint the
members took great offence. Evidently Jackson's animad-
versons upon the character of words set to music were
sadly wanted. At a rather later period followed the Glee
Club, which lasted from 1787 to 1857, and consisted
only of musicians; and the Concentores Sodales, 1798 to
1847, at which every member was a composer.

A leading musician of the later eighteenth century may be predicated certainly a composer of glees, and this branch of composition was the only one in which good work was done. From about 1780 to 1810 was on the whole the weakest period of English music, as regards *production ;* in execution there are very important matters to chronicle, and the general level of vocal music seems to have been high. Throughout the century the Italian Opera remained a fashionable resort in London.

When the Catch Club began its operations, Arne, Boyce, Stanley, etc., were still working, and they were among the prize-winners at various periods; but the accepted model of glee had not then been evolved.

Edmund T. Warren, secretary to the Catch Club, published a great collection of glees, madrigals, canons, and catches, in thirty-two volumes. A large part of the edition was destroyed by fire, and complete sets are rare. They were printed in score, a novelty. The first volume, which appeared in 1763, contained canons by Byrd, Ives, and some from *Pammelia*; with madrigals by John Bennet and Orlando Gibbons, and a number of pieces then new. G. W. Budd published a detailed index in 1836.

The earliest-born composer of the true glee was Dr. BENJAMIN COOKE, the son of a London music-publisher, and born in 1734. He was distinguished at an early age, being Pepusch's successor at the Academy of Ancient Music, conducting it 1752–89. He became organist of Westminster Abbey in 1762, and died September 14th, 1793; on his tomb in the cloisters of the Abbey is a splendid canon in double augmentation. A great collection of Cooke's autograph compositions is at the Royal College of Music, including good ecclesiastical music, Collins's Ode on the Passions, and a great number of glees, canons, and catches. Forty were printed by Warren, and many by Cooke himself. As might be expected in a pupil of Pepusch, Cooke was a learned theorist, and something of a musical antiquary.

The most gifted amateur of the period was certainly LORD MORNINGTON, father of the great Duke of Wellington. He was born at Dangan Castle. Meath, on July 19th,

1735, and showed extraordinary precocity. The office of Professor of Music at Dublin University was created for him in 1764; but he resigned in 1774, and a successor was not appointed till 1847. A double chant in E by Lord Mornington was once everywhere familiar; and his glee, 'Here in cool grot,' equally so. (See Dickens's *Bleak House*, chap. xxxii.) He composed very many glees, and also church and instrumental music; and died at Kensington, May 22nd, 1781.

LUFFMAN ATTERBURY (d. 1796) composed an oratorio, *Goliah*, as well as a popular glee, 'Come, let us all a-Maying go,' and many others; there are thirty pieces in Warren, and some were published by himself.

JONATHAN BATTISHILL was perhaps the most gifted composer of the weak period, and but for a series of sad mischances might have done work sufficient to redeem its character altogether. He was born in London, May, 1738, and educated in St. Paul's Choir. Having been harpsichordist at Covent Garden Theatre for a time, he joined Arne's son in composing the opera *Almena*, which did not live owing only to the poverty of the libretto. Afterwards he became a City organist, and composed several fine anthems, of which 'Call to remembrance' is the best, and is still much performed. The death of his wife in 1777 so affected him that he composed no more, and occupied himself with reading. Battishill died Dec. 10th, 1801, and was buried in St. Paul's. His works show that he possessed considerable latent powers, which scarcely had a fair chance to develop; his glees are of the best.

The musician who is recognised as the typical glee-composer was SAMUEL WEBBE. His father was an officer stationed at Minorca, where Webbe was born in 1740. The sudden death of his father left the family in distress; Webbe was accordingly apprenticed to a cabinet-maker; during this period he taught himself six languages. Having to repair the case of a harpsichord, he tried his fingers on it whenever he was alone. Barbandt, organist to the Bavarian ambassador, accidentally overheard him, and offered to teach him. Thus Webbe became a musician. In 1766 he won one of the Catch Club's prizes, and subsequently twenty-six others. He was a Roman Catholic, and published motets and easy masses of no importance. In composing for unaccompanied male voices he was exactly at home; he wrote altogether about 300 glees, of which he published nine volumes. The most famous of Webbe's glees—'When winds breathe soft,' 'Discord, dire sister,' 'Thy voice, O Harmony,' 'Swiftly from the mountain's brow'—exhibit the 'mosaic' style at its very best. Of his many canons and catches, 'Would you know my Celia's charms?' has deservedly remained popular, and is one of the few old catches now bearable. Webbe was secretary to the Catch Club after 1784, and librarian to the Glee Club. For the latter Society he composed a glee (or rather a part-song), 'Glorious Apollo,' which ever after opened their programmes. It is his most popular work, though slight, and lends itself well to choral rendering. Dickens's *Old Curiosity Shop*, chap. xiii, gives evidence of its popularity. Webbe died May 25th, 1816. His eldest son, also named Samuel Webbe, was a good glee-composer and organist; he settled at Liverpool, where he died, November 25th, 1843.

STEPHEN PAXTON (d. 1787), JOHN DANBY (1757–98), MICHAEL ROCK (1753–1809), and his brother, WILLIAM ROCK, all won prizes and composed glees which became stock pieces; but they were far inferior in talent to JOHN WALL CALLCOTT, who was the son of a small builder, and was born at Kensington, November 20th, 1766, Callcott seems to have been a very Micawber—sanguine, unsteady, and vacillating, though no one could work harder when he had a distinct task before him. He won three of the Catch Club's prizes in 1785; in 1787 he sent in nearly one hundred pieces to the competitions, which caused a rule to be made restricting the number to twelve in all, three each of serious glees, cheerful glees, canons, and catches. In 1789 he carried off prizes in all four departments. Callcott graduated in 1800, published a 'Musical Grammar,' and made collections for a Dictionary of Music; but he suddenly lost his reason in 1807, and though he regained it in 1813, madness again seized him till his death, May 15th, 1821. Dr. Callcott's unquestionable industry and abilities might have produced greater results if he had been under some restraining influence which would have kept him settled in one direction; the prizes offered by the Catch Club alone were a steady incentive, and only by the work done for them is he remembered. But we still hear his glees, 'Queen of the valley' and 'Father of heroes'; and his catch on the rival histories of music is not forgotten.

Though born rather earlier than Callcott, JOHN STAFFORD SMITH and R. J. S. STEVENS lived and worked much longer. J. S. Smith was the son of the organist at Gloucester, where he was born in 1750; he was a pupil of Boyce and Nares, and a choir-boy of the Chapel Royal, where he subsequently was organist and Master of the Children. He published anthems, and was a zealous and learned antiquary, obtaining a great number of ancient MSS., including the Mulliner Book. The sad fate of this library is mentioned elsewhere. Stafford Smith, besides his most important historical publications (which have been so frequently alluded to in earlier chapters), issued sacred music, and some glees of the highest and most ambitious kind. He lived till September 20th, 1836. Smith's spirited tune, 'To Anacreon in Heaven,' was a favourite in America, and will be preserved by its union with Scott Key's national hymn, 'The Star-spangled Banner,' which was written to it, September 14th, 1814.

RICHARD JOHN SAMUEL STEVENS was born in London in 1757, and was a choir-boy of St. Paul's. In 1786 he became organist of the Temple Church, and in 1796 of Charterhouse also; he was made Gresham Professor in 1801. Stevens's glees are always to good poetry; his treatment of Shakespearian words was particularly happy, and in 'Ye spotted snakes' he succeeded in adapting the sonata-form to the glee. The fragmentary style was less cultivated by him. He died September 23rd, 1837.

It is now necessary to mention others who were distinguished in various branches. Dr. SAMUEL ARNOLD, though a sound musician, had little invention. He was born in London, August 10th, 1740, and became a Chapel

Royal choir-boy, and afterwards a composer of music for dramas, and also of oratorio. After Nares's death he was organist of the Chapel Royal. His most important work was an edition of Cathedral Music published in 1790, and intended as a continuation of Boyce's edition. It contains nineteen Services (or parts of Services) by Patrick, Child, King (five), Croft, Aldrich (two), Goldwin, Greene, Bryne, Travers (two), Boyce, Nares, Hall, and Hine; and eighteen full anthems, by Tallis (two), Child (two), Aldrich (three), Kent, King (three), Goldwin, Weldon, Boyce (two), Nares (three); and twenty-one verse-and-solo anthems by Purcell, Croft (two), Weldon, Greene (eight), Tudway, Boyce (four), Aldrich, Travers (two), and King; with chants, etc.

It will be seen that the composers are mostly of a later period than Boyce had used; but the publication of Nathaniel Patrick's fine Service was a distinct gain to Elizabethan music. Arnold also edited the works of Handel in score; he issued forty volumes, which contained all the choral and instrumental works then known, but only four of the operas. He joined Linley in the oratorios after Stanley's death, was the third and last conductor of the Academy of Ancient Music, 1789–92; helped to found the Glee Club, and died October 22nd, 1802.

A further addition to the English ecclesiastical music in score was issued in 1800 by John Page, a tenor singer, who had been a lay clerk at Windsor, and was afterwards a vicar-choral of St. Paul's Cathedral. His work entitled *Harmonia Sacra* consists entirely of anthems, containing altogether seventy-four. Of these, thirty-nine are solo-anthems, by Croft (six), Weldon, Boyce (two), Purcell (three), Kent (two), Greene (five), Clarke (two), Dupuis, Arnold, Battishill, the brothers Wesley, King, Goldwin, Holmes, Linley, Henley, and Hine, with arrangements from Handel and Marcello; twenty-four are anthems with verses, by Blow, Clarke, Battishill (three), Aldrich, Stroud, Dupuis, Goldwin, Mason, Reynolds, King (two), Attwood, Nares, Blake, Baildon, Travers, Wood, Busby, Banks, and Handel; and eleven full anthems, by Tye ('From the depth I called'), Farrant ('Lord, for Thy tender mercies' sake '), Marenzio, Rogers, Tucker, Boyce (Burial Service), Richardson, King, Greene, Battishill, and Marsh. These composers are mainly Page's contemporaries, and the work is thus a happy continuation of Boyce and Arnold. The two Elizabethan anthems are of the highest importance; and it is strange that they had not been included by Boyce or Arnold. Concerning the authorship of 'Lord, for Thy tender mercies' sake ' I have already repeatedly spoken. It will be seen, however, that neither Boyce, nor Arnold, nor Page had included anything by Tye's contemporaries, Caustun and Whyte, although the latter had been recently prominently put forward by Burney.

So far no Englishman had written a history of music; and the subject had received scarcely any attention except in Germany, where, as previously mentioned (see p. 62), Venzky had proposed to celebrate the tercentenary of Dunstable's invention of composition. Padre Martini, in Italy, now began to treat the subject scientifically, and at the same time two different Englishmen formed the same plan. Little could then be found in books; the materials had all to be collected. Neither of the Englishmen was quite fitted for the task. Sir JOHN HAWKINS, whose work appeared in 1776, was an amateur, and destitute of literary skill also; while his compeer, Dr. CHARLES BURNEY, though a good practical musician, had not eclectic taste, and both writers were very much under the sway of eighteenth-century prejudices, and thought the Middle Ages barbarous. Burney had also a singular dislike to madrigals and to all English secular music before Purcell, while his reverence for Italian performers and contempt for French were unbounded. In spite of these and other defects, and the labour required to collect, sift, and digest the enormous mass of facts, both works are most valuable. Closer research has corrected many of their statements and guesses. A carefully edited reprint, especially of Burney, embodying later discoveries, would be useful.

Hawkins had acquired many mediæval works that had belonged to Pepusch; he subsequently presented them to the British Museum. His antiquarian researches, the most valuable part of his work, were but little added to by Burney, whose first volume also appeared in 1776. Three other volumes, in which Hawkins's complete work was freely used, followed in 1782–9. Burney's was the more successful, but has never been reprinted. Burney gave considerable attention to his contemporaries; Hawkins mentioned no musicians then living. Hawkins bequeathed to the British Museum a copy with additions and corrections, which have been inserted in reprints; Burney, unfortunately, troubled himself no further after his last volume appeared in 1789, though he lived till 1814. A supplement with additions and corrections was especially called for in his case.

Many musicians warmly resented Burney's sneers at our old secular music. William Hawes and Dr. Busby, and afterwards William Chappell and Ouseley, all gave expression to this feeling, sometimes with unreasoning exaggeration. Burney's 'History' should be judged only in connection with his 'Travels' and 'Account of the Handel Commemoration.' These supply omissions in the treatment of Handel's works, even of Bach's.

The omissions of Burney and Hawkins were partly rectified by JOHN STAFFORD SMITH, the glee composer, who in 1779 had printed a collection of Ancient Songs, mainly from the Fayrfax MS.; in 1812 appeared his most important collection, *Musica Antiqua*, containing 190 pieces, principally English. There is, unfortunately, practically no description of the works or letterpress, and the examples are without proper arrangement; yet this is the finest collection of ancient music that has been printed. The whole of the virginal pieces from Appendix to Royal MSS. 58 are included, also some of the songs. Smith had a magnificent library, including the Mulliner MS. (which he lent to Hawkins) and others, which have been described in previous chapters; it was, unfortunately, sold in 1844 by an auctioneer ignorant of its value, and the musical and antiquarian public had not been informed, with the result that many priceless relics may have been lost altogether. Some of the MSS. were acquired by the British Museum about 1880. The Old Hall MS. (see p. 67) came to light in 1900.

The works of the quarrelsome antiquary Ritson were of use to the musical art in several respects, and deserve remembrance as such. He discovered Wynkyn de Worde's Songbook (1530), and several valuable MSS.

Many important and useful institutions were established towards the end of the eighteenth century. The Academy of Ancient Music closed its honourable career in 1792. Its place was supplied by a different institution, The Concert of Ancient Music, commonly called the ANCIENT CONCERTS, an aristocratic society which lasted from 1776 to 1848. It was directed by noble amateurs, each of whom managed a concert in turn. They helped to keep alive the taste for Handel's and Purcell's music, and for madrigals. The rule was that no music composed during the previous twenty years should be performed. The published programmes and lists of performers are interesting as showing how the taste for choral singing gradually caused the voices to equal the band in numbers, and afterwards even to surpass it. The programmes were put together with singular lack of taste; sacred and secular pieces were intermingled quite casually, often with ludicrous results.

The Professional Concerts began in 1783, and the works of Haydn were enthusiastically received there. An excellent German violinist, Salomon, had disagreed with the directors, and started concerts on his own account. In 1786 he performed symphonies by Haydn and Mozart, whom he endeavoured to bring to England. Mozart was ready enough to come, but his cautious father dissuaded him. Haydn could not come until Prince Nicholas Esterhazy died; he crossed to Dover on New Year's Day, 1791, and produced six Grand Symphonies at Salomon's concerts; the players numbered between thirty-five and forty. Their success was so great that Haydn remained for another year; and again visited England in 1794, finally leaving in August 1795. His two visits were the principal musical events of the last decade of the eighteenth century. But he himself learnt much while he was in England; he appeared not only at

2E

Salomon's concerts, but also at several other societies. He became acquainted with much more choral music than was to be heard anywhere in Germany at the time; and the many performances * of old and modern unaccompanied music must have been a large increase of his experience. All the works by which Haydn is now remembered date from his stay in England, or subsequently. He was deeply affected with the singing of the Charity Children at St. Paul's; and, above all, he heard the last Handel Commemoration at Westminster Abbey.

Handel was born February 23rd, 1684–85; the old style of reckoning time confused the date, which was described as 1684, and it is so engraved on his monument. As the centenary of his birth approached, three of the leading amateurs—Lord Fitzwilliam, Sir Watkin W. Wynne, and Joah Bates—conceived the idea of celebrating the occasion by performances of his works on an unprecedented scale. Three were originally intended, but five were given; four in Westminster Abbey and one at the Pantheon, May 26th to June 5th, 1784. An organ and orchestra were erected at the west end of the nave; the conductor sat at a keyboard in the middle, with the stringed basses round him; the voices were placed in front of the band. The relative strength of the performers was so unlike modern practice, and is so instructive, that it is here appended:

Voices (including principals).			*Instruments.*	
Sopranos (boys and six ladies)	59	Violins		95
Male Altos	48	Violas		26
Tenors	83	Violoncellos		21
Basses	84	Double Basses		15
Total	274	Flutes		6
		Oboes		26
		Bassoons		26
		Double Bassoon		1
		Trumpets		12
		Horns		12
		Trombones		6
		Drums		4
		Conductor at the organ		1
		Total		251

* See especially Pohl's 'Haydn and Mozart in London.'

A detailed account of this Commemoration was published by Burney, who feared posterity would find the story incredible! It was repeated in several subsequent years; in 1789 the performers numbered 829. At the last repetition, in 1791, there were 1,068 performers; Haydn was present. The celebrity of this Festival inspired J. Adam Hiller to a grand performance of *Messiah* at Berlin, when all the vocalists procurable numbered 118; the instrumentalists 186.

£6,000 of the profits in 1784 was given to the Royal Society of Musicians, which the next year gave a performance of the *Messiah* for its benefit, and the performance has ever since been annually repeated. This admirable charity has benefited very largely from this source.

In 1785 a number of residents in the City, who were in the habit of meeting weekly at each others' houses to practise hymns and anthems, organised themselves into the Cecilian Society, which for many years remained the only amateur association of the kind. It soon grew able to perform Handel's oratorios; the concert-room was originally in Friday Street, Cheapside, finally at Albion Hall, London Wall. It lived on till 1861.

Ashley (a bassoonist), in Lent, 1795, started at Covent Garden a rival speculation to Arnold's oratorio performances at Drury Lane. For a time Handel's works formed the main attraction; but it was known that Haydn was composing an oratorio on a libretto which had been intended for Handel. It was performed at Vienna in 1798 and 1799, but did not appear in print till 1800. Salomon was still giving his concerts, and hoped to produce the new work; but Ashley bribed a King's Messenger to bring a copy, and only a week after he arrived, Ashley gave the first English performance of the *Creation*, March 28th, 1800, repeated twice during the next week. Salomon followed on April 21st, Wesley playing between the parts. In the autumn the oratorio was also given at Worcester by the Three Choirs. It thus entered on a long lease of popularity, which culminated some forty years later. *The Seasons* never equalled it in popular estimation.

The Lenten 'Oratorios' gradually changed into concerts with miscellaneous programmes. Ashley died in 1805; his son continued the Covent Garden performances.

Poor as the productions of the later eighteenth century were, the standard of performance was high; and English musicians seem to have been thoroughly satisfied with their deeds. In Jackson's *Present State of Music in London* (1791) occurs the interesting passage:

'Instrumental music has been of late carried to so great perfection in London, by the consummate skill of the performers, that any attempt to beat the time would be justly considered as entirely needless.'

At the Handel Commemoration, Hayes came forward to beat time; but F. Cramer, the leader, refused to begin until Hayes retired. Burney exulted over the perfect time kept 'without the measure being beaten in the usual clumsy manner.'

A certain vein of complacency runs throughout the musical literature of the period. Burney, in his last volume (1789), spoke of the enormous improvement in taste, during the previous twenty years, 'as different as civilised people from savages.' Yet Burney recorded his delight at the attentive silence of the audience during the Handel Festival; while elsewhere 'the best operas and concerts are accompanied with a buzz and murmur of conversation equal to that of a tumultuous crowd or the din of high 'Change.' J. Stafford Smith, in the preface to his selection of songs from the Fayrfax MS., said that in England music was then (1779) 'thought to be in greater perfection than among even the Italians themselves.' Where now are all the huge piles of English music produced and published then? No one sings the oratorios; no one acts the operas; no one plays the harpsichord music or the concertos. A few of the glees are sung; and there are some unforgotten songs still to be mentioned.

WILLIAM SHIELD was born at Swallwell, Durham, about 1748, learnt music from his father and Avison, and in 1772 gravitated to London, where he remained. He became first viola at the opera and the principal concerts, and composed the music for a great many dramas at

Covent Garden. In 1791 he learnt much from Haydn, and also made an excursion to France and Italy. He retired in 1807, but lived on till January 25th, 1829, and was buried in the cloisters of Westminster Abbey.

Shield had a splendid talent for natural and vigorous English melody, and has written most beautiful songs. He published a little instrumental music and some glees (including 'O happy fair,' which was very popular), with two theoretical treatises; but it is by some of his ballads that he is remembered. 'The saucy Arethusa,' his special contribution to the patriotic ditties, was originally a folk-dance, 'The Princess Royal.' 'Tom Moody,' 'The Wolf,' and, above all, 'The Thorn,' are his most famous melodies; and it will be long before they are forgotten.

CHARLES DIBDIN was born at Southampton on or before March 4th, 1745. He was educated at Winchester College, being intended for the Church; but he joined the Cathedral choir and had some lessons from Kent and his future successor Fussell. By 1761 Dibdin was in London, and appeared at Covent Garden as a singing-actor; in 1763 he wrote and composed a pastoral, *The Shepherd's Artifice*, himself taking the principal part. This was the first of a very long series of dramatic works, in which Dibdin proved himself a very Jack-of-all-Trades, ready to act as librettist, or composer, or actor, or singer, or accompanist, or general manager. He published an account of his tour through England; and started for a tour in India, but desisted on the vessel being driven into Torbay by a gale. Next he started Table Entertainments, into which he introduced musical features, and it was for these Table Entertainments that he wrote and composed the famous nautical songs for which he was pensioned by Government. He also became musical publisher; lost his pension for a time; was relieved by public subscription; and ended his eventful and disreputable career July 25th, 1814.

Dibdin, to some extent, represented the English side of the popular folk-song movement which, at the same time, was producing Burns's songs and Moore's 'Irish Melodies'; but he both wrote and composed his own ballads, while they wrote words to existing tunes. The nautical ballads have dropped one by one into oblivion; 'Tom Tough,' 'The Sailor's Journal,' 'Poor Jack,' and others so popular in their day and long afterwards, have gradually faded from remembrance, and one alone remains, 'Tom Bowling,' more sentimental than the others, but not falling into the theatrical affected pathos natural to the Irish and French. Two of Dibdin's 'operas,' as they were called (that is, plays introducing ballads), are preserved—*The Waterman* and *The Quaker*—though neither is given in entirety or frequently.

An Italian contrabassist named Storacé, who settled in England, had two children born in London who were prominent musicians for some years. They went together to Italy, and then to Vienna, where the sister, Anna Storacé (1766–1817) was the original Susanna in Mozart's *Figaro*, and her brother, STEPHEN STORACÉ (1763–96) produced two operas. They returned to England in 1787, and soon abandoned Italian Opera. Stephen Storacé was evidently a highly gifted musician, and his operetta, *No Song no Supper*, is still occasionally heard. Owing to his continental training and his friendship with Mozart his instrumentation is much in advance of the English Opera of the time; and he introduced here the finale-in-several-movements. His melodies are thoroughly English, and his early death was a great loss. Anna Storacé became a leading singer, and died rich.

JAMES HOOK, born June 3rd, 1746, at Norwich (and father of Theodore Hook), composed some thousands of songs, catches, and other vocal pieces, besides concertos and sonatas, music for many dramas, and even an oratorio in 1776. 'The Lass of Richmond Hill ' and ' Within a mile ' are still sung. He died in 1829 at Boulogne. JOHN DAVY, of Exeter (1765–1824), a pupil of Jackson's, composed some ballads, including 'Just like love is yonder rose' and 'The Bay of Biscay.' WILLIAM REEVE (1757–1815), an organist and an actor, shared with Davy and others in setting the music for many dramas.

We have now reached the end of the eighteenth-century composers, and can see how evanescent their larger works were. Not one of the English composers, not even Arne, is a *personality* to us such as is Handel, or Bach, or Gluck, or Haydn, or Mozart. The great merit of the English music was melody, which seems to have been a common gift; but the only strong feeling was patriotic enthusiasm, and the compositions that survive are almost all short ballads expressing this sentiment, or connected with it by their nautical subjects. It has been common enough to speak of the Court and the nobility as patronising Italian Opera only and neglecting native art; but this was not so. If any native composer had appeared with genius he would have received patronage enough, too much patronage probably. George III and all his sons were musical—directed the Ancient Concerts, supported the Catch Club; it was the timid mediocrity of the composers that prevented great works appearing. Among the leading amateurs was the dissipated Earl of Sandwich. Viscount Fitzwilliam, who died in 1816, studied music thoroughly, and formed an immense collection of Italian and English music, which formed part of his munificent bequest to Cambridge University. The great Virginal Book found its resting-place here, and there are interesting MSS. of Purcell, Blow, Croft, and especially of Handel. How the aristocracy in those patriotic times would have rejoiced at the appearance of an English Mozart! But he did not appear.

As regards keyboard music, the standard of execution was apparently not high, and Handel's passing the thumb under the other fingers was talked of as a curiosity long after his time. The change in the method of marking fingering took place probably in this period. The ancient English plan was (see p. 172) to indicate the right thumb by 1, and the left by 5, so that the figures in one hand were reversed in the other. At what time this method was replaced by the violin-fingering long used here (× 1 2 3 4) I have not ascertained. Another matter, the change in the mode of marking accidentals, assumed in England its very worst form. Purcell, Bach, and Handel marked accidentals every time they occurred; but in the weak period which followed, the innovation of marking them only once in a bar was adopted, and in England this was exaggerated into making one accidental serve for all notes of the same name, even those in a different octave. The pianoforte was announced as a 'new instrument' in a Covent Garden playbill dated May 16th, 1767; but it very quickly came into general use. Specimens of the best (least feeble) keyboard music were republished by Josiah Pittman, and in 1919 by Alec Rowley. John James's prelude and fugue in A minor, Stanley's in C minor, and Battishill's Suites, are not quite negligible. A. Moffat has edited some tuneful violin pieces, by Joseph Gibbs and others. Fashionable teachers published sonatas, by subscription; a set by Maria Hester Reynolds (1785) deserves mention as the first serious attempt by a woman, and they are not below the average.

Almost the entire chapter has been occupied with the doings of London musicians. Yet country towns were still of importance, and the county families made society there in the winter; but we cannot conceive that an English genius in any department should live a long life without ever going twenty miles from his native provincial town, as was the case with Kant at Kœnigsberg. The Scottish and Irish capitals (especially Dublin, during the time of 'Grattan's Parliament') maintained their ancient character, but their annals present nothing of general musical interest except the visit of Handel to Dublin in 1742. The Scottish and Irish folk-music, however, calls for more description. In Smollett's *Humphrey Clinker* there are references to the concerts, the Psalmody teacher, and daily carillon at Edinburgh; and to Highland pipers. (Letters dated August 8th and September 3rd.)

The eighteenth century up to the last decade was probably the most peaceful time ever known in Ireland. Good musicians—the Rosingrave family, the violinist Dubourg, and others settled there; Handel, Geminiani, Arne visited the country. The introduction of foreign art brought a decay in the old folk-music, which Irish antiquaries attempted to maintain. Burke Thumoth in

1720 published the first collection of Irish tunes. Congresses of harpers were held in Limerick, at Granard, and finally, in 1792, at Belfast; Edward Bunting, of Armagh (1773–1843) was present on the last occasions, and began to make collections of the ancient music, which he published in 1796 and subsequently.

A frequent phase of the mock classicism, windy sentiment, and shallow ethics so characteristic of the prosaic eighteenth century, was an exaltation of country retirement above the artificial town life, which produced so many singular effects in French life and literature. There was much in England, and one of the forms it assumed was a tendency to express poems on such sentiments in the Scottish dialect, by which a 'rustic' flavour was imparted. Even existing poems were altered to suit this fancy; as, for instance, Percy's 'O Nancy, wilt thou go with me?' which the glee composers changed into 'O Nanny, wilt thou gang wi' me?' The feeling is a natural and advisable one, quite apart from the more musical nature of the Scottish dialect. Poetry is so much a matter of style, words become so laden with associations, that the fitting epithets must be chosen; thus Coleridge called his masterpiece 'The Ancient Mariner' instead of 'The Elderly Seaman.' A poem proclaiming rustic inartificial sentiments naturally calls for a provincial dialect; and the Scottish is peculiarly favourable to such, quite apart from its glorification in the poems of Burns. We hear of 'northern tunes' in the seventeenth century; and Scottish songs became popular in England during the eighteenth. Very many were composed by James Hook and others in obedience to this demand. In 1787 Johnson, an Edinburgh publisher, issued a 'Musical Museum' of Scottish airs with poems; Burns entered warmly into the scheme, and sent a long succession of beautiful poems to any tunes he could find. Many of them were doubtless 'sham antiques' by the London composers of the day, while 'Robin Adair' is Irish; but Burns has conquered all alike for Scotland, with many others not written-for by him; and though 'Auld Lang Syne,' 'Ye banks and braes,' and 'Comin' thro' the rye' may possibly enough have been English tunes originally, they are, at any rate, Scottish tunes now.

The most famous of the country Scottish fiddlers was NIEL GOW (1727–1807), who published several collections of tunes, many of them—including 'Caller Herrin''— being his own composition. The bagpipe was still restricted to the Highland Kelts, but before the end of the century the world began to imagine that all Scots were Highlanders.

The Welsh music had been also cared for. Parry and Williams had published a collection of 'Ancient British Music' in 1742; Edward Jones another, with historical accounts, in 1794.

The English folk songs were more neglected; though a great number of melodies were produced. Only in distant corners was the ancient folk-music preserved. Bewick's *Autobiography* gives charming references to the continuance of the ancient pipes and warlike songs in Northumberland. The leading composers, particularly Dibdin, contributed most of the new additions to English folk-melody; and it is significant that no one thinks of writing nautical songs in the Scottish dialect, still less in the Irish. A Scot wrote 'Ye mariners of England!' another Scot wrote 'A wet sheet and a flowing sea,' where the good ship 'leaves Old England on the lee.'

A vulgar Scottish ballad, 'The Blue Bells of Scotland,' was rewritten by the Irish actress, Dorothy Jordan (1762–1816), and fitted to a new tune of her own com- posing. Lady Anne Lindsay's poem, 'Auld Robin Gray,' was set by a Somersetshire clergyman, William Leeves (1748–1828). Both these songs have become national possessions.

Among the real English folk-tunes of the eighteenth century must be mentioned 'The Vicar of Bray,' 'O dear, what can the matter be?' 'The tight little island,' 'The Mermaid.' Not one of the English poets has sought in- spiration in our folk-tunes, as Burns did in the Scottish and Moore in the Irish.

Lastly, the popular religious music requires some consideration. A great change began early in the century when Watts christianised the Psalms, and also published original hymns. His new psalms were received with enthusiasm, and both his psalms and hymns were immediately adopted by most Dissenters; there were, however, exceptions, and in the Established Church Tate-and-Brady's Psalter was adhered to even into the nine-teenth century. The singing of hymns is now so much a part of ordinary worship that it is difficult to conceive that their introduction was a startling novelty in Watts's days, and that the Evangelical leader Romaine in 1775 lamented the practice of hymn-singing, and vigorously denounced Watts's paraphrases. In Scotland the old metricised psalms remained in exclusive favour, and hymns were quite unknown. The Church of England psalmody, though lining-out fell into disuse, appears to have become very dull and uninteresting, and to have been left to the clerk and the charity children. Burney said the Lutheran chorales were played *almost* as slowly as English psalm-tunes; and any one who has heard the pace at which the Germans still drawl their hymns can imagine how tedious the English psalmody sounded. Scarcely a single writer of the eighteenth century has a good word to say for it; and several point to the enthusiasm of the Methodist psalmody as successful in attracting crowds to their meetings. Organs were general in town churches only, and were usually relegated, with the charity children, to the west gallery; they still had no pedals. The German Chapel in the Savoy had an organ with pedals in 1772; about twenty years later the organ at Westminster Abbey adopted this improvement, and other churches gradually followed. But as yet there were no independent pedal-pipes.

A new style of hymn-tune arose in the second half of the century. In 1708 appeared *Lyra Davidica*, a small anonymous work with a preface pleading for a more animated form of melody than the usual psalm-tune, and pointing to the universal practice of chorale-singing in Germany; the Easter Hymn is given as a specimen attempt. The only known copy of *Lyra Davidica* is in the British Museum; it was unheeded, and the old simple

psalm-tunes continued in use a generation longer. Then
Wesley's meetings at the Foundry Chapel began a
religious movement which among other changes brought
in a new kind of music, vehement, florid, tuneful, often
vulgar; the multitude sang the new tunes with enthusiasm
such as the plain syllabic tunes never aroused. There
were also 'set pieces,' popular hymns composed throughout to a connected tune; they were of little musical value,
but they were known and relished. Then came 'repeating'
tunes, with points of imitation; these, if carelessly used,
may produce ludicrous effects, and several instances are
proverbial. But *Miles's Lane*, composed by William
Shrubsole (1760–1806), first published 1779, exhibits the
advantages of repetition, and will not be superseded.
Tunes in tranquil triple time were another addition.
Isaac Smith's *Abridge* (1770), Dr. Miller's *Rockingham*
(1790), and afterwards Wesley's *Bethlehem*, display the
beauties of this style, and are permanently established.
They suggest the sober family devotions of Cowper's
'Winter Evening,' sincere and earnestly pious, however
restrained, formal, even genteel. Whitefield's Taber-
nacle, where the sexes sat apart, created yet another
form of hymn and tune, the question-and-answer, best
remembered by the refrain, 'What, never part again?
No, never part again!' All these novelties, beginning in
Methodist chapels, in due time reached the Established
Church also; Burney in 1789 declared the only new
tunes admitted in churches were the Easter Hymn,
'Hanover,' and Howard's 'St. Bride's; the change then
came quickly.

Besides Croft's tunes, 'St. Anne's and 'St. Matthew,'
and those just instanced, John Wainwright's 'Christians,
awake!' for Christmas Day, and William Knapp's
'Wareham' are still alive. One special favourite, 'Lo,
He comes,' has been decried as much as it is loved; it is
sung all over England on Advent Sunday. Its origin is
still unsettled; it has been claimed as a hymn-tune
composed by John Olivers, one of Wesley's evangelists;
also as an arranged ballad; even as a dance, 'Miss Catley's
hornpipe.' Musicians have frequently denounced this

tune as essentially secular, even vulgar; but all attempts to replace it have entirely failed, and it represents a part of the historical life of the Church, while it is undeniably melodious.

Another feature of the eighteenth century ecclesiastical music was the invention of Double Chants, which is ascribed to the Rev. Luke Flintoft, who was at Lincoln 1704–14, and afterwards in the Chapel Royal till his death in 1727. The chants, both single and double, suffered like the hymn-tunes from the florid style; there is an interesting reference to this in Cowper's essay, 'Mr. Village to Mr. Town.'

WILLIAM MASON (1724–97), canon of York, active in musical as well as literary and political life, and composer of the favourite florid anthem, 'Lord of all power and might,' published *Essays* which throw light on the condition of sacred music in the Established Church:

> 'Psalmody is become not only despicable to persons of a refined taste, but is now hardly tolerable to our Village Practitioners. . . . For these, since the rage for Oratorios has spread from the Capital to every Market Town in the Kingdom, can by no means be satisfied unless they introduce chants, Services, and Anthems, into their parish churches.'

And to the worthy canon's horror, orchestral instruments were added. Thus arose the 'village orchestra,' which lasted well into Victorian times.

Summing up the story of English music in the eighteenth century, it will be seen to be a fair type of the age —solid, prosaic, respectable, dull. On one side alone did the eighteenth century show enthusiasm—in patriotism; and on this one side fine, noble, immortal music was achieved.

CHAPTER IX
THE NINETEENTH CENTURY

Infant Prodigies.—Samuel Wesley.—Field and his Nocturnes.—Song-Composers.—The Philharmonic Society.—Choral Societies.—Hullah's Classes.—Tonic Sol-fa.—The Handel Festivals.—Choral Services become general.—English Opera.—Sterndale Bennett and Macfarren.—A dull period.—Organist-Composers.—Performers.—Concert Institutions.—Sullivan.—Fresh activity.—Defects to be amended.

THE story of our nineteenth-century music was not very different from that of the eighteenth century, and largely consists of biographical details. In both periods there were occasional intervals of self-satisfaction, which soon afterwards appeared singularly unjustifiable; in both periods there were very remarkable performances; in both periods there were composers with admirable faculty in producing tunes that have become part of the national life, who yet could produce nothing larger than tunes. But at last came a real awakening, though it is still too near to judge its importance fairly.

As the nineteenth century opened there were several young men who had already attained considerable reputation as composers, and three had evinced such singular precocity that expectations were formed of them such as Mozart had aroused and had so gloriously fulfilled. None of these three, however, produced very special results, in one case certainly owing to misfortune.

The oldest and perhaps the most gifted was CHARLES WESLEY, son of the younger of those wonderful brothers whose purifying enthusiasm and energy revolutionised English religious life during the eighteenth century. When the father was engaged on his mission in Bristol his eldest son was born there, December 11th, 1757. At two years and three quarters the child could play 'a tune on the harpsichord readily and in just time,' and put a correct bass. Yet he was not educated as a musician, and though he eventually became one, he attained no excellence either as a performer or composer. He lived till May 23rd, 1834.

His brother SAMUEL WESLEY far surpassed him; Samuel was born (also at Bristol) on February 24th, 1766, and was less precocious than Charles had been, but could play a tune at three years old, having also the advantage in infancy of hearing his brother's performances. He thus grew up in a more musical atmosphere, and had remarkable intellectual powers also. Samuel accordingly far outshone Charles in later years, but ill-fortune prevented his obtaining his due position. During his teens he became a fine violinist and a magnificent improviser on keyed instruments; he was further distinguished by literary taste and scholarship. All pointed to a career of highest success and noblest results; but all was frustrated in 1787 by an accident which severely injured his skull. He lived fifty years more, sometimes disabled for years together, then recovering and working for a time, but with the brain permanently affected. Samuel Wesley was the finest English organist of his time, and on becoming acquainted with Bach's 'Forty-Eight' studied and played them with the greatest enthusiasm; to him their diffusion in England was due, and in 1812 he and a German named Horn joined in publishing an English edition. He had already performed choral works of Bach's. Of his compositions, the Latin motets are the finest; he attempted all styles, but apparently none of his published efforts was equal to his wonderful improvisations. Yet he reached sublimity in his grandest effort, 'In exitu Israel de Ægypto.' Samuel Wesley died Oct. 11th, 1837.

WILLIAM CROTCH was son of a Norwich carpenter, who was an amateur musician; he was born July 5th, 1775. The child at the age of two could play on his father's organ, and when four years old he was brought to London. An account of his precocity was drawn up by Daines Barrington, and another by Dr. Burney. The boy was afterwards educated by the Cambridge Professor, Dr. Randall, and had an oratorio performed in 1789; removing to Oxford he became organist of Christ Church, graduated Mus.Doc., and in 1797 succeeded P. Hayes as

University Professor. Nothing remarkable came of
Crotch's early promise; his best work was an oratorio,
Palestine, performed in 1812, good, sound, unoriginal
music in Handel's style. One number, 'Lo, star-led
chiefs,' is still used as an anthem at Epiphany. As a
theorist, Dr. Crotch was doubtless the first Englishman
of his time; and he was a good all-round practical
musician, also a cultivated man, and had much skill in
drawing. He gave lectures on music, the illustrations
being published in three volumes; and his Oxford lectures
of 1831 also were printed. The latter contain some just
and profound thoughts on the limits of musical expression,
and are still worthy of consultation; but they also afford
sad evidence that at that time the English musicians
were as usual behind the age. The puzzlingly inappreciative remarks upon Mozart's instrumental music may be
cited as a striking instance, for Mozart had then been
dead forty years; Crotch thought Mozart's symphonies
and quartets laboured in comparison with Haydn's, and
especially as regards the themes! In deciding who was
the very greatest composer, Crotch declared the choice
must be between Handel, Purcell, Hasse, Leo, Graun,
and Jomelli. On the establishment of the Royal Academy
of Music in 1822–3, Dr. Crotch was appointed Principal;
but he was no disciplinarian, and was compelled to resign
in 1831. He died suddenly, December 29th, 1847.

These three infant prodigies certainly did not fulfil
expectations. In Charles Wesley's case the reason is not
apparent; Samuel Wesley's unlucky fall accounted for
his comparative failure; Crotch, however, had every
opportunity. The only reason of his poor achievements must have been abstinence from invention; he did
not try to advance the art, but used only the previously
perfected forms and resources, and his powers were
accordingly wasted.

Yet another young prodigy who did not fulfil expectations was George Frederick Sanders, a Londoner;
his mother's parents were Italian and German. Young
Sanders, born 1786, showed splendid talent for all
branches of music. He shone as violinist and composer,

taking his grandfather's name PINTO. Through him Samuel Wesley learned to appreciate Bach. Pinto had already issued several large works when his health failed through excesses, and he died in 1806.

Contemporary with them was THOMAS ATTWOOD, born in London, November 23rd, 1765, and educated in the Chapel Royal; afterwards he was sent by George IV (then Prince of Wales) to Naples, and finally spent some time under Mozart, returning to England with the Storacés in 1787. He became organist of St. Paul's in 1795, then composer to the Chapel Royal, in 1821 organist to George IV at the Brighton Pavilion, and in 1836 of the Chapel Royal. He died March 28th, 1838, and was buried in St. Paul's. From 1792–1801 Attwood contributed the music to many dramas; and his songs, glees, and sonatas were much performed. Afterwards he composed ecclesiastical music. For the coronation of George IV he composed an anthem with full and independent orchestral accompaniments, and another in 1830 for the coronation of William IV; he had begun a third for the coronation of Queen Victoria, when he died. These and his other anthems and services are of distinct value; they introduced a new and dramatic element into the Anglican cathedral style. This infusion of dramatic feeling and orchestral brilliancy was evidently suggested by the ecclesiastical music of Haydn and Mozart; and though the resulting style has little in common with Anglican traditions, Attwood certainly used it well.

One other musician must be mentioned here, though he composed comparatively little and lived through two-thirds of the century. This was GEORGE SMART (son of a London music-seller), born May 10th, 1776, and educated in the Chapel Royal. After 1791 he was an organist and violinist; being in Salomon's orchestra when Haydn was rehearsing, he once took the place of the absent drummer, and received a practical lesson from Haydn in drumming. After some years he began to conduct, which was still done at the pianoforte or organ; and having gone to Ireland, he was knighted by the Lord-Lieutenant in 1811. On his return to London he took a leading place in the direction of concerts and oratorios. He introduced several new works of Beethoven's, and also Mozart's additional accompaniments to Handel, for which he was warmly attacked in the *Gentleman's Magazine* and elsewhere. For many years longer Sir George Smart was a leading figure in musical performances and musical doings of all kinds. In his old age he was considered the special authority for the Handelian traditions, as he had turned over for Joah Bates at the Handel Commemoration in 1784, and used to relate how Bates put in occasional chords into the accompaniment of the songs, saying that he had seen Handel himself do it. Smart had also received Handelian traditions from his father. He composed some vocal music. After a very long and honourable life, Sir George Smart died February 23rd, 1867.

We now reach a generation of musicians specially prominent in our history, and the first is a composer and performer of European celebrity, JOHN FIELD. Here at last we meet with a musician who *invented*, who had a style of his own. He was born at Dublin, where his father was at the time a violinist at the theatre; the family returned to England, and the boy was placed in London under Clementi, who used him to show off the pianofortes in his factory. In 1802 Clementi took Field to the Continent, through Paris and Vienna to Russia. There Spohr saw the lad, whom he describes as shy and awkward, wearing clothes so old that his arms came out even to the elbows; and Field himself afterwards declared that he nearly perished from cold and hunger in the first winter. When Clementi left Russia in 1804 Field broke loose from his hard master, and became the fashionable teacher at St. Petersburg, whence he removed to Moscow. He revisited England in 1832 and subsequently went to Italy, where he fell into sickness and poverty and was rescued by a Russian family named Raemanow, who took him back to Moscow, where he died, December 11th, 1837. Dessauer has written a full biography.

As a player, Field is reckoned among the very greatest that ever lived. He is said to have kept the fingers almost perpendicular, and his touch was distinguished by an unprecedented richness and *sostenuto*, and by the subtlest details of expression. Clementi had trained him in the severest style, and he was celebrated in early life for his perfect rendering of fugues. The style which is peculiarly Field's own is quite different, depending upon the use of the pedal to sustain a bass-note while the left hand is engaged elsewhere. Field's compositions were few; and the largest—the seven concertos—are old-fashioned, and are only useful as technical practice. But he made an important addition to existing means of expression by his new form, the *Nocturne*. His new pianoforte style, the harmonies widely spread and diffused over the keyboard, yet sustained (as far as pianoforte vibrations permit) by means of the pedal, is more than any preceding style adapted to express the performer's inner sentiment; and there has since been a constant and increasing stream of compositions which are suitable for the performer's pleasure rather than to be played to an audience. This is one of the chief uses of the pianoforte, and we owe it entirely to Field. Chopin, a man of far greater intellectual power, applied deeper science and richer poetry to the *Nocturne*; but he did not altogether eclipse Field, the original inventor   To this day, Field's Nocturnes are very much played in Russia, Germany, and France; Liszt edited a selection with a charmingly-written preface.   Field's concertos are also much used abroad as teaching-pieces. At home his works are much less known.

In Schumann's criticisms there are fanciful references to the supposed English character of Field's works, the rhapsodical notice of Field's seventh Concerto being especially interesting; while other writers, finding that he was born at Dublin, have attempted to point out Irish characteristics. The gifts of tone and expression, for which the Kelts have always been justly celebrated, seem again to be displayed in Field's performances and compositions; but there is an entire lack of dramatic feeling, while his shy awkwardness in youth, and rough vulgarity in manhood, are not Irish faults. Little is known of his descent.

Another musician who, though he has not made a great mark on the world's musical history, has left a large number of most charming works, was HENRY ROWLEY BISHOP, born in London, November 18th, 1786, and taught by an Italian named Bianchi. Bishop's career in several respects resembled Arne's; and the two used their powers in a similar way and with similar results. Neither had the usual cathedral education, and neither was a great executant. Both passed their lives in 'English Opera'—that is, a play with occasional musical interpolations; both occasionally attempted higher flights with but little success, Bishop even less so than Arne

At the age of eighteen Bishop began his connection with the stage by writing some music for a little piece, *Angelina*, produced at Margate; and in 1806 he was entrusted with the music of a ballet for the King's Theatre, then for other pieces at the King's Theatre and at Drury Lane, all produced before he was twenty years old. In 1810–11 he was engaged to compose and direct the music at Covent Garden Theatre, and for fifteen years he produced a great number of pieces with music. Many of these were adaptations from foreign operas by Mozart, Rossini, Boieldieu, etc.; some were adaptations of Shakespeare's works, with new and old music; some were entirely new. Bishop showed himself to be, like Shakespeare, 'an absolute Johannes Fac-totum,' ready to bring out anything at all likely to be successful. These adaptations have been unsparingly denounced by some who forget that a temporary adaptation of a drama or opera in no way destroys the original, which remains untouched for those who wish it. It must be confessed that many of Bishop's arrangements exhibit alterations and cuttings which seem needless and capricious. He re-harmonised the part-writing of some old madrigals.

In 1825 Bishop was engaged at Drury Lane. The manager, fearing the attractions of the new opera which Weber was writing for Covent Garden, resolved also to produce a grand opera. Bishop accordingly set *Aladdin*, which had as bad a libretto as *Oberon*, and was not successful. His next engagement was at Vauxhall Gardens;

he finally returned to Covent Garden Theatre, and there he concluded his long connection with the stage. His last work was *The Fortunate Isles*, produced on the occasion of Queen Victoria's wedding in 1840.

In 1842 he was knighted, and as Sir Henry Bishop he is best known at the present day. He had been in 1841–3 Professor at Edinburgh; in 1848 he succeeded Crotch as Professor at Oxford. On April 20th, 1855, he died; he was buried at Finchley. The final account of Bishop's works was contributed by Mr. F. Corder to *The Musical Quarterly*, January, 1918.

Among the works of Sir Henry Bishop were a few large works—one oratorio, one cantata, and one grand opera; none was important. Instrumental music he avoided, except as regards overtures to dramas; and these, though musical and spirited (sometimes approximating to Cherubini's), are not of lasting value. Everything of Bishop's is forgotten except some of the pieces written for dramas; and a few detached glees and songs. The glees are of the best, but require no special mention. The dramatic music calls for some description.

It was in the pieces written for 'plays with music' that Bishop created a novelty, and consequently did his best work. He added a chorus to the principal 'singing characters,' and wrote pieces resembling glees, but with more continuity and development of form than glees usually showed. These pieces are indeed frequently called glees; from these they differ essentially in having orchestral accompaniment, as well as in using a chorus either entirely or partly. They can be detached from the context without any loss,* and consequently have been much used as concert and domestic music.

Most of Bishop's songs are forgotten, though the neglected include a great many worth an occasional hearing; while some are as familiar as Arne's Shakespearian songs. Above all, the household melody, 'Home, sweet home,' which occurs in *Clari, the Maid of Milan* (produced 1823), was at once seized upon as the typical

---

* Except that in some cases the words then become incomprehensible a defect which never troubles the British public.

representative of English sentiment, exactly displaying the individualism characteristic of the Anglo-Saxon all over the world. It was published as a 'Sicilian Air,' but is almost certainly Bishop's own, though melodies resembling it exist in several countries.

One may regret that, after all, Bishop's long and active life and splendid natural talents left so little permanent result; he was apparently content in his smaller sphere, and had little ambition to rise to higher and wider productive activity. As the composer of 'Home, sweet home,' 'Tell me, my heart,' and 'Bid me discourse'; of the glees, 'Sleep, gentle lady,' and 'Where art thou?' and of the accompanied pieces, 'The chough and crow' and 'Stay, prithee, stay,' he is assured of remembrance. He had the knack of writing vocally, which was doubtless part of the acquisition from Bianchi's teaching.

WILLIAM HORSLEY's long life began also in London, November 15th, 1774, and lasted till June 12th, 1858. He held various organ appointments, and composed much vocal and instrumental music, from songs and glees to sonatas and symphonies. He is one of the greatest of glee composers, and 'By Celia's arbour' is one of the most melodious of glees; he used good poetry, and set it tastefully. He edited Byrd's 'Cantiones Sacræ' (1589) for the Musical Antiquarian Society, writing a most unappreciative preface. The occasional harsh collisions in Byrd shocked an ear accustomed to the polished smoothness of glees. Horsley married Dr. Callcott's daughter; their son, Charles Edward Horsley (1822-76) showed great promise for music, and was very carefully educated; but on attaining manhood he wrote only imitations of Mendelssohn, and invented nothing.

Other musicians, partly of the eighteenth, partly of the nineteenth centuries, were DR. CLARKE-WHITFELD (1770–1836), an organist, and Cambridge Professor; C. S. EVANS (1786–1849); BENJAMIN JACOB (1778–1829), organist of Surrey Chapel; Thomas Simpson Cooke, better known as TOM COOKE, a versatile Irishman (1782–1848), who could sing well, act well, and play every instrument well. These and many others, including the wealthy amateur, SIR JOHN LEMAN ROGERS (1784–1847), were all glee-composers. The more serious attempts of CHARLES STOKES (1784–1839), organist and composer of real merit, though unassuming and little known; of the blind GEORGE DRUMMOND, organist of Paddington, who published fugues, chorale-preludes, and editions of Bach; and of GEORGE HEPWORTH, who settled in Germany as organist of Schwerin Cathedral, and produced pianoforte Etudes—all deserve mention.

During the long wars which began in 1793 and ended with Waterloo in 1815, communication with the Continent was difficult; and after 1806 it was actually contraband. Yet there seems to have been no tardiness in making acquaintance with foreign masterpieces, though it does not appear how they arrived. The competition for Haydn's *Creation* has been mentioned. Many of the principal performers lived here; Clementi had come in 1766; his pupil, J. B. Cramer, was also brought in boyhood; and these long-lived musicians were the leading pianists for many years. Dussek had been in London, 1788–1800; Steibelt, Ries, Berger, and Woelfl were much here. Viotti escaped to England during the Reign of Terror, and remained as the leading violinist. Clementi, Cramer, and Dussek all speculated in music-publishing.

Kollmann, organist of the Lutheran Chapel, announced an edition of Bach's 'Forty-Eight' in 1799; but renounced the design, as Nægeli's Zurich edition appeared. Birchall, a leading publisher, issued the 'Forty-Eight' in 1809, and also the six organ sonatas; Wesley and Jacob helped to make them known. Beethoven's music reached England very quickly. W. Gardiner, of Leicester, an enthusiastic amateur, tells us in *Music and Friends* that a Bonn refugee brought specimens as early as 1795! In 1807 a symphony was played at Brighton, and Clementi bought the English copyright of several of Beethoven's works, ordering three new sonatas. Thomson, of Edinburgh, sent Beethoven many Scotch airs for arrangement in 1806 and later. In 1812 J. Stafford Smith wrote that—

'The superior knowledge of instrumental effect possessed by Haydn, Mozart, Beethoven, and others, by no means compensates for the

want of that manly, open, clear, vocal melody which characterised
the work of Mr. Handel.'

An old story, ever new, is this. That Haydn, Mozart,
and Beethoven were deficient in melody sounds amusing
enough now, but not one whit more amusing than the
similar accusations against Wagner will sound in a few
years' time.* Is is, of course, not easy to state precisely
whether J. S. Smith's opinions represented average taste
of the time; probably they did. In the same year (1812)
Don Giovanni was first performed in London, and had
an immense success; its production had been most
strenuously opposed by an Italian cabal, which all but
prevailed. *The Gentleman's Magazine* introduced regular
reviews of new music in 1813, in one of which it is
mentioned that many musicians considered Beethoven
the greatest composer living. In the same year we find
that three performances of his Symphonies took place in
London; these were given, with his Septet and other
pieces, by a new institution—the PHILHARMONIC SOCIETY.

The honourable career of the Philharmonic Society
began with a circular issued by J. B. Cramer, P. A. Corri,
and W. Dance, from the house of the latter, on January
17th, 1813; on the 24th a meeting was held at Messrs.
Chappell's, and the Society was constituted. The first
concert took place at the Argyll Rooms, Regent Street,
on March 8th, Salomon leading, and Clementi at the
pianoforte. The concerts were then longer than at present,
containing two symphonies and also chamber music.
Cherubini was invited, and came in 1815. Beethoven
was also invited in 1817, and again in 1824; he always
had the warmest appreciation for the English, from
Shakespeare downwards, and looked forward with immense pleasure to the journey, but various circumstances
prevented it each time. A new symphony was commissioned, in response to which Beethoven composed
the Choral Symphony, which was performed by the
Philharmonic Society on March 21st, 1825; it had been
already performed in Vienna, and was there published
with a dedication to the King of Prussia. At this period

* This prediction, written in 1894, has long since been fulfilled.

it was common to use different dedications for different editions of the same work; English editions of the Choral Symphony should always bear Beethoven's dedication to the London Philharmonic Society. Two years afterwards a fresh symphony was ordered, and £100 was sent for it, which reached Beethoven just before his death. Mayseder relates that some Viennese amateurs were once arguing with him that the English were unmusical, upon which he appealed to Beethoven, who immediately declared that the English were the only people who appreciated himself, adding, with his usual boisterous laughter, that a nation which appreciated his works must evidently know nothing about music. Whether Beethoven would have been cured of his Anglomania if he had visited England is another matter; and the same may be said of Schumann, equally fond of everything English. In 1820 Spohr was invited, and conducted his D minor Symphony; he insisted on beating the time, and, after some opposition, prevailed. In spite of the manifest advantage, the change did not become settled for some years. Weber conducted in 1826. In 1829 Mendelssohn made his first appearance; the band were offended at his requiring certain passages of his C minor Symphony to be tried through more than once. This dislike soon changed to the very opposite feeling. In 1844 (when the Society was in a failing condition, the novelty having worn off) Mendelssohn was engaged as conductor and saved the institution; but the band disgraced itself bv treating Schubert's Symphony in C with such contempt that Mendelssohn refused to go on with it. A regular unchanged conductor was appointed in 1846; and in 1868 the concerts were removed to St. James's Hall, and to the still larger Queen's Hall in 1894.

Very noteworthy, though of little influence on the general musical life, were the private concerts given by the nobility. These were the Eldorado of Italian singers; opera-managers looked to these engagements for their real profit. A glance through the volumes of the *Quarterly Musical Magazine and Review* (issued by Kollman, 1818–28) will show how numerous these concerts were, and how they were almost monopolised by Italians; they remained in full prosperity till the second half of the century. As aristocracy became less exclusive, private concerts began to decay; and larger concert-halls enabled singers to raise their terms enormously, until a private concert by operatic artists is now unknown. Through the cessation of these concerts, the existence of Italian Opera was seriously jeopardised.

No performances on an exceptional scale having taken place since the Handel Commemorations in 1784–91, the proposal to revive them in 1834 was well received. The performances were on this occasion not restricted to Handel. The proportion of vocal and orchestral forces was entirely altered, and showed the tendency towards that drowning the orchestra altogether which characterises modern English performances. In 1784 there had been 274 vocalists to 251 instrumentalists; in 1834 the band was reduced to 222, and the chorus raised to 356. In 1834 there was also a conductor beating time. These two changes were warmly resented by an old amateur, the Earl of Mount-Edgcumbe, whose *Musical Reminiscences* contain an account of both celebrations; his book is one of the best ever written upon musical matters by an English amateur.

The Ancient Concerts lingered on until 1848; in 1826 an extensive selection from Mozart's works was performed, and later programmes were more varied. A similar institution would be useful everywhere; especially if the rule should be that all music performed must be at least 200 years old. The rule enforced at the Ancient Concerts (that the music should be twenty years old) would be sufficient if the programmes were drawn up with wide knowledge and eclectic taste. During the first third of the nineteenth century the principal London performances of oratorio were those of the Cecilian Society.

Prince Albert, from his childhood a skilled practical musician and composer, had excellent influence on public taste in the middle portion of the century; and he caused Bach's *Matthew-Passion*, Schubert's Symphony in C, and Wagner's *Lohengrin* to be performed at Court. His own

Service in C major is still sung. By his command the Philharmonic Society in 1855 introduced Schumann's *Paradise and the Peri* to London audiences. It was just at this time that English musical taste had again lagged far behind the age, and it remained so till after 1870. From about 1820–50 the general average of taste seems to have been fairly advanced, in spite of some passages I have quoted, and others such as the obituary notices of Beethoven. Weber's *Freischutz* had immense popularity in 1824; and Weber was invited to England, and died here. Rossini had previously visited this country; though disappointed at the Opera, he took away £7,000 earned at public and private concerts. Spohr, already famous, about 1830–40 became over-valued by many musicians; but his renown was speedily eclipsed by the extraordinary popularity of Mendelssohn. Especially in sacred music Mendelssohn was the only model followed for many years. Schumann was long in getting a hearing; and only towards the end of his life did he have the pleasure of knowing that some of his works had been performed in the country he so much loved. They were not appreciated, and were strongly opposed by some. At this time, and for long after, public opinion followed the lead of J. W. Davison, critic of the *Times*, and H. F. Chorley, critic of the *Athenæum*, both of whom had never advanced beyond the tastes of their youth, and appreciated neither the fine ancient English music nor the new works produced after Mendelssohn. An article in *All the Year Round* for October, 1864, sneering at Schumann and attacking Wagner as a conscious charlatan, shows the average taste of the time. After 1870, and especially from the performance of Wagner's *Lohengrin* in 1875,* there was a rapid change for the better; and now all new works of importance are performed in London as soon as they are published.

Returning now to biographical details, some musicians celebrated early in the century must be noticed. Among the original members of the Philharmonic Society was

* At the first London performance of *Lohengrin* the chorus during the arrival of the Swan was encored and repeated!

CHARLES NEATE (1784–1877), and of the original associates
CIPRIANI POTTER (1792–1871). These young pianists
both visited Vienna in the quiet times after Waterloo,
to make acquaintance with Beethoven. They were both
London-born. Neate, though a fine player, published
little; but Cipriani Potter was at once recognised by
Beethoven as a talented composer. The two pianists
introduced the concertos of Beethoven and Weber to
the Philharmonic audiences. Few musicians have so
thoroughly kept pace with the advancements of the art
as Potter did. Towards the end of his life Sullivan
brought under his notice the works of Schumann, for
which the octogenarian conceived such enthusiasm that
he grew indifferent even to his own works; and only
two months before his death he took part in a private
performance of Brahms's *Requiem*. Potter composed
instrumental music of all kinds, including several symphonies; his pianoforte studies are still used.

GEORGE ASPULL was another highly-gifted performer
who aroused great expectations which were frustrated by
his early death. He was born at Manchester in June,
1813, and played in public at the age of eight, then before
King George IV; and in 1824 toured through the
country. At Brighton at the end of the year he played
Weber's 'Concertstück' for the first time in England.
He visited Paris in April, 1825, and was looked upon
as a coming genius, but caught a cold at Clementi's
funeral, and died of consumption, August 19th, 1832.
Aspull's early death was a great loss to English music,
as his posthumous compositions prove.

Burney had proposed that the Foundling Hospital
should be organised as a music-school on the plan of the
Naples and Venice Conservatorios. His suggestion had
not been adopted, and the need of a central academy
was now felt. This led to the establishment of the Royal
Academy of Music, the real founder of which was Lord
Burghersh, afterwards Earl of Westmorland. A number
of the aristocracy met him at the 'Thatched House
Tavern' on July 5th, 1822; subscriptions were obtained,
and on March 24th, 1823, the first lessons were given.

The Royal Academy was unprosperous financially for many years, until at last the professors got a share in the management; and since 1867 the institution has been uniformly prosperous. At first the foundation scholars and some others lived in the building, a custom given up in 1853. The Principals have been: Dr. Crotch, who resigned in 1831; Cipriani Potter, who also resigned in 1859; Charles Lucas, 1859–66; Sir Sterndale Bennett, 1866–75; Sir G. A. Macfarren, 1875–87; and Sir A. C. Mackenzie. All except the first two had been pupils.

Outside London there is practically nothing to notice except the local 'Music Meetings,' which were formerly more numerous than at present; many of the performers had to be imported from London. Beethoven's first symphony was introduced at Birmingham in 1817; at that Festival the band numbered 83, the chorus 130. In 1820 the second and fifth symphonies were played. The conductor always sat at the organ, until 1832. The first Edinburgh Festival was held in 1815; there were 128 performers, mostly imported, as the chorus 'could not be found in Scotland.' A valuable account of these celebrations was published by Crosse (of York) in 1825. In those days, and for long after, there was never any question of commissioning novelties for a Festival.

Before 1840 the practical knowledge of music was confined to comparatively few. Nevertheless these, being real amateurs, in many respects attained a higher average of skill than was the case a generation later. Glee-singing was especially well cultivated, and probably more appreciated than any other form of music. Byronically gloomy young men not infrequently affected flute-playing; and entire operas and oratorios were printed in arrangements for flute solo! In 1837, when Macfarren was in the Isle of Man, he found the available musical resources there consisted of a few violins, one violoncello, one clarinet, and sixteen flutes.

Ladies generally learnt the harp; the pianoforte also was much studied, though it was still costly. It was considered not a man's instrument, and the Oxford undergraduates once hissed a male pianist off the

platform.   The English makers had made the important
improvement of deeper notes than the FF to which the
older instruments were restricted; and they had tried
higher notes also, a pianoforte made by Broadwood in
1804 reaching f^{iv}, probably only as an experiment.   The
usual compass was that of the pianoforte sent to
Beethoven in 1817, and consisted of six octaves, CC to
c^{iv}.   The first cottage pianoforte was made by Wornum
in 1811.   At this time there was still a school of English
violin-makers, which died out almost entirely in the
middle of the century.

The great cultivation of choral singing now claims
attention.   In 1832 the Sacred Harmonic Society was
founded, and gave miscellaneous selections in a Dissenting chapel; the first of these performances took place
Jan. 15th, 1833, and was mainly from Handel's works.
Next year the Society removed to Exeter Hall; and in
1837 increased its band and chorus to 500, using the
large hall.   There were then so few amateur performers
that singers were brought from Yorkshire and Lancashire
to strengthen the chorus, and were found employment in
London.   The Society was fortunate in appearing just as
Mendelssohn was coming into notice; and his works,
with Handel's, were always the mainstay of the programmes.   Complete oratorios, a quasi-novelty, replaced
the selections commonly heard since the Lenten performances had been vulgarised by Ashley; and the two
patent theatres disused these speculations.   All Handel's
principal works were revived by the Sacred Harmonic
Society, which speedily found imitators all over England.
Most of the local 'Music Meetings' were disused,
doubtless partly owing to the decrease in importance of
county towns consequent on the opening of railways,
which gave the finishing touch to English centralisation
and the finishing blow to English music.

The uprising of amateur choral societies is not unconnected with the religious features of English social
life.   The middle classes had always remained essentially
Puritan in spirit; thousands of respectable families
shunned the theatre as they would have shunned a plague-

stricken house, and their dislike was then justified by certain practices since abolished.* These precisians now found that there was an entertainment which appealed at once to their religious and musical tastes, in which they could take part either as performers or auditors without experiencing scruples of conscience. Sala's *Twice Round the Clock* has an instructive chapter on the subject. Nor should it be forgotten that since Dissent and the Low Church party began to lose their narrowness and weaken, many choral societies have languished, and secular music has been prominent in their programmes. The Sacred Harmonic Society, comically enough, admitted *Acis and Galatea* into its selections. In time the original religious feeling was lost, there as elsewhere, and it was simply a concert-giving Society like others, except in its restricted programmes. The zealots at the head of the Young Men's Christian Association accordingly ousted it from Exeter Hall in 1880, and it was dissolved in 1882, various attempts to revive it all failing. During its fifty years' life it had accumulated a magnificent library, containing many rarities and MSS.; exhaustive catalogues were prepared by W. H. Husk and published.

Just when the Sacred Harmonic Society was arousing imitators, the movement received an enormous impetus from the establishment of classes for choral singing. JOHN HULLAH, an earnest and cultivated young man, already associated with Dickens as an opera-composer, started classes in 1840, and in 1841 began to teach schoolmasters at Exeter Hall. This was the first attempt in England to diffuse a general knowledge of music, and as such deserves great credit. Hullah was also a skilful voice-trainer and conductor, and speedily brought his upper classes into a condition which justified his giving concerts with them. So little printed music was then available that Hullah issued large collections for his choir, and his wide knowledge and judicious taste were fully displayed in the singularly admirable selections he made

---

* See the conclusion of Scott's *Essay on the Drama*. Prince Pückler-Muskau's indignant description of London theatres is still more significant.

His work excited great interest, and, above all, it showed
that every one might learn to sing. For two centuries
(compare pp. 206, 228) singing had denoted *artistic vocalisation*; the idea of every one learning to sing *somehow* was
new, and was attacked by John Barnett and others.

But Hullah made one fatal mistake, which spoiled
his promising attempt to found a popular system; he introduced the Italian nomenclature. When the Guidonian
hexachords were disused in the seventeenth century the
ancient letter-notation was in Italy disused with them,
and C, D, E, etc., were called *ut*, *re*, *mi*, etc., and are so
in the south of Europe to this day, except that *ut* was
exchanged for the more sonorous *do*. Hullah introduced
this nomenclature, which was known in England as the
Fixed *Do*; in this he departed from the practical English
plan (based on the Guidonian) of regarding the tonic
as *do*. The Hullah system accordingly, in spite of its
splendid success at first, was found unsuitable to the
generality of learners, and fell into disuse; as the Wilhem
method, from which it was borrowed, had already done
in France. Italians, who use only the fixed *do*, sing
almost entirely by ear, and have an extraordinary and
general gift for remembering and repeating a long passage
heard only once;* the English very seldom have this
power, and require a perfect mastery of the notation.
The unpractical Hullah system accordingly is unsuitable
to ordinary persons with no good sensation of absolute
pitch.

Its place was taken by a further development of the
old English plan, adapted to the modern octave scale;
which was called the *Norwich Sol-fa Ladder*, since its
invention was due to a Norwich lady, Miss Sarah Anna
Glover (1785–1867). In 1841 a conference of Dissenting
ministers at Hull discussed the question of congregational
singing, and selected JOHN CURWEN (born at Heckmond-
wike, Yorkshire, on November 14th, 1816) to investigate
the subject and discover the easiest method of teaching
singing. John Curwen finally adopted Miss Glover's
plan, farther developing it as the *Tonic Sol-fa Method*

* See Spohr's *Autobiography*.

into a system suitable for the most elaborate as well as the most simple vocal music. Tonic Sol-fa had much to contend with: it had a new notation; it was not brought forward by a recognised artist, but by a Dissenting minister; and Hullah's system was at the height of its celebrity. In addition, nothing but elementary music was attempted at first, and a prejudice was excited in many minds, which is even yet by no means dispelled. But it was so much easier than the fixed-*do* system that in a few years it began to attract attention. The first decided approbation from a high authority came from the acoustician Helmholtz in 1863, who spoke with the greatest surprise of the results attained; and Sir John Herschel was emphatic on the same side. Oratorios and other large works were issued in the Tonic Sol-fa notation. In 1872 Hullah was appointed Inspector of Elementary Schools; and finding his own method being superseded, he prepared a report in which he acrimoniously attacked Tonic Sol-fa. The higher ranks of the profession were in general unaware of the extent to which the new system had spread; and Hullah's repeated attacks drew general attention to it. John Curwen died May 26th, 1880, having lived to see the movement he had set on foot successful beyond all his intentions; from England it spread to America and the Antipodes, and missionaries have taught it to savage tribes in all quarters of the world. Upon Hullah's resignation, Dr. Stainer succeeded him as Inspector of Schools; Stainer's advocacy of Tonic Sol-fa gave the final blow to the Hullah system.

John Curwen at first did not know the latent possibilities of Tonic Sol-fa; nor, had he known them, would he have regarded them as anything but secondary to the religious question which originally brought him his commission to examine the matter. Still, one cannot help regretting that many workers in the movement persistently aimed low; and that nothing was for a long while done to notify prominently the fact that Tonic Sol-fa is equally adapted to the most elementary and the most advanced forms of vocal music. Consequently many leading musicians came to look upon the method only as a pandering to laziness and uncultivated taste; for instance, W. S. Rockstro could write, and Sir George Grove could insert in his *Dictionary*, that Tonic Sol-fa 'could never be used for any other purpose than that of very commonplace part-singing,' and this preposterous assertion was made at a time when the largest choral works were being continually performed all over the country by singers who knew no other notation.   Something similar has happened in France, where the Galin-Chevé method (which is in fundamentals like Tonic Sol-fa but differs in detail) was first suggested by Rousseau, and subsequently developed by provincial amateurs; nor are instances wanting in the history of other sciences than music where, outside the 'Inner Circle' of bigwigs, some quick and easy method of work has been discovered and brought into general use long before it received academical sanction.

In 1891 a Jubilee was held at the Crystal Palace; and though the opportunity of displaying the higher developments of the system was missed, the results displayed were wonderful.   The public performance of a single chant just composed by Stainer, then taken down by ear and immediately sung in harmony by a vast choir, though a familiar test at Tonic Sol-fa competitions, much astonished London critics.   That it should have astonished them, and that the ridiculous blunder previously quoted should have found its way into Grove's Dictionary (though corrected in the second edition), are yet again results of the centralisation to which I have so frequently referred, and which makes those who should be authorities upon musical matters concentrate their attention upon performances in the West-end of London, ignoring the musical life of the nation.

Tonic Sol-fa has now spread to other countries. Over five millions of children are learning it here, and its victory is won, though here and there a musician of repute still remains ignorant of it. In the near future the Tonic Sol-fa method will be the recognised portal admitting to the realm of music. It is (by my own and others' experience) particularly useful in developing musical memory. A recent development is the lack of preparation, on the part of student-teachers, to teach music in the elementary schools, and the shortage of trained teachers is another difficulty. Sight-singing is consequently neglected, and singing by rote, which Tonic Sol-fa supplanted, is being reverted to; only for a time, let us hope.

Having been told of some distinct advantage to the world, a philosopher will proceed to inquire what disadvantages have thereby been caused. As I have now detailed how class-singing was invented and brought into use, beginning in 1840, and ever increasing down to the present day—to the enormous increase of musical knowledge and appreciation—this is the place to state the drawbacks which have arisen in consequence. One result of a general cultivation of singing has been to make our choirs so large that the public is accustomed not to hear the orchestra, which is drowned by the excessive predominance of the voices. Another result has been to diminish the average skill. The half-trained vocalists who had learned by some system to sing easy music, naturally wished to join choral societies and partake in oratorio performances. This has led to a heavy, tedious, unexpressive rendering of the choral numbers. Handel's music, frequently very florid and requiring trained singers, has suffered considerably from this cause; and a *brilliant* rendering of the brilliant numbers is now never heard. The music of Bach, being more difficult, suffers yet more. Modern composers dare not employ the rapid divisions which are such a prominent feature of Handel's choral writing, and even of the popular songs of Bishop and his contemporaries; but Handel also sometimes used simple and broad effects, and then the weight of the numbers in a huge modern choir is effective.

All these peculiarities may be heard in full vigour at our biggest musical celebrations—the Triennial Handel Festivals held at the Crystal Palace, Sydenham. These, after a preliminary trial in 1857, began in 1859, the centenary of Handel's death. The chorus numbered 2,700; the band 460; the arrangements were made by the

Sacred Harmonic Society, under Costa. The Festival was repeated in 1862, and triennially till 1883; the next was in 1885 to celebrate the bicentenary of Handel's birth, after which the triennial repetition was resumed. The programme until 1909 remained the same—a public rehearsal on Friday, *Messiah* on Monday, a miscellaneous selection (slightly varied at each Festival) on Wednesday, and *Israel in Egypt* on Friday. The attendance has generally amounted to over 80,000. In 1909 Mendelssohn was also represented. After 1912 the World-War prevented the Festivals; a fresh start was made in 1920. *Messiah* now concludes.

The original strength of the performers has been enlarged; the chorus now numbers about 3,000, and the band about 500. It is evident that this disproportion between the vocal and instrumental forces must lead to effects quite diverse from Handel's intentions; but this is in accordance with our usual methods. Lord Mount-Edgcumbe objected to the proportion employed in 1834, when the choir was half as large again as the band; what would he have said to these performances? But the huge aggregate of performers, producing such enormous sound-waves in such a vast space, has shown certain acoustical results which have not attracted the attention they deserve. As I have alluded to the matter in the *Overture* for June, 1891, and the *Quarterly Musical Review* for May, 1894 (with additions from further experience in the *Musical Herald*, July, 1920), I need say nothing further on this subject.

To sum up, these monster performances are musical curiosities rather than ideal reproductions of immortal masterpieces; but there are passages, even entire numbers, where the multitudinousness of the orchestra, with its sixty double-basses, and of the thousands of voices, will impress the listener as nothing else will. Such a passage is the unison in the 'Hallelujah Chorus'; another is the 'Holy, holy, holy,' of the *Dettingen Te Deum*; and for entire pieces, 'Envy! eldest-born of hell,' and especially the antiphonal, 'Thy right hand, O Lord, is become glorious,' may be cited as by their breadth of conception splendidly exhibiting the actual strength of the army of performers.

On the earlier occasions the altos were men singing falsetto; they are now principally women. The sopranos were formerly nearly all boys; they are also now women. In 1784 (compare p. 386) there were twenty-six oboes and twenty-six bassoons; there are now less than half so many, the strings being five-sixths of the whole instrumentalists.

For comparison, and to show the change in taste, a list of the performers on three different great occasions is here subjoined:

	Westminster Abbey, 1784	Westminster Abbey, 1834	Crystal Palace, 1894
Sopranos	60	124	733
Altos	47	68	793
Tenors	83	64	683
Basses	84	100	788
Total Choir..	274	356	2,997
Total Band ..	251	222	519
	525	578	3,516

Throughout the nineteenth century the instrumental music was far inferior to the vocal. In 1824, when Weber's *Freischutz* was at the height of its popularity, it was performed at Brighton with the assistance of some members of George IV's private band, the manager advertising that this was the only theatre out of London where it was 'possible to play the celebrated overture.' The instrumentalists at the 'Music Meetings' came from London. There were, however, village bands coarsely accompanying in church; the Oxford Movement caused the disuse of these, and the general introduction of organs or harmoniums. As late as 1885 I visited an East Sussex church where no instrument was visible except a flute, and there was even in 1895 a Dorsetshire church where a clarinettist had played for more than fifty years. Dissenting congregations gradually overcame their prejudice against instrumental music in their services. In Presbyterian Scotland and Ireland the struggle has been very bitter; an attempt (speedily relinquished) to introduce an organ was made at Aberdeen about 1800; another followed in 1806 at Glasgow, and was repelled; and though an organ was actually used there on August 23rd, 1807, it was then withdrawn. The first permanent erection was perhaps at Dumfries about 1837. An attempt was made at the Greyfriars, Edinburgh, in 1864. Then progress, though slow, was steadily successful. There was no organ at Regent Square, London, until 1902. In the Free Church the organ was opposed with intense violence, and is far from universal even yet.

Pedals were long used only to pull down the lower octave of the manuals, the lowest note of which was GG or FF; Dr. Gauntlett succeeded in introducing independent pedal-pipes and a CCC compass after 1840. The meantone temperament remained in use till, in 1852, Mr. Herbert was appointed at Farm Street Chapel, and immediately had the organ tuned to equal temperament, which had been strongly advocated by Dr. Crotch. The lead was quickly followed everywhere. The pneumatic action was first tried in 1827 by Josiah Booth of Wakefield. The finest of the older organists was THOMAS ADAMS (1785–1858), who was also a remarkable improviser and good composer; his works have fallen into disuse from their unsuitableness to the CCC organ.

Another result of the Oxford Movement was the re-introduction of the Gregorian tones, and the gradual decay of the Double Chant. In ordinary parish churches the Psalms had been read; and the return to chanting them was much opposed as a Popish innovation, and even occasioned riots.* The increasing reverence for externals acted beneficially upon cathedral services, where more care and dignity have since been observed; the choirs have been restored to their due numbers, and the music has been less florid. A good view of the defective state of ecclesiastical music may be seen in the three volumes of the *Parish Choir*, published by the Society for Promoting

---

* Notably at St. George's-in-the-East, 1859–60. The rector had introduced harmonised responses and chanted canticles; a crowd of opponents assembled at every evening service, and drowned the music by speaking the sung portions as loudly as possible. Choral Services were nicknamed 'Sunday Opera.'

Church Music; in the first number (February, 1846) occurs the assertion:

'Not many weeks since, in a chapel in the most wealthy and fashionable part of all London, the clergyman was obliged to put a stop to the singing in the middle of the psalm, because it was so horribly bad.'

In the second volume a Cambridge correspondent wrote that only five colleges there had choral service; that Caius College had recently sold its organ, and several other colleges possessed lofts where organs had once been. The *Parish Choir* had good influence, and many anthems and Services by sixteenth and seventeenth-century composers appeared in its issues, including anthems from Day's publication (1565) by Heath, Hasilton, and Okeland, and various works by Tallis, Fox, Gibbs, Whitbroke, Shepherd, and many Stuart composers, especially Batten.

One feature of that renewed appreciation of the Middle Ages which produced the romanticism of early nineteenth-century literature, the revival of Gothic architecture, and in part the Oxford Movement, was a revival of interest in sixteenth-century music. This was less noticeable in England (where the madrigals had remained in use, and the sacred music had never been quite neglected) than on the Continent, where brilliant orchestrally-accompanied sacred music was used almost everywhere except in the Papal Chapel; but here also there were some results which must not be omitted. Several societies were formed; some are still existing, the principal being the Western Madrigal Society, founded in 1840. The Motet Society published three volumes of ancient English, Italian, and Flemish music arranged for the Anglican service, and well chosen, though not always well adapted. The Musical Antiquarian Society was founded in 1841, and published in score nineteen volumes of important works by Elizabethan composers and Purcell; it was limited to 950 members, and was complete in the second year, but had to dissolve in 1848. A similar attempt to publish Handel's complete works in score also soon failed.

Vincent Novello published all the then known sacred

music of Purcell in 1829–32, and was just in time to preserve some pieces which would have been for ever lost in the fire at York Minster in 1829. The Purcell Club was founded in 1836, and met once a year; in the morning performing sacred music at Westminster Abbey, in the evening giving a concert. A special bicentenary celebration was held in 1858; the Club dissolved in 1863. The Purcell Society, for the complete publication of his works, was founded in 1876; it has met with small support, but has continued its task.

One important publication, an outcome of the Oxford Movement, was issued by Dr. Jebb in 1847–57, and is entitled *The Choral Responses and Litanies of the Anglican Church*. It contains a very large number of pieces, responses, psalm-chants, and litanies, by sixteenth and seventeenth-century composers, from Cranmer's Litany (1544) and the preces of Tallis, down to the Restoration music. There is an extensive selection from the Peterhouse MSS. in the second volume, including the Latin litanies.

Oliphant, an enthusiastic lover of our old music, had conducted two performances of Tallis's forty-voiced motet by the Madrigal Society; he also published *La Musa Madrigalesca*, the first attempt towards drawing general attention to the wealth of fine poetry written and used by the Elizabethan composers. A catalogue of the musical MSS. in the British Museum (published in 1842) was prepared by Oliphant; it is unfortunately most unsystematic, some important Royal MSS. being quite cursorily mentioned, while others are elaborately detailed, and the absence of all allusion to J. Stafford Smith's publications is a serious defect. [It is now superseded.]

I must here allude to a strange ignorance of music and musicians which is perceptible in the writings of some leading authors about the middle of the century. A very striking instance occurs in Macaulay's *History of England*, published in 1848. The famous third chapter contains a most elaborate account of the state of England in 1658, describing the conditions of life at that date, with the learning, sciences, and arts then cultivated. The poetry, drama, painting, sculpture, and architecture of the period are all discussed with full details; music is not once mentioned, although the period in question was exactly the one in which England's greatest composer was in full maturity. One might easily imagine that Macaulay had never heard of the existence of such an art as music. Similar instances may be cited from the works of Carlyle; while Landor spoke with the greatest contempt of musicians. Fortunately some musical writers of eminence appeared about the same time.

The principal of these was WILLIAM CHAPPELL (1819–88). He occupied himself with old English poetry and music; and in 1855–9 issued his *Popular Music of the Olden Time*. A vast amount of original research is contained in this work, the standard authority on the subject; the airs were harmonised by G. A. Macfarren. The book deals, however, only with English songs, and a distinct animus against everything Scottish is perceptible; there are also absurdly exaggerated attacks upon Burney. A thoroughly revised edition, with some of the airs reharmonised, was published by H. E. Wooldridge in 1892. Two other writers—E. F. Rimbault and John Hullah— were both so inaccurate that they have done considerable harm; the former, indeed, deserves harsher epithets than *inaccurate*, yet he did much useful historical work, besides preserving the Mulliner MS. and many rarities. Hullah, already mentioned, wrote two histories which are amazingly inaccurate in details, especially in dates; they might, however, be easily corrected and made really valuable by a competent editor. Some of Hullah's opinions, *e.g.* on Bach and on Wagner, have proved wrong. John Bishop, of Cheltenham, was active in research.

None of the great poets at the beginning of the century had much appreciation of music, excepting Coleridge. Scott was even singularly unmusical; nor was there any warm love for the art shown by Keats, Byron, Wordsworth, or Shelley himself. Neither does the lyrical work of these poets seem to yearn for music, and it is far less easy to set than the songs of Goethe and Heine. Not a single English lyric of the Shelley period has passed into the nation's life as a song to be *sung*. In consequence, all these poets put together wielded no influence by their writings; while Tommy Moore, a good amateur musician, used the tremendous weapon they neglected, invented the downtrodden and weeping Erin, and set his poems to national Irish tunes. In publishing these (1808–18) he was helped in the harmonising by J. A. Stevenson, of Dublin (knighted in 1803), and afterwards by Sir H. Bishop. The old saying concerning the ballads and the laws of a nation was never better exemplified than in the case of Moore's *Irish Melodies*, which had and may continue to have enormous political consequences; while the political, social, and religious opinions of his immeasurably greater English contemporaries do not influence a single mind. The popular English song-writer was T. Haynes Bayly; and J. P. Knight (1812-87) set Bayly's 'She wore a wreath of roses,' which still lives, with ' Rocked in the cradle of the deep.'

JAMES SANDERSON (*c.* 1770-1840), and afterwards GEORGE H. B. RODWELL (1800–59), were very active in the old style of English theatrical music.

In the first half of the century Italian Opera still represented high-class music, in the public conception of the term; and the Opera-house was always the resort of the noble and the genteel. Lord Mount-Edgcumbe's account is very instructive. In 1831-2 Chélard (a Parisian, then conductor at Munich) brought a German Opera company, which introduced *Fidelio* and other works; this visit had the result of permanently replacing the conductor at the pianoforte by the conductor beating time. Lord Mount-Edgcumbe, who disliked Rossini's music, finding it 'noisy,' 'unvocal,' and 'overloaded with accompaniment,' speaks with great appreciation of the German performances. A few years subsequently the Italian Opera was more fashionable than ever; and the period about 1835-70 constitutes what is called the 'palmy days.' The repute opera then had may be seen in Carlyle's famous essay (1852), from which one might judge that Carlyle had never heard of oratorios or instrumental music, and supposed that all modern tone-art consists of Italian Opera followed by ballet-divertissement. At this time the singers had serious rivals in the dancers Taglioni, Cerito, and Ellsler, who made the ballet (after the opera) as distinct an attraction as the music.

There was an important attempt to raise English Opera to a higher level. The first success was made by JOHN BARNETT, born of foreign parentage at Bedford, July 15th, 1802; his *Mountain Sylph* (August, 1834) was a pretty and taking work, and a real opera, not a play with music. Barnett wrote other operas, but retired to Cheltenham about 1840, where he lived as a singing-master till 1890.

A far greater success was scored by an Irishman, MICHAEL WILLIAM BALFE, born at Dublin, May 15th, 1808; he was an infant prodigy, composing and scoring at seven, and at nine appearing in public as a violinist. Balfe was a true Irishman, brilliant and versatile; he was taken to Italy by Count Mazzara, studied singing, and appeared at the Paris Grand Opera in 1828, then at Palermo, Milan, and through Italy till 1835, when he returned to England.

Balfe's career as a composer of English Opera began with *The Siege of Rochelle*, produced at Drury Lane, October 29th, 1835; *The Maid of Artois, Catherine Grey*, and *Joan of Arc* followed. The success of these operas led to Balfe's composing an Italian opera (*Falstaff*) for Her Majesty's Theatre, where it was produced, July 19th, 1838; the only precedent for a native composer's work being performed by Italians had been Arne's *Olimpiade* in 1765. Several abortive attempts were made about this time to establish a National English Opera; the one showing most promise was made by Balfe in March, 1841, at the Lyceum. It began with *Keolanthe*, written for Mrs. Balfe, a Hungarian. Other native composers had been commissioned to produce new works. For a long time previously a strong controversy had been going on as to the chances of success of an English Opera House, but the worst forebodings were fulfilled, as Balfe quickly became bankrupt and left England. He composed for the Opéra Comique; but his greatest and most lasting success followed at Drury Lane, November 27th, 1843, when *The Bohemian Girl* entered on its hitherto unfading brilliance of success. It was immediately performed everywhere, and has been translated into almost every European language. The simplest of stories—a plot familiar to ancient Athens, told in the baldest commonplace—has here found an exactly adequate musical setting, in tunes which appeal on a first acquaintance to all hearers. With this opera Balfe visited Vienna, Berlin, and St. Petersburg; everywhere receiving all possible honours. He also produced several new operas in London and Paris, ceasing his wanderings in 1856; in 1864 he retired to a small estate in Hertfordshire, called Rowney Abbey, where he died, October 20th, 1870.

Balfe may be considered the typical Irish composer, fully at home in the theatre, and especially skilled in the effective setting of sentimental words. Higher and deeper art were alike beyond his powers; but he knew how to appeal to all by tasteful commonplace. And though nearly all his thirty operas are entirely forgotten, his memory is safely preserved by *The Bohemian Girl*, which still shows no signs of diminishing popularity.

All the operas ever written by English composers have together not achieved a tenth part of *The Bohemian Girl's* success, though there were several which at that time secured temporary favour. Among the principal composers were MACFARREN, who will be mentioned later; H. LAVENU (1818–59); and EDWARD JAMES LODER, born at Bath in 1813. Loder was a pupil of F. Ries; his best work was *The Night Dancers*, produced at the Princess's Theatre (where he was conductor) in 1846. Afterwards he conducted at Manchester, where his *Raymond and Agnes* was performed in 1855; this is almost the only case on record of an English opera having been produced outside London. That it should be so is a sufficient proof of the centralisation which is the unconquerable opponent of English music. Loder had to retire owing to cerebral disease; he died April 5th, 1865.

A success comparable even to Balfe's was attained by another Irish-born composer (of Scottish descent), WILLIAM VINCENT WALLACE, who was born at Waterford, in 1812 or 1814, the son of a bandmaster. During Wallace's childhood his gift for music became noticed, and he soon played in the Dublin Theatre. In time he matured into a fine violinist, and played a concerto of his own in 1834. He left Ireland in 1835, and entered upon the most singular life of adventure that ever befell a musician. Ten years afterwards he turned up at London, having in the meantime visited every part of the world and gone through perils and escapes of all kinds. He now entered upon his career as an opera-composer, and his first work, *Maritana* (produced at Drury Lane, November 15th, 1845), has been nearly as great a favourite as *The Bohemian Girl*. After more wandering, Wallace had another great success in 1860 with *Lurline*, although this opera has not secured permanent favour. Wallace composed much tasteful but rather superficial pianoforte music, which was popular all over Europe. He died in the Pyrenees, October 12th, 1865, and was buried (as was Balfe) at Kensal Green.

The Irish nature of Balfe and Wallace produced results differing so fundamentally and entirely from the works of English musicians of all periods, that they throw very great light on the diversity between the two nations. Balfe and Wallace were born dramatic composers, with plenty of natural gift but little learning, and exactly that kind of gift which is not benefited by learning, being described rather by the convenient term *inspiration*, though in their cases it was of a shallow kind. They did exactly what they were capable of doing, and with the most advantageous circumstances would hardly have done more than they did. That only one opera by each remains, the popularity of which is in each case enhanced by the effective libretto; that these two—*The Bohemian Girl* and *Maritana*—are each easy of performance, and contain detachable ballads; and that both composers wrote their works for London and Paris—are matters which will all repay a little meditation.

Barnett and Balfe deserve the credit of advancing English Opera to a far higher level than the old play with songs which was all Bishop had attempted. None

of the later school had musical talent at all approaching
Bishop's; but they used theirs in the best way, he in the
worst, and the results in each case have been good tunes
and nothing more. All the musical dramas of the first
third of the nineteenth century, and all the operas which
were produced for thirty years after Barnett had led the
way with *The Mountain Sylph*, are now summed up in
a number of short pieces which might have been written
as drawing-room pieces, excepting only *The Bohemian
Girl* and *Maritana*.

It should be mentioned that Balfe conducted several
series of National Concerts at Her Majesty's Theatre;
but the enterprise was not well supported. For nearly
twenty years Jullien gave Promenade Concerts with a
large orchestra all over the British Islands.

The Royal Academy of Music speedily produced a
number of most promising young composers. In 1834
the Society of British Musicians was formed, and till its
decease in 1865 brought forward many important works,
especially instrumental. A similar attempt had been
made in 1823. Among the composers the principal was
the renowned WILLIAM STERNDALE BENNETT.

Bennett was born at Sheffield on April 13th, 1816,
the son and grandson of musicians. The family came
from Ashford-in-the-Peak. The grandfather, a lay clerk
of King's College, Cambridge, took charge of the boy
on the death of the father in 1819; and afterwards he
was a choir-boy at the College till, in April, 1826, he
was sent to the Royal Academy as a violin-student. There
he remained ten years. Bennett, like Arne and Bishop,
did not have the Chapel Royal training which has produced so many of the best English musicians; but he
occasionally assisted in St. Paul's choir. At the Academy
he soon came to the front, both as a pianist and a composer; his teachers were Lucas and W. H. Holmes,
afterwards Crotch and Cipriani Potter. It was in 1833
that he first attracted general attention; then he played
a concerto of his own which was so well received that
Mendelssohn, who was present, invited him to Germany,
and the Academy authorities had the concerto printed.

Before Mendelssohn's invitation was accepted, Bennett had composed three symphonies, four concertos, and three overtures, besides smaller pieces, of which several had been published. In September, 1836, he finally left the Academy, and spent nine months at Leipzig. He was warmly welcomed by Schumann, who introduced him to a publisher; three of his works immediately appeared. For the new year Schumann wrote one of his best articles, introducing the new composer. Bennett played his third concerto at the Gewandhaus concerts on the 19th January, and subsequently conducted his *Naiads* and *Parisina* overtures. In June he returned to England, and was appointed professor at the Royal Academy. In 1838–9 he was again at Leipzig, and played his fourth concerto; and he paid a third visit in 1842.

Then he broke down, and turned drudge. He had already published his Op. 25, and though he lived another thirty years he never reached Op. 50. But already signs of weakness were apparent; Schumann said of his Caprice, Op. 22, 'We begin to fear that Bennett appears to be spinning himself up into a mannerism, from which he finally will not emerge. Of late he says always the same thing, only in varying form; and the more perfectly he has learnt to master the form, the more the real invention seems to diminish in him.' The result was even worse than Schumann's forebodings. Instead of composing in a fixed mannerism, Bennett composed almost nothing of any kind for years, and the actual few works published were far inferior to his early works. Continuing the story of his life, it should be mentioned that he was married in 1844, and was an unsuccessful candidate for the Edinburgh Professorship. In 1849 he lent valuable assistance to the advancement of art by the establishment of the Bach Society, which helped much to diffuse a knowledge of the great master's works, and might have done much more had Bennett been an energetic man. In 1854 and subsequently he conducted the *Matthew-Passion*; the *Christmas Oratorio* and part of the *High Mass* were performed before the Society dissolved in 1870.

A great honour was paid to Bennett in 1853 when he was asked to conduct the Gewandhaus Concerts for the following winter. This, to his infinite regret, he was obliged to decline, as Cipriani Potter (whom he would have asked to take his place in various engagements) was then on the Continent. In 1856 Bennett became conductor of the Philharmonic Society and Professor at Cambridge.

After a long interval Bennett once more roused himself to compose a large work, at the request of the Committee of the first Leeds Festival in 1858. *The May Queen*, to a ridiculous libretto by Chorley, was the result; it was performed with splendid success, and is a charming secular cantata, the most frequently performed of his larger works. The Cambridge students asked him for a new work, and an arrangement of *Ajax* was prepared for him, but the music was never finished. A new orchestral work—a fantasia-overture on *Paradise and the Peri*—was indeed completed in 1862; but in that year Bennett's wife died, and he was never quite himself again. A symphony in G minor bears evident signs of his increasing weakness. A short oratorio, *The Woman of Samaria*, produced at Birmingham in 1867, had some vigorous numbers from an early attempt, and is one of Bennett's more important achievements. In 1871 he was knighted; he was now devoting himself entirely to the Royal Academy of Music. He died, after only a week's illness, on February 1st, 1875, and was buried near Purcell in Westminster Abbey.

Sir Sterndale Bennett's influence on English music, though wide, was not lasting; his opinions were not those of the present day, and have long since been relinquished. As a composer he was beyond all question capable of greater things than he actually accomplished. What was wanted in his case was an over-ruling will forcing him to compose and to invent. The timidity which is one great curse of English music never worked direr mischief than in Bennett's case. Here we had a composer with splendid gifts, admirable training, a European reputation, and apparently every advantage; but he would not dare to invent anything. In his compositions he never attempted to advance the art, either in resources or forms. There were indeed some exceptions to this rule in his early works; he wrote characteristic pieces with titles, and a ' Barcarolle ' and concert-overture (a form which had then been only just invented by Mendelssohn), but these were youthful escapades, and for the rest of his life he paid devoutest obedience to Mrs. Grundy, composing only (when he composed at all) in the most respectable and prosaic style. It is inexpressibly sad that such a beautiful talent should have been so entirely wasted. At the age of twenty, Beethoven and Schumann had composed almost nothing; at the same age Bennett had composed the *Naiads* overture, the four published concertos, the ' Three Musical Sketches ' —in short, almost everything of his which still lives. Then he made no improvement, and practically abandoned composition when in the prime of life. So must it ever be with a musician who will not invent.

A number of young contemporaries and friends of Bennett emulated his early attempts at symphony and concerto. Among them were T. M. MUDIE (1809–76), one of the first scholars elected at the Royal Academy; HENRY WESTROP (1812–79); the younger Horsley; and, above all, Bennett's successor at the Royal Academy, G. A. Macfarren. J. W. Davison was also one of this band of young composers, who were all much under the spell of Mendelssohn. What they produced is forgotten already; but, as regards style, it was far in advance of older English instrumental works.

A special account must be given of GEORGE ALEXANDER MACFARREN, so complete a contrast to Sterndale Bennett. Macfarren possessed the talents, denied to Bennett, of strong will, fixed purpose, steady energy, and patient endurance. The two conjoined would have made a great composer; alone, either was insufficient. Bennett, sufficiently musical, had too weak a character; Macfarren, far stronger as a man, was insufficiently musical.

Macfarren was born in London, March 2nd, 1813, the son of a gifted versatile man who had turned dramatist and was an amateur musician, having vocal and instrumental

performances at home. These aroused a love of the
art in his son, a delicate and weak-eyed boy. Probably
the latter might have achieved more permanent work if
he had devoted himself to literature instead of music.
Having learnt under his father and C. Lucas, he entered
the Royal Academy in 1829, remaining till 1836. He
at once distinguished himself by industry, and quickly
composed symphonies and other works, the first work
ever performed by the Society of British Musicians being
a symphony of his. In conjunction with his father,
Macfarren also composed *The Devil's Opera* (performed
1838), *Don Quixote* (1846), and several others which
never came to a hearing. Macfarren and Davison shared
an enthusiasm for Shelley, and endeavoured to put some
of the poet's theories into practice. They gave chamber
concerts together in 1843–4, though neither was a virtuoso,
and both began to make essays in journalism, to which
Davison soon devoted his entire attention. Macfarren
also took an active interest in musical theory, and warmly
supported a system of harmony promulgated by a
physician named Alfred Day. For a time he in consequence left his post at the Royal Academy, but returned
in 1851. His eyesight continued to weaken as he continued
to compose works in all styles, from glees to operas; and
it failed altogether in 1860, when he produced his most
successful opera, *Robin Hood*.

At this time there had been a revival of the interest
in English Opera. From 1856 to 1862 two leading
vocalists—Louisa Pyne and William Harrison—had maintained a permanent company, and had produced several
new works, including Balfe's *Satanella* and Wallace's
Lurline; Macfarren's *Robin Hood*, though not written for
them, was also added to their repertory.

Macfarren had written many able criticisms and
analyses, and had produced treatises intended to apply
Day's system to the exigencies of students. He had not
had a church-choir training, nor was he an organist,
having indeed little executive skill; and his principal
work had been opera, until in 1872 he turned to oratorio.
His first and most successful oratorio was *St. John the*

Baptist, produced at Bristol in 1873; it contains a splendidly original and effective fugal treatment of Croft's psalm - tune 'Hanover.' Unbounded commendations were bestowed on this oratorio; and three others followed, but all proved much less interesting. Two secular cantatas, *May-day* and *Christmas*, had fair success.

It should not be forgotten that Macfarren, who was well learned in musical history, deserves the credit of being the first to deny the old slanders upon the Puritans. He could not go as far as I have done in their defence, as he was unacquainted with much of the evidence I have collected, and could only quote the publications and the operatic performances during the Commonwealth as evidence that the Puritans did not suppress the art. On later music his opinions were prejudiced; and his *Musical History* (from the *Encyclopædia Britannica*) is of little value. He succeeded Bennett as Cambridge Professor and Principal of the Royal Academy, was knighted in 1883, and died October 31st, 1887. Of his many works, a cantata for female voices (to Miss Rossetti's *Songs in a Cornfield*), with some fine settings of Shakespeare songs, may possibly prove the longest-lived.

With Bennett and Macfarren may be placed the names of two foreigners. These were Michael Costa (1809–84) of Naples, and Jules Benedict (1804–85) of Stuttgart. Both had the art of thriving in the world. Costa was conductor of the opera at twenty-two, when some of the band sent him a packet of toy razors; but he was a rigid disciplinarian, and stopped the childish jokes and carelessness which had become usual under the lax rule of his predecessors. From 1846 to 1854 he conducted the Philharmonic Society, after 1848 the Sacred Harmonic Society, the Handel Festivals, and some of the provincial Festivals. Benedict, who had been a pupil of Weber's, came to England in 1835, and was an opera-conductor and fashionable teacher for many years, besides making a great deal of money as accompanist at the private concerts of the aristocracy. Benedict and Costa, who were both knighted, were eminently adaptable men, and learnt to compose for the English taste of their time; their lives may be taken as instances of the successful career which lies open to a clever foreigner who, either by 'boo-ing' and complimenting everybody as Benedict did, or by imperturbable self-confidence like Costa, will (with good luck) at once take a leading position in London. Especially after 1850 there was an evident depression of English music and musicians; great exertions had been made in the previous decade, but the reaction was so strong that 1850–70 was one of the most uninteresting periods in our history.

A few other composers and performers contemporary with Bennett remain to be mentioned. HENRY SMART, an excellent organist, was nephew of Sir George Smart, and was born in London, October 26th, 1813. He was organist at Blackburn, 1831–6, afterwards in London till his death, July 6th, 1879. An extremely interesting account of the services at which he played was included in Curwen's *Studies in Worship Music*, vol. i.* Among H. Smart's compositions were operas and cantatas, but he is principally remembered by graceful part-songs and organ pieces. GEORGE COOPER (1820–76), though not distinguished as a composer, was superior to Smart as an organist. Both Smart and Cooper were distinguished by practical capabilities; the former for engineering, the latter for natural science.

A great renown for musical learning was attained by SIR F. A. G. OUSELEY (son of the eminent Orientalist), born in London, August 12th, 1825, and an infant prodigy, with an ear as wonderful as Mozart's. He entered the Church in 1849, but continued his study of music, graduated Mus.Doc. in 1854, and next year became Oxford Professor. Ouseley founded a college at Tenbury, where he accumulated a splendid library and maintained grand choral services. He was a fine organist and improviser, and a profound theorist; as a composer he tried most styles, with respectable results only. Ouseley died on April 6th, 1889.

THOMAS ATTWOOD WALMISLEY was the son of an able

* Now out of print.

composer of glees, Thomas Forbes Walmisley (1783–1866), and was born January 21st, 1814, in London. He became a fine performer at an early age, and was taught composition by his godfather, Attwood. He had also fine talents for literature and mathematics, and distinguished himself at Cambridge University, where he became Professor in 1836. Both as an organist and a composer Walmisley was well skilled, and his madrigal, 'Sweet flowers, ye were too fair,' is likely to live. He died January 17th, 1856; after his death, a volume of his Cathedral Music was published by his father.

John Goss was born at Fareham, where his father was organist, on December 27th, 1800. His uncle belonged to the Chapel Royal, where the boy also entered in 1811; completing his education under Attwood. Some new glees by John Goss were sung by the Concentores Sodales in 1827; one of them, 'There is beauty on the mountain,' subsequently became a great favourite. Goss was organist of St. Paul's Cathedral, 1838–72, when he retired and was knighted. The principal compositions of Sir John Goss are for the church, and include remarkably fine anthems composed for the Duke of Wellington's funeral, the bicentenary of the Sons of the Clergy, and the Thanksgiving for the Prince of Wales's recovery. He died May 10th, 1880.

Samuel Sebastian Wesley, the last of this gifted family, was the third son of Samuel Wesley, and was born in London, August 14th, 1810. He was for a time in the Chapel Royal; subsequently an organist. In 1832 he was appointed at Hereford, afterwards at Exeter, next at Leeds, in 1849 at Winchester, and finally at Gloucester, where he died, April 19th, 1876. He was buried at Exeter. Wesley's improvisations were wonderfully grand; and his compositions are of special importance for the Anglican service. He indicated full details of expression in his church music, a novelty. The new dramatic style, originating with Attwood, is commonly typified by 'Wesley in E'; and many of his anthems are masterly. He inherited, alas, the eccentricities which his father's accident had brought; among them was a preference for the meantone temperament and the G or F compass, besides personal oddities and dogmatisms.*

ROBERT LUCAS PEARSALL was descended from an ancient Gloucestershire family, and was born at Clifton, March 14th, 1795. He was scarcely more than an amateur, yet he composed with singular success in the unaccompanied style, for which he had great enthusiasm. Much of his life was spent in Germany, where he finally settled in 1837 at the castle of Wartensee, on the lake of Constance. Pearsall was an enthusiast in archæology, and (like many students of mediæval romanticism) turned Romanist; and called himself 'de Pearsall.' Both in tuneful part-songs and contrapuntal madrigals he has produced works which have met with immense and lasting success; his sacred music is mostly unpublished. Pearsall died at his castle, August 5th, 1856.

JOHN LIPTROT HATTON was born at Liverpool, October 12th, 1809, and was mainly self-taught. He had a good gift of tune, with little skill in deeper forms. Many of his songs and part-songs are familiar to all. Hatton came to London in 1832; in 1844 he succeeded in producing *Pascal Bruno* at the Vienna Opera. He composed much dramatic music, and another opera was performed at Covent Garden in 1864. An attempt in oratorio was less successful, as the necessary science was lacking. He died at Margate, September 20th, 1886. Hatton belonged rather to the school of Shield and Bishop than to that of Bennett; and he was happiest in producing tunes. This was partly the result of his character, for he was as lighthearted as a child, and took nothing seriously.

Another musician who in many respects resembled Pearsall but composed in quite a different style was HENRY HUGH PEARSON, who was born at Oxford, April 12th, 1815. He was educated at Harrow and Cambridge, then turned to music, and had some instruction from Attwood. In 1839 he went to Germany, and settled there, changing his name to Hugo Pierson, also using the pseudonym Edgar Mansfeldt. Schumann wrote

* *Cf.* W. Prendergast in the publications of the International Musical Society, July 1912

appreciatively of his songs. Pearson died at Leipzig, January 28th, 1873; he was buried at Sonning, Berkshire. Among his works were two operas performed at Hamburg, oratorios written for the Norwich Festivals of 1852 and 1869, and many other ambitious works distinguished by poetic intention and some power of expression but with a total lack of constructive skill. They are already forgotten, though some of the 'New German School' of his time had reckoned them among the great works only to be sufficiently valued by posterity. Some music to the second part of Goethe's *Faust* (which I have heard in the Leipzig Theatre) is a fair specimen of Pearson's works.

There have been many fine English singers, including Catherine Stephens (1794–1882), who became Countess of Essex in 1838; Mary Anne Paton (1802–64), an infant prodigy, singing, playing, and composing at eight years old, and subsequently a fine operatic soprano; Ann Goward, who, as Mrs. Keeley, told till 1899 how she sang the Mermaid's Song at the original production of Weber's *Oberon* in 1826; Clara Novello, particularly grand in Handel's music; and Mary Postans (Mrs. Shaw), contralto; a splendid array of singers, followed later by Charlotte Birch and Louisa Pyne. The leading male alto was William Knyvett (1779–1856), also a fair composer. Contralto singing was brought into vogue by Charlotte Dolby (1821–85), subsequently Madame Sainton; this grand singer founded a really new school of vocalisation which has considerably affected not only performance, but also composition. The contralto solos of Mendelssohn's *Elijah* were especially intended for her, and contralto solos have been since prominent features of every large English work, while the male alto is relegated to choirs. The earlier tenors were Charles Incledon (1763–1826), and the famous John Braham (1774–1856), born of Jewish parents named Abraham, whose voice lasted till he was an octogenarian. He actually sang in public till 1852. He appeared for a number of years in the dramas-with-music then usual; and always composed his own songs, which were, and still are, remarkably popular. 'The Death of Nelson,' the best-known of all, is, comically enough, annexed from a French tune— Méhul's 'Chant du Départ.' His successor was William Harrison, 1813–68. The baritone, James Bartleman (1769–1821), was another singer of the very highest merit; Henry Phillips (1801–76) was little inferior.

The English instrumentalists have, on the whole, been inferior to the vocalists. The pianists have mostly been already mentioned among the composers. Field was undeniably the greatest. Besides Neate, C. Potter, and Sterndale Bennett, there was a very fine lady pianist, Mrs. Anderson (Lucy Philpot, 1790–1878), almost self-taught. Of violinists there have been few of eminence; Henry Blagrove (1811–72) was perhaps the best. Robert Lindley (1776–1855) was a remarkably fine violoncellist. Henry Litolff, the son of an Alsatian prisoner and an Englishwoman, was a pianist of importance, and not without merit as a composer.

In one direction only can England claim to have materially advanced modern musical technique; this was in the invention of new execution on the harp. Elias Parish-Alvars, born at Teignmouth, of Hebrew parents (1816–49), was the first to perceive the novel effects producible by the addition of pedals; and it is through his example (though he did not remain long in England) that English harpists have kept fully equal at the least to those of other countries. No English player on other instruments deserves special mention, except Thomas Harper, a highly skilled trumpeter.

Having now passed the middle of the century we have to examine the beginnings of various institutions prominent in late Victorian days. No composers of mark appeared before 1860–70, when a new generation began to be noticed.

Earliest, and most important of these institutions, came the Crystal Palace Saturday Concerts, established in 1855 under August Manns; the concert-room was opened in 1860. Next, in 1859, followed the Monday Popular Concerts in the new St. James's Hall, to which the Saturday Popular Concerts were added in 1865. By the

Crystal Palace Concerts the highest orchestral music was made more accessible, as was chamber-music by the Monday Popular Concerts. The latter scarcely ever gave a hearing to an English composer; and the same practice had been followed by an earlier and very aristocratic institution, the Musical Union, founded and conducted from 1844 to 1880 by John Ella. The Crystal Palace Concerts, on the contrary, were celebrated for their continual introduction of young composers to the public. Another institution of importance was the famous choir formed by Henry Leslie in 1855, which for many years was probably without an equal in the world for the performance of Bach's motets and other *a capella* music. Among the works Leslie revived was Tallis's forty-voiced motet. The choir was finally dissolved in 1887; its place has never been filled. The dissolution of the Sacred Harmonic Society has already been told; its place has been filled by the Royal Albert Hall Choral Society, performing the standard oratorios on a still larger scale to larger audiences. The Albert Hall was opened in 1871; the first conductor of its Choral Society was Gounod (then resident in England), succeeded soon after by Joseph Barnby, until 1896, when Sir Frederick Bridge was appointed.

The Bach Society had been dissolved in 1870. The two *Passions* were then given at St. Anne's, Soho, under Barnby's direction; they have since become tolerably familiar to many London congregations, and we may even say popular. In 1876 a complete performance of Bach's High Mass in B minor was attempted by a body of amateurs, subsequently consolidated as the Bach Choir. At their concerts a large number of most important choral works of various schools have been introduced.*

The closing of Exeter Hall was very prejudicial to London music for some ten years; then, towards the end of 1893, the Queen's Hall in Langham Place, a model concert-hall in nearly every respect, was completed. The Philharmonic Society and the Bach Choir

---

* The extraordinary diffusion of Bach's works in the twentieth century is told in the Appendix.

removed there, followed by other societies. There are also suburban concerts of significance.

In the northern counties there is a very general enthusiasm for music, and the rich sonorous voices of the people are highly celebrated. Choral societies flourish everywhere there, and the workmen of the factories very commonly join in brass bands, of which there are an immense number, holding contests which are reckoned important local events. Our composers, unfortunately, ignore these opportunities.

Before further alluding to music in the provinces it will be necessary to proceed with the story of English Opera—the darkest page in our musical history. After the Pyne-Harrison management (1856–62) had ceased, English Opera was at an absolute standstill for some time.* Ten years later a revival came through a German violinist named Carl Rosa, who organised a company in 1875, which appeared in London during the spring, and afterwards toured round the provinces. Many an Englishman became acquainted with grand operas through the performances of this company; and it is surely better for the public to hear a few operas, with second-rate performers and a makeshift orchestra, than never to hear operas at all. Carl Rosa in 1883 began to commission new works; the first and most successful of these was *Esmerelda*, composed by ARTHUR GORING THOMAS, who in 1885 contributed *Nadeschda*. Thomas (1851–92) was born at Ratton Park, near Eastbourne, and was of French education and tastes. F. Corder produced both libretto and music of *Nordisa* (1887).

Carl Rosa was already turning his attention to light opera when he suddenly died in 1889; but his services to English music deserve affectionate remembrance. He did all he could, and it was not a little; through him several new works were composed, and performed both in England and on the Continent, and our provincial public got some chance of dimly guessing what grand operas are like.

---

* An English Opera Association (Limited) was announced in 1864, but apparently effected nothing.

His success excited the ambition of others; there was a very general feeling that English Opera should be permanently established in London on a grand scale. A theatre was built in the most luxurious style on a commanding site at Cambridge Circus; and it opened on January 31st, 1891, with all possible brilliancy of pride, pomp, and circumstance. Sir Arthur Sullivan had composed a version of Scott's *Ivanhoe*, which was performed for several months; after a holiday a French light opera was substituted. Then the Royal English Opera-house was closed altogether; and after some months Sir Augustus Harris took it and turned it into a 'variety theatre.'

Such has been the fate of the most thorough and most promising of all the vain attempts which have been made to establish a national opera. London, with five millions of inhabitants, could not support the attempt; and it has hitherto been made only in London. The English musical public does not even apprehend the fact that on the Continent opera is a permanent institution in every fairly large city, thus providing regular work for resident orchestras and singers. Here lies the fundamental difference between English and Continental musical conditions.

With the ever-increasing rapidity of communication came ever-increasing centralisation; the provincial theatres gave up stock companies, the last disappearing about 1880. There was no longer any opportunity for local opera, even if the public had shown any inclination for it. Here, however, improvement is perceptible as regards both drama and opera.

The result of this want is that our provincial towns, even the largest, have no complete musical resources, and must bring performers from London. Local orchestras have been almost impossible; and our music has acquired a totally different character from the music of other countries. Our small army, with its few regimental bands, has also acted unfavourably upon the supply of wind instrument players. Here and there persistent attempts have been made to establish a complete local orchestra,

finally accomplished in the largest towns and some
pleasure resorts. From 1880 to 1885 a fashion for
violin-playing set in among ladies, and helped the for-
mation of amateur orchestras.

Among the additions to the list of provincial musical
festivals the most important has been the Leeds, begun
in 1858, and signalised by the production of Bennett's
May Queen; in 1874 they became triennial. The chorus
of the Leeds festivals is specially famous. Another
festival of mark is the Bristol, begun in 1873. The
celebrations at Birmingham still maintain their pride of
place, and the works originally produced there include
Mendelssohn's *Elijah*, Gounod's *Redemption*, and Dvořák's
Spectre's Bride. A serious attack was made upon the
Three Choirs Festivals, on the ground that they dese-
crated the Cathedrals; at Worcester, in 1875, the authorities succeeded in changing the performances into
ecclesiastical music intermixed with prayers, but general
opposition caused this instance to be the only one.
Nearly every festival now boasts a new work; and choral
music of English composers hardly gets its first hearing
elsewhere.

An objection has been brought against these festivals,
on the ground that they hinder the appreciation of the
art at ordinary times and with local means; that they do
this to some extent is undeniable. In the towns where
triennial festivals are most firmly established, music, in
the three years between each grand celebration, is less
supported than might be expected. The three largest
northern cities—Glasgow, Liverpool, and Manchester—
all have regular winter concerts instead of an occasional
week's music, and do better so.

As another direct result of the want of opera, English
singing is entirely directed to concert-music, and is more
concerned with tone-production than dramatic expression.
Technically it is among the best in the world, though
suffering from much indistinct pronunciation; but
Italians, Germans, Americans, and especially French,
often complain of its dullness. Domestic music naturally
exaggerates the defects of the public performers; and in

drawing-room singing no one expects to hear expressive feeling, or to understand the words. As one result of the lack of dramatic expression our concerts exhibit the strangest incongruities; audiences do not in the slightest degree resent the performance by great female singers of words intended for a man, a barbarism which no French audience would tolerate. The beautiful words of Herrick's 'Cherry ripe' have been stupidly altered in C. E. Horn's setting for the same reason. There has, however, been a galaxy of really grand singers in Janet Patey, a magnificent contralto; Sims Reeves, a tenor of the greatest; his successors, Joseph Maas (who died young) and Edward Lloyd; and the baritone, Charles Santley, at one time distinguished upon the stage. The others were all concert-singers, though Reeves and Maas for a time 'walked through' a few operas. The sharp contrast between our musical conditions and those of the Continent is here evident, for a Continental singer goes on the stage as a matter of course. Among specially remarkable successes of English singers may be mentioned Edward Lloyd's beautiful rendering of the songs in Wagner's *Meistersinger*; Santley's grandly dramatic performance in Wagner's *Flying Dutchman* at Drury Lane in 1870; and what has been perhaps the greatest achievement of any English singer, Sims Reeves's delivery of the Narrator's recitatives in the *Matthew-Passion* when performed by the Bach Society under Sterndale Bennett on May 24th, 1862.

As distinguished instrumentalists, Arabella Goddard, pianist, and John Tiplady Carrodus, violinist, must be mentioned. The former, though purely English, happened to be born near St. Malo, on January 12th, 1838; she did much to familiarise London audiences with Beethoven's later sonatas from 1853 onwards, under the guidance of J. W. Davison, whom she married in 1860. After touring round the world she retired about 1880. Carrodus, born at Keighley on January 20th, 1836, was a pupil of Molique; and in his best time was a very fine classical soloist and orchestral leader. He died July 13th, 1895.

In one department of execution we can challenge

comparison with the world. Our organists are quite equal
to any. There is so much more church-going, and there
are so very many more places of worship of all kinds
in England than on the Continent, that there are more
organists' posts; and almost all our professional instrumentalists study the organ rather than the pianoforte.
The great performers, W. T. Best, Sir John Stainer, and
Sir Walter Parratt, have not been surpassed anywhere.

As organs became all but universal, a change took place
in congregational singing. Instead of diatonic psalm-
tunes, chromatically-harmonised sentimental melodies
were brought into use; frequently they become cloying
successions of chords only, evidently intended to be
played rather than sung in parts. At the same time
psalms began to be neglected for hymns: in 1861 appeared
Hymns Ancient and Modern, which speedily pushed out
all rivals, and many millions of copies have been sold.
Much of the harmonising is not of a high order, while
some settings have been taken from Bach's choral works,
and are quite unsuited for congregational singing. The
marching-tunes prove the most generally popular, and we
may take Wesley's 'Aurelia' as the type of a good modern English hymn-tune. A practical composer may yet
find an artistic use for this form of tune, and his works
will in that case attain extraordinary popularity. The
introduction of hymns is still opposed by some Presbyterians.

After the dull period which set in about the middle
of the century, no new composer appeared till 1862.
Then came the world-renowned ARTHUR SEYMOUR
SULLIVAN, who was born in London, May 13th, 1842.
Sullivan, though Irish by his father's and partly Italian by
his mother's side, was English by birth and training, and
had the invaluable experience of a Chapel Royal choir-
boy. In 1856, when at the Royal Academy, Sullivan won
the Mendelssohn scholarship after a tough struggle with
Barnby. In 1858 he was sent to Leipzig, and made
his first acquaintance with the works of Schumann,
who speedily became his idol. He returned in 1862,
bringing his promising music to *The Tempest*, which was

performed twice at the Crystal Palace; a Symphony in E soon followed, and a cantata, *Kenilworth*. In 1867 he composed a good and successful short oratorio, *The Prodigal Son*, but Sullivan had now relinquished the domain of abstract music, in which he never seemed quite at home. In 1870 Tennyson wrote a song-cycle, *The Window*, on the model of those set by Schubert and Schumann; for this Sullivan composed some of his very best music, and though these songs are German rather than English in style, they are the finest specimens of 'songs for voice and pianoforte' that any English composer had ever produced. Among his other works may be mentioned *The Light of the World*, an ambitious oratorio performed at Birmingham in 1873, but seldom heard since; *The Martyr of Antioch*, and a very popular cantata, *The Golden Legend* (both produced at Leeds), and some admirable music for dramas, especially *Macbeth*. None of these, not even *The Golden Legend*, nor even his many popular smaller pieces—sacred and secular, songs and hymn-tunes—would have made his music familiar all over the world. This he accomplished by inventing a new kind of opera, which deserves detailed notice.

When collaborating with W. S. Gilbert, Sullivan had the advantage of setting libretti of literary value, written for real actors, not for concert-singers. As in a Wagnerian music-drama, so in the Gilbert-Sullivan operas, the music is only one of the factors all uniting in the total effect. The topsy-turvy satire, the importance given to the chorus, and the necessity of adapting the music to the powers of speaking actors, all called for a style of music not exactly analogous to any operatic style previously existing. Sullivan rose to his new task splendidly, and set the libretti in a thoroughly artistic manner, yet keeping in view the popular garb which was requisite, and not forgetting the necessity of letting the *words* be paramount. It cannot be said that Sullivan entirely succeeded in 'writing down' to popular taste, for most of the music is too graceful in melody and too refined in harmony to be appreciated by the absolutely uncultivated; but it is exactly adapted to that very large class which knows a little, while the extraordinary skill displayed is the envy of musicians. The operas have had an unprecedented success with the whole English-speaking race; but attempts to introduce them to other countries have usually been unsuccessful, as the dramas are not suited to foreigners. The great exception has been *The Mikado*, which has a plot not dealing with English life, and had a very special success in Germany. It is strange that Gilbert should have so persistently prevented the operas from Continental success; but he could not refrain from satirising English institutions, and making the stories incomprehensible or uninteresting except to the English and their kindred. In 1889 the series ceased. The latest, especially *Yeomen of the Guard*, had become small regular operas. Subsequent attempts had little success.

There have been some who thought Sullivan was degrading the art by composing such works; and who would doubtless have said the same of Mozart when he composed *Die Zauberflœte*, and of Shakespeare when he introduced Lear and the Fool together. But Sullivan did in 1891 produce one grand opera, *Ivanhoe*, already mentioned as written for the ill-fated Royal English Opera-house. It was not altogether successful, as the short pieces, such as Sullivan had used in his comic operas, proved too tiny for the large framework of a grand opera; and there were frequent over-refinements of harmony, notably in the refrain of Friar Tuck's song, emasculated by secondary sevenths. Sullivan produced no other great work; he died suddenly 22nd November, 1900, and was buried in St. Paul's. A technical matter of interest is Sullivan's use of the second inversion of the dominant seventh to finish a clause; see Fairfax's song in *Yeomen of the Guard*, at the word *June*; in the first chorus of *The Martyr of Antioch*, at *pursue*; in *The Golden Legend*, at *to the music of the sea*; in ' O hush thee, my babie,' at *to thee*; etc. etc.

No young composer, except F. H. Cowen, attracted attention for some fifteen years after Sullivan had come forward. Then three appeared about the same time: C. Hubert H. Parry, C. Villiers Stanford, and A. C.

Mackenzie. These three long remained with Sullivan at the head of English musicians. Parry's masterly oratorio *Judith* is generally conceded the topmost place in their achievements as regards choral music; in instrumental music Mackenzie has been very successful. As none of them has invented an original style, it is not necessary to examine their works. (See Appendix.)

Before concluding, one very unpleasant matter must be touched upon. A bandmaster from Hamburg, named Felix d'Albert, whose father was French and mother was German, settled in England and married a Newcastle lady. Their son, Eugène d'Albert, was born at Glasgow, April 10th, 1864. He showed great talent for music, and was carefully educated at the National Training School; and in 1881 he was sent to Vienna, having won the Mendelssohn Scholarship. On arriving in Germany he immediately called himself Eugen d'Albert, pretended he was not English, and abused his native country, to which he would not return even for his father's funeral. He made a very great name as a pianist, and takes a high place among German composers; with the fury of a renegade he adopted ultra-German eccentricities. He occasionally revisited his native country, but continued his Teutomania until the World-War, when he was naturalised a Swiss. Another musician, somewhat resembling d'Albert but with far less talent, was George Marshall-Hall, who settled and died at Melbourne; he gave vent to somewhat similar utterances, though without the *suppressio veri* (to use the mildest term) which has stained the words of Eugène d'Albert. In each case ignorance has been the moving cause; neither d'Albert nor Marshall-Hall was aware of the state of music in Germany, and judged that nation to be fairly represented by the few exceptional geniuses it has produced in the eighteenth and nineteenth centuries. The feeling that everything German was musically good, and everything English has been musically bad, unfortunately may also be traced elsewhere; many who should be better informed apparently imagine that there is no vulgar music except in England. Just as every Italian opera or opera-singer

seemed to Burney deserving of careful mention, while
madrigalists were not, so every tenth-rate German composer seemed to some people more important than our
own very greatest musicians.

The National Training School, founded by the Society
of Arts, was subsequently merged into the Royal College
of Music, opened on May 7th, 1883. This institution has
magnificent endowments, and has acquired the libraries
of the Ancient Concerts and of the Sacred Harmonic
Society.* Its first director was Sir George Grove, a
well-known enthusiastic amateur who had edited a very
elaborate *Dictionary of Music and Musicians*; this work,
though affording the strongest contrasts of careful schol-
arly research side-by-side with careless hackwork, has
done much for the cultivation of professors, and is the
best contribution to musical literature which England has
hitherto made. The articles on English music, especially
of the earlier periods, are unfortunately among the least
valuable parts of Grove's Dictionary; the biographical
notices are more satisfactory.†

Every possible provision is made for teaching, and
everything is made easy for a talented man to come
forward. The public would be ready enough to welcome
a native composer or performer of absolutely the first
rank, and everybody is perfectly ready to agree with the
idea that thorough training and long hard study are
necessary for musical eminence. All these matters are
pleasant enough, but there are some other stern facts
which must not be ignored. Worst of all is the apparent
hopelessness of permanent English Opera. What England
most needs, musically, is the establishment of a complete
grand opera company in every large town; and that need
is precisely the one which seems to have least probability
of fulfilment. It must also be remembered that the
social conditions of English life are very different from
those on the Continent; especially the living away from
business in scattered suburbs is very unfavourable to
entertainments of all kinds. And another matter is not

* For its achievements so far, see Appendix.
† For the second edition, see Appendix.

without importance. The part which England has played in the world's history has been so magnificent and imposing, that both Englishmen and foreigners do not realise that England is quite a small country; that France is much more than twice the size of Great Britain, that the German Empire is yet larger even now. With our small distances and rapid communications, local life has no opportunity to assert itself; and London is everything, while itself too huge for artistic life. The result is only too evident when a post outside London has to be filled. High salaries, fortunes to a Continental artist, may be offered at Edinburgh, Dublin, or Melbourne; but nothing will induce an English musician, with a made reputation, to settle out of London.*

Again, our composers are not sufficiently practical. They do not recognise what the conditions around them are. None of them (except in some degree Sullivan) has studied the use of resources, and the varying treatment required by varying resources. The influence of the moribund German school has had a very deleterious effect upon some of our best composers; German music since Beethoven has been abstract and unpractical, and these defects are copied here. Consequently all the fertile resources awaiting cultivation are neglected, and our composers persist in lazily using those which have long ago been provided for, and in repeating the old forms. They even produce orchestral works, though they perfectly well know that there are scarcely any orchestras in England. At the same time musicians of a very low class, who address themselves to the problems before them, achieve enormous success; while our leading musicians produce works which nobody wants, and which go almost immediately on the shelf for ever, because they are practically uncalled-for. The great geniuses of the past would have rejoiced with exceeding great joy had they but once enjoyed such opportunities as are open to a present-day musician all his life long; but they were practical men, writing for particular performances by particular resources, while a modern composer, both in

---

* This paragraph, written in 1894, still holds good in essentials.

England and Germany, thinks only of his inner consciousness and his artistic conscientiousness, and has his
works published before thay have been heard. As
Ruskin's and William Morris's views of art extend, they
may some day reach our best composers, and cause them
to give their attention to works which are practically
useful and actually needed. Then we shall perhaps have
original art-works.*

Neither is the condition of the lower provinces of
music at all satisfactory. The best feature is the enormously improved character of the pianoforte music
learnt by school-girls; since 1880 the prevalence of local
examinations has caused a complete change. Good vocal
music is also more frequently heard. *Per contra*, music
has come to be looked upon rather as a task than a pleasure,
as something to be conscientiously studied until a certifi-
cate has been obtained, not as a delight for the hearer
and the performer. And as usual the lower tendencies
of taste, repressed by authority, have found a new vent;
during the nineties songs of low life took the place of the
feeble drawing-room sentimentalities dear to past generations. The enormous success of variety entertainments at
so-called music-halls † is among the most powerful of the
forces making against music; and the nuisance of street-
performers grows ever worse and worse. All these
unpleasancies show that the evil spirit of bad taste has
not been effectually exorcised; and if he re-enter, our
last state will be worse than the first. At present we are
going in the direction which has done so much harm to
German music—the entire separation of the artistic and
the popular. A great artist's duty is to master all styles
and to supply works for all tastes; if he be a Shakespeare,
he will create a Dogberry and a Hamlet, and will mingle
base mechanicals among the quarrels of Oberon and
Titania, every motley addition increasing the supremacy
of their creator. Nothing is common or unclean to the
truly creative mind. But our best composers would

---

* This paragraph now fortunately requires considerable qualification. Academic influence has long since been set aside, and originality is sought.

† This feature has, in the twentieth century, been remarkably altered.
See Appendix

scorn to compose anything for the general public, and imagine they are elevating the art by holding altogether aloof from uncultivated taste, and using just those resources and forms which have received the sanction of great names. This Grundyism is a terrible enemy to English music; and our most ambitious composers are completely under its sway.*

The increased attention given to the cultivation of the art has brought music out of the disrepute from which it formerly suffered; and its study at our Universities is one of the most cheering signs. A number of interesting contributions to musical literature have appeared; but this branch has also been sadly degraded by amateurs, who have perpetrated most amazing farragoes of ignorance and nonsense, even publishing instruction-books crammed with childish blunders. Among the cultivated amateurs who have produced really valuable works are Messrs. W. H. Beatty-Kingston, Morton Latham, E. J. Dent, Arthur Balfour, and Sir Henry Hadow. It is pleasant to find something in this department worthy of praise, for one can hardly write coolly of certain meddling impostors, whose publications are perhaps the worst disgrace which stains English music.

Hearty praise and recommendation must be bestowed upon the *Old English Edition* of Mr. G. E. P. Arkwright, who has done most useful work in making rare or unpublished early music generally accessible; and Mr. Barclay Squire, Mr. J. A. Fuller-Maitland, and Mr. H. E. Wooldridge have also distinguished themselves in this direction. Yet even here some meddling half-instructed amateurs have done mischief.

Even in the worst of these facts we may find something cheering. Regrettable as it is that utterly ignorant or deceptively half-learned writers should succeed in getting their contemptible books published, and even widely circulated, yet the fact that the public buys these books shows that the public has an interest in the subject. It is hard to discover a soul of goodness in the evil deeds

* This paragraph also now requires much qualification; since 1895 there has been distinct improvement.

of some bungling amateurs who have attempted to edit early music, yet we must remember that their zeal is praiseworthy, even if it be not according to knowledge.

I cannot refrain from expressing my regret that our cathedrals, colleges, and principal other churches do so little in the way of performing the magnificent poly- phonic anthems of the Elizabethan composers. Besides the special masterpieces which no choir can blamelessly neglect, each choir could cherish a reverent remembrance of its *own* past musicians. To take a striking instance, has not Ely Cathedral as much right to be proud of the compositions of Tye, Whyte, Fox, and Amner, as of the architecture designed by Alan of Walsingham and John of Wisbech? Nearly every cathedral and college can boast of its own great sixteenth or seventeenth- century composers. Thus King's College educated Tye, Gibbons, and Loosemore; Magdalen College had a splendid succession of organist-composers, from Richard Davy through John Mason and Sheppard down to Dr. Rogers; Worcester Cathedral can boast of Nathanael Patrick and Thomas Tomkins; Lichfield, of Michael East; Chichester, of Thomas Weelkes; Lincoln, of Byrd. If each choir maintained special remembrance of its own worthies there would be a distinct individuality in each choral service which could not fail to have a beneficial effect upon each choir as well as upon English music generally. Unfortunately too many of our precentors and organists prefer to introduce pieces from oratorios, quite unsuited to a cathedral choir and an organ; but whose modern (and generally sentimental) phraseology satisfies their uncultivated tastes, for which the poly- phonic style is too severe. I am referring, as those who remember my remarks in Chapter IV will know, to anthems rather than to Services.

The art of music has received full attention in the poetry of Browning (long in doubt whether he should not become a musician); and his 'Abt Vogler,' 'Parleying with Charles Avison,' and some shorter pieces, are among the noblest passages inspired by the tone-art. George Eliot and Swinburne have written appreciatively.

In Herbert Spencer's philosophy, music plays a not un-important part; and the historians Lecky and Fyffe have given music its due share of notice. Such ignorance as Macaulay's or Landor's will be impossible in future. Our publishers not infrequently issue translations of foreign works on music which are entrusted to literary hacks who make the strangest mistakes in technical terms; even historical and critical works of the very first im-portance are sometimes thus disgraced. Adaptations of foreign poems and word-books are very rarely executed even reasonably well; our excess of monosyllables, and paucity of double rhymes, are hopeless stumbling-blocks.

With the knowledge that music is now held at least equal to the other arts, that any Englishman of real musical genius will at once find encouragement and support from all sides, that every opportunity for study is given, that the demand for printed music is im-measurably greater than in the time of Bach and Handel or even of Beethoven, that before 1700 the condition of English music was most brilliant, we ought apparently to expect with confidence the speedy arrival of a great composer. There are considerations, however, which may lead us to think less hopefully. It is to be feared that the conditions are a little too comfortable to bring forth the due ripening of genius; furthermore, that a highly-gifted young musician will be misled (as so many have already been, both in Germany and England) into an attempt to do again what has been done already. If a composer uses the old resources and old forms, he must use them better than any one has done before; if he writes symphonies on the plan of Beethoven's, they must be better than Beethoven's, or they will be played once but very seldom twice, loudly applauded, and declared an honour to English art, and never be heard again. Young composers should be carefully taught that great works have been achieved only by taking resources or styles previously neglected, and treating them artistically. Plenty of such resources and styles lie around us, urgently needing artistic treatment, but abandoned to the un-inventive. A very obvious case is what may be called the

'Congregational Oratorio'; a work suited to the capacity of an average church or chapel choir, with a share for the congregation. Let, therefore, a young composer be encouraged to devote himself to the strictly practical; and let musicians endeavour to apprehend the idea that thus and thus only the art will be enlarged, that a composer who invents a new form, or ennobles a neglected resource, is doing a more artistic work than the composer who writes a symphony in exact imitation of Beethoven. Working upon given models is the task of students; a man who wishes to make a business of composing ought to produce something new in each successive work; either in detail or design novelty should always be present.*

The principal defects in the present state of English music have now been alluded to, and I may here tabulate the following propositions as an embodiment of the chief improvements which I believe are required and are feasible:

I. The establishment of a complete permanent Grand Opera company in every large town should be continually held up as the ideal to be striven after.

II. Our leading musicians should occupy themselves with the production of those works which are absolutely needed, which the incompetent must supply if the competent will not.

III. More enthusiasm, and a wider acquaintance with the masterpieces of the art, must be cultivated by (and expected in) the great body of our professional musicians. This involves the reverent preservation and study of the great deeds achieved by English composers from 1400 to 1700; frequent performances of the madrigals by our societies, of the anthems by our choirs, of the songs by our vocalists, and even of the instrumental and dramatic works.

IV. The public, and the profession also, should understand that every country alike has its high-class music and its low-class music; that where the high-class is highest, there the low-class will probably be lowest. Thorough apprehension of this idea would be a very considerable

* Here also distinct progress is perceptible since 1895.

improvement in English musical knowledge; but the improvement must begin at the top.

V. Ignorant amateurs who presume to publish lucubrations on the art, or to edit existing music, should be sternly repressed by all our critics.

VI. If we must not hope to put down the noisy vulgarities of street music, let us at least strive to make them as little mischievous as possible. Even if barrel-organs and church bells were only required to be in tune a very great advance would have been made.

VII. All children should learn our best old folk-tunes, for which some born song-poet should write suitable words. At present there is a general ignorance of the words even of the most familiar tunes—'Rule, Britannia,' for instance. An English melody, such as 'Come back to Erin' (composed by Mrs. Barnard), or 'Auld Robin Gray' (composed by William Leeves), should have distinctively English words on a distinctively English topic. An Irish melody, such as Mrs. Jordan's 'Blue Bell of Scotland,' should have Irish words.

A few words on the further study of the musical history of England may be useful. Writers who wish to take up the subject will do well to begin by verifying all my statements and collating all my quotations before inserting materials I have overlooked and fresh discoveries, or adding the great future deeds which we hope for. In the meantime very much work remains to be done with the known materials; many part-books, both printed and MS., have still to be scored; many anonymous works may yet be identified; and many imperfect sets of part-books may yet be completed. Permanent institutions of various kinds might contribute enormous assistance in this direction; they might attach to their harmony competitions the condition that each prizeman should contribute to the library a motet or madrigal scored by himself from the ancient part-books. Something similar might be done at cathedrals; and still more by our university colleges, where the work would be particularly in keeping with the surroundings, and would especially stimulate historical knowledge. A sufficiency of material remains to occupy many decades; to take one instance, Add. MSS. 17,802–5 (so often referred to in Chap. IV) contains ninety-six works.*

Less need be done in publishing, unless any specially fine masterpiece should come to light, which could pass into the ordinary repertory; such might be the case with the historical madrigals partly preserved in the Egerton MSS. 2009–12. Otherwise, good and accessible MS. scores would be sufficient; and a musician who devotes his spare hours to the completion of several such volumes will be more likely to leave a footprint on the sands of time than he will by composing an orchestral work, even though it should reach a public hearing.

Further work may also be done in practical performance, especially with our immortal madrigals, which every English musician should know, love, and exhibit to the world. The anthems and motets should never be neglected, though we cannot expect them to be as much appreciated by the public as the madrigals are. As regards the early instrumental music, Mr. Arnold Dolmetsch has already given us a splendid example of what can be done.

Should it be deemed worth while to issue a grand national monument of the splendid achievement of the English nation in creating first vocal, afterwards instrumental, musical composition, then such a publication might take the form of a selection of works by every known composer from John Dunstable to Purcell, with 'Sumer is icumen in' as a frontispiece. There could be three series—a sacred, an instrumental, a secular—and each composer should be represented by his one best work in each department. Such a publication would be a *practical* History of English Music; and should be issued with a splendour worthy of its purpose, and also in a generally attainable form. It would be an immense undertaking, as a selection would have to be made from several thousands of pieces; and hundreds of composers would claim representation, many of them in all three

* Dr. R. R. Terry has shown that this appeal was justified; he has even brought many of these works into practical use.

departments. But it would be an additional jewel of rare brilliancy in England's crown of glory; and the cost of such a work would be cheerfully borne by any continental nation, while in the United States rich men would contend for the honour of issuing such a national memorial. In England we are less fortunate. In this case also the depression and disrepute of English music since 1700 have created a suspicion which will be long ere it is eradicated, in spite of the plainest evidence.

Though the highest pinnacles of musical composition were reared by Germans, the foundations were laid by Englishmen. No light thing is it, that John Dunstable certainly solved the problem of vocal composition, and Hugh Aston apparently solved the problem of instrumental composition. Let us ever reverence these men; the English musicians of the fifteenth and sixteenth centuries have dowered the whole world with a glorious new art unknown before, *structural music*, an art complete in itself, which can bear analysis as can poetry, architecture, and the graphic arts.

APPENDIX

RECENT MUSICAL HISTORY

SINCE this work appeared in 1895 the course of musical events has led to many important developments; the the features demanding special notice are:

1. Changes in public taste.
2. Advances in the study of musical literature and science.*
3. The present social position of the art and its professors.
4. The alterations and developments in surroundings.
5. Choral concerts and Church oratorio.
6. Orchestral concerts.
7. Chamber music.
8. Opera and operetta.
9. Great performers, vocal and instrumental.
10. Composers and compositions.

---

1. On the whole, the changes in public taste have been in the direction of improvement, and very perceptibly so—in several departments even remarkably and quite unexpectedly. An institution I had not thought worthy of mention, the Promenade Concerts, suddenly assumed a position of highest importance, and requires particular discussion. Equally extraordinary has been the improvement in the concerts at pleasure resorts, most influential upon general culture. Formerly a 'selection' from some old-fashioned opera, with solos for the principal performers, was the central item among a series of dance-pieces and the like; now an entire programme of Beethoven and other classical masters is frequent and attractive, every other concert including one or more pieces such as a serious musician would select.

The principal change which has come over our musical thought is the great decline in the worship of

---

* The French use the convenient terms *musicologie, musicologue*. We require them.

Handel, though it can only be temporary. His choral works, sacred and secular, are almost forgotten in central musical life; while his violin sonatas and many operatic airs have reappeared. There had been writers whose idolatry of Handel—the man and the musician—had been scarcely sane; Samuel Butler pronounced him the greatest of all men, as much above Shakespeare as Shakespeare is above the rest of mankind! J. F. Runciman, more accurately judging his powers as the first of all song-writers, also was inclined to think him the greatest of men, for 'the man was immeasurably greater than his music.' Rockstro, Hullah, and H. H. Statham gave full utterance to the older belief in Handel's uncontested supremacy as a composer. The verdict, both English and German, that Handel is for the public, Bach for the scholar, was usual, practically unanimous. When Bach's style became familiar and his works more frequently heard, many critics turned against Handel, with deplorable ignorance declaring him a purely English possession unvalued elsewhere. Even where solid information was to be expected—in the *Oxford History of Music*, for instance—this strange ignorance is displayed; and generally our professional musicians are astounded when they hear of the Handel performances on the Continent, where all his great choral works are on the repertory.

In the meantime Bach has, in our musicians' estimation, taken the place formerly occupied by Handel. The concert-going public has learnt to appreciate Bach's instrumental style; his concertos and 'overtures' are now stock pieces, and had they been written for modern resources no orchestral works would be more frequently performed. Bach's choral works are also much in demand; there still remains some feeling that such renderings are instructive attempts or *tours de force* rather than normal performances of beautiful music. The two *Passions* are naturally free from such suspicion; and, with the *Christmas Oratorio*, are familiar to many choirs. At St. Anne's, Soho, the weekly Lenten performances of the *John-Passion* are really popular. There, as elsewhere in England, the congregation joins in the chorales, often with imposing effect, whether justifiable or the reverse; dynamic shadings also, quite alien to Bach's style, are employed.

The Mendelssohn-worship of early Victorian times, and the Schumann-worship which succeeded, have died out. Of all the post-Beethoven school, Brahms alone retains a certain following. Beethoven himself is rather less idolised than in the nineteenth century; Mozart and Haydn have reasserted their immortality. The popularity of Slavonic composers began with Dvorák; then Tschaikovski and many other Russians were appreciated, and have taken the place of German romanticists in public estimation. In opera, Wagner and the later Italians reign supreme. The lighter French school is still influential; the severer composers who followed César Franck's lead are respected.

2. In recent musical literature the first place must be accorded to the new edition of Grove's *Dictionary*. Not free from the worst faults of the original publication, from neglect of native music, careless proof-reading, strange want of proportion in the articles—Spontini and Steibelt being allotted as much space as all the principal English composers put together, and Weber six times as much as Bach!—from unrestrained expression of individual opinions, and defective knowledge, yet this second edition is a decided improvement on the first. Many very important articles had originally been intrusted to W. S. Rockstro, and were quite behind the age. Rockstro had opposed Wagner's works, and afterwards confessed he had been practically ignorant of them. In general his tastes and knowledge were only early Victorian.* The new edition has been improved by omitting or shortening many of his worst articles. A number of highly competent new contributors were called in to assist; and should a third edition be ever attained, a well-informed editor, who will take his task seriously, may make Grove's *Dictionary* a compilation equal to any work of the kind in existence.

* He wrote the article 'Madrigal' without knowing even Chappell's researches!

The Oxford Musical History was an attempt to give a detailed account of the rise and progress of the art, under the auspices of Oxford University. Professor Wooldridge, Sir Hubert Parry, and Dr. (now Sir) W. Henry Hadow took three periods; Mr. Fuller-Maitland the fourth; and Dannreuther, an American-German, the last. Wooldridge, on the polyphonic centuries, is often lucid and informing; Parry's account of the seventeenth century is, but for the unlucky omissions of Viadana and the Prince of Venosa, the final word on this transitional period; and Hadow's volume on the Viennese period is distinguished by charm of style. All the writers alike confine themselves almost entirely to criticising particular compositions; performance, performers, general musical life, resources, advances in musical practice, are but slightly touched upon. This latter deficiency is frequent in British works on music.

Of older writers who, like Rockstro, belonged in the main to the Handel-Mendelssohn worshippers, Joseph Bennett and the diligent investigator F. G. Edwards have passed away. Vernon Blackburn and J. F. Runciman expounded the literary man's views towards music, which are continued by Ernest Newman and Cecil Forsyth. C. A. Barry and J. S. Shedlock were worthy men, highly esteemed as historical and general authorities. On abstract questions William Wallace's *Threshold of Music* deserves special appreciation, with Sir Hubert Parry's works. Dealing with particular composers, P. Robinson's very clever attempt to justify Handel from the charge of 'borrowing,' and R. A. Streatfeild's fine volume on Handel, are noteworthy; also Parry's study of Bach. F. Niecks, Reid professor at Edinburgh, has produced a similarly important work on Chopin, and several exhaustive monographs. D. F. Tovey, his successor, showed in the *Encyclopædia Britannica* that he may with unremitting research, careful verifying, and a wide unrestricted outlook, produce historico-æsthetic work of the very first importance. E. J. Dent has specialised on Italian music; his book on A. Scarlatti is conclusive. W. H. Cummings, a leading singer, became a zealous antiquary.

Percy A. Scholes does much meritorious journalistic work.   Dr. Ralph Dunstan's *Cyclopædic Dictionary* is a remarkably complete and trustworthy epitome of musical knowledge in details.

Except for some useful antiquarian research by Mr. Barclay Squire, British musicology was not strongly represented in the publications of the International Musical Society.   Dr. Maclean was the English editor, and misused his opportunities by inserting whole articles of literary paradox and political diatribe, often neglecting music entirely.

We are fortunate in possessing a distinguished body of musical antiquaries whose researches have very materially facilitated the study of our own musical history.   E. W. B. Nicholson arranged the publication, under the title *Early Bodleian Music*, of the relics preserved in the Bodleian Library; the cumbrous volume contains facsimiles and translations, and is of the highest importance.   Robert Steele edited a full list of early English printed music for the Bibliographical Society. *The Musician* in the late nineteenth century, and *The Chord*, contained some important articles; *The Musical Antiquary*, from 1909 to 1913, in its twelve numbers, was a storehouse of historical learning.   Mr. Godfrey E. P. Arkwright continued his most useful *Old English Edition* to the twenty-fifth volume, making accessible a fine collection of the most representative musical works from Tye to Blow, with much accurate historical research. The Rev. E. H. Fellowes has done valuable work for the madrigal school, editing Morley's, Gibbons's, Wilbye's, and Farmer's collections in practically convenient form, and discovering the biography of Wilbye.   Miss Janet Dodge claims remembrance for editing Elizabethan 'Ayres' in modern notation.   Mr. W. Barclay Squire has distinguished himself in bibliography.   The publication of Purcell's works has materially advanced, and the goal is in sight.

Mr. Cecil Sharp has devoted himself to our folk-songs; Miss Lucy Broadwood has published a selection, and now great numbers from all quarters are printed, mechanism being used for recording. Some think over-much stress is laid on the matter, and insufficient allow-ance made for uneducated singers' unsteadiness in tune and still more in time. Mrs. Kennedy Fraser has been equally assiduous in collecting and performing songs from the Hebrides.

Mr. F. W. Galpin's book on *Old English Musical Instruments* deserves all recognition; Mr. W. W. Cobbett has studied and endeavoured to revive the oldest instru-mental forms. Mr. Frank Kidson still remains the unwearied student and connoisseur of folk-melody and antiquarian research. Of particular importance for the study of English compositions have been the per-formances of early sacred music at Westminster Cathedral under Dr. R. R. Terry. He has brought to a hearing, as part of the regular services, the works, not only of the sixteenth century, but also of the fifteenth, even to the beginnings in Dunstable, Power, and King Henry the Sixth. Fayrfax and Ludford have found a permanent home in the repertory; the mature works of Tye, Tallis, Byrd, Philipps, and Deering are among the staple, and have become really familiar. Secular art is cultivated by the Oriana Madrigal Society. The Plainsong and Mediæval Music Society, not fortunate in guidance from its beginning, rather missed its opportunities; yet it issued some valuable facsimiles. Many curious old English and other compositions have been performed as illustrations to the lectures of the Gresham Professor, Sir Frederick Bridge. Miss Nellie Chaplin and her sisters give de-lightful performances on the older keyed and stringed instruments. All these efforts have resulted in a know-ledge of our musical history far greater than even recluse scholars could attain in mid-Victorian times.

Of publications dealing with the general subject, the most important has been Dr. Ernest Walker's *History of Music in England*, published 1907. His work is occupied almost entirely with criticisms upon compositions; the general story of national musical life is but little discussed. Performers, even the greatest, are ignored altogether; Sims Reeves and W. T. Best alike are not mentioned.

Dr. Walker's criticisms not infrequently betray peculiar and personal tastes; his carpings at Handel would revolt foreign musicians; Arne is slightingly dismissed; Sullivan's 'Lost Chord' and 'Sailor's Grave' are termed 'disgraceful rubbish.' But Dr. Walker can be illuminating, incisive, and appreciative when treating the polyphonic schools, from Tye to Wilbye and Gibbons; or Purcell, Greene, S. Wesley, Pearsall, and Elgar.

Dr. J. S. Bumpus published a *History of Cathedral Music*, an exhaustive treatment of this important branch of English art. Useful summaries of the general story have been issued by Percy A. Scholes and C. Antrobus Harris. Mr. Orsmond Anderton has now joined the movement. But there have also appeared works for which any word of praise can seldom be said. One specimen is Ernest Ford's *Short History of English Music*, which, among other peculiarities, never mentions Arne; and it occupies fourteen pages with the doings of Charles Hallé and Wilma Norman-Néruda! Of contributions by foreign writers, the completion of Dr. Willibald Nagel's *Geschichte der Musik in England* claims first notice. Acknowledging that my own work had already accomplished his intended bibliographical purpose, he changed his plan and confined his second volume to criticisms, stopping at Purcell. C. Van den Borren's discussion of Elizabethan virginal music unfortunately suffers from imperfect knowledge of the existing remains, which mars what might have been a really valuable disquisition; and the same defect is only too perceptible in Max Seiffert's *Geschichte den Klaviermusik*, which has an admirable account of the remains he knew. A trustworthy summary is contained in Albert Soubies's *Histoire de la Musique*. J. Didiot, F. de Ménil, and V. Lederer have been mentioned in Chapter II. Dr. A. Schering, speaking at Berlin in 1912, predicted that the oratorio of the future will probably be developed in England, and the poet must lead the way; so far the prediction has hardly been fulfilled. The poet has not yet done his share.

3. The contemning of musicians had died out long before this History originally appeared. Since the

multiplication of concerts—choral, ballad, instrumental—
our performers had been freed from the disreputable
theatrical associations which still taint the musical profession, especially the singer, in other countries. A
British public singer, soprano or contralto, is expected
to live as honest and reputable a life as any other British
lady, and she does. Without blatant Podsnappery, we
may be proud of this. Any British concert artist, male
or female, is received as gentle. But is the Art properly
respected? There have been, and are, unpleasant facts
which cannot be neglected in considering the position
of the musical art. The attendance at football matches
may outnumber fiftyfold the attendance at concerts,
but stress need not be laid on such occurrences. Does the
British public respect the music it patronises? Yes,
more than formerly; while there is still much room for
improvement. In theatres, the behaviour of audiences
during music is disgracefully inattentive, even in the
leading metropolitan theatres, frequented by the highest
classes. When Sir Henry Irving planned an elaborate
revival of *Macbeth*, he asked Sullivan to supply a new
overture; Sullivan rose to the occasion, composing a poetic
inspiration which by general consent was his finest
instrumental work. The Lyceum audience, then the
most distinguished and intellectual in London, paid not
the slightest attention, chattering noisily, to Sullivan's
bitter disappointment. For the opening of an exhibition
at Liverpool, Cowen had been engaged to compose and
conduct a new overture. He duly composed it, rehearsed
it, and started the performance; but soon the Mayor
went to him and asked him to stop! A generation has
since elapsed, and even now people who will be attentive
listeners to concert programmes will treat music in a
theatre as only accompaniment to conversation. Nor is
a musician, even the highest, honoured by men, as he
may be by women. The painter, even the poet, indeed
shares this neglect. The average Englishman, whether
high, middle, or low class, is quite indifferent to any form
of culture, alike to literature, to art, or even to science.
But as regards music there are signs of improvement.

Our novelists, from Dickens and George Eliot downwards, blunder most amusingly when they touch on musical matters. Mr. Galsworthy, in *The Island Pharisees*, has described a fashionable wedding, in which 'the organ began rolling out the Wedding March' as the bride *arrived*; 'once *again* the organ played the Wedding March' at the conclusion. Where is the girl, of any class, who could not have enlightened him? If the characters in a novel visit an opera, the author will attempt to introduce and use the story, with astonishing results. Charles Reade, in *A Woman-Hater*, describes a visit to Gounod's *Faust*, and criticises the singing of the Marguerite and the Siebel in the *first* act, where neither sings a note, and Siebel is not even seen! H. G. Wells makes King Marke appear in the first act of *Tristan*; twists the second act into hopeless confusion; and supposes the shepherd plays on the piccolo! These perfectly gratuitous blunders are quite average specimens. In Frankfort Moore's *Food of Love*—the story of a musical genius born into a stolid county family—technical details are delightfully muddled.

And authors remain childishly ignorant of musical life. Macaulay and Buckle knew nothing of its past. R. H. Gretton, whose *Modern History of the English People* is a storehouse of accurate facts, is equally ignorant of the present state, hardly mentioning Sullivan, not at all Parry or any living composer, even Elgar. Of our continual orchestral, chamber, and choral concerts Mr. Gretton had apparently never heard; he chronicles the wild enthusiasm over Paderewski, which 'did, nevertheless, make music a subject of common interest, and prepared the way for a removal of the reproach that England as a nation cared nothing for it.' In the great reviews articles on music are rare, and usually the work of amateurs, whose ignorance in matters of fact and defects of taste are often lamentable.

4. In surrounding circumstance there has been decided improvement. The 'variety shows' have almost entirely altered their style and programmes; what I wrote of them on p. 491 of my first edition is no longer true. Great singers

have been heard at 'music-halls'; variety 'numbers' have developed into connected pieces; orchestral interludes of important works are customary, and usually a programme has at least one purely musical 'turn,' often of the most technically brilliant character. Rampant vulgarity and impudent suggestiveness were formerly the staple attractiveness of the songs; in the twentieth century these defects have nearly disappeared, the audiences being so entirely changed that what were rowdy, vicious drinking-dens in which no decent citizen ever ventured, are become the most fashionable resorts. This is a very hopeful and inspiring improvement.

The multiplication of 'picture theatres,' which use continuous musical accompaniment, must eventually have considerable influence on popular taste; but their establishment is recent, and the effect is as yet uncertain. The perpetually increasing migration to distant and scattered suburbs at present hinders music; its ultimate development, when convenient concert-halls are built, may be favourable. The Queen's Hall affords an unexceptionable model; imitations on a suitable scale would give each suburb of large towns a nucleus for the zealous cultivation of music.

Sunday concerts began in the late nineteenth century at Glasgow, and in the eighties at Liverpool. Then by a legal subterfuge they were made possible at Queen's Hall in 1895, and have since become very numerous, giving performances of familiar works, which do not require rehearsal, at less than usual prices. Large numbers who would have but little chance of attending ordinary concerts benefit by these opportunities. But all the concert halls and theatres of every kind touch, after all, only a fraction of the nation. If all Londoners wished to attend the Queen's Hall, six or seven years of daily concerts would only allow each inhabitant a single attendance. Adding places of worship, which are in a way concert halls, still only perhaps a quarter of the nation has opportunity for musical culture.

5. Choral music, at least in London and the South, suffers from the increasing cultivation of orchestral music.

One special branch, the Church oratorio, flourishes. The introduction of Bach's *Passions* suggested similar works intended for Anglican choirs with organ accompaniment. A. R. Gaul's *English Passion* was published in 1879; Stainer's *Crucifixion* (1882) quickly became a favourite, and every Lent the performances may be counted by hundreds; C. Lee Williams's *Gethsemane*, Dr. Ferris Tozer's *Way of the Cross*, and W. S. Vinning's *Passion* deserve mention; J. H. Maunder (1858-1920) addressed himself to average taste and skill. In *The Atonement* Coleridge-Taylor produced a similar work of a more ambitious order, inclining to the concert-oratorio. Many works intended for other seasons of the ecclesiastical year are now also composed and published. These Church oratorios, in spite of their limitations, have great possibilities. Ordinary choral compositions favour secular rather than sacred themes. Granville Bantock has attacked the task of inventing new methods of choral writing, borrowing resources of tone-colour from the orchestra. Cantatas for soloists, chorus, and accompaniment are produced in great numbers; a few are heard for several winters.

The Festivals have survived the Great War; 1920 saw a revival of the Handel Festivals. The Three Choirs Festivals are also now revived. The future of other provincial Festivals is still uncertain. In central London concerts, oratorios are hardly to be heard. Mr. A. R. Fagge endeavours to keep the flag flying, and performs new large works at Queen's Hall. Northern England, Wales, and the South-west, still cherish their delight in all forms of choral singing; every style, from oratorio to part-song, is cultivated and appreciated by all classes. A most complicated work will be prepared and performed under an uninstructed man, who asks visitors to tell him if the rendering is correct, as he has never heard it; often such renderings are brilliant though unrefined. For London performances of special significance complete societies have been brought from Yorkshire.

Yet for finished delicate perfection of rendering by smaller numbers, the Church music at St. Paul's Cathedral, Westminster Abbey, and the Temple Church in London, or the principal colleges at Oxford and Cambridge, cannot be surpassed. Nor should the Oriana Madrigal Society be forgotten. There is, however, little prospect of a revival of choral singing in the South.

An important addition to musical celebrations is the Competitive Festival, which adds the interest of emulation and prize-winning to performances of various kinds. As in the case of local examinations, domestic music is favourably affected by these festivals. They began at Stratford, East London, in 1883, directed by the late Mr. J. Spencer Curwen, and have since become widespread. The Eisteddfodau of Wales further the progress of music but little; prize-hunting and speechmaking absorb too large a share of their efforts. The English form of competitive festival, on the other hand, is concerned only with music, and is usually organized by representative musicians embracing a wide district, and not denominational or parochial. A zealous worker from 1885 was Miss A. M. Wakefield, of Westmorland (1853-1918), especially for competitive and combined singing of choirs. The movement is now federated and progressing rapidly.

6. Orchestral concerts have increased considerably, both in London and the provinces; though complete orchestras are still but few, owing to the lack of permanent local opera. Even yet the Britons who have ever once heard a full modern orchestra of strings, wood, brass, and percussion are a small minority of the nation. A very decided improvement, greater here than in any other department of music, has been in progress; there is room for much more. It is highly encouraging to find that the increased opportunities for hearing the best instrumental music have brought a corresponding improvement in the appreciation of the best. When a distinctly popular appeal is made, the highest classical works are not excluded. In May, 1919, Robert Newman completed his twenty-fifth year of management at Queen's Hall, and was granted a week of 'benefit concerts'; the programmes, entirely instrumental, consisted mainly of Beethoven, Bach, and other classics!

A very special feature of London musical life is contributed by the Promenade Concerts given every autumn
in Queen's Hall. Promenade Concerts began in 1841 at
Covent Garden, and continued, gradually worsening
musically and morally, for half a century. They always
encouraged dissipation rather than art, and were the resort
of the lounger and the profligate of both sexes. Latterly
they became a bear-garden, and on the last night of the
season it was customary for the mob to invade the
orchestra and smash all the instruments. Quite un-
regretted, the enterprise came to an end in 1891. But
then the Queen's Hall was opened. The Promenade
Concerts were resuscitated there. Perhaps through the
severance from the theatrical associations a new era
began. The audiences listened attentively to the music.
Soon, with misgiving, the directors tried classical items,
whose cordial reception encouraged further experiment.
Wagnerian excerpts, still not unanimously accepted,
proved a great attraction. In the third season, 1895, it
was already established that Monday night should be
devoted to Wagner; Friday, which was then the 'off-
night,' to classical works, including a Beethoven symphony; and there were many pieces of the highest class
on the other nights also. The Russian school was much
favoured. The classical Fridays quickly proved specially
attractive. So matters have remained; and for ten weeks
in the autumn fine orchestral performances have been
attainable every evening. A noteworthy occurrence was
the first introduction of a work by Bach in 1910. The
Third Brandenburg Concerto was announced; only the
first half was played, but the result was most extraordinary. Encores were strictly forbidden in the first
part of the programme; but this time the audience
simply refused to let the concert proceed till the piece
had been repeated. It was realised that Bach also is a
popular composer, acceptable to the general concert-
going public; and Bach has since become as necessary
to the classical Fridays as Beethoven. The Great War
did not suppress the Promenade Concerts; and the
season has since been lengthened. These performances,

giving grand renderings of grand music through the holiday season, have a wide influence on national musical life. The programmes are not beyond criticism as regards the use of native music and the slighter vocal pieces.

Other orchestral speculations have prospered; and the oldest societies keep a vigorous life. Sir Thomas Beecham's enterprise replaced and absorbed the Richter and Henschel concerts. The Great War gave hundreds of thousands, even millions, of Britons opportunities of knowing what concerts may be, and increased the supply of wind instruments. In quality and quantity alike, London orchestral performances have greatly advanced; though the Crystal Palace Concerts ceased in 1901.

Outside London, orchestral concerts are fast increasing. Bournemouth has for many years set a fine example in regular orchestral programmes under Dan Godfrey, who gives especial opportunities to native composers. Brighton had to overcome difficulties of locality, but its orchestras have flourished. Harrogate, Buxton, Llandudno, and Hastings compete for favour. Manufacturing towns are zealously struggling against the difficulties which obstruct the establishment of complete orchestras. The great popularity of Sunday concerts is an important factor. London has very many, every available hall being used. Grand Sunday concerts are regularly given on the Brighton Piers. Since the Peace, extensive plans have begun to bear fruit in Birmingham. In Manchester the old Sunday-worship was strong, and fought hard before it was defeated. Popular appreciation of instrumental performances by concert orchestra or military band can be reckoned upon; the problem is to find permanent daily work for orchestral players.

7. Chamber music, however, has suffered from the increased popularity of orchestral music. The Monday and Saturday Popular Concerts at once languished when the Queen's Hall opened; the former ceased in 1898, and the entire enterprise soon failed. For nearly forty years the success of these concerts had been boasted as a proof of English musical taste. The sluggish policy which year after year put forward the same familiar works rendered

by the same artists has been alleged the real cause of the
decline and fall of this institution, apparently quite
permanently established. A contributory cause it may
have been. Many straggling chamber music concerts are
still given in London; but nothing so imposing, representative, and complete as the Monday and Saturday
Popular Concerts of Victorian times. The London String
Quartet has made a valiant attempt to fill the gap, and
its concerts already may be counted in three figures. At
Leighton House, and afterwards at Wigmore Hall, the
London Chamber Concert Society has worked on the
social lines of the Musical Union, and its delightful
meetings are safely established.

Vocal chamber music is hardly prospering; concerted
practice is but little cultivated. Songs with pianoforte
accompaniment are a flourishing branch of the art; and
the most opposite kinds find favour, if the accompaniments be not difficult. Dramatic expression, and especially
gesture, are still neglected, and would be considered out
of place in a drawing-room. In construction and harmonic richness the advance upon Victorian song-writing
is very great.

One independent branch of performance, the organ
recital, may be counted among chamber music. It is a
modern growth. In July, 1870, the *Musical Times* rejoiced
that two recitals had been given at Kensington, as 'organ
performances are so seldom heard in London.' They are
now given at least daily, and are particularly useful in
occupying the noontide leisure hour of workers far from
home. Nor are the programmes inartistic. The ancient
churches in the City of London have found their function
here. And all over the kingdom formal organ recitals,
with vocal or violin solos as relief, are very frequent.
Some large towns maintain a corporation organist, who
gives daily recitals in the town hall. This flood of organ
performance has occasioned a demand for new organ
compositions, a noteworthy department of native work.

The People's Concert Society was started by aristocratic amateurs in 1878, to bring music into poor neigh-
bourhoods. Beginning with ballads, it found higher

flights of composition also welcome; and still works steadily. The Sunday Chamber Concerts at South Place, Finsbury, have maintained a very high standard since their beginning in 1886. Battersea and other London suburbs are following this lead. Of provincial under- takings, Midgley's free concerts at Bradford deserve mention.

Speculations with short programmes, such as the 'Tuesday Twelve o'clocks' at Manchester and the duet- recitals of the Misses Foxon at Sheffield, help to dissemi- nate good music. Their success has naturally brought imitation.

The British Music Society strives to advance native art, both by publication and performance. Its aims are of the best.

Domestic instrumental music is still considerably affected by local examinations. The pianoforte solos generally learnt are academic. Technical skill and musical knowledge advance, with hardly a corresponding increase in the pleasure brought by the home-circle performances. One material improvement has lately been effected: suitable test-pieces by native composers are used. The fashion for ladies' violin playing proved a fashion only; and has left little more trace than the craze for coster- songs and coon-songs which ruled in the nineties. Yet all these passing fancies had more colour than the inane sentimentalities of earlier generations. Let it never be forgotten that 'the suburban amateur's cottage piano' and the church choir have wider influence than Queen's Hall.

The multitudes of camp and hospital concerts must leave memories everywhere of vocal and instrumental performances; on the whole it seems to have been found that the level of taste was distinctly higher than had been expected. Performers' experiences varied remarkably; as a rule really good selections were appreciated. Our millions of fighting and serving men have all heard much music, and this is an asset in general culture.

8. Opera, small and great, has made some progress. Sir Thomas Beecham, complaining loudly that his efforts

are not appreciated in London, has met with great success in London as well as in the North of England. The Carl Rosa Company keeps a high efficiency, and ventures seasons in central London. Other touring companies give makeshift performances in suburban London and the provinces, adapting the largest works of Wagner and other modern writers to unsuitable small theatres where there is insufficient space on the stage or in the orchestra; yet most useful work is done towards conveying some idea of complete performances to the minds of many thousands who would otherwise remain ignorant. Saint-Saëns's *Samson et Delila* having been permitted, a further and more daring step was taken. An operatic version of Mendelssohn's *Elijah* has been ventured, and received with much favour. Some details of the music were improved by stage rendering with a small chorus; but many others were sacrificed or obscured. Another singular operatic experiment was an arrangement of Bach's cantata, *Phœbus and Pan*, with an interpolated ballet founded on the French Suites; dramatically, this was still less successful than Mendelssohn's oratorio. From these introductions, it may be gathered that real new operas have not been found attractive ; further, that approval of such arrangements is not creditable to the dramatic sense of a public which knows *Tristan* and *Meistersinger*, whatever it may say for the musical taste.

On the lighter side of the art, the operettas, Stanford's *Shamus O'Brien* and Sullivan's *Rose of Persia*, were produced before the nineteenth century closed. 'Musical comedy' is the title now degraded by its application to the least artistic class of hotch-potch.

A prize was offered in 1908 for a light opera. It was awarded to Dr. E. W. Naylor for *The Angelus*, which was too obviously affected by organ-loft traditions to be a complete success; it was good music, and was performed fairly often. In 1921 it was revived.

9. Conducting, which was long almost monopolised by foreigners, is now entrusted also to Britons. F. H. Cowen was a pioneer. Some of the performances under Sullivan were remarkably fine. Sir Henry J. Wood, and afterwards

Landon Ronald and Adrian G. Boult, have long been successful. Albert Coates, an Anglo-Russian, showed at Stockholm, then at Petrograd, and finally in London, splendid talent. Sir T. Beecham took charge of opera.

Singin₂ is well represented in every department. In Clara Butt we have an artist who for power and richness of tone is beyond compeer. Muriel Foster, now unfortunately silenced, was distinguished for declamatory intellectual delivery; Carrie Tubb, Agnes Nicholls, Phyllis Lett, Dorothy Silk, Edna Thornton, maintain the traditions of English concert-singing; as Kirkby Lunn of dramatic; Louise Dale and Ursula Greville of brilliant vocalisation. Ben Davies, in oratorio; Frank Mullings, John Coates, and Tom Burke, replace Sims Reeves and the retired Edward Lloyd. Gervase Elwes, who had especially cultivated Bach, is now lost to us. We have Robert Radford and Murray Davey for the aged Santley. And very special success has been gained by singers from the Colonies: Albani from Canada, and Melba from Australia, have justly earned world-wide renown; Donalda, Stralia, Rosina Buckman, and Ada Crossley are the most prominent among many others.

We have very many competent pianists and violinists with complete mastery of technics and a finished style, even if they lack that last and crowning gift of creative individuality which makes the world's virtuoso, the Busoni, Kubelik, Paderewski, or Moiseiwitsch. Only the renegade Eugène d'Albert attained such rank. Among the leading performers, we can boast of Marie Hall, Marjorie Hayward, Margaret Fairless, Albert Sammons, violinists; Tertis, unsurpassed on the viola; Borwick, Katherine Goodson, besides pianists named among the composers, where the violinist, Frank Bridge, must also be placed. Australia claims Daisy Kennedy and Percy Grainger; and New Zealand sent us Arnold Trowell, violoncellist.

A proportion of the best instrumentalists bear names which betray their foreign extraction. The names Adela Verne, Myra Hess, Eugène Goossens, and Irene Scharrer, among pianists, and Isolde Menges, violinist, are typical. As in the days when Flemish chapel-masters ruled all over the Continent, and later during the long dominance of Italian art, a performer finds it advisable to adopt a suitable appellation; an international prima donna requires an international convenient name: Albani, Melba, are improvements.*

10. 'Where there are ten musicians there are nine composers' has been asserted. Every musician must be a performer or teacher or director; the world requires only a comparatively small number of composers, but they should all be of special powers. Performers die off and must be replaced by a new generation; composers' productions can be preserved and repeated and, if sufficiently good, are immortal. The mass of absolutely first-class music already in existence can suffice us without any additions; unless some resource, hitherto unprovided for, is brought into notice, new compositions seldom remain on the repertory. Nevertheless a huge stream of novelties continually appears in every country. England is very well supplied with these; though one cannot select any specimens likely to be heard a century hence. A brief mention of the leading composers is necessary.

In the original edition of this History, Sullivan alone among composers then living was discussed. Among workers of his generation a word is due to EBENEZER PROUT (1835–1909), as he produced, besides many theoretical works, the regulation English cantatas and symphonies, two organ concertos, and a duet-sonata for pianoforte and harmonium; the sonata is still heard not infrequently, though published in the early seventies. No other English chamber work since Bennett and F. E. Bache has lingered so long. WILLIAM THOMAS BEST (1826–97), greatest of organists, left church music, still on the repertory. Sir JOSEPH BARNBY (1838–93), a successful composer, but most prominent as a choral conductor; and Sir JOHN STAINER (1840–1901), whose writing exactly fitted the Anglican service, and who distinguished himself in general musical culture, were leading men in late Victorian times, each in his sphere.

* So in the eighteenth century were Mara for Schmeling; Bernasconi for Wagele; Venturino for Mysliweczek.

Young composers who had shown talent but left the world early were Erskine Allon (1864–97) and the still-remembered WILLIAM YEATES HURLSTONE (1876–1906). Hamish McCunn (1868–1916) aroused expectations hardly fulfilled; his opera, *Jeanie Deans*, reached performance, and two Scottish overtures are still played. Stanley Hawley (1868–1916) specialised in accompaniment to recitations; his limited technique, though they are interesting at first, soon makes them pall.

Before turning to the principal composers of the twentieth century, a few words on smaller productions are necessary. The hymn-tunes composed by WILLIAM HENRY MONK (1823–89) and JOHN BACCHUS DYKES (1823–76) include many settings of popular hymns which are familiar all over the English-speaking world, and will hardly be displaced. Their worth is strangely various, but some are entirely successful, and adventitious circumstances have given personal interest to several, including 'Nearer, my God, to Thee,' played by the band on the deck of the sinking 'Titanic'; 'Abide with me,' in which the martyred Edith Cavell joined while her voice held out; and 'Lead, kindly Light.' All these tunes and words alike have found their homes in the hearts of millions. Secular tunes can show no recent instances of success at all comparable to these, and their influence on general taste can hardly be over-estimated. A thoroughly revised edition of *Hymns Ancient and Modern* appeared in 1904; it is scarcely an improvement on the original, either on the poetical or musical side. A singular success was made by Dr. Bunnett's 'Unison Service'; as publishers refused to pay £5 it was issued on 'sharing terms,' and many hundreds of thousands of copies have been sold! Thus sacred compositions can bring wealth, which, however small in comparison with the rewards brought by popular operetta, are beyond anything the great composers ever expected. The drawing-room ballad, nautical or sentimental, of late Victorian days, is fortunately now unknown in our concert-rooms.

Sir C. HUBERT H. PARRY (*b.* 1848) claims first notice

among our recent leading composers. After adding considerably to his output of choral works, he died rather
suddenly at his Sussex seaside retreat, 7th October, 1918.
His symphonies, concertos, and sonatas are already forgotten; among his larger instrumental productions only
his ' Characteristic ' Variations for orchestra show signs of
vitality. His oratorios, cantatas, and especially his odes,
remain on the repertory, with a few exceptions; the *Magnificat* was a failure and immediately fell into neglect. His
second oratorio, *Job* (1892), was ill-planned and disappointed the world, expectant of another such success as
Judith; it soon dropped into oblivion. *King Saul* had a
rather better reception. But Parry's fame must in future
depend mainly upon his smaller choral works. *Blest Pair
of Sirens* has from its production (1887) enjoyed special
popularity; and, though usually rated perhaps quite high
enough, is a noble work revealing all Parry's merits. He
never again produced music so completely satisfying. His
motet, *Voces clamantium*, and his *Love that casteth out fear*,
a scena on an original plan, will long retain their attraction
for the serious musician. Many of his songs possess
intellectual merits to the full, while just lacking the one
essential quality of musical charm; this judgment may,
indeed, be passed on almost everything Parry has left
us; intellectually blameless, musically just short of
perfection.

It is a singular feature of Parry's deeds that in early
life he produced work which suffered from immaturity
but approached the innermost source of beauty nearer
than any of his mature compositions. His first cantata,
Prometheus Unbound, puzzled critics and the provincial
public who attended the original performance, 7th September, 1880; and it has seldom been heard since, though
treasured by many, for it contains passages of absolute
beauty, to which the musician can return again and again,
although the composer's inexperience is patent. And in
that early period he published a set of pianoforte pieces,
Seven Ages of Mind, founded on Schumann's methods,
yet almost completely successful in avoiding Schumann's
faults while partaking his merits; and these pieces also

do not wither. Near the end of his life Parry published a collection on the model of the Bach and Handel Suites, entitled *Hands across the Centuries*; nearly all are dull, artificial, and quite ungrateful to the player. Similarly the charm of many a page in *Prometheus Unbound* has no counterpart in the solidly constructed latest cantatas. The first oratorio *Judith*, and *Blest Pair of Sirens*, remain the central and most satisfying of Parry's productions, having still a plentiful admixture of the first sprightly running and an assured touch in the construction. Some attempts to treat English hymn-tunes in the style of Bach's chorale-preludes were among his latest successes.

Parry also laboured zealously in the field of musical literature. Both in history and æsthetics he achieved enduring work. He wrote many of the most important articles in Grove's *Dictionary*; those on 'Sonata' and 'Variations' were of the highest value. Occasionally his articles betray the limited knowledge and opinions of the eighties; and, most unfortunately, the second edition reprints them without systematic revision or even due additions. *Studies of Great Composers, The Art of Music, The Seventeenth Century*, and a smaller handbook, were volumes treating musical history in an effective and interesting manner. It should be noted that Parry, more than any other writer, discussed musical history as a succession of compositions; musical practice he almost ignored; many unimportant and forgotten composers are mentioned in his *Summary*, but not Farinelli, Malibran, Lablache, or Sims Reeves.

Still more important were Parry's contributions to æsthetics, in a volume, *Style in Musical Art*, which displayed splendid originality of thought and charming literary style. A remarkable study of Bach, though not quite impeccable on the historical side, is most valuable for its appreciative insight. The many-sided activity which Parry displayed ranks him in the same class with G. A. Macfarren, whom, however, he surpassed entirely.

SAMUEL COLERIDGE-TAYLOR (1875–1912) achieved a brilliant and enduring success with one large work. He was of half-Negro, half-English descent, London-born, brought up in poverty, noticed and taught by Beckwith, a violinist, and finally trained at the Royal College. While still a pupil his ' Ballade ' for orchestra brought him celebrity, and his ' Scenes ' from Longfellow's *Hiawatha* (1898–1900) placed him among the first living composers ; but he never again reached that level. The work is still performed by choral societies, and its solo, ' Onaway! awake beloved,' is in the repertory of all English tenors. Several other vocal and instrumental works continue familiar.

Of older composers still living, ALEXANDER CAMPBELL MACKENZIE (*b.* 1847) has maintained his high position without reaching still higher. His best works, including *La Belle Dame sans merci*, and *Britannia*, for orchestra ; Pibroch for violin solo ; *The Story of Sayid*, a cantata ; *The Rose of Sharon*, and *Bethlehem*, oratorios ; and especially his opera, *Colomba*, were all produced in early or middle life, before this History was originally printed. Many of Mackenzie's smaller works are constructed on charming themes ; unfortunately he has not the gift of writing naturally for the keyboard, and his beautiful early pianoforte pieces are little known. His most successful attempt is the fine ' Scottish Concerto,' first introduced by Paderewski. A ' Benedictus ' for violin is probably played more often than all Mackenzie's other instrumental works put together.

C. VILLIERS STANFORD (*b.* 1852) has continued his fertile production in a great variety of departments, adding to his reputation. His *Shamus O'Brien* (1896) showed his powers in light opera ; he might have been Sullivan's successor had he found a collaborator. Liturgical music to Latin words has inspired some of Stanford's best choral music ; in secular art he has never surpassed his early setting of Tennyson's *Revenge*, and his instrumental works speedily fall into neglect.

F. H. COWEN (*b.* 1852), who in early life published six symphonies,* besides oratorios and operas, has achieved his most lasting successes in lighter forms ; *The Language of Flowers* and *The Butterfly's Ball* are still played by our

* No. 3, the ' Scandinavian,' was much played in the eighties.

orchestras, their graceful dance-rhythms, melodies, and orchestration finding sure appreciation.

After Sullivan, the leading British composers in 1895 were Parry, Mackenzie, Stanford, and Cowen; all received the honour of knighthood. Deep influence on all departments of musical culture has been exercised by FREDERICK CORDER; besides his important compositions, his many and varied contributions in musical literature have been warmly appreciated in England and America.

Quite suddenly a new star appeared, and his life-history proves that it is still possible for a composer of the first importance to remain in obscurity till he is well into middle life.

EDWARD ELGAR, like Dvořák and like César Franck, was unheard-of for many years; and in all three cases the long obscurity is inexplicable. Elgar, born near Worcester, 2nd June, 1857, was brought up in music, his father being organist at the Roman Catholic church, a violinist, and proprietor of a music-selling business. Instead of systematic training young Elgar had practical experience of a singularly miscellaneous kind. Vocal music, organ, violin, wind instruments, orchestral leading and conducting, all fell to his lot, and special circumstances caused exceptional intimacy with every kind of instrument. At the age of thirty-two he married and came to London, where he could obtain no notice, and after two years' hopeless struggle he went to Malvern and remained in obscurity till 1896. At last, in his fortieth year, his opportunity arrived: his *King Olaf* and his oratorio *The Light of Life* both came to a hearing. They won an immediate success, drawing general attention on the unknown composer. A series of large works, including the 'Enigma' Variations, added to Elgar's fame in the next four years; then his *Dream of Gerontius* fell rather flat and did not meet with full appreciation till it had been acclaimed in Germany. Established now among the leading English composers, Elgar has ever since issued large and important choral and instrumental works; some have dropped off the repertory, but others are repeated regularly. And he has succeeded, as no other of our leading composers has done, in reaching the universal soul in short unambitious pieces; a tune from the march *Pomp and Circumstance*, wedded to patriotic verses by W. E. Henley, became at once almost a national song; and a slight melody, 'Salut d'Amour,' takes a place among the sentimentalities dear to solo performers. A very fine song-cycle, *Sea Pictures*, for contralto and orchestra, is conspicuous among Elgar's shorter works. His highest recent flights include a remarkably imposing orchestral picture, *Carillon*, inspired by the agony of Belgium; two symphonies, the first being acclaimed everywhere; a violin concerto; and finally, original and delightful chamber music. Since producing *The Apostles* and *The Kingdom* (1906) he has neglected oratorio; both contain inspired pages. A knowledge of orchestration unsurpassed among composers is one of Elgar's most obvious merits.

It has been pleaded that none of Elgar's greater works is quite completely satisfying; and this may be admitted. We find certain numbers of every standard masterpiece less interesting than the rest; but separate independent numbers can be omitted. With continuous strains, 'unending melody,' any uninspired passages leaven the whole lump. When all deductions are made, we may be proud to have as compatriot a musician who has given to the world *The Dream of Gerontius*, *The Apostles*, *The Kingdom*, the Symphony in A flat, the Violin Concerto, the 'Enigma' Variations, *Carillon*, the overtures *Cockaigne* and *In the South*, the song-cycle *Sea Pictures*, and the tune to 'Land of Hope and Glory.' He was knighted in 1904.

EDWARD GERMAN (German Jones originally), born 1862, has earned a special place among our composers; being, next after Sullivan, the representative of graceful and artistic light music. He also began with a training at the Royal Academy; but the Church was not his nursing-mother, and he completed his education in theatre orchestras. We owe to German the tuneful operetta *Merrie England* and a brilliantly effective 'Welsh Rhapsody.' He was the eldest of a long succession of clever musicians born during the sixties and seventies.

GRANVILLE BANTOCK (*b.* 1868), established at Birmingham since 1900, also a Royal Academician, has attempted a novel kind of choral technique, employing effects intended to reproduce the varieties of orchestral colouring. His instrumental writing is masterly; some of his smaller pianoforte pieces, particularly in a set of twelve, have singular charm and real originality, attaining beauty which will long endure. Among Bantock's larger choral works *Vanity of Vanities* and *Omar Khayyam* must not be omitted.

Among the many other gifted composers who have passed through the Royal Academy are William Henry Bell (*b.* 1873), who has settled in South Africa; Adam Carse, Harry Farjeon, and Joseph Holbrooke (1878); Paul Corder (1879); Hubert Bath (1883); York Bowen (1884); Arnold Bax (1885), distinguished in descriptive orchestral music; and Benjamin Dale, whose D minor sonata is specially remarkable. J. B. McEwen has devoted himself mainly to chamber music. All these were pupils of Frederick Corder, who instructed them not only in musical attainments, but also in the knowledge adapted to the requirements of a practical career; and all, without scarcely an exception, have profited.

The Royal College has equally fulfilled the task of sending out well-equipped composers. Henry Walford Davies (*b.*1869) followed the accustomed Church organist's career till he settled as University professor in Wales; then came R. Walthew and Vaughan Williams (1872); Nicholas C. Gatty and G. T. Holst (1874); T. Dunhill and H. Balfour Gardiner (1877). Frank Bridge (1879) is prominent in chamber composition; Edgar L. Bainton (1880), James Friskin (1886), and Herbert Howells (1892) continue the line. John Ireland has been successful in prize competitions. George Butterworth died for his country, but his 'Shropshire Rhapsody' lives yet.

All these are fine performers as well as composers; York Bowen as a pianist, and Frank Bridge as a violinist, are executants of the first rank.

Composers * who were not trained at either institution include the older Arthur Hervey and A. M. Goodhart.

* Frederick Cliffe, who started splendidly, failed to continue.

F. Delius (1863), of German parentage, is highly esteemed
by many. Roger Quilter (1877) has scored one great
success with a song; Hamilton Harty (1879) and Norman O'Neill well represent the sister isle; Cyril Scott,
the most revolutionary of our composers, has a distinct following. Waldo Warner and Montague Phillips
must not be omitted; nor the Australian-born Percy
Grainger.

Lady composers have been active. Frances Allitsen
(died 1912) nearly achieved a national song in 'There's
a land, a dear land.' Ethel M. Smyth was warmly praised
by Tchaikoffski, and has succeeded in operatic composition. Marian Arkwright, Ethel Harraden, A. E. Horrocks,
Throsby Hutchison, Katherine Eggar, and Emma Lomax
have shown their ability to use the highest forms and
resources. Great deeds are expected from Dorothy
Howell.

Organ-playing, which has so very great a share in
British musical life, has been decidedly ennobled by the
Royal College of Organists, founded in 1864. Performances and programmes have alike improved considerably,
and fine original compositions are numerous. The blind
ALFRED HOLLINS and W. WOLSTENHOLME are specially distinguished both as performers and composers. It may be
assumed that an organist of every cathedral or any important church has published some solid compositions,
and not liturgical only, and has taken a musical degree.
But this catalogue would be incomplete without particular
mention of Dr. C. Harford Lloyd (1849–1919) and the
living Basil Harwood, Ernest Walker, and Alan Gray; each
of these cultivated artists has been an ornament to the
Anglican Church.

RUTLAND BOUGHTON has boldly explored an independent
path, and his laudable endeavour must be mentioned,
though the Fates have not yet been propitious. He has
tried to emulate Wagner on a small scale, giving dramatic
performances in a room at Glastonbury. Sufficient
support has not been forthcoming, but interest has been
aroused and future attempts on a well-considered plan
may have better success.

Isidore de Lara (Cohen), of Hebrew race, began as a popular singer and purveyor of drawing-room ballads; he has developed into an opera-composer; his *Messalina* and *Naïl* have been performed in London and Paris. During the World-War he was energetic in arranging concerts with exclusively British programmes.

Our ambitious young composers prefer to devote their energies to orchestral music; and their large choral works are usually secular, upon exotic or primitive themes. Their few dramatic attempts show the same tendency. We have nothing analogous to Charpentier's *Louise*, a story of contemporary Parisian life. When such themes are used it is for humorous stories, as in Miss Smyth's *Boatswain's Mate*.

Very much has been done towards creating opportunities for composers to bring their works to a hearing. Sir Ernest Palmer has established a Patron's Fund for the performance of new music. Valuable prizes have been offered for competition; John Ireland, and especially York Bowen, have been successful. The Carnegie Trust has helped in publishing. We have fortunately passed out of the days when the secretary of the Philharmonic Society could call the performance of an English work 'a dangerous precedent.'

Over fifty composers, even among the living, have been named above, and many, many more call for insertion: Julius Harrison, Alick Maclean, Cyril Jenkins, Gerrard Williams, have all been justly successful. Lord Berners well represents the talented amateur. Arthur Bliss, Havergal Brian, Eugène Goossens, have won recognition. Martin Shaw shows a gift for sacred music, little cultivated by younger leaders. Shall we, then, not look for a great native genius in the immediate future? There exists a general belief that such a genius is likely to appear; the sole ground for the belief is apparently the desire. We also desire an artist equal to Titian or Raphael; and still more, a poet equal to Shakespeare; but the desire alone will not effect its fulfilment. Nor is it by any means certain that there will ever be any more music of the highest rank, unchangeable by time. At present there is

no composer anywhere in the world at all likely to rank
with the greatest geniuses of the past. We may justly
claim that our best living men are equal to any others
now living. The technics of composition are now so
systematised, the opportunities of hearing the best models
are so favourable, that composers must multiply continually. But though so many are called, few, very few
are chosen.

Oliver Goldsmith's 'Citizen of the World' tells how he
had read in English newspapers of 'twenty-five great men,
seventeen very great men, and nine very extraordinary
men, in less than the compass of half a year. These,
say the gazettes, are the men that posterity will gaze
at with admiration; these the names that fame will be
employed in holding up for the admiration of succeeding
ages. . . . Ninety-two (sic!) in a year. I wonder how
posterity will be able to remember them all?' So of
our composers. And we may be sure that the list
will be continually lengthening. Contemporary composers now meet with appreciation and can reap some
emolument, and fortunately are no longer so un-
reasonably exalted as Hubert Parry was a generation
since, or Sterndale Bennett and G. A. Macfarren rather
earlier. In all soberness, our leading critic told Macfarren that his first oratorio was 'a really great thing,'
'one that will be handed down among the heirlooms
of the nation'; and the success of another oratorio made
an enthusiast congratulate him on 'the tribute of praise
which the lovers of the true and good in Art shall pay
you in the time to come, as you take your just place
with the worthies whose names are remembered when
the wearers of crowns are forgotten and dynasties have
crumbled to dust.' Even Elgar is not so belauded now;
good and clever temporary work is duly valued and rewarded, yet not confused with great and enduring work.
This we may count an advance. The days of general
contentment prove eventually to be the days of weakness;
I have quoted specimens of such ungrounded self-
satisfaction on pages 261, 304, and 388. In Purcell's day
we do not find them. Our own time does not display the

individual genius, but the multitude; it is a time, not of Much, but of Many, in all countries alike.*

Let us, then, not be too sanguine of future deeds. Rather should we do what we can towards extending and deepening general knowledge and appreciation of music; towards perfecting the finish of public performances, improving the repertory and renderings of our domestic music, giving the young composer opportunities for hearing and publishing his works; towards advancing orchestral and chamber and dramatic and ecclesiastical music of every description, not looking for an immediate reward in the appearance of some really great genius, yet making ready the surroundings suitable for his advent.

* This holds good outside music. But we are less easily deceived now. Within living memory, when Alexander Smith's dreary *Life-Drama* appeared 'he was hailed as a second Shakespeare'; Lewis Morris's *Epic of Hades*, another forgotten work, was enthusiastically appreciated for a time. A truer perspective has been established.

ADDENDA

CHAPTER II, page 62: A paper by Van den Borren, supporting Dunstable's priority, was read before the Musical Association in March, 1921.

CHAPTER III, page 83: According to Mr. Grattan Flood (*Musical Times*, March, 1921), the Hygons of the Eton choir-book was Master of the Choristers of Wells Cathedral; he was succeeded by R. Bramston in 1507. Page 97: An inventory of the choir-books at King's College, Cambridge, was prepared in 1529. The catalogue remains and was printed in the *Ecclesiologist* for 1863. Forty-two books are mentioned, with a few details. The composers named are Cornys, Coper, Taverner, Turges, Lambe, Horwud, Hacomplaynt, Dunstabyll, Morgan, ffarfax, Wylkynson, Pygot, and Davys. None of the compositions is known, except 'Masse Regale.'

CHAPTER IV, page 126, paragraph 2, line 9: Sternhold's selection, published about the same date, contains no music.

CHAPTER V, page 174: Addit. MS. 34800 contains three-part Fancies by Morley, E. Blankes, O. Gibbons, H. Loosemore, and M. Este; with vocal music.

CHAPTER VI, page 252: 'T. F., Minister of Exon,' was Thomas Ford (1598–1674). Page 258: N. Hookes's *Amanda* (1653) contains verses boasting of the Cambridge musicians, 'If not the best, as good as anywhere.'

CHAPTER VIII, page 396, line 7: Confusion has arisen through the various names given to many hymn-tunes. By the one here called 'Bethlehem' I intended 'Carey's' (or 'Yarmouth,' or 'Brighthelmstone'), published already by John Church, in 1723, and possibly the earliest specimen of a hymn-tune in tranquil triple time.

CHAPTER IX, page 407: Add that Thomas Busby (1755–1838) published a *History of Music* in 1819, mainly intended to controvert Burney's attacks on Elizabethan madrigals, but with some additions. Haydn is ridiculed, with every one who should presume to compete with Handel by attempting to compose oratorios!

INDEX

Abbot, Archbishop, 155, 182, 230–1, 246

Aberdeen, Music at, 149–50, 307, 422

Abyngdon, Henry, 76

Academy of Ancient Music, 362–363, 224, 325, 385

Accidentals, 33, 127, 153, 366, 391

Acoustical discoveries, 302

Adams, R., 123

——, Thomas, 422

Adamus Dorensis, 36

Additional MSS., British Museum, 7, 26–8, 36, 37, 43, 53, 64, 84–6, 91–7, 101, 107–13, 119–26, 129, 132–41, 161–5, 172–5, 181, 211, 234, 255, 267, 276, 284, 308, 350, 489

Adson, J., 168

Ailred of Rievaulx, 16, 17

Alain, de L'Isle, 19, 29

——, John, 55

Albani, Madame, 477–8

Alcock, Dr., 372

Alcuin, 10, 28

Aldhelm, 8, 9, 11, 38

Aldrich, Dean, 319–20

Allison, R., 158, 173, 182, 207

Allitsen, Fr., 486

Allon, Erskine, 478

Allwoode, Richard, 89, 119, 141

Alphredus Anglicus, 36

Ambros's *Geschichte der Musik*, 46, 65, 68, 141, 148, 196, 225

Ancient Concerts, 385, 410

Angus, Dean John, 149

Anmer, John, 159, 218

Anthems, 117–20, 124, 128–31, 135–7, 139–42, 146, 186–9, 191, 205, 215–20, 228, 231–4, 238–42, 283–4, 310–20, 329–32, 339–46, 355, 360–2, 372, 374, 379–83, 397, 399, 401, 437, 454

Anthem, The National, 333, 368–369

Appleby, T., 91, 139

Arber, Professor, 160

Arbuthnot, Dr., 340

Arkwright, Godfrey P. E., 119, 132, 147, 177, 205, 208, 313, 464

——, Miss Marian, 486

Arne, Dr., 369–71

Arnold, Dr., 381; *Cathedral Music*, 382

Arundel Collection. *See* Royal MSS.

——, MSS. (British Museum), 11, 25–7, 110, 129

Ashley, John, 387

Ashmole MSS., 26, 63, 66

Ashwell, T., 89–91, 97

Aspull, G., 412

Aston, Hugh, 1, 72, 103–5, 148

Atterbury, Luffman, 379

Attey, J., 159

Attwood, T., 400

Avison family, The, 373

'Ayres,' 157–66, 194, 208 ff., 227–8, 253, 263–6, 291, 464

Bachelor, D., 174, 194, 213

Bagpipe, The, 13, 41

Bainton, Edgar L., 485

Baldwin, John, 90, 124, 146, 148, 163, 172, 187

Bale's *Scriptores*, 34, 36, 61, 68, 106

Balfe, 427–30

Ballad Opera, 366, 389

Ballads. *See* Folk-Music.

Ballet, W., 175

Baltzar, violinist, 260

Banastir, Gilbert, 75

Banister, John, 292, 320

Bantock, Granville, 484

Barber, R., 123

Barcroft, G., 141

DATE DUE

MAR 0	

GAYLORD   PRINTED IN U.S.A.